**EXPLORER**

C000147095

# Dubai

## LIVE WORK EXPLORE

www.liveworkexplore.com

# Where Water Meets Wonder

Atlantis is the majestical focal point of Palm Jumeirah, a man-made island that has captured the world's imagination with its magnificent scale and ingenuity. The resort offers relaxation and thrills for couples and families alike, including Aquaventure the largest water-themed attraction in the Middle East, over 20 marine exhibits in Lost Chambers, 17 bars & restaurants, a private 2km beach, an indulgent spa and over 30 cosmopolitan boutiques.

ATLANTIS
THE PALM, DUBAI

**Dubai Explorer  2010/14th Edition**
First Published 1996
2nd Edition 1997
3rd Edition 1998
4th Edition 2000
5th Edition 2001
6th Edition 2002
7th Edition 2003
8th Edition 2004
9th Edition 2005
10th Edition 2006
11th Edition 2007
12th Edition 2008
13th Edition 2009
**14th Edition 2010    ISBN 978-9948-442-52-3**

**Copyright © Explorer Group Ltd,** 1996, 1997, 1998, 2000, 2001, 2002, 2003, 2004, 2005, 2006, 2007, 2008, 2009, 2010.
All rights reserved.

Front Cover Photograph – Dubai Marina – Victor Romero

Printed and bound by Emirates Printing Press, Dubai, United Arab Emirates.

**Explorer Publishing & Distribution**
PO Box 34275, Dubai
United Arab Emirates
**Phone**      +971 (0)4 340 8805
**Fax**        +971 (0)4 340 8806
**Email**      info@explorerpublishing.com
**Web**        www.explorerpublishing.com

While every effort and care has been made to ensure the accuracy of the information contained in this publication, the publisher cannot accept responsibility for any errors or omissions it may contain.
No part of this publication may be reproduced, stored in a retrieval system, or transmitted, in any form or by any means, electronic, mechanical, photocopying, recording or otherwise, without the prior permission in writing of the publisher.

# Welcome...

...to the all new **Dubai Explorer – Live Work Explore**, the ultimate insiders' guide to moving to, living in and loving one of the world's most exciting cities. From red-tape to restaurants, housing to hobbies, entertainment to exploring and shopping to socialising, this book gives you the lowdown on all aspects of life in Dubai.

Plus, this year we are giving you a special gift – the **Explorer Member Card** (tucked away in the back of this book), which gives you access to a whole host of fantastic discounts. Just log on to www.liveworkexplore.com and register your card, then check out the offers, from food and drink to exploring and leisure, and everything in between.

Also online you will find up-to-the minute events, company listings for all manner of needs, great competitions, and the chance to give us your insights on life in Dubai – whether it's a restaurant review or an expat experience.

And if all that wasn't enough we also have our **lifestyle magazine** of the same name – liveworkexplore – available around the UAE. A must-read, it includes travel features on far-off places, weekend breaks to the best of the GCC, real life issues on being an expat and the best of things to see and do in the Emirates.

And don't forget – whether it's dining out or driving off-road, shopping or snorkelling, working in the gulf or whizzing off for a weekend break, Explorer has a guide for you. Check out all our guides, photography books and maps at www.explorerpublishing.com.

Enjoy Dubai, enjoy this book, and if you're not already an explorer let's hope you soon will be!

**The Explorer Team**

More than 100,000 spectators and over 600 million viewers watched history being made as Yas Marina Circuit played host to the first Formula 1™ Etihad Airways Abu Dhabi Grand Prix.

Now the world's most spectacular motorsports venue is operating year round.

## "Seeing is Believing..."

Whether for business or pleasure, Yas Marina Circuit's state of the art facilities, must be seen to be believed.
Embrace the future. Be part of the vision.

FOR MORE INFORMATION CALL OUR BUSINESS DEVELOPMENT TEAM ON 800 YMC
OR EMAIL: corporate@eaa.gov.ae

yasmarinacircuit.ae

**Forthcoming Events**
- GP2 Asia Series
  5-6 FEBRUARY 2010
- V8 Supercars
  19-20 FEBRUARY 2010

**Driving Packages**
- F1 2-Seater
  Experience
- Corporate Driving
  Experience

**Additional Facilities**
- Events
- Conferences
- Corporate Hospitality
- 7 Hotels
- 18 Hole, Links Golf Course

YASMARINACIRCUIT

Official Partner

NATIONAL BANK OF ABU DHABI
The Number One Bank

*Ernie Els*

Golf Course Architect
Monday, November 16, 2009
2.52pm, Hole 9
Second shot.

**Links Golf Magazine** "Best New International Course 2008"   **Golf Inc.** "Best Golf Development of the Year 2008" - Finalist
**Troon Golf** "Best New Facility of the Year 2008"   **CNBC Arabian Property Awards** "Best Golf Course, Dubai 2009"

# THE PERFECT CLUB FOR YOUR GAME

The Els Club at Dubai Sports City is the first golf course in the Middle East designed by US Open and Open Champion, Ernie Els. Set on undulating slopes of native desert vegetation, it is a links style layout combining traditional classic design. In essence the golf course combines the best of all the great clubs Ernie has played worldwide over the last 20 years. It creates an extraordinary experience by providing superior service and superb, tournament-spec playing surfaces.

Members and Guests have access to two restaurants including Dubai's first Big Easy Bar & Grill, exceptionally appointed professional shop, full service locker facilities with oversized whirlpool spa and sauna rooms, Founders Club and a choice of meeting and conference facilities. Tee-times can be booked by contacting the Reservations Team on +971 4 425 1010 or reservations@elsclubdubai.com

www.elsclubdubai.com

## THE ELS CLUB
### DUBAI SPORTS CITY

# THE ![crest] TIMES

The world's most respected newspaper, printed daily in the Gulf

# The armchair explorer's guide to the world.

Explore the world from the comfort and safety of your armchair. Get global news on your doorstep daily. Subscribe to the world's most respected newspaper and enjoy the finest in cutting edge journalism, incisive commentary, features, business and sport. To subscribe now simply email subscribe@sab-media.com

www.thetimesme.com

# BIGGEST CHOICE OF BOOKS

## BORDERS ®

### YOUR PLACE FOR KNOWLEDGE AND ENTERTAINMENT

Mall of the Emirates 04 3415758, Mall of the Emirates Metro Link 04 3996729
Dubai International Financial Centre 04 4250371,
Deira City Centre 04 2943344, Oasis Centre 04 3397752
Ibn Battuta Mall 04 4341925, Dubai Marina Mall 04 4342501
Sharjah City Centre 06 5330645
Muscat City Centre 00968 24558089 & Qurm City Centre 00968 24470491

**Nothing stops you here!**

Ras Al Khaimah Highway,
through Emirates Road, Exit 103
Tel: 06 7681888 | www.dreamlanduae.com
Fridays, Saturdays & public holidays are family days

Take a break. There is something for
everyone at Dreamland Aqua Park.
Induige in absolute fun at the amazing
250,000 sq.m. fun land. Over 30 thrilling
rides, crazy slides, go-karts and unlimited wet &
dry attractions. So, splash. Play. Get recharged!

" Today a Reader
Tomorrow a Leader "

 **JASHANMAL BOOKSTORES**

Dubai: Mall of the Emirates, Tel: 3406789, The Village Mall, Jumeirah, Tel: 3445770,
Caribou Coffee, Uptown Mirdiff, Tel: 2888376, Dubai Marina Walk, Tel: 04 4222504,
Abu Dhabi: Abu Dhabi Mall, Level 3, Hamdan Street, Tel: 6443869, Sharjah: Sahara Centre, Tel: 5317898
Bahrain: Seef Mall, West Wing, Tel: 17581632, Al Aali Shopping Complex, Tel: 17582424

INCA/JNC/1191

# THE A TO Z OF GOOD HEALTH

❖Anaesthesiology  ❖Antenatal  Classes  and  Breast-Feeding  Clinics  ❖Cardiology  (Interventional  &  Non-Interventional)  ❖Cosmetic  Reconstructive and Hand Surgery  ❖Dentistry, Periodontics, Orthodontics, Oral Surgery and Dental  Implantology  ❖Dermatology and Laser Skin Surgery  ❖Dietetics  ❖Endocrinology and Diabetology  ❖ENT, Audiology and Speech Therapy  ❖Gastroenterology  ❖General and Laparoscopic Surgery  ❖General Practice  ❖Internal  Medicine  ❖Nephrology and Dialysis  ❖Neurology  ❖Neurosurgery  ❖Nuclear Medicine  ❖Obstetrics and  Gynaecology  ❖Oncology  ❖Ophthalmology  and Laser Eye Surgery  ❖Orthopaedics  and  Physiotherapy  ❖Paediatrics  and  Neonatology  ❖Pathology  ❖Pulmonology  ❖Radiology  and Imaging & Interventional Radiology  ❖Urology

**AL ZAHRA**
THE HEALING TOUCH

Al Zahra Hospital,  Sharjah, U.A.E
Tel: 06 5619999, Fax: 06-5616699
Appointments: 06  5167080/81

Al Zahra Medical Centre, Dubai, U.A.E
Tel:  04-3315000, Fax: 04-3313865
Appointments:  04  3311155/44

Email:  alzahra@alzahra.com  www.alzahra.com

MOH 2746/2/11/28/12/09

Mall of the Emirates 04 3414353    Mercato 04 3446971    Deira City Centre 04 2958599    JBR 04 4230715

# Royal
## EVENTS & WEDDINGS

WEDDINGS
LADIES EVENTS
VIP EVENTS
THEME EVENTS

www.royalevents.com • e-mail:info@flyingelephant.com

**Contents**

# making it **easy every step** of the way

# Move *One*
## R E L O C A T I O N S

> Dedicated to simplifying moving and relocation process, Move One Relocations provides comprehensive customized services - all through a single point of contact.

> Worldwide moving   > Relocation services   > Fine art shipping   > Pet transportation

**mail** dubai@moveonerelo.com   **tel** 800 MOVEONE   **web** www.moveonerelo.com

# UAE:

# A Country

# Profile

# UNITED ARAB EMIRATES

Located in the heart of the Middle East, the United Arab Emirates (UAE) is home to over 150 nationalities. While proud and protective of its Islamic culture, it is also one of the most progressive, cosmopolitan and open-minded countries in the region. From the brash metropolis of Dubai to the desert wilderness of the Empty Quarter, its many landscapes lie waiting to be explored. Whether you're new to this remarkable land or have been living here for years, there's always something new to discover.

## Location

Situated on the eastern side of the Arabian Peninsula, the UAE borders Saudi Arabia and the Sultanate of Oman, with coastlines on both the Arabian Gulf and the Gulf of Oman. The country comprises seven emirates – Abu Dhabi, Ajman, Dubai, Fujairah, Ras Al Khaimah, Sharjah and Umm Al Quwain. Abu Dhabi is by far the largest emirate, occupying over 80% of the country with the emirate of Dubai the second largest, although they have similar populations (p.6).

The country is best known for the modern, rapidly expanding metropolis of Dubai, but visitors may be surprised by the variety of landscapes when they venture beyond the city. The coast is littered with coral reefs and more than 200 islands, most of which are uninhabited. The interior of the country is characterised by sabkha (salt flats), stretches of gravel plain, and vast areas of sand desert. To the east rise the Hajar Mountains, (hajar is Arabic for rock). Lying close to the Gulf of Oman, they form a backbone through the country, from the Musandam Peninsula in the north, through the eastern UAE and into Oman. The highest point is Jebel Yibir at 1,527 metres. The Rub Al Khali, or Empty Quarter, occupies a large part of the south of the country. Stretching into Saudi Arabia, Oman and Yemen, it's the largest sand desert in the world, covering an area roughly the same size as France, Belgium and the Netherlands. This stark desert is interrupted by salt flats and occasional oases, and its spectacular sand dunes rise to more than 300 metres.

## Climate

Dubai has a subtropical and arid climate. Sunny blue skies and high temperatures can be expected most of the year. Rain falls on an average of only 25 days per year, mainly in winter (December to March). It rarely rains very heavily or for long periods. However, in the Hajar Mountains the amount of rainfall can be much higher and flash floods in the wadis are not unheard of.

Although infrequent, when it comes, heavy rainfall can really take its toll on the city within a relatively short period. Not all roads have adequate drainage, and even those that do are not designed for massive downpours

so drains get blocked by sand. In addition, many of Dubai's drivers are not accustomed to wet conditions, and tend to respond by putting their hazard lights on, which can be confusing for other drivers. January 2008 saw two days of flooding which resulted in many schools and businesses closing due to impassable roads, and even a number of homes had water damage.

During winter there are occasional sandstorms when the sand is whipped up off the desert. This is not to be confused with a shamal, a north-westerly wind that comes off the Arabian Gulf and can cool temperatures down. Sandstorms cover anything left outside in gardens or on balconies and can even blow inside, so make sure your doors and windows are shut.

Temperatures range from a low of around 10°C (50°F) in winter to a high of 48°C (118°F) in summer. The mean daily maximum is 24°C (75°F) in January, rising to 41°C (106°F) in August. Humidity is usually between 50% and 65%, however, when combined with the high summer temperatures, even 60% humidity can produce extremely uncomfortable conditions. The most pleasant time to visit Dubai is in the cooler winter months, when temperatures are perfect for comfortable days on the beach and long, lingering evenings outside. For up to date weather reports, log on to www.dubaiairport.com/dubaimet, or www.das.ae, or call Dubai Meteorological Services' automated system on 04 216 2218.

# HISTORY

Dubai's early existence is closely linked to the arrival and development of Islam in the greater Middle East region, although it traces its trading routes back as far as the Kingdom of Sumer in 3000BC. Islam developed in modern-day Saudi Arabia at the beginning of the seventh century AD with the revelations of the Quran being received by the Prophet Muhammad. Military conquests of the Middle East and North Africa enabled the Arab empire to spread the teachings of Islam from Mecca and Medina to the local Bedouin tribes. Following the Arab Empire came the Turks, the Mongols and the Ottomans, each leaving their mark on local culture.

---

**UAE Fact Box**

Coordinates: 24°00′ North 54°00′ East
Borders: 410km with Oman and 457km with Saudi Arabia
Total land area: approx. 83,000 sq km
Total coastline: 1,318km
Highest point: 1,527m
Total land area: 3,885 sq km
Total Dubai coastline: 60km, but new offshore projects will add over 1,000km

---

After the fall of the Muslim empires, both the British and Portuguese became interested in the area due to its strategic position between India and Europe, and for the opportunity to control the activities of pirates based in the region, which earned it the title the 'Pirate Coast'. In 1820, the British defeated the pirates and a general treaty was agreed by the local rulers, denouncing piracy. The following years witnessed a series of maritime truces, with Dubai and the other emirates accepting British protection in 1892. In Europe, the area became known as the Trucial Coast (or Trucial States), a name it retained until the departure of the British in 1971.

In the late 1800s Dubai's ruler, Sheikh Maktoum bin Hasher Al Maktoum, granted tax concessions to foreign traders, encouraging many to switch their base of operations from Iran and Sharjah to Dubai. The city's importance as a trading hub was further enhanced by Sheikh Rashid bin Saeed Al Maktoum, father of the current ruler of Dubai, who ordered the creek to be dredged, thus providing access for larger vessels. Dubai came to specialise in the import and re-export of goods, mainly gold to India, and trade became the foundation of this emirate's wealthy progression.

In 1968, Britain announced its withdrawal from the region. The ruling sheikhs of Bahrain, Qatar and the Trucial Coast realised that by uniting forces as a single state, they would have a stronger voice in the wider Middle East region. Negotiations collapsed when Bahrain and Qatar chose independence, however, the Trucial Coast remained committed to forming an alliance, and in 1971 the federation of the United Arab Emirates was born.

## Emirs Or Sheikhs?

While the term emirate comes from the ruling title of 'emir', the rulers of the UAE are called 'sheikhs'.

The new state comprised the emirates of Dubai, Abu Dhabi, Ajman, Fujairah, Sharjah, Umm Al Quwain and, in 1972, Ras Al Khaimah (each emirate is named after its main town). Under the agreement, the individual emirates each retained a certain degree of autonomy, with Abu Dhabi and Dubai providing the most input into the federation. The leaders of

## UAE TIMELINE

| | |
|---|---|
| 1760 | The Baniyas Tribe finds fresh water in Abu Dhabi and settles on the island |
| 1833 | The Maktoum family settles in Dubai |
| 1835 | Maritime Truce signed between the Trucial States and Britain |
| 1890s | Dubai and Abu Dhabi fall under the protection of Britain |
| 1950s | Oil is discovered in Abu Dhabi and production begins |
| 1963 | Maktoum Bridge is built, becoming the first bridge across Dubai Creek |
| 1966 | Commercial quantities of oil discovered off the coast of Dubai. HH Sheikh Zayed bin Sultan Al Nahyan becomes ruler of Abu Dhabi. Dubai's first hotel, The Carlton (now The Riviera), is built |
| 1967 | The Shindagha Tunnel is built, providing an alternative to Maktoum Bridge for crossing the creek |
| 1971 | Britain withdraws from the Gulf and Dubai becomes independent. The United Arab Emirates is born, with HH Sheikh Zayed bin Sultan Al Nahyan as the leader. The UAE joins the Arab League |
| 1972 | Ras Al Khaimah joins the UAE |
| 1973 | The UAE launches a single currency, the UAE dirham |
| 1981 | The Gulf Cooperation Council is formed, with the UAE as a founding member |
| 1985 | Emirates Airline is founded |
| 1990 | After the death of his father, Sheikh Rashid bin Saeed Al Maktoum, Sheikh Maktoum bin Rashid Al Maktoum becomes the ruler of Dubai |
| 1999 | The doors of the Burj Al Arab, the tallest hotel in the world, open to the public for the first time |
| 2001 | Construction starts on Palm Jumeirah |
| 2002 | The freehold property market is opened up to foreigners |
| 2004 | Sheikh Zayed bin Sultan Al Nahyan dies and is succeeded as ruler of the UAE by his son, Sheikh Khalifa bin Zayed Al Nahyan |
| 2006 | Sheikh Maktoum bin Rashid Al Maktoum dies and is succeeded as Ruler of Dubai and Prime Minister of the UAE by his brother, Sheikh Mohammed bin Rashid Al Maktoum |
| 2007 | The first residents move on to the Palm Jumeirah |
| 2008 | Atlantis on the Palm opens its doors; in the wake of global economic crisis, Dubai's property market crashes to around 50% of its peak value |
| 2009 | Abu Dhabi hosts its inaugural grand prix at Yas Marina Circuit. Dubai Metro, the region's first public mass-transit system, is launched |
| 2010 | The tallest building in the world, the Burj Dubai, opens |

## Modern UAE

Trade and commerce are still the cornerstones of the economy, with the traditional manufacturing and distribution industries now joined by financial, construction, media, IT and telecom businesses. With so many world-class hotels, and leisure and entertainment options, the UAE is also becoming an increasingly popular tourist destination.

the new federation elected the ruler of Abu Dhabi, His Highness Sheikh Zayed bin Sultan Al Nahyan, to be their president, a position he held until he passed away on 2 November, 2004. His eldest son, His Highness Sheikh Khalifa bin Zayed Al Nahyan, was then elected to take over the presidency. Despite the unification of the seven emirates, boundary disputes have caused a few problems. At the end of Sheikh Zayed's first term as president, in 1976, he threatened to resign if the other rulers didn't settle the demarcation of their borders. The threat proved an effective way of ensuring cooperation, although the degree of independence of the various emirates has never been fully determined.

The formation of the UAE came after the discovery of huge oil reserves in Abu Dhabi in 1958 (Abu Dhabi has an incredible 10% of the world's known oil reserves). This discovery dramatically transformed the emirate. In 1966, Dubai, which was already a relatively wealthy trading centre, also discovered oil.

Dubai's ruler at the time, the late Sheikh Rashid bin Saeed Al Maktoum, ensured that the emirate's oil revenues were used to develop an economic and social infrastructure, which is the basis of today's

modern society. His work was continued through the reign of his son, and successor, Sheikh Maktoum bin Rashid Al Maktoum and by the present ruler, Sheikh Mohammed bin Rashid Al Maktoum.

# GOVERNMENT & RULING FAMILY

The Supreme Council of Rulers is the highest authority in the UAE, comprising the hereditary rulers of the seven emirates. Since the country is governed by hereditary rule there is little distinction between the royal families and the government. The Supreme Council is responsible for general policy involving education, defence, foreign affairs, communications and development, and for ratifying federal laws. The Council meets four times a year and the rulers of Abu Dhabi and Dubai have power of veto over decisions.

The Supreme Council elects the chief of state (the president) from among its seven members. The current president is the ruler of Abu Dhabi, Sheikh Khalifa bin Zayed Al Nahyan. He took over the post in November 2004 from his late father, Sheikh Zayed bin Sultan Al Nahyan.

The Supreme Council also elects the vice president of the UAE, currently Sheikh Mohammed bin Rashid Al Maktoum, ruler of Dubai. The president and vice president are elected and appointed for five-year terms, although they are often re-elected time after time, as was the case with Sheikh Zayed. The president appoints the prime minister (currently Sheikh Mohammed bin Rashid Al Maktoum) and the deputy prime ministers (currently Sheikh Sultan bin Zayed Al

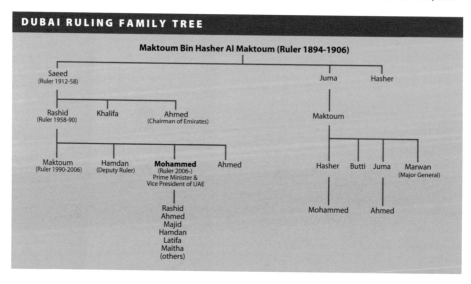

**DUBAI RULING FAMILY TREE**

Nahyan and Sheikh Hamdan bin Zayed Al Nahyan).

The emirate of Dubai is currently ruled by Sheikh Mohammed bin Rashid Al Maktoum, vice president and prime minister of the UAE (who is considered the driving force behind Dubai's exponential growth) and his brother Sheikh Hamdan bin Rashid Al Maktoum, the UAE Minister of Finance & Industry.

### Girl Power

Following elections in 2007, a number of women were voted in to government positions. Today over 40% of government employees are women, one of the highest rates in the world.

The Federal National Council (FNC) reports to the Supreme Council. It has executive authority to initiate and implement laws and is a consultative assembly of 40 representatives. The Council currently monitors and debates government policy but has no power of veto.

The individual emirates have some degree of autonomy, and laws that affect everyday life vary between them. For instance, if you buy a car in one emirate and need to register it in a different emirate, you will have to export and then re-import it. All emirates have a separate police force, with different uniforms and cars.

Downtown Burj Dubai

# INTERNATIONAL RELATIONS

The UAE remains open in its foreign relations and firmly supports Arab unity. HH Sheikh Khalifa bin Zayed Al Nahyan is very generous with the country's wealth when it comes to helping Arab nations and communities that are in need of aid.

The UAE became a member of the United Nations and the Arab League in 1971. It is a member of the International Monetary Fund (IMF), the Organisation of Petroleum Exporting Countries (Opec), the World Trade Organisation (WTO) and other international and Arab organisations. It is also a member of the Arab Gulf Cooperation Council (AGCC, also known as the GCC), whose other members are Bahrain, Kuwait, Oman, Qatar and Saudi Arabia.

All major embassies and consulates are represented either in Dubai or in Abu Dhabi, or both. See Embassies & Consultates, Inside Back Cover).

## SHEIKH MOHAMMED: A PROFILE

Sheikh Mohammed bin Rashid Al Maktoum is ruler of Dubai and vice president of the UAE. He acceded to both positions in 2006 following his brother Sheikh Maktoum bin Rashid Al Maktoum's death. Born in 1948, he is father to 19 children including Rashid, the deputy ruler of Dubai and Hamdan, crown prince and future ruler of Dubai.

Widely accredited with the vision of modern day Dubai, Sheikh Mohammed has been a major driving force in the completion of some of the emirate's elaborate construction projects such as the Burj Al Arab and Palm Jumeirah. He is also attributed with fostering the progressive, cosmopolitan society that exists in Dubai today.

Among Sheikh Mohammed's passions are poetry and horse racing; the latter nowhere more evident than in the emirate's hosting of the richest horse race in the world, the Dubai World Cup (p.26). Dubai's ruler is a patron of the ancient poetic form, Nabati (also known as Bedouin poetry), and has published volumes of his own verses.

To find out more about the ruler of Dubai visit www.sheikhmohammed.co.ae or visit his Facebook profile www.facebook.com/HHSheikhMohammed.

# FACTS & FIGURES

Jumeira Mosque

## Population

The population of the UAE stood at 4.77 million at the end of 2008, an increase of 6.49% on 2007. Of the 2008 total, 1.596 million lived in the city of Dubai and 1.559 million in Abu Dhabi. Following the global economic crisis in 2009, it was forecast that Dubai would experience its first population decline in many years. A new UAE census is planned for April 2010 after which official statistics will be published, but experts estimate a decline of anywhere between 8% and 17% for the emirate. As Abu Dhabi was hit less severely than Dubai by the financial downturn, it is expected that new figures will show a proportion of the departing population migrating to the UAE capital.

There are an estimated 150 nationalities living in Dubai today and expats make up more than 80% of the population.

## Local Time

The UAE is four hours ahead of UTC (Universal Coordinated Time – formerly known as GMT). Clocks are not altered for daylight saving in the summer, so when Europe and North America gain an hour, the time in the UAE stays the same. During this period the time difference is one hour less, so when it is 12:00 in the UAE it is 09:00 in the UK instead of 08:00 during the winter. The table below shows time differences between the UAE and various cities around the world (not allowing for any daylight savings in those cities).

### Time Zones

| | | | |
|---|---|---|---|
| Amman | -2 | Los Angeles | -12 |
| Athens | -2 | Manama | -1 |
| Auckland | +8 | Mexico City/Dallas | -10 |
| Bangkok | +3 | Moscow | -1 |
| Beijing | +4 | Mumbai | +1.5 |
| Beirut | -2 | Munich | -3 |
| Canberra | +6 | Muscat | 0 |
| Colombo | +2 | New York | -9 |
| Damascus | -2 | Paris | -3 |
| Denver | -11 | Perth | +4 |
| Doha | -1 | Prague | -3 |
| Dublin | -4 | Riyadh | -1 |
| Hong Kong | +4 | Rome | -3 |
| Johannesburg | -2 | Singapore | +4 |
| Karachi | +1 | Sydney | +6 |
| Kuwait City | -1 | Tokyo | +5 |
| London | -4 | Toronto | -9 |
| | | Wellington | +8 |

## Social & Business Hours, Weekends

Working hours differ greatly in the UAE, with much of the private sector working a straight shift (usually from 08:00 to 17:00 or 09:00 to 18:00, with an hour for lunch), while a minority work a split shift (working from 09:00 to 13:00, then taking a long lunch break before returning to work from 16:00 to 19:00). It's not uncommon for working hours in private companies in the UAE to be longer than in other cities. Government offices are generally open from 07:30 to 14:00, Sunday to Thursday. Embassies and consulates operate similar hours, but may designate specific times and days for certain tasks (such as passport applications), so it's best to call before you go. Most embassies take a Friday/Saturday weekend. All will have an emergency number on their answering service, website or on their office doors.

The majority of larger shops and shopping centres are open throughout the day and into the evening, generally closing at 22:00 or midnight. Traditional shops and smaller street traders often operate under split shift timings, closing for three or four hours in the afternoon. Some food outlets and petrol stations are open 24 hours a day.

Friday is the Islamic holy day and therefore a universal day off for offices and schools; most companies and schools have a two-day weekend over Friday and Saturday. Some companies still require a six-day week from their staff, while others operate on a five and a half day system. Consumer demand means that the hospitality and retail industries are open seven days a week.

### Ramadan Hours

According to the labour laws, all companies are obliged to shorten the working day by two hours during Ramadan. Even though this is to assist Muslim employees who are fasting, the law makes no distinction in this regard between Muslim and non-Muslim employees. So technically, even expats are entitled to a shorter working day. However, many international companies do not follow this principle, and labour lawyers would advise you not to make a fuss if you are not given a shorter working day. Some lucky expats do get to work shorter hours during Ramadan, and many businesses, schools and shops change their hours slightly.

Dubai's traffic has a totally different pattern during Ramadan; instead of being gridlocked in the mornings and quiet in the afternoons, the mornings are almost jam-free and you'll sail through all the usual trouble spots, while in the afternoons the roads are totally clogged. Night-time activity increases during Ramadan, with many shops staying open later (until midnight or even 01:00) and the city's many shisha cafes and some restaurants stay open until the early hours.

## Public Holidays

The Islamic calendar starts from the year 622AD, the year of Prophet Muhammad's migration (Hijra) from Mecca to Al Madinah. Hence the Islamic year is called the Hijri year and dates are followed by AH (AH stands for Anno Hegirae, meaning 'after the year of the Hijra').

As some holidays are based on the sighting of the moon and do not have fixed dates on the Hijri calendar, Islamic holidays are more often than not confirmed less than 24 hours in advance. Most companies send an email to employees notifying them of the confirmed holiday date. Some non-religious holidays are fixed according to the Gregorian calendar. It should be noted that the public sector often gets additional days off for holidays where the private sector may not (for example on National Day the public sector gets two days of official holiday, whereas private sector companies take only one day). This can be a problem for working parents,

as schools fall under the public sector and therefore get the extended holidays, so your children will usually have more days off than you do. No problem if you have full-time home help, but if not then you may have to take a day's leave.

### Lunar Calendar

The Hijri calendar is based on lunar months; there are 354 or 355 days in the Hijri year, which is divided into 12 lunar months, and is thus 11 days shorter than the Gregorian year. There are plenty of websites with Gregorian/Hijri calendar conversion tools, so you can find the equivalent Hijri date for any Gregorian date, and vice versa. Try www.rabiah.com/convert.

Below is a list of the holidays and the number of days they last. This applies mainly to the public sector, so if you work in the private sector you may get fewer days per holiday.

The main Muslim festivals are Eid Al Fitr (the festival of the breaking of the fast, which marks the end of Ramadan) and Eid Al Adha (the festival of the sacrifice, which marks the end of the pilgrimage to Mecca).

Mawlid Al Nabee is the holiday celebrating the Prophet Muhammad's birthday, and Lailat Al Mi'raj celebrates the Prophet's ascension into heaven.

### Public Holidays 2010

| | |
|---|---|
| **New Year's Day (1)** | Jan 1 (Fixed) |
| **Mawlid Al Nabee (1)** | Feb 26 (Moon) |
| **Lailat Al Mi'raj (1)** | Jul 9 (Moon) |
| **Eid Al Fitr (3)** | Sep 10 (Moon) |
| **Eid Al Adha (4)** | Nov 16 (Moon) |
| **UAE National Day (2)** | Dec 2 (Fixed) |
| **Islamic New Year's Day (1)** | Dec 7 (Moon) |

Media City

# UAE: Facts & Figures

## Mobile UAE

The World Bank estimated that in 2008, 86% of the UAE population were internet users, but that for every 100 people there were 209 mobile phone subscriptions.

## UAE Free Zones

There are more than 30 free zones in the UAE. Incentives for setting up business in a free zone include 100% foreign ownership, 100% repatriation of profit and 0% tax.

### Dubai GDP By Sector

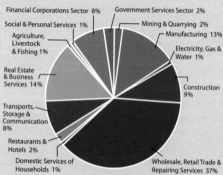

Financial Corporations Sector 8%
Government Services Sector 2%
Social & Personal Services 1%
Mining & Quarrying 2%
Manufacturing 13%
Agriculture, Livestock & Fishing 1%
Electricity, Gas & Water 1%
Real Estate & Business Services 14%
Construction 9%
Transports, Storage & Communication 8%
Restaurants & Hotels 2%
Domestic Services of Households 1%
Wholesale, Retail Trade & Repairing Services 37%

Source: Dubai Statistics Centre, 2007

### UAE GDP By Sector

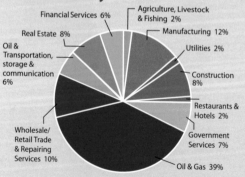

Financial Services 6%
Agriculture, Livestock & Fishing 2%
Real Estate 8%
Manufacturing 12%
Oil & Transportation, storage & communication 6%
Utilities 2%
Construction 8%
Restaurants & Hotels 2%
Wholesale/Retail Trade & Repairing Services 10%
Government Services 7%
Oil & Gas 39%

Source: UAE Yearbook, 2009. Figures shown are for 2007.

### UAE GDP By Emirate

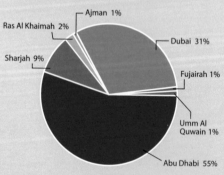

Ajman 1%
Ras Al Khaimah 2%
Dubai 31%
Sharjah 9%
Fujairah 1%
Umm Al Quwain 1%
Abu Dhabi 55%

Source: Minsitry of Economy, 2008

## Temperature & Humidity

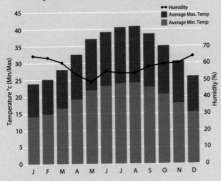

## Rainfall

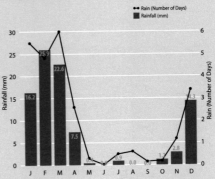

## Education Levels

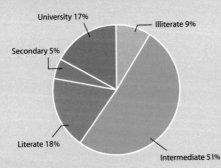

Source: www.tedad.ae and Dubai Statistics Centre

## Population By Emirate

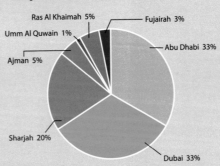

Source: Ministry of Economy, 2007

## Dubai Population Age Breakdown

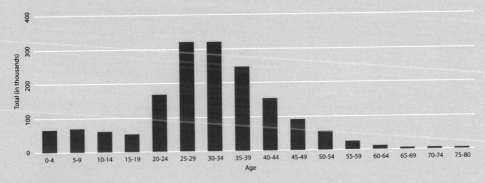

Source: Dubai Statistics Centre, 2008

## Currency

The monetary unit is the dirham (Dhs.), which is divided into 100 fils. The currency is also referred to as AED (Arab Emirate dirham). Notes come in denominations of Dhs.5 (brown), Dhs.10 (green), Dhs.20 (light blue), Dhs.50 (purple), Dhs.100 (pink), Dhs.200 (yellowy-brown), Dhs.500 (blue) and Dhs.1,000 (browny-purple).

The denominations are indicated on the notes in both Arabic and English. To see examples of the UAE's banknotes, visit the website of the Central Bank of the UAE (www.centralbank.ae) and click on 'currency' on the left.

There are only three coins in circulation in the UAE but distinguishing them is tricky because the amount is written in Arabic only. The Dhs.1 coin is the largest, the 50 fils is smaller but seven-sided, and the 25 fils is of a similar size to the 50 fils but is circular. All are silver in colour.

The dirham has been pegged to the US dollar since 1980, at a mid rate of $1 to Dhs.3.6725.

### Exchange Rates

| Foreign Currency | 1 Unit FC = xv Dhs | Dhs1 = xFC |
| --- | --- | --- |
| **Australia** | 3.39 | 0.29 |
| **Bahrain** | 9.74 | 0.1 |
| **Bangladesh** | 0.05 | 18.84 |
| **Canada** | 3.47 | 0.29 |
| **Denmark** | 0.74 | 1.36 |
| **Euro** | 5.48 | 0.18 |
| **Hong Kong** | 0.47 | 2.11 |
| **India** | 0.08 | 12.65 |
| **Japan** | 0.04 | 26.26 |
| **Jordan** | 5.18 | 0.19 |
| **Kuwait** | 12.87 | 0.08 |
| **Malaysia** | 1.08 | 0.92 |
| **New Zealand** | 2.71 | 0.37 |
| **Oman** | 9.54 | 0.10 |
| **Pakistan** | 0.04 | 22.72 |
| **Philippines** | 0.08 | 12.77 |
| **Qatar** | 1.01 | 0.99 |
| **Saudi Arabia** | 0.98 | 1.02 |
| **Singapore** | 2.65 | 0.38 |
| **South Africa** | 0.49 | 2.04 |
| **Sri Lanka** | 0.03 | 31.11 |
| **Sweden** | 0.54 | 1.87 |
| **Switzerland** | 3.63 | 0.28 |
| **Thailand** | 0.11 | 9.03 |
| **UK** | 6.14 | 0.16 |
| **USA** | 3.67 | 0.27 |

Rates correct as of November 2009
Source: www.xe.com

### Exchange Centres

**Al Ansari Exchange** 04 341 4005,
*www.alansariuae.com*
**Al Fardan Exchange** > *p.129* 600 52 2265,
*www.alfardanexchange.com*
**Al Ghurair Exchange** 04 295 5697,
*www.alghurairexchange.com*
**Al Rostamani Travel** 04 353 0500,
*www.alrostamanitravel.com*
**First Gulf Exchange** 04 351 5777, *www.fgb.ae*
**UAE Exchange** 04 341 8822, *www.uaeexchange.com*
**Wall Street Exchange Centre** 04 226 9871,
*www.wallstreet.ae*

# ENVIRONMENT

## Flora & Fauna

While the variety of flora and fauna in the UAE is not as extensive as in some parts of the world, a number of plants and animals have managed to adapt to a life in arid conditions. In addition, the Dubai Municipality has an extensive greening programme in place and areas along the roads are unusually colourful for a desert environment, with grass, palm trees and flowers being constantly maintained by an army of workers and round-the-clock watering. The city also boasts a large number of well-kept parks (see p.246).

### See Them for Yourself

Get out of the city and into some natural habitats. In the sand dunes, mountains and wadis you'll find hardy creatures that survive despite harsh conditions. Don't forget to take a copy of the *UAE Off-Road Explorer* with you – it's the ultimate guide to the best off-road routes in the region.

The region has about 3,500 native plants, which is perhaps surprising considering the high salinity of the soil and the harsh environment. The most famous is, of course, the date palm, which is also the most flourishing of the indigenous flora. In mountainous regions, flat-topped acacia trees and wild grasses create scenery not unlike that of an African savannah. The deserts are unexpectedly green in places, even during the dry summer months, but it takes an experienced botanist to get the most out of the area.

Indigenous fauna includes the Arabian leopard and the ibex, but sightings of them are extremely rare. Realistically, the only large animals you will see are camels and goats (often roaming dangerously close to roads). Other desert life includes the sand cat, sand fox and desert hare, plus gerbils, hedgehogs, snakes and geckos.

Recent studies have shown that the number of species of birds is rising each year, due in part to concerted greening efforts. This is most apparent in the parks, especially in spring and autumn, as the country lies on the route for birds migrating between central Asia and east Africa. You can also see flamingos at the Ras Al Khor Wildlife Sanctuary at the southern end of Dubai Creek.

Off the coast of the UAE, the seas contain a rich abundance of marine life, including tropical fish, jellyfish, coral, the dugong ('sea cow') and sharks. Eight species of whale and seven species of dolphin have been recorded in UAE waters. Various breeds of turtle are also indigenous to the region including the loggerhead, green and hawksbill turtles, all of which are under threat. Sightings are not uncommon by snorkellers and divers off both coasts, particularly at places such as Snoopy Island (p.294) and Khor Kalba (p.292) on the East Coast.

## Environmental Issues

### Water Usage & Desalination

Demand for water from the UAE's growing population means that natural water sources are being depleted faster than their rate of replenishment. As the water table decreases (it has dropped by an average of one metre a year for the past 30 years), saltwater moves inland to fill the gap. This contaminates fresh water, especially near the coast where the increasing salinity of the ground affects the fertility of the soil, hampering farming. It has even affected places as far inland as the Hajar Mountains, where inland freshwater wells have started to dry up in areas close to Masafi, home of the country's most famous brand of bottled water.

The UAE currently has the highest water consumption per capita in the world; UAE residents use an average of 550 litres per person per day compared to 85 litres in Jordan, which has a similar climate. To meet this demand, water desalination complexes have been built around the country (the biggest in the world operates in Jebel Ali), but while solving one issue, desalination creates new problems of its own. As well as the large quantities of highly saline water which are released back into the sea to the detriment of marine life, water desalination plants require vast amounts of energy to operate and are thus major contributors to the UAE's sky-high energy demands.

The UAE has the highest ecological footprint in

---

**Dolphin Friendly?**

2008 saw the opening of two dolphinariums, Dubai Dolphinarium at Creek Park and Dolphin Bay at Atlantis the Palm. Animal welfare organisations have been critical of how the star attractions were acquired, contending that no dolphinarium could ever be big enough to house these magnificent marine creatures, who can swim up to 100km per day in the wild. There was also huge controversy about the addition of sand tiger sharks to Dubai Aquarium and a rescued whale shark who was found a new home in Atlantis' Ambassador Lagoon aquarium, and has yet to be released into the wild. To find out more about dolphins in captivity, log on to www.wdcs.org.

---

the world per capita, according to the WWF's (World Wide Fund for Nature) Living Planet Report 2008. The energy and water consumption levels are also some of the highest in the world, and its residents are among the highest waste producers.

Despite high level support for ecological issues (the late Sheikh Zayed was awarded the WWF's Gold Panda Award in 1997 for his environmental efforts), at ground level there is still a long way to go before environmental awareness and action reaches the levels of developed countries in Europe and around the world.

Conservationists assert that the massive construction for projects in the Arabian Gulf, such as the Palm Islands and Dubai Waterfront, will destroy coral reefs and fish stocks, as well as damage breeding grounds for endangered species such as the hawksbill turtle. The developers, however, argue that the sites will attract sealife, and point to the recent increase in fish and marine life witnessed around the crescent on the Palm Jumeirah. One strange by-product of this development is that due to the crescent being six kilometres out to sea, certain species of shark that wouldn't normally come so close to the land have been spotted around the beaches. Similarly, developments like Dubailand are impacting the desert landscape and its wildlife. Of the animals that can survive in this naturally harsh environment, those that disappear from the area due to construction work will be very difficult to reintroduce. It remains a contentious issue though as, arguably, the greening of new residential areas has resulted in an increase in vegetation and a rise in bird and insect life in these areas.

---

**WATER RETENTION**   Habiba Al Marashi chairperson, Emirates Environmental Group

*There is an urgent need for all sectors to save water. The solutions vary from simple to complicated ones like checking for leaks, turning taps off, using a pail of water for washing cars, using water saving fixtures and recycling water to name a few. However saving water requires a conscious effort on our part that we are saving a precious and expensive resource.*

# Going Green

## Responsibility

Perhaps as a result of living in a nation inhabited by a vast majority of expatriates, the average UAE resident feels little responsibility towards the country's environment. Expats from countries where 'green' initiatives, such as household recycling, are commonplace may be surprised by the lack of awareness and facilities for similar schemes in the UAE. Government efforts, such as the ban on plastic carrier bags, are heading in the right direction but are slow to take effect. In the meantime, there is a pressing need for all residents to start making a personal contribution to reduce the impact of their presence.

## Recycling

On the recycling front, UAE residents are becoming more proactive. The Emirates Environmental Group (p.319) has reported a large increase in its schools, corporate and community recycling drives which collect paper, plastic, glass, aluminium and toner cartridges. Mobile phones, broken computers and all kinds of electronic equipment can be recycled through the EnviroFone campaign (www.enviroserve.ae/envirofone) or at your nearest Plug-ins store (800 758 4467). Emirates Hills is one of Dubai's few residential areas to have an official recycling collection service for glass, paper, cans and plastic bottles (800 732 9253, www.zenathrecycling.ae). If your area doesn't have a recycling scheme, it can involve rather a lot of administrative wrangling with the developer or community management company, but it's worth bringing the issue to the attention of your residents' committee to build support and put pressure on the developers. In the meantime, you can always take your own waste to the recycling bins dotted around Dubai. The municipality has installed recycling bins for paper, glass and plastic at petrol stations and bus stops, and some supermarkets like HyperPanda (p.392) and Spinneys (p.392) have recycling bins outside. In addition, large cages for collecting recyclable materials have been installed on Al Wasl Road near Safa Park, at Mirdiff Recycling Centre and on the service road near to the Shangri-La on Sheikh Zayed Road. Keep your eyes peeled – your nearest bins won't be far away.

If everyone in the world was to live like the average UAE resident, calculations suggest that 4.5 planets would be needed to provide the natural resources. Indisputably, the UAE is living beyond its ecological means and habits have to change.

## Small Efforts For Big Changes

The first step towards a greener way of life in the UAE is simply to consider the three Rs – Reduce, Reuse and Recycle. Look for a positive and practical change that you can make to a routine – like switching off the lights when you leave a room – and make it a habit. Once you've done that, don't rest on your laurels – find the next change that you can make, and the next. You'll soon find that looking for ways to use the three Rs becomes habit in itself, influencing your buying decisions, your product consumption and usage levels.

> *Consider the three Rs – Reduce, Reuse and Recycle. Look for a positive and practical change that you can make to a routine and make it a habit. Once you've done that, don't rest on your laurels – find the next change that you can make, and the next.*

## Getting Started

It's easy to start making positive environmental changes in your own home which contribute to a greener Dubai. Here are a few suggestions to get you on your way:

- It is estimated that 35% of Dubai's waste is organic matter – kitchen and garden waste. Cut down on wasted produce in your own household by planning your meals for the week ahead, before you head to the supermarket. Write a shopping list and only buy items which are on the list so that you know you'll be able to use them up before they go bad.
- The average resident of the UAE consumes more than double the amount of energy of citizens in countries such as France and the UK, and more than even America, traditionally the worst ecological offender. Simple actions such as turning your air conditioning up by a few degrees or replacing traditional light bulbs with energy efficient ones can have a big impact on your energy usage. Find energy saving inspiration and work out your carbon and money savings at www.heroesoftheuae.ae.
- Opt for water coolers rather than buying bottled water – a 5 gallon bottle contains nearly 19 litres, meaning you will only use a fraction of the number of plastic bottles over the course of a year – and most water companies recycle or re-use water cooler bottles as well.
- Do you really need that litre of milk right now, or can you pick one up on your way to somewhere else later? Think twice before jumping in the car for small errands, and try to combine trips to cut car usage and emissions.
- Cover your pool in the summer. An uncovered pool loses up to 3,785 litres of water per month through evaporation.
- Unplug your phone charger. Between 65% and 95% of the energy used by mobile phone chargers is wasted by leaving them plugged in when not in use.
- Create your own desert oasis and choose native plants for your back yard to cut down on the volumes needed for daily watering.
- Make the most of Dubai's arid climate and dry your laundry in the open air rather than using the tumble dryer.
- By 2013, plastic bags will be outlawed in Dubai. Invest in reusable carriers or trendy jute bags for your weekly shop and save on the millions of plastic bags which go into landfill every year.
- If you've got some time on your hands why not get involved with a volunteer programme. See p.124 for more details.
- Dubai Municipality's 'Bulky Waste Collection Service' (04 206 4231) will pick up old home appliances and dispose of them in a safe and environmentally friendly manner. If there's still life in your appliances, extend their useful life by selling them at the flea market (p.395) or online at www.dubizzle.com.
- All aboard! The launch of Dubai Metro is the perfect chance to switch to public transport and cut down on your car usage. Find out more on p.55.

### Environmental Initiatives & Organisations

On the positive side, the UAE government and the local municipalities have started making efforts towards reducing waste and consumption and raising environmental awareness. Masdar City in Abu Dhabi is being hailed as a ground-breaking green project and will be the world's first waste-free, carbon-neutral city (www.masdarcity.ae). By 2012, plastic carrier bags will have been phased out across the country. There are various green building codes in place and in 2009, the Dubai Department of Tourism and Commerce Marketing (DTCM) announced an initiative to reduce carbon emissions in the hospitality industry by 20% by 2011.

The government effort is being accelerated by various environmental organisations who aim to protect the environment, as well as to educate the population on the importance of environmental issues. The Environment Agency Abu Dhabi (www.ead.ae) assists the Abu Dhabi government in the conservation and management of the emirate's natural environment, resources, wildlife and biological diversity.

Sir Bani Yas Island, which is part of the Abu Dhabi emirate, is home to an internationally acclaimed breeding programme for endangered wildlife. Created as a private wildlife sanctuary by the late Sheikh Zayed, it is now an exclusive eco-resort (02 801 5400, www.anantara.com).

Emirates Wildlife Society is a national environmental NGO that operates in association with the WWF (www.panda.org/uae). In addition, The Breeding Centre for Endangered Arabian Wildlife (06 531 1212) at Sharjah Desert Park, has a successful breeding programme for wildlife under threat, particularly the Arabian leopard. The breeding centre

is off-limits to visitors but the Arabian Wildlife Centre (p.281), also at the Desert Park, is open to the public. See also Environmental Groups (p.319).

# BUSINESS & COMMERCE

## Overview

The UAE is considered the second richest Arab country, after Qatar, on a per capita basis. The country has just under 10% of the world's proven oil reserves (most of it within Abu Dhabi emirate) and the fourth largest natural gas reserves.

Prior to the crash of 2008-09, the UAE enjoyed the benefits of a thriving economy growing at a rate of over 7% a year. In 2008, the UAE economy was worth Dhs.535.6 billion, with Abu Dhabi contributing 57% and Dubai 32% of the GDP.

Successful economic diversification means that the UAE's wealth is not solely reliant on oil revenue and in 2007, over 64% of the GDP was generated by non-oil sectors. In Dubai, the most economically diverse of the Emirates, oil revenues accounted for around half of Dubai's GDP 20 years ago, whereas in 2007 the oil sector contributed just 3%. It is expected that by 2010, oil will account for less than 1% of total GDP.

Across the country, trade, finance, manufacturing, tourism, construction, real estate and communications are playing an increasingly important part in the national economy. Other sectors such as publishing, recruitment, advertising and IT, while not as developed in terms of size, have been steadily growing in Dubai and Abu Dhabi, aided in part by the various free zones.

Media City

However, don't be fooled by the high national income into thinking that the average expat coming to work in Dubai will automatically be on a huge salary. The wealth isn't spread evenly and even before the financial crisis, the salaries for most types of jobs, with the exception of highly skilled professionals, were dropping. This downward trend is attributed in part to the willingness of workers to accept a position at a very low wage. While the UAE GDP per capita income was estimated at Dhs.93,000 in 2007, this figure includes all sections of the community and the average labourer, of which there are many, can expect to earn as little as Dhs.600 ($165) per month.

While the unemployment level of the National population in the UAE is lower than that of many other Arab states, there are still a significant number of Emiratis out of work (over 30,000, according to some estimates). This is partly due to a preference for public sector work and partly because of qualifications, and salary expectations, not matching the skills required in the private sector. However, the government is trying to reverse this scenario and reduce unemployment in the local sector with a 'Nationalisation' or 'Emiratisation' programme (which is common to countries throughout the region). The eventual goal is to rely less on an expat workforce, which will be achieved by improving vocational training and by making it compulsory for certain types of companies, such as banks, to hire a set percentage of Emiratis.

Traditional architecture

## Trade

A long trading tradition, which earned Dubai its reputation as 'the city of merchants' in the Middle East, continues to be an important consideration for foreign companies looking at opportunities in the region today. It is reflected not just in an open and liberal regulatory environment, but also in the local business community's familiarity with international commercial practices and the city's cosmopolitan lifestyle. Strategically located between Europe and the far east, Dubai attracts multinational and private companies wishing to tap the lucrative Middle Eastern, Indian and African markets (which have a combined population of over two billion). The country's main export partners are Saudi Arabia, Iran, Japan, India, Singapore, South Korea and Oman. The main import partners are Japan, USA, UK, Italy, Germany and South Korea.

Annual domestic imports exceed $116 billion and Dubai is the gateway to over $150 billion (annually) in trade.

## Tourism

The UAE is well ahead of many other cities in the Middle East in terms of travel and tourism. Boosting tourism plays a central part in the government's economic diversification plans and is a major driving force behind the array of record-breaking tourism, infrastructure and hospitality developments announced over the past few years.

The development of these high-end tourist amenities and visitor attractions, in conjunction with an aggressive overseas marketing campaign, means that Dubai is swiftly becoming a popular holiday destination. It is striving to reach its target of attracting 15 million visitors a year by 2010 and 40 million by 2015 and despite tough economic conditions, the number of tourists coming to Dubai is still on the rise. The city's hotels and hotel apartments accommodated 7.5 million guests in 2008, an increase of 7.7% on the previous year. During the first half of 2009, Dubai International Airport was the only one of the world's top 20 airports to report any growth in traffic and the number of guests staying in Dubai's hotels grew by 5% in comparison to the same period of 2008.

Abu Dhabi's sights are set on 3.3 million tourists by 2015 and 7.9 million tourists by 2030, and over the last few years has followed Dubai's lead, announcing multi-billion dollar tourism developments. These include Yas Island, the venue for the 2009 Abu Dhabi Formula 1 Grand Prix, and Saadiyat Island, home to a proposed Louvre Gallery, a Guggenheim Museum and a host of other cultural attractions.

In Dubai, work on some key tourism developments is still going ahead, despite the gloomy economic conditions and in 2009, major projects such as Dubai Metro (p.55) were completed. Work continues on some of Dubai's most ambitious ventures including the world's tallest construction, Burj Dubai, Palm Jebel Ali – the second of the three Palm Islands, Meydan – an urban community centred around a new horseracing track, the vast Dubai Sports City and the residential district of Al Furjan. Other developments have fallen victim to the credit crunch and are either delayed, cancelled or on indefinite hold (see Main Developers, p.73).

## Growth & The Crash

The pace of economic growth in Dubai over the last 20 years has been incredible. Trade alone has grown at more than 9% per annum over the past 10 years and the population has almost doubled since 1990.

Over the last decade, legislation and government institutions have been honed to reduce bureaucracy and create a constructive business environment. Free zones, such as Internet City, Media City and Healthcare City, offering financial incentives to encourage international business, flourished and multiplied (see Free Zones, p.120) and multi-billion dollar mega project proposals such as the three Palm Island projects, Dubai Sports City and Burj Dubai, were the result of the government's active promotion of investment in Dubai.

### Really Tax Free?

Do taxes exist in the UAE? Yes and no. You don't pay income or sales tax, except when you purchase alcohol from a licensed liquor store – when you'll be hit with a steep 30% tax. The main tax that you will come across is the municipality tax of 5% on rent and 10% on food, beverages and rooms in hotels. The rest are hidden taxes in the form of 'fees', such as your car registration renewal, visa/permit fees and Salik (road toll).

When the financial crisis hit in late 2008, the UAE, along with the rest of the world, seemed caught unawares. Within a few short months, the country was reeling with Dubai feeling the full brunt of the crisis, while Abu Dhabi's oil revenues shielded it from the worst of the effects. Daily reports of mass redundancies, cancelled projects, company closures and absconding business owners sent shock waves through the economy and the property market all but collapsed. By September 2009, house prices in Dubai were at 48% of their peak, with some experts forecasting a decline of a further 20% by the year end. A report by research company Proleads estimated that 29% of construction projects in the UAE were either on hold or cancelled by September 2009.

At the end of 2009, the future remained uncertain. The economy is expected to post negative growth

for the first time in recent history and analysts predict that Dubai's population will contract as a result of mass redundancies. However, what many see as the green shoots of recovery are starting to be seen. The International Monetary Fund (IMF) expected the UAE's GDP to contract by 0.2% in 2009, but to grow again in 2010 by around 2.4%. Inflation, which was spiralling out of control in the years running up to the crash, reaching a bloated 12.3 % in 2008, is expected to fall to an all time low of 2.5% in 2009, before normalising at around 3.3% in 2010.

Feelings of positivity have been buoyed by both Abu Dhabi and Dubai successfully staging major world firsts in the closing months of 2009, with the inaugural Abu Dhabi Formula 1 Grand Prix and the opening of Dubai Metro. Some companies have started hiring again, and, in both of the UAE's major cities, construction work continues on many key projects.

Rental prices in Dubai have dropped significantly, allowing many expats to upgrade their accommodation to standards well beyond expectation, and if nothing else, the mass exodus has meant that traffic on inner city roads has improved dramatically.

With its vast oil reserves to buffer the impact, it's likely that the UAE's economy is resilient enough to recover in the long-run. Popular opinion maintains that the country's unbridled ambition needed a healthy does of realism and that the economy will be all the stronger for it in the long run. Although Dubai was the most effected of the seven emirates by the global credit crunch, it remains part of a successful federal economy, and despite the financial downturn, the UAE is still one of the world's richest countries on a per capita basis. For its own part, Dubai will doubtlessly bounce back, albeit in a little more humble fashion.

# CULTURE & LIFESTYLE

## Culture

The UAE manages what some Arab cities fail to achieve: a healthy balance between western influences and eastern traditions. Its culture is still very much rooted in the Islamic customs that deeply penetrate the Arabian Peninsula and beyond. However, the country's effort to become modern and cosmopolitan is proof of an open-minded and liberal outlook.

Islam is more than just a religion; it is a way of life that governs even mundane everyday events, from what to wear to what to eat and drink. Therefore, the culture and heritage of the UAE is closely linked to its religion. However, the UAE is tolerant and welcoming; foreigners are free to practise their own religion, alcohol is served in hotels and the dress code is liberal. Women face little discrimination and, contrary to the policies of neighbouring Saudi Arabia, are able to

Arabian heritage

# Culture & Lifestyle

drive and walk around uncovered and unescorted.

The rapid economic development over the last 30 years has changed life in the Emirates beyond recognition. However, the country's rulers are committed to safeguarding their heritage. They are therefore keen to promote cultural and sporting events that are representative of their traditions, such as falconry, camel racing and traditional dhow sailing. Arabic culture in poetry, dancing, songs and traditional art and craftsmanship is encouraged.

## Cross Culture

The Sheikh Mohammed Centre for Cultural Understanding (04 353 6666, www.cultures.ae) was established to help bridge the gap between cultures and give visitors a clearer appreciation of the Emirati way of life. It organises tours of Jumeira Mosque where you can learn about Islam.

Courtesy and hospitality are the most highly prized virtues, and visitors are likely to experience the genuine warmth and friendliness of the Emirati people. Luckily, the negative view of Islam that has affected many Muslims living abroad has not had an impact on Dubai, where you'll find people of various nationalities and religions working and living side by side without conflict. In Islam, the family unit is very important and elders are respected for their experience and wisdom. It's common for several generations to live together in the same house. Polygamy is practised in the UAE, with Islam allowing a man to have up to four wives at one time, providing he has the financial and physical means to treat each of them equally. However, a Muslim man taking more than one wife is more the exception than the norm, and most Muslim families resemble the traditional western family unit: mum, dad and kids.

Weddings are important cultural occasions; the men and women celebrate separately with feasting and music. They are usually very large affairs; however, the government has placed a ceiling of Dhs.50,000 on dowries, and overly lavish weddings can result in a prison sentence or Dhs.500,000 fine. The government-sponsored Marriage Fund, based in Abu Dhabi, assists Emiratis with marriage, from counselling and financial assistance (long term loans up to Dhs.70,000 for a UAE National man marrying a UAE National woman) to organising group weddings to keep costs down. With so many UAE Nationals studying abroad, and so many expats in Dubai, inter-cultural marriages are increasingly common. The Marriage Fund strongly encourages Nationals to marry fellow Nationals (in an effort to preserve the culture and reduce the number of UAE spinsters), although it is easier for a National man to marry a non-National woman than it is for a National woman to marry a non-National man.

When you first arrive you may find many aspects of the local culture seem very strange to you. Take time to observe and understand before you pass judgement; you'll soon realise that the many different nationalities living here make it a sometimes-frustrating but ultimately fascinating city.

## Language

Arabic is the official language of the UAE, although English, Hindi, Malayalam and Urdu are commonly spoken. Arabic is the official business language, but English is so widely used that you could conduct business here for years without learning a single word of Arabic. Most road signs, shop signs and restaurant menus are in both languages. The further out of town you go, the more you will find just Arabic, both spoken and on street and shop signs.

Arabic isn't the easiest language to pick up, or to pronounce. But if you can throw in a couple of words here and there, you're more likely to receive a warmer welcome or at least a smile – even if your pronunciation is terrible. See the box on the right for a list of useful Arabic phrases, and p.19 for Arabic language courses.

## Religion

Islam is the official religion of the UAE, and is widely practised. The Islamic holy day is Friday. The basis of Islam is the belief that there is only one God and that Prophet Muhammad is his messenger. The faith shares a common ancestry with Christianity and many of the prophets before Muhammad can be found in Christian as well as Muslim writings. There are five pillars of Islam which all Muslims must follow: the Profession of Faith, Prayer, Charity, Fasting and Pilgrimage. Every Muslim is expected, at least once in his or her lifetime, to make the pilgrimage (Hajj) to the holy city of Mecca (also spelt Makkah) in Saudi Arabia.

## Arabic Family Names

Arabic names have a formal structure that traditionally indicates the person's family and tribe. Names are usually taken from an important person in the Quran or someone from the tribe. This is followed by the word bin (son of) for a boy or bint (daughter of) for a girl, and then the name of the child's father. The last name indicates the person's tribe or family. For prominent families, this has Al, the Arabic word for 'the', immediately before it. For instance, the President of the UAE is His Highness Sheikh Khalifa bin Zayed Al Nahyan. When women get married, they do not change their name.

Additionally, a Muslim is required to pray (facing Mecca) five times a day. The times vary according to the position of the sun. Most people pray at a mosque, although it's not unusual to see people kneeling by the side of the road if they are not near a place of worship. It is considered impolite to stare at people praying or to walk over prayer mats. The modern-day call to prayer, transmitted through loudspeakers on the minarets of each mosque, ensures that everyone knows it's time to pray.

While the predominant religion is Islam, the UAE is tolerant of many other denominations, and the ruling family has, on numerous occasions, donated plots of land for the building of churches. Christian churches of various denominations have been built in clusters on Oud Metha Road and in Jebel Ali, and there is a Hindu temple in Bur Dubai (see Churches, p.45).

# National Dress

On the whole, Emiratis wear traditional dress in public. For men this is the dishdasha or khandura: a white full length shirt dress, which is worn with a white or red checked headdress, known as a gutra or sifrah. This is secured with a black cord (agal). Sheikhs and important businessmen may also wear a thin black or brown robe (known as a bisht), over their dishdasha at important events, which is equivalent to the dinner jacket in western culture.

In public, women wear the black abaya – a long, loose black robe that covers their normal clothes – plus a headscarf called a sheyla. The abaya is often of very sheer, flowing fabric and may be open at the

## BASIC ARABIC

### General

| | |
|---|---|
| Yes | na'am |
| No | la |
| Please | min fadlak (m) |
| | min fadliki (f) |
| Thank you | shukran |
| Please (in offering) | tafaddal (m) |
| | tafaddali (f) |
| Praise be to God | al-hamdu l-illah |
| God willing | in shaa'a l-laah |

### Greetings

| | |
|---|---|
| Greeting (peace be upon you) | |
| | as-salaamu alaykom |
| Greeting (in reply) | |
| | wa alaykom is salaam |
| Good morning | sabah il-khayr |
| Good morning (in reply) | |
| | sabah in-nuwr |
| Good evening | masa il-khayr |
| Good evening (in reply) | |
| | masa in-nuwr |
| Hello | marhaba |
| Hello (in reply) | marhabtayn |
| How are you? | |
| | kayf haalak (m) / kayf haalik (f) |
| Fine, thank you | |
| | zayn, shukran (m) |
| | zayna, shukran (f) |
| Welcome | ahlan wa sahlan |
| Welcome (in reply) | |
| | ahlan fiyk (m) / ahlan fiyki (f) |
| Goodbye | ma is-salaama |

### Introductions

| | |
|---|---|
| My name is... | ismiy… |
| What is your name? | |
| | shuw ismak (m) / shuw ismik (f) |

| | |
|---|---|
| Where are you from? | |
| | min wayn inta (m) / |
| | min wayn inti (f) |
| I am from… | anaa min... |
| America | ameriki |
| Britain | braitani |
| Europe | oropi |
| India | al hindi |

### Questions

| | |
|---|---|
| How many / much? | kam? |
| Where? | wayn? |
| When? | mataa? |
| Which? | ayy? |
| How? | kayf? |
| What? | shuw? |
| Why? | laysh? |
| Who? | miyn? |
| To/for | ila |
| In/at | fee |
| From | min |
| And | wa |
| Also | kamaan |
| There isn't | maa fee |

### Taxi Or Car Related

| | |
|---|---|
| Is this the road to... | hadaa al |
| | tariyq ila... |
| Stop | kuf |
| Right | yamiyn |
| Left | yassar |
| Straight ahead | siydaa |
| North | shamaal |
| South | januwb |
| East | sharq |
| West | garb |
| Turning | mafraq |
| First | awwal |

| | |
|---|---|
| Second | thaaniy |
| Road | tariyq |
| Street | shaaria |
| Roundabout | duwwaar |
| Signals | ishaara |
| Close to | qarib min |
| Petrol station | mahattat betrol |
| Sea/beach | il bahar |
| Mountain/s | jabal/jibaal |
| Desert | al sahraa |
| Airport | mataar |
| Hotel | funduq |
| Restaurant | mata'am |
| Slow Down | schway schway |

### Accidents & Emergencies

| | |
|---|---|
| Police | al shurtaa |
| Permit/licence | rukhsaa |
| Accident | haadith |
| Papers | waraq |
| Insurance | ta'miyn |
| Sorry | aasif (m) / |
| | aasifa (f) |

### Numbers

| | |
|---|---|
| Zero | sifr |
| One | waahad |
| Two | ithnayn |
| Three | thalatha |
| Four | arba'a |
| Five | khamsa |
| Six | sitta |
| Seven | saba'a |
| Eight | thamaanya |
| Nine | tiss'a |
| Ten | ashara |
| Hundred | miya |
| Thousand | alf |

## Dressing Down

Sharjah has a less liberal attitude to dress code and moral behaviour. 'Indecent dress' includes anything that exposes the stomach, back, shoulders or legs above the knees. Tight-fitting, transparent clothing is also best avoided, as are acts of vulgarity, indecent noises or harassment.

front. Some women also wear a thin black veil hiding their face and/or gloves, and older women sometimes still wear a leather mask, known as a burkha, which covers the nose, brow and cheekbones. Underneath the abaya, women traditionally wear a long tunic over loose, flowing trousers (sirwall), which are often heavily embroidered and fitted at the wrists and ankles. However, these are used more by the older generation and modern women will often wear the latest fashions from international labels under their abayas.

# Food & Drink

You can eat your way around the world in Dubai – it is home to every cuisine imaginable, from European and American to Indian and Asian. Alongside a glut of fine-dining options, you can find cheaper fare at the many street cafes, independent restaurants and fast-food chains.

In terms of food shopping, supermarkets stock a range of products from around the world to keep their multinational client base happy. Waitrose is a luxury British supermarket; Spinneys and Park n Shop stock British and South African products including Waitrose-branded items, Safestway sells more American items, and Choithram has a mix of both. Carrefour, HyperPanda and Géant are huge and stock products from just about everywhere (see Supermarkets & Hypermarkets, p.391). Fruit and vegetables are imported from around the world, and so can be a bit more expensive than buying local produce. Look out for locally grown cucumbers, tomatoes, aubergines, courgettes, green peppers and potatoes, all of which are extremely cheap. For a more colourful food-buying experience, head to the fruit and vegetable market off Emirates Road where you can bulk buy various fruits and vegetables at bargain prices (p.395). The fish market in Deira offers a seemingly unlimited range of fresh fish and seafood at low prices, and the buzzing atmosphere is worth the trip in itself (p.395).

## Arabic Cuisine

Culturally speaking, eating in the Middle East is traditionally a social affair. Whether eating at home with extended families, or out with large groups, the custom is for everybody to share a veritable feast of various dishes, served in communal bowls. Starters are generally enjoyed with flat Arabic bread, and main courses are often eaten with the fingers.

The Arabic food available in Dubai is based predominantly on Lebanese cuisine. Common dishes are shawarmas (lamb or chicken carved from a spit and served in a pita bread with salad and tahina), falafel (mashed chickpeas and sesame seeds, rolled into balls and deep fried), hummus (a creamy dip made from chickpeas and olive oil), and tabbouleh (finely chopped parsley, mint and crushed wheat). Drinking Arabic coffee (kahwa) is an important social ritual in the Middle East. Local coffee is mild with a distinctive taste of cardamom and saffron. It is served black without sugar, but is accompanied by dates to sweeten the palate between sips.

## Emirati Cuisine

There are also opportunities to sample Emirati food while in Dubai. The legacy of the UAE's trading past means that local cuisine uses a blend of ingredients imported from Asia and the Middle East. Dried limes are a common ingredient, reflecting a Persian influence; they impart a distinctively musty, tangy, sour flavour to soups and stews. Spices such as cinnamon, saffron and turmeric along with nuts (almonds or pistachios) and dried fruit add interesting flavours to Emirati dishes. Look out for Al Harees, a celebratory dish made from meat and wheat, slow-cooked in a clay pot or oven for hours, and Al Majboos, in which meat and rice are cooked in a stock made from local spices and dried limes. Fish is widely used in local cuisine, both freshly caught and preserved. Al Madrooba is a dish which uses local salted fish, prepared in a thick, buttery sauce. Use the Cuisine Finder on p.438 to find the pick of Arabic and Emirati restaurants.

## Pork

Pork is taboo in Islam. Muslims should not eat, prepare or serve pork. In order for a restaurant to serve pork on its menu, it should have a separate fridge, preparation equipment and cooking area. Supermarkets are also required to sell pork in a separate area and Spinneys, Park n Shop, Waitrose and Choithram all have a screened-off pork section. As pork is not locally produced you will find that it's more expensive than many other meats. In restaurants, where bacon appears on a menu, you will usually be served beef or veal bacon. All meat products for Muslim consumption have to be halal, which refers to the method of slaughter.

## Alcohol

Alcohol is only served in licensed outlets associated with hotels (restaurants and bars), plus a few leisure clubs (such as golf clubs and sports clubs) and associations. Restaurants outside of hotels that are not part of a club or association are not permitted to serve alcohol. For more information on liquor licences see p.42.

# Cultural Dos & Don'ts

You'll find that in general, people in the UAE are patient when it comes to cultural etiquette and are keen to explain their customs to you. However, there are a few cultural dos and don'ts that you should be aware of to avoid causing offence to others.

## PDAs

Not a reference to the latest handheld gadget but to public displays of affection: these are a no no in the UAE and anything more than an innocent peck on the cheek will at best earn you disapproving looks from passers by.

## Appropriate Attire

While beachwear is fine on the beach, you should dress a little more conservatively when out and about in public places. If in doubt, ensuring that your shoulders and knees are covered is a safe bet. That said, when out at bars and clubs in the evening, pretty much anything goes. A pashmina is always useful for the journey home or in case the air conditioning is set to 'deep freeze'. .

## Photography

Dubai is full of snap-worthy sights and normal tourist photography is fine. Like anywhere in the Arab world, it is courteous to ask permission before photographing people, particularly women. In general, photographs of government and military buildings should not be taken.

## Arabic Coffee

It's likely that you'll be served traditional Arabic coffee (kahwa) during formal business meetings. This is an important social ritual in the Middle East so be polite and drink some when offered. Cups should be taken in the right hand and if there is a waiter standing by, replenishing your cup, the signal to say that you have had enough is to gently shake the cup from side to side.

## Meeting People

Long handshakes, kisses and warm greetings are common when meeting people in the Middle East. It's normal to shake hands with people when you are introduced to them, although if you are meeting someone of the opposite sex, be aware that a handshake may not always be welcome. It's best to take your cue from the other person and not offer your hand unless they first offer theirs. It's polite to send greetings to a person's family, but can be considered rude to enquire directly about someone's wife, sister or daughter. You may see men greeting each other with a nose kiss; this is a customary greeting in the Gulf region but is only used between close friends and associates and you should not attempt to greet someone in this way.

## Out On The Town

Dubai has a good variety of nightlife and alcohol is widely available in hotel bars, pubs and clubs (see Going Out, p.430). Remember, however, that you're in a Muslim country and drunken or lewd behaviour is not only disrespectful but can lead to arrest and detention.

## Business Etiquette

Business meetings in the region will usually start with introductions and small talk before you get down to business. Business cards will be exchanged – you should treat them with respect as an extension of the person who gave them. Punctuality to meetings is important and arriving late is considered to be very bad mannered. Do not assume, however, that your meeting will start at the appointed time or that once started it will not be interrupted.

## Home Values

When visiting an Emirati home it is customary to remove your shoes, however, it's best to take your cue from your host. Traditionally, men and women dine separately and meals are eaten while seated on floor cushions. When you sit, be carefully not to point your feet at anyone or to show the soles of your feet. Mealtimes are long and leisurely and as a guest your plate will be heaped high. Try everything offered but if you're not sure you'll like something, take a small amount that you can finish. If you invite a Muslim to your home, you should not offer pork or alcohol, as this may cause offence.

Nevertheless, permanent residents who are non-Muslims can get a liquor licence (p.42) which allows them to obtain alcohol for consumption at home.

## Shisha

Smoking the traditional shisha (water pipe) is a popular and relaxing pastime enjoyed throughout the Middle East. It is usually savoured in a local cafe while chatting with friends. They are also known as hookah pipes or hubbly bubbly, but the proper name is nargile. Shisha pipes can be smoked with a variety of aromatic flavours, such as strawberry, grape or apple, and the experience is unlike normal cigarette or cigar smoking. The smoke is 'smoothed' by the water, creating a much more soothing effect (although it still causes smoking related health problems). QD's (p.514) and Chandelier (p.466)

### Dates

One of the very few crops that thrive naturally across the Middle East, date palms have been cultivated for around 5,000 years. It's said that in some countries the Bedouin way of life was sustained primarily by dates and camel milk up until as recently as the mid 20th century. High in energy, fibre, potassium, vitamins, magnesium and iron, with negligible quantities of fat, cholesterol and salt, dates are a cheap and healthy snack. Just five dates per day provide enough nutrition for one recommended daily portion of fruit or vegetables.

## Tipping

It is entirely up to the individual whether to tip for services and it is not a fixed expectation as you find in other countries. Some people in Dubai choose not

to tip at all, but for those who feel that the service was worth recognising, the usual amount is 10% and tips are greatly appreciated. An increasing number of restaurants now also include a service charge on the bill, although it's not clear whether this ever sees the inside of your waiter's pockets, so some people add a little extra. Tips in restaurants and bars are often shared with other staff. See Going Out for more information (p.430).

For taxi drivers, it is regular practice to round up your fare as a tip, but this is not compulsory, so feel free to pay just the fare, especially if his driving standards were poor. For tipping when collecting your valet-parked car at hotels, around Dhs.5 is average. At petrol stations, especially when you get your windows cleaned, it's common practice to give a few dirhams as a tip. In beauty salons, spas and hairdressers, tipping is at your discretion but around 10% of the treatment price is an acceptable amount.

# LOCAL MEDIA

## Newspapers & Magazines

The UAE has a number of daily English language broadsheets – the cream of the crop is definitely *The National*; arguably the region's first national newspaper offering quality journalism, intelligent editorial and meaty lifestyle pieces. Other titles include *Gulf News*, *Khaleej Times* and *Gulf Today*.

In most areas of Dubai, you can also pick up a free copy of *7Days*, a tabloid-size newspaper published five days a week that features local and international news, business and entertainment news, and a sports section. An international edition of British publication *The Times* is also printed and distributed in Dubai.

There are plenty of local magazines, including a range of Middle Eastern editions of international titles that are produced here (examples include *OK!*, *Grazia*, *Harpers Bazaar* and *Stuff*). Keep an eye out for expat titles like *liveworkexplore* (Explorer's bi-monthly lifestyle magazine targeted directly at expats), *Connector* and *Aquarius*, as well as for listings magazines such as *TimeOut Dubai* and *What's On*.

### Censorship

International magazines are available in bookshops and supermarkets, at greatly inflated prices. All international titles are examined by the censor. You'll also notice that kissing scenes are usually cut from shows and films, both at the cinema and on TV, which can turn a raunchy romance into a fleeting affair. In contrast the censorship of violent scenes and swear words are little more sporadic.

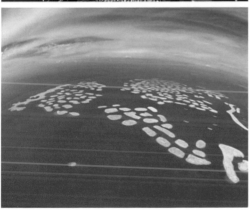

2009 Winner "Cover ot the Year award", International Printed Publication Awards, Moscow
2009 Winner "Book Cover Advertising Professional", PX3 Prix de la Photographie Paris
2009 Winner Architecture, PX3 Prix de la Photographie Paris
2009 Winner Travel and Tourism, PX3 Prix de la Photographie Paris
2009 Winner Gold Lux Interiors. Spain National Photography Awards, Barcelona

t. +97150 844 85 64     e. contact@vromero.com     w. www.vromero.com

## Local Media

### Radio

The UAE has a number of commercial radio stations broadcasting in a range of languages. The leading English stations operate 24 hours a day:

**Dubai 92:** current music, competitions and popular DJs, 92.00FM, www.dubai92.com

**Dubai Eye:** quality talk radio, 103.8FM, www.dubaieye1038.com

**Virgin Radio:** Hit music along the lines of Virgin Radio in other cities, 104.4FM, www.virginradiodubai.com

**Channel 4:** contemporary music for a younger audience, 104.8FM, www.channel4FM.com

**The Coast:** Middle of the road and classic hits throughout the day, 103.2FM, www.1032thecoast.com

**Radio 1:** hit music broadcast across the country, 104.1FM, www.gulfnews.com/radio1

**Radio 2:** contemporary music broadcast throughout the UAE, 99.3FM, www.gulfnews.com/radio2

### Television

Local TV is in a state of continuous improvement – gone are the days when all you could watch was early episodes of *ER* and *Mad About You*, with all kissing scenes cut out. Channels like Dubai One and MBC4, despite being free-to-air, are doing a good job of securing the rights to some fairly mainstream international shows, and Fox Movies, also free-to-air, was the first Middle Eastern TV channel to buy the rights to air 2008 smash hit *Slumdog Millionaire*.

Satellite or cable TV is a staple in most expat homes

> ## Always On The Box
>
> Orbit Showtime offers a Showbox service, with which you can pause live television and record your favourite shows on a digital box. You can also watch special previews of forthcoming movies, or virtual 'boxsets' of popular series. See www.orbitshowtime.com for more info.

– although it can be a bit hit and miss when judged by international standards. Some shows are aired just a few days later than they are in the US or UK, while others are delayed by a few months.

Where you live in Dubai may affect what channels are available to you – if you live in one of the freehold residential communities, such as Emirates Hills, Arabian Ranches, JBR or International City, you will have your satellite package installed and maintained by telecom provider du, which may offer a slightly different specification than if you deal directly with the satellite providers.

### Internet

Although they sometimes comes under criticism for being expensive and slow in comparison with what is available in other cities around the world, internet services in Dubai are fairly modern and easy to install. Etisalat and du both offer a range of packages, from the practically prehistoric dial-up option to high-speed broadband solutions.

You will probably find that using the internet

## USEFUL WEBSITES

**Dubai Information**

| | |
|---|---|
| **www.7days.ae** | Local newspaper |
| **www.dubaidonkey.com** | Free listings website – jobs, property, cars and more |
| **www.dubaikidz.biz** | Great site for kids' info |
| **www.dubaitourism.ae** | Department of Tourism & Commerce Marketing |
| **www.dubizzle.com** | Dubai's largest website for classifieds and community |
| **www.expatwoman.com** | General information on living in UAE, woman's perspective |
| **www.gulfnews.com** | Local newspaper |
| **www.khaleejtimes.com** | Local newspaper |
| **www.liveworkexplore.com** | Essential info on living in Dubai from Explorer Publishing |
| **www.sheikhmohammed.co.ae** | His Highness Sheikh Mohammed Bin Rashid Al Maktoum |
| **www.sheikhzayed.com** | A site dedicated to the life of the late UAE President |

**Business/Industry**

| | |
|---|---|
| **www.dm.gov.ae** | Dubai Municipality |
| **www.dubaipolice.gov.ae** | Dubai Police Headquarters |

**UAE Information**

| | |
|---|---|
| **www.ameinfo.com** | Middle East business news |
| **www.das.ae** | Weather info from the Department of Atmospheric Studies |
| **www.government.ae** | UAE Government 'e-portal' – lots of good info |
| **www.thenational.ae** | Local newspaper |
| **www.uaeinteract.com** | UAE Ministry of Information & Culture |

while in Dubai has a few quirks that can take some getting used to, not least the much-despised proxy that blocks access to any sites deemed offensive. What is or isn't offensive is at the discretion of the Telecommunications Regulatory Authority (TRA), which supposedly applies the same rules to both Etisalat and du subscribers. While living in a Muslim community, you can certainly expect sites containing pornography or dubious religious content to be blocked; however, the TRA has been criticised for blocking access to VoIP sites such as Skype, meaning that you can't use the internet to make those cheap calls back home. If you do want to speak to friends and family abroad, you either have to use the actual telephone (and pay the comparatively expensive rates), or access VoIP sites such as Skype illegally with the help of a proxy blocker. It's a frustrating conundrum, made even more so by the lack of valid reason (apart from financial, of course) for blocking such sites in the first place. Being able to make a cheap internet call to wish your granny a happy birthday can hardly be classed as offending religious or moral values, but rules are rules. Other sites that you will not be able to access include online dating sites, sites dealing with gambling or drugs, and, oddly, some photo-sharing sites such as Flickr.

# UAE CALENDAR 2010

Throughout the year, the UAE hosts a wide variety of public events, some of which have been running for years. Whether you choose to chill out to international jazz performances, show off your prized pooch, raise money for charity or watch the world's best tennis stars, the emirate offers some unforgettable experiences.

### Abu Dhabi Golf Championship  January
**Abu Dhabi Golf Club**
www.abudhabigolfchampionship.com
With $2 million in prize money and some of the biggest names in golf appearing annually, the Abu Dhabi Golf Championship is one of the UAE capital's biggest sporting events.

### Al Ain Aerobatic Show  January
**Al Ain Airport**
www.alainaerobaticshow.com
A five-day annual air show with flying dare-devils from around the world performing aerobatic displays.

### Capitala World Tennis Championship  January
**Zayed Sports City, Abu Dhabi**
www.capitalawtc.com
An international tennis tournament featuring the world's top seeded players competing for a $250,000 prize fund.

### Dubai Marathon  January
**World Trade Centre**
www.dubaimarathon.org
This charity event attracts all types of runners aiming to fundraise or work off that festive tummy in either the 10km road race, 3km charity run or the full 42km.

### Dubai Shopping Festival  January – February
**Various Locations**
www.mydsf.com
Dubai Shopping Festival is a great time to be in the city with bargains galore for shoppers and entertainers, prize draws and kids' shows held in participating malls.

### Dubai Bike Week  February
**Dubai Festival City**
www.dubaibikeweek.com
Over 20,000 bikers attended last year's event, enjoying stunt shows, motorbike displays and test rides.

### Dubai Desert Classic  February
**Emirates Golf Club**
www.dubaidesertclassic.com
This longstanding PGA European Tour fixture has been won in the past by golfing legends such as Ernie Els and Tiger Woods and is a popular event among Dubai's golfing community.

### Dubai Pet Show  February
**Festival Centre**
www.dubaipetshow.com
A popular family outing and the only show of its kind in the Middle East, with pedigree and crossbreed shows, a police dog unit demonstration and the uncanny 'Dog Most Like its Owner' competition.

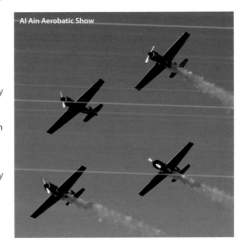
Al Ain Aerobatic Show

## Dubai Tennis Championships    February
**Aviation Club**
www.barclaysdubaitennischampionships.com
Firmly established on the ATP and WTP circuit, this $1
million tournament attracts the world's top men's and
women's seeds.

## Gourmet Abu Dhabi    February
**Various locations in Abu Dhabi**
www.gourmetabudhabi.ae
This annual culinary and arts festival features free
master classes from Michelin-starred chefs, industry
insights from experts in the hospitality field, and
gourmet dinners hosted by various Abu Dhabi hotels.

## International Property Show    February
**Dubai International Convention &
Exhibition Centre**
www.internationalpropertyshow.ae
Featuring everything to do with buying international
property, this show is particularly popular among
expats who are looking to invest overseas.

## Terry Fox Run    February
**Wonderland**
www.dubaiterryfoxrun.com
Each year, thousands of individuals run, jog, walk,
cycle, and rollerblade their way around an 8.5km
course for charity. The proceeds go to cancer research
programmes at approved institutions around the
world. For more information about the Abu Dhabi
Terry Fox Run email abudhabiterryfoxrun@gmail.com.

## Abu Dhabi Desert Challenge    March
**Empty Quarter, Abu Dhabi**
www.uaedesertchallenge.com
This high profile motorsport event attracts some of
the world's top rally drivers and bike riders to race Abu
Dhabi emirate's challenging desert routes. 2010 will
see the event's 20th anniversary.

## Abu Dhabi International Triathlon    March
**Various locations in Abu Dhabi**
www.abudhabitriathlon.com
A new event for 2010, this is set to be one of the
world's richest triathalons with a prize purse of
$250,000.

## Abu Dhabi International Book Fair    March
**Abu Dhabi National Exhibition Centre**
www.adbookfair.com
A joint venture between Frankfurt Book Fair and Abu
Dhabi Authority for Culture and Heritage, the Abu
Dhabi International Book Fair is the Middle East's
largest-growing book fair. In 2009, there were 482
exhibitors from 42 countries, and 600,000 titles on
display.

---

### Out & About

Bars, pubs, clubs and restaurants around town
host a spectrum of annual events. For New
Year's Eve and Christmas celebrations, The Cellar
(p.466), Jumeirah Beach Hotel (p.234) and Madinat
Jumeirah (p.234) always put on a festive show.
Oktoberfest at the Grand Hyatt (p.232) is an
authentic, boot-slapping, lederhosen-clad replica
of the Munich original, Sir Bob Geldof's yearly St
Patrick's Day performance at Irish Village (p.510)
is a good excuse to raise a jar, and The Lodge's
legendary Halloween fancy dress party (p.509)
is enough to frighten the fiercest of fiends. Visit
www.liveworkexplore.com to find out what's
coming up next.

---

## Art Dubai    March
**Madinat Jumeirah**
www.artdubai.ae
An international art exhibition. Running alongside it
is the Global Art Forum lecture and discussion board
programme.

## Dubai International Boat Show    March
**DIMC**
www.boatshowdubai.com
You don't have to have big bucks to enjoy the Boat
Show. The largest marine industry exhibition in the
Middle East, showcases yachts and boats from both
local and international builders, together with the latest
innovations in marine equipment and accessories.

## Dubai International Jazz Festival    March
**Dubai Media City**
www.dubaijazzfest.com
The Jazz Festival attracts a broad range of artists from
all around the world to a chilled and pleasant setting
in Dubai Media City. Courtney Pine, John Legend,
James Blunt and David Gray have all taken to the stage
in previous years.

## Dubai International Poetry Festival    March
**Various Locations**
www.dipf.ae
Embracing an important part of Arabic culture, this
annual event, new in 2009, hosts seminars, workshops
and readings by international and local poets.

## Dubai World Cup    March
**Meydan City**
www.dubaiworldcup.com
The world's richest horserace will take place in it's new
venue at the brand new Meydan City in 2010. The
huge prize fund (last year's was over $20 million) and
a buzzing, vibrant atmosphere, ensure it's one of the
year's big social occasions.

## Emirates Airline International Festival of Literature — March
**Dubai Festival City**
www.eaifl.com
Back in 2010 after the success of the inaugural 2009 event, over 70 authors including Jacqueline Wilson, Alexander McCall Smith, Martin Amis, Kate Adie and the UK's Poet Laureate Carol Ann Duffy, will give readings and participate in literary debates.

## Powerboat Racing — March
**Dubai International Marine Club**
www.dimc.ae
The UAE is well established on the world championship powerboat racing circuit – in Abu Dhabi with Formula One (Inshore) and in Dubai and Fujairah with Class One (Offshore). Check the DIMC website for dates of Dubai races.

Off-road adventures

## Bride Show Dubai — April
**World Trade Centre**
www.thebrideshow.com
A must-do before you say 'I do', this is the largest bridal exhibition in the region, and brings the whole wedding industry together, showcasing dresses, photographers, entertainment, honeymoon destinations and wedding organisers.

## Dragon Boating Festival — April
**Festival City**
www.festivalcentre.com
Open to social, school and corporate groups this is a fun, competitive and sociable team building event.

## Gulf Film Festival — April
**Festival City**
www.gulffilmfest.com
Promoting the work of filmmakers from the GCC, this week-long festival also hosts a number of international films and a competition for Emirati short films.

## Red Bull Air Race — April
**Abu Dhabi Corniche**
www.redbullairrace.com
Abu Dhabi is the starting fixture of the Red Bull Air Race World Series. Spectators can view the action close up from the Corniche as the pilots race through the air just metres above the water.

## WOMAD Abu Dhabi — April
**Abu Dhabi Corniche**
www.womadabudhabi.ae
2009 was the inaugural year for the Abu Dhabi arm of this world music festival which attracted 80,000 spectators over 3 days to see music and dance acts, plus art installations, workshops and food stalls from all over the globe.

## Dubai Summer Surprises — June – August
**Various Locations**
www.mydsf.com
Held in shopping malls around the city, with fun-packed, family-orientated activities and big shopping discounts, it's a popular event with Dubai residents looking to escape the heat during the summer months.

## Summer In Abu Dhabi — June – August
**Abu Dhabi National Exhibitions Centre**
www.summerinabudhabi.com
A family carnival held in the air-conditioned comfort of ADNEC. The exhibition halls are home a host of games, sports and educational experiences to keep kids busy and active during the summer months.

## Dubai Fashion Week — October
**InterContinental Dubai**
www.dfw.ae
One of the glitziest events on the annual calendar, in which regional fashion designers to present their collections to the world's fashion media.

## Dubai World Game Expo — October
**Dubai International Convention & Exhibition Centre**
www.gameexpo.ae
A calendar highlight for all gaming fans wanting to try out the latest software and hardware in the market. Includes the Dubai World Game Championship.

## GITEX — October
**Dubai International Convention & Exhibition Centre**
www.gitex.com
The five-day IT exhibition, will celebrate its 30th year in 2010. The event is renowned for its Gitex Computer

UAE: A Country Profile

Shopper where the public can snap up some great deals on technology and gadgets.

## Middle East International Film Festival    October
**Various cinemas across Abu Dhabi**
www.meiff.com
Growing rapidly since its inception in 2007, MEIFF brings more films, more awards, and more stars to the capital year on year, giving a huge boost to the country's developing film industry.

## Camel Racing    October – April
**Nr Al Ain Road**
This popular local sport is serious business with racing camels changing hands for as much as Dhs.10 million. Morning races take place throughout the winter between 07:00 and 08:30. Admission is free.

## Abu Dhabi Classics    October – May
**Various locations in Abu Dhabi and Al Ain**
www.abudhabiclassics.com
A series of classical music concerts by international artists and orchestras which takes place at venues across the capital and at Al Jahili Fort in Al Ain. The festival runs from October to May and gets bigger, lasts longer, and becomes more adventurous every year.

## Dhow Racing    October – May
**Dubai International Marine Club**
www.dimc.ae
This is a great traditional Arabic spectator sport. Fixed races are held throughout the year as well as on special occasions, such as National Day. Check the DIMC website for upcoming events.

## Abu Dhabi Formula 1 Grand Prix    November
**Yas Marina Circuit, Abu Dhabi**
www.yasmarinacircuit.com
The newest fixture on the F1 racing calendar is held only 90 minutes away from Dubai. Abu Dhabi put on a great show for the race weekend in 2009, with a fanzone in the city and live music from the likes of Beyonce and Kings Of Leon.

## Exhibitions
With its increasing emphasis on MICE (meetings, incentives, conferences, exhibitions) tourism, Dubai has two large, state-of-the-art exhibition spaces showcasing a variety of exhibitions each year. These are the Airport Expo and the exhibition halls at the Dubai World Trade Centre. For details of exhibitions in Dubai, contact the Department of Tourism & Commerce Marketing (04 223 0000, www.dubaitourism.ae).

## Gala Celebrations
There's always an excuse to get dressed up with a number of annual gala events in the UAE. Most are open to members of the general public and are usually attended by a round-up of international celebrities. The CNCF gala dinner in aid of the Christina Noble Children's Foundation, kicks off the Dubai Rugby Sevens (www.urbanevents.ae). The Chequered Flag Ball is a key event of the Abu Dhabi F1 weekend (www.chequeredflagball.com), while the Oil Barons Ball is the calendar highlight for the oil and gas sector (www.theoilbaronsball.com). St George's Day balls are held in both Abu Dhabi and Dubai (www.rssgauh.com, www.dsgs.org); St Andrew's Day is marked by the Scottish St Andrew's Society (www.scottishsocietyabudhabi.com) and the annual Kiwi Ball brings New Zealand expatriates and their friends together (www.kiwiball.com).

## Desert Rallies    November
**Various locations**
www.emsf.ae
There are numerous desert rally events taking place throughout the year, the biggest being the Abu Dhabi Desert Challenge (above). Check the Emirates Motor Sports Federation website for listings.

## Dubai World Championship – Race To Dubai    November
**Jumeirah Golf Estates**
www.dubaiworldchampionship.com
The world's best golfers congregate in Dubai for the final fixture of the PGA European Golf Tour and a shot at a share of the $7.5 million prize fund.

## Sharjah World Book Fair    November
**Sharjah Expo Centre**
www.swbf.gov.ae
One of the oldest and largest book fairs in the Arab World showcases thousands of titles in Arabic, English and other languages, displayed by private collectors, publishers, governments and universities.

## Swim The Burj    November
**Burj Al Arab**
www.swimburjalarab.com
A charity race to swim a one kilometre route around the spectacular Burj Al Arab hotel. Both competitive swimmers and fundraisers can take part. All proceeds go to Medecins San Frontieres.

## Whatever Floats Your Boat    November
**Festival Marina, Dubai Festival City**
This charity race invites schools and businesses to build boats from recycled materials to raise awareness

of recycling and take part in a fun day on the water. For more info email kmueller@igymarinas.com.

### Abu Dhabi Art
November – February
**Emirates Palace, Abu Dhabi**
www.abudhabiartfair.ae
A new event for 2009, this international art fair is expected to take place again in 2010 with a full programme of exhibitions, lectures, debates and workshops.

### Horse Racing
November – April
**Meydan Racecourse**
www.dubairacingclub.com
Horseracing in Dubai is moving to the brand new, state-of-the-art track in Meydan City. Racing takes place at night under floodlights (see the website for race dates) and competitions to select the winning horses are held, with the ultimate aim of taking home prizes or cash.

### Dubai Rugby 7s
November/December
**The Sevens Stadium**
www.dubairugby7s.com
Over 130,000 spectators descend on the 7s stadium over the course of three days to watch top international teams compete for the coveted 7s trophy

and Gulf teams contesting the local competition. With friendly rivalry between competing nations and prizes for the best fancy dress, the party atmosphere carries on until the small hours.

### FIFA Club World Cup
December
**Sheikh Zayed Sports City Stadium, Abu Dhabi**
www.fifa.com
The champions of each continent, plus the host nation's team, battle it out on the pitch to take the coveted trophy.

### Dubai International Film Festival
December
**Madinat Jumeirah**
www.dubaifilmfest.com
A hotly anticipated annual event showcasing Hollywood and international arthouse films, as well as work from the region. Premieres are generally held at Madinat Jumeirah, while screenings take place across the city.

### Fun Drive
December
**Dubai Autodrome**
www.gulfnews.com
Spread over two days, the Fun Drive is a very sociable, guided off-road trip through the wilderness of the UAE with around 500 other 4WDs.

### The Etisalat Sharjah Water Festival
December
**Al Majaz Park**
www.sharjahtourism.ae
Sharjah hosts an annual family extravaganza at Al Majaz Park, as part of the Powerboat Formula One Grand Prix. The festival kicks off with a parade on National Day (2 December), and for the next 10 days kids can enjoy a variety of entertainment. Entry is Dhs.5 per person, Dhs.20 per family. The grand prix will take place in early December on Khalid Lagoon.

### Mother, Baby & Child Show
December
**Dubai International Convention & Exhibition Centre**
www.motherbabyandchild.com
Mums and kids will love this show, featuring exhibits by child-friendly companies and lots of entertainment for the little ones, plus endless samples and giveaways.

### Abu Dhabi Adventure Challenge
December
**Various locations in Abu Dhabi**
www.abudhabi-adventure.com
The Abu Dhabi Adventure Challenge is a multi-sport endurance that sees racing over six consecutive days through the varied terrain of urban and rural Abu Dhabi. The disciplines include sea kayaking, camel hiking, mountain biking and adventure running.

Dhow racing

Role ☑  Sector ☑  Location ☑
Salary ☑  Environment ☑

At iQ selection we tick all the boxes

Sales & Marketing • Advertising, Media & PR • FMCG • Banking & Finance • Human Resources • Emiratisation
Executive Secretarial • IT & Telecommunications • Construction & Engineering • Oil & Gas

At iQ selection we are passionate
about selecting the right job for you.
Tel: + 971 4 324 4094 **www.iQselection.com**

iQ selection

# Dubai: Becoming A Resident

# CITY PROFILE

There are certain descriptions of Dubai that are frequently used: pearl of the Gulf, sleepy fishing village transformed into modern metropolis, tax-free expat haven, headquarters of luxury living, and so on.

The truth is that, behind these cliches, Dubai is for most people a wonderful place to live, with some excellent career opportunities, a readily available network of social contacts, some unique activities and, apart from a few sweaty months in summer, brilliant weather. Most expats will tell you that their standard of living is better here than it was back home, they can travel more, spend more time with family, enjoy outdoor living and make more friends.

### And In 77th Place...

Dubai ranked number 77 in Mercer's 2009 Quality of Living survey (www.mercer.com). It was the top ranking city in the Middle East and Africa region.

This chapter is here to help you, whether you are making the decision to move or not, you've just arrived and don't know where to start, or you find yourself faced with an overwhelming amount of red tape. Just remember, procedures and laws do change regularly, often in quite major ways. While these changes are generally announced in newspapers, they are often implemented quickly so it's a good idea to be prepared for the unexpected.

### Drinking In DXB

While drinking alcohol is forbidden for Muslims, it is served in the many bars, clubs and restaurants throughout Dubai. You won't find a booze aisle in your local supermarket, although some people have made the mistake of stocking up on the 0% alcohol beers that line the shelves. Two companies operate liquor stores, but you'll need a licence to buy alcohol (see p.42).

# DUBAI'S ECONOMY & TRADE

Whereas 20 years ago oil revenues accounted for around half of Dubai's GDP, in 2007 the oil sector contributed just 3%. It is expected that by 2010 oil will account for less than 1% of total GDP. Knowing that oil will eventually run out, great investment in other industries has been made. Trade, manufacturing, transport, construction and real estate are now the main contributors to the economy. Of course, during the global recession of 2008/2009, Dubai's economy took some hard knocks; some say it was one of the hardest-hit economies in the world. While this may be true when looking at the real estate market, in which property values plummeted by up to 50%, it can be argued that Dubai had a strong trade economy before the property market opened up, and therefore the economy will survive the crash.

When the economy was growing towards its peak in 2008, there were concerns about the rate of inflation. Factors such as rising rents meant that the cost of living increased rapidly for residents. In fact, inflation in 2007 was the highest it had been in two decades, at 11.8%. The drop in rents and other cost of living indicators has been one of the silver linings of the recession.

Historically, Dubai has enjoyed a long tradition of trading, and continues to be an important location for foreign companies looking at opportunities in the region. Dubai's strategic location, liberal regulatory environment and cosmopolitan population are all factors that attract foreign business. Annual domestic imports exceed $17 billion and Dubai is the gateway to over $150 billion annually in trade.

Employment levels are fairly good in Dubai, although by some estimates there are up to 30,000 Emiratis out of work. This is partly due to a preference for public sector work and partly due to qualifications and salary expectations not matching the skills required in the private sector. Emiratisation programmes aim to improve these figures. In 2009 there have been significant redundancies made in the private sector, resulting in many expat professionals leaving Dubai to return to their home countries or take up employment in regional markets that were less affected by the recession, such as Qatar and Abu Dhabi.

One of the main effects of the recession was the cancellation of many major projects that had been announced during Dubai's period of rapid growth. Some of the projects that are said to be still going ahead include:

**Al Furjan:** A luxurious residential and commercial site with freshwater streams, cycle paths and a golf course designed by Greg Norman. www.alfurjan.com

**Business Bay:** Built around an extension to the creek, this self-contained city within a city will become the commercial and business capital for the region. www.businessbay.ae

**Creek Crossings:** Two more bridges across the creek are planned, one near Shindagha Tunnel and one between the Shindagha Tunnel and Maktoum Bridge.

**Dubai Metro:** The Red Line opened in September 2009, and the Green Line is due to open on 10 October 2010. Other lines are at the planning stage.

**Dubai Sports City:** DSC will be home to a mass of sporting venues and facilities, and is set to be a key part of Dubai's 2020 Olympic bid. www.dubaisportscity.ae

**Dubai World Central:** This will be a self-contained urban centre based around a new airport with six runways, expected to handle 120 million passengers a year by 2050. www.dwc.ae

**Jumeirah Garden City:** Older sections of Satwa have been demolished to make way for this residential and commercial development that will link up to the Business Bay development. www.meraas.com

**Meydan:** Aspiring to be a 'horseracing city' with a business park, residential areas, shopping arcades and a major racecourse, Meydan will be linked to the creek by canal, and have its own marina. www.meydan.ae

**Palm Islands:** Work continues on the three Palm Islands, with 70% of the Palm Jumeirah now complete. Each island will feature villas and apartments, luxury hotels and numerous leisure attractions. www.thepalm.ae

# CONSIDERING DUBAI

Sunny days, great shopping, outdoor living and tax-free salaries sum up the Dubai dream. Of course there are red-tape hassles and everyday annoyances, but for many expats these are far outweighed by the positives.

Costs of living in Dubai reached a peak towards the end of 2008, when rents were sky-high, and prices for everything were increasing as a result. If there has been any positive side to the global recession, it's that prices have stabilised to a more normal, affordable level, and as long as your job is secure, you're actually better off in 2009 than you were before.

The job market is still in recovery, however, so before you jump on the first plane, make sure you test the waters by contacting potential employers, monitoring newspaper appointments pages and scouring international recruitment websites.

You should also consider how you will enter the city and stay here. To stay in Dubai long-term, you need a residency visa, and for this you need a 'sponsor'. Your sponsor is usually your company, or your spouse if you are not working (see p.37). If you don't have work lined up, you can enter on a visit visa, but will only be allowed to stay for a limited time (p.34).

# BEFORE YOU ARRIVE

If you're coming to Dubai to work, or even just to look for work, you should have any qualification certificates and important documents (such as your marriage certificate, and kids' birth certificates) attested in your home country. This can be quite a lengthy process, and involves solicitors and the UAE foreign embassy.

Property owners may consider selling up before the move, but don't be hasty. It may be wise to test the water and give yourself a year before you commit

One of Dubai's new Metro stations

long-term – although many people have come for a year or two and are still in the country five years later.

You also need to get your financial affairs in order, such as telling banks and building societies, and the tax office – tax rules differ from country to country, so check whether you have to inform the tax office in your home country of any earnings you accrue while in Dubai. Speak to your pension company too – moving abroad could have implications on your contributions (see Work, p.111).

## Stare Wars

As annoying and infuriating as it is to have someone blatantly stare at you, the good news is that these stares are not really sexual in nature – they are more the result of curiosity. The bad news is that there is little you can do to stop this strange little quirk of living in the region. Your best defence is to avoid wearing tight or revealing clothing, particularly in certain areas such as the Gold Souk.

If you've got kids you should start researching schools as soon as possible. There are fortunately a lot more schools in Dubai today than there were a few years ago, although it can still be tough to get a guaranteed place at the school of your choice. The earlier you get your child's name on the waiting list, the better.

When it comes to choosing an area of Dubai to live in, take your time to explore the different residential areas (see p.80 for a head start). It's a good idea to arrange temporary accommodation for when you first arrive (try to negotiate this with your employer), so that you can look for your perfect home. Speak to shipping companies about bringing your stuff over, and try to book as far in advance as possible.

If you're coming to Dubai on a 'look-see', do your homework before you arrive. Contact recruitment agencies in advance, sign up with online job sites, and visit agencies in your home country that specialise in overseas recruitment. Check also that your qualifications or industry experience are in demand here. See Work (p.111) for more information.

## Customs

Before you fly into Dubai, be aware that several prescription medications are banned, especially anything containing codeine or temazepam. The UAE maintains a strict zero-tolerance policy on recreational drugs, and even microscopic amounts could land you in jail. Your bags will be scanned on arrival to ensure you have no offending magazines or DVDs. Each passenger is allowed 2,000 cigarettes, 400 cigars or two kilograms of tobacco. Non-Muslims are also allowed four 'units' of alcohol; a unit is either one bottle of wine, one bottle of liqueur or spirits, or a half-case of beer.

# WHEN YOU ARRIVE

As you can expect during an international move to any new city, you're very likely to find a long 'to-do' list waiting for you when you arrive in Dubai. You'll be doing a lot of driving around, form filling, and waiting in queues in government departments. Just keep your sense of humour handy and soon all the boring red tape will be a distant memory.

The first thing you'll probably need to sort out is visas – you may be lucky enough to have a company PRO who does this all for you; if not, see p.36.

House-hunting will also be on your agenda – see p.74 for advice on finding your ideal home, and then getting electricity, water, phones and furniture.

You'll probably need a car – while the bad news is that driving seems a little scary here at first, the good news is that cars are cheap. See p.60.

As for paperwork, you'll need to get your driving licence, and your liquor licence if you're planning on buying alcohol. See p.42.

And once you've got the administrative stuff out of the way, it's time to put your feelers out and start meeting your fellow expats – a task which some find challenging, but most find easier than expected. See p.44.

# GETTING STARTED

## Entry Visa

Visa requirements for entering Dubai vary greatly between different nationalities, and regulations should always be checked before travelling, since details can change with little or no warning. GCC nationals (Bahrain, Kuwait, Qatar, Oman and Saudi Arabia) do not need a visa to enter Dubai. Citizens from many other countries (including the UK, USA, Australia, Canada and many EU countries) get an automatic visa upon arrival at the airport (p.36). The entry visa is valid for 30 days, although you can renew for a further 30 days at a cost of Dhs.620.

Expats with residency in other GCC countries, who do not belong to one of the 33 visa on arrival nationalities but who do meet certain criteria (professions such as managers, doctors and engineers) can get a non-renewable 30 day visa on arrival – check with your airline before flying.

People of certain nationalities who are visiting the Sultanate of Oman may also enter Dubai on a free-of-charge entry permit. The same criteria and facilities apply to Dubai visitors entering Oman (although if you have Dubai residency you will pay a small charge).

All other nationalities can get a 30 day tourist visa sponsored by a local entity, such as a hotel or tour operator, before entry. The fee is Dhs.100, and the visa can be renewed for a further 30 days for Dhs.620.

## eGate Card

The eGate service allows UAE and GCC nationals, as well as people with a valid residence permit, to pass through both the departures and arrivals halls of Dubai International Airport without a passport. Swipe your smart card through an electronic gate and through you go, saving a great deal of time otherwise spent in long queues. Applications for a card are processed within minutes at Dubai International Airport, in the DNATA buildings (one on Sheikh Zayed Road and one in Deira near Deira City Centre), or the DNRD office on Trade Centre Road. You'll need your passport, containing the valid residence permit and you will be fingerprinted and photographed. The eGate card costs Dhs.200 and is valid for two years. Payment can be made by cash or credit card. For further information, contact 04 316 6966 or see www.dubai.ae.

"We've moved so many times that we were used to arriving at our new home and discovering some of our belongings were broken during the move. Not this time. With Crown we finally discovered packers who can do the job right."
-Mr. Michael Martin, Corporate Transferee

Crown Relocations provides international and domestic moving and settling in services for transferees and their families. With over 150 locations in 50 countries, Crown's customers are Well connected. Worldwide.™

**Household Shipment • Online Tracking • Insurance
Immigration Assistance • Home and School Search
Orientation Tours • Intercultural Training**

*Dubai*
*Call us at* **(971) 4 289 5152**
*or visit* **crownrelo.com** *for details.*

**CROWN**
R E L O C A T I O N S

2008SG_NOV_I7IDUBAI

# Getting Started

## Visa On Arrival

Citizens of the following countries receive an automatic visit visa on arrival: Andorra, Australia, Austria, Belgium, Brunei, Canada, Cyprus, Denmark, Finland, France, Germany, Greece, Hong Kong, Iceland, Ireland, Italy, Japan, Liechtenstein, Luxembourg, Malaysia, Malta, Monaco, Netherlands, New Zealand, Norway, Portugal, San Marino, Singapore, South Korea, Spain, Sweden, Switzerland, United Kingdom, United States of America and Vatican City.

Citizens of eastern European countries, countries that belonged to the former Soviet Union, China and South Africa can get a 30 day, non-renewable tourist visa sponsored by a local entity, such as a hotel or tour operator, before entry into the UAE. The fee is Dhs.100 for the visa and an additional Dhs.20 for delivery.

Other visitors can apply for an entry service permit (exclusive of arrival/departure days), valid for use within 14 days of the date of issue and non-renewable. Once this visa expires the visitor must remain out of the country for 30 days before re-entering on a new visit visa. The application fee for this visa is Dhs.120, plus an additional Dhs.20 delivery charge.

For those travelling onwards to a destination other than that of the original departure, a special transit visa (up to 96 hours) may be obtained free of charge through certain airlines operating in the UAE.

A multiple-entry visa is available to visitors who have a relationship with a local business, meaning they have to visit that business regularly. It is valid for visits of a maximum of 14 days each time, for six months from date of issue. It costs Dhs.1,000 and should be applied for after entering the UAE on a visit visa. For an additional Dhs.200, a multiple entry visa holder is eligible for the eGate service (see p.34). Companies may levy a maximum of Dhs.50 extra in processing charges for arranging visas. The DNATA (Dubai National Airline Travel Agency) visa delivery service costs an extra Dhs.20.

### Fully Fledged Resident

After entering Dubai on an employment or residency visa, you have 60 days to complete all of the procedures involved in becoming a resident – although it's unlikely to take anywhere near that long. If you need to leave the country again before the process is completed, you should be able to do so as long as you have the entry visa that was stamped in your passport when you first entered. It's probably best though if you avoid booking any holidays in those first few weeks.

## Sponsorship

### Residence Permit

In order to live in Dubai, you need to have a residence permit. There are two types of permit, both of which require the individual to be sponsored: one is for those sponsored for employment, and the other for residence only (for example when you are sponsored by a family member who is already sponsored by an employer). There was a property-owner visa for a while, which fell into the latter category with the developer acting as sponsor for as long as you own the property, but without employment rights. However, this law ceased to exist in 2008, meaning buying a property no longer entitles you to a residency permit – although property owners are still able to apply for investor-based residency, and are entitled to an initial

**EMBASSY INSIGHT**   Yacoob Abba Omar, South African ambassador to the UAE

*The main role of the embassy is to promote South Africa to our host country. Aside from consular services, we also deal with signing agreements, arranging for various delegations to visit SA, and meeting with industry and government representatives.*

*Despite the current economic climate, the business ties between South Africa and the UAE have been growing from strength to strength, with bilateral trade between the two countries reaching Dhs.6.14 billion in 2008. I believe that we will be seeing more South African initiatives in the future, as South African businesses are resilient and innovative and have the reputation of adhering to high standards and quality.*

*We encourage the South African citizens to register with the Embassy. This would come in handy especially during emergencies, but we also connect citizens with the South Africa Business Council so they can network with fellow-South Africans.*

*Our flagship event is the Freedom Day celebration on 27 April, which is aimed at key contacts of the Embassy. We also support SABCo in hosting the South Africa Family Day, which the South African community attends in droves to celebrate Freedom Day. My advice to first timers is to begin by learning some of the culture and traditions of our host country. Use the opportunity of being here to visit many countries in the region.*

*For a full list of embassies in Dubai, see inside back cover.*

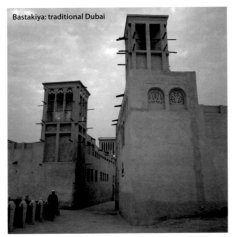
Bastakiya: traditional Dubai

To be accepted by the authorities here, your education certificates must be verified by a solicitor or public notary in your home country and then by your foreign office to verify the solicitor as bona fide, then the UAE embassy. It's a good idea to have this done before you come to Dubai, but Empost does offer a verification service at a cost of Dhs.500 per degree. The minimum turnaround time you can expect for this service is two weeks.

## Sponsoring A Maid

To sponsor a maid you must have a salary above Dhs.6,000 per month, and be able to provide the maid with housing and the usual benefits including an airfare home at least every two years. The process is very similar to sponsoring a family member (see below), the main differences being the additional costs involved – you have to pay a 'maid tax' of around Dhs.5,200 per year. If you are processing a health card for a maid, driver or cook, you will need to pay an additional fee (Dhs.60-100) to have him or her vaccinated against hepatitis. There will also be a small typing fee (see Domestic Help, p.106).

six-month multiple entry visa (renewable for Dhs.2,000 provided the owner leaves and then re-enters the country; see www.dubai.ae for more details).

Residency permits are valid for three years, but once you become a resident, if you leave the UAE it can only be for a period of less than six months at any one time, otherwise your residency will lapse. This is particularly relevant to women going back home to give birth, or children studying abroad. If the residency is cancelled, the original sponsor can visit the Immigration Department and pay Dhs.100 for a temporary entry permit which will waive the cancellation and allow the person to re-enter Dubai. You'll need their passport copy, and will have to fax them a copy of the permit before they fly back.

## Employer Sponsorship

If you have moved to Dubai to take up a job offer, your employer is obliged to sponsor you. Your new company's PRO (personnel relations officer) should handle all the paperwork, meaning you probably won't have to visit the Immigration Department yourself. They will take your passport, employment visa (with entry stamp), medical test results, attested education certificates, copies of your company's establishment immigration card and trade licence, and three passport photos. For a fee of Dhs.300 (plus typing fees) the Immigration Department will process everything and affix and stamp the residency permit in the passport. This may take up to 10 days, during which time you'll be without your passport, but for an extra Dhs.100 they can do it on the same day. Your company must pay these fees for you. When arranging your residency, the company will apply directly for your labour card (see p.38). The Ministry of Labour website (www.mol.gov.ae) has a facility for companies to process applications and transactions online.

## Family Sponsorship

If you are sponsored and resident in Dubai you should be able to sponsor your family members, allowing them to stay in the country as long as you are here. To sponsor your wife or children you will need a minimum monthly salary of Dhs.3,000 plus accommodation, or a minimum all-inclusive salary of Dhs.4,000, although there are rumours this amount may rise to as high as Dhs.10,000 – check www.dubai.ae for the latest regulations. Only what is printed on your labour contract will be accepted as proof of your earnings, so make sure you're happy with this before starting the job. To apply for residency visas for your family, you'll need to take your passport, the passport of the family member(s), and your labour contract to the Family Entry Permit counter at the Immigration Department. Your company PRO may help you with this process, but in most cases you will need to do it

## Older Children

For parents sponsoring children, difficulties arise when sons (not daughters) turn 18. Unless they are enrolled in full-time education in the UAE they must transfer their visa to an employer, or the parents can pay a Dhs.5,000 security deposit (one-off payment) and apply for an annual visa. Daughters can stay on their father's sponsorship until they get married.

# Getting Started

(and pay for it) on your own. After submitting all the documents, return after a couple of days to collect the visa. Once the visa is processed, your family member must apply for a health card and take the medical test.

With the medical test out of the way, you then return to the Immigration Department with all the essential documents as before, plus the medical test result and the attested birth certificate (if sponsoring a child) or attested marriage certificate (if sponsoring your spouse). For Dhs.300 (plus typing) the application will be processed and around five days later the passport – with the residency permit attached – will be ready for collection (for an additional Dhs.100, you can have the process completed on the same day).

If the family member is already in Dubai on a visit visa you can still apply for residency as above. Once processed, the family member must exit the country and re-enter with the correct visa, or you can pay Dhs.500 to have the visa swapped. If you have family sponsorship and then get a job, you don't need to change to employer sponsorship, but the company will need to apply for a labour card on your behalf.

## Labour Card

Once you have your residency permit, either through your employer or family sponsor, you need a Labour Card. If you are on a family residency and decide to work, your employer, not your visa sponsor (usually your husband), will need to apply for a labour card. You'll need to give your employer the usual documents including a letter of no objection (NOC) from your sponsor (husband/father), your passport with residency stamp, attested certificates, passport photos, and a photocopy of your sponsor's passport. The Labour Card will cost your employer Dhs.1,000, and must be renewed annually. See Work, p.111.

It is common to hear that women can't sponsor their husbands unless they are doctors, nurses or teachers. While this used to be the rule at one stage, today it is possible for working women to sponsor their husbands and children, provided they meet the minimum salary requirements. If you are in this situation you should speak to the Immigration Department and present your case. The main disadvantage of a wife sponsoring her husband is that the spouse's visa must be renewed annually, while if a husband sponsors his wife, the spouse's visa only needs to be renewed every three years.

There are constraints when Dubai residents want to sponsor their parents – a special committee meets to review each case on an individual basis, usually to consider the age and projected health requirements of the parents.

## PROs & NOCs

In Dubai, a PRO is your company's 'man who can' – he liaises with various government departments and carries out admin procedures. The PRO will take care of all visa, residency, health card, and labour card applications. An NOC is a no objection certificate, and is essentially a letter stating that the person in question permits you to carry out a particular procedure. You'll find you need one of these in a variety of situations, whether it's from your employer allowing you to switch jobs, or your own NOC permitting a family member to work.

## Medical Test

You need to pass a medical test in order to get your residence visa – you will be tested for communicable diseases such as tuberculosis and HIV. To take your test, you will need the test form filled out in Arabic (there are typing offices near the government hospitals who can do this for you for around Dhs.20), two passport photos, a receipt for the Dhs.310 that you paid for your health card, and the test fee of Dhs.210. Blood will be taken and if your tests are positive you will be deported to your home country; if you are at all nervous about the possibility of testing positive it may be a good idea to get tested by your doctor in your home country before you arrive in Dubai. You will also need to undergo a chest x-ray to test for TB. After all your tests are finished, collect your receipt, which will tell you when to return to collect your results (usually around three days later).

You may find the government testing centres chaotic, which can be a little bit scary if this is your first experience of Dubai's healthcare system. Rest assured that, despite appearances, medical hygiene standards are followed and test results are processed efficiently. A good tip is to go wearing a plain, pale-coloured T-shirt: this way you should not have to remove your clothes or wear a hospital gown (which may have been used by someone else before you) for your x-ray.

You can have your medical test done at a private clinic, but not all private clinics are authorised to perform government health tests, so your employer should inform you of your options and whether they will cover the extra cost.

## Health Card

Once you have passed your medical test, you are able to get a health card, which entitles you to subsidised health care at government-run hospitals and clinics. The health card must be renewed each year, but you only need to take a new medical test when your visa is up for renewal. See Health, p.181, for how to get your card.

# Redefining **Relocations** in the **United Arab Emirates**

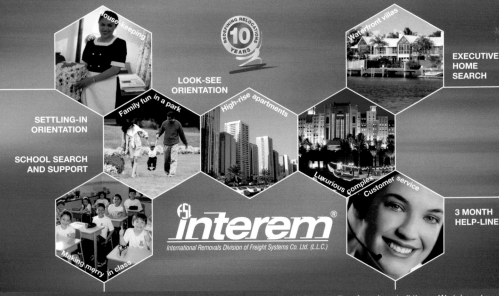

Housekeeping

LOOK-SEE
ORIENTATION

Family fun in a park

High-rise apartments

Waterfront villas

EXECUTIVE
HOME
SEARCH

SETTLING-IN
ORIENTATION

SCHOOL SEARCH
AND SUPPORT

Luxurious complex

Customer service

3 MONTH
HELP-LINE

Making merry in class

## *interem*®
International Removals Division of Freight Systems Co. Ltd. (L.L.C.)

At Interem, we are absolutely committed to giving your customers the highest quality of service at all times. We take extra care and walk that extra mile to ensure an absolutely hassle-free experience for both you and your customers. Our state-of-the-art relocation procedures, precise planning and co-ordination, and the resources of a global network, enables us to handle everything from packing, documentation, customs formalities and finally unpacking and setting up your customer's new home.
**Move with us and you'll never take a chance with your customer's sentiments.**

## NEVER TAKING A CHANCE WITH YOUR CUSTOMER'S SENTIMENT

International Credentials:

**FIDI** GLOBAL ALLIANCE

**Omni**

WORLDWIDE ERC°

Memb. No. F414.

**IAM**

**lacma**

DUBAI QUALITY GROUP

Plot M-00539, Street 732, Near Lipton Round 13, P.O.Box 61243, Jebel Ali Dubai, UAE
Tel: +9714 8070581 / 584, Fax: +9714 8070580  E-mail: albert@freightsystems.com  Website: www.freightsystems.com

**INTERNATIONAL PACKAGING SERVICES • COMPREHENSIVE RELOCATION SERVICES • SHORT & LONG TERM STORAGE FACILITIES**
OUR INTERNATIONAL NETWORK NOT AFFILIATED TO FIDI: QATAR • KUWAIT • DELHI • MUMBAI • CHENNAI • BANGALORE • KOLKATTA • HYDERABAD • PUNE

## Improved Service

The Department of Health & Medical Services is embracing the digital age; results of medical tests can now be retrieved online and health cards can be renewed using the Express HC service. You will need to register at www.dohms.gov.ae to use this service.

## ID Card

The UAE is in the process of implementing an ambitious countrywide ID card programme, which, when complete, will require all nationals and residents to register for and carry the card.

So far the project has had several some major hiccups, including various deadline delays, low turnouts for registering, and administrative problems. By the end of 2009, the deadline for professional expats to apply for their UAE ID card had passed, but only a small number of people can actually say that they are ID card carriers. On top of this, those that did get the card were still puzzled over what it's actually for, with some even saying that, when trying to use it to identify themselves when banking or receiving registered deliveries, the ID card is not recognised as an official form of identification.

It is early days for such a complex scheme, however, so in case the ID card swings into full action in 2010 and beyond, here's what you need to know:

All residents, both nationals and expats, must be in possession of a UAE ID card, the purpose of which is to secure personal identities and cut down on fraud and identity theft. The card will eventually replace all other cards, such as health cards or labour cards. UAE Nationals must pay Dhs.100 for their ID cards; expat residents should pay a fee that is linked to the validity of their residence visa, paying Dhs.100 per year of validity left (so, for example, if your residence visa expires in two years, you will pay Dhs.200 for your ID card).

To register for your card, download the pre-registration form from www.emiratesid.ae, then take the completed form to a registration centre with the fee, your passport and your residency visa. Once it has been processed, your card will be delivered to you (for an additional fee of Dhs.20).

You can find more up-to-date information as well as a list of registration centres at www.emiratesid.ae and www.dubai.ae.

## Driving Licence

If you are in Dubai on a visit visa and wish to drive a hire car, you need a valid international licence (although you can only do this if your nationality is on the transfer list on p.42). A standard driving licence from your country of origin is not enough on its own.

If you want to drive a private vehicle, you will need to get a temporary or permanent Dubai driving licence – you are not allowed to drive a privately owned Dubai car on just an international driving licence. As soon as your residence visa comes through, then you will need to switch to a Dubai driving licence, which is valid for 10 years. If you are not a citizen of one of the licence transfer countries, then you will need to take a driving test, which is an arduous process by all accounts. Obtaining a motorcycle licence follows the same procedure. For more information, see p.57.

### Eye Tests

To get your eyes tested, visit one of the many opticians around Dubai and tell them you need an eye test certificate for the driving licence. Many have signs in the window indicating that they do eye tests for driving licences. It costs around Dhs.30 and you'll need to take along two passport photos.

Driving in Dubai

# Expat Women

## Helping Women Living Overseas

### Real-Life Experiences
200+ Stories
Confessions
900+ Blogs

### Interviews
Success Stories
Business Ideas
Expat Authors

### 1,000+ Pages
Country Resources
City Experiences
Expat Clubs

### Inspiration
Newsletters
Giveaways
Articles

## www.ExpatWomen.com

Media City freezone

and earn more than Dhs.4,000 a month. Pick up an application form from any branch of A&E or MMI (the two licensed liquor store chains in Dubai). Complete the form, including details and a photograph of your spouse if you need them to be able to use the licence too, have it signed and stamped by your employer, and return to the outlet for processing. You will need to provide the following documents: passport copy, residence permit copy, labour contract copy (the Ministry of Labour one, in Arabic and English), tenancy contract copy or ownership of residency documents (or a letter from your employer, if you are in company accommodation), a passport photo and the fee (Dhs.160 at time of writing). A&E and MMI usually have special offers whereby they give you back the value of the licence fee in vouchers to spend in their outlets.

## Automatic Licence Transfer

Citizens with licences from the following countries are eligible for automatic driving licence transfer: Australia, Austria, Bahrain, Belgium, Canada*, Cyprus, Czech Republic*, Denmark, Finland, France, Germany, Greece*, Iceland, Ireland, Italy, Japan*, Kuwait, Luxembourg, Netherlands, New Zealand, Norway, Oman, Poland*, Portugal*, Qatar, Saudi Arabia, Singapore, Slovakia, South Africa, South Korea*, Spain, Sweden, Switzerland, Turkey*, United Kingdom, United States.
*Citizens of these countries will require a letter of approval from their consulates and an Arabic translation of their driving licence (unless the original is in English).

### Traffic Police

- **Traffic Police HQ:** near Galadari Roundabout, Dubai-Sharjah Road (04 269 2222)
- **Bur Dubai Police Station**: Sheikh Zayed Road, Junction 4 (04 398 1111)
- **Al Quoz Police Station:** near Dubai Police Academy, Umm Suqeim Street (04 347 2222)

## Liquor Licence

Dubai has a relatively liberal attitude towards alcohol. You can't buy alcohol in supermarkets, but you can buy it from licensed liquor shops for home consumption if you have a liquor licence. Only hotels and sports clubs are allowed to serve alcoholic drinks in their bars and restaurants. Independent restaurants do not serve alcohol. To drink in a bar or restaurant you need to be 21 or older.

Applying for a liquor licence is straightforward, as long as you are non-Muslim, a resident of Dubai

### Get The Red Card

There are many benefits of getting your liquor licence, and not just because it can keep you out of trouble. MMI offers preferential treatment at events it sponsors, such as at the Rugby 7s, where you can use an express queue as long as you have your licence with you. You also get vouchers back to spend on alcohol, as well as gifts and special offers throughout the year.

The liquor store will then process your application through the Dubai Police on your behalf. Once approved, you will get a specified amount (based on your monthly salary, and determined at the discretion of the police) to spend on alcohol each month. The limit is usually enough to last you a month, although if you've got a big party planned you might need to stockpile over a few months, since you can't overspend on your limit. It should take around 10 days to process your licence.

Once you have your licence, you can buy alcohol from any branch of A&E or MMI throughout Dubai. However, it can work out expensive thanks to a 30% tax that is added to the marked price at the till. The range and service, however, is excellent. For a list of branches, see www.mmidubai.com and www.africanandeastern.com.

You can also buy alcohol from shops in neighbouring emirates, such as the Al Hamra Cellar in Ras Al Khaimah, the 'hole in the wall' near the Ajman Kempinski, and the Barracuda Beach Resort in Umm Al Quwain. To buy from these shops you do not need to show your liquor licence, but you do need to have a licence on you when transporting alcohol. It is also illegal to buy alcohol for home consumption unless you have a licence, so it is wise to keep your licence updated, even if you only ever buy your alcohol from 'non-licence' shops.

# JO'BURG HAS NO COASTLINE, IN DUBAI WE HAVE MILES OF GOLDEN BEACHES.

## FOR MANY MORE REASONS TO BE CHEERFUL TAKE ADVANTAGE OF ALL THE GREAT OFFERS IN STORE FOR YOU AT MMI.

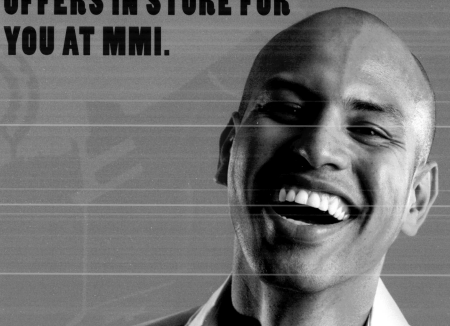

**VISIT OUR SHOPS AT** TRADE CENTRE RD • AL WASL • IBN BATTUTA MALL • BUR DUBAI • GREEN COMMUNITY • DEIRA
MALL OF THE EMIRATES • KARAMA • SHEIKH ZAYED ROAD • DUBAI SILICON OASIS • FESTIVAL CITY **Shop finder** www.mmidubai.com

# How To Make Friends

Getting to know new people is one of the most important things you can do to settle in – here are some ways to get connected.

Moving to a new country is a major upheaval in many ways, particularly as you've probably left a big network of friends and family behind. If you don't know anyone in your new home town, it's important to get out and about as soon as you can to meet people and make friends. Not only will these acquaintances be able to offer you loads of help in terms of cutting through red tape and getting word-of-mouth recommendations for a good school, doctor or hairdresser, some of them may also end up becoming life-long friends. Dubai's transient nature means people tend to come and go more frequently than in other places, but it generally follows that expats here are more sociable, amenable and open to friendship as a consequence – and the relationships you do make could last long after you've moved on to new pastures.

## Social Groups

Meeting new people early on is one of the keys for dealing with culture shock and starting the settling-in process. Talking to people you meet at work and in social situations will help you discover the lie of the land a lot more quickly – you'll be able to get advice on where to live, how to get things done, coping with the differences between your home country and the UAE.

To help you get started, there are numerous nationality-based and other social groups in Dubai, and these are handy for broadening your network of acquaintances, and ultimately your circle of friends:

**American Women's Association Of Dubai:** A group of volunteers offering information programmes, social functions and common interest groups to American women. www.awadubai.org

**Dubai Caledonian Society:** Provides a social network for Scottish expats and organises several major events each year, including the St Andrew's Ball in November

and the Chieftan's Ball in May. www.dubaicaledoniansociety.com

**Dubai Irish Society:** Promotes Irish culture, social events and sporting interests, as well as organising several events throughout the year. www.irishsocietydubai.com

**Dubai Manx Society:** This non-profit social and cultural organisation is dedicated to bringing the traditions of the Isle of Man to Dubai. www.dubaimanxsociety.com

**Dubai Toastmasters Club:** The Dubai branch of this worldwide, non-profit organisation provides a supportive environment that promotes self-confidence and personal growth. They meet twice a month. www.dubaitoastmasters.org

**Anza UAE:** This social and community group welcomes all Australians and New Zealanders living in the UAE, organising various events and functions throughout the year. www.anzauae.org

**Dubai St George's Society:** Serving the British expat community, the DSGS focuses mainly on fun and social activities, but also raises money for various charities. www.dsgs.org

There are also several web-based groups that will help you get settled too. Expatwoman is like a permanent virtual coffee morning, where you can log on to discuss anything from cleaning your dog to irritating husbands with fellow Dubai females, as well as more serious issues. The group organises real-life get-togethers too (so just be careful what you say about other posters in case you end up meeting them face to face). There are several Dubai groups on Facebook and Twitter as well (see Websites, p.24, for more ideas).

If you're a full-time parent there are a number of friendly mother and toddler groups in Dubai, which are great to break up those long days and help both mum and junior make new friends (see p.145).

> *If you don't know anyone in your new home town, it's important to get out and about as soon as you can to meet people and make friends.*

## Leisure

Joining a sports team is not only a fun means of staying in shape, it's also a great way to meet lots of new people and mix in new circles. Organisations such as Duplays (www.duplays.com) run a number of leagues and teams year-round which anybody can sign up to. See the Activities chapter (p.308) for details of some of the other clubs and societies that operate in Dubai.

## Network

Networking is one of the easiest ways to make new business contacts, so it makes sense that it is a good way to increase your social circle too.

With strict laws against dating and matchmaking services here in Dubai, these social networking groups are purely for meeting like-minded people in a friendly, social setting.

Below is a selection of some of the social networking groups that operate in Dubai. See Work, p.111, for a list of business networking groups.

**Rendezvous:** Billing itself as a 'dinner party without the dinner', Rendezvous meets in various locations to discuss monthly topics such as 'how do we achieve a balanced life?' or 'how can we make a positive difference?' www.rendezvousdubai.com

**Match:** Match meetings offer the opportunity to try 'speed networking' – mainly for creative groups. At Match you get two minutes to talk to each person before the buzzer goes and you have to move on. match.dubai@gmail.com

**Social Circles Dubai:** A well-organised social community that focuses on meeting new people and networking for business or pleasure. www.socialcirclesdubai.com

## Churches

The UAE has a fairly liberal and welcoming attitude to other religions, and as a result there are several active churches established in Dubai. Even if you're not a regular church-goer, these places also act as good community hubs.

**Church of Jesus Christ of Latter-Day Saints**
Oud Metha, 04 395 3883

**Christ Church Jebel Ali**
Jebel Ali, *www.christchurchjebelali.org*

**Dubai Evangelical Church Centre**
Jebel Ali, 04 884 6630, *www.deccc.com*

**Emirates Baptist Church International**
Jumeira, 04 349 1596, *www.ebci.org*

**Holy Trinity Church (Church of England)** Oud
Metha, 04 337 0247, *www.holytrinitychurchdubai.org*

**New Covenant Church**
Oud Metha, 04 335 1597, *www.nccuae.org*

**St Francis of Assisi Roman Catholic Church**
Jebel Ali, 04 884 5104, *www.stfrancisjebelali.ae*

**St Mary's Church Dubai** Oud Metha,
04 337 0087, *www.saintmarysdubai.com*

Dubai Media City

# BEFORE YOU LEAVE

Leaving already? Whether your time in Dubai lasts a few months, a few years or longer, there are a few things you should take care of before you jump on the plane. In the wake of the global recession, 2009 was full of tales of expats fleeing debts, abandoning cars at the airport and walking away from unmanageable negative property equity. Ideally, when you leave, you should have wrapped up all your financial affairs so that you don't end up 'doing a runner'. Some other things you will probably need to take care of include:

- Get your electricity, water and other utilities disconnected. You should remember that most providers (DEWA, Etisalat, du) will need at least two days' notice to take a final reading and return any security deposits you have paid. You'll need to settle the final bill before you get your deposit, and make sure you keep hold of the original deposit receipt to smooth the process. You'll also need to go through the official channels to close any bank accounts you have here. Banks (p.128) have been known to freeze an individual's account once they have been informed by the sponsor of a visa cancellation, so it's a good idea to get your finances in order first. See *Dubai Red-Tape* for full step-by-step procedures.
- Settle your debts – you can get into serious trouble if you try to leave the country without paying off all your loans and outstanding bills, so be sure to keep on top of payments to avoid large sums complicating your exit.
- If you are leaving rented accommodation, make sure the place is spick and span so that you can reclaim your entire security deposit. The landlord may also require a clearance certificate from DEWA to prove you've paid all your bills, so make sure you leave enough time for all the administration

involved. If you own a property you may choose to either sell or rent out your home – see Housing, p.70, and www.dubai.ae for more information.
- Sell your car. This has been a tricky one recently, with many people owing more than they can sell the car for, but persevere and be prepared to take a financial knock if you need to offload it quickly with a dealer. See p.62.
- Organise your shipping: Shop around for good rates and give as much notice as possible to the shipping company. See p.96.
- Sell the stuff you're not taking with you. Have a garage sale, list your items on www.dubizzle.com or www.expatwoman.com, or put photos up on supermarket noticeboards. Dubai Flea Market (p.395) and the car boot sale at Dubai Autodrome (www.carbootuae.com) are both good options for last-minute clearouts.
- If you've got any pets, and you are taking them with you, you will need to make sure their vaccinations are up to date, particularly the rabies vaccination. There are other procedures to be followed when exporting pets (p.148), and ideally you need around six months to prepare. If you can't take your pets with you, you should rehome them with a new family – Dubai has a dreadful problem with abandoned pets.

## Cancelling Your Visa

Your visa and how you cancel it will depend on the type of document you have. If you're on a residence visa that has been sponsored by your employer, as soon as your employment ends, so does your privilege to a work visa. Just as your employer would have been responsible for sorting out your paperwork, it is their responsibility to cancel it.

There's not much paper work involved, you'll have to submit your passport and sometimes sign a waiver or a memorandum of understanding clarifying that you have received all monies owed to you and so on. Once your visa has been cancelled, you have a grace period of 30 days to leave the country, after which time you will be fined at a rate of Dhs.25 per day for the first 6 months, Dhs.50 per day for the next 6 months, and Dhs.100 per day after that.

If you are in Dubai on a spousal visa, and have – for example – separated or just need to leave, you will need the help of your husband or wife to cancel your status. Again your spouse's company will have completed the paperwork, and they will accordingly get their employee (your husband or wife) to sign off on the cancellation papers.

The whole process takes about five days – whichever visa you happen to be on – and is reasonably smooth sailing.

Emirates Towers

# Reflections On Modern Dubai

Sultan Sooud Al Qassemi, an Emirati social commentator and writer, looks at the rich, cross-cultural influences on the city that has grown up around him.

## Recent Beginnings

In autumn of the year 2000, I was sat at home watching television when I saw Sheikh Mohammed bin Rashid, the then Crown Prince of Dubai, giving a speech in which he launched Dubai Internet City. At the time I, like others, was still coming to grips with the fallout of the recent internet bubble burst. I asked myself how an entire Internet City could be launched just a few short months after this crisis.

Today, many believe that it was this speech that signalled the race for Dubai to make its mark on the global map. Massive infrastructure projects were quickly launched and within a few years Dubai started counting tourists by the million, competing with other regional destinations such as Egypt and India.

## Dubai's Ancient Appeal

It would be a mistake to believe that Dubai's appeal for travellers started only recently. In fact many of its inhabitants and citizens today are the sons and daughters of immigrants, some of whom believed they were visiting for a short stay of a few weeks or a few months before settling here for good.

At the turn of the last century a large contingent of Persian merchants were attracted by Dubai's open, transparent trade policies and decided to establish a base on either side of the creek. So large was that influx that one of the most magical areas of Dubai, Bastakiya, takes its name from Bastak, the region in southern Persia from where these travellers came. Even today many of my friends carry that name, some of whom aren't from Bastak but adopted the name because of the area they were raised in. Bastakiya's location only a few hundred yards from the royal residence, Fahidi Fort, signifies the tolerant nature of the ruling Al Maktoum family, who welcomed their guests to settle in their immediate vicinity.

## Influences From Afar

Dubai's mosaic of ethnic origins has added to the city's charm, architecture, cuisine, vocabulary, trade links and diversity – ultimately enriching this already fascinating city. Today when I walk in Bastakiya I can't help but notice the melange of pan-Gulf cultures that can be seen in one street.

The barjeel, for instance, is a centuries-old windtower that can be found on both shores of the Gulf. I was personally so inspired by Bastakiya's barjeels that I chose that architectural icon as the name of my own brokerage firm in Dubai. My late father told me that the small windows on the exterior of these buildings allow privacy for the inhabitants and serve to keep out the sun light out, helping the rooms remain cool.

Down the creek in Shindagha the guest house of Sheikh Saeed Al Thani (p.241), a member of the ruling family of Qatar, displays very clear Hijazi architecture such as the mashrabiya, a crisscrossing wooden window panel that allows the inhabitant to peer out but blocks outsiders from looking in. Mashrabiyas can be found in Jeddah and Bahrain but their origins lie in the ancient streets of Cairo's Islamic quarter. My mother used to visit her friends in that very house on the creek to play and observe through mashrabiyas the boats on the creek carrying goods from lands afar. In addition to the rich Persian influence on Dubai, African,

DIFC: Dubai's changing face

Levantine, Bedouin, south Asian, Balouchi and central Asian cultures merge in this city and lend their names and traits to its neighbourhoods and streets. On one of our weekend drives around the city many years ago my father told me that, according to popular legend, the Port Saeed area of Dubai, in which there is no port at all, was thus named in honour of the Arab and Egyptian traders who relocated there many decades ago from the Egyptian port city with the same name.

## Early Dubai

Dubai's appeal was not unexpected; although the city's ancient history extends many thousands of years, its modern history was shaped by the ancestors of the current ruler in 1833. Then, Sheikh Maktoum bin Bati bin Suhail, who was a cousin of the respected Al Nahyan ruling family of Abu Dhabi, decided to establish his own emirate a hundred miles north of Abu Dhabi by the borders of Sharjah, then a formidable maritime empire and the city of my own ancestors.

Sheikh Hasher and his descendants realised that in order for the emirate to have a better chance of survival, demographic clout was essential, hence Dubai's open policy of welcoming travellers was born, and the city has not looked back since. The Al Maktoums went about securing their new emirate, establishing strategically positioned lookout posts that can still be seen dotted strategically around Dubai today if one knows where to look.

In order to appreciate the distances and the treacherous terrain that the former inhabitants had to cover in Dubai one must only travel a short distance from Al Fahidi Fort to Majlis Ghorfat Um Al Sheef, the former ruler's resting point in Jumeira. This journey would take us less than 15 minutes today from the creek but then it would have been covered in as long as half a day, even with the advent of the automobile, due to the lack of roads, as my father explained.

## Echoes Of The Past, Visions Of The Future

The Majlis Ghorfat Um Al Sheef is a simple house which, even today, offers an escape from the hustle of this global metropolis and transports its visitors back into a bygone era. The small well in the grounds served to quench the thirst of the ruler, his men and guests, as well as the visitors who were making their way from across the Gulf and inner Arabia to trade.

Dubai's own magical kingdom is the beautiful settlement of Hatta (p.282), which has been blissfully frozen in time for visitors to enjoy. I noticed how the architecture of this wondrous mountain village differs completely from the arches of Bastakiya. Here, echoes of Omani architecture are prevalent in the preserved houses, farms and forts.

I and other UAE Nationals experienced one of the proudest moments when the Dubai government started building hotels and monuments that would preserve the architecture of our coastal towns. Jumeirah's Al Qasr and Mina A'Salam remain two of the most sought after hotels by tourists and UAE Nationals, and Emaar's wonderful Old Town district has already established itself firmly in the hearts and minds of residents and tourists. I was personally glad to see Emaar's chairman Mohammed Al Abbar create an open air museum within Old Town by hosting statues and sculptures by the celebrated Colombian painter and sculptor Fernando Botero and Kuwaiti master artist Sami Al Saleh, whose Ghaf sculpture honours one of the most underappreciated trees in the deserts of Dubai. All of these developments are testament that you can draw inspiration from the past to engage with the present, which will continue to propel this magnificent city into greater success in the future.

# Car Accessories
# Auto Maintenance

### Car Accessories Available

Audio/Video Entertainment Systems
Navigation and Handsfree Gadgets
Alloy Wheels
Performance Tires
Window Tint Film
4x4 and Off-Road Equipment
Safety and Emergency Gear
Brake Discs
Performance Grade Suspension Kits
Sports Style Interior Upgrades
Interior and Exterior Accent Lighting
Car Care and Cleaning Products
Touch up and restoration kits
Car Interior Accessories

### AutoMaintenance Services Offered

Lube Services
Car Wash Services
Car Detailing Services
Window tinting
Paintless Dent Removal
Paint Protection film
Tire fitting and balancing
Wheel Alignment
Tire repair
Battery testing & replacement
Brakes Maintenance

**YellowHat**
*Japan*

Times Square Center Branch
Tel: 04 341 8593

Email: info@yellowhat.ae
www.yellowhat.ae

Nad Al Hamar Branch
Tel: 04 289 8060

Getting Around

# Getting Around

# GETTING AROUND IN DUBAI

Private cars and taxis have long been the primary means of transportation for many of Dubai's residents, and the government has made great strides in improving the city's infrastructure to accommodate all of the drivers. Traffic is still a major problem, but Dubai's public transportation options are also getting better, especially with the opening of the beautiful new Metro and a much improved bus network.

Many residents of Dubai are crazy about cars and you'll see every make and model imaginable cruising down the highway. Buying, insuring, registering and maintaining your car is fairly easy and straightforward, but getting a driving licence can be a drawn-out nightmare for some. Dubai's roads can be dangerous if you're not careful, but if you avoid speeding, pay attention at all times and learn how to drive defensively you will gain confidence in no time.

## Dubai's Road Network

When you arrive in Dubai, the extensive, expanding network of roads can be intimidating, but once you find your bearings and become familiar with the city's layout, you'll find things easier. The creek divides Bur Dubai (to the south) and Deira (to the north), and has five main crossing points: Shindagha Tunnel, Maktoum Bridge, Garhoud Bridge, Business Bay Bridge and the Floating Bridge.

The main thoroughfare through the city is Sheikh Zayed Road, which runs from Sharjah, parallel to the sea, all the way to Abu Dhabi. Three bypass roads have been constructed inland towards the desert to ease the city's congestion problems. All run parallel to the coast and Sheikh Zayed Road. Al Khail Road

Wafi Roundabout

(E44) is the closest bypass to the coast and runs from Sports City to Ras Al Khor, where it turns east and heads towards Hatta and Oman. Emirates Road (E311) is the next furthest from the coast and connects Abu Dhabi directly to Sharjah and the northern emirates. The Outer Ring Road (E611) sits outside of Emirates Road and runs roughly from the southern border of Dubai to the northern border of Sharjah, although it is currently being expanded. There are also a few main east-west roads, including Umm Suqeim Road (D63), the Dubai-Al Ain Road (E66), Doha Street (D71), and Muscat Street (D69).

Despite all the road expansions, traffic is still a problem in Dubai, and the worst rush-hour bottlenecks usually form at the creek crossings. Within the city, the roads in older parts of town such as Bur Dubai and Deira are smaller and more congested, while the road networks in newer developments such as Downtown Burj Dubai tend to accommodate greater traffic flow.

## Traffic Regulations

While the infrastructure is superb, the general standard of driving is not. The UAE has one of the world's highest death rates per capita due to traffic accidents. Basic driving discipline is often a problem, and aggressive driving, swerving, pulling out suddenly, lane hopping, tail-gating and drifting happen far too regularly. As a result, you must take extra caution when driving on Dubai's roads.

It is important to note is that you drive on the right side of the road in Dubai, and you should overtake on the left – people often ignore this rule but if you are caught you could receive a fine (see p.58).

Speed limits are usually 60 to 80kph around town, while on main roads and roads to other emirates they are 100 to 120kph. The speed limit is clearly indicated on road signs. Both fixed and movable radar traps, and Dubai Traffic Police, are there to catch the unwary violator.

### Parking

Most street parking in Dubai is now governed by parking meters. You pay Dhs.1 or Dhs.2 for one hour, depending on how busy the area is. After feeding your coins into the machine, you get a printed ticket that you must display on your dashboard. The price increases steeply the longer you park in a spot, so you'll pay Dhs.5 for two hours, Dhs.8 for three hours, and Dhs.11 for four hours (the maximum). Parking is free from 13:00 to 16:00 and 21:00 to 08:00 daily and on Fridays and public holidays. Several Dubai neighbourhoods now support the mParking system (www.mpark.rta.ae), which allows drivers to pay parking tolls through SMS. Vehicles with Dubai licence plates do not need to register for the system, but non-Dubai registered vehicles must register online

## Maps

With new roads popping up on a weekly basis, finding your way around Dubai can be difficult. Explorer Publishing produces several of the most up-to-date street maps available, including the fully indexed *Dubai Street Atlas* and the pocket-sized *Dubai Mini Map*.

first. Areas where mParking is supported will have an orange sign displaying the parking code and a step-by-step guide on how to use the system. To use mParking, send an SMS to PARK (7275) with your car licence plate number (including the first letter), a space, the area parking code listed on the sign, a space, and the number of hours you wish to pay for (one to four). The system will then send you a confirmation SMS, and the parking fee plus a 30 or 40 fils service charge will be deducted from your Etisalat or du phone credit. Ten minutes before your time has expired, the system will send an SMS reminder and ask if you'd like to add more time.

## Road Signs

Signposting in Dubai is generally good once you understand the system. Blue or green signs indicate the roads, exits or locations out of the city, and brown signs show heritage sites, places of interest and hospitals. Dubai's new signage system relies more heavily on street names and compass directions, compared to the older system which relied more on local area names. If the signage gets confusing, remember that Abu Dhabi is south of Dubai, Sharjah is north of Dubai, the beach is to the west and the desert is to the east.

## Address System

All roads are numbered to aid navigation, but the numbers are gradually being phased out and replaced with official road names. In Jumeira 3, where a successful pilot of this scheme was run, all of the roads are named. Although all roads in the city have an official name or number, many roads are referred to by a different moniker. For instance, Al Jumeira Road is often known as Beach Road, and Interchange One, on Sheikh Zayed Road, is invariably called Defence Roundabout. Dubai Municipality has started a more formal road-naming process to help eliminate confusion, and many of the city's main roads have been given the names of prominent Arab cities, such as Marrakech Road. Street signs now also include the direction of travel, so you know whether you are travelling north or south of Dubai.

This lack of consistency makes locating an address difficult. Companies often only list their building name, road and nearest landmark when writing

their address. The *Dubai Street Atlas* makes locating particular buildings much easier with an index of over 13,000 roads and buildings.

## People With Disabilities

Dubai is starting to consider the needs of disabled visitors more seriously and services for disabled residents are improving. Dubai International Airport is well equipped for disabled travellers, with automatic doors, large lifts and all counters accessible by wheelchair users, as well as several services such as porters, special transportation and quick check-in to avoid long queues. Dubai Transport has a few specially modified taxis for journeys from the airport and around town. Some Metro stations have disabled access and its trains are have wider doors and are flush with the platform making access easier for wheelchair uses. There are also talks that the Metro will be free for disabled commuters in the near future. Disabled parking spaces do exist, there are ignorant drivers who don't need the facility; however, police do monitor these spaces and hand out fines to offenders.

Most of Dubai's five-star hotels have wheelchair access, but in general, facilities for disabled guests are limited, particularly at tourist attractions. Wheelchair ramps are often really nothing more than delivery ramps and therefore have steep angles. When asking if a location has wheelchair access, make sure it really does – an escalator is considered 'wheelchair access' to some.

The Dubai Department of Tourism and Commerce Marketing (DTCM) is responsible for improving access for the physically challenged visit the website www. dubaitourism.ae for more information.

## Cycling

Although the RTA has often talked about the benefits of cycling in the city's most congested districts, not much has been done to promote this form of transportation. You cannot cycle on Dubai's highways and even riding within city neighbourhoods can be dangerous. Also, summer temperatures can reach 45°C, which makes riding a bike to work a very sweaty option.

## Walking

Cities in the UAE are generally very car oriented and not designed to encourage walking. Additionally, summer temperatures of over 45°C are not conducive to spending any length of time walking through the city. The winter months, however, make walking a pleasant way to get around and people can be found strolling through the streets, especially in the evenings. Most streets are lined with pavements and there are pedestrian paths either side of the creek, along the seafront in Deira and Jumeira, as well as in the parks throughout the city.

Police have vowed to crack down on jaywalking in Dubai in an effort to encourage people to cross roads at designated pedestrian crossings only. If you cross the road in an undesignated area, you could face a fine.

# PUBLIC TRANSPORT

In an effort to ease the city's congestion problems, the government has made a serious commitment to improving public transportation. The Metro is the centrepiece of its efforts and, when it is fully operational by the end of 2010, it should reduce the overall number of daily drivers. Dubai's bus system has also seen major improvements over the past few years with the introduction of air conditioned bus stops, new buses and an increase in the number of routes. To join these systems, as well as the city's water-bus system, the Roads and Transport Authority (www.rta.ae) implemented an automatic payment system called 'Nol', which is now the only method of payment accepted on Dubai's public transportation.

## Air Travel

Currently, more than 150 airlines take advantage of Dubai's open skies policy, operating to and from nearly 200 destinations. The airport's three terminals are a 15 to 30 minute taxi ride apart, depending on the traffic, and there's also a shuttle bus. All terminals offer car rental, hotel reservations and exchange services. Most of the better-known airlines use Terminal 1, while Terminal 2 is used primarily by Flydubai and airlines serving former Soviet countries and central Asia. Terminal 3, which opened in 2008, is the newest and most luxurious of the three and is dedicated for the use of Emirates Airlines. Both Terminal 1 and Terminal 3 have a vast selection of drinking and dining venues, plus the famously large Duty Free shopping section. For up-to-date flight information from Dubai International Airport, call 04 216 6666.

Dubai's official airline, Emirates (www.emirates.com), operates scheduled services to almost 100 destinations in over 50 countries. Newcomer, Flydubai (www.flydubai.com), is a low-cost carrier based in Dubai that flies mainly to other Arab cities such as Damascus and Alexandria, however expansion plans are underway. Both airlines use the Dubai International Airport as their hub of operations. Two other airlines are based in the UAE. Etihad Airways (www.etihadairways.com) is based in Abu Dhabi and low-coast carrier Air Arabia (www.airarabia.com) is based in Sharjah. Abu Dhabi airport is a 90 minute drive from Dubai, and Sharjah airport is 45 minutes away. For more information on travelling from Dubai, see the Out of the City chapter on p.273.

All three terminals have both short and long-term parking facilities, as well as busy taxi ranks. There are Metro stations at both Terminal 1 and Terminal 3 that any traveller can access. The stations are part of the Red Line, which runs throughout Deira, under the creek and along Sheikh Zayed Road all the way to Jebel Ali. Keep in mind that check-in-sized luggage is not permitted on the Metro.

An airport buses operates to and from Dubai International Airport every 30 minutes, 24 hours a day. There are two routes: Route 401 services Deira, while 402 serves Bur Dubai. The fare is Dhs.3. Call 800 9090 for details, or log on to www.rta.ae.

## Airlines

**Aeroflot** 04 222 2245, *www.aeroflot.ru*
**Air Arabia** 06 508 8888, *www.airarabia.com*
**Air France** 04 602 5400, *www.airfrance.ae*
**Air India** 04 227 6787, *www.airindia.com*
**Air Mauritius** 04 221 4455, *www.airmauritius.com*
**Air New Zealand** 04 335 9126, *www.airnewzealand.com*
**Air Seychelles** 04 286 8008, *www.airseychelles.com*
**Alitalia** 04 282 6113, *www.alitalia.com*
**American Airlines** 04 393 3234, *www.aa.com*
**Austrian Airlines** 04 294 1403, *www.aua.com*
**Bangladesh Biman Airlines** 04 222 0942, *www.bimanair.com*
**British Airways** 04 307 5777, *www.britishairways.com*
**Cathay Pacific** 04 204 2888, *www.cathaypacific.com*
**China Airlines** 02 626 4070, *www.china-airlines.com*
**CSA Czech Airlines** 04 294 5666, *www.czechairlines.com*
**Cyprus Airways** 04 221 5325, *www.cyprusairways.com*
**Delta Airlines** 04 397 0118, *www.delta.com*
**Egypt Air** 02 228 9444, *www.egyptair.com*
**Emirates Airline** 04 214 4444, *www.emirates.com*
**Etihad Airways** 800 2277, *www.etihadairways.com*
**Flydubai** 04 301 0800, *www.flydubai.com*
**Gulf Air** 04 271 3222, *www.gulfair.com*
**Iran Air** 04 224 0200, *www.iranair.com*
**Japan Airlines** 04 232 5799, *www.jal.com*
**KLM Royal Dutch Airlines** 04 319 3777, *www.klm.com*
**Kuwait Airways** 04 228 1106, *www.kuwait-airways.com*
**Lufthansa** 04 316 6642, *www.lufthansa.com*
**Malaysia Airlines** 04 397 0250, *www.malaysiaairlines.com*
**Middle East Airlines** 04 223 7080, *www.mea.com.lb*
**Olympic Airlines** 04 221 4455, *www.olympicairlines.com*
**Oman Air** 04 351 8080, *www.oman-air.com*
**Pakistan International Airlines** 04 222 0913, *www.piac.com.pk*

Qantas 04 316 6652, *www.qantas.com*
Qatar Airways 04 229 2229, *www.qatarairways.com*
Royal Brunei Airlines 04 351 9330,
*www.bruneiair.com*
Royal Jet Group 02 575 7000, *www.royaljetgroup.com*
Royal Jordanian Airlines 04 4 216 6810, *www.rj.com*
Saudi Arabian Airlines 04 229 6111,
*www.saudiairlines.com*
Singapore Airlines 04 316 6888,
*www.singaporeair.com*
South African Airways 04 397 0766, *www.flysaa.com*
Sri Lankan Airlines 04 316 6711, *www.srilankan.aero*
Swiss Air 04 294 5051, *www.swiss.com*
Thai Airways 04 268 1702, *www.thaiair.com*
United Airlines 04 316 6942, *www.ual.com*
Virgin Atlantic 04 406 0600, *www.virgin-atlantic.com*

# Boat

Crossing the creek by abra is a common method of transport for many people in Dubai, with the number of passengers in 2008 estimated at over 20 million. The fare for a single journey across Dubai Creek is Dhs.1, and the abras run from 05:00 to midnight. There are four recently renovated abra stations, two on the Deira side near the souks and two on the Bur Dubai side near the Ruler's Court.

## ┌─ Abra Ka Dabra ─────────

Unique to the region, an abra is a wooden, single engine boat used to carry passengers across the creek. Long before the construction of Dubai's four bridges and one tunnel, abras were the primary method of crossing the creek. Each covered abra can carry around 10 seated passengers. Abras don't run on a regular schedule, as they tend to depart as soon as all of their seats have been filled.

The RTA also manages a fleet of air-conditioned water buses costing Dhs.4 per trip. There are four waterbus routes running up and down the creek, from Bur Dubai to Deira and all the way down to Creekside Park. There is also a waterbus route aimed at tourists that runs the length of the creek, costs Dhs.24 and takes 45 minutes. The route starts and stops at the Shindagha station.

It is possible to travel from Dubai, Sharjah and Ras Al Khaimah to several ports in Iran by hydrofoil or dhow cost. Prices between Dhs.130 and Dhs.250, and the journey time can be up to 12 hours depending on the travel option chosen. For more information, contact the Oasis Freight Agency on 06 559 6320.

The RTA is developing a new water taxi project in a bid to help clear congestion on major routes. Due for completion in mid 2010, the scheme will see 20 stations dotted along Dubai Creek and coastline which will be served by a fleet of luxury water taxis

that customers can book over the telephone, similar to a regular taxi. Taxi stations will include four at the marina, with further stops catering to the hotels along the Jumeira stretch.

# Bus

There are currently more than 70 bus routes servicing the main residential and commercial areas of Dubai. While all of the buses and most of the bus shelters are air-conditioned and modern, they do tend to be rather crowded. In conjunction with the unveiling of the Metro, the RTA is taking concrete steps to increase usage of the city's bus system, which now stands at roughly 6% of the population. Many of the bus stations now display better timetables and route maps and a host of double-deck and articulated buses have helped with the crowding problem.

The main bus stations are near the Gold Souk in Deira and on Al Ghubaiba Road in Bur Dubai. Buses run at regular intervals, starting between 05:00 and 06:00 and going until midnight or so, and a handful of Nightliner buses operate from 23:30 till 06:00. The front three rows of seats on all buses are reserved for women and children only. Cash is not accepted so you need to purchase a Nol card (see above) before boarding.

Buses also go further to Khawaneej, Al Awir, Hatta, and even Oman, for very reasonable prices – a one-way ticket to Hatta, which is 100 kilometres away, is Dhs.7, while Dubai to Muscat takes six hours and costs Dhs.50. The E1 service links Dubai and Abu Dhabi. From early morning to late at night, buses operate every 40 minutes between Al Ghubaiba and Abu Dhabi Central bus stations, and the two-hour journey costs Dhs.15 each way. There is also a service to and from Al Arouba Road and Al Wahda in Sharjah to both Bur Dubai and Deira, which runs every 10 minutes and costs Dhs.5. For a complete list of the RTA's inter-emirate routes, check the website (www.rta.ae).

# Metro

The Dhs.28 billion Dubai Metro opened in September 2009, bringing public transport to the masses. At launch, only 10 of 29 stations of the Red Line were open, with the rest due to follow by February 2010. The Red Line runs from Rashidiyah to the airport, and down Sheikh Zayed Road, terminating at Jebel Ali (see pull-out map). The Green Line, running from Al Qusais on the Sharjah border to Jaddaf, is due to open in March 2010, with Blue, Purple and Pink lines planned or rumoured up to 2020. Trains run from around 06:00 to 23:00 everyday except Friday (14:00 to 23:00) at intervals of 3 to 4 minutes at peak times. Each train has a section for women and children only, and a first or 'Gold' class cabin. The fare structure operates as a pay-as-you-go system in which you touch your prepaid 'Nol' card (see below) to the gates at the entrances and exits of stations.

# Public Transport

The RTA has developed a feeder bus system to transport passengers from stations to local destinations. The feeder buses are free if boarded within 30 minutes of exiting the Metro. Each station is also slated to have a taxi rank outside the exit to help travellers reach destinations that aren't accessible by bus. Check the RTA's journey planner (see below) for travel options.

## Plan Your Trip

The best way to work out your public transport options is to use the Road & Transport Authority's (RTA) online journey planner (http://wojhati.rta.ae). For further assistance, call the RTA on 800 9090.

A monorail runs the length of Palm Jumeirah from the Gateway Towers station on the mainland to Atlantis hotel. Trains run daily from 08:00 to 22:00 and cost Dhs.15 for a single fare or Dhs.25 for a return. Work has also begun on a tramline along Al Sufouh Road which will eventually service Dubai Marina, Media City and Knowledge Village, linking to the Metro system and the Palm Monorail.

## Nol

Introduced with the opening of the Metro, Nol cards are rechargeable travel cards which can be used to pay for public transport and street car parking in Dubai. The card is meant to help streamline the Metro, bus and water bus systems, and fares are calculated by the number of zones travelled through on a single journey, regardless of what form of transportation you use. Single journeys start at Dhs.1.80 for up to 3km, rising to Dhs.6.50 for travel across two or more zones. The red Nol card is a paper ticket aimed at tourists and occasional users. It can be charged for up to 10 journeys, but is only valid on one type of transport – bus, Metro or water bus. The silver Nol card costs Dhs.20, including Dhs.14 credit. It can be recharged up to Dhs.500 and is a better option if you plan to use different types of public transport or travel extensively while in town. The gold card is identical to the silver, except that holders are charged first class prices (usually double the standard fare) and can travel in the Gold Class cabins of the Metro. Nol cards can be purchased and topped up at Metro and bus stations and at selected stores including Carrefour and Spinneys supermarkets. Information on the Nol fare structure and a map of the different zones can be found at www.nol.ae.

## Taxi

If you don't have a car, taxis are still the most common way of getting around. There are nearly 7,000 metered taxis in Dubai with a fixed fare structure. The cars are all beige with different coloured roofs. A fleet of 'ladies taxis' was launched in 2007, with distinctive pink roofs. These cars have female drivers and are meant for female passengers or mixed-gender groups only.

Taxis can be flagged down by the side of the road or you can make a Dubai Transport taxi booking by calling 04 208 0808. If you make a booking, you will pay a slightly higher starting fare. The DTC automated phone system stores your address after the first time you call. Each subsequent time you ring from that number, just listen to the prompts, hit 1, and a cab will be dispatched automatically, (or hit 2, then enter a later time using the phone's keypad). All DTC taxis now have GPS too, so the nearest car can reach you in the shortest time. Unfortunately, the dispatch centre never gives approximate wait times, so the cab could arrive in five minutes or 30. Waits are usually longer on weekends.

Dubai Creek

The minimum taxi fare is Dhs.10, and the pickup fare ranges from Dhs.3 to Dhs.7, depending on the time of day, and whether or not you ordered by phone. The starting fare inside the airport area is Dhs.20. Taxis are exempt from Salik tolls, but crossing the border into Sharjah adds another Dhs.20 to the fare. The rate for stoppage or waiting is 50 fils per minute, so don't be surprised when the meter keeps running in standstill traffic. Taxis can be hired for six hours for Dhs.300 or for 12 hours for Dhs.500.

Dubai taxi drivers occasionally lack a decent knowledge of the city and passengers may have to direct them. Start with the area of destination and then choose a major landmark, such as a hotel, roundabout or shopping centre. Then narrow it down as you get closer. It's helpful to take the phone number of your destination with you, in case you and your driver get lost. At a last resort, you can ask the driver to radio his control point for instructions.

Finding a taxi in congested areas can be difficult, and in their frustration, many people are using illegal cabs. Be warned though that unlicensed taxis haven't had to meet the safety standards for their cars that legal cabs do. As these cabs are difficult to trace, there have also been cases where drivers have either been the victim of crimes or have perpetrated them.

## Passenger Rights

Taxi drivers are obliged to accept any fare, no matter the distance. They are also obliged to drive in a safe manner, so don't be timid about asking them to slow down. If a driver refuses to pick you up because of your destination or refuses to drive responsibly, you can call the RTA complaint line and report the driver. The RTA takes complaints seriously and will most likely call you back to let you know how the situation was handled.

# DRIVING
## Getting A Driving Licence

Once you have your residence permit you can apply for a permanent (10 year) Dubai licence. Nationals of the countries listed below can automatically transfer their driving licence, as long as the original is valid. Take your existing foreign licence, your passport (with residency stamp), an eye test certificate (available from any optometrist), two passport photos, and a Dhs.100 fee to any of the RTA Customer Centres (www.rta.ae). The process is quite easy and you should have your licence that same day.

If your nationality is not on the automatic transfer list you will need to sit a UAE driving test to be eligible to drive in Dubai. Much of the process has been handed over to the five authorised driving institutes listed below, so you can apply for a learner's permit

at the driving school directly, instead of going to the Traffic Police.

┌─ **Traffic Jam Session** ────────────

Avoid a traffic jam by tuning in to any of the following radio channels: Al Arabiya (98.9 FM), Al Khallejiya (100.9 FM), Dubai 92 (92.00 FM), Channel 4 FM (104.8 FM), and Emirates 1 FM (99.3FM, 100.5 FM). Regular updates about the traffic situation on main roads are provided throughout the day, forewarning you if a certain road is blocked so you can take an alternative route.

Some driving institutions insist that you pay for a set of prebooked lessons. In some cases, the package extends to 52 lessons and can cost up to Dhs.4,000. The lessons usually last 30 to 45 minutes during the week, or longer lessons can be taken at weekends. Other companies offer lessons on an hourly basis, as and when you like, for around Dhs.35 per hour. Women are generally required to take lessons with a female instructor, at a cost of Dhs.65 per hour. You will take three different tests on different dates. One is a Highway Code test, another includes parking and manoeuvres, and the third is a road test. You also have to take an assessment prior to doing the final test. Before you are issued with your permanent driving licence you will have to attend a number of road safety lectures, the cost of which is incorporated into the price of your lessons. It is not uncommon to fail the road test multiple times. Each time you fail, you will need to attend and pay for another set of lessons before you can take the test again.

Always carry your licence when driving. If you fail to produce it during a police spot check you will be fined. You should also ensure you have the car's registration card in the car.

┌─ **Automatic Licence Transfer** ─────────

Australia, Austria, Bahrain, Belgium, Canada*, Cyprus, Czech Republic*, Denmark, Finland, France, Germany, Greece*, Iceland, Ireland, Italy, Japan*, South Korea*, Kuwait, Luxembourg, Netherlands, New Zealand, Norway, Oman, Poland*, Portugal*, Qatar, Saudi Arabia, Singapore, Slovakia, South Africa, Spain, Sweden, Switzerland, Turkey*, United Kingdom, United States. *Citizens of these countries require a letter of approval from their consulates and an Arabic translation of their driving licence (unless the original is in English).

The rules for riding a motorbike in Dubai are similar to driving a car. If you have a transferable licence from your home country, you can get a six-month

# Driving

temporary licence or a 10 year permanent one (as listed previously).

## Driving Schools

**Al Ahli Driving Center** 04 341 1500, *www.alahlidubai.com*
**Belhasa Driving Center** 04 324 3535, *www.bdc.ae*
**Dubai Driving Center** 04 345 5855, *www.dubaidrivingcenter.net*
**Emirates Driving Institute** 04 263 1100, *www.edi-uae.com*
**Galadari Motor Driving Centre** 04 267 6166, *www.gmdc.ae*

### Safe Driver

If you've had a drink, don't even think about getting behind the wheel of your car. Instead, call Safe Driver (04 268 8797, www.saferdriver.ae), which will send a driver to pick you up and drive your car home for you. Rates vary depending on distance, but the minimum charge is Dhs.120. Money well spent.

## Renewing A Driving Licence

Licences can be renewed at any of the RTA Customer Centres (www.rta.ae). The procedure costs Dhs.110 and you will need to take your UAE ID card (see p.40), an eyesight test and the expired driving licence. The process is usually quick if there isn't a queue.

## Car Pooling

In an effort to reduce rush-hour congestion, the government has introduced an online lift sharing programme (www.sharekni.ae). After registering online, a passenger can search for a driver that lives nearby and is heading to the same destination. Drivers can also register for the programme to request passengers. The programme aims to legalise carpooling while minimising the number of illegal cabs in the city. Cash is not to be transferred from passenger to driver, but passengers can pay for petrol. Co-workers do not need to register with the programme to share rides.

## Salik

Salik is an automated toll system for Dubai's roads. There are currently four gates: one at Garhoud Bridge, another on the Sheikh Zayed Road after Mall of the Emirates, one at Safa Park on Sheikh Zayed Road (between interchanges one and two), and another on Maktoum Bridge. The Maktoum Bridge crossing is free between 22:00 and 06:00 and 22:00 and 09:00 on Fridays, when the Floating Bridge is closed. There are no booths, and no need to stop as you drive through. Instead, drivers stick a tag to their windscreen, which is read by radio frequency as they pass through.

Drivers must initially buy a 'welcome pack' costing Dhs.100: Dhs.50 for the tag and Dhs.50 credit. It costs Dhs.4 each time you pass a toll gate, but if you travel between the Al Barsha toll gate and the Al Safa toll gate during one trip (and in the space of an hour) you will only be charged once. The maximum you will be charged in one day is Dhs.24. If your Salik card is out of credit you will be fined Dhs.50 for each gate you pass through. The Salik system will send you an SMS when your account balance runs low or when you pass through a gate without any balance. The kit can be bought from Emarat, EPPCO, ENOC, and ADNOC petrol stations, Dubai Islamic Bank and Emirates Bank. Salik fees do not have to be paid by passengers in taxis. For more information about the toll gates, visit the Salik website, www.salik.ae, or call 800 72545 (800 SALIK).

## Traffic Fines & Offences

In an effort to help combat bad driving, the Dubai Police initiated a black points system to go along with the existing fines system. You are issued a certain number of black points against your licence according to the particular violation. For example, the fine for allowing a child under 10 years of age to sit in the front of a car is Dhs.100 and the driver will be given four black points. If you get 24 points you will lose your licence for a year, but any points you acquire will expire 12 months after they are issued. Parking fines start at Dhs.200, and speeding fines start at Dhs.400 for driving up to 10kph over the speed limit and go up from there. Driving in a reckless manner or racing will earn you 6 points, as will parking in a handicapped zone or in front of a fire hydrant. Black points aren't usually awarded for speeding violations, unless you are driving more than 50kph over the speed limit; in which case you will be given six black points along with a Dhs.900 fine. An outline of the black point system can be found on the Dubai Police website (www.dubaipolice.gov.ae).

Average-speed and stopping-distance traps were recently introduced to try to catch speeding drivers who only slow down when they see speed cameras, and to discourage tailgating. On-the-spot traffic fines for certain offences have been introduced, but in most cases you won't know you've received a fine until you check on the Dubai Police website or renew your vehicle registration. Most fines are paid when you renew your annual car registration. However, parking tickets that appear on your windscreen must be paid within a week; the amount increases if you don't pay within the time allotted on the back of the ticket.

Dubai Police exercises a strict zero tolerance policy on drinking and driving. This means that if you have had anything to drink, you are much better off taking a taxi home or getting a lift. If you get into an accident, whether it is your fault or not, and you fail a blood-alcohol test you could find yourself spending a night in a police cell before a trial in Dubai Courts, after which a jail sentence will most likely be applied. In addition, your insurance is automatically void. Police have increased the number of random drink-driving checks. You should also be aware that alcohol still in your system from the night before will get you in just as much trouble.

## Blood Money

As the law currently stands, the family of a pedestrian killed in a road accident is entitled to Dhs.200,000 diya (blood) money. The money is usually paid by the insurance company unless there's any whiff of the driver having been under the influence of alcohol. However, an amendment to the law is being considered to put a stop to the terrible trend among desperate lower-income workers of killing themselves to provide for their family. This will mean blood money is not automatically due if the victim was walking across a road not intended for use by pedestrians, such as Sheikh Zayed Road.

## Breakdowns

In the event of a breakdown, you will usually find that passing police cars will stop to help, or at least to check your documents. It's important that you keep water in your car at all times so you don't get dehydrated while waiting. Dubai Traffic officers recommend, if possible, that you pull your car over to a safe spot. If you are on the hard shoulder of a highway you should pull your car as far away from the yellow line as possible and step away from the road until help arrives.

The Arabian Automobile Association (AAA) (04 266 9989 or 800 4900, www.aaauae.com) offers a 24 hour roadside breakdown service for an annual charge. This includes help in minor mechanical repairs, battery boosting, or help if you run out of petrol, have a flat tyre or lock yourself out. Mashreq Bank Visa card holders receive free AAA membership. The more advanced service includes off-road recovery, vehicle registration and a rent-a-car service. Other breakdown services that will be able to help you out without membership include IATC (www.iatcuae.com), Dubai Auto Towing Services (04 359 4424) and AKT Recovery (04 263 6217). Some dealers offer a free breakdown and recovery service for the first few years after buying a new car. Be sure to ask the dealership about this option when purchasing a new car.

## Traffic Accidents

If you are involved in an accident call 999. If the accident is minor and no one has been hurt you need to agree with the other driver where the blame lies and move your cars to the side of the road to avoid obstructing the flow of traffic. You can be fined Dhs.100 for failing to do so even if the accident wasn't your fault. If blame has been clearly decided and the accident is minor, the 999 dispatcher may ask you to drive yourself to the nearest Traffic Police station to fill out the necessary paperwork. The Dubai Police Information Line (800 7777, Arabic and English) gives the numbers of police stations around the emirate.

If blame cannot be decided without police intervention, an officer will be dispatched to assess the accident and apportion blame. The officer will then give you a copy of the accident report, if it is green then the other party is at fault but if it is pink then you are to blame for the accident and you will receive a Dhs.200 fine from the attending officer. You will need to submit the accident report to the insurance company in order to process the claim, or to the garage for repairs. Keep in mind that garages rarely repair vehicles without a police report.

Stray animals are something to avoid on desert roads. If the animal hits your vehicle and causes damage or injury, the animal's owner should pay compensation, but if you are found to have been speeding, you must compensate the animal's owner.

## Petrol Stations

Petrol is subsidised in the UAE and generally inexpensive. Within Dubai you will find Emarat, ENOC and EPPCO stations and the price of unleaded petrol (Dhs.6.25 or Dhs.6.75) is the same at all of them. The octane rating of unleaded petrol in the UAE is high – 'Special' is rated at 95 octane and 'Super' at 98 octane. Many of the stations have convenience stores and some have small cafes or fast food restaurants attached to them. Every station is manned by attendants that will pump your petrol for you. You can't use credit or debit cards to purchase fuel or shop items, and many stations don't have ATMs, so make sure you have enough cash before the pump starts.

## Cash Only

In 2007, petrol stations adopted a 'cash only' policy whereas before you could pay for your petrol by debit and credit card. So make sure you have cash to hand before you fill up, and don't rely on there being an ATM at all petrol stations.

# GETTING A CAR

## Hiring A Car

New arrivals to Dubai often find that they have no other option than to hire a vehicle until their residency papers go though. Most leasing companies include the following in their rates: registration, maintenance, replacement, 24 hour assistance and insurance. All the main car rental companies, plus a few extra, can be found in Dubai. It is best to shop around as the rates vary considerably. The larger, reputable firms generally

# Getting A Car

have more reliable vehicles and a greater capacity to help in an emergency (an important factor when dealing with the aftermath of an accident). Find out which car hire agent your company uses, as you might qualify for a corporate rate. Most rental companies will keep track of how many times you pass through Salik gates (p.58) and charge you at the end of the month, along with a Salik service charge.

Leasing is generally weekly, monthly or yearly. Monthly lease prices start at around Dhs.1,500 for a small vehicle such as a Toyota Yaris, and go up from there. As the lease period increases, the price decreases, so if you're considering keeping the car for a long period, it may not work out that much more expensive than buying.

Before you take possession of your leased car, check for any dents or bumps. To hire any vehicle you will need to provide a passport copy, credit card and a valid driving licence. Those with a residence visa must have a UAE driving licence to drive a hired car, while those on a visit visa can use a licence from their home country as long as it is at least one year old. Comprehensive insurance is essential; make sure that it includes personal accident coverage, and perhaps Oman cover if you're planning on exploring.

## Car Hire Companies

**Autolease Rent-a-Car** 04 282 6565, *www.autolease-uae.com*
**Avis** 04 295 7121, *www.avisuaecarhire.com*
**Budget Rent A Car** > *p.61* 04 295 6667, *www.budget-uae.com*
**Diamond Lease** 04 343 4330, *www.diamondlease.com*
**Discount Rent A Car** 04 338 9060, *www.discountcardubai.com*
**Dubai Exotic Limo**, 04 286 8635, *www.dubaiexoticlimo.com*

**EuroStar Rent-a-Car** 04 266 1117, *www.eurostarrental.com*
**Hertz** 04 282 4422, *www.hertz-uae.com*
**Icon Car Rental** 04 257 8228, *www.dubairentacar.ae*
**National Car Rental** 04 283 2020, *www.national-me.com*
**Thrifty Car Rental** 800 4694, *www.thriftyuae.com*
**United Car Rentals** 04 285 7777, *www.unitedcarrentals.com*

## Buying A Car

Aside from the horrendous traffic, the UAE is a motorist's dream. Petrol is cheap, big engines are considered cool and the wide highways stretching across the country are smooth and perfect for weekend drives.

Most of the major car makes are available through franchised dealerships in Dubai, with big Japanese and American brands particularly well represented. Expat buyers are often pleasantly surprised by the low cost of new cars compared to their home countries. For many, this lower initial cost, coupled with cheaper fuel and maintenance, means they can afford something a little more extravagant than they might drive at home.

There is a large second-hand car market in the UAE. Dealers are scattered around town but good areas to start are Sheikh Zayed Road and Al Awir, behind Ras Al Khor. Expect to pay a premium of between Dhs.5,000 and Dhs.10,000 for buying through a dealer (as opposed to buying from a private seller), since they also offer a limited warranty, insurance, finance and registration.

The Al Awir complex houses several smaller used-car dealers and it's easy to spend a whole day walking around the lots speaking with salesmen. Al Awir is also home to Golden Bell Auctions

Sheikh Zayed Road

# Going places?

When it comes to getting more value for your money, there's just one name, Budget. Whether it is daily, weekly or monthly rentals, short or long term leasing, you can be assured of the quality of service that has consistently earned us the vote as "Best Car Rental Company in the Middle East".

**For Reservations:**

Dubai: +971 4 295 6667
Jebel Ali: +971 4 881 1445
Abu Dhabi: +971 2 443 8430
Sharjah: +971 6 530 4455
Ras Al Khaimah: +971 7 244 6666
Fujairah: +971 9 244 9000
Email: reservations@budget-uae.com
**or book on-line at**
**www.budget-uae.com**

Car and Van Rental    ISO 9001 Certified

A member of the UAE-based Liberty Investment Co. (Liberty Group) (www.goldenbellauctions.com), with sales held each Wednesday evening. All cars up for auction have to undergo a test at the nearby Eppco/Tasjeel garage, and all outstanding fines will have been cleared. There's a Traffic Department office on the site so buyers can register their new vehicles on the spot.

## Tinted Windows

Currently, the government allows you to avoid the sun somewhat by tinting your vehicle's windows up to 30%. Some areas have facilities where you can get your car windows tinted but don't get carried away – remember to stick to the limit. Random checks take place and fines are handed out to those caught in the dark. Tinting in Sharjah is allowed for a fee of Dhs.100 and Ajman residents may tint for Dhs.200 per annum, but only if they are women.

For private sellers, check the classifieds in Gulf News and Khaleej Times. Supermarket noticeboards are another good option for finding a deal. Online classifieds such as www.dubizzle.com and expat forums such as www.expatwoman.com are also good places to look.

## New Car Dealers

**Autostar Trading** Skoda 04 269 7100
**AGMC** BMW, Rolls Royce, Mini, 04 339 1555, www.bmw-dubai.com
**Al Futtaim Motors** Lexus, Toyota, 04 228 2261, www.toyotauae.com
**Al Ghandi Automotive** Fiat, Lancia, Ssangyong, 04 266 6511, www.alghandi.com
**Al Habtoor Motors** Aston Martin, Bentley, Mitsubishi, 04 269 1110, www.alhabtoor-motors.com
**Al Majid Motors** Kia, 04 269 5600, www.kia-uae.com
**Al Naboodah Automobiles – Audi Showroom** Audi, 04 347 5111, www.nabooda-auto.com
**Al Naboodah Automobiles – HQ** Volkswagen, Porsche, 04 338 6999, www.nabooda-auto.com
**Al Rostamani Trading Company** Suzuki, 04 295 5907, www.alrostamani.com
**Al Tayer Motors** Ferrari, Ford, Jaguar, Land Rover, Lincoln, Maserati, Mercury, 04 201 1001, www.altayer.com
**Al Yousuf Motors** Chevrolet, Daihatsu, 04 339 5555, www.aym.ae
**Arabian Automobiles Nissan** Nissan, Infinity, Renault, 04 295 1234, www.arabianautomobiles.com
**Galadari Automobiles** Mazda, 04 299 4848, www.mazdauae.com
**Gargash Enterprises – Mercedes Benz** Mercedes Benz, 04 209 9777, www.gargash.mercedes-benz.com
**Gargash Motors** Alfa Romeo, Saab, 04 266 4669, www.gargashme.com

**Juma Al Majid Establishment** Hyundai, 800 498 6324, www.hyundai-uae.com
**Liberty Automobiles Co.** Cadillac, Opel, Hummer, 04 282 4440, www.libertyautos.com
**Swaidan Trading Co** Peugeot, 04 266 7111, www.swaidan.com
**Trading Enterprises** Chrysler, Dodge, Honda, Jeep, Volvo, 04 204 7160, www.alfuttaim.ae

## Used Car Dealers

**4x4 Motors – HQ** One of the largest used-car dealers in the UAE, sells all types of vehicles, not just 4WDs. Al Awir, 04 706 9666, www.4x4motors.com
**Al Futtaim Automall > p.63** Al Futtaim Automall has three sites in Dubai, and each car comes with a 12 month warranty and a 30 day exchange policy. Al Quoz, 04 340 8029, www.automalluae.com
**Auto Plus** Al Quoz, 04 339 5400, www.autoplusdubai.com
**Boston Cars** Al Awir, 04 333 1010
**Dynatrade** Al Awir, 04 320 1558, www.dynatrade-uae.com
**Exotic Cars** Al Quoz, 04 338 4339, www.exoticcarsdubai.com
**House of Cars** Sheikh Zayed Road, 04 343 5060, www.houseofcarsgroup.com
**Jumeirah Motors** Al Wasl, 04 343 4449
**Motor World** Al Awir, 04 333 2206
**Offroad Motors** Al Quoz, 04 338 4866, www.offroad-motors.com
**Quartermile – HQ** Sheikh Zayed Road, 04 339 4633, www.quartermile.net
**Reem Automobile** Al Wasl, 04 343 6333, www.reemauto.com
**Sun City Motors** Al Barsha, 04 269 8009, www.suncitymotors.net
**Target Auto** Al Wasl, 04 343 3911, www.target-auto.com
**Western Auto** Deira, 04 297 7788, www.westernauto.ae

## Vehicle Finance

Many new and second-hand car dealers will be able to arrange finance for you, often through a deal with their preferred banking partner. Previously this involved writing out years and years worth of post-dated cheques, but most official dealers and main banks will now set up automatic transactions. Always ask about the rates and terms, and then consider going directly to one of the banks to see if they can offer you a better deal. It's often easier to get financing through the bank that receives your salary.

## Vehicle Insurance

Before you can register your car you must have adequate insurance. The insurers will need to know the usual details such as year of manufacture, and

# UAE's Largest Used Automobile Retailer

Al-Futtaim automall
★★★★★
DRIVEN BY TRUST

## The second-hand car that makes a first impression.

Al-Futtaim Automall is proud to have the world's

most comprehensive used car warranty up to 3 years.

• The world's most comprehensive Used Car Warranty up to 3 years • Mileage Certificate
• 99-Point Check • Fully Reconditioned • 30-day Exchange Pledge

**Dubai** Airport Road (04) 295 4123, Shaikh Zayed Road (04) 340 8029, Al Awir Municipality Complex (04) 333 6870
**Abu Dhabi** Mina Centre, Mina Zayed (02) 673 3504 **Sharjah** (06) 532 2322 **Ajman** Next to Safeer Mall (06) 711 3351
e-mail: automall@alfuttaim.ae    www.al-futtaim.ae

An Al-Futtaim group company

CALL US NOW ON
**800** AUTOMALL 28866255

www.automalluae.com

# Getting A Car

## Second Opinion

When buying a used car it's well worth having it checked over by a garage or mechanic. EPPCO/Tasjeel, AAA and Max Garage offer a checking service. Alternatively, speak to the service department at the dealership where the car was originally bought. A thorough inspection will cost about Dhs.250.

value, as well as the chassis number. If you got a real bargain of a car and feel it's worth much more than you paid, make sure you instruct the insurance company to cover it at the market value. Take copies of your UAE driving licence, passport and the existing vehicle registration card.

## Personal Loans

The interest rates for personal loans are often lower than those for car loans. Be sure to compare the two rates and to check with your bank to see if you qualify for a personal loan.

Annual insurance policies are for a 13 month period (this is to cover the one-month grace period that you are allowed when your registration expires). Rates depend on the age and model of your car and your previous insurance history, however, very few companies will recognise any no-claims bonuses you have accrued in your home country. The rates are generally 4% to 7% of the vehicle value, or a flat 5% for cars over five years old. Fully comprehensive cover with personal accident insurance is highly advisable, and you are strongly advised to make sure the policy covers you for 'blood money'. For more adventurous 4WD drivers, insurance for off-roading

accidents is also recommended. Young or new drivers might need to call a few insurance companies before finding one that is willing to insure them, especially if they own a sports car. If you have no claims for three years, you will probably qualify for a reduction in your insurance rates.

### Car Insurance Providers

**Al Khazna Insurance Company** 04 294 4088, *www.alkhazna.com*
**Arab Orient Insurance Company** 04 295 3425, *www.al-futtaim.com*
**AXA Insurance – UAE** > *p.65* 04 324 3434, *www.axa-gulf.com*
**Emirates Insurance Company** 04 299 0 655, *www.eminsco.com*
**Greenshield Insurance** 04 397 4464, *www.greenshield.ae*
**Nasco Karaoglan** 04 352 3133, *www.nascodubai.com*
**National General Insurance** 02 667 8783, *www.ngi.ae*
**Oman Insurance** 04 398 1710, *www.tameen.ae*
**RSA** 04 302 9800, *www.rsagroup.ae*

## Registering A Vehicle

All cars must be registered annually with the Traffic Police. There is a one-month grace period after your registration has expired (hence the 13 month insurance period), but after that there'll be a Dhs.110 fine for each month the registration has expired. Along with the Dubai Traffic Police, both EPPCO and Emarat run full registration services under the names of Tasjeel (www.eppcouae.com) and Shamil (www.shamil.ae) respectively. Both Tasjeel and Shamil have several locations throughout Dubai.

The process is relatively straight forward. You will need to bring your old car registration, your driver's licence, proof of car insurance for the coming year

Deira

# Why should you ask when choosing car insurance?

do they offer you a 24 hour claims service? **/ we do**

if your car is in the workshop,
do they offer you a replacement? **/ we do**

if you have an accident, will they bring
a replacement car to the accident location? **/ we do**

will they let you open a claim with just one call? **/ we do**

do we honestly believe that AXA gives
you the best service and cover available? **/ we do**

can we prove it? **/ we just did**

**redefining** / insurance
رؤية جـديدة / للتأمين

**AXA**

*For a motor quote call 8004845*

*www.axa-gulf.com*

(although you can sometimes purchase the insurance on site), Dhs.50 for the car inspection and Dhs.385 for the registration. You must also pay all outstanding fines before the car can be re-registered. The fines can usually be paid at the registration centre, but try to check how much you owe beforehand (you can do so on www.dubaipolice.gov.ae), as some of the larger fines cannot be paid at the test centre. New cars don't need to be inspected for the first two years, but still need to be re-registered every year.

### To Oman & Back

It is wise to check whether your insurance covers you for the Sultanate of Oman as, within the Emirates, you may find yourself driving through small Oman enclaves (especially if you are off road, near Hatta, through Wadi Bih and on the East Coast in Dibba). Insurance for a visit to Oman can be arranged on a short-term basis, usually for no extra cost.

Both EPPCO Tasjeel and Emarat Shamil offer pick-up and drop-off registration services for an extra charge, usually around Dhs.200. Call 800 4258 to make an appointment with Tasjeel or 800 4559 to make an appointment with Shamil. The RTA recently launched a service offering vehicle registration online; to sign up to the service visit www.rta.ae.

# Vehicle Repairs & Maintenance

By law, no vehicle can be accepted for major 'collision' repairs without an accident report from the Traffic Police, although very minor dents can be repaired without a report. Your insurance company will usually have an agreement with a particular garage to which they will refer you. The garage will carry out the repair work and the insurance company will settle the claim. Generally, there is Dhs.500 deductible for all claims, but check with your insurance company for details of your policy.

If you purchase a new vehicle your insurance should cover you for 'agency repairs', that is, repairs at the workshop of the dealer selling the car, although this is not a guarantee and you may have to pay a premium. It's worth it though as your car's warranty (two to three years) may become invalid if you have non-agency repairs done on it. Even if you buy a fairly new second-hand car (less than three years old) it may be beneficial to opt for agency repairs in order to protect the value of the car.

Besides accidents and bumps, you may also have to deal with the usual running repairs associated with any car. Common problems in this part of the world can include the air-conditioning malfunctioning, batteries suddenly giving up and

tyres blowing out. With the air-con it may just be a case of having the system topped up, which is a fairly straightforward procedure. Car batteries don't tend to last too long in the hot conditions, and you may not get much warning (one day your car just won't start), so it's always handy to keep a set of jump leads in the boot.

If you do manage to get your car started then it's worth taking a trip to Satwa; before you know it, your car will be surrounded by people offering to fix anything. Haggle hard and you can get a bargain for simple repairs and spares – including a new battery.

When buying a used vehicle, many shoppers like to see a history of agency maintenance, especially for relatively new cars. It may seem ridiculous to have your oil change at the dealership every 5,000km, but it often pays in the long run when selling your car.

### Vehicle Repairs
**4x4 Garage** Al Quoz, 04 339 2020, *www.4x4motors.com*
**House Of Cars** Al Quoz, 04 339 3466, *www.houseofcarsgroup.com*
**Icon Auto Garage** Al Quoz, 04 338 2744, *www.icon-auto.com*
**Max Garage** Al Quoz, 04 340 8200, *www.maxdubai.com*
**X Centre** Al Quoz, 04 339 5033

4WD

# The ultimate boating guide

**Dubai Yachting & Boating**
Guaranteed to float your boat

DUBAI MARITIME CITY AUTHORITY

www.explorerpublishing.com

EXPLORER

# Minimum spending

## *Maximum Flexibility*

**EXPRESSIVE LIVING**

### Set up your home in the UAE for under AED 1,000*

Indigo Living offers furniture rental across our entire range with flexible lease options from one month to two years. Pay as you go with low monthly installments. Delivery & maintenance included in our full professional service package.

Come to Indigo Living and discover why some of our best customers never buy a thing!

*Basic inventory for studio apartment on long term lease

**INTERIOR AND FURNISHING SOLUTIONS:** HONG KONG . SHANGHAI . MACAU . DUBAI . DELHI

The Walk at Jumeirah Beach Residences (Sadaf Plaza Level) . T: 04 428 1350 . jbr@indigo-living.com
Showroom 45, Road 8, Street 19, Al Quoz Industrial 1 (near Times Square Mall) . T: 04 341 6305 . dsr@indigo-living.com
At Home Design - Level One, Mall of the Emirates, Dubai (above Carrefour) . T:04 323 3370 . moe@indigo-living.com . www.indigo-living.com

# Housing

# HOUSING

Apart from securing your new job, getting your accommodation satisfactorily sorted out is probably the most crucial factor in making your move to Dubai a success. The first thing to decide is what type of accommodation you want (and can afford) to live in, and in what part of town. This chapter provides a detailed run down on the different residential areas in Dubai (p.82), focusing on the type of accommodation available, the amenities, and the general pros and cons. There are sections on the procedures and practicalities involved in both the rental (p.71) and owning (p.73) markets too, discussing what you need to do to secure your dream pad. Once you've found somewhere to live, this chapter also tells you how to get settled in, covering everything from getting your TV and electricity connected to sprucing up the garden. Happy house hunting.

# ACCOMMODATION OPTIONS

## Hotel & Serviced Apartments

Hotel apartments are expensive, but ideal if you need temporary, furnished accommodation. There's a large

Jumeirah Beach Residence

concentration in Bur Dubai, but more and more are cropping up out of town, especially in Al Barsha. They can be rented on a daily, weekly, monthly or yearly basis. Water and electricity are also included in the rent.

**Al Bustan Centre & Residence** Al Qusais, 04 263 0000, *www.al-bustan.com*

**Al Deyafa Hotel Apartments 1** Deira, 04 228 2555, *www.aldeyafa.com*

**Al Faris Hotel Apartment 3** Oud Metha, 04 336 6566, *www.alfarisdubai.com*

**Al Mas Hotel Apartments** Bur Dubai, 04 355 7899, *www.almashotelapartments.com*

**Arjaan – Dubai Media City** Al Sufouh, 04 436 0000, *www.rotana.com*

**Bonnington, Jumeirah Lakes Towers** > *p.229* Jumeirah Lakes Towers, 04 356 0000, *www.bonningtontower.com*

**BurJuman Arjaan by Rotana** Bur Dubai, 04 352 4444, *www.rotana.com*

**Capitol Residence Hotel Apartments** Bur Dubai, 04 393 2000, *www.capitol-hotel.com*

**Chelsea Tower Hotel Apartments** Trade Centre 1, 04 343 4347, *www.chelseatowerdubai.com*

**City Centre Residence** Deira, 04 294 1333, *www.accorhotels.com*

**Crystal Living Courts** Al Barsha, 04 420 2555, *www.livingcourts.com*

**Dar Al Sondos Hotel Apartments by Le Meridien** Bur Dubai, 04 393 8000, *www.starwoodhotels.com*

**Desert Rose Hotel Apartments** Bur Dubai, 04 352 4848

**Golden Sands Hotel Apartments** 04 355 5553, *www.goldensandsdubai.com*

**Grand Hyatt Hotel Apartments** Umm Hurair, 04 317 1234, *www.dubai.grand.hyatt.com*

**Khalidia Hotel Apartments** Deira, 04 228 2280,

**Marriott Executive Apartments Dubai Creek** Deira, 04 213 1000, *www.marriottdubaicreek.com*

**Marriott Executive Apartments Dubai Green Community** Jebel Ali, 04 885 2222, *www.marriott.com*

**Number One Tower Suites** Trade Centre 1, 04 343 4666, *www.numberonetower.com*

**Nuran Greens Serviced Residences** Emirates Hills, 04 422 3444, *www.nuran.com*

**Nuran Marina Serviced Residences** Dubai Marina, 04 367 4848, *www.nuran.com*

**Oasis Beach Tower** > *p.237* Dubai Marina, 04 399 4444, *www.jebelali-international.com*

**The Radisson Blu Residence** Dubai Marina, 04 435 5000, *www.radissonblu.com*

**Ramee Hotel Apartments** 04 396 3888, *www.rameehotels.com*

**Residence Deira by Le Méridien** Deira, 04 224 1777, *www.starwoodhotels.com*

**Rihab Rotana Suites** Garhoud, 04 294 0300, *www.rotana.com*

**Rose Rayhaan by Rotana** Trade Centre 2,
04 323 0111, *www.rotana.com*
**Savoy Crest Exclusive Hotel Apartments**
Bur Dubai, 04 355 4488, *www.savoydubai.com*
**Villa Rotana** Al Wasl, 04 321 6111,
*www.rotana.com*
**Wafi Residence** Umm Hurair,
04 324 7222, *www.wafiproperties.com*
**World Trade Centre Residence** Trade Centre 1,
04 511 0000, *www.jumeirahliving.com*

## Owning A Property

Since 2002, foreigners have been allowed to purchase property in certain areas of Dubai. Property prices soared for six years until the end of 2008, when everything came crashing down and mortgages from banks dried up. Prices have now levelled out a bit, and buying a house is once again becoming a viable option for people planning on staying in Dubai for the long term. It's not a decision to be taken lightly though, and it pays to really do your research. For more information on the procedures and pitfalls involved in buying a property, see p.73.

## Standard Apartments

Dubai apartments come in various sizes, from studio to four-bedroom, with widely varying rents to match. Newer apartments usually have central air conditioning (C A/C) and older ones have noisier air conditioner units built into the wall. C A/C is usually more expensive, although in some apartment buildings your air-conditioning costs are built into the rent. Many of the newest developments utilise district cooling, a system in which all of the buildings within an area receive cold water from a central cooling plant. Residents living in apartments with district cooling will need to sign an agreement with the local cooling company and pay that company monthly.

Top of the range apartments often come semi-furnished (with a cooker, fridge and washing machine), and have 24 hour security, covered parking, private gym and swimming pool.

One downside to apartment living is that you're at the mercy of your neighbours to some extent, especially those upstairs. Depending on the area, parking may be a problem too – check to see if you get a space with your apartment.

## Villa Sharing

Sharing a large villa is a popular option with young professionals for economic and lifestyle reasons. The downside is the lack of privacy and the chore of finding new housemates when someone moves out. If you're looking to share an abode, the noticeboards at local supermarkets or property classifieds in Gulf News or www.dubizzle.com are good places to start. See p.72 for information on the legality of accommodation sharing.

Old Town

## Villas

The villa lifestyle doesn't come cheap, and smart villas are snapped up pretty quickly. The good news is that if you look hard enough and use the grapevine, you might find the perfect villa that won't break the budget. Depending on the location, size and age of the property it may be cheaper than some apartments, even if air-conditioning costs will be higher.

Villas differ greatly in quality and facilities. Independent ones often have bigger gardens, while compound villas are usually newer and often have shared facilities like a pool or gym.

# RENTING A HOME

New residents arriving in Dubai to start a new job may be given accommodation or a housing allowance as part of their package. The housing allowance may not always be high enough to rent a place in an ideal area, so many expats choose to cover the costs out of their own pockets. If your contract provides specific accommodation but you would prefer the cash equivalent, it is worth asking as most employers are willing to be flexible.

Thanks to the global economic crisis, rents in Dubai fell up to 45% in 2009 and many believe they will continue to fall in 2010. This is good news for residents and, for the first time in several years, renters now have the upper hand in lease negotiations.

## Finding A Rental Home

There are a number of ways to find suitable accommodation, the most obvious of which is via a real estate agent (see p.73). Agents will be able to show you several properties, but if that agent also represents the landlord, they might not have your best interests in mind. If you have the time it is worth checking classified ads in Gulf News or on www. dubizzle.com, although this works better when trying to find a shared accommodation.

Most of the listings in Dubai's classifieds are done by real estate agents anyway. An even better bet is to drive around a few areas and look out for 'To Let' signs displayed on vacant villas; these will display the phone number of either the landlord or the letting agent.

If you find a particularly attractive apartment building, try asking the security guard on duty if there are any vacant properties. Often this extra effort when looking for a home can result in a 'real find' and many proud barbecues to come. It also helps to ask colleagues and friends to keep an eye out for vacancies in shared villas.

## Sharing

There is some confusion as to the legality of villa or apartment sharing in Dubai. The topic reached its pinnacle in 2008 when tenants of several shared villas were handed eviction notices. In some cases, the electricity and water to those villas was cut off in order to force the tenants out. Things calmed down in 2009 and the Dubai Municipality clarified its stance. According to them, the main issue was overcrowding and defiance of health codes. It is now generally understood that unrelated singles of the same sex are allowed to share a villa as long as that villa is not in a neighbourhood designated for families and is not overcrowded. Sharing villas should still be approached with caution as the rules could change at any time. Areas designated as family-only include, but are not limited to, Al Barsha and Jumeira. As a rule, villa sharing among singles is looked down upon in areas with a high concentration of local families.

## The Lease

Your lease is an important document and, in addition to the financial terms, will state what you are liable for in terms of maintenance as well as what your landlord's responsibilities are. Therefore it is important that you read the contract and discuss any points of contention before you sign on the dotted line. Now that rents are dropping, negotiating power is in the hands of the tenant. Since rents are expected to keep dropping, avoid signing a multiple-year lease. This will allow you to renegotiate once the lease is up for renewal. The following points are often open to negotiation:

- Tenants usually pay rent via a number of post-dated cheques. Although one or two cheques used to be standard, it is now possible to pay with 12 cheques. If you can afford to provide fewer cheques, you can use that as a bargaining chip to lower the rent.
- Make sure you agree who is responsible for maintenance. Some rents might be fully inclusive

of all maintenance and repairs, while you could negotiate a much cheaper rent (particularly on older properties) if you agree to carry out any maintenance work.
- While not common, some landlords will include utility expenses in the rent.
- The amount of the security deposit can sometimes be negotiated, but Dhs.5,000 to Dhs.10,000 is standard.
- The landlord must give written notice of any rent increase at least one month in advance. If your landlord does try to increase the rent unfairly then there are government channels through which you can dispute rent matters.

It is important to have the official lease registered with the Dubai Land Department (www.rpdubai.ae). This procedure should be taken care of by the real estate agent. The Land Department will only work to resolve rent disputes in which the original lease was registered at the time of signing. Keep in mind that for a lease to be registered, the landowner must have an official title deed for the property. Not all properties in Dubai have title deeds.

## Other Rental Costs

Extra costs to be considered when renting a home are:
- Water and electricity deposit (Dhs.2,000 for villas, Dhs.1,000 for apartments) paid directly to Dubai Electricity & Water Authority (DEWA) and fully refundable on cancellation of the lease (p.100).
- If your accommodation is in an area that uses district cooling, you will need to pay a deposit to the cooling company (usually Palm District Cooling, www.palmutilities.com). The deposit amount varies depending on the size and location of the property.
- Real estate commission is around 5% of annual rent and is a one-off payment.
- Maintenance charges vary, but could be around 5% of annual rent, and are sometimes included.

You may also find that your monthly DEWA bill includes a 'Housing Fee'. Over the course of 12 months, the fee will add up to 5% of your yearly rent. If you're renting a villa, don't forget that you may have to maintain a garden and pay for extra water. It's worth asking the landlord or the previous tenants what the average DEWA bills are for a particular property.

## The Rent Committee

In an effort to better regulate Dubai's rampaging rental market, the Real Estate Regulatory Agency (RERA) was set up a couple of years ago to release a quarterly rental index that lists the top and bottom of the average market value of a rental property based on size and location. The rental index was introduced to control the huge rental increases that had been taking place in the previous years, and put a cap on increases. Any tenants that have disputes with a rent increase, or indeed evictions, can take their case to the Dubai Municipality Rent Committee (04 221 5555), and in many cases the committee finds in favour of the tenant.

Ironically, shortly after the RERA rental index was brought in, the global recession hit hard and rental prices dropped naturally. This, combined with the many new apartments and villas that are still being released, has meant that recently tenants have had little problems with increasing rents – and in fact many rental contracts have found prices reduced at renewal time, or at least frozen.

While an economic recovery and associated population increase may turn the tables once more in the future, it is unlikely that the 50-200% increases that were seen previously will be back again.

### Real Estate Agents

**Al Futtaim Real Estate** 04 285 9460, www.afrealestate.com
**Arenco Group** 04 355 5552, www.arencore.com
**Asteco Property Management** 04 403 7700, www.astecoproperty.com
**Betterhomes** 04 344 7714, www.bhomes.com
**Cluttons** 04 334 8585, www.cluttons.com
**Dubai Property Group** www.dubaipropertygroup.com
**Dubai Real Estate Corporation** 04 398 6666, www.realestate-dubai.gov.ae
**Landmark Properties** 04 331 6161, www.landmark-dubai.com
**Links Gulf Real Estate** 800 54657, www.links-realestate.com
**Oryx Real Estate** 04 399 0202, www.oryxrealestate.com
**The Property Shop** 04 345 5711, www.propertyshopdubai.com
**Sherwoods** 04 343 8002, www.sherwoodsproperty.com
**The Specialists** 04 329 5959, www.thespecialistsdubai.com

# BUYING A HOME

The UAE property buying process is unlike that of any other established market. Dramatic price inflations in 2007 and 2008 were followed by equally dramatic falls in 2009, while new laws and reforms are being introduced all the time.

Buying or selling a property here is a complex affair, but navigating the minefield is made easier by having a clear idea of the costs, procedures, laws and expectations of all involved.

Despite the recent instability, if you choose your property carefully there is still the potential to make a sound investment, for either rental income or to live in, but it pays to be cautious.

However, unless you are planning a long-term use of your property as your main home, you may need to think twice about snapping up a 'bargain', which could be difficult to sell on due to market saturation.

It is important to select your 'property partners' wisely (from agents to developers) in order to ensure that the process will be a little smoother.

One key thing to note is that non-UAE nationals can only buy in areas designated specifically for expatriate freehold and leasehold sales. In some areas of Dubai, only Emiratis or other GCC nationals can purchase property, most notably Jumeira, Umm Suqeim, Al Barsha and most parts of 'old Dubai'. See the Where To Buy box, p.79, for areas where expats can purchase.

Most property in Dubai available for purchase by non-nationals is freehold, although there is some availability of 99 year leasehold properties.

If you buy leasehold, you need to be aware that your lease will stipulate who is responsible for maintaining and repairing different parts of the property and any conditions you must meet as a resident. You must also pay a ground rent to the owner of the land (the freeholder), which is usually a small annual fee. It is important to check that the seller is up to date with ground rent payments before you take over the contract.

## Residential Developments

If you are buying off-plan or are the first owners of a new property, you will purchase directly from a developer. As the market matures, more purchases are being sold on a secondary basis, but although you will buy from the owner via an agent, as a freeholder you are still subject to the maintenance fees, rules and regulations of the master developer.

There was a lot of controversy surrounding the major players in real estate development in 2009, with big redundancies, and rumours of financial difficulties and mergers. What will happen moving forward is anyone's guess, but what can be expected is a higher level of accountability and more major shake-ups. It pays to do your research and keep an eye on news stories concerning developers you are considering buying from.

Some of the major players include the following:
**Nakheel** (www.nakheel.com). Built, sold and is responsible for maintaining several large developments, including: Palm Jumeirah, Jumeirah Islands, International City*, Discovery Gardens, Jumeirah Village*, Palm Jebel Ali, Palm Deira, The World and Al Furjan Community.
**Emaar** (www.emaar.com). Emaar's flagship property is the Burj Dubai; its portfolio of freehold real estate projects includes: Dubai Marina*, Arabian Ranches, Emirates Living (Emirates Hills, The Views, The Meadows, The Springs, The Lakes, The Greens), Emaar Towers and Downtown Dubai (Burj Dubai, Burj

Residence, Old Town, South Ridge).
*Master developers with some buildings built by sub-developers.*
**Dubai Properties** (www.dubai-properties.ae). Dubai Properties' flagship freehold properties are Jumeirah Beach Residence (p.227) and Business Bay. It also has a big residential development called The Villa.
**Union Properties** (www.up.ae) Responsible for The Green Community and Motor City.
**Damac** (www.damacproperties.com) Develops apartment buildings and commercial office towers, including Ocean Heights, Marina Terrace and The Waves in Dubai Marina; Palm Islands; and Lake View and Lake Terrace in JLT.
**Sama Dubai** (www.sama-dubai.com) Has retail, commercial and residential projects in the Lagoons and Dubai Towers.

Within the residential apartments market, notably in areas such as Dubai Marina, Jumeirah Lakes Towers and Business Bay, there are numerous sub developers building towers that are either finished or near to completion.

Generally all of the developers are reputable; however the level of finish and facilities management capability will vary. By buying from one of the larger known developers, you are also buying the piece of mind that comes with purchasing from a reputed organisation.

Since the recession hit in late 2008 the off-plan property market has slowed almost to a halt. Buyers and investors are understandably far more cautious, and the preference has shifted to buying finished property. However, just because a property is finished doesn't mean moving in is immediate. Handovers are notoriously delayed and protracted and can be costly due to extended rents or mortgage payments on properties that cannot yet be moved into.

## Legal Issues

By law, there might be no requirement to have a solicitor act for you when buying property in Dubai, but doing so provides extra piece of mind. Inheritance issues are something you must consider before buying Dubai apartments or villas too; succession is based on a number of factors, such as whether the owner is a non-Muslim and whether a will exists (see p.133).

## House Hunting

Real estate agencies in Dubai are many. The choice may have lessened in the course of the downturn, but this is definitely a positive. All agents in Dubai now have to be registered and 'trained' via RERA (Real Estate Regulatory Authority), which, along with the Dubai Land Department, formulates, regulates, manages and licenses various real estate-related activities in Dubai.

Despite a choice of big-name agencies available, the experience you'll have usually depends on the individual agent you end up dealing with.

While new laws have made processes more transparent and regulated, and levels of professionalism and service within the real estate industry have largely improved from a couple of years ago, not everything is up to perfect standards just yet.

Be sure to only use a registered broker, and ask to check their Broker ID card.

An excellent website that collates all relevant, laws, fees and information is www.rpdubai.ae.

In the UAE, the purchaser must pay a fee to the agency that finds and secures their desired property; estate agents and brokers in Dubai are not entitled to a commission or fee for service until the sale is settled and completed. The fee is usually around 2% of the purchase price of the property.

To get an idea of the players on the estate agent market, see Real Estate Agents, p.73. It's also worth checking the Freehold section of Gulf News, as well as www.dubizzle.com. The online version of Gulf News classifieds (www.gnads4u.com) is also updated daily.

### Going It Alone

You can, of course, always cut out the middle man and attempt to buy a property privately. Private sales are not very common in Dubai unless it is an arrangement between friends or business associates. It is very rare to see properties advertised in Dubai as private sale. When they do crop up, they are usually advertised via notice boards in community centres or supermarkets locally, listed as classified adverts in Gulf News, or featured online at www.dubizzle.com or www.gnads4u.com.

## Maintenance Fees

Maintenance fees payable by the owner encompass the costs to the developer of maintaining all the facilities and communal areas. Fees are typically paid annually, although some developers, such as Emaar, are now accepting quarterly payments.

Potential purchasers should also factor in the maintenance fees when deciding where to buy. Not only do fees vary from developer to developer but also from one development to the next. These fees are rarely mentioned in any of the developers' contracts, and if they are, the fine print will nearly always read 'subject to change.'

If you live in an apartment, communal facilities may include a gym, changing areas, and a swimming pool. Full time security and cleaning personnel will also be employed to service communal areas. In a villa, communal responsibility will extend to more security personnel manning the way to gated communities and all communal landscaping. Both will include rubbish collection, and villa communities may also enjoy pools and tennis court areas.

Moving back to
Boston with husband,
daughter, three dogs
and two containers
of treasured
possessions.
When?
Tomorrow.

Simplify your life

Relocating can be a trying experience with so much to plan, organize and accomplish. There is also less time to spend on things that really matter like friendships or special places you've enjoyed. This is why Writer Relocations provides unparalleled move support so that you can continue to enjoy life right until the time you leave.

Writer Relocations
P.O. Box 34892
Dubai, UAE
Phone: 04 340 8814  Fax: 04 340 8815
writerdubai@writercorporation.com
www.writercorporation.com

WRITER
RELOCATIONS

# Dubai's Property Market

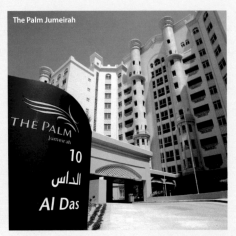

The Palm Jumeirah

Between mid 2006 and the second half of 2008, the price and scope of property developments in Dubai went through the roof. Then the taps of freely obtainable credit were turned off globally, and the crazy, unsustainable bubble that was the local housing market burst in spectacular fashion, causing a steep price correction of an over-inflated market – good news for renters and potential purchasers, bad news for those that had already invested.

The boom was largely driven by speculators. The process of 'flipping' was so widespread it became a phenomenon. Investors would buy up individual off-plan properties, whole floors, or even the whole building, and immediately sell on at a profit to a new buyer before the next payments became due to the developers.

In the first quarter of 2008, it was impossible to find a villa in Dubai to buy for less than $1 million – and even then, this would only have got you a regular-sized place in a new Dubai development, usually without any landscaping. Completed properties were scarce and snapped up immediately by potential landlords keen to cash in on exorbitant rental rates.

The returns were good, but for many the ultimate price was high. In the second half of 2008, credit dried up affecting not only new purchases but also the ability for investors to pay subsequent instalments on off-plan properties. The industry spiralled into a panic, and property sales all but stopped. Investor confidence was non-existent and access to funds, for any potential purchasers was just as scarce. Distress sales took place with desirable homes being sold on for 50% or less of their 'worth' at the height of the bubble. By the time buyers began to dip their toes back into the market in 2009, average prices were down 30% to 40% from the 2008 peak.

At the end of 2009, life had begun to creep back into the property market, albeit in a tentative, wary fashion. The press, both locally and internationally, report on the changing property outlook on a daily basis, with opinions varying from predictions of a rosy future with a return to the dizzy heights of 2008 to a further crash of up to another 33%, depending on the paper and the day of the week.

Caution remains the watchword. Some things will remain in Dubai's favour as a place to buy: its central location, its popularity with expats, its global hub position and its tax-free status will always be appealing to property buyers. However, despite the recent price falls, it's still not a cheap place to buy. As prices stand at the end of 2009, the lowest priced completed properties on the market were studio flats of approximately 650-800 sq ft, which started at Dhs.400,000 and go up to Dhs.1,250,000 for a luxury, serviced version in a five-star block overlooking the Burj Dubai.

One and two bedroom apartments were starting at anything from Dhs.750,000 in recently built properties in areas such as Motor City or

The Dubai property boom led to an increasingly speculative market that shot prices up to levels never imagined. And then the recession hit.

Jumeirah Lakes Towers, rising to Dhs.2,000,000 and beyond for larger units in parts of Downtown Burj Dubai and Jumeirah Beach Residence, The Palm Jumeirah, or serviced apartments within hotels. Apartment living is where prices vary massively, depending on location, developer and quality of finish.

Villa prices are affected by location, size and any cosmetic upgrades. Master planned communities by the major developers consist of hundreds of villas of the same style floor plan, with a few variations on the theme. This means that if you decide on a particular area to live, regardless of an advertised price, you would get a good feel for the average offer as there is guaranteed to be more than one of its kind available.

When headlines cry of 50% drops in Dubai property prices, they are certainly correct when it comes to villas on the flagship Palm Jumeirah. Here 'garden villas' that cost Dhs.14 million at the beginning of 2008 became valued at Dhs.7 million just six months later. Their larger 'signature villa' cousins now advertise for Dhs.14 million as opposed to a previous Dhs.21 million.

Other popular, established villa-only communities are Emirates Living, Arabian Ranches, Green Community and the 'almost there' Victory Heights. In these places two bedroom houses can range from Dhs.1.5 million up to over Dhs.3 million, with three bedroom or larger villas starting from Dhs.3.2 million and going up to more than Dhs.8 million. These communities saw a price reduction just like everywhere else, with current figures approximately 30% to 40% less than the height of the over-inflated bubble.

What happens next in Dubai's property market remains to be seen, but it is most likely that recovery from the global recession will be fraught with ups and downs.

Jumeirah Beach Residence

## Strata Committees

Brought in at the beginning of 2008, Dubai Strata law requires the proper division of property according to the Strata plan. This, along with a drawing which marks out the boundaries of lots, entitlement of these lots and other required documents, should be registered with the registrar.

Strata law is designed to settle disputes over issues like parking, keeping pets that disturb other owners, privacy, and alteration or maintenance of common areas.

It relates to the management of common property and shared facilities such as parking, fire services, air conditioning, lifts, pools, gyms, walkways, roadways and gardens. Under the law, an association of owners should be established as a regulatory framework to maintain the quality of the shared facilities.

The law, which clearly defines the relationship between developers and owners, should help remove ambiguities about who is responsible for common property management and aims to reduce scepticism among investors. Though Strata law cannot stop these disputes altogether, it can help in solving them before these quarrels can escalate.

## Mortgages

The UAE mortgage industry is still in its relative infancy compared with other countries. Dubai is home to many of the world's international finance houses, as well as local banks and lenders, but although familiar names such as HSBC, Lloyds TSB, Barclays, Standard Chartered and Citibank sit alongside local entities, sophisticated borrowing structures are difficult to secure and can take significantly longer to complete than in other parts of the world.

> ### Lend Some Advice
>
> A mortgage consultancy or broker will conduct all the legwork for you. Upon assessing your circumstances, choice of property and financial eligibility, they will gain pre-approval on your behalf and cut out the middleman of the banks and all the running around that goes with it, holding your hand until the keys are handed over. The fee will either be a percentage of the purchase price (approximately 0.5%) or a set price agreed from the outset.

The financial crisis that began in late 2008 also saw a lot of banks in the region suspend or severely curtail their mortgage lending activities. Some banks began to lend again in 2009, but on a much more cautious basis than in the gung-ho pre-recession days.

The mortgage process is slightly more convoluted in Dubai. Banks and lenders will only provide mortgages on a select number of developments, which vary from institution to institution. Additionally, each bank and lender has different acceptance criteria and mortgage processes, which change frequently.

> ### Shariah Compliant
>
> Shariah compliant or Islamic mortgages are an alternative financing option which are available to non-Muslims. The term 'home finance' is used as opposed to mortgages. Complying with Islamic beliefs, the bank purchases the asset on behalf of the buyer who then effectively leases it back from the institution. The bank owns the title deeds of the purchased property.

Interest rates vary massively from approximately 6.5% up to 9.5%, much higher than in many parts of the world, and many lenders will insist on life insurance on the loan amount. This is often a stumbling block if overlooked and not addressed before the transfer date. In addition many lenders will only finance up to 85% of the property price (100% finance mortgages do not currently exist in the UAE and are unlikely to appear anytime soon). The amount financed by the lender also varies and depends on whether the property is a villa or an apartment and where they are and who built them.

Equity release and mortgage transfers have recently been introduced to the market, offering investors the opportunity to release equity and secure better rates. To combat price sensitive customers moving their loans, most banks have introduced exit fees but there are still completely flexible mortgages available. New innovations also include international mortgages, which offer loans in currency denominations other than dirhams. This offers clients the ability to structure their loan in a preferred currency, with the ability to switch.

### Mortgage Application

It is possible for prospective buyers to seek a mortgage pre-approval before beginning their property search, which can give the buyer confidence when entering the market.

For a mortgage application you will need original and copies of your passport, six months of bank statements, salary confirmation from your employer and six months of salary slips.

A mortgage 'approval in principle' should only take up to four working days to come through upon submitting the correct paperwork. Generally, employed applicants can borrow a higher percentage of income than self employed. Most lenders will offer mortgages of up to 50% of disposable monthly income, based on the applicant's debt burden ratio – your realistic ability to service the monthly payments from your income, minus your other financial commitments. The larger the deposit placed, the better your terms are likely to be.

Mortgage terms are usually for 25 years. Age restrictions are in place and vary, but lenders will normally finance individuals up to 65 years of age.

The next step is for the lender to provide an unconditional approval on the basis that any conditions noted in the pre-approval are satisfied. This enables you to be sure that no more requirements are to be fulfilled in order for you to get your mortgage. The lender will then issue a letter of offer followed by the mortgage documentation. This will provide the terms and conditions of the mortgage and, once signed and sent back to the lender, the settlement process is started.

The process is settled when the lender has transferred the mortgage payment to either the seller or to the existing lender who has the first charge over the property. This will usually occur on the day of transfer or as per the conditions of the lender.

## Other Purchase Costs

On top of the purchase cost and deposit required, charges incurred by the property purchaser securing a home with a mortgage are as follows:
• Real estate agents/brokers fee: 2% of purchase price.
• Mortgage arranged via bank or lender: 1% to 1.25% mortgage processing fee based on value of loan.

### Valuation

Your mortgage lender will arrange a valuation of your chosen property via an independent source. This is to determine the market worth against the selling price and the lenders loan to you. The cost to the buyer is Dhs.2,500 to Dhs.3,000. Additional obligatory costs to the mortgaged property buyer equate to approximately an extra 6% on top of the purchase price, not including any cash deposit required.

### Optional Costs

It is not required to secure the use of a lawyer for property transactions in the UAE, but you may wish to employ legal help to see you through the process. Legal costs in this arena vary depending on whose services you used. If employing the services of a mortgage consultancy or broker, the typical cost is 0.5% of the property price.

## Land Registry

The government of Dubai Land Department is the Emirates' registry and land transactions agency. The department requires that all new real estate transactions are registered with them, and establishes legal ownership of the land or property, thus safeguarding the owner from future dispute, and provides the owner with the title deeds to their property or land. Fees levied by the Dubai Land

Department are dependent on whether the property purchase is covered by a conventional mortgage, an Islamic (Sharia compliant) mortgage or a cash purchase. All fees are payable by the buyer.

## Selling A Home

Contrary to many international press reports, property transactions in Dubai are steady and can be viewed at their actual selling value via www.rera.ae.

When selling, your first and most important task is to find yourself a preferred agent. Remember that private property sales are very rare so finding the right agent is key. Some real estate agencies charge 'marketing' fees of between 1-2% of the sale price. This is essentially to cover the costs of print and online advertising, open days and brochures. There is no legal need in Dubai for a property survey, assessment or solicitor, so all of these fees are negated.

## Real Estate Law & RERA

The Real Estate Regulatory Authority (RERA) is a subsidiary agency under Dubai Land Department. It is a government organisation that, aside from setting the rental index (p.72), regulates the real estate market, and aims to maintain healthy property investment Dubai.

The agency's responsibilities include the following: licensing all real estate activities; regulating and registering rental agreements, owners' associations, and real estate advertisements in the media; regulating and licensing real estate exhibitions; and publishing official research and studies for the sector.

RERA has instigated regulations on contractors, developers and agencies involved within Dubai real estate industry in a bid to safeguard the investor and regulate any disputes that may occur. This is particularly important for those buyers investing in properties yet to be completed or 'handed over'.

Any potential property dispute can be taken directly to RERA in the first instance, and there are comprehensive and clear rules on issues such as payments, escrow accounts and more with which developers are obliged to comply. To find out more about RERA, visit www.rera.ae or call 04 222 1112.

---

### Where To Buy

The areas within Dubai that expats can purchase property are: Discovery Gardens, Dubai Marina, Jumeirah Beach Residence, Jumeirah Lakes Towers, Emirates Hills, The Meadows, The Springs, The Lakes, The Greens, Palm Jumeirah, Arabian Ranches, Falcon City, The Villa, Al Barari, Sports City, Motor City, Green Community, Downtown Burj Dubai, Old Town, Business Bay, International City, IMPZ, Jumeirah Village and Jumeirah Islands.

# Residential Areas Map

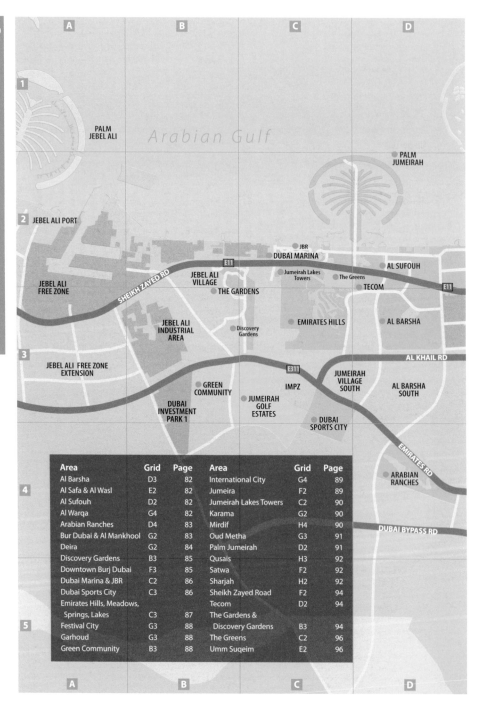

**Arabian Gulf**

PALM
JEBEL ALI

PALM
JUMEIRAH

JEBEL ALI PORT

JBR
DUBAI MARINA

AL SUFOUH

E11

JEBEL ALI
VILLAGE

Jumeirah Lakes
Towers

The Greens

JEBEL ALI
FREE ZONE

SHEIKH ZAYED RD

THE GARDENS

TECOM

E11

JEBEL ALI
INDUSTRIAL
AREA

Discovery
Gardens

EMIRATES HILLS

AL BARSHA

AL KHAIL RD

JEBEL ALI FREE ZONE
EXTENSION

E11

GREEN
COMMUNITY

IMPZ

JUMEIRAH
VILLAGE
SOUTH

AL BARSHA
SOUTH

DUBAI
INVESTMENT
PARK 1

JUMEIRAH
GOLF
ESTATES

DUBAI
SPORTS CITY

EMIRATES RD

ARABIAN
RANCHES

DUBAI BYPASS RD

| Area | Grid | Page | Area | Grid | Page |
|------|------|------|------|------|------|
| Al Barsha | D3 | 82 | International City | G4 | 89 |
| Al Safa & Al Wasl | E2 | 82 | Jumeira | F2 | 89 |
| Al Sufouh | D2 | 82 | Jumeirah Lakes Towers | C2 | 90 |
| Al Warqa | G4 | 82 | Karama | G2 | 90 |
| Arabian Ranches | D4 | 83 | Mirdif | H4 | 90 |
| Bur Dubai & Al Mankhool | G2 | 83 | Oud Metha | G3 | 91 |
| Deira | G2 | 84 | Palm Jumeirah | D2 | 91 |
| Discovery Gardens | B3 | 85 | Qusais | H3 | 92 |
| Downtown Burj Dubai | F3 | 85 | Satwa | F2 | 92 |
| Dubai Marina & JBR | C2 | 86 | Sharjah | H2 | 92 |
| Dubai Sports City | C3 | 86 | Sheikh Zayed Road | F2 | 94 |
| Emirates Hills, Meadows, | | | Tecom | D2 | 94 |
| Springs, Lakes | C3 | 87 | The Gardens & | | |
| Festival City | G3 | 88 | Discovery Gardens | B3 | 94 |
| Garhoud | G3 | 88 | The Greens | C2 | 96 |
| Green Community | B3 | 88 | Umm Suqeim | E2 | 96 |

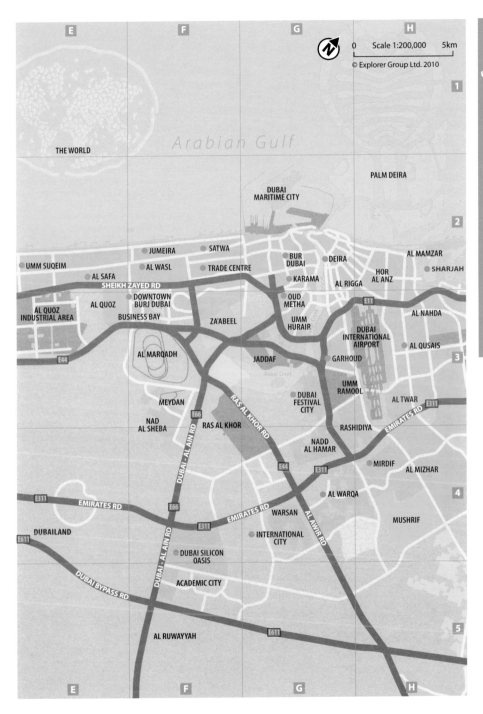

Scale 1:200,000    5km
0                  5km
© Explorer Group Ltd. 2010

*Arabian Gulf*

THE WORLD

PALM DEIRA

DUBAI
MARITIME CITY

JUMEIRA          SATWA
                              BUR              AL MAMZAR
UMM SUQEIM       AL WASL      DUBAI   DEIRA
                 TRADE CENTRE                 SHARJAH
    AL SAFA                   KARAMA  HOR
SHEIKH ZAYED RD                      AL ANZ
                                     AL RIGGA
AL QUOZ    AL QUOZ  DOWNTOWN         OUD              AL NAHDA
INDUSTRIAL AREA    BURJ DUBAI        METHA
           BUSINESS BAY    ZA'ABEEL  UMM
                                     HURAIR       DUBAI
AL MARQADH                                        INTERNATIONAL
                             JADDAF              AIRPORT    AL QUSAIS
                                     GARHOUD
                      *Dubai Creek*
MEYDAN                              UMM
                                   RAMOOL          AL TWAR
NAD        RAS AL KHOR    DUBAI
AL SHEBA                 FESTIVAL               RASHIDIYA
                         CITY                            EMIRATES RD
              RAS AL KHOR RD
                         NADD
                         AL HAMAR
                                          MIRDIF
              E44      E11                        AL MIZHAR
EMIRATES RD      E66                AL WARQA
DUBAILAND        E311   EMIRATES RD WARSAN              MUSHRIF
E611                          INTERNATIONAL
                              CITY
DUBAI - AL AIN RD   DUBAI SILICON
                    OASIS
DUBAI BYPASS RD     ACADEMIC CITY

AL RUWAYYAH              E611

# RESIDENTIAL AREAS

## Al Barsha

Map **1 Q5** Metro **Mall of the Emirates**

Al Barsha has two distinct zones, each with its own accommodation options. The main area offers large villas with big gardens and is popular with local families. New apartment blocks closer to Mall of the Emirates are popular with Media and Internet City workers.

### Accommodation

Accommodation is mainly in the form of fairly new, three to five-bedroom villas. Around 75% of the houses are locally owned and inhabited. Prices for villas start at Dhs.150,000 for a three bedroom and go up to Dhs.300,000 for larger options. Apartments in Al Barsha 1, near the mall, start from around Dhs.40,000 for a one-bedroom and Dhs.80,000 for a two-bedroom, but get snapped up quickly.

### Shopping & Leisure

The area's proximity to Mall of the Emirates means it has plenty of accessible amenities, including a Carrefour and Lulu Hypermarket, a popular cinema, and plenty of restaurants. The Kempinski Hotel at Mall of the Emirates has licensed restaurants and bars and Al Barsha is just across Sheikh Zayed Road from Madinat Jumeirah, and a short drive from the Marina.

### Healthcare & Education

There is a GP and paediatrician in the area at the Medical Specialist Centre (04 340 9495, www. mscdubai.com) in the Khoury Building near Sheikh Zayed Road, but the nearest emergency room is in the Medcare Hospital in Al Safa (04 407 9100). The Dubai American Academy (p.158) and Al Mawakeb are located in Al Barsha, and Wellington International School (p.166), Dubai College (p.160) and Jumeirah English Speaking School (p.162) are nearby.

## Al Safa & Al Wasl

Map **2 C4** Metro **Business Bay**

These residential areas are separated from the beachside districts of Jumeira and Umm Suqeim by Al Wasl Road. Everything between Safa Park and Satwa is officially known as Al Wasl, while Al Safa 1 and 2 lie between Safa Park at the north and Al Manara Street, which comes off Interchange 3. Th e area is safe, well lit and popular with families. Traffic within the communities is rarely a problem, but Al Wasl Road tends to get congested during rush hours. Its proximity to Sheikh Zayed Road makes it easy to get to other places in the city quickly. The area's openness is great for evening strolls when the weather is nice, and the low traffic means kids can ride their bikes and play outside without fear.

### Accommodation

Al Safa consists mostly of three-bedroom villas starting at Dhs.150,000, but bigger villas are available. All of the villas are locally owned, so renting is the only option. Both independent villas and older compounds with established greenery populate the areas. There are a few older bungalows to be found, but most are home to local families.

### Shopping & Leisure

Its central location means shopping is a breeze, and the Mazaya Centre, Spinneys Centre, a Choithram and Park n Shop are all within 10 minutes by car. The restaurants and cafes lining Beach Road, as well the licensed venues at Madinat Jumeirah are close as well.

### Healthcare & Education

Al Wasl Road and nearby Jumeira Road (Beach Road) have plenty of private medical centres, specialist doctors and dentists. The private Medcare Hospital (04 407 9100) near Safa Park has an emergency room, and the excellent value Iranian Hospital is just down Al Wasl Road towards Satwa.

Al Safa 1 has several schools including Jumeirah English Speaking School (p.162), The English College (p.160), Jumeirah English Speaking School (p.162), Jumeirah College (p.162) and Jumeirah Primary School (p.162) as well as nurseries including Jumeirah International Nursery School (p.152) and Kangaroo Kids (04 395 5518). The proximity to Sheikh Zayed Road makes Wellington International School (p.166) a popular choice, and the highway means access to other schools is easy too.

## Al Sufouh

Map **1 P4** Metro **Dubai Internet City**

Located between Knowledge Village and Umm Suqeim, this tiny collection of compounds is in high demand and the villas, which start at Dhs.150,000 for a three-bed, are hard to come by. Some of the villas are old by Dubai standards but the area is largely finished, so construction is not a problem. The facilities within the Marina, Mall of the Emirates and Umm Suqeim are a short drive away. There's plenty of parking outside the villas and the Media City Interchange from Sheikh Zayed Road makes accessing the area a breeze. Dubai College (p.160), the International School of Choueifat (p.160) and the Wellington International School (p.166) are all in Al Sufouh.

## Al Warqa

Map **2 M12** Metro **Rashidiya**

Directly south of Mirdif, Al Warqa has a lot of big (expensive) villas belonging to local families, as well as many new apartment blocks where one-bedrooms start at around Dhs.40,000. Many of the apartment blocks are still under construction, as are many of the roads, so residents will often have to drive over dirt to reach their parking space. Aside from the tiny corner shops, there is a big Mars supermarket in the area and the drive to Uptown Mirdif takes about five minutes. There are a few schools in Al Warqa, including the Sharjah American International School (04 280 1111). Mirdif's many nurseries, including Small Steps (04 288 3347), Super Kids (p.156) and Emirates British Nursery (p.152) are also close. The Al Warqa Medical Centre (04 280 0899, www.drmoopensgroup) has a paediatrician and GP, but the nearest government A&E unit is Rashid Hospital (p.188) near Garhoud bridge.

## Arabian Ranches
Map **1 Q12**

The quiet, curving, grass-lined lanes of the Arabian Ranches development are located away from the centre of town, off Emirates Road near Dubai Autodrome. This is an all-villa project set among lush greenery, lakes and the Arabian Ranches Golf Course, with a range of luxury facilities that all add up to some pretty fine living. It was one of the first freehold residential areas to be completed and there is certainly a neighbourhood feel to the place.

### Accommodation

Arabian Ranches villas range from two-bedroom town houses to seven-bed mansions. The starting price for a three-bedroom villa is around Dhs.120,000, although most of the people who bought villas in the development still live in them, so finding one that suits your needs can be difficult.

### Shopping & Leisure

There are several pools, basketball and tennis courts, barbecue pits and grassy areas throughout, plus the Village Community Centre, which houses Le Marche

supermarket, a chemist, liquor store and several cafes, restaurants and takeaways. Although a bit out of town it is still just a 15 minute drive from shopping and dining options in Madinat Jumeirah. The Arabian Ranches Golf Course (p.324) is home to a clubhouse and restaurant and bar. The Autodrome and licensed Dubai Polo & Equestrian Club are nearby too.

### Dubai Sports City

Although several of the sports facilities in this sports-centric development have been completed, only a few of the villas and apartments are ready to be lived in. Dubai Sports City is located in Dubailand off Emirates Road. It is already home to The Els Club (www.elsclubdubai.com) and many of the Victory Heights villas that surround the course are finished.

### Healthcare & Education

There's only one medical centre in the development, Village Medicentre (04 360 8866), and the nearest emergency room is Cedars Jebel Ali International Hospital (p.186). The Jumeirah English Speaking School (p.162) is the only school in the Ranches, but it isn't too far to options in Al Barsha and Emirates Hills.

## Bur Dubai & Al Mankhool
Map **2 L3** Metro **Khalid Bin Al Waleed**

This older, traffic-laden area of Dubai is a bit of a concrete jungle, with mid-size apartment blocks and virtually no green spaces. Many of the newer apartments have excellent facilities and spacious interiors, and the area itself is always humming with activity. The dense population means traffic and parking can often be a problem. It also means the

Bur Dubai

# Residential Areas

streets are always full of people, and women may feel uneasy walking the streets, especially in the evening when many men seem to be loitering.

One of the most popular areas is Al Mankhool (also known as Golden Sands), but there are also some nice apartment blocks in the Al Hamriya area (across Bank Street from the BurJuman Mall). Nearer the creek and further west towards the sea, the buildings are generally a lot older with fewer facilities and limited parking, although those with balconies facing in the right direction do have beautiful views of the creek.

## Accommodation

The area is dominated by apartments in a mix of new and old medium-rise buildings, from studios to large flats with several bedrooms. Some of the larger apartments are used as company flats. Rents in the newer buildings have risen to nearly the same as in other areas of Dubai, but the older the accommodation the cheaper it gets. A two-bedroom apartment in a new building could set you back around Dhs.120,000 but for that you should expect excellent facilities. A one-bedroom apartment in an older building starts at Dhs.50,000 while a two bedroom will be around Dhs.80,000, depending on the age of the building and range of facilities offered.

## Shopping & Leisure

There are two large Spinneys supermarkets in the area, as well as a Union Co-Op on Trade Centre Road, a Choithram on Mankhool Road and a huge Carrefour in Al Shindagha near the mouth of the creek. On and around Bank Street (Khalid Bin Al Waleed Road), there are a number of banks and ATMs, some smaller food stores, clothing shops and sports stores. BurJuman (p.398) provides a huge range of shops as well. The souk area of Bur Dubai and the markets in Karama are good for picking up funky gifts.

The hotels on and around Bank Street house some great dive bars and inexpensive licensed restaurants, including expat-favourite Waxy's (p.516). There are also many small independent eateries on Bank Street and further into Bur Dubai. Bur Dubai's central location also means it's easy to find a cab to take you a short distance to nearby nightspots in Downtown Burj Dubai and on Sheikh Zayed Road.

## Healthcare & Education

Both in Bur Dubai and in neighbouring Karama you can find a number of small medical centres. The emergency room at Rashid Hospital (p.188) is just a stone's throw away in Umm Hurair, as is the private American Hospital (p.186). If that weren't enough, the expansive Healthcare City is only a few minutes away by car.

There are no schools in the area, but the central location means that there is plenty of choice nearby.

## Deira

Map **2 N3** Metro **Baniyas Square**

Although it's not very popular with expats in higher income brackets, Deira's heavily lived-in atmosphere and traffic-laden, bustling streets have been made more accessible by the introduction of the Metro. The heart of Deira is densely built up with a mix of old apartment blocks, while nearer the creek there are several new buildings offering modern apartments, many with spectacular views across the water. Rents are relatively low in some of the more built up areas, while the creekside dwellings cost much more. Once you get past the horrible traffic and lack of parking that plagues it, Deira's best attribute is its walkability.

### Deira Is Not Dead

This is the oldest and one of the most atmospheric parts of town. Many might have forgotten its charms as Dubai expands, but it's a great place to explore along the bustling corniche, through the souks, in heritage sites and creekside restaurants and bars.

## Accommodation

Although Deira does have some areas with villas (Abu Hail, Al Wuheida), they are almost exclusively inhabited by Emiratis, with the areas closer to the creek full of apartments where most expats in the area congregate. In the heart of Deira, you'll pay around Dhs.40,000 for a one-bedroom apartment and Dhs.100,000 for two bedrooms, but these are often in older buildings and are not what you might call salubrious. The creekside area just north of Maktoum bridge offers a great standard of accommodation and is used by professional expats of all nationalities. There are many executive apartments with great views over the creek, impressive landscaping and good facilities – but prices here tend to be high, with a standard two-bedroom costing around Dhs.110,000.

## Shopping & Leisure

Deira is home to several popular malls including Al Ghurair City (p.410) and Deira City Centre (p.400). Both have good supermarkets (Spinneys and Carrefour respectively) as well as many other shops. Being an older area of town, there are also plenty of smaller groceries, pharmacies, dry-cleaners and laundry services within walking distance. Deira's main post office is close to Al Ghurair Centre and there are many banks on Al Maktoum Road.

Within a small area, there's also a choice of hotels, including the InterContinental, Hilton and Sheraton Creek, the JW Marriott, Renaissance, Traders and Metropolitan Palace, all of which offer a great choice of dining outlets, bars and nightclubs.

For cheap eats, Al Rigga Street has a great range of independent restaurants, including the famed Automatic Lebanese restaurant (p.457). Al Ghurair Centre also has some particularly nice cafes on the terrace. There are some pleasant walking areas by the creek and along the corniche towards Mamzar Park, which is huge and great for weekends, especially with the beach chalets available for daily rental.

### Healthcare & Education
Local healthcare is provided by the government-run Dubai Hospital (p.186) near the corniche, while Dubai's foremost emergency hospital, Rashid Hospital (p.188), is just across Maktoum bridge in Umm Hurair. There are also many small private medical clinics, although the larger private hospitals tend to be located on the Bur Dubai side of the creek (p.444). Since the area tends to attract less families, Deira doesn't have many expat schools within its borders, so most children in Deira attend school in nearby Garhoud.

## Discovery Gardens
Map **1 H6** Metro **Nakheel**
Made up of hundreds of seemingly identical low-rise apartment blocks, Discovery Gardens is surprisingly green. Rents tend to be lower here and apartments easy to come by. The buildings only contain studios and one-bedroom apartments. A one-bedroom can

be found for around Dhs.50,000. Although there aren't any shops within the development, Ibn Battuta is conveniently close and contains a large Géant hypermarket, a cinema and several restaurants. The Marina and Al Barsha are both nearby, so going out for a drink or nice dinner isn't a hassle. Traffic is rarely a problem and there is plenty of parking around the buildings. There is also a Red Line Metro stop outside Ibn Battuta, but you need to take the F43 feeder bus to access it.

## Downtown Burj Dubai
Map **2 F6** Metro **Burj Dubai**
Dubai's newest residential area, Downtown was designed to foster a community. Children's play areas, hubs of coffee shops, souks and elegant swimming pools all encourage residents to spend time outside and mix with their neighbours. On top of this, the wide promenades, Arabian passageways and palm-lined streets that link the different residential quarters encourage residents to get around on foot. The massive development is made up of a mixture of high and low rise residential units, with landmark buildings – The Address, Dubai Mall, The Palace Hotel, Emaar Square and the Burj itself – as the cornerstones. At one end, near to Burj Dubai, are the Burj Residence towers and 8 Boulevard Walk, while at the opposite end, on the border with the Business Bay development, are

Downtown Burj Dubai

the Southridge high-rises. In between these is the distinctive Arabian architecture of Old Town. Traffic throughout the area is constantly being improved with the opening of new roads, and the entire development sits between Sheikh Zayed Road and Al Khail Road (E44), making it very accessible. There is also plenty of parking within each of the residential complexes.

## Accommodation

Options range from tiny studios to expansive four-bedroom flats. All of the buildings are new and the finishing is of a high spec throughout. A small one-bedroom in one of the residential towers can be found for around Dhs.80,000, while apartments in Old Town tend to be larger and cost a bit more. Most residential towers come with incredible facilities including game rooms, libraries, barbecue areas, child care, gyms, swimming pools, and sports courts.

## Shopping & Leisure

Downtown Burj Dubai is a shopper's dream with both Dubai Mall (p.402) and Souk Al Bahar (p.396) within walking distance of all of the area's residential districts. For day-to-day shopping needs, Dubai Mall has both a Waitrose supermarket and an Organic Foods & Café, and there are several small Spinneys outlets scattered throughout the residential areas. Many residents tend to shop at the Union Co-op on Al Wasl road to avoid the high prices found in the local supermarkets. Pretty much all of the banks are covered on the ground floor of Dubai Mall, along with plenty of pharmacies and opticians.

Right next door to Dubai Mall is the more low-key Souk Al Bahar, which houses a few boutique shops and is fast becoming a nightlife hub with several licensed bars and restaurants, including Hive (p.510), Left Bank (p.512) and Mirai (p.485). Dubai Mall has

quite a few unlicensed restaurants along with one of the largest food courts in the city. If that weren't enough, there's also the Address hotel, which is home to the gorgeous Neos sky bar (p.513) on the 63rd floor.

## Healthcare & Education

Apart from pharmacies dotted round the Old Town, Dubai Mall and the Residences, there is the large Dubai Mall Medical Centre (p.181). The closest hospitals are Medcare Hospital (04 407 9100) in Al Safa and the Iranian Hospital (04 344 0250) on Al Wasl Road in Satwa. While there are no primary or secondary schools in Downtown Burj Dubai, those in Jumeira and Al Quoz are an easy drive away. There are however, a few nursery facilities for pre-school aged kids. The newly opened Old Town Nursery, part of Raffles International School, is in the Qamardeen district of Old Town. Kangaroo Kids' bright and colourful nursery is in the Burj Residences, and Cello Kids Club (04 422 1303) is located in the Al Manzil Club.

## Dubai Marina & JBR

Map **1 K4** Metro **Dubai Marina**

The high-rise apartment towers of the Marina and Jumeirah Beach Residence have quickly become one of the most desirable places to live in Dubai. The many hotels that dot the area are home to several popular restaurants and bars and the JBR Walk is packed every evening with couples and families socialising and strolling. Road access in and out of the area is fairly efficient now, the main exceptions are the roads leading to The Walk on weekend evenings, which can get congested, while many parts of the neighbourhood are now walkable so residents rarely need to venture outside the area to access amenities. There is also a great open beach and an incredible marina to round out the package.

Dubai Marina

## Accommodation

Apartments in Dubai Marina vary greatly in quality, and a studio in one of the less luxurious towers can be found for around Dhs.45,000 a year, while a three-bedroom in a building with great facilities and impressive finishing might go for as much as Dhs.170,000 a year. Apartments in one of JBR's many identical towers go for a bit less and a one-bedroom can be found for as little as Dhs.80,000 a year. All of the buildings in the district are freehold, and most of the apartments are owned by expats.

## Shopping & Leisure

Shopping options in the area received a boost with the opening of the Dubai Marina Mall (p.411) in 2009. The mall isn't huge, but it holds a Waitrose supermarket and a few highstreet shops. On Marina Walk, alongside all the restaurants, there's a Spinneys supermarket, a pharmacy, a bookshop, a florist, and a liquor store, plus a number of ATMs. The Walk along JBR is also home to a thriving shopping scene, with clothing boutiques and furniture stores. Both Mall of the Emirates and Ibn Battuta are only a short drive away.

Several large hotels line the beach outside JBR and each has a decent selection of bars and licensed restaurants. The Walk around JBR is now teeming with places to eat, many of which are open until the early morning. The Marina Walk also has a number of popular restaurants, including Chandelier (p.466) and The Rupee Room (p.492). The hotels along the beach all have bars and restaurants too, including the popular Mai Tai bar (p.516) and Frankie's Italian restaurant (p.473) at Oasis Beach Tower.

## Healthcare & Education

The nearest government clinic is Umm Suqeim, and The Neuro Spinal Hospital (04 315 7777) opposite Jumeira Beach Park has the closest emergency room, as well as its own ambulance. In the other direction, the Cedars Jebel Ali International Hospital (p.186) also offers 24 hour emergency care. There's a Welcare Clinic (04 366 1030) in nearby Knowledge Village, and Drs Nicolas & Asp (p.181) dental and medical clinics in JBR.

There are a few nurseries in the Marina, but no schools. However, Al Sufouh is only five minutes away by car and is home to Wellington International School (p.166) and the International School of Choueifat (p.160). Its location along Sheikh Zayed Road means all of the schools on this side of town are easily accessible.

# Emirates Hills, Meadows, Springs, Lakes

Map **1 L6** Metro **Nakheel**

Emirates Hills is a desirable address with a range of villa-style houses in The Springs, The Lakes and The Meadows. Tree-lined streets and pathways, attractively landscaped lakes, gardens and recreation areas make it perfect for those who want to enjoy the peace and quiet of suburbia. Located between Sheikh Zayed Road and Al Khail Road, across from Media City, each individual zone of Emirates Hills (for example Springs 6, Meadows 5) has its own gated security entrance. The gated-community feel runs throughout each neighbourhood, as kids play in the streets and parks, while adults in expensive jogging gear pound the pavements. Traffic within each community is not a problem, although the intersections near the highways gets clogged at rush hour.

## Accommodation

Generally, the style and quality of all houses in Emirates Hills is good, although they all look the same. The smallest villas available are located in The Springs, where a two-bedroom townhouse can be found from around Dhs.80,000. Prices go up from there, and a six-bedroom mansion in the Lakes will cost around Dhs.500,000 a year. Emirates Hills was one of the first freehold villa complexes in Dubai and many of the properties are owned by expats.

## Shopping & Leisure

There are three supermarkets within the various compounds. There's a Choithram at the Springs end, a large Spinneys at Spinneys Town Centre in the middle and a Spinneys Market in the Meadows. Each centre has a Hayya! gym, a beauty salon, a pharmacy and ATMs. Between them all, you should find everything you need, from laundry services to fast food and fine dining, or coffee shops to video rentals.

Other nearby supermarkets include Spinneys and Waitrose at Dubai Marina, Géant at Ibn Battuta and Carrefour at Mall of the Emirates.

The Hayya! Club in the Lakes has a licensed restaurant and bar, as does the Montgomerie Golf Club for evenings where you want to stay local. Other than that, you'll have to venture to the Marina or Al Barsha for a better selection of dining venues. Both Ibn Battuta and Mall of the Emirates are only 10 minutes away in either direction.

## Healthcare & Education

The Rosary Medical Center is located at Springs Town Centre in Springs 7, while nearby facilities include a private medical centre in Al Barsha, Medical Specialist Centre (04 340 9495), the Cedars Jebel Ali International Hospital (p.186), and Welcare Clinic in Knowledge Village (04 366 1030).

There are several education options for families based in the area, but waiting lists for a place in the most sought-after schools and nurseries are long, and it is best to sign up well in advance. Schools already open include Emirates International School in The Meadows (p.161), Dubai British School (p.158), Dubai

# Residential Areas

International Academy (p.160) in The Springs, and Dubai American Academy (p.158) at the Emirates Hills entrance near The Lakes. As for nurseries, Raffles International School (p.162) operates several nurseries in The Springs, Springs Town Center, Emirates Hills and The Lakes.

## Garhoud

**Map 2 N7** Metro **Emirates**

With its central location, range of villas and suburban feel, it's no surprise that Garhoud is such a popular residential area. It's handy for both central Dubai and downtown Deira, although this does mean that traffic can be a problem at peak times. Finding available accommodation isn't always easy, and there's not much in the way of new construction. Being only two minutes away from the airport means it's popular with airline staff and frequent travellers. It also means there is a chance of aircraft noise depending on the wind direction. Parking is a problem and finding a spot on the street, even with the introduction of parking meters, can often be difficult.

### Accommodation

Garhoud has some nice, older villas, usually with well-established gardens and plenty of character. They are also relatively cheap considering the central location. The price for a three bedroom ranges anywhere from Dhs.115,000 upwards, and will depend on the age of the villa. The biggest problem is finding somewhere vacant. Away from the airport, there are some newer villas, predominantly in large compounds, that are similar in standard and price to villas in other areas of Dubai. The usual size is four-bedroom, which should rent for around Dhs.200,000 per year. There are also a few apartment blocks near the Aviation Club where a one-bedroom can be found for at little as Dhs.50,000.

Festival City

---

### Festival City

Residential homes in the Festival City area are all fairly new, and this is a desirable area to live with all apartments and villas being situated around a golf course. Apartments and villas in the Festival City complex are quite luxurious and in high demand, and therefore not cheap, but if you have a good budget then it's your only chance this side of town to experience golf course living.

### Shopping & Leisure

There is one main shopping street in Garhoud which has two supermarkets, as well as a laundry, pharmacy and ATM. Other than that, both Carrefour in Deira City Centre (p.400) and HyperPanda in Festival City (p.401) are less than a 10 minute drive away. Garhoud may be the best location for nightlife-lovers. The many licensed restaurants and bars in The Al Bustan Rotana, Le Meridien Dubai, Millennium Airport Hotel, Century Village and Aviation Club are all within walking distance, and a taxi to the hotels on Sheikh Zayed Road shouldn't set you back more than Dhs.30. Festival City is also just around the corner and has a large selection of licensed and unlicensed restaurants to choose from.

### Healthcare & Education

Although there are no government clinics in the area, there are good private facilities such as Welcare Hospital (p.188), and two of the main government hospitals, Al Wasl (p.186) and Rashid (p.188), are only a short distance away across the creek.

Several schools are located along the road on the southern edge of Garhoud including Deira International School (p.158), American School of Dubai (p.158) and Cambridge International School (p.158). Many other schools are accessible in areas like Umm Hurair, Al Twar and Festival City. Yellow Brick Road Nursery (p.158) and Montessori Nursery (p.152) are in the neighbourhood as well.

## Green Community

**Map 1 F9** Metro **Energy**

An oasis of green in the desert, this new development is good for families, and homes are hard to come by. The area is made up of villas with large front gardens, as well as spacious, low-rise apartment blocks set among lakes and green parks. There's plenty of room for kids to play in and the place has quietly developed a strong community feel. It's a bit out of the city, but a good choice for people working in the Jebel Ali Free Zone. At the moment, the community has only one road leading into and out of it, so rush-hour traffic is often a problem. Its location away from the rest of Dubai also means that taxis can be expensive for nights when the car needs to be left at home.

## Accommodation

There is a wide variety including villas, townhouses, and apartments. The original Green Community was so well received that the developer built a new phase – Green Community West. For a four-bedroom villa you can expect to pay around Dhs.180,000 in rent, and you should be able to find a one-bedroom apartment for around Dhs.60,000. The developer, Union Properties, has a good reputation and the finishing in all of the units is of a high quality.

## Shopping & Leisure

The area is serviced by The Market shopping centre, which houses a large Choithram supermarket, as well as a jewellers, clothes shops, and home furnishing outlets. There's also a pharmacy, a florist, a dry cleaners, an optician, and a branch of Ace Hardware. If that's not enough, Ibn Battuta mall is not far away.

There are a few good licensed restaurants within the Courtyard by Marriott and The Market is home to a number of coffee shops and good unlicensed restaurants. For a better selection, the Dubai Marina is about 15 minutes by car.

## Healthcare & Education

The private Green Community Medical Centre (04 885 3225) is upstairs in The Market, while the nearest government-run clinic is at Jebel Ali. For emergencies, the Cedars Jebel Ali International Hospital (p.186) within the Jebel Ali Free Zone is nearest. For government A&E care it's quite a trip to Rashid Hospital.

The Children's Garden (04 349 8806) offers a primary bilingual curriculum in English/German or English/French, and there are various primary and secondary schools in Emirates Hills and Jebel Ali.

## International City

East of Mirdif, Map **2 Q12**

This collection of hundreds of nearly-identical low-rise apartment blocks is finally coming into its own. New shops and unlicensed restaurants seem to open daily and many of them are receiving favourable reviews. Rents in International City are some of the lowest in Dubai, and a one-bedroom apartment can go for as little as Dhs.40,000 a year. Located at the intersection of Emirates Road and the Dubai-Hatta Road, the development is a bit out of the way, but a trip to Festival City shouldn't take more than 10 minutes by car, and the Trade Centre is never more than a half hour away, even in rush hour traffic. Both Carrefour and Spinneys have outlets within International City and there are smaller groceries and cornershops underneath nearly every building. A few small private clinics have opened within International City, as have some pharmacies. There are no schools within the development, but options in Mirdif and Al Warqa are only 10 minutes away.

## Jumeira

Map **2 F3** Metro **Business Bay**

The actual area of Jumeira occupies a prime nine-kilometre strip of coastline stretching south-west from the port area, but the name has been hijacked to such an extent that new residential and commercial developments bearing the Jumeira tag are cropping up for miles around. Even the Palm Jumeirah doesn't connect with Jumeira, but actually extends from the area of Al Sufouh. Jumeira itself is characterised by quiet streets lined with sophisticated villas, golden beaches, and good access to lots of shopping. Traffic and parking on the back streets is never a problem, but Al Wasl Road and Jumeira Road can get clogged during peak hours.

## Accommodation

Although prices have dropped considerably, Jumeira villas still attract some of the highest rents in the city. There's a mixture of huge 'palaces', independent villas, and villas in compounds with shared facilities. For a three-bedroom, stand-alone villa you can expect to pay around Dhs.220,000 depending on the age and specific location. You can, however, get the odd villa in an older compound for around Dhs.180,000.

### Jumeira or Jumeirah?

According to the 'official' spelling used by Dubai Municipality, it's Jumeira, so that's what we use when referring to this area. However, many hotels, parks, clubs, schools, and residential developments have added an 'h' to the end, so don't be surprised if you see the two different spellings side by side throughout the book.

## Shopping & Leisure

Jumeira Road has long been home to several boutique retailers selling art and fashion. For groceries, there are two Spinneys, a Union Co-op and two Choitrams all within a five-minute drive. There is also the popular Mercato (p.406) on Jumeira Road, along with several smaller shopping centres.

Jumeira Road also hosts several independent restaurants and takeaways, as well as many fast-food joints. The Jumeirah Beach Hotel and Madinat Jumeirah are both packed with impressive licensed restaurants and bars and the restaurant-filled hotels that line Sheikh Zayed Road are nearby as well. Best of all, the city's most popular beaches are all within walking distance, including Jumeirah Beach Park (p.246).

## Healthcare & Education

Al Safa Clinic (04 394 3468) opposite Safa Park is the nearest government health clinic. Emirates Hospital (p.188), opposite Jumeirah Beach Park, has a 24 hour walk-in clinic to deal with common ailments, but they

**Housing**

do not accept emergency cases. The Neuro Spinal Hospital (04 315 7777) in the same building does have a 24 hour emergency department though. Medcare (p.188), near Safa Park, is a popular new private hospital. Jumeira is known for being home to countless beauty salons and private medical facilities, including dentists, physiotherapists and cosmetic surgery centres.

There are numerous nurseries in Jumeira, and Jumeirah Primary School (p.162), Jumeirah College (p.162) and Jumeirah English Speaking School (p.162) are all in the neighbourhood. Easy access to road networks means outlying schools are easy to reach.

## Jumeirah Lakes Towers

Map **1 K4** Metro **Jumeirah Lakes Towers**

JLT is a high-rise community made up of 79 towers, both residential and commercial. It is located directly across Sheikh Zayed Road from the Marina, and is serviced by two Metro stations. The nearest supermarkets are in nearby Ibn Battuta mall (p.404) and Emirates Hills. The quality of housing is comparable to the Marina, but prices are still quite a bit less. When the lakes are completed there will be a promenade around them with cafes and shops. Getting in and out of the area by car can be quite tedious due to the huge one-way loop that revolves around the development, and there is still quite a bit of construction going on, so residents often wake to the sound of machinery.

## Karama

Map **2 L4** Metro **Karama**

Near the heart of downtown Dubai lies Karama. Its convenient location means it is a thriving commercial area with plenty of amenities. The price you pay is a lack of peace and quiet and lots of traffic. There are many low-cost restaurants, supermarkets and shops as well as the Karama Market (p.388), which sells a wide range of goods. Reasonable rents make Karama a good choice for Dubai residents on a budget.

### Accommodation

Most accommodation is in low-rise blocks with apartments ranging from studios to three-bedrooms. Prices can be as low as Dhs.30,000 for a one bedroom in the older buildings, but those tend to get snapped up quickly through word of mouth. The most desirable buildings are along Zabeel Road or in the area along Trade Centre Road, opposite Spinneys. A two-bedroom in one of those neighbourhoods can be found for around Dhs.80,000. If you can find a flat in a newer building with a full set of facilities, rent for a two-bedroom could be as high as Dhs.140,000.

### Shopping & Leisure

Everything is on your doorstep here. On Trade Centre Road there is a Spinneys and a Union Co-Op. There are plenty of small grocery shops, a fish market

and the well known Karama Market. The recently expanded BurJuman Mall (p.398) provides good shopping, while cheap-and-cheerful Avenue and Sana department stores are nearby. There are also beauty salons, barbershops, laundries, video rental shops and independent fitness clubs all within walking distance. The central post office and several banks are also in the area.

For daytime leisure, the gorgeous Zabeel Park and amazing Stargate (p.254) children's area is within walking distance. Karama is also home to some of the finest inexpensive dining venues in Dubai and you'll have access to takeaways from the many Arabic, Indian, Filipino, Sri Lankan and Pakistani restaurants that populate the area. There are several three-star hotels in the area, most of which house a few dive bars that are a blast for a down-and-dirty night out. Otherwise, the licensed restaurants and bars of Downtown Burj Dubai, Sheikh Zayed Road and Bur Dubai are only a short cab ride away.

### Healthcare & Leisure

Karama is convenient for many reasonably priced medical centres, doctors and dentists and is also just a few minutes away from Rashid Hospital (p.188) for emergencies. Although there are no popular schools or nurseries in the area, there are plenty of options close by in Garhoud and along Sheikh Zayed Road, and reaching them should be relatively easy.

## Mirdif

Map **2 Q12** Metro **Rashidiya**

Aside from the apartments in the Uptown Mirdif complex, Mirdif is made up of stand-alone villas and small, shared-facility compounds. It's a popular place for families and a good place for children to ride their bikes in and parents to socialise. Although it was once one of the least expensive areas to find a villa, prices have risen to match other villa-based communities. Traffic in and out of the area can be annoying during rush hour, but the streets within the individual neighbourhoods are free-flowing, and there are usually enough speed-bumps to prevent speeders.

### Accommodation

If you can find one, a decent three-bedroom villa should cost around Dhs.120,000 to Dhs.200,000 a year and, depending on whether it's a stand-alone or in a compound, it may have a little garden or shared pool. When searching for a place in Mirdif, be sure to take your time and see as many houses as possible. Since this is not a freehold development like Arabian Ranches or Emirates Hills, the quality of construction and finishing varies greatly between properties, and Dhs.200,000 could either get an old dilapidated three-bedroom or a new, spacious four-bedroom with a garden and pool.

Mirdif

## Shopping & Leisure

There is a large Spinneys supermarket in Uptown Mirdif, along with several shops, a pharmacy, hairdressers and restaurants. Mirdif also has many small shopping areas throughout that usually contain a small grocery, a convenience store and at least one cafeteria or takeaway. There is also a Westzone and Lifco supermarket within the area. The massive Mirdif City Centre should be open by the end of 2010 and will contain a Carrefour, among many other shops. Further down Airport Road is the Arabian Center shopping mall (p.410), which is a popular destination.

There aren't any hotels or licensed restaurants or bars within Mirdif, but Uptown Mirdif has a number of sit down restaurants and a food court full of fast food places. There are also several independent restaurants scattered throughout the community that offer delivery. Festival City is the nearest destination for licensed restaurants and bars and a cab ride to Sheikh Zayed Road takes about 15 minutes.

## Healthcare & Education

Welcare Clinic is in Uptown Mirdif and offers a wide range of medical services (04 288 1302). Drs Nicolas & Asp Dental Clinic is also in the area (04 288 4411). Over Airport Road in Mizhar there is a branch of Dubai London Clinic (04 287 8530). Rashidiya Clinic (04 285

7353) is the nearest government health facility. The nearest government hospital is Rashid (p.188), with 24 hour emergency services. There is a choice of nurseries in Mirdif including Small Steps (04 288 3347), Super Kids (p.156) and Emirates British Nursery (p.152). Uptown Primary (p.166) is recommended. Other new schools include Star International Academy (p.164) in Mirdif, the Sharjah American International School (04 280 1111) in Al Warqa, Royal Dubai School (p.164) in Muhaisnah, and the American Academy for Girls (p.158) in Mizhar.

## Oud Metha

Map **2 L5** Metro **Oud Metha**

Oud Metha is centrally located and within easy reach of the highways. There are plenty of shops and restaurants within walking distance or just minutes by car, as well as Lamcy Plaza (p.412) and the Wafi (p.409) complex of shops and restaurants. Accommodation is mainly in low-rise apartment blocks, which are not as densely packed as in other 'inner-city' areas. Oud Metha is quite popular and vacant apartments often get snapped up quickly. If you're lucky, you can find a one-bedroom for Dhs.65,000, but apartments in newer buildings with good facilities usually cost more. The apartments in Oud Metha are often larger than their freehold counterparts in the Marina or JLT. A large three-bedroom could go for as much as Dhs.150,000. Wafi, the Movenpick Hotel and the Grand Hyatt all have a good selection of licensed restaurants and fun bars. Many of the city's best independent restaurants, including Lemongrass (p.479) and Lan Kwai Fong (p.479) are also in the area. There are several private clinics and hospitals in Healthcare City (p.186), and both the American Hospital (p.186) and the Canadian Specialist Hospital (04 336 4444) are very close. Oud Metha is also home to Dubai English Speaking School (p.160) and the Indian High School.

## Palm Jumeirah

Map **1 M3** Metro **Nakheel**

The Palm Jumeirah is synonymous with Dubai's extravagance, and the price of housing on the man-made island matches the reputation. The trunk of the island is made up of large one to four-bedroom apartments, and a one-bedroom goes for around Dhs.80,000 a year. The fronds are covered in nearly identical three to six-bedroom villas which start at Dhs.250,000 and go as high as Dhs.550,000 for one of the massive 'Signature Villas'. Traffic onto the island isn't a problem and there is plenty of parking underneath the apartment buildings and next to the villas. Aside from the fine-dining options at the Atlantis, there are a few licensed restaurants and bars in the Shoreline Apartments on the trunk. The hotels in the Marina are less than five minutes away, as is Madinat Jumeirah. Nearby Al Sufouh has several schools popular expat schools.

# Residential Areas

## Qusais
Map **2 R8** Metro **Al Qusais 1**

Situated right on the border with Sharjah, apartments in Qusais tend to cost much less than the rest of Dubai. Despite the newly-widened Dubai-Sharjah Road, traffic is still a problem and commutes to other parts of Dubai can be a nightmare. A one bedroom in Al Qusais shouldn't cost more than Dhs.40,000 and large four-bedrooms can be found for around Dhs.70,000. The area has several larger supermarkets, including a Lulu Hypermarket, and Union Co-op, as well as several smaller corner groceries, shops and pharmacies. There are plenty of inexpensive Indian, Pakistani and Arabic restaurants that deliver, but you'll have to travel closer to the centre of Dubai to find a bar or licensed restaurant. The private Zulekha Hospital (p.190) has an emergency room and is located in Al Qusais, as are a few private clinics.

## Satwa
Map **2 H4** Metro **Trade Centre**

Despite having large sections demolished for the now-on-hold Jumeirah Garden City project, Satwa is still a desirable place to live for singles looking for a vibrant area. The main street, Diyafah, buzzes with pedestrians and is home to several of the city's favourite Arabic restaurants as well as plenty of fast food venues. There are a number of low-rise apartment blocks on Diyafah Street and Al Hudeiba Street (Plant Street). There are also several villas on the outskirts of the area that are popular for sharing. A two-bedroom on Diyafah Street shouldn't cost more than Dhs.90,000 and if you can find a villa in good condition, expect to pay around Dhs.170,000 for a three-bedroom. Rydges Plaza has long been a nightlife hub and there are several three-star hotels in the area that are home to intimate licensed restaurants and bars. Shoppers will be able to find everything they need along Diyafah Street and Plant Street and the larger supermarkets in Jumeira are less than 10 minutes away by car. Traffic can be horrendous at rush hour and street parking is hard to come by, but once the car is parked, the large pavements and many crosswalks make walking easy. In case of emergency, the Iranian Hospital (p.188) on Al Wasl Road has a very good A&E unit and Rashid Hospital (p.188) is nearby. There are no schools in Satwa, but several in neighbouring Jumeira and Al Wasl.

## Sharjah
Map **2 U5** Metro **Stadium**

Dubai's neighbouring emirate is an attractive location for many mainly due to the lower rents, which can be up to half what you'd pay in Dubai. As you'd expect in any city, there's a wide range of options, from small apartments to big villas. Unfortunately, rush-hour traffic in and out of Sharjah is a nightmare and finding a parking spot in some areas is almost impossible

## Silicon Oasis

Silicon Oasis, located off the Academic City Road, is a development containing hundreds of beautiful villas with gardens. Many of the villas are lived in by Emirates pilots. This area is considered to be quite far out of town, although it is just a 10 minute drive from Mirdif. There are a few small restaurants inside Silicon Oasis and in the nearby Academic City, and the Outlet Mall is just a quick trip over the other side of the Dubai-Al Ain Road. For more information, check out the community forum www.siliconoasis.org.

### Accommodation
Downtown it's all high-rise apartment blocks. Some have been around a few years so facilities are a little basic. Newer blocks command higher rents. As you venture out of town there are some big independent villas, and smaller, older villas too. For a new, large one-bedroom apartment in town with good facilities you could pay as little as Dhs.40,000, while a three-bedroom villa can be found for Dhs.110,000.

### Shopping & Leisure
Sharjah City Centre, Sharjah Mega Mall, and the Sahara Centre all feature a host of international brands and stores (such as M&S and Debenhams), and there are plenty of smaller shopping centres catering to all tastes and budgets. For a slightly more traditional shopping experience, the big Central Souk (aka Blue Souk) has rows of jewellery shops and stores selling Arabian knick-knacks and pretty much anything you could imagine. The Souk Al Arsah (p.396), in the Heritage Area, is a traditional Arabian market. Sharjah also has fruit, vegetable and fish markets in Al Jubail beside the water, with many stalls offering a variety of fresh produce.

For your everyday shopping needs, there's a big Carrefour in City Centre mall and a Spinneys in the Sahara Centre. You'll also find plenty of small grocery stores dotted around the residential areas, as well as dry cleaners and laundries.

Sharjah has a reputation for being quiet and the emirate is dry. That being said, Sharjah has some of the best independent restaurants in the country, many of which have been popular for decades. There is one licensed club in Sharjah, the Sharjah Wanderers Sports Club (www.sharjahwanderers.com), which is popular with expats in need of a local drink.

### Healthcare & Education
Sharjah has a number of government health clinics for subsidised medical care, plus private clinics and hospitals. The two government hospitals with emergency facilities are the Qassimi (06 538 6444) and Kuwaiti (06 524 2111) hospitals, while Al Zahra

Grand villas

Dubai Marina

Springs living

Emirates Hills

(06 561 9999), Zulekha (06 565 8866), and the Central Private (06 563 9900) are the main private hospitals with 24 hour emergency care.

Sharjah English School is a primary school for English-speaking children (06 552 2779), and Wesgreen International School (06 537 4401) teaches the British curriculum. There is also The Sharjah American International School (06 538 0000), Lycée Georges Pompidou de Sharjah (06 552 3430), and the German School Sharjah (06 567 6014). The Australian International School (06 558 9967) is on the Sharjah-Dubai border, just five minutes from Sharjah Airport.

## Sheikh Zayed Road
Map **2 J4** Metro **Al Jafiliya**

The strip between Trade Centre Roundabout and Interchange One is home to some of Dubai's biggest, brightest and boldest towers, both residential and commercial, plus some of the most impressive hotels in town. Being so close to all the action it's a popular area, and rents are high as a result. A one-bedroom with a good view will cost around Dhs.70,000 a year, and a three-bedroom in a newer building could cost upwards of Dhs.150,000. With the Dubai Mall, Mazaya Centre and the supermarkets of Jumeira (p.89) nearby, residents never have to travel far to get what they need. Both sides of Sheikh Zayed Road have pharmacies and smaller shops for daily needs, and there are plenty of takeaway restaurants for when you don't want to leave the apartment.

The strip is a popular nightlife destination with several bars and licensed restaurants in The Shangri-La, The Fairmont and The Towers Rotana. In other words, if you live here you should purchase a comfortable couch for friends who can't make it home after a night on the town.

Sheikh Zayed Road

### Defence Roundabout

You'll often hear Sheikh Zayed Road's Interchange One referred to as Defence Roundabout, as the army HQ was previously situated nearby. The current overhaul of this busy junction includes bridges, flyovers, and a new name – Burj Dubai Interchange – although the old Defence title will no doubt live on for many years.

Al Zahra Medical Centre (04 331 5000) in Al Safa Tower has a number of departments including family medicine and dentistry. The nearest emergency care is either Rashid Hospital (p.188) near Garhoud Bridge or the Iranian Hospital on Al Wasl Road.

There aren't any schools in the direct area, but as Sheikh Zayed Road is the city's main thoroughfare, several schools in Jumeira and beyond are only a short drive away.

## Tecom
Map **1 N5** Metro **Dubai Internet City**

Next to The Greens (p.96), Tecom is made up primarily of residential towers. Since each plot in the area was sold to a different developer, there is still a lot of construction going on, very few of the roads have been finished, and you can't walk anywhere. As a result, rents tend to be a bit cheaper than in neighbouring Al Barsha or The Greens, and a one-bedroom can be found for around Dhs.50,000. The quality of apartments varies, and traffic in and out of the neighbourhood is awful during peak hours. There is a Metro stop in front of the area, which is useful for anyone working on Sheikh Zayed Road. There are no shops within Tecom, but The Greens has a Spinneys and several other amenities. Nightlife destinations such as the Marina and Al Sufouh are just across Sheikh Zayed Road and the Media Rotana in Tecom is home to local pub Nelson's (p.513).

## The Gardens
Map **1 G5** Metro **Ibn Battuta**

The Gardens is somewhat of an anomaly for Dubai real estate. The entire development is fully owned by Nakheel and, unlike the rest of the city, rents here haven't seemed to grow since its opening. Located directly behind Ibn Battuta, the collection of low-rise apartment blocks is characterised by large trees and

# making it **easy every step** of the way

# Move *One*

# R E L O C A T I O N S

> Dedicated to simplifying moving and relocation process, Move One Relocations provides comprehensive customized services - all through a single point of contact.

> Worldwide moving    > Relocation services    > Fine art shipping    > Pet transportation

**mail** dubai@moveonerelo.com    **tel** 800 MOVEONE    **web** www.moveonerelo.com

fully-matured gardens. If you can find an apartment here, which isn't an easy task, expect to pay around Dhs.50,000 for a decent-sized one-bedroom. Residents of The Gardens tend to do their shopping at Ibn Battuta (p.404), and spend their nights at the licensed restaurants and bars at the nearby Marina. Traffic is rarely a problem within the development and its location is great for anyone working in Jebel Ali. For emergencies, Cedars Jebel Ali International Hospital (p.186) has a 24 hour emergency room and is very close.

## The Greens
Map **1 N5** Metro **Dubai Internet City**

The Greens, on the edge of Emirates Hills, offers a range of one to four-bedroom apartments, which are well appointed but a bit small for the money. A one-bedroom rents for around Dhs.60,000 and a three-bedroom for around Dhs.130,000. The shopping centre in the middle of the neighbourhood has a range of shops, including a Choithram and an Organic Foods & Café, as well as a few unlicensed restaurants. The area shares the same educational and healthcare facilities as Tecom and Emirates Hills. The Greens is especially convenient for those working in Media or Internet City, as there is a direct flyover connecting the two sides of Sheikh Zayed Road.

## Umm Suqeim
Map **1 T4** Metro **Al Quoz**

This is a desirable area mainly because it is close to the beach and has all the amenities you could wish for, while still remaining relatively peaceful. There are only villas in the area. Umm Suqeim is within easy reach of the major road networks and midway between the old centre of Dubai in Deira and the new Dubai emerging further along the coast towards the marina. This is an ever-popular choice for expats with kids but the rents are on the steep side. There is hardly any traffic on the residential streets, but Al Wasl Road and Jumeira Road can get clogged in the evenings.

### Accommodation

Villas range from traditional, old single-storey dwellings and smart multi-bedroom villas to palatial mansions. If you're extremely lucky you may hear about an old (perhaps run-down) villa going for Dhs.170,000, but for this price you can expect to have to pay for any maintenance and repairs. In fact, you hear stories of people spending a fair amount to make their cheap villa more liveable, only for the owner to then up the rent once they see how nice it is. For a detached four or five-bedroom villa, you'll be paying at least Dhs.300,000.

### Shopping & Leisure

There are several supermarkets in the area, including a large Choithram on Al Wasl Road, which has a dry cleaners, a good florist and a pharmacy. There is also a new Aswaaq supermarket (04 423 4431) in Umm Suqeim 3. Jumeira Road is littered with clothing boutiques and small takeaways, and Madinat Jumeirah sits right on the border between Umm Suqeim and Al Sufouh. Mall of the Emirates (p.405) is less than five minutes away by car and has a large Carrefour.

With the Burj Al Arab, Jumeirah Beach Hotel, and Madinat Jumeirah all on the doorstep, the entertainment and dining options are plentiful. There are also several independent restaurants on Jumeira Road. The nearest cinema is in Mercato (p.406) or Mall of the Emirates, and the entire community is within walking distance to the beach.

### Healthcare & Education

The nearest hospital with a 24 hour emergency room is the private Neuro Spinal Hospital opposite Jumeirah Beach Park in Jumeira 2. For general medical care there is the government-run Umm Suqeim Clinic (04 394 4461). Jumeira Road has several specialist clinics as well. The Medcare hospital (p.188) by Safa Park is also nearby. The largest secondary schools is Emirates International School (p.160). Umm Suqeim is also home to two Raffles International campuses (p.162), and there are several other schools in neighbouring Jumeira and Al Sufouh. There are plenty of nurseries including Emirates British Nursery (p.152) and Alphabet Street Nursery (p.152).

# SETTING UP HOME
## Moving Services

When hiring from abroad, Dubai employers sometimes offer help (such as a shipping allowance or furniture allowance) but the city is also well served by relocation specialists. If you're planning to arrive with more than a suitcase, you'll need to send your belongings by air or by sea. Air freight is faster but more expensive. Sea freight takes longer but it's cheaper, and containers can hold a huge amount.

### Smooth Moves

- Get more than one quote – some companies will match lower quotes to get the job.
- Make sure that all items are covered by insurance.
- Ensure you have a copy of the inventory and that each item is listed.
- Don't be shy about requesting packers to repack items if you are not satisfied.
- Take photos of the packing process, to use for evidence if you need to make a claim.
- Carry customs restricted goods (DVDs, videos or books) with you: it's easier to open a suitcase in the airport than empty a box outside in the sun.

# moving?

## relax.
## we carry the load. <sub>SM</sub>

Door to door moving with Allied Pickfords

Allied Pickfords is one of the largest and most respected providers of moving services in the world, handling over 50,000 international moves every year.

We believe that nothing reduces stress more than trust, and each year thousands of families trust Allied Pickfords to move them. With over 800 offices in more than 40 countries, we're the specialists in international moving and have the ability to relocate you anywhere anytime. Move with Allied to Allied worldwide.

Call us now on +971 4 408 9555
www.alliedpickfords.com
general@alliedpickfords.ae

 Your Chance to Earn Airmiles for using Allied Pickfords

**ALLIED PICKFORDS**
*The Careful Movers*™

# Setting Up Home

Everything you ship will need to be checked by customs and you must be present to collect your goods. Air freight must be picked up from Cargo Village in Garhoud and sea freight from Jebel Ali Port. Be sure to have your own copy of the inventory so that you know exactly what is in each box. And be patient.

Shipping goods by air can be expensive, so it may be worth only sending your bare essentials. Most of the big relocation companies will have warehouses at Cargo Village, so the entire process can be handled there. Head to the warehouse and fill out the customs information, and pay any applicable fees. You will then have to go across to Customs where you will pay any duty, plus a processing fee. Once this has been done, you can go back to the warehouse and collect your shipment. Before you can leave, you will have to head back over to Customs to have your goods x-rayed.

The process for sea freight is a little longer but some agencies will do the customs clearing for you, and arrange delivery to your home. This is also true for some air freight companies.

Once your sea freight is ready for collection (you'll get a call or letter), go to the agent's office and pay the administration and handling charges. Keep these documents. The Bill of Lading number must be marked on all paperwork and entered into the customs computer system.

Then go to Dubai Customs House, on Al Mina Road. The staff are helpful and the procedure is fairly straightforward, so ignore the touts outside. When the papers have been stamped and the Port Clearance received (there are fees at each stage) head down to Jebel Ali Port.

Now that rents are dropping, many people are moving within Dubai. If your possessions are valuable, you will want to hire an insured company to do the packing and moving for you. If not, you may benefit from packing your belongings yourself and hiring an uninsured 'man with a van'. There are several trucks-for-hire companies in the city and the best way to find a good one is to ask a friend or colleague. Otherwise, go to large furniture places such as Dragon Mart (p.411) or IKEA (p.371) where these unlicensed movers often congregate. A quick drive through an industrial area such as Al Quoz will also turn up some results. The trucks will usually have a mobile number written on the side of the door. Call the number and try to negotiate a good price (usually around Dhs.60 an hour) for the truck, driver and moving labour.

## Relocation & Removal Companies
**Allied Pickfords** > *p.97* 04 408 9555, *www.alliedpickfords.com*
**Crown Relocations** > *p.35* 04 289 5152, *www.crownrelo.com*
**Gulf Agency Company (GAC)** > *p.99* 04 881 8090, *www.gacworld.com/dubai*

**Interem (International Removals Division of Freight Systems)** > *p.39* 04 807 0583, *www.freightsystems.com*
**Move One Relocations** > *p.95* 04 299 3006, *www.moveonerelo.com*
**Writer Relocations** > *p.75* 04 340 8814, *www.writercorporation.com*

## Furnishing Accommodation
Most properties, including rentals, are unfurnished, and don't even have basic white goods such as a cooker or fridge. Not all villas have fitted cupboards and wardrobes. Dubai is home to many furniture shops, ranging from Swedish simplicity at IKEA (p.371) to rich Indian teak at Marina Gulf Trading (p.408). Alternatively, head to one of the carpentry workshops on Naif Road or in Satwa. See p.370 for more information on where to buy furniture, and p.373 for white goods.

### Second-Hand Furniture
The population of Dubai is still fairly transitory. As a result, finding second-hand furniture in good condition is quite easy. There are a number of small shops, mainly in Karama, Naif and Satwa that sell second-hand furniture, but you might find even better bargains from scouring online classifieds. Try www.dubizzle.com, www.expatwoman.com, www.websouq.com, or www.dubaidonkey.com. They have quite large followings and everything from white goods to living room furniture can be picked up. The Expat Woman website will often have notices for garage sales, where it's quite often possible to buy in bulk and prices can be negotiable. Supermarket noticeboards also carry listings for garage sales, or individual items with photos so you have a good idea what to expect before you view. Safa Park and Mamzar Park both have regular flea markets (www.dubai-fleamarket.com). Held the first Saturday of every month at Safa Park and every third Saturday at Mamzar Park, the markets are open between 09:00 and 15:00.

### Furniture Leasing
Setting up a new life and home is an expensive business. Aside from rental or mortgage costs, it is unlikely that many expats will have shipped their entire home contents over here. Furniture rental, from firms such as Indigo Living (p.100), provides a solution for new arrivals. Having the option of renting furniture means it's possible to move into your new home earlier, and there is no initial rush to have the entire house furnished before you can move in.

## Curtains & Blinds
Finding the right blinds or curtains can add a finishing touch to your room, ensure privacy if the house is overlooked, or stop you waking up with the sun. Some properties have windows built to standard

**GAC International Moving**

| Abu Dhabi | ▶ |
| Bahrain | ▶ |
| Dubai | ▶ |
| Kuwait | ▶ |
| Oman | ▶ |
| Qatar | ▶ |

# Click GAC International Moving

## for peace of mind in every move

Relocation in itself is a challenge. And we believe that you already have enough to do without worrying about your forthcoming move. That's why when it comes to moving your home or office, GAC treats each item with care and every move with pride.

With more than 30 years of experience in moving household goods in and out of the Middle East, GAC provides comprehensive high quality door-to-door services for any relocation need. Moves are professionally planned, starting with a free initial survey and recommendations on the most efficient shipment mode. It's another world-class solution from GAC – available in over a thousands locations on earth.

www.gacworld.com

**GAC Abu Dhabi**
moving.abudhabi@gacworld.com
Tel: +971 2 673 0500
Fax: +971 2 673 1328

**GAC Dubai**
moving.dubai@gacworld.com
Tel: +971 4 881 8090
Fax: +971 4 805 9342 / 805 9323

**GAC Bahrain**
moving.bahrain@gacworld.com
Tel +973 17 339 777
Fax +973 17 320 498

**GAC Oman**
moving.oman@gacworld.com
Tel: +968 2447 7800
Fax: +968 2447 7891

**GAC Kuwait**
moving.kuwait@gacworld.com
Tel: +965 222 64 164
Fax: +965 248 36 375

**GAC Qatar**
moving.qatar@gacworld.com
Tel +974 420 5600
Fax +974 420 5601

sizes, which means you can buy ready-made options from shops such as IKEA (p.372) and THE One (p.372). If these don't measure up though, there are several companies that will tailor and install curtains and blinds to fit your property. IKEA also has a fabric store and offers a tailoring service for basic curtains and roman blinds at bargain prices.

Many community notice boards will have notices for second-hand blinds or curtains that were made to fit the strange window sizes found in many freehold developments.

**Dubai Blinds** > *p.101* Trade Centre, 04 312 4086, *www.dubaiblinds.com*
**Home Centre** Al Barsha, 04 341 4441, *www.homecentre.net*
**IKEA** Festival City, 800 4532, *www.ikeadubai.com*
**Indigo Living** > *p.68* Al Quoz, 04 339 7705, *www.indigo-living.com*
**Pan Emirates** Barsha, 04 383 0800, *www.panemirates.com*
**Sedar** Satwa, 04 345 4597, *www.sedaremirates.com*

## Interior Design

Moving into a new, empty apartment can be a hassle if you have arrived without any furnishings – but there are several good interior design firms in the city that can make the decorating process easier.

### 3 Square

Number One Tower Suites, Sheikh Zayed Road
Trade Centre **04 321 5592** www.3square.ae
Map **2 G5** Metro **Financial Centre**
A firm that provides both design consultancy and complete concept through to installation solutions.

### House Of The World

Warehouse 3, Umm Suqeim Rd Al Quoz **04 323 3482**
www.houseoftheworld.com
Map **1 S3** Metro **First Gulf Bank**
Tailored interior design for apartments and villas, drawing heavily on eastern influences.

### Indigo Living > *p.68*

Showroom 45, Street 19 Al Quoz **04 341 6305**
www.indigo-living.com
Map **1 U5** Metro **Al Quoz**
Along with interior design consulting, this store offers furniture rentals. Also has a branch on The Walk.

### KLC Interior Architecture

Gold & Diamond Park Al Quoz **04 341 3030**
www.klc-dubai.com
Map **1 S5** Metro **First Gulf Bank**
Interior architects with a focus on home audio and visual, lighting and home automation, as well as garden landscaping.

## Household Insurance

Crime and natural disasters are not generally a big concern for Dubai's residents, but insuring your household goods against theft or damage is still wise. To create a policy, the insurance provider will need your home address, a list of household items and valuation, and invoices for anything worth more than Dhs.2,500.

Cover usually includes theft, fire and storm damage. You can also insure personal items outside the home. As a guideline you can expect to pay around Dhs.1,500 per 1.2 sq m for building insurance, Dhs.250 for up to Dhs.60,000 worth of home contents and Dhs.850 for up to Dhs.60,000 worth of personal possessions.

**AXA Insurance** > *p.65*
800 4845, *www.axa-gulf.com*
**Greenshield Insurance**
04 397 4464, *www.greenshield.ae*
**HSBC Bank Middle East**
800 4560, *www.hsbc.ae*
**Millienium Insurance Brokers Co**
04 335 6552, *www.mibco-uae.com*
**National General Insurance**
04 222 2772, *www.ngi.ae*

# UTILITIES & SERVICES

## Electricity & Water

Dubai Electricity and Water Authority (DEWA) is the sole provider of water, electricity and sewerage. When you sign up for connection to your new home you will need to pay a deposit (Dhs.2,000 for a villa and Dhs.1,000 for an apartment), which is fully refundable when you leave the property. DEWA charges a standard rate per unit, currently 20 fils per unit for electricity, 3 fils per unit for water and 0.5 fils per unit for sewerage. If you use too much electricity or water, DEWA will increase your rates. For example, if you use over 2,000kWh of electricity in a month the rate increases to 24 fills per unit. Your DEWA bill also includes the municipality housing tax, which, over the course of twelve months, adds up to 5% of the rental value of the property. The 'housing fee' covers refuse collection and utilities maintenance.

If you have a garden it will probably need watering twice a day in summer. It might be possible to have a borehole installed in your garden, meaning that, after the initial expense, you have access to free groundwater. Installation will set you back around Dhs.1,000. Once it's done you should notice a marked decrease in your DEWA bill. Be sure to get permission from the landlord before starting the process. See Gardens, p.108, for more details.

# Utilities & Services

## Electricity

The electricity supply in Dubai is 220/240 volts and 50 cycles, and the socket type is the same as the three-pin British system. Many appliances are sold with two pin plugs which can either be changed or used with an adaptor which can be bought for a couple of dirhams from any hypermarket.

### Apartments Are Cool

You can expect a higher A/C bill in a villa – not only is it probably bigger than your average apartment, but many apartment buildings include air-conditioning costs in the rent.

## Water

Tap water is desalinated sea water and is generally considered safe to drink – although the government's Food & Environment Laboratory does warn of contaminated water in buildings which have poorly maintained pipes. Most people opt for mineral water, mainly because it tastes better. Bottled water is cheap, but most people end up buying a water cooler or pump (available from most large supermarkets), or leasing one from a water supplier and using the four or five-gallon bottles of purified water to drink at home. Prices vary per company; some charge a deposit of around Dhs.30 for each re-useable bottle, and then Dhs.7 per refill, while Masafi recycles its bottles rather than re-using them and charges Dhs.12 per new bottle (plus one free bottle for every 10 you buy). Companies will deliver the bottles to your door, and collect your empties.

### Hot Water

The water in your cold taps can get so hot in summer that you can turn off your water heaters. You know winter's coming when you have to turn the water heater on again.

## Water Suppliers

**Al Madina Drinking Water Supply** 04 267 0710
**Culligan International** 800 4945
**Desert Springs** 800 6650
**Falcon Spring Drinking Water** 04 396 6072
**Masafi** 800 5455, www.masafi.com
**Nestle Pure Water** 04 800 4404
**Oasis Drinking Water** 04 884 5656, www.oasisuae.com

## Gas

There are still no gas mains in Dubai, and individual gas canisters need to be purchased and attached to the cookers. There are a number of gas suppliers that will deliver the canisters and connect up the supply. Supply companies tend to slip stickers or flyers under doors on a regular basis and they're all essentially the same. A few of the largest companies include Honest Hands (04 285 6586), Oasis (04 396 1812) and New City (04 351 8282). Gas bottles come in three sizes: most houses use the medium size, the small are better in apartments and the large are really only for industrial use – they are enormous. The canisters initially cost around Dhs.350 and refills are usually Dhs.60 (keep your receipt so that you can get some of your deposit back). There is usually a gas van around your area at all times so chances are that if you run out of gas in the middle of cooking your chips, one call to your local gas man and he can be with you in less than 20 minutes.

## Sewerage

Much of Dubai now has mains sewers but there are areas where houses and apartment buildings are still serviced by septic tanks. These are regularly emptied by municipality contractors, but should you have a problem, contact your landlord or local municipality office. All sewage has to be treated, hence the charges on the DEWA bill even for houses not on the main sewer network.

## Rubbish Disposal

Dubai's per capita domestic waste rate is extremely high, with some estimates saying that each household generates over 1,000kg of rubbish per year. Fortunately, rubbish disposal is efficient, with municipality trucks driving around each area and emptying the skips daily. Just empty your household bins into the skips (there is usually one on every street). If you don't have a skip on your street, contact the municipality on 04 206 4234 to request one. Certain areas, such as Emirates Hills, have wheelie bins outside each house, where waste is collected from. Recycling efforts are poor but slowly improving. For more information on recycling and environmental issues, see p.11.

## Telephone

There are two telecommunications companies in the UAE, Etisalat and du. Both are government-owned.

To install a landline with Etisalat you must apply directly with a completed application form, a copy of your passport and residence visa, a no objection letter from your sponsor, and Dhs.125 (inclusive of first quarterly rental). Taking the number of the landline closest to your house can help pinpoint your location. Telephone calls between landlines in Dubai are free, but there is a nominal charge for calls to Jebel Ali. Depending on the time of day, calls to elsewhere in the UAE cost between Dhs.0.12 and Dhs.0.24 per minute; calls to mobiles cost between Dhs.0.18 and Dhs.0.24. The tariffs for international calls vary from country to country but there is some variation in peak timings, depending on country. For more information

**THE MORE CARDS YOU SEND,
THE MORE LIVES YOU CHANGE.**

There are millions of children who need the things we take for granted everyday.
This holiday season, you can help make a difference in a child's life
by simply buying UNICEF cards.
To view the collection of cards and gift items, please go to www.unicef.org/gao and contact
us to place your orders. Remember, every card you buy goes towards helping a child in need.

unite for children

aramex
delivery unlimited

Tel. +971.4.3680703 E-mail: rasfour@unicef.org

ilevel

on phone services with Etisalat, including peak and off-peak timings, see www.etisalat.com.

du's landline service offers pay-by-the-second landlines and flat rates on long-distance calls. du provides services to many Emaar and Nakheel properties, both business and residential (such as Dubai Marina, Arabian Ranches, Emirates Hills, the Greens/Springs/Lakes, and International City). Villas and apartments in these areas are equipped with multiple sockets for telephone, internet and TV signals. To apply, you will need a copy of your passport and tenancy agreement. The fees include a one-off installation charge (Dhs.200) plus line rental of Dhs.15 per month. For more information on phone services with du, check their website: www.du.ae.

### Mobile Phones

Mobile phone users can choose between du (prefix 055) and Etisalat (prefix 050 or 056). Both providers offer monthly or pay-as-you-go packages. You can register for a pay-as-you-go line and pick up a SIM card for either Etisalat or du from any of the company kiosks located in malls or from any of the many mobile phone shops scattered throughout the city. To get a line, you will need your passport with residency visa. A du pay-as-you-go line costs Dhs.55 and includes Dhs.10 credit. An Etisalat pay-as-you-go line costs Dhs.165 and also includes Dhs.10 credit. Both du and Etisalat require you to renew your line every year. The renewal fee for a du line is Dhs.55 and Dhs.100 for an Etisalat line.

Both companies also offer monthly post-paid services. To sign up for a post-paid plan through du, you will need to bring your passport and residency visa as well as either a UAE credit card, a recent utility bill with your physical address, your tenancy agreement or a salary certificate that shows a minimum salary of Dhs.2,500 per month. For an Etisalat post-paid mobile line you will need to bring your passport with residency visa as well as a salary certificate showing a minimum salary of Dhs.2,500 per month. A new du post-paid line costs Dhs.62 plus a Dhs.30 service charge every month, while an Etisalat line costs Dhs.125 plus Dhs.20 every month.

---

#### Cheap Calls Not Allowed

Downloading certain voice over internet protocol (VoIP) services such as Skype can be difficult within the UAE due to the sites being blocked here. However, if you have downloaded it in a different country, or within an area where the restriction is lifted, such as in some freezones, it will still work when calling another computer, but not when calling landlines or mobiles.

---

## Internet

Internet services in the UAE are provided by either Etisalat or du. All internet usage, however is regulated by the Telecommunications Regulatory Authority (TRA). This means that many sites that are deemed to be offensive, either religiously, culturally or politically, are blocked and can't be accessed.

Etisalat has various packages available based on speed. For a 1Mbps broadband connection with unlimited usage you pay a Dhs.200 installation fee plus Dhs.249 per month. Check www.etisalat.ae for more details.

If you live in a new development, your internet will most likely be provided by du (www.du.ae). It offers a range of 'always on' internet packages, ranging from 256kbps (Dhs.149 per month) to 2mbps (Dhs.349 per month). There is a Dhs.200 installation fee. Check www.du.ae for details.

---

#### du Installation

All of du's home telecommunication services, including cable TV, are routed through the same sockets. As a result, du recommends you sign up for all of your services at the same time. The installation fee for all du services is Dhs.200, regardless of how many services you have installed at one time.

---

### Dial & Surf

This facility allows you to surf without subscribing to the Etisalat internet service. All that's needed is a computer with a modem and a regular Etisalat phone line – no account number or password is required. In theory, you then simply dial 500 5555 to gain access. However, in practice it may not be quite so straightforward, since there are different set-ups depending on your software. If you have difficulties, contact the helpdesk (800 5244). The charge of 12 fils per minute is made for the connection and billed to the telephone line from which the call is made.

---

#### Area Codes & Prefixes

| | | | |
|---|---|---|---|
| Abu Dhabi | 02 | Jebel Ali | 04 |
| Ajman | 06 | Ras Al Khaimah | 07 |
| Al Ain | 03 | Sharjah | 06 |
| Dubai | 04 | UAE country code | 971 |
| Fujairah | 09 | Umm Al Quwain | 06 |
| Hatta | 04 | | |

---

## Postal Services

There is currently no postal delivery service to home addresses, and everyone has their mail delivered to a PO box. Mail is first delivered to the Central Post Office and then distributed to clusters of PO boxes in various

# Enjoy your visit to the UAE and Maximise your mobile savings.

Etisalat's Visitor's Mobile Package "Ahlan" ensures that all your communication needs are taken care of during your visit to the UAE.
What's more, call back home at a flat rate of AED 1.25/minute* and make the most of Super Off Peak rates.

* Call 125 to subscribe to the Super Off Peak plan & enjoy discounted rates from 1 am to 7 am.

For more information call 101 or visit www.etisalat.ae/ahlan

 Reach...  Value  Convenience  Coverage Innovation

areas. To get your own PO box, fill in the application form at your nearest post office and pay the annual fee (Dhs.150); you will be given a set of keys (Dhs.10 per key) to access your own box. Many people have mail delivered to their company's PO box.

Empost will send you notification by email when you receive registered mail or parcels in your PO box. For an extra Dhs.9 you can have the item delivered to your door. However, you might have to pay customs charges on international packages.

Letters and packages do occasionally go missing and, if the item has not been registered, there's little that you can do apart from wait – some turn up months after they are expected.

Empost offers a courier service for both local and international deliveries. Delivery times are guaranteed and packages can be tracked. Registered mail is a relatively inexpensive alternative, and can also be tracked via a reference number.

All of the major international courier services deliver to Dubai, including DHL (299 5333), FedEx (800 4050), UPS (800 4774) and Aramex (04 286 5000), and all of them will deliver to your door. If you are expecting a package, make sure the person sending it has included the correct phone number, as that is often the only way for the courier to find your location.

### Sending Gifts Home

If you would rather not chance the post, Gift Express provides a selection of gifts that can be sent to most countries (www.giftexpress.ae).

## Carpet Cleaners & Laundry Services

Wall-to-wall carpets are rare in this part of the world, but many homes do sport loose rugs and carpets. When they're looking a bit grubby, the companies listed below can pay you a visit, give you a quote, and take the carpets away to be cleaned, returning them a couple of days later. All of the carpet services listed below, will also come to your house to clean upholstery.

There are no self-service launderettes, but laundry shops are everywhere. Some of the largest chains in the city include Butler's (04 366 3359) and Champion Cleaners (04 224 6403). As well as dry cleaning and laundry, they all offer ironing services. If you have specific instructions, make sure these are noted when you drop off your laundry – creases in trousers are standard, so if you don't want them, speak up.

Compensation policies for lost or damaged items vary, but losses are rare, even in the places that look most disorganised. Large chains normally have a free pick-up and delivery service. Expect to pay Dhs.12 for a shirt, Dhs.45 for a suit and Dhs.40 for a quilt.

## Carpet Cleaners

**Churchill** 04 800 7076, *www.churchill-gulf.com*
**Modern Cleaning Methods**
04 285 1668, *www.modernmethodsco.com*
**Royal Carpet Cleaning & Painting** 04 393 5038
**Spotless** 04 331 8827

## Domestic Help

Domestic help is readily available in Dubai, whether full or part-time, and there are a number of options available. Legally, a housemaid may only be employed by the individual who sponsors her, but in practice many maids take on cleaning or babysitting for other families; if you are caught you face a hefty fine but the law seems rarely to be enforced. If you are looking for someone part time, but want to stay within the law, there are many companies in Dubai that provide cleaners and maids on an hourly basis, and for around Dhs.20 to Dhs.30 per hour they'll take care of all your sweeping, mopping, dusting, washing, and ironing. Most companies stipulate a minimum number of hours, usually two or three per visit.

**Home Comfort Services** 04 272 2135
**Home Help** 04 355 5100, *www.homehelp.ae*
**Molly Maid** 04 339 7799,
*www.mollymaidme.com*
**Ready Maids** 04 294 8345,
*www.readymaidsdubai.com*
**Sky Maid Services** 04 332 4600

# HOME IMPROVEMENTS

## Maintenance

Whether you're a home owner or live in rental property, are responsible for your property's general maintenance or have an assigned company, housing in Dubai requires constant maintenance – not in small part thanks to the climate.

Air conditioning units can be temperamental and need regular servicing, plumbing problems aren't uncommon, electrics can go haywire and creepy crawlies like to pay a visit.

Most homeowners and tenants employ the services of a maintenance company. Annual contracts don't come cheap, but the benefit is it will cover you for most of your maintenance needs. The contract should include regular scheduled servicing of air conditioning units and boilers, seasonal pest control protection, basic masonry works and 24 hour emergency call out services. Most companies offer extra services such as swimming pool maintenance and gardening for an add-on fee.

# ACE
NE STORE. MANY LIFESTYLES.

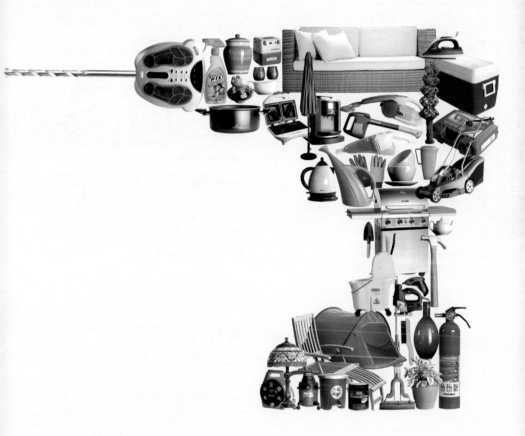

# Thinking hardware? Think again.

here's certainly more to ACE than just a hardware store. From automotive accessories to kitchen appliances. amping gear to Barbeques. Indoor decor to outdoor furniture. Paints to plants. Gardening items to et accessories. There's so much to choose from all under one roof. **ACE. One Store. Many Lifestyles.**

**bai:** Dubai Festival City, Tel: 800 ASK ACE (800 275 223), Sheikh Zayed Road, Tel: (04) 338 1416, Fax: (04) 338 6151, The Market Mall, Green Community, : (04) 885 3208, Fax (04) 885 3209 **Sharjah:** Al Qasimia Road, Tel: (06) 532 2600, Fax (06) 532 2911 **Abu Dhabi:** Mina Road, Tel: (02) 673 1665, x (02) 673 0415 **Al Ain:** Sultan Bin Zayed Road, Bawadi Mall (03) 784 0561 **e-mail: ace@alfuttaim.ae or www.al-futtaim.ae**

An **Al-Futtaim group** company                    www.**ace**uae.com

# Home Improvements

Typical costs for such maintenance contracts go from Dhs.7,000 up to Dhs.11,000 per year. Companies that offer maintenance services include Emrill (covering Emaar Properties, www.emrill.com), Howdra (www.howdra.ae), Jim Will Fix It (www.jimwillfixitservices.com), and Hitches & Glitches (www.hitchesandglitches.com).

Whichever community you live in, your developer will have standard rules and regulations relating to noise, parking, and general upkeep of your property. These will be detailed on the developers' website and local security guards perform regular checks. If you live in a villa, a dirty or messy garage may be frowned upon, and you could be fined for such things as parking on the street rather than in a designated bay, so it's worth making yourself aware of what is required of you as either a tenant or homeowner.

## Builders

The law is constantly changing when it comes to making alterations to your property, and has so far been very restrictive. In Nakheel and Emaar developments, you are not allowed to build any higher than your perimeter wall, so should you wish for the popular addition of an outside extensions or garden house, you would have had to dig down and build upwards to avoid the structure being higher than the wall.

To build an extension, you need to apply for permission via your master developer, who would need to approve the plans and receive a deposit of Dhs.5,000. An inspector will make a site visit during the works and then carry out a final assessment on completion of the building, after which your deposit will be returned if you have met all the guidelines. Developers also determine the colour of the paint you may use on the exterior of your property and also the particular design and style of any doors, gates or decorative iron fencing.

All this may change though as the Planning & Engineering Department of Dubai Municipality is currently working to centralise all structural work carried out on residential buildings in Dubai, effectively taking the responsibility out of the hands of the developers. The anticipation is that when the new laws are passed, rules on extension plans and designs will be more lenient.

If you are intending to make some structural changes to your property you should always use a licensed and experienced contractor. Options include Cygnet (04 324 1785), Rustom General Maintenance (06 749 1702) and Stallron Services (04 342 0822).

## Painters

Once you own your property you are free to paint the insides any style you choose. If you rent, the likelihood is that your landlord will not mind on the basis that he has your deposit, and will be happy to keep hold of it should you not leave the villa or apartment in its original state. Many Dubai landlords do not need much of a reason to hold back security deposits though, so it's worth checking and getting something in writing before you get the roller out.

An excellent range of paints and associated implements can be found at Jotun Paints and Ace Hardware (p.414). Companies like Cygnet (04 324 1785), Jim Will Fix It (www.jimwillfixitservices.com) and Cairo Maintenance (050 6452160) all offer painting services. The cost of internally painting a whole villa can vary between Dhs.3,000 and Dhs.8,000, depending on size, materials and contractor.

## Gardens

For a city on the edge of the desert, Dubai boasts a lot of lush greenery – but with very little annual rainfall and rapidly diminishing groundwater, plenty of hydration is required to create your own little garden oasis.

Gardens need watering twice a day ideally, and you will notice a huge difference in the quality of your plants and lawns if this routine lessens – green can turn brown within a matter of days. You can install a timed irrigation system or employ the services of a gardener, while boring a well in your garden to access natural supplies is also an option.

For houses further in from the coast (such as in the Dubailand area) you'll need to drill down approximately 25 metres before you hit groundwater, whereas houses in areas nearer the sea such as Al Barsha or Jumeira will access water after only a couple of metres. The level of salt in the water will vary, and it is possible to pump the water into a mixed tank to desalinate it for your domestic use. The cost for drilling and finding should be approximately Dhs.1,000 if you secure the expertise of any of the landscaping companies found in the Plant Street area of Satwa (see p.92).

If maintaining a grassy garden seems like too much hassle you can always opt for astroturf. Fake lawns are increasingly popular; they stay green throughout the year and need no watering (although you do need to hose them down every few weeks). You can buy astroturf (in varying degrees of quality) in Ace Hardware, while Clearview (www.clearview.ae) and Cape Reed (www.capereed.com) both install fake lawns. Another option is to go for block paving or decking. Again, you can purchase decking in Ace Hardware (p.414), while Alomi (www.alomirealwoodflooringllc.com) is a wood merchant that has carpenters with experience in laying decks.

For apartment dwellers or those who wish to add to, or beautify their existing outside areas, sourcing individual plants, trees, shrubs, decorative pots, soil and composts is a relatively simple search. The Dubai Municipality Nursery recently relocated to the

Jadaf area, next to Business Bay crossing. Prices are reasonable and discounts based on quantity will be given. Dubai Garden Centre (04 340 0006) sells pretty much everything you could need for your outdoor space, while Plant Street in Satwa has a number of basic nurseries, but choice here can be limited.

Larger retailers such as Spinneys (p.392), Carrefour (p.391) and IKEA (p.371) sell plants, pots and smaller sized gardening implements, while Ace Hardware (p.414) is a one stop shop for the outdoor enthusiast selling everything from fauna to furniture, tools to trees and plants to pergolas.

If you are buying a brand new house, the developers may have left you with no more than a sandpit plot, so you will need to start your garden from scratch, and landlords are not obliged to landscape the gardens of new villas before they rent them to you either.

If the DIY is not for you, Dubai Garden Centre offers a full landscaping service, while Royal Gardenscape (www.royalgardenscape.com) provides all you need in the way of paving and gravel. Plant Street is a great place to start for cheap labour and materials, while Terraverde (www.terraverde.ae), Cre8tive (www. cre8tive4u.com) and Bespoke Concepts (www. bespokeconcepts.ae) all offer full service design and

installation for gardens. For more information on garden furniture see Shopping, p.370.

## Swimming Pools

A lot of properties in Dubai have private pools or access to a shared pool. If you don't have one in your villa, you can always pay to have one installed – but it doesn't come cheap. One option is to have a custom-made, free-form fibre glass and ceramic tiled pool fitted. As tough and durable as a concrete version, these are effectively portable. Delivery of one of these usually takes around four weeks, with an onsite installation period of approximately 10 days. Prices for such a pool start at around Dhs.110,000 and includes all labour, pumps and filtration. Try Pools by Design (050 754 6852).

Aside from cleaning, your pool will also need the water to be changed and chemical levels balanced on a regular basis. Those Pool Guys (www. thosepoolguys.com) or Island King (04 334 6555) are both well established in Dubai and can take care of maintenance, while word of mouth can turn up other companies such as Aquamani (04 360 3593) and Hennessy (050 453 6214). Most pool maintenance companies will also be able to perform repairs of things such as broken lights and filters.

Settle into your Dubai home

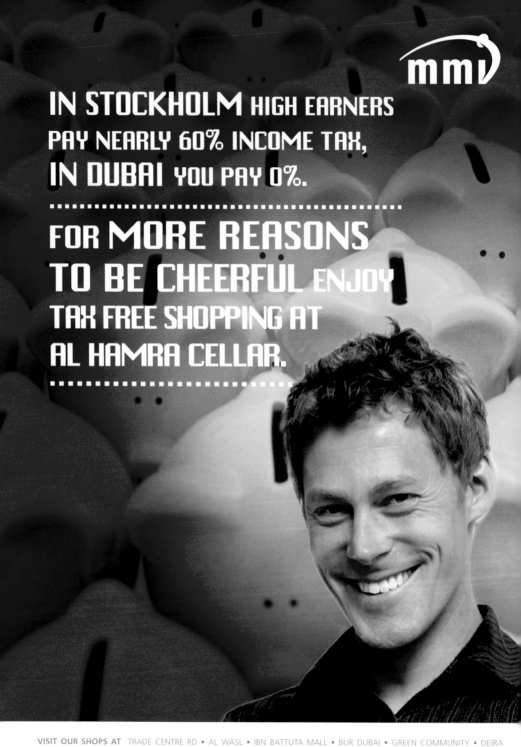

IN STOCKHOLM HIGH EARNERS PAY NEARLY 60% INCOME TAX, IN DUBAI YOU PAY 0%.

FOR MORE REASONS TO BE CHEERFUL ENJOY TAX FREE SHOPPING AT AL HAMRA CELLAR.

mmi

VISIT OUR SHOPS AT TRADE CENTRE RD • AL WASL • IBN BATTUTA MALL • BUR DUBAI • GREEN COMMUNITY • DEIRA
MALL OF THE EMIRATES • KARAMA • SHEIKH ZAYED ROAD • DUBAI SILICON OASIS • FESTIVAL CITY Shop finder www.mmidubai.com

# Work, Finance & The Law

# WORKING IN DUBAI

Expat workers come to Dubai for a number of reasons: to advance their career, for a higher standard of living, to take advantage of new opportunities or, most commonly, for the lifestyle and the experience of living and working in a new culture. Whatever the reason, there are various advantages to working here.

While the biggest bonus of working in Dubai may seem to be tax-free salaries, the cost of living (or your newly acquired lifestyle) can somewhat balance out this benefit.

In addition, the instability of the world's economy has had an effect on the job market in Dubai, and there has been a shift from the fervent recruitment drive of past years. However, the situation is constantly changing. At the very senior end of the scale, there remain some idyllic opportunities and huge packages that attract the big players, and these are predominantly in the construction, aviation and finance industries.

However, for less senior positions, the image of a cushy expat life in the Gulf is changing, with much more competition in all areas of the market and an increasing number of people looking for work in Dubai. Not so long ago foreign expats could walk into jobs that they could only dream of back home, but these days the market is much more competitive, not least because of the effects of the global economic downturn. All-inclusive packages with accommodation and education allowances are also not as common, although basic benefits still apply (such as annual flights home and 30 calendar days leave).

Work-wise, Dubai is still a land of opportunities for skilled professionals. It is easier to change industries, as skill sets are less 'pigeon-holed' than in other countries and jobs in certain industries (such as construction) are more available.

One of the main differences about working in Dubai, as opposed to your country of origin, is that you need to be sponsored (see p.37) by an employer, which often leaves people feeling tied or uncomfortably obligated to their employer. If you leave the company, your current visa will be cancelled and you will have to go through the hassle of getting a new residency permit (for you and your family, if they are on your sponsorship).

## Labour Card

To work in the UAE you are legally required to have a valid labour card. The labour card can only be applied for once you have residency and is usually organised by the company PRO.

If you are recruited from your home country, your company will have to get approval from the Ministry of Labour. You will then enter on an employment visa, get a health card, take the medical test, and get the residency stamp in your passport. The company PRO then takes all of the relevant paperwork to the Ministry of Labour where the actual labour card will be issued (even though it has 'work permit' printed on the back). The card features your photo and details of your employer. You're supposed to carry the card with you at all times but it is highly unlikely that you will ever be asked to produce it. The process can also be quite slow, and it's possible you may not receive your card for a few weeks, or even months, after starting work. The labour card costs Dhs.1,000 (paid by your company) and is usually valid for three years. It must be renewed within 60 days of expiry. Failure to do so will result in a fine (which your company will be liable for) of Dhs.5,000 for each year the card has expired.

If your employer is arranging your residency, you will need to sign your labour contract before the labour card is issued. This contract is printed in both Arabic and English. It's not necessarily your agreed 'contract' as such – most employees will sign a more comprehensive contract. Unless you read Arabic it may be advisable to have a translation made of your details, since the Arabic is the official version in any dispute. However, if there is any discrepancy, the judge would want to know why your company got the details wrong in the first place (see Employment Contracts, p.116).

## Working Hours

Working hours differ dramatically between companies; straight shifts vary from 07:30 to 14:00 for government organisations to the common 09:00 to 18:00 for private companies. Most retail outlets tend to be open from 10:00 to 22:00 but often operate shifts. Teachers start early at around 07:30 and classes finish around 14:00, although their hours aren't as predetermined as other roles. Although less common nowadays, some offices and shops operate split shifts, which allow for a longer break in the afternoon (hours are usually 08:00 to 13:00 and 16:00 to 19:00).

The maximum number of hours permitted per week according to UAE Labour Law is 48, although some industries, such as hospitality and retail, have longer stipulated hours. Annual holiday allowance starts at one calendar month per year, or roughly 22 working days. Some employees, especially those in management, have more than this and long service usually adds to holiday allowance.

Friday is the Islamic holy day and therefore a universal day off for offices and schools. Consumer demand means that the hospitality and retail industries are open seven days a week. Saturday is the second day of the weekend; some companies work five and a half days a week and some operate a six-day week, taking only Friday as a rest day.

Public holidays (see p.7) are set by the government, while the timing of religious holidays depends on the sighting of the moon. This can mean that it is difficult to plan holidays, as confirmation of public holidays can come just days before the event. The labour law states that all employees (even non-Muslims) are entitled to a shorter working day during Ramadan, although labour lawyers would advise you not to insist on this if you are non-Muslim or not fasting.

## Business Culture

Like anywhere in the world, doing business in the UAE has its unique idiosyncrasies. Even if you work for a western company, the chances are that some of your business transactions will be with Emiratis, whether on a customer or client basis. While you're likely to find that Emiratis are open to different styles of business and are generally keen to explain their customs, understanding some of the local business etiquette can help you keep one step ahead of the competition.

It's a good idea to dress conservatively for meetings, particularly if you are female, and it is advisable to cover your knees and arms. You may also have a meeting with a woman wearing a hijab (a veil which leaves the face uncovered), or some women choose to wear a niqab which covers the full face.

Don't be surprised if greetings are more tactile in the UAE than in your home country; long handshakes, kisses and effusive compliments are common. While it's normal to shake hands with people of the same sex, if you are meeting someone of the opposite sex it's best to take your cue from the other person and not offer your hand unless they offer theirs.

It's polite to send greetings to a person's family, but can be considered rude to enquire directly about someone's wife, sister or daughter. A nose kiss is a customary greeting in the Gulf region but is only used between close friends and associates and you should not attempt to greet someone in this way.

Business meetings will usually start with numerous greetings and an exchange of business cards – you should take time the time to read the card as a sign of respect. Punctuality is important and arriving late to meetings is considered very impolite – however, don't assume that your meeting will start at the appointed time or that it will not be interrupted.

If you're attending a business meeting at an Arab-owned company, it's likely that you'll be served traditional Arabic coffee, or kahwa. Sharing coffee is an important social ritual in the Middle East so you should drink some when offered. Cups should be taken in the right hand and if there is a waiter standing by, replenishing your cup, there are two ways to signal that you have had enough: either leave a small amount of coffee in the bottom of your cup or gently tip the cup from side to side.

DIFC & Emirates Towers

# Working in Dubai

While not so much a matter of etiquette, patience is the ultimate virtue for doing business in the UAE. Things may move more slowly and decisions take longer than you may be used to. Keeping in regular contact with your clients and customers helps to maintain genial relations and picking up the phone rather than relying on email can make the world of difference.

## Finding Work

Until the financial crisis hit, Dubai's economy was booming and therefore the recruitment market was extremely buoyant. Things have slowed down a great deal and a large majority of companies made redundancies, forcing many expats to return home. However, the UAE remains optimistic and during the end of 2009, the job market began to look more positive. Opportunities are out there, however, the competition for good positions is greater which means there is a stronger focus on what skills employees will bring to the table.

There are numerous recruitment agencies in Dubai but employers also use local newspapers and head-hunters to advertise job opportunities. It is undoubtedly easier to look for a job once you are in Dubai. Your first step should be to get your hands on the *Gulf News* appointments supplement (www. gnads4u.com), published everyday except Fridays and Saturdays, or the *Khaleej Times* Appointments (www.khaleejtimes.com) everyday except Friday – also available online. *The National* has a careers section that is available to those who subscribe online.

It is also beneficial to check listings on online versions of international newspapers as companies within the UAE often post jobs on these sites. Websites for the *Guardian* (www.guardian.co.uk) and *The Times* (www.timesonline.co.uk) newspapers in the UK and *The Washington Post* (www.washingtonpost.com) in the US are often a good resource. You can also upload your CV to sites like www.monstergulf.com, www. naukrigulf.com, www.bayt.com and www.gulftalent. com. Job advertisements are also posted on Dubizzle (www.dubizzle.com).

It is also a good idea to register with a recruitment agency (p.114) and to contact companies directly and start networking (p.116). Networking sites like www. linkedin.com should also be useful. Thanks to Dubai's relatively small size, the more people you meet the more likely you are to bump into someone who just happens to work somewhere that has a vacant position that you might be able to fill. Many large Dubai-based companies have vacancy listings on their websites, so if you have a company in mind, it's up to you to keep checking its site for updated listings.

Advertisements in Dubai can be more direct than in other countries and, while it isn't always acceptable to specify candidate requirements like nationality in other countries, advertisements here will often detail whether they are looking for a 'western applicant' for example.

Most recruitment agencies accept CVs via email, but you can check whether they accept walk-ins. The agency will then set up an interview where you are usually required to fill out a form summarising your CV, you will also need a few passport photos. The agency takes its fee from the registered company once the position has been filled. It is illegal for a recruitment company to levy fees on candidates for this service, although some might try.

Headhunters (also known as executive search companies) will usually contact desirable candidates directly to discuss opportunities, but this is normally for more senior positions.

Should you be suitable for a job, a recruitment agency will mediate between you and the employer and arrange all interviews. However, don't rely too heavily on the agency finding a job for you. More often than not, agencies depend on candidates spotting one of their advertised vacancies. You can sign up with more than one agency but they may both try to put you forward for the same job. In this case it is at your discretion which agency you want to represent you. Below is a list of recruitment agencies based in the UAE. Some of these agencies specialise in certain industries so do your research and register accordingly. One to investigate if you have come to Dubai as a result of your partner or spouse's job is the Xpat Partners agency (www.xpatpartners.com), which specialises in finding part-time and flexible work, particularly for expat women.

For external advice on changing jobs or improving your long-term employment prospects, contact Sandpiper Coaching (www.sandpipercoaching.com), a career coaching company based in Dubai that provides coaching programmes for people who have lost their jobs, those who are looking for a change of job, and people returning to work after a career break.

## Recruitment Agencies

**BAC Middle East** > *p.115* 04 337 5747,
*www.bacme.com*
**Bayt** 04 391 1900, *www.bayt.com*
**Charterhouse Partnership** > *p.123* 04 372 3500,
*www.charterhouseme.ae*
**IQ Selection** > *p.121* 04 324 4094,
*www.iQselection.com*
**Kershaw Leonard** 04 343 4606,
*www.kershawleonard.net*
**Manpower Professional (Clarendon Parker)** > *p.125*
Al Sufouh, 04 323 3723, *www.manpower-me.com*
**SOS Agency** 04 396 5600, *www.sosrecruitment.net*
**Talent Management Consultancy** 04 335 0999,
*www.talentdubai.com*

# We've seen a lot of changes since 1979. (Thankfully!)

*Technology, interior design, style*; many things about the office environment have changed since 1979.

One thing that hasn't changed is the commitment and excellent service that has kept BAC at the forefront of the UAE's recruitment industry for over 30 years.

We were the first recruitment consultancy in the world to obtain ISO 9001 quality certification, and have successfully placed over 20,000 candidates. We work closely with the best employers and recruit across all major sectors. Whether you're new to Dubai, or are looking for your next career move, please visit our website or forward your CV to jobs@bacme.com

 EST. 1979

Your Search Partner | ISO9001:2000 Certified

BAC
Middle East

EXECUTIVE RECRUITMENT

Tel: +971 4 3375747   Fax: +971 4 3376467   Email: jobs@bacme.com        www.bac.ae

## Networking & Events

With Dubai still being a relatively small city, made up of communities that are smaller still, networking is critical, even across industries. Everyone seems to know everyone and getting in with the corporate 'in-crowd' definitely has its plus points. Business acumen here can, at times, be more important than specific industry knowledge so it pays to attend business events and trade shows. Make friends in government departments and this will often land you in the front line for opportunities. Likewise, bad news is rarely made public here, so staying in tune with the grapevine can help prevent wrong decisions. Social networking sites like LinkedIn (www.linkedin.com) are a great resource when looking for new jobs or contacts, while groups like Social Circles Dubai (www.socialcirclesdubai.com) arrange regular meet-ups.

### Business Councils

**American Business Council** Al Barsha, 04 340 7566, *www.abcdubai.com*
**Australian Business Council** Al Sufouh, 04 367 2437, *www.abc-dxb.com*
**British Business Group** Oud Metha, 04 397 0303, *www.britbiz-uae.com*
**Canadian Business Council** Bur Dubai, 04 359 2625, *www.cbc-dubai.com*
**Finnish Business Council** Trade Centre, 050 457 9118, *www.fbc.org.ae*
**French Business Council** Trade Centre, 04 312 6704, *www.fbcdubai.com*
**German Business Council** Bur Dubai, 04 397 3208, *www.gbc-dubai.com*
**Indian Business & Professional Council** Trade Centre, 04 332 4300, *www.ibpcdubai.com*
**Iranian Business Council** Oud Metha, 04 335 9220, *www.ibcuae.org*
**Italian Business Council** Al Wasl, 04 321 3082, *www.ibcdubai.ae*
**Malaysia Business Council** Oud Metha, 04 335 5538
**Netherlands Business Council** Al Wasl, 050 559 2272, *www.nbcdubai.com*
**Pakistan Business Council Dubai** Oud Metha, 04 335 9991, *www.pbcdubai.com*
**Singapore Business Council** Deira, 04 393 7758, *www.sbcuae.org*
**South African Business Council** Al Sufouh, 04 390 0433, *www.sabco-uae.org*
**Spanish Business Council** Trade Centre, 04 427 0379, *www.spanishbusinesscouncil.ae*
**Swedish Business Council** Oud Metha, 04 336 7705, *www.swedenabroad.com*
**Swiss Business Council** Al Wasl, 04 321 1438, *www.swissbcuae.com*

## Employment Contracts

An employment contract should list the full details of your employment, including the name of the employer, details of your salary and a breakdown of your responsibilities. Accepting an expat posting can have its pitfalls, so before you sign your contract pay special attention to things such as probation periods, accommodation, annual leave, travel entitlements, medical and dental cover, notice periods, and repatriation entitlements.

There is often confusion over the offer letter and the contract. An offer letter should give details of the terms of the job you are being offered, such as salary, leave, hours and other benefits; if you accept the terms of this offer, it becomes a legally binding contract. You may be asked to sign an additional Ministry of Labour contract that accompanies your residency application, but the initial offer letter is, in effect, your contract. If you receive your employment contract in both English and Arabic, it's a good idea to have the Arabic translated to ensure they match – the Arabic version will prevail in the UAE courts.

The UAE labour law allows for an end-of-service gratuity payment for employees. The rules are a bit convoluted, but basically, an employee on a fixed-term contract, who has completed one or more years of continuous service, will be entitled to 21 days pay for each of the first five years of service, and 30 days pay for each additional year. If the employee is on an 'unlimited duration' (open-ended) contract and terminates it of his own accord, he will get a third of the gratuity for a service period of between one and three years, two thirds for three to five years, and the full amount if service exceeds five years. Leaving before the end of your fixed-term contract or being fired for breaking the UAE Labour Law, could result in the loss of your gratuity payment. Gratuity payments are worked out according to your basic salary, but note that your salary will be split into various categories (basic, housing, transport and utilities). You will still get the same cash salary at the end of every month, but because your basic salary is much lower than your total salary, your gratuity payment is lower.

The UAE Labour Law states that probation periods can be set for a maximum of six months. Some companies may delay the residency process illegally until the probation period is up, which can make settling in difficult – no residency means you can't sponsor family members, buy a car or get a bank loan.

By law, employees are not entitled to paid sick leave during their probation period and most companies do not permit annual leave to be taken during this time – you will continue to accrue annual leave over the course of the year. Discuss these matters with your future employer before signing your contract.

# 110,000 buildings

# 3,000 streets

# 300 pages

# One Atlas

This large scale street atlas features a comprehensive A to Z of Dubai's ever-growing road network, with a thorough index giving the exact location of every street, hotel, shopping centre, landmark, and every major residential and commercial building.

Also available for Abu Dhabi and the UAE

www.explorerpublishing.com

EXPLORER

# Exhibitionist Tendencies

With financial uncertainty rocking businesses throughout the UAE, but exhibitions still in the work diary, should you still be putting yourself out there? Is it better to conserve cash or continue to showcase?

The Middle East is an internationally renowned hub for conferences, trade shows and exhibitions but the economic shockwaves are leading local companies to doubt the merits of intense marketing. Budgets have been slashed across the board, from in-house advertising costs and PR contracts to international travel and salaries, but could exhibiting be the outlay that brings the most worthwhile returns?

Exhibitions offer opportunities for businesses to interact with, talk (and listen) to new prospects, demonstrate products and services in real life instead of in a catalogue and check out the competition. By meeting a high volume of contacts in a short amount of time, exhibitions are actually a cost-effective way of boosting trade – providing you follow up on those many business cards you accumulate. Even better, with hotel occupancy down and airlines reducing prices, there are travel deals to be done; by sending more company representatives to attend, opportunities can be maximised further. If you can dominate in these times, you can prosper at the expense of competitors. If contacts are in place, your brand remains strong and you manage to retain staff then you could be ideally placed to capitalise once the market shows signs of upturn. A recent survey by industry research company Exhibit Surveys Inc. revealed that up to 66% of trade show visitors plan to purchase one or more products as a result of attending an exhibition. Exhibiting may thus be the wisest spend in securing both long and short term business goals.

Alex Heuff, PALME exhibitions director at IIR Middle East explains: 'Trade shows are still the most cost-effective root to market for local and international firms. In times of financial constraint, for companies big and small, taking part in a trade-related exhibition or event remains the best way of using tighter resources to stay directly in front of customers. I expect the events sector to play a critical role during 2009 as the catalyst to stimulate the investment climate and boost economic growth, while playing a major role in driving up visitor traffic in the region. Some sectors will always do well in an economic downturn, such as IIR's Arab Health Show, Middle East Electricity and PALME, where secondary shows targeting hobbies and lifestyle may not weather the storm and personal buying habits shift. When times are good you should exhibit, when times are bad, you must exhibit.'

As many European trade shows and conferences shift their attention – and budgets – to Asia and emerging markets such as India, China and Russia, the Middle East is often the location of choice. Thanks to its unique position, transport links, and the potential for a few, post-exhibition, relaxing days on the beach to celebrate a deal being done, the UAE find itself in prime position and is poised to capitalise on this trend.

# Major Exhibitions In Dubai & Abu Dhabi

**January**

| | | |
|---|---|---|
| 25-28 | Arab Health | www.arabhealthonline.com |
| 26-29 | International Real Estate & Investment Show | www.realestateshow.ae |
| 28-28 | Dubai Shopping Festival | www.mydsf.com |

**February**

| | | |
|---|---|---|
| 02-04 | Dubai International Property Show | www.internationalpropertyshow.ae |
| 03-06 | Dubai International Children's Book Fair | www.dicbf.ae |

**March**

| | | |
|---|---|---|
| 02-07 | Abu Dhabi International Book Fair | www.adbookfair.com |
| 09-11 | Gulf Education Supply Show | www.gesseducation.com |
| 09-11 | WETEX 2010 | www.wetex.ae |
| 22-24 | Map Middle East | www.mapmiddleeast.org |
| 28 Mar-01 Apr | Careers UAE 2010 | www.careersuae.ae/ |
| 29-31 | Offshore Arabia | www.offshorearabia.ae |
| 29-31 | Interiors UAE 2010 | www.interiorsuae.com |
| 29-31 | Gulf Incentive, Business Travel & Meetings Exhibition | www.gibtm.com |

**April**

| | | |
|---|---|---|
| 12-15 | Aviation Outlook Middle East | www.terrapinn.com |
| 18-21 | Cityscape Abu Dhabi | www.cityscapeabudhabi.com |

**May**

| | | |
|---|---|---|
| 04-07 | Arabian Travel Market | www.arabiantravelmarket.com |
| 18-20 | The Hotel Show | www.thehotelshow.com |
| 04-06 | Franchise Arabia | www.franchisearabia.info |
| 17-19 | MECOM 2010 | www.mecomexpo.com |

**June**

| | | |
|---|---|---|
| 01-03 | Beautyworld Middle East | www.beautyworldme.com |
| 08-10 | Gifts & Premiums – Dubai 2010 | www.premium-dubai.com |
| 17 Jun-7 Aug | Dubai Summer Surprises | www.mydsf.com |
| 21-23 | Expo World Middle East | www.gameexpo.ae |

**October**

| | | |
|---|---|---|
| 04-07 | Cityscape | www.cityscape.ae |
| 16-23 | GITEX Computer Shopper & Home Electronics | www.gitexshopperdubai.com |
| 17-21 | GITEX Technology Week 2010 | www.gitex.com |
| 25-26 | Business Travel Show | www.businesstravelshowdubai.com |
| 31 Oct-02 Nov | Sweets Middle East | www.sweetsmiddleeast.com |
| 31 Oct-02 Nov | Light Middle East | www.lightme.net |
| 07-16 | Sharjah World Book Fair | www.swbf.gov.ae |

**November**

| | | |
|---|---|---|
| 07-09 | Middle East Business Aviation | www.meba.aero |
| 21-24 | Big Five Exhibition | www.thebig5exhibition.com |
| 29 Nov-01 Dec | Dubai World Game Expo | www.gameexpo.ae |
| 23-27 | International Automobile Show | www.int-autoshow.com |

**December**

| | | |
|---|---|---|
| 04-06 | Mother, Baby & Child Show 2010 | www.motherbabyandchild.co |
| 15-19 | Abu Dhabi International Motor Show | www.admotorshow.com |
| 16-20 | Dubai International Motor Show | www.dubaimotorshow.com |

## Free Zones

It was way back in 2001 when Dubai Media City first opened its doors to regional and international media companies, and since then, not only has the free zone concept expanded rapidly across several industries, but there has also been the arrival of several other creative free zones. Unique laws regarding taxation, recruitment of labour, and income repatriation apply to these areas. These benefits make free zones ideal for companies wishing to establish a distribution, manufacturing and service base for trade outside of the UAE.

Employees of companies in free zones have different sponsorship options depending on the free zone. For example, in Jebel Ali you can either be sponsored by an individual company or by the free zone authority itself. Whether you are in the Jebel Ali Free Zone, Dubai Internet City, Media City, Knowledge Village, Healthcare City or the Dubai Airport Free Zone, the respective authority will process your residency visa/permit directly through the Immigration Department, without having to get employment approval from the Ministry of Labour. This speeds up the process significantly, and residency permits can sometimes be granted in a matter of hours. Once Immigration has stamped your residence permit in your passport, the free zone will issue your labour card – this also acts as your security pass for entry to the free zone. A big advantage of working in a free zone is the lack of red tape encountered if you move jobs to another free zone company. This is because the free zone is actually your sponsor, so when you switch jobs to another employer you won't be switching sponsors.

If you want to work as a consultant or you wish to set up a small business, free zones are the best bet. The process and fees for getting a visa varies between each free zone, and the cost of commercial property can be quite high in popular free zones, such as Dubai Media City and the Jebel Ali Free Zone.

A free zone residency permit is valid for three years, and the labour card for either one or three years, depending on the free zone. Designed to encourage investment from overseas, free zones allow 100% foreign ownership and offer exemption from taxes and customs duties. An added attraction is the relative lack of red tape. For more information on setting up a business in a free zone, refer to the Business chapter of the *Dubai Red-Tape Explorer*.

## Labour Law

The UAE Federal Law Number 8 for 1980 on regulation of labour relations (otherwise know as the UAE labour law) outlines information on employee entitlements, employment contracts and disciplinary rules. The law is employer friendly, but it also clearly outlines employee rights. You can download a copy of the document from the Ministry of Labour website (www.mol.gov.ae); the document has not been fully updated for some time but, amendments and additions are often posted on the site.

Labour unions and strikes are illegal, although there have been some protests by labourers in the past. The labourers achieved some results and the employers concerned were forced to pay wages immediately or remedy living conditions, and a hotline was set up for other unpaid workers to report their employers. Also, an amended federal labour law looks likely to allow the formation of labour unions (trade unions have long existed in some other Gulf countries). If you find yourself in the situation where you have not been paid, you can file a case with the UAE Labour Department who will take the necessary action. You could also get a lawyer to deal with the claim on your behalf (see p.133 for a list of law firms). Although lawyers are expensive in Dubai, the employer will have to bear the cost if the case is settled in your favour.

---
### Maternity Leave

Under UAE Labour Law, women are entitled to 45 days maternity leave, on full pay, once they've completed one year of continuous service – fathers are not entitled to paternity leave. Maternity leave can only be used directly before and after the birth. Those who have been with their employer for less than a year can claim 45 days on half pay (see p.141 for more information).

---

## Changing Jobs

Until recently, anyone leaving a job and cancelling their visa faced the possibility of being 'banned' for six months. Fortunately, the banning rules have been relaxed, so as long as you remain on good terms with your employer, and you are given permission to leave your job (in the form of a no objection certificate or NOC), you should be able to switch to a new job.

It is important to review whether a non-compete clause was added to your contract, particularly if your new role is with a direct competitor to your current employer. This clause could mean that you are restricted to taking an unrelated role before returning to your current field.

To change sponsors, pick up the relevant forms from the Ministry of Labour and get them typed in Arabic. Get the forms signed and stamped by both your previous and new employers, and submit them along with the trade licence and establishment card of your new company. Everything goes to the Immigration Department who will amend your visa. In most cases your new employer will take care of this procedure for you.

Role ✓ Sector ✓ Location ✓
Salary ✓ Environment ✓

## At iQ selection we tick all the boxes

Sales & Marketing • Advertising, Media & PR • FMCG • Banking & Finance • Human Resources • Emiratisation
Executive Secretarial • IT & Telecommunications • Construction & Engineering • Oil & Gas

At iQ selection we are passionate
about selecting the right job for you.
Tel: + 971 4 324 4094 **www.iQselection.com**

DIFC

There are some exceptions where you can transfer your sponsorship without the approval of your current sponsor, such as death of your sponsor, change of company ownership, company closure and cancellation of your company's trade licence. If your company has closed, it is important to note that you will receive an automatic labour ban unless the company has cancelled its trade licence.

Regulations differ in the free zones, as you are technically sponsored by the free zone authority (FZA) rather than the company. Therefore if you move to another company within the free zone, there is no need to transfer your visa.

## Banning

The notorious 'ban' is a topic of frequent discussion in Dubai, however the details of when and for how long you can be banned change from case to case. There are two types of ban: an employment ban that restricts employment for a period (usually six months to a year), or a visa ban (which restricts entry or departure from Dubai).

A visa ban is often imposed if you have committed a serious criminal offence, or you have absconded (p.122). Theoretically, it is possible for your employer to ban you from working with another company for a short period of time, even if you have served the correct notice period and have left on good terms. However, this is less likely since a new fee was introduced and employers now have to pay to ban an employee.

A six month employment ban can also be imposed by the Ministry of Labour, with no instruction from your previous employers, but this is indeterminate and can often be resolved. If you do receive a ban, all is not lost, it may be possible to pay for your ban to be lifted.

The laws regarding banning change frequently and revisions are occasionally posted online without any announcements to the general public; check the Ministry of Labour website (www.mol.gov.ae) for updates.

## Absconding

Anyone leaving the country without cancelling their residence visa with their sponsor will be classed as 'absconding' and may receive a ban (p.122), though employers have to wait six months to report absconders who have left the country. Anyone who leaves their employment and remains in the country without notifying their employer can be reported as having absconded after a period of seven days. Absconders are reported to the Ministry of Labour, who then pass information on to Immigration and the police.

Under Article 120 of the Labour Law, if you leave the country or are unaccountable for seven days in a row or 20 days in total, your company can terminate your employment contract without awarding you gratuity pay or any outstanding benefits.

During the economic downturn, there were reports of residents leaving the city at short notice to avoid the ramifications of defaults on bank loans and debts. If you default on a loan and the bank files a case against you, you could receive a visa ban which restricts you from either entering or leaving the country. Details of this claim are filed with the Immigration Department, the police and the Ministry of Labour, which means you could be identified and detained when your visa is scanned at the airport on departure or arrival.

## NOC

A No Objection Certificate is a letter of confirmation awarded by your former employer or the Ministry of Labour giving you permission to work for another employer. If you have an NOC from your previous employer, and the Ministry of Labour approves the move, your visa transfer should be hassle-free. But this is one area where laws change frequently so it's best to check with the Labour Department or a lawyer first.

# KNOW THE RIGHT
# MOVE

Banking

Compliance

Construction

Corporate Strategy

Finance

Hospitality

Human Resources

Information Technology

Insurance

Legal

Marketing

Professional Support

Sales

Supply Chain & Logistics

## STRATEGIC CAREER DEVELOPMENT

**Dubai**
Tel: +971 4 372 3500
Fax: +971 4 332 8062

**Abu Dhabi**
Tel: +971 2 406 9819
Fax: +971 2 406 9810

PO Box 75972, Suite 502, Al Moosa Tower 1, Sheikh Zayed Road, Dubai, UAE.
PO Box 113100, Office MB1, 1st Floor, Al Bateen Business Centre, Al Bateen C6, Abu Dhabi, UAE.

Middle East – Australia – Europe – Asia
www.charterhouseme.ae

## CHARTERHOUSE
PARTNERSHIP
MIDDLE EAST · AUSTRALIA · EUROPE · ASIA

## Redundancy

Redundancy can be a serious blow to your personal life and finances, particularly in a city like Dubai where you may only be here as long as you have a job. If you are made redundant, try not to dwell on feelings of self doubt about your performance or likeability and focus on the financial reasons for your termination. The first thing to discuss with your employer is whether they are prepared to be flexible with you visa status. If you have a good relationship with your company, you should have room to negotiate the terms under which you are leaving, and it's a good idea to request a few months leeway so you have the opportunity to find a new employer and sponsor. If this is not possible and your company wishes to cancel your visa immediately, you have a standard 30 day grace period within which to leave the country before incurring any fines for overstaying your visa. Similarly, if you are in company accommodation, try to negotiate the date on which you need to move out. If your company has paid for your villa or apartment up front, they may let you stay for a fixed period.

As there are no overdraft facilities in Dubai, it is always a good idea to plan for every eventuality by putting money aside to act as a buffer should you lose your job; rather than incur large credit card debt, this money can help pay for key bills like rent and car loans.

## Company Closure

Employees who face the unlucky situation of company bankruptcy or company closure are entitled under, UAE Labour Law, to receive their gratuity payments and holiday pay, but you will need to speak to the Labour department for the proper process as it is rather complex. An employee of a firm that has been closed is allowed to transfer sponsorship to a new employer if they are able to find a new job, but if

not, their visa will be cancelled and they will have to leave the country. To transfer the visa they'll need an attested certificate of closure, issued by the court and submitted to the Ministry of Labour & Social Affairs (04 269 1666). If your company were to close without cancelling their trade licence you could receive a short time ban from taking a new role with a new employer. Consult the appropriate government offices to get your paperwork right, or consider investing in the services of a lawyer who specialises in labour issues (see p.133 for a list of lawyers).

## Voluntary & Charity Work

There are a number of opportunities to do voluntary or charity work in Dubai and the organisations listed below are always looking for committed volunteers. If it's environmental voluntary work you're after, the Emirates Environmental Group (www.eeg-uae.org) organises regular campaigns.

### Volunteer Organisations

**All As One**
www.allasone.org
A non-profit organisation, staffed by volunteers, whose primary concern is to care for the abandoned, disabled, abused and destitute children of Sierra Leone in the All As One Children's Centre. It depends on donations, child sponsorship, and fundraising events to fund operating costs.

**Feline Friends**
050 451 0058
www.felinefriendsuae.com
This non-profit organisation, with volunteers who rescue and re-home stray cats and kittens, promote the control of street cats by sterilisation and provide care and relief to sick and injured cats and kittens. Volunteers are needed for rescues and also for fostering cats until homes can be found for them.

**Foresight**
04 364 3703
www.foresightrp.com
Foresight was formed to raise funds for research and to improve the lives of visually impaired people in the UAE and throughout the world.

**K9 Friends** > *p.151*
04 885 8031
www.k9friends.com.
K9 Friends is run by a dedicated group of volunteers who care for and re-home unwanted dogs from all over the UAE. Running costs are met entirely through donations from the public, as well as corporate sponsors. If you are interested in volunteering, contact them on the number above or visit their website.

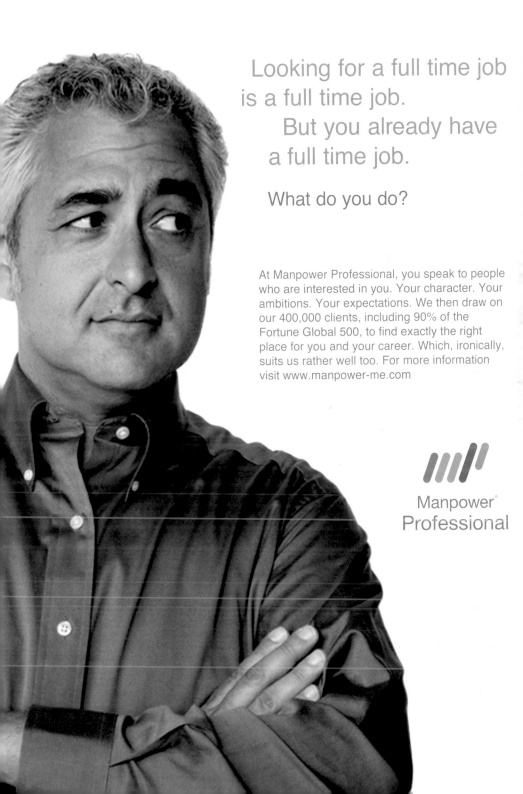

### Médecins Sans Frontières (MSF) > *p.178*
04 345 8177
www.msfuae.ae
This is an international, independent, non-profit emergency medical relief organisation that relies on volunteers to provide aid in any way they can. Volunteers can become involved locally with their fund-raising or awareness campaigns.

### Riding for the Disabled
www.rdad.ae
An organisation that provides physical and mental stimulation through gentle horse riding for children with special needs. They are always on the lookout for reliable, committed volunteers to lead the horses and assist the riders. For more information visit the website.

## Working As A Freelancer Or Contractor
It is possible to obtain a visa to work in Dubai on a freelance basis. This kind of visa is linked to the various 'free zones' that exist, such as Dubai Media City, Jebel Ali Free Zone and Knowledge Village. Your profession needs to be related to the free zone you wish to set up in so, artists, editors, directors, writers, engineers, producers, photographers, camera operators and technicians in the fields of film, TV, music, radio and print media can only set up in Dubai Media City.

If you fall into one of the categories, and meet all the relevant criteria, you will get a residence visa and access to 'hot desk' facilities. There are a number of fees involved in this process, and obtaining a visa in this way will cost somewhere between Dhs.20,000 and Dhs.30,000. For more information, contact the appropriate free zone (see Free Zones, p.120).

An alternative option, depending on your line of work, may to be set up or register your own company (see setting up a small business p.126). The Department of Economic Development (www.dubaided.gov.ae) is the place to contact for further information on how to do this.

## Working Part-Time
It is difficult to organise part-time work in the city and many companies favour those who are already in Dubai under their partner's sponsorship. Expats who have student visas are not permitted to work, which can be a problem if you want to get your teens out of your hair during the holidays, or at the weekend. There are reports that legislation that will allow residents to work part-time in Dubai will be introduced in the

# Flying Solo
If you do decide to freelance, here's what you need to know:
- You need to apply for a freelance permit, which at present is only offered by Dubai Media City (www.dubaimediacity.com).
- Only media professionals of the following categories are eligible: artists, editors, directors, writers, engineers, producers, photographers, camera operators and technicians in the fields of film, TV, music, radio or print media.
- The permit includes a residence visa, access to 10 shared work stations, and a shared PO Box address and fax line.
- A minimum of three hours per week and no more than three hours per day must be spent at the hot desk.
- A business plan, CV, bank reference letter and portfolio must be submitted along with your application.
- Costs at DMC include:
  Dhs.5,000 security deposit (refundable)
  Dhs.5,000 joining fee (one-off payment)
  Dhs.8,000 annual permit fee
  Dhs.4,000 annual membership fee

future, but until then, expat students who wish to work during the holidays or at the weekend should apply to the Department of Naturalisation & Residency (near the Galadari roundabout, 04 313 9999) for a permit allowing them to work legally.

## Setting Up A Small Business
Since the global economic meltdown, the business climate in the UAE has quickly changed from one of hope and optimism to one of uncertainty for many. However, small and medium sized businesses are still starting up in the region and many are finding success.

Starting a business in the current economy requires meticulous market research, a stricter and more realistic business plan and responsive action to take advantage of fleeting openings in the market. Recent high-profile cases have also made it clear that there are serious risks involved in doing business in the country. Bankruptcy laws are not as defined as in other countries and mismanagement of funds could result in harsh repercussions, including deportation or even jail time.

**BUSINESS MATTERS** Tammy Urwin, Urban Events www.urbanevents.ae, 04 428 0814

*I have been in Dubai now for 15 months and have been amazed by the support from people, they are more than happy to pass on contacts and help you grow the business. There is a very dynamic feel to the region, especially in the world of sport.*

# MacKenzie Art

## ART, MURALS & SPECIALIST DECORATION

## ENHANCE YOUR ENVIRONMENT

Specialist Finishes

Artworks

Murals

Trompé L'Oeil

For that unique finishing touch to your space, we provide original paintings and faux-finishes for both homes and commercial projects.

For a free estimate, please contact us.

**04 341 9803 • info@mackenzieart.com • www.mackenzieart.com**

# Financial Affairs

The government and ruling families have passed legislation and formed organisations that aid the start-up process in the UAE. In August 2009, the UAE Ministry of Economy removed the minimum capital requirements for new businesses, which used to be Dhs.300,000 in Dubai.

One of the major hesitations that entrepreneurs have about starting a business here is the requirement of having a local sponsor control a majority stake of the company. The increasing number of free zones (p.120) in the region eliminate that rule and allow full private ownership. The licensing process for opening a business in a free zone is also more streamlined and helped by the free zone organisation.

Government and private-sponsored initiatives are also helping spur growth and educate potential business owners. The Mohammed Bin Rashid Establishment for SME Development (www.sme.ae), was set up to help entrepreneurs understand the procedures and potential costs of setting up in Dubai. The organisation provides guidance and information to Emiratis and expats hoping to start their own business.

There are various business groups in Dubai that help facilitate investments and provide opportunities for networking with others in the community. Some business groups and councils provide information on trade with their respective countries, as well as on business opportunities both in Dubai and internationally. Most also arrange social and networking events on a regular basis.

Before you set up, contact the Dubai Chamber of Commerce & Industry (www.dubaichamber.ae) and the Ministry of Economy (www.economy.ae). Both can offer excellent advice. Embassies or consulates can also be a good business resource and may be able to offer contact lists for the UAE and the country of representation.

For information and details, refer to the *Dubai Red-Tape Explorer*, the *Dubai Commercial Directory*, or the *Hawk Business Pages*.

# FINANCIAL AFFAIRS
## Bank Accounts

There are several reputable banks in Dubai, including well-known names like HSBC, Barclays Bank and Lloyds TSB Bank. Banks that operate internationally rarely have connections with their counterparts in other parts of the world, so you won't be able to view or manage accounts held in other countries through your Dubai account.

Most banks offer online banking, so you can check your balance, transfer money and pay bills online. There are plenty of ATMs (cashpoints) around Dubai and most cards are compatible with the Central Bank network (some also offer global access links). You may pay a small fee for using another bank's ATM but it should never be more than a few dirhams.

To open an account in most banks, you need a residence visa or to have your residency application underway. To apply, you will need to submit your original passport, copies of your passport (personal details and visa) and an NOC from your sponsor. Some banks set a minimum account limit – this can be around Dhs.2,000 for a deposit account and as much as Dhs.10,000 for a current account. This means that at some point in each month your account balance must be above the minimum limit, many people avoid this complication by having their monthly wage deposited into their accounts. Although credit cards are widely available, Dubai banks don't provide an overdraft facility. Banks are exercising more caution than they have been in the past, due to the global credit crisis of 2008, particularly where loans are concerned. If you don't have a residence visa, meBANK (an offshoot of Emirates Bank) will open an account for you and provide an ATM card, but not a chequebook. meBANK also allows you to apply online for an account (www.me.ae).

---

### Valuable Information

If you have some precious items that you would like to give a little extra protection to, JFT Safe Deposit Lockers, based in Al Qusais, offers secure storage boxes in monitored premises on a monthly or annual basis. Visit www.jftlockers.com or call 04 258 2992 for details.

---

A number of laws have been introduced to combat money laundering. The UAE Central Bank monitors all incoming and outgoing transfers, and banks and currency exchanges are required to report transfers over a certain limit. Additionally, if you need to send more than Dhs.2,000 by international transfer you may have to show a valid passport.

### Main Banks

**ABN AMRO Bank** 04 351 8480, *www.abnamro.com*
**Abu Dhabi Commercial Bank** 800 2030, *www.adcb.com*
**Arab Bank** 04 295 0845, *www.arabbank.ae*
**Bank of Sharjah** 04 282 7278, *www.bankofsharjah.com*
**Barclays Bank Plc** 04 362 6700, *www.barclays.ae*
**BNP Paribas** 04 424 8200, *www.bnpparibas.ae*
**Citibank – Middle East** 04 324 5000, *www.citibank.com/uae*
**Dubai Islamic Bank** 04 295 9999, *www.alislami.ae*

**fastest remittance to any destination in the world**

## Our unmatched service range

Demand Draft • Courier Draft • Foreign Currency Sale & Purchase

Electronic Pay Order • Bank-to-Bank Delivery • Door-to-Door Delivery

SWIFT Transfer • Money Gram • Al Ahli Filahza • Instant Transfer

• Cash Against Credit Card • Kwarta Bilis

## خدماتنا القيمة

حوالات بريدية • إرسال حوالات • بيع و شراء العملات الاجنبية

طلب دفع الكتروني • حوالات سويفت • تحويل من بنك الى بنك

خدمة توصيل إلى الباب • خدمة الموني جرام • تحويل فوري

سحب نقدي على بطاقات الائتمان • كوارتا بيليس

## الفردان للصرافة
## AL FARDAN EXCHANGE
*It's about service*

Abu Dhabi: Liwa Street, Amin Tower, Abu Dhabi, Tel: 02-6223222 Opp. Abu Dhabi Mall, Tourist Club,Tel: 02-6454111 Bada Zayed (Madinat Zayed) Branch Tel: 02-8844406 , Musaffah, Industrial Area, Abu Dhabi, Tel: 02-5555928,Ruwais, Tel: 02-8774877,Gayathi, Tel: 02 8742700 ,Al Wahda Mall, Tel: 02-4437444,Zenith Super Market Bldg, Baniyas, Tel: 02-5834997,Shangrila Shopping Complex - 02-5581127 ,Old Shahama , Tel : 02-5634281,Mirfa Market ,Tel : 02 8835454 Dubai : Khalid Bin Waleed Street, BurDubai,Tel: 04-3513535,Al Maktoum Street,Deira, Tel: 04-2280004 Gold Land, Deira -Tel: 04-2266442 Dubai Festival City Mall- Tel: 04-2325588, Jebel Ali Tel: 04-8814455 Satwa, Al Diyafa Street Tel: 04-3988852, Dubai Mall - 04-4340404. Al Qusais : Tel:04 2578303 HealthCare City. Tel:04 4255355 , Mall of Emirates - Tel: 04 3233004,Al Quoz, Tel: 04-3237700.  Sharjah: Sharjah Clock Tower,Tel: 06-5635581,5635371,Al Arooba Street, Rolla,Tel: 06-5695999,Al Fardan Center, Tel: 06-5561955 Abu Shagara - Tel: 06-5534833 National Paints R/A :Tel:06 5344466 Ajman: Hamdan Center, Near GMC Hospital Tel: 06-7468866 Al Ain Al Takhtit Street, Tel: 03-7554325, 7555934 Souk Branch: 03-7661010 Sanaya,Lulu Centre - Tel: 03-7211123 Al Yahar North- Tel: 03 7827001 Ras Al Khaimah: Sheikh Saqr Street AL Nakheel, Tel: 07-2275777

Call centre number - 600 522265  ٦٠٠ ٥٢٢٢٦٥  رقم مركز الاتصال – ٦٠٠ ٥٢٢٢٦٥

E-mail: exchange@alfardangroup.com  or  log on to www.alfardanexchange.com

# Financial Affairs

**Emirates Islamic Bank** 04 316 0101,
*www.emiratesislamicbank.ae*
**Emirates NBD Bank** 04 316 0316,
*www.emiratesbank.ae*
**Habib Bank AG Zurich** 04 221 4535,
*www.habibbank.com*
**HSBC Bank Middle East** 600 554 722, *www.hsbc.ae*
**Lloyds TSB Bank Plc** 04 342 2000, *www.lloydstsb.ae*
**Mashreqbank** 04 424 4444, *www.mashreqbank.com*
**National Bank of Abu Dhabi** 800 2211,
*www.nbad.com*
**National Bank of Dubai (NBD)** 04 310 0101,
*www.nbd.com*
**RAKBANK** 04 224 8000, *www.rakbank.ae*
**The Royal Bank of Scotland** 04 351 2200,
*www.rbsbank.ae*
**Standard Chartered Bank – Middle East**
04 352 0455, *www.standardchartered.com*
**Union National Bank** 800 2600, *www.unb.co.ae*

## Financial Planning

Many expats are attracted to Dubai for the tax-free salary and the opportunity to put a little something away for the future. However, Dubai's alluring lifestyle can quickly steer you away from your goal. It is often necessary for residents to get credit cards and bank loans to finance their life in Dubai and it is easy to slip further into debt – you'll find there is little or no support if you do (see Debt p.133). It is therefore more important to plan your finances and arrange a safeguard in case your finances take a turn for the worse.

When choosing a financial planner in Dubai, you should ensure that they are licensed by the Central Bank of the UAE (04 665 2220, www.centralbank. ae), so that you have some recourse in the event of a dispute. You should also consider the company's international presence – you'll still want the same access to advice, information and your investments if you return home. It may also be better to use an independent company or advisor who is not tied to a specific bank or savings company, and therefore will objectively offer you the full range of savings products on the market.

Before leaving your home country you should contact the tax authorities to ensure that you are complying with the financial laws there. Most countries will consider you not liable for income tax

## Financial Advice

There seems to be overabundance of financial advisors in the city who may contact you over the phone and advertise their services. Most advisors won't ask for money initially, however they may ask you for contact details of your friends and family members so that they can continue to spread the word.

once you prove you're a UAE resident (a contract of employment is normally a good starting point). However, you may still have to fulfil certain criteria, so do some research before you come (if you are already here, check with your embassy). You may be liable for tax on any income you receive from back home (for example if you are renting out your property).

If you have a pension scheme in your home country, it may not be worth continuing your contributions once you come to Dubai, but rather to set up a tax-free, offshore savings plan. It is always advisable to speak to your financial adviser about such matters before you make any big move.

### Financial Advisors

**Holborn Assets** Dubai Internet City, 04 336 9880,
*www.holbornassets.com*
**KPMG** Trade Centre, 04 403 0300,
*www.ae-kpmg.com*
**Mondial** Al Barsha, 04 399 6601,
*www.financial-partners.biz*
**PIC Middle East** Trade Centre, 04 343 3878,
*www.pic-uae.com*
**Prosperity Offshore Investment Consultants**
Trade Centre, 04 312 4334, *www.prosperity-uae.com*

## Credit Cards

The process for obtaining a credit card is fairly straightforward and is usually offered by the bank connected to your payroll account. If you are eligible, you'll often receive phone calls from your bank offering credit cards – if you opt for one, a representative will often offer to meet you to set up the account. Banks will usually ask that you have a minimum salary (dependant on the credit amount), a salary certificate, which details your earnings (this should be provided by your employer), and a copy of your passport with your residence visa and work permit.

**SPULRGE NOW, PAY LATER** Holborn Assests, www.holbornassests.com, 04 336 9880

*The biggest pitfall for expats in the UAE is the lack of social security, pension provision and comprehensive medical cover. Though some employers provide certain benefits, if yours doesn't you are on your own. You may need to set aside 15% of your salary to take of these issues – more if you are older. It's your choice, but sooner or later you are going to find yourself wishing you had taken care of things earlier. 15% is less than you might pay in income tax elsewhere.*

# Top Tips For Healthy Personal Finance

**Don't Neglect Your Credit Cards**: They are great to bail you out in emergencies, but unless you are self-disciplined when using them, credit cards can land you in trouble. Leave them in a secure place at home where you won't be tempted and always make the minimum repayments on time to avoid late fees.

**Try To Live Off Half Your Salary**: Really examine your expenses and be brutal when it comes to deciding what you can live without – manicures, double lattes, fancy restaurants and gym memberships are all luxuries, and cutting them out of your budget could mean surprising savings at the end of the month.

**Entertain At Home:** Eating out in Dubai's lavish restaurants is so alluring, but it doesn't come cheap. In tough financial times, master the art of 'cocooning' – staying in and inviting friends round for dinner or a movie night.

**Shop Smart:** Certain supermarkets may be convenient and stock all your favourites from back home, but are much more expensive than other, more basic supermarkets. You'll save much more if you buy your everyday items from a larger hypermarket (p.391). Decide on a grocery budget at the beginning of the month, and make it last.

**Don't Pay Full Price For Anything:** Shops in the city regularly offer promotions, sales and buy-one-get-one free promotions. Shop around to find the best bargains; you'll be amazed at what you can save.

**Get Packing:** There's no such thing as a free lunch, but packing your own sandwiches is the next best thing. It's healthier and the savings you'll make do add up at the end of the month.

**Avoid Salik:** No matter where you're going, there's usually a way around the Salik toll gates. If you often pass under a Salik gate on your way to and from work, avoid them for a month and you'll save nearly Dhs.200.

**Take Advantage Of Exchange Rates:** Certain items can work out much cheaper when buying from Amazon, even when you factor in the shipping, simply because of the exchange rate. You can get a current CD for over dhs10 cheaper than what you'd pay in a retail outlet here – so if you're ordering a few, you could save a bundle. If you've got visitors coming over, get your Amazon order delivered to them (most orders ship free locally), and get them to bring it with them.

**Buy Second-hand:** Visit Dubai Flea Market for a browse through other people's unwanted items (it is held indoors at Safa School Hall from June to September; www.dubai-fleamarket.com). House of Prose sells a huge range of second-hand books (04 344 9021), and supermarket noticeboards are cluttered with great pre-owned items looking for new homes.

**Reduce Costs Over Summer:** If you are planning to be away for some time over the summer, look into downgrading your satellite TV and internet packages for a few months. That way you can usually upgrade again come September without having to pay any reconnection fees. Better yet, if you only have satellite TV so you can watch the premier league football, cancel it completely over summer. You can always resubscribe when the season kicks off again.

## Cost Of Living

| | |
|---|---|
| **Bottle of wine** (off-licence) | Dhs.40 |
| **Burger** (takeaway) | Dhs.12 |
| **Can of soft drink** | Dhs.1 |
| **Car rental** (per day) | Dhs.100 |
| **Cigarettes** (pack of 20) | Dhs.7 |
| **Cinema ticket** | Dhs.30 |
| **Cleaner** (per hour) | Dhs.25 |
| **Dozen eggs** | Dhs.8 |
| **House wine** (glass) | Dhs.25-40 |
| **Loaf of bread** | Dhs.4.5 |
| **Milk** (1 litre) | Dhs.5.5 |
| **Mobile to mobile call** (local, per minute) | 30 fils |
| **New release DVD** | Dhs.85 |
| **Newspaper** (international) | Dhs.15 |
| **Petrol** (gallon) | Dhs.6.25 |
| **Pint of beer** | Dhs.20 |
| **Six-pack of beer** (off-licence) | Dhs.25 |
| **Taxi** (10km journey) | Dhs.20 |
| **Text message** (local) | 18 fils |
| **Water 1.5 litres** (supermarket) | Dhs.1.5 |

# Financial Affairs

Most shops, hotels and restaurants accept the major credit cards (American Express, Diners Club, MasterCard and Visa). Smaller retailers are sometimes less likely to accept credit cards and if they do you may have to pay an extra 5% for processing (and it's no use telling them that it's a contravention of the card company rules – you have to take it or leave it). Conversely, if you are paying in cash, you may sometimes be allowed a discount – it's certainly worth enquiring.

## Cash For Gas

Strangely, you are no longer able to use your credit card to buy petrol at garages in Dubai. Garages only accept cash at petrol pumps and in their forecourt convenience stores.

If you lose your credit or debit card, you must contact the bank as soon as possible and report the missing card. Once you have reported the loss it is highly unlikely that you will be held liable for any further transactions made on the card. As a consequence of ATM fraud, banks have now set a limit on the amount of cash you can withdraw per day in order to limit the financial damage of stolen credit cards (the amount varies from card to card). In addition to these measures, banks also advise the public on how to prevent credit card crime. A frequent problem is that people do not change their pin when they get the card. This is vital for secrecy, and banks also suggest you continue to change your pin on a regular basis.

## Offshore Accounts

While offshore banking used to be associated with the very wealthy or the highly shady, most expats now take advantage of tax efficient plans.

An offshore account works in much the same way as a conventional account, but it can be adjusted specifically for you. Money can be moved where it will produce the best rewards, and cash accessed whenever and wherever you need it, in your desired currency. Offshore accounts allow for management through the internet, and over the phone, in a range of currencies (most commonly in US dollars, euros or pounds sterling). If you are travelling outside the UAE, try to make sure that your account comes with 24 hour banking, internationally recognised debit cards, and the ability to write cheques in your preferred currency. To open an account, there is usually a minimum balance of around $10,000. Do some thorough research before opening an account, and check the potential tax implications in your home country. It is important to seek independent financial advice, and not just the opinion of the bank

offering you an account. Lloyds TSB (www.lloydstsb.ae) and HSBC (www.hsbc.ae) both offer good offshore services, but will of course, only advise on their own products. To open your account, you may have to produce certain reports or documents from your chosen country. However, for those willing to do the research and undertake the admin, offshore banking can prove to be a lucrative investment.

## Taxation

The UAE levies no personal income taxes or withholding taxes, but there are talks that income tax and VAT may be introduced in the future. There are no firm dates for implementation at present, and it would no doubt be unpopular, and could hamper attempts to attract foreign investment, but the IMF is advising Middle Eastern governments to introduce tax reforms in order to diversify their resources.

## Taxing Issues

You may need to register your residency in the UAE with the government in your home country to avoid paying income tax or capital gains tax. It's best to check with your consulate for exact details. There are also rumours that income tax will be introduced in the UAE however, at present, nothing concrete has been announced by the government.

The only noticeable taxes you pay as an expat are a 5% municipality tax on rental accommodation, a 30% tax on alcohol bought at Dubai liquor stores and 50% tax on tobacco (although cigarettes are still comparatively cheap). The municipality tax is included in your DEWA bill, and if you don't pay your utilities will be cut off. This has resulted in some complaints – the tax is meant to cover refuse collection, street lighting and community road networks, but people renting freehold properties also pay maintenance to cover these things so it's understandable why some people have objections. There is also a 10% municipality tax and a 10% service charge in hotel food and beverage outlets, but you'll find that these are usually incorporated into the displayed price. In 2007, the Salik road toll system (p.58) was introduced for the purpose of 'traffic management'. Many residents are unhappy about the efficiency of the system while others feel that Salik is effectively a road tax.

## Cheques

Cheques aren't commonly used as a method of payment in Dubai. Most residents will only have to organise them when organising post-dated cheques for rental agreements. The most important thing to remember is that issuing a cheque when you have insufficient funds in your account to cover the amount is considered a criminal offence. If your cheques bounce and a complaint is filed with the authorities you could be arrested without warning. When writing a post-dated cheque it is important that you are sure of your finances; you should also encourage the beneficiary to deposit the cheques as soon as possible (if that is best). A cheque cannot be cancelled, unless it is mislaid or stolen, so a cheque you wrote several months ago could land you in big trouble, if cashed unexpectedly.

## Debt

In a city that seems to run on credit cards and post-dated cheques, it can be quite a shock (and a major inconvenience) when severe penalties are dealt out for late or missed payments. While you may be forced to take large loans to purchase vehicles or for annual rent, it is important to note that if you are suddenly made redundant and your finances spiral out of control there is no safety net.

Unlike some countries, where you will receive several reminders for missed payments, if you are late paying for basic household bills such as electricity or water, your services may be disconnected without much warning – even if you regularly pay your bills. Missed payments on credit cards bills will often incur fines or restrictions to services, and it is also considered a criminal offence to write a cheque when you have insufficient funds to cover the balance (see cheques p.132). In some cases, failure to meet payments can lead to prosecution, a visa ban (p.122) and jail time.

The economic downtown of 2009 highlighted this issue when several residents, who were made redundant, made a swift departure from Dubai to avoid prosecution (see Absconding p.122). Banks are subsequently more cautious about who they will offer loans and credit cards to. There are also rumours that debt collectors are increasingly being employed to recover outstanding debts from residents who have returned back to their home countries.

The best way to avoid any unpleasant situations is to try and avoiding getting into debt in the first place – plan well, and always keep some money in reserve.

### Don't Bank On It

There are no bankruptcy laws in the UAE, so individuals who fall into financial difficulties are fully liable for their debt. If you are unable to keep up with repayments for your bank loans, and your bank files a complaint against you, you may be faced with a visa ban or an extended term in jail.

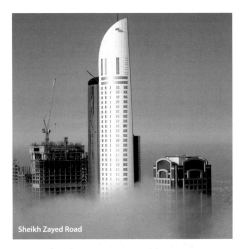
Sheikh Zayed Road

# LEGAL ISSUES

## Sharia Law

The country's constitution permits each emirate to have its own legislative body and judicial authority. Dubai has thus retained its own judicial system, including appellate courts (courts of appeal), which are not part of the UAE federal system. There are three primary sources of UAE law, namely federal laws and decrees (applicable in all emirates), local laws (laws and regulations enacted by the individual emirates), and Sharia (Islamic law). Generally, when a court is determining a commercial issue, it gives initial consideration to any applicable federal and/or local laws. If such federal and local laws do not address the issue, Sharia may be applied. Moreover, Sharia generally applies to family law matters, particularly when involving Muslims.

### Law Firms

**Afridi & Angell** 04 330 3900, *www.afridi-angell.com*
**Al Sharif Advocates & Legal Consultants** 04 262 8222, *www.dubailaw.com*
**Al Tamimi & Company** 04 364 1641, *www.tamimi.com*
**DLA Piper** 04 438 6100, *www.dlapiper.com*
**Hadef & Partners** 04 429 2999, *www.hadalaw.com*
**Musthafa & Almana Associates** 04 329 8411, *www.musthafa-almana.com*
**The Rights Lawyers** 04 390 3646, *www.therightslawyers.com*
**Trench Associates** 04 355 3146, *www.trenchlaw.com*

## Wills & Estate Law

Having a valid will in place is one of those essential things that everybody should do. It is especially important to seek legal advice when drawing up your

# Legal Issues

will if you become a property owner in Dubai. This is one area where the law is rather complicated – under Sharia law, the basic rules as to who inherits property after someone's death differ to 'western' rules. For example, in the event of your death it may be the case that your sons (or brother, if you don't have any sons) are first in line for inheritance and your wife could end up with nothing. Therefore it is better to make sure that you have a clear last will and testament in place. A Dubai-based lawyer will be able to assist you with a locally viable will. See the table on p.133 for a list of law firms, or contact Just Wills (www.just-wills.net), part of a UK-based estate planning organisation that has a presence in the UAE.

## Family Law

In accordance with the constitution of the UAE, family law (which governs matrimonial matters such as divorce) will either be governed by UAE law – which is Sharia law – or by the laws of the individuals' originating country. If the parties are from different countries, the law applicable will be the law under which their marriage was solemnised.

Normally, the court will look into the possibility of reconciliation before granting a divorce. This means that before filing for divorce, you can approach the Family Guidance and Reformation Centre which functions under the Department of Justice at Dubai Courts (04 334 4447). Anyone experiencing marital problems or any family dispute is able to approach this organisation. The other party in the dispute will be called in and the counsellors will try to help you reach an amicable settlement. If the matter is not resolved, the Guidance Centre may refer the matter to the court for legal proceedings to take place.

In deciding on the custody of any children, the court's paramount concern will be the child's welfare. In Sharia law and most other laws, the custody of the child will be the mother's right while the child is a minor, unless there are compelling reasons to decide otherwise. For more information on divorce see p.142.

## Crime

Dubai is known for having a low crime rate – in fact for many expats it is still the number one benefit of living here. However, it would be naive to think that there was no crime, as there are cases of theft, rape and even murder, but these occur on such a small scale that they rarely affect the quality of life of the average expat.

The most common reason for expats getting on the wrong side of the law is driving under the influence of alcohol. In the UAE there is a zero-tolerance policy drinking and driving. If even a sip of alcohol has passed your lips, you are not allowed to drive. While there are few spot checks, if you have even a minor accident, and even if you were not at fault, you might be breathalysed and the consequences can be serious.

Even driving the morning after a heavy night is risky, since you will still have alcohol in your system. You will be arrested, and the usual penalty is a minimum 30 days in prison, although it can vary from case to case. You should bear in mind too that your insurance company is likely refuse to pay the claim if you were in an accident, even if you were not to blame. It's just not worth the risk – cabs are cheap and there are plenty of them. It also pays to keep your cool if you are involved in altercation on the road obscene gestures can result in a prison sentence or a fine and even deportation.

Harming others, whether physically or verbally, will get you into trouble – at the very least a heavy fine, but if the other person was injured a jail term may be in order. If the victim chooses to drop the charges then you will be released. If you are detained for being drunk and disorderly you may spend a night in the cells, but if you are abusive you could be looking at a fine or longer sentence.

In a very high profile case in 2008, two Britons were charged with public indecency (after it was alleged they were having sex in public) and being under the influence of alcohol. Apart from having their exploits publicly broadcast by the world's media and being fired from work (in the case of the female), the pair received a three-month suspended sentence, fines and deportation, although legally the punishment could have been much stronger. This case should serve as a warning for all visitors and residents in the UAE, and a reminder that the authorities will extend the full arm of the law if you are caught breaking it.

## Police

Dubai Police are generally very calm and helpful – if you stay on the right side of the law. There is a visible presence of the police in the city, albeit not as prominent as other larger cities; you can recognise the police by their green army-style uniform and green and white saloon cars or 4WD.

You are most likely to be stopped by the police for a traffic offence; you must always carry your driving licence and vehicle registration – failure to do so could result in a fine. If you are stopped by the police, it is important to appear helpful and co-operative at all times. Even if you are positive you are in the right, arguing your case aggressively or being impolite could help land you in further trouble. If you are being charged with a very serious offence it is advisable to contact your embassy for more advice (see p.136).

In an effort to better serve Dubai's visitors, the Dubai Police Dubai has launched the Department for Tourist Security. It acts as a liaison between you and Dubai Police, although in general police officers are extremely helpful. Its website (www.dubaipolice.gov.ae) is easy to navigate, helpful and has extensive information on policies and procedures. For assistance, call the toll fee number (800 4438).

# Laws To Remember

**Licence To Imbibe:** There are several places you can go to buy alcohol if you don't have a liquor licence, but the fact of the matter is that, if you want to enjoy a few drinks in Dubai, you should really have a 'red card'. The good news is that it is so easy to get a licence: just head down to any branch of MMI or A&E, fill in the form, pay Dhs.160 (which you get back as a voucher to spend on booze), and wait a few days. See Getting An Alcohol Licence p.42.

**Crimes Of Cohabitation:** You would have to be pretty unlucky to get pulled up on this, but the UAE law states that men and women who are not related to each other can not live together If you are worried about the risk, however low it may be, the choice is to get married, or live apart.

**Illegitimate Bumps:** Getting pregnant if you are not married is a big no-no here. If you are having your prenatal checkups at a government hospital, you will be asked for your marriage certificate when you register. If you are at a private clinic, you won't have to show your marriage certificate until the baby is born. Either way, you need to have that crucial piece of paper before giving birth here, or you could be looking at a spot of bother that transcends sleepless nights and dirty nappies.

**Remain Orderly:** Drinking in public view (unless you are at a licensed venue or event), is illegal. Being drunk and disorderly in public is against the law no matter where you are. Be careful when you are ordering that seventh cocktail – if that's the one that's going to make you lose your decorum, think about the consequences and make sure there is someone responsible for getting you home safely (apart from the taxi driver).

**Keep The PDAs In Check:** Holding hands won't land you in any trouble, but think twice before kissing, hugging and other public displays of affection. It may be acceptable in some places (like in airport lounges), but it has been known to get people into trouble, particularly if the kissing and hugging is on the more amorous side. Beware in nightclubs: a seemingly innocent kiss, even between married couples, can result in a bouncer giving you a rather firm warning.

**Bounce Into Jail:** It is a criminal offence to bounce a cheque in the UAE and can result in jail time, so make sure you have enough money in your account to honour it. And don't rely on post-dating here: there are many reports of funds being cleared from your account long before the date that is written on the cheque.

**Don't Have One For The Road:** It goes without saying that drinking and driving is illegal. But what many people fail to understand is that there is no such thing as a safe, legal limit when it comes to drinking and driving here. Even a sip of wine or a strong brandy pudding can put you over the limit, because the limit is zero. If you are driving, you should stick to soft drinks, and only soft drinks, all night. If you are drinking, it's best to leave the car keys at home and get a cab.

**Over The Counter But Outside The Law:** Codeine is widely available in over the counter medications in countries like the UK, and Temazepam is a commonly prescribed sleep aid. However, they are illegal substances in the UAE, and possessing them could result in arrest. You can't buy them here, but it's a good idea to tell your overseas visitors not to stock up on the Tylenol or Restoril before they arrive. If they do need these medications, they should carry a doctor's prescription, translated into Arabic if possible.

**Respect Ramadan:** In the UAE, it is illegal to eat, drink or smoke in public view during Ramadan fasting hours. 'In public view' includes your car, the beach, and even the gym. You should not chew gum either. Many restaurants have closed off sections where you can eat lunch out of sight, and most offices set up a little area where non-Muslims can eat and drink during the day. If these options are not available to you, then you should wait for Iftar (the breaking of the fast) before eating, drinking or smoking.

**Look Mum, No Hands:** It's one of the most widely flouted laws in the history of the legal system, but it is absolutely illegal to drive while talking on your mobile handset. Apart from being dangerous, not just for you but for your fellow road users, it is punishable with hefty fines and black points. Invest in a hands-free kit, or better yet, switch your phone off while driving – it may be one of your few opportunities to enjoy some peace and quiet in the midst of a typical busy day.

# Legal Issues

In 2007, a new hotline number was launched for people suffering problems in the beach such as sexual harassment (04 203 6398). For other emergency services call 999 for the police or ambulance and 997 for fire department.

## Neighbourhood Watch

In their efforts to maintain and promote a safe community, the Dubai Police launched Al Ameen, a confidential toll free telephone service where you can report anything suspicious. For example, if you have seen someone hanging around your property or loitering at cashpoints you can pass the information on anonymously by call 800 4888 or emailing alameen@eim.ae.

## If You Are Arrested

If you are arrested you will be taken to a police station and questioned. If it's decided that you must go to court the case will go to the public prosecutor who will set a date for a hearing. For a minor offence you may get bail, and the police will keep your passport and often the passport of another male resident who is willing to vouch for you. Police stations have holding cells, so if you don't get bail you'll be held until the hearing. All court proceedings are conducted in Arabic, so you should secure the services of a translator. If sentenced you'll go straight from court to jail.

Upon being arrested you are advised to contact your embassy or consulate. They can liaise with family, advise on local legal procedures and provide a list of lawyers, but they will not pay your legal fees. The consulate will try to ensure that you are not denied your basic human rights, but they cannot act as lawyers, investigators, secure bail, or get you released.

## If You Are Detained

Most prisoners will be detained in the new Central Jail near Al Awir, which was moved from its old location in Al Wasl. Short-term or temporary male prisoners may be held in an 'Out Jail', while long-term prisoners are likely to go to the main Central Jail.

Conditions inside the old jail were described as basic but bearable, but the new complex has much improved conditions, with the reported overcrowding in the old jail a thing of the past.

Inmates are given three meals a day, and there's a small snack shop with limited opening hours. Prisoners are allowed occasional access to payphones, so if you are visiting an inmate a few phone cards will be appreciated.

Prisoners are generally allowed visits once a week. Thursdays are reserved for visits to Arab detainees, and Fridays are for other nationalities. Men and women are not allowed to visit together – men can visit from 10:00 to 11:00 and women from 16:00 to 17:00. If you are a woman you may not be allowed to visit a man who is of no family relation to you.

Visiting times are subject to change so it's best to check by calling the Department of Punitive Establishments (04 344 0351).

## Victim Support

There are some support services available to those who have been victims of crime. Women and children, who are victims of domestic violence, can seek shelter at Dubai Foundation for Women and Children (800 111, www.dfwac.ae); the organisation also offers counselling and advice for women and their partners. The National Committee to Combat Human Trafficking (02 404 1000, www.nccht.gov.ae) assists those who are the victim of sexual abuse. Its website also provides information on other support services in the UAE. Dubai Police www.dubaipolice.gov.ae) offer a victim continuity service that offers support and provides updates on the progress of cases.

## Tips For Women

The following general tips are useful for women in Dubai:
- Stick to the dress code; tight, revealing clothing equals unwanted attention.
- Be careful when out alone at night, especially after a few drinks.
- Never get into an non-metered taxi; and always take down the taxi number.
- As long as you exercise due care and attention Dubai is a safe place for women.

## Prohibited Items

Taking illegal narcotics is an absolute no-no – even the smallest amounts of marijuana or hashish could earn you a prison sentence of four years or more. This will almost certainly be followed by deportation. If you are found guilty of dealing or smuggling, you could be looking at a life sentence, or even the death penalty (although this is uncommon).

Some medications that are legal in your home country, such as codeine, temazepam and prozac, may be banned here – check with the UAE embassy in your home country before you leave, and if you are in any doubt, try and find an alternative. If you must bring this medication with you, keep a copy of the prescription with you and obtain a medical report from your doctor – this may help explain your case if you are questioned. You can see a list of approved drugs on the Ministry of Health website (www.moh.gov.ae) although it is not known how frequently this list is updated or how reliable it is.

DIFC

# Kids Club

# Club Rush

Children aged four to twelve can enjoy the Atlantis Kids Club where they will discover an array of exciting activities from movies in the underwater theatre to rock climbing, computer games, and arts and crafts.

Teenagers will enjoy the only club in Dubai exclusively for them! Club Rush is full of energy playing the latest video games, catching a newly released movie or surfing the web. Club Rush is the new hot spot for teens to hang out in a safe, supervised, and alcohol free environment.

Entrance cover charge applies.
For information call +971 4 426 1295
or email activities@atlantisthepalm.com
atlantisthepalm.com

# ATLANTIS
THE PALM, DUBAI

Family &
Education

# FAMILY

Family is a huge part of life in Dubai, as well as an integral part of Emirati culture. From birth to high education bringing up your family here is a rewarding and enjoyable experience. The facilities, from the practical to the pleasurable, are world class and Dubai has so much to offer families of all nationalities. However, while the nurseries, play centres and facilities for babies and toddlers are very good, and the primary and secondary schools of an extremely high standard, older children may have more of a struggle settling into life in the Emirates. However, with improved education facilities, especially at university level, and an ever-expanding leisure industry, teens have a lot to keep them occupied. The challenges are transport – although the new Dubai Metro will hopefully alleviate this – as driving your teenagers to and from malls can be a bit of a chore. Also, chores need to be enforced for older kids in order to avoid 'expat brat' syndrome – unfortunately there is little in the way of Saturday jobs in Dubai but you may want to encourage your older children to volunteer (p.124).

Children are rarely expected to be seen and not heard in Dubai, and many restaurants are abuzz with kids running around. (There are however many places where kids will be less welcome so you should always call before you turn up). Cinemas also seem to have a pretty open door policy – although often to the annoyance of other patrons. Parks (p.246), beaches (p.248) and amusements centres (p.252) keep families happy and childcare options are available (p.143), although more in the form of paid babysitters than parent run babysitting circles.

Whether you come with your family or have a family here, Dubai is a great place to call home.

## Getting Married

A few years ago, organising a wedding in Dubai could be a bit of a challenge, but thanks to the trusty rules of supply and demand, weddings are now big business.

While many hotels offer wedding packages, they mainly extend to the reception – The One&Only Royal Mirage (04 399 3999) and The Ritz-Carlton (04 399 4000) are the hot favourites, and the Radisson Blu also offers a tailored wedding service (04 205 7047) as does the Park Hyatt (04 602 1234). Most Dubai hotels will offer a wedding service (see p.140 for a list of hotels).

A wedding planner could be your fairy godmother (especially when your family support network is miles away), check out Royal Events & Weddings for bespoke weddings (www.royalevents.com). Sarah Feyling is an expert wedding planner based in Dubai who will help you every step of the way – from the paperwork to the seating plan (www.theweddingplanner.ae). Jennifer Mollon is a freelance wedding planner who offers reasonable packages; she also runs the first second-hand wedding dress agency in Dubai (050 804 2585, www.myprelovedbridal.com). Upscale & Posh offers a tailored service for flowers and wedding reception decorations (www.upscaleandposh.com).

Brides needn't worry about missing out on the princess treatment, since most spas offer tailor-made services for them. See p.211 for a list of spas. For more information on wedding dresses and accessories, as well as cakes and invitation cards, see p.386 in the Shopping section.

### The Paperwork

Before going ahead with a wedding you should consult your embassy or consulate for advice, especially regarding the legality of the marriage back home. In nearly all cases, a marriage that is performed in Dubai will be legally recognised elsewhere in the world, but it's always best to check. In addition, you may need to inform your embassy of your intention to marry. The British Embassy in Dubai, for example, will display a 'notice of marriage' in the embassy waiting room for 21 days prior to the marriage (along the same lines as 'the banns' being published in a parish newsletter for three successive Sundays). Afterwards, providing no one has objected, they will issue a 'certificate of no impediment' that may be required by the church carrying out your ceremony.

Christ Church Jebel Ali can offer further assistance regarding marriage between two Christians (http://christchurchjebelali.org).

### Shotgun Weddings

It is illegal to have a baby out of wedlock in the UAE. If you are unmarried and fall pregnant, you have two choices: march down the aisle asap or leave Dubai. You'll be asked for your marriage certificate when you give birth (and even earlier if you are having your prenatal checks at a government hospital). If there is a significant discrepancy in the dates, you will probably face many questions and a lot more paperwork.

A Muslim marrying another Muslim can apply at the marriage section of the Dubai Courts, next to Maktoum Bridge. You will need two male witnesses and the bride should ensure that either her father or brother attends as a witness. You will require your passports with copies, proof that the groom is Muslim and Dhs.50. You can marry there and then. A Muslim man can marry a non-Muslim woman, but a non-Muslim man cannot marry at the court. The situation is more complicated for a Muslim woman wishing to marry a non-Muslim man and this may only be possible if the man first converts to Islam. Call the Dubai Courts (04 334 7777) or the Dubai Court Marriage Section (04 303 0406) for more information.

Christians can either have a formal church ceremony with a congregation, or a small ceremony that must take place in a church, followed by a blessing at a different location, such as a hotel.

Your church may require that you have someone witness you signing a 'legal eligibility for marriage' document (a legal paper signed under oath) at your embassy or consulate. You may also need to attend at least three sessions of premarital counselling.

At the official church ceremony you will need two witnesses to sign the marriage register and the church will then issue a marriage certificate. You will need to get the certificate translated into Arabic by a court-approved legal translator. Take this, and the original, along with your essential documents to the Notary Public Office at the Dubai Courts. They will certify the documents for a fee of about Dhs.80. Next you will need to go to the Ministry of Justice (http://ejustice.gov.ae) to authenticate the signature and the Notary Public seal. Just when you think it's all over, you still have to go to the Ministry of Foreign Affairs (behind the distinctive Etisalat building in Deira) to authenticate the seal of the Ministry of Justice. Now you just need to pop back to your embassy for final legal verification.

Catholics must also undertake a marriage encounter course, which usually takes place at the busy St Mary's Church in Oud Metha (04 337 0087) on a Friday. At the end of the course you are presented with a certificate. You should then arrange with the priest to undertake a pre-nuptial ceremony (which will require your birth certificate, baptism certificate, passport and passport copies, an NOC from your parish priest in your home country and a donation, and the filling out of another form). If you are a non-Catholic marrying a Catholic you will need an NOC from your embassy/consulate stating that you are legally free to marry. A declaration of your intent to marry is posted on the public noticeboard at the church for three weeks, after which time, if there are no objections, you can set a date for the ceremony. Anglicans should make an appointment to see the chaplain at Holy Trinity Church (04 337 0247). You will need to fill out forms confirming that you are legally free to marry and take your essential documents along (passports, passport copies, passport photos, residence visa). If you have previously been married you will need to produce either your divorce certificate or the death certificate of your previous partner. Fees differ depending on your nationality and circumstances but are around Dhs.1,000 for the ceremony and an additional Dhs.1,000 if you wish to hold the ceremony outside the church. You'll pay Dhs.50 for any additional copies of the marriage certificate that you want. If you're not overly concerned about sticking to a particular doctrine, but want a church wedding, the Anglican ceremony is simpler to arrange and less time consuming than the Catholic equivalent.

## Wedding Photographers

Rates vary depending on where your wedding is and how long you will require a photographer for. Try the following photographers: Sue Johnston (www.imageoasisdubai.com), Charlotte Simpson (www.hotshotsdubai.com), Darrin James (www.djphotography.net).

These marriages are recognised by the government of the UAE but must be formalised. To make your marriage 'official', get an Arabic translation of the marriage certificate and take it to the Dubai Court. Filipino citizens are required to contact their embassy in Abu Dhabi before the Dubai Court will authenticate their marriage certificate.

Hindus can be married through the Hindu Temple and the Indian Embassy (04 397 1222). The formalities take a minimum of 45 days.

## Having A Baby

In many ways, having a baby while you are living in Dubai as an expat is very easy. The standard of maternity healthcare, whether you choose to go private or government, is excellent, and as long as you have insurance or the means to pay for healthcare, there is absolutely no reason to return to your home country to give birth (more on maternity healthcare on p.192). There is more of a chance that you can get away with one income in Dubai, meaning that many mothers get to stay at home with their new babies, rather than having to return to work. And you will have access to cheap childcare and babysitting services here, so you may find that you can be a little more independent than your counterparts back home.

Of course, there are some disadvantages too. If you are pregnant and working, then you've got some pretty paltry maternity leave to look forward to: just 45 days paid leave, and absolutely nothing for dads. You can take another month unpaid, as long as your employer agrees, and if you need some extra time for medical reasons, you can take up to 100 days, although this is only granted upon production of a medical certificate from your doctor. Having an understanding employer can obviously result in these maternity leave rules being slightly more flexible.

Another big disadvantage of living here and having a baby is the absence of the family support network you may have had back home – grandparents and other family members, who would normally muck in to help you with mundane tasks like cooking, cleaning and babysitting are now thousands of miles away. Fortunately, many women who have babies here find themselves a strong network of other mums who meet up regularly and offer plenty of support to each other.

## Pregnant Out Of Wedlock

If you fall pregnant but are not married then there is no reason to panic, but there are several decisions that you will need to make fairly quickly. It is illegal to have a baby out of wedlock while you are a resident in the UAE and if you deliver your baby at any hospital here, private or public, and can't produce a marriage certificate, you will most likely face a prison sentence. Therefore, as soon as you see the blue lines on the pregnancy test, you need to sort a few things out. The easiest solution is to have a quick wedding, after which you can go on to have antenatal care in a government or private hospital without any fear of punishment. If this is not an option, you can stay in Dubai until a reasonable time before you are due to give birth, and even have your antenatal check-ups in a private hospital, but you will need to ensure that you return to your home country to actually deliver the baby. Once you have delivered you can return to Dubai with the baby: there are no rules against being a single mother here (see p.143 for more information on single parents).

### Babies Born Back Home

Babies born abroad to expatriate mums with UAE residency are required to have a residence visa or a visit visa before entering the UAE. The application should be filed by the father or family provider, along with the essential documents, a salary certificate and a copy of the birth certificate.

## Birth Certificate & Registration

The hospital that delivers the baby will prepare a 'notification of birth' (which will be in Arabic) upon receipt of hospital records, photocopies of both parents' passports, your marriage certificate, and a fee of Dhs.50.

To get the actual birth certificate, take the birth notification to the Birth Certificate Office at Al Baraha Hospital (04 271 0000).

Every expat child born in the UAE should be registered with their parents' embassy. If the parents are from different countries, you will probably be able to choose which nationality your child adopts, and in some cases he or she may be able to take on dual nationality. Check with your embassy for further details.

The important thing to remember is that your baby needs to get a UAE residency visa within 120 days of birth, and in order to do this you need to have received his or her passport, so you should start the process as soon as possible. If you don't get the residency within that time, you will have to pay a fine of Dhs.100 for every day that you go over the limit.

If you feel like you've got enough on your hands with your new arrival, MEDI-Express offers a service, for a fee, that will take much of the administration and hassle out of arranging the birth certificate for your baby. The firm is based at Baraha Hospital. See www.mediexpress.ae or call 04 272 7772 for more details.

## Adoption

While you can't adopt a UAE National baby, many couples in Dubai adopt children from Africa, Asia and Far Eastern countries. Adoption regulations vary according to which country the child comes from, but once you clear the requirements of that country, and complete the adoption process, you will have no problems bringing your new child into the UAE on your sponsorship. Check with your embassy about the procedure for applying for citizenship of your home country for your new child.

If you are considering adopting a child, a good place to start is the Adoption Support Group Dubai. Join their Yahoo group (http://groups.yahoo.com/group/asgdubai), or email asgdubai@yahoogroups.com.

# Getting Divorced

Statistics show that the UAE has one of the highest divorce rates in the Arab world. To counter this, bodies such as the State Marriage Fund have launched schemes offering education and counselling services to National couples. Expats can get divorced in Dubai, and in some cases the procedure can be relatively straightforward. However, expat couples wishing to divorce may also be governed by the laws of their home country (if the couple has mixed nationalities, the home country of the husband applies), so it is advisable to seek legal advice. A husband who sponsors his wife has the right to have her residence visa cancelled in the event of divorce. See p.133 for a list of law firms.

If you do decide to get divorced whilst living in Dubai and are an expat couple, you will be governed by the law of the country which issued your marriage licence. It can be challenging getting divorced whilst living abroad, especially if the situation isn't amicable. If you are the one filing for divorce and you have legal representation in your home country it is likely that you will also need a solicitor here to serve the divorce papers to your spouse. In addition, whilst you may be living in Dubai and therefore think custodial issues are not relevant, it may still be a good idea to arrange for a residence and access order or similar through the courts in your home country in order to clarify your parental rights for when you do intend to return. If the relationship between you and your spouse has deteriorated it is a good idea to try and meet with a mediator, Dr Ruth McCarthy at the Counselling & Development Clinic Dubai (www.drmccarthypsychologyclinic.com) specialises in marriage counselling.

## Single Parents

It is possible to live in Dubai and sponsor your children as a single parent, even if you are a woman. There will be extra requirements that you need to meet, including a minimum salary level and a letter of no objection from the other parent (or a death certificate, in the case of a deceased spouse). You may also need to show your Divorce certificate but it is best to visit the Immigration Department to find out the exact requirements, as these may change from time to time. Being a working single parent in Dubai may seem daunting for a number of reasons. Firstly as an expat, your support system may not be as great as back home, where friends and family can help out, and secondly in a country where marriage and family are so important you may feel a little like the 'odd one out'. However, once you get used to people enquiring where your husband is (if you have a child with you people assume you're married), there are actually lots of advantages of living in Dubai as a working single parent. The nurseries (p.150) in Dubai are very good, and a few offer full day care, and are generally much more affordable than in your home country, there is also the option of having a live-in nanny (see Sponsoring a Maid, p.37), which means that you can not only work as a single parent but also still have a social life.

## Babysitting & Childcare

Dubai may be a great place to raise children, but it can be a challenging task to find reliable childcare here. Many families choose to hire live-in, full-time maids (nannies) to assist them with childcare and babysitting; however, this can work out to be quite expensive due to the sponsorship fees, and you also need to have an apartment or villa with suitable accommodation.

If both you and your spouse work full time then a live-in maid is really your best option as there is no official network of childminders, although you will find the occasional expat mum offering her services underneath the radar, so to speak.

Finding the right person to live-in can certainly be a challenge. There are a number of agencies around Dubai they don't have the greatest reputations, so it is best to interview them before you interview any of their candidates. It is preferable to recruit someone who is already in the country and therefore your best bet would be to find someone who is leaving the country and therefore no longer needs their maid, so speak to other parents and check/put up notices on Spinneys and community noticeboards as well as

Safa Park

on www.expatwoman.com, www.dubizzle.com and www.trixabell.com.

Depending upon the nationality of your live-in maid (the majority of whom are Sri Lankan and Filipina) you may have to visit their local embassy to get a contract drawn up before beginning the sponsorship process (see Sponsoring A Maid, p.37).

Domestic help agencies (p.106) can provide part-time babysitters, although there is no guarantee that you will get the same babysitter every time.

Ask around your neighbourhood to see if any of the local maids or teenagers are available for ad hoc evening babysitting, or try your child's nursery, as classroom assistants are often up for a bit of extra work and they will already know your children.

If you do manage to find someone for part-time babysitting, the rate ranges from Dhs.15 to Dhs.30 per hour. Western childminders are most likely to charge more than this.

## Activities For Kids

During the cooler months (October to May), Kids can enjoy the many parks (p.246) and beaches (p.248) around Dubai which house playgrounds for varying ages (Safa Park p.248 and Dubai Creek Park p.246 have excellent play areas for both toddlers and older kids), as well as tennis and basketball courts. There are also a number of waterparks (p.248) in and around the city, however, while swimming is obviously popular, there are few public pools. Mushrif park (p.246) does have separate women's and men's pools, however, outside the hotels and health clubs the only other options are villa compound pools or the beach. Unless your child is an extremely strong swimmer it is unwise to let them swim unsupervised at the public beaches as there are undercurrents.

# Family

Family fun

During the warmer months (June to September) the many amusement centres (p.252) and kids' play areas keep your brood from getting bored. Fun Corner is a soft play centre with a few arcade games and small rides located in Bin Sougat Centre (p.410) Al Ghurair City (p.410) and the Spinney's Centre on Al Wasl Road. Fun City (www.funcity-fec.com) offers similar facilities as well as scheduled classes and can be found in the Arabian Center (p.410), Oasis Centre (p.412), Reef Mall (p.413), Ibn Battuta (p.404), Mercato (p.406) and BurJuman (p.398). Dubai Festival City (p.401) has a play area beneath Toys R Us called Cool Times which has the usual ball pit and soft play as well as some arts and crafts.

There are various sports and activity clubs that run after school activities (p.146) and summer camps (p.145) and most hobbies are covered (see the Activities chapter, p.145).

## Active Sports Academy
050 559 7055
www.activeuae.com
Running for 13 years, the Active Sports Academy organises various sports coaching classes in multiple venues around Dubai, including after school at various campuses. They teach tennis, soccer, cricket, basketball, swimming and gymnastics and run various tournaments, as well as holiday camps through all school break periods, including Spring, Eid, Christmas and Summer.

## DuGym Gymnastics Club
Various Locations 050 553 6283
www.dugym.com
DuGym offers gymnastics and trampoline coaching to children of all ages and abilities. Established by Suzanne Wallace in 2000, the club now operates at

15 locations including the GEMS World Academy, Jumeirah English Speaking School and Emirates International School. Classes are held from Sunday to Thursday. Contact Suzanne on the above number for more details.

## Favourite Things
Dubai Marina Mall Dubai Marina 04 434 1984
www.dubaimarinamall.com
Map 1 K4 Metro Dubai Marina
The perfect place to leave your kids happily playing for an hour or two, Favourite Things in Dubai Marina Mall has more than enough options to keep the rug rats happy. There's everything from a toddlers soft play area to a mini race track, jungle gym and dressing up area. Parents can join in, watch from the comfort of the cafe, or even leave the tots in the centre's capable hands while they go shopping.

## Junior Gym Bus
Off Tunis St, Exit 60 Al Qusais 04 254 3070
www.juniorgymbus.com
Map 2 S10
Junior Gym Bus is a unique and stimulating innovation promoting fitness in children and encouraging them to partake in sports activities. A converted school bus is driven to the daycare centre or preschool, and parked outside for certified instructors to teach gymnastics and basic motor skills to the children. The floors and walls are padded with foam and carpeted for safety. Rates include monthly payments of Dhs.200 per month as a member or a fee of Dhs.65 per session as a non-member. An annual registration fee of Dhs.120 per child is also applicable.

## Kids' Theatre Works
Dubai Community Theatre & Arts Centre (DUCTAC)
Al Barsha 04 341 4777
www.kidstheatreworks.com
Map 1 R5 Metro Mall of the Emirates
Running classes in creative drama, musical theatre, acting, dance, youth theatre, music and scene work for ages 6 and up, if you're kids are budding superstars, Kids Theatre Works is a good start. They run classes at DUCTAC, Uptown Mirdif Primary, Jebel Ali, DESS and American School of Dubai.

## My Gym
Jumeira Rd, Villa 520 Jumeira 04 394 3962
www.mygymuae.com
Map 2 B3 Metro Al Quoz
If you are looking for innovative ways to get the kids active, My Gym offers a variety of event. Programmes range from 'Mommy and Me' for babies aged six weeks up to gymnastics, dance and general fitness alongside fun-filled private birthday parties and camps; children up to the age of 13 can participate.

A two hour per week class and play session will cost Dhs.1,000 for 10 weeks. Parents can also participate in classes with their children if preferred, but independent classes are offered.

### Physical Advantage
**Club House 2 Al Manhal, Shoreline Apartments, Palm Jumeirah** Palm Jumeirah **04 311 6570**
www.physicaladvantage.ae
Map **1 N2** Metro **Nakheel**
If your kids seek a challenge, try out Physical Advantage's Military Bootcamp Programmes which are designed for 6 to 15 year olds. The Cadets Bootcamp programme will test all aspects of your child's health and fitness while teaching them discipline and health education. Timings and locations for courses vary according to the age group your child belongs to. A single session costs Dhs.100, and a two week course (four sessions) costs Dhs.300.

### Tickles and Giggles
**Sadaf 1, Plaza Level, JBR 04 432 8681**
www.ticklesandgiggles.com
Map **1 K3** Metro **Dubai Marina**
Tickles and Giggles has a kids salon and spa as well as offering unique classes such as baby yoga, etiquette classes, arts and crafts and nursery rhymes. They also host ultra trendy parties for kids (no bears or tank engines in sight), and will match decorations and the menu to your chosen theme. You can become a member on their website, where you can order their party supplies as well as make online bookings.

# Mother & Toddler Activities
Dubai is a great place for young families, and while you may not have the helpful hand of family close by, there are lots of mother and baby groups (see below) as well as support groups (p.146) to keep you and your baby happy. There are of course also the many parks (p.246) which make great spots for mothers to meet and many of them have walking tracks which are excellent for a bit of pram pushing exercise. As pavements are a rarity in Dubai, going for a stroll with your pushchair may be a challenge – malls are of course an option and The Walk at Jumeirah Beach Residence (p.389) has nice wide walkways and Uptown Mirdif's pedistrianised area is another good spot. For more on places to walk see p.53.

Look out for Gymboree Play & Music which is due to re-open in Dubai soon (www.gymboreeclasses.com).

### Deira Mums And Tots
**Reef Mall** Deira **050 678 1168**
www.deiramums.blogspot.com
Map **2 N4** Metro **Salahuddin**
You can register for classes on the website. They hold arts and craft classes on Mondays between 17:00 and 18:00 and singing classes on Saturdays between 14:30 and 15:30. Classes cost Dhs.250 for a set of six and are held at Fun City in Reef Mall.

### Kidz & Mumz
Arabian Ranches **050 451 0225**
Map **2 N7**
The aim of this group is to allow mums and their children to engage together in creative and educational activities such as arts and crafts, games, reading, writing, story telling, and cooking and baking. The 'MumZ Forum' also allows the grown-ups to discuss different aspects of their children's development. The current age group of the 'kidz' is between 2 and 5.

### Mirdif Mums
Mirdif **050 654 8953**
www.mirdifmums.com
As Mirdif has a strong family population it is only fitting that the mums got together to share coffee mornings, afternoons in the park and various activity days. The group also has some social outings without the kids and it is a great way to make new friends.

### Mums & Tots Group
**Wafi** Umm Hurair **050 656 5837**
Map **2 L6** Metro **Healthcare City**
This group organises coffee mornings either at members houses or out and about in Dubai, as well as activities from arts and crafts to music.

### Power Buggies
**050 544 1062**
www.powerbuggies.net
A fun group of mums who get together in Safa and Umm Suqeim Parks for cardiovascular classes that incorporate their buggies, as well as power walking and jogging. They have 60 minute beginners (on Tuesdays and Thursdays) and advanced (on Mondays and Wednesdays) classes.

# Summer Camps
With more and more kids in Dubai during the summer holidays, many hotels, clubs and organisations have added summer camps and activities to their annual schedule. Most language schools run summer courses for kids (see Language Schools, p.176), if you want your kids to put their time off to good use. If you'd rather see them having fun over the holidays, many leisure clubs offer summer camps that focus on sports, arts and crafts, so if you have a leisure club in your area, contact them to see what they have on offer. Alternatively, contact Active Sports Academy (see Kids Activities p.143), as they arrange sporty summer camps at various venues around the city.

# After-School Activities

Many schools will run ECAs (Extra Curricular Activities) from Kindergarten upwards. Generally, the younger years only have one ECA a week for around 30-60 minutes directly after school, while the older years may have multiple classes at various times. School-run ECAs are often included in the school fees, however, independent companies also hold classes at schools during the afternoons and evenings and charge term fees (which are far from cheap). Many school campuses are utilised by various sports academies and dance schools in the afternoons, weekends and holidays, and you are likely to receive a multitude of flyers in your kids' school bags from such companies.

Turning Pointe (p.316) run ballet classes for all ages in various schools around Dubai, as do Kids Theatre Works (p.144), and Kids Active have a range of sports classes. If you're kids are sports players (or you want them to be) there are a number of academies that can develop their talents – would-be Federers should sign up with Clark Francis Tennis Academy (p.341), budding Beckhams can hone their skills with the International Football Academy (p.321) or UAE English Soccer School of Excellence (p.321), wanna-be olympic gold medalists should dive in with Arabian Gulf Swimming Academy (p.340) or Australian International Swim Schools (p.158) and potential Bruce Lees can kick it with various clubs around Dubai (see Martial Arts, p.328).

Many parents also get together in the many parks (in the winter) and play centres (in the summer) around Dubai for their own impromptu after school activities so new families shouldn't worry about long afternoons and bored kids.

# Support Groups

Starting a new life in a different country away from your normal support network of family and friends can be challenging, but there are a number of support groups to help you through the difficult patches. In addition to the groups listed below, the Human Relations Institute offers a range of support group workshops (p.205) and Dubai Community Health Centre (p.205) provides space for support group meetings.

## Adoption Support Group
04 360 8113
Meetings are held once a month for parents who have adopted children or who are considering adopting. For more information on the meetings call Carol on the number listed above.

## Alcoholics Anonymous
Various Locations **050 744 8092**
www.aaarabia.org
This organisation spans the GCC and wider Middle East with regular AA meetings held in various

locations. They also offer a 12-step programme which allows AA members to join a 'closed' workshop. Check out the website for the classes and workshop schedule.

## All 4 Down Syndrome Support Group
Various Locations **050 880 9228**
www.downsyndromedubai.com
All 4 Down's Syndrome provides support to families whose lives have, in some way, been affected by Down's Syndrome. The group is part of an awareness raising campaign, and offers advice on health, education and care for people with Down's. Social mornings are held every Sunday between 10:00 and 12:00.

## Bullying Support
050 657 0866
If you're child is having problems at school, in addition to contacting the school itself, you can turn to this group who help bullied children and their parents deal with bullying as a family. Call Salomi on the above number for more details.

## Dubai Dyslexia Support Group
04 344 6657
This group holds occasional meetings for people with dyslexia and may be able to assist you if you suspect that your child is suffering from dyslexia.

## Genesis International Ventures Ltd
Oud Metha, Nr Russian Hospital 04 335 5578
This non-profit organisation offers support to caregivers of those living with ADHD, autism and other disabilities, through educational workshops and parent forums. The online group http://uk.groups.yahoo.com/group/genesis_autism/ has information about upcoming events.

## Mothers Of Children With Special Needs
050 659 1707
A support group run by parents of special needs children offering support and information, as well as get togethers with their children. Call Lilly for details of monthly meetings.

## SANDS Support group
04 348 2801
www.dubai-sands.org
SANDS Support Group. A UK-based charity for those families experiencing pregnancy loss, either through still birth, neonatal death or late miscarriage. Contact Angela on 04 482 2801, Anita on 050 644 7903 or Paula on 055 393 2804. SANDS also offers hospital and home visits.

## Special Families Support
04 360 5654
www.sfs-group.net
Special Families Support has monthly meetings for the families of special needs children. It also runs a summer camp. Contact Gulshan for more details.

## Twins, Triplets Or More Of UAE
www.ttomdxb.com/forum
This is an online support group offering a forum for parents of multiples to exchange advice and ask questions. Also, many parents get together for play dates and activities with their children.

## UAE Down Syndrome Support Group
04 367 1949
www.uaedssg.com
This active group organises day trips and events for and offers support to people with Downs' Syndrome in the UAE and their families. The organisation also runs conferences and workshops and publishes a regular newsletter for members. Call Dr Eman Gaad on the above number at extension 1949.

# Death
In the event of the death of a friend or relative, the first thing to do is to notify the police by dialling 999. The police will fill out a report and the body will be taken to Rashid Hospital (p.188) where a doctor will determine the cause of death and produce a report. The authorities will need to see the deceased's passport and visa details. Dubai Police will investigate in the case of an accidental or suspicious death, and it's likely that an autopsy will be performed at a government hospital. If you're unhappy with the outcome of an investigation you could hire a private investigator, but this is a bit of a grey area so seek advice from your embassy or consulate.

## Certificates & Registration
On receipt of the doctor's report, the hospital will issue a death certificate declaration, for a fee of Dhs.50. Take the declaration and original passport to the nearest police department, which will issue an NOC addressed to Al Baraha (Kuwaiti) Hospital (p.184). You should also request NOCs addressed to the mortuary for embalming, the airport for transportation and the hospital for the release of the body. This letter, plus death declaration, original passport and copies should be taken to Al Baraha Hospital, Department of Preventative Medicine, where an actual death certificate will be issued. You will also need to cancel the deceased's visa at the Department of Naturalisation and Residency.

If you are sending the deceased home you should also request a death certificate in English (an additional Dhs.100) or appropriate language – check this with your embassy. Since Islam requires that the body be buried immediately, the death certificate and registration procedures for deceased Muslims can be performed after the burial.

## Returning The Deceased To Their Country Of Origin
To return the deceased to his or her country of origin, you will need to book you own ticket with the airline of your choosing as well as make shipping arrangements through DNATA (04 211 1111), which will handle the body at Cargo Village and process any required documentation. The deceased will need to be embalmed before reaching cargo village, and you will need the original death certificate, the NOC from Dubai Police, an NOC from the embassy of the deceased (which must be the same as the destination to which they are being sent), the cancellation or the passport and visa and a copy of the air tickets specifying flight details. You will also need to purchase a coffin in accordance with the size of the deceased. Embalming can be arranged through the Dubai Health Authority and will cost around Dhs.1,000, which includes the embalming certificate. The body must be identified before and after embalming, after which it should be transferred to Cargo Village for shipping. Cargo fees will range from Dhs.1,000 to Dhs.10,000 and a coffin costs about Dhs.750.

## Local Burial Or Cremation
Before the deceased can be buried or cremated locally, you will need the following documentation: original passport (cancelled from the embassy), death certificate, proof that the visa was cancelled and an Non Objection Certificate (NOC) from the sponsor stating that all debts have been settled. For Hindu cremation, you must also provide written permission from the next of kin, as well as that person's passport. The procedure for local cremation and burial can be complicated and changes often, so you will need to contact the Dubai Municipality (04 264 3355, www.dm.gov.ae), the Christian Cemetery (04 337 0247), or the Hindu Temple in Bur Dubai (04 353 5334) for the latest information.

## Local Burial
A local burial can be arranged at the Muslim or Christian cemeteries in Dubai. The cost of a burial is Dhs.1,100 for an adult and Dhs.350 for a child. You will need to get a coffin made, as well as transport to the burial site. Cremation is also possible, but only in the Hindu manner and with the prior permission of the next of kin and the CID.

# Pets

The attitude towards pets in Dubai is mixed so it's sensible to keep your pet under control. Pets are prohibited from parks and beaches, and there aren't many places where you can walk your dog, other than the streets in your area. While uncommon, animal abuse is a problem in the city, and can be reported to the municipality (04 289 1114).

You should check with your landlord what the pet policy is before you move in. When walking your dog, keep it on a short leash, as many people are frightened of them. Be sure to keep your pet indoors or within your garden to avoid contact with strays and to prevent any problems with frightened neighbours. Dubai has a significant problem with strays, although both Feline Friends (050 451 0058) and K9 Friends (04 885 8031) are hard-working animal charities that take in as many as they can. The Dubai Municipality is also hard at work fixing the stray problem.

You should inoculate your pet annually against rabies, and register it with the municipality (04 289 1114), who will microchip cats and dogs and provide plastic neck tags. If the municipality picks up an animal without a tag, it is treated as a stray. Also Vets will not treat your cat or dog if it isn't microchipped.

While rare, there have been reports of dogs being stolen, either to be sold to unscrupulous pet shops, or for dog fighting. Ensure your garden is secure and don't let your dog roam around on the street.

## Bringing Your Pet To Dubai

Pets may be bought into the UAE without quarantine as long as they are microchipped and vaccinated with verifying documentation, including a government health certificate from the country of origin. However, you cannot import cats and dogs under four months old and all pets must arrive as manifest cargo and must have a valid rabies vaccination no less than 21 days before their arrival. For more information check out http://petimport. moew.gov.ae and create an account.

### Cats & Dogs

Feline Friends (050 451 0058) is a non-profit organisation, aiming to improve the lives of cats by rescuing and rehoming stray cats and kittens. It has a 24 hour telephone answering service as well as a comprehensive website, www. felinefriendsuae.com. K9 Friends (04 885 8031) helps to rehome stray and injured dogs, many of which are abandoned family pets looking for a second chance. See www.k9friends.com for more information. Another useful website for pet owners in the Emirates is www.petdubai.com.

## Taking Your Pet Home

Dubai is part of the international pet passport scheme and therefore a pet can be sent out of Dubai either accompanied by their owner on the same flight or unaccompanied as cargo depending on the airline and destination, you need to contact the airline cargo department to find out the regulations. Dubai Kennels & Cattery (04 285 1646) and IAL Pet Express (04 310 9455) offer an export service, as does The Doghouse (www.dubaidoghouse.com). You need to check the laws of the country you are exporting your pet to as they each have varying quarantine stipulations – the UK requires a rabies blood test (RNATT) to be done six months in advance of departure.

### Sleek Salukis

The saluki is the breed of dog most commonly associated with the region; they are used in traditional forms of hunting. The Arabian Saluki Center (www.arabiansaluki.ae) can provide information on all aspects of the care of these animals. Many 'desert dogs' descend from the saluki. If you'd like to adopt your own desert dog, contact K9 Friends (www.k9friends.com).

## Vets, Kennels & Grooming

Standards of care at Dubai's veterinary clinics are reasonably high. Prices do not vary dramatically, but the Deira Veterinary Clinic and Al Barsha Veterinary Clinic are a little cheaper than the rest. Dubai Municipality has a veterinary services department (04 289 1114), which treats and vaccinates animals and issues identity tags. It is located next to Mushrif Park. The Nad Al Shiba Veterinary Hospital (04 340 1060) not only treats cats and dogs but also more exotic animals and birds.

Kennels are generally of a good standard, although spaces are limited during peak times (summer and Christmas). An alternative is to use an at-home pet-sitting service – someone will come into your house at least once a day to feed and exercise your pet for a reasonable fee (for a bit extra they might even water your plants). For information on Pet shops see p.148.

In terms of grooming there are a number of companies, see p.150, that offer a variety of grooming treatments from the basic shampooing, medicated baths and nail clipping to the more indulgent, like fashion advice.

## Pet Boarding

**Dubai Kennels & Cattery (DKC)** > *p.149* Al Rashidiya, 04 285 1646, *www.dkc.ae*
**Petland Resort** Al Quoz, 04 347 5022,
**Poshpaws Kennels & Cattery** Sharjah, 050 273 0973, *www.poshpawsdubai.com*

**Dubai Kennels & Cattery**

# Just come 'n meet us
## (owners welcome too.)

**Global Relocations & Transit Care**
**Boarding & Daycare**
**Collection & Delivery**

horses, dogs, cats, birds, rabbits . . .
and other creatures, too . . . since 1983

**04 285 1646** • info@dkc.ae • www.dkc.ae

DKC is a member of AATA, IPATA and PCSA

## Pet Sitting

**Creature Comforts** 050 695 9480,
*www.creaturecomfortsdubai.com*
**Eve's Home Comforts Pet Sitting Service** Sharjah,
06 524 4111
**Pet Partner** 050 774 2239, *www.pet-partner.com*
**Pets At Home** Jumeira, 04 331 2186,
*www.petsathomedubai.com*

## Pet Grooming & Training

**Al Safa Veterinary Clinic** Umm Suqeim, 04 348 3799
**Creature Comforts** 050695 9480,
*www.creaturecomfortsdubai.com*
**Poshpaws Kennels & Cattery** Sharjah, 050273 0973,
*www.poshpawsdubai.com*
**Shampooch Mobile Pet Grooming** Various
Locations, 04 344 9868, *www.shampooch.ae*
**Snoopy Pets** 04 420 5348
**Tail Waggin Mobile Pet Spa** 050 366 6622
**Paws Canine Training Centre** 050784 5350,
*www.pawstraining.com*

## Veterinary Clinics

**Al Barsha Veterinary Clinic** Al Barsha, 04 340 8601,
**Al Safa Veterinary Clinic** Umm Suqeim, 04 348 3799,
*www.alsafavetclinic.com*
**Animal Care Centre** Various Locations, 050 646 7792,
*www.animalcarecentre.biz*
**Deira Veterinary Clinic** Deira, 04 258 1881,
**Energetic Panacea** Jumeira, 04 344 7812,
*www.energetic-panacea.com*
**European Veterinary Center** Trade Centre,
04 343 9591
**Jumeirah Veterinary Clinic** Jumeira, 04 394 2276
**Modern Veterinary Clinic** Umm Suqeim, 04 395 3131
**Nad Al Shiba Veterinary Clinic** Nad Al Sheba,
04 340 1060, *www.nadvethosp.com*
**Veterinary Hospital** Umm Suqeim, 04 344 2498,
*www.vet-hosp.com*

# EDUCATION

There is no cause for concern that your child's
education will suffer as a result of going to school
in Dubai; on the contrary, many parents report
satisfaction with the way a multicultural upbringing
results in well-rounded, worldly wise children.

Something you can't escape, unfortunately, is
paying high school fees – as an expat, your child
will have to go to private school, and it will cost you
a pretty penny. So before you hand over wads of
your hard-earned cash, it is really worth doing your
research and picking a school that suits the needs
of your child best. Have a chat with other parents
for word-of-mouth recommendations, or ask your

company's HR departments which schools they are
used to dealing with. And as Dubai traffic can be a
nightmare, it makes sense to look at schools near your
home or office as a starting point.

School terms run to a similar calendar to education
systems in the UK and USA, with the academic year
starting in September after a long summer holiday.

## Nurseries & Pre-Schools

Some nurseries accept babies from as young as 3
months, although most prefer to take on children
who are at walking age (around 12 months). Fees and
timings vary dramatically so it's best to call around and
visit a few nurseries to get an idea of what's available.
As a general rule of thumb, most nurseries are open
for four or five hours in the morning and charge
anything from Dhs.3,000 to Dhs.12,000 per year.

The more popular nurseries have long waiting lists
so you should enrol your child before he or she is even
born. Some of the bigger primary schools also have
nursery sections – if you've got a primary school in
mind for your child, it's worth checking to see if they
have a nursery, as this may help you secure a place a
few years down the line.

There are a number of factors to consider when you
are looking for a nursery and it is always a good idea
to take your time to visit a number of schools.

Try to drop in during the day so that you can have a
look at the facilities while there are children in school.
Many of the nurseries in Dubai operate morning hours
which may rule them out if you are working. However,
many also run late classes for an extra fee, while a
number of them have early-bird drop-offs as well
as running term break classes and summer school.
Another factor worth thinking about when selecting
your child's nursery is whether or not the school
provides meals – having to make a packed lunch every
morning when you're trying to get ready for work may
not be suitable for you.

### The Montessori Way

Montessori is a popular teaching method that
encourages a more flexible approach to learning
than a strict academic curriculum. Children are
encoraged to discover new things through
imaginative play, social interaction and physical
activity. The method encourages children to
develop their own instinct to learn and is a good
foundation for the International Baccalaureate
curriculm. There are numerous Montessori
nurseries in Dubai including: Baby Land (p.152),
Gulf Montessori Dubai (p.152), Yellow Brick Road
(p.156), Tiny Home (04 349 3201), First Steps (p.152),
Ladybird Nursery (p.154), and Little Land (p.154).

Associated member of

**RSPCA**

**WSPA**
World Society for the Protection of Animals

# K9 FRIENDS

K9 Friends is a voluntary organisation that rescues and rehomes stray and abandoned dogs here in the UAE. Our finances are solely dependent on fund raising and donations kindly given by the general public.

**If you can:**

- Give a dog a home
- Foster a dog until a permanent home can be found for it
- Help with fundraising and marketing or organising events
- Give some of your time to help with our rescue dogs
- Sponsor a kennel or a dog on an annual basis to help pay expenses

Please give us a call on 04 885 8031 or email us at k9@emirates.net.ae

Our proud supporter

www.k9friends.com

# Education

## Alphabet Street Nursery

Al Manara St, Rd 8A Umm Suqeim **04 348 5991**
www.alphabetstreetnursery.com
Map **1 U4** Metro **First Gulf Bank**
Alphabet Street employs a mix of the Montessori
teaching method and the Early Years & Foundation
Stage Programme (UK), to develop each child's
communication, control, and coordination. It offers
flexible early morning drop off, with the possibility of
a 07:30 start, and also provides holiday care outside of
term time. Late class available until 17:30.
Age range: 14 months to 5 years.

## Baby Land Nursery

Nr Choithram Al Wasl Rd Umm Suqeim **04 348 6874**
www.babylandnursery.com
Map **1 T4** Metro **First Gulf Bank**
Baby Land uses Montessori methods to encourage
learning through play and exploration. Children
participate in a series of practical activities specially
designed to improve independence, concentration,
hand-eye coordination, fine motor skills, patience
and judgement. Baby Land offers late classes until
16:00 and a summer school. Age range: 12 months to
4.5 years.

## The Blossom Nursery

28-30 Umm Al Sheif Road Jumeira **055 687 7379**
www.blossomdubai.com
Map **2 B4** Metro **Al Quoz**
Opened in 2009, The Blossom Nursery focuses on
all-round development of children through varied
methods of learning. Based on the International
Early Years Curriculum, structured play programmes
are set to include dance, drama, music, water play,
and foreign languages. A 'smartbook' record will
keep parents informed of their child's development,
and there's a high priority placed on parent-staff
interaction.

## British Orchard Nursery

Villa 20A, St 33, Al Mankool Bur Dubai
**04 398 3536**
www.britishorchardnursery.com
Map **2 K4** Metro **Karama**
This nursery follows the British national curriculum,
and the guidelines of OFSTED, the schools regulator
in the UK. Timings are from 08:00 to 12:30 and there
are two out-of-school daycare clubs, Little Apples and
Breakfast Club, which run from 07:30 to 17:00. Parents
can also log on to a secure website and see what their
children are up to through the in-class CCTV. There's
another branch in Jumeira (04 395 3570).

## The Children's Garden

Green Community Dubai Investment Park
**04 885 3484**
www.childrensgarden.ae
Map **1 H9**
Offering early years education to pre-schoolers from
2 to 5 years, Children's Garden features an innovative
curriculum which focuses on the attainment of
knowledge through creativity. Languages form an
integral part of this and children will be taught in at
least two languages, becoming fluent in both after
three years. A Taaleem school, The Children's Garden is
located in the Green Community, in custom-
built premises.

## Emirates British Nursery

Off Al Wasl Rd Umm Suqeim **04 348 9996**
www.ebninfo.ae
Map **1 S5** Metro **First Gulf Bank**
Emirates British Nursery regards playtime as an
important factor in a child's early development. Both
locations (the other is in Mirdif, 04 288 9222) are
spacious and well planned, with multilingual staff and
an in-house nurse. A summer school (a lifesaver for
working mums) is available during July and August.
Late class available until 15:00.
Age range: 11 months to 4 years.

## First Steps Nursery School

Opp Burj Al Arab Umm Suqeim **04 348 6031**
www.firststepsdubai.ae
Map **1 S4** Metro **Mall of the Emirates**
Previously known as Fantasy Land this Montessori
nursery opens from 07:30 to 18:00 and caters for
ages 18 months to five years. They encourage child
development through arts and crafts, reading,
educational videos and indoor and outdoor play
areas. They open on Saturdays when they also accept
children up to the age of 10. In addition they run
summer camps.

## Gulf Montessori Dubai

Garhoud Village Garhoud **04 282 7046**
www.gulfmontessori.com
Map **2 N7** Metro **GGICO**
Gulf Montessori Nurseries have fully equipped
Montessori classrooms, an art room, swimming pool
and large outdoor play area. They accept children
between 2 and 5 years and children are required to
wear a uniform.

## Jumeirah International Nursery School

Nr Jumeira Post Office, St 13 Jumeira **04 349 9065**
www.jinschools.com
Map **2 F4** Metro **Financial Centre**
One of the oldest nurseries in Dubai, Jumeirah
International Nursery follows the standards set by the

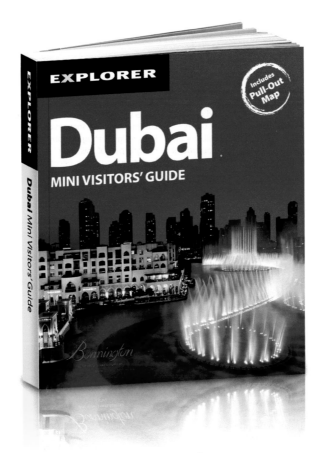

Pocket sized
and plentiful

**Dubai Mini Visitors' Guide**

Maximising your holiday, minimising your hand luggage

www.explorerpublishing.com

# Education

UK Ofsted, and individual care and attention is given in a safe and balanced environment. Classes run from 08:00 to 12:30. Another branch off the Al Wasl Road near Jumeirah Primary School offers early drop-offs at 07:30 and late classes until 17:00 (04 394 5567). Age range: 18 months to 4.5 years.

## Kids Island Nursery
**Off Beach Rd** Umm Suqeim **04 394 2578**
www.kidsislandnursery.com
Map **2 B3** Metro **Al Quoz**
Kids' Island aims to create a relaxed and caring atmosphere, in which children follow the British curriculum. The nursery is open all year round, thanks to the summer school. There are large, shaded outdoor play areas, an activity room and playroom. Late class available until 13:30. Age range is 13 months to 3 years. Another branch in Jumeira 3 called Cocoon Nursery (04 394 9394) is aimed at children between 3 and 4 years.

## Kids Cottage Nursery School > *p.155*
**Off Beach Rd** Umm Suqeim **04 394 2145**
www.kids-cottage.com
Map **2 B4** Metro **Al Quoz**
This cheerful nursery with good facilities offers an activities-based curriculum for children over the age of 12 months. Parents can check up on their kids via a webcam (access is password protected). Early class is available from 07:30. Age range: 12 months to 4 years.

## The Knightsbridge Nursery School
**Burj Bungalow 24, St 17** Umm Suqeim **04 348 1666**
www.theivychild.com
Map **1 S4** Metro **First Gulf Bank**
The Knightsbridge Nursery School was founded in 2006. Located near Jumeirah Beach Hotel, it takes children from 4 months to 4.5 years old. Classes are based on the British curriculum and run for 50 weeks of the year. Opening hours of 07:30 to 18:00 make it convenient for working parents to drop off and pick up.

## Ladybird Nursery
**Nr Post Office** Al Wasl **04 344 1011**
www.ladybirdnursery.ae
Map **2 E4** Metro **Business Bay**
Ladybird strikes an interesting balance between a traditional nursery and a Montessori school, by providing the usual bright and cheerful environment, toys, dressing up clothes and soft play. Late class available until 13:30. Age range: 18 months to 4.5 years.

## Little Land Montessori
**Beach Rd** Umm Suqeim **04 394 4471**
www.littleland-montessori.net
Map **1 U3** Metro **First Gulf Bank**
Jointly owned by a neonatal specialist and a qualified Montessori teacher, this professional team has created a relaxing environment. The six classes are split according to age. A late class is available until 14:00. Age range: 15 months to 4 years.

## Little Woods Nursery
**St 4C, Villa 82** Al Safa **04 394 6155**
www.littlewoodsnursery.com
Map **2 A4** Metro **Al Quoz**
Catering for infants aged 40 days to 4 years, this well-equipped Safa-based nursery has a strong emphasis on child learning through interaction with others and individual development, within a structured framework. Early morning drop-off and late pick-up are offered.

## The Palms Nursery
**Villa 45 St 25B** Jumeira **04 394 7017**
www.palmsnursery.com
Map **2 C4** Metro **Business Bay**
Now in its new spacious home on Street 25B, Palms Nursery has six classrooms and seven outdoor play areas. The curriculum is intended to help children acquire the skills and values that enable them to develop socially, physically and emotionally. Late class available until 13:30. Age range: 22 months to 4 years.

## Safa Kindergarten Nursery
**Nr Shangri-La, off Sheikh Zayed Rd** Al Safa
**04 344 3878**
www.safanurseries.com
Map **2 F5** Metro **Burj Dubai**
This nursery follows the British curriculum with Montessori principles. Activities include educational play, singing, playhouse activities and water play. Arabic or French as a second language are introduced to children above the age of 3. Field trips to various locations are arranged throughout the year, and there are annual event days. Late classes run until 14:00. Age range: 2 to 4 years.

## Seashells Nursery
**Nr Mall of the Emirates** Al Barsha **04 341 3404**
www.seashellsnursery.com
Map **1 R6** Metro **Mall of the Emirates**
Seashells follows the British curriculum, has two indoor playrooms, an indoor gym, a project room for cooking and fun experiments, and outdoor shaded play areas. The children can join in library, show and tell, recycling activities and field trips. A holiday school programme is available. Age range: 18 months to 4 years.

**Kids CottageNursery**
*early years matter*

**Did you know that 85% of brain development occurs by the age of 5?**

- **Our Guiding Philosophy**
  the first 5 years of life are critical to a child's development and lifetime success.

- **Our Approach**
  A holistic programme that offers relationships and experiences which greatly influence all round development.

nformative nursery tours are conducted on request....come and experience our 'enabling environment'

• 04 3942 145     • www.kids-cottage.com     • kcndubai@eim.ae

# Education

## Small World Nursery

**Rd 16, Nr Jumeirah Beach Rd** Jumeira **04 349 0770**
www.smallworldnurserydubai.com
Map **2 H3** Metro **Al Jafiliya**
Small World offers a balanced educational structure,
combining academic learning with physical education.
The well-equipped facilities include a sandy play
space, discovery garden, swimming pool and outside
play area. There is a late class until 13:30. There is
another branch in Umm Suqeim called Child's Play (04
348 0788) which offers a mixture of the UK curriculum
and Waldorf-Steiner philosophy, a swimming pool,
and a late class until 15:00. Age range: 1 to 4.5 years.

## Super Kids Nursery

**Off Street 15, St 23C** Mirdif **04 288 1949**
www.superkidsnursery.com
Map **2 Q12** Metro **Rashidiya**
Super Kids is a small but popular nursery that serves
the growing Mirdif community. The focus is on
providing a warm, cosy 'home away from home'
environment. Facilities include a large, shaded outside
play area, an activity gym and a music room. Hot lunch
and transport are optional extras. Early bird class from
07:30 and late class available until 17:00. Age range: 11
months to 4.5 years.

## Tender Love & Care

**Dubai Media City** Al Sufouh **04 367 1636**
www.tenderloveandcare.com
Map **1 M4** Metro **Nakheel**
A popular option for people working in Internet and
Media cities, this nursery has weekly activity plans and
parents are notified of the monthly theme. Facilities
include a gymnasium and garden. The nursery has a
daily 'drop in' service, and a late class until 17:00. Age
range: 18 months to 4.5 years.

## Yellow Brick Road Nursery

**Nr Irish Village** Garhoud **04 282 8290**
www.yellowbrickroad.ws
Map **2 N7** Metro **GGICO**
This huge and very popular nursery (with a long
waiting list) accommodates 180 children in nine
classes and a dedicated baby room. Children are
taught the British nursery curriculum as well as
enjoying outdoor play and swimming in the paddling
pool. A cooked breakfast and lunch are provided. Late
class available until 18:00. There is another branch in
Jumeira 2 called Emerald City Nursery (04 349 0848).
Age range: 4 months to 4.5 years.

# Primary & Secondary Schools

As an expatriate in Dubai, you most likely have no
choice but to enrol your child in private education –
government schools are for UAE Nationals and Arab
expats only. When planning your child's education,
there are several golden rules that will help ease the
process: firstly, if you have a school in mind, get your
child's name on the waiting list as soon as possible,
since the demand for spaces at the more popular
schools is high. Secondly, consider the 'school run'
when choosing your school – Dubai's rush-hour traffic
can turn a short journey into a tedious hour-long trek
every morning. Thirdly, pick a school that offers the
best curriculum for your child: if you are British and
are planning to return home after a couple of years, it
might be best to find a school that offers the English
National Curriculum; similarly, if you think you might
end up elsewhere on another expat assignment after
you leave Dubai, it might be better to choose the
International Curriculum, which will help your child
slot into a wide range of curriculums.

Kids here start school as early as 3 years old (in
schools that offer a foundation or reception year), and

usually graduate from secondary school at around 18 years. Most schools are open from 08:00 to 13:00 or 15:00, from Sunday to Thursday. Ramadan hours are shorter – usually starting an hour or so later and finishing an hour earlier.

## Homeschooling

One of the main reasons for homeschooling in the UAE is to avoid the hefty private school fees. There are very few private schools in Dubai that offer home schooling curriculums. K12 in Knowledge Village offer someone online courses (www.k12.com/int/arabian_gulf). Schools in your home country will be able to provide you with the curriculum, materials and online testing, for a fee. The Ministry of Education do offer home-schooling for all nationalities but the curriculum is only in Arabic. Many expats who have multiple children find that whilst nurseries tend to be more affordable than in their home countries, when it comes to schooling it makes more financial sense to return home where education is often offered by the government for no fee.

School fees are a contentious issue: private education doesn't come cheap. For a good school, you can expect to pay Dhs.25,000 plus per year for KG years, Dhs.30,000 and up for the middle primary years, and as much as Dhs.60,000 per year for secondary school. Ouch. If you're lucky, your company may offer school fees as part of your package. On top of this, you will usually need to pay around Dhs.500 to put your child's name on a school's waiting list, and a registration fee (around Dhs.2,000), which comes off your fees.

Be prepared to accept that there are a lot of school holidays here in Dubai. The summer holidays stretch for 10 long weeks over the hottest months of July and August, when many kids return to their home countries for extended holidays, or attend summer camps. There are also holidays in April and December. Schools close for at least a week twice a year for Eid Al Fitr and Eid Al Adha, and will most likely also open for reduced hours during the month of Ramadan. If one of you is a stay at home parent then this poses few problems in terms of childcare; however, if both of you work, you will need to make sure that you have alternative arrangements for childcare during school holidays and random days off.

## School Inspections
Education standards in private schools are high. The Knowledge and Human Development Authority (KHDA) has been set up to ensure that education in Dubai is delivered consistently and to an acceptable standard. In 2008 and 2009, the KHDA conducted a first round of school inspections, in which a team of international inspectors visited all Dubai private schools and rated them on a number of issues. Of four possible results (Outstanding, Good, Acceptable and Unsatisfactory), just four schools received an outstanding rating. The results achieved by each school determined the amount by which that school could raise its fees, with those schools rated outstanding raising their fees the most, and those rated unsatisfactory raising their fees the least. See www.khda.gov.ae for more information and for a breakdown of each school's result. A new round of inspections began at the end of 2009.

## Which Curriculum?
Choosing the right curriculum for your child can be obvious – for example, if you're planning on being here for a year or two before returning to your home country, it makes sense to pick the curriculum that is offered back home, such as the English National Curriculum or the American Curriculum. However, if you are not sure what your future plans are, you may want to consider the International Baccalaureate Programme (IB), which is compatible with most curriculums worldwide.

There are distinct differences between each curriculum; it is a good idea to do plenty of research before deciding which one is best for your child.

## School Uniforms
Most private schools here in Dubai will insist on students wearing the official school uniform. Each school will use a particular uniform supply shop, and this will be the only place where you can buy official school items. Before heading out and spending a fortune on uniforms, check with the school and with other parents which items are compulsory and which are not: a sturdy pair of black school shoes and a pair of non-marking trainers are usually essential items, whereas a branded school bag is often not.

Uniforms bought from the official suppliers are usually priced very highly, and can often be of poor quality, so if your school offers any flexibility on the uniform issue (such as your child wearing a plain white collared shirt as opposed to a white shirt with the school badge on the pocket), you may want to take it.

A final word on uniforms: if you leave your uniform shopping until the last few days before the beginning of term, chances are you'll get to the uniform shop to find several items have sold out. This is definitely one task where it pays to shop in advance. Find out from your school who their uniform supplier is, and stock up on uniforms as early as possible.

## School Transport
If for whatever reason you are not able to do the school run every morning and afternoon, you can make use of the bus services offered by most schools.

# Education

The advantages are that the bus driver, not you, gets to deal with the traffic every day, and, since school transport has to abide by some strict regulations, you can rest assured that your child will reach school safely. The disadvantages are that it can be a very expensive option: you will pay the same fee whether you live 500 metres or 10 kilometres from the school. Also, if your child is one of the first on the pick-up roster, it will mean a very early start and then a very long ride on the bus as it drives round to pick up all the other kids.

Still, for parents who work or don't drive, school transport is a godsend and you should speak to your school directly about costs and arrangements.

## Al Mizhar American Academy For Girls
11A St, Mizhar 1 Mirdif 04 288 7250
www.aag.ae
Map 2 S12 Metro Etisalat
American curriculum, all-girls' school in Mizhar (near Mirdif) for pupils from Kindergarten to Year 12. The school is equipped with a range of facilities including swimming, basketball, football, volleyball, drama and a band. A swimming pool, gymnasium, well-resourced library, computer labs, interactive whiteboards, art studios, music studios, science labs, and a mini auditorium are all present. KHDA Inspection rating: Acceptable.

## American Community School of Sharjah (ACSS) > p.159
Sharjah 06 522 7583
www.acssharjah.org
ACS offers the American Curriculum and the IB Diploma Programme from its purpose-built campus in Sharjah. It also features the POLARIS programme for gifted, ESL and special needs children. When it opens in 2010, ACS will accept children from nursery to grade 4; it will subsequently phase in other years up to grade 12.

## American School Of Dubai
Street 53B, Building 30 Al Wasl 04 344 0824
www.asdubai.org
Map 2 G3 Metro Financial Centre
This is a non-profit, American curriculum school with primary and secondary sections. The huge campus includes around 70 classrooms as well as two separate buildings for kindergartens. Other facilities include a media centre, swimming pool, computer labs, art rooms and two gymnasiums. The school also partners with external companies to provide a range of recreational activities such as skiing, horse-riding, surfing and sailing. The school is moving to a new location in 2010. KHDA Inspection rating: Good.

## Australian International School
Opp Shj University, Malihard Rd, Dubai-Sharjah border Sharjah 06 558 9967
www.ais.ae
This school is run in partnership with the State of Queensland, offering the Australian curriculum to primary school children. Facilities include large activity rooms, teaching areas for art and music, computer labs, a comprehensive library, conference rooms, a swimming pool and a multi-purpose hall and gym area.

## Cambridge International School
5th Rd Garhoud 04 282 4646
www.gemscis-garhoud.com
Map 2 N8 Metro Emirates Head Office
Cambridge offers the English National Curriculum to primary and secondary level students, including foundation year. The campus is equipped with excellent recreational facilities including a kindergarten playground, a swimming pool, tennis and volleyball courts, science and computer labs, and music and art studios. KHDA Inspection rating: Acceptable.

## Deira International School
Festival Centre Festival City 04 232 5552
www.disdubai.ae
Map 2 M8 Metro Emirates Head Office
Based in Dubai Festival City, DIS offers GCSE/IGCSE, A-levels and the International Baccalaureate programme. Primary, middle and secondary levels, including a foundation year. Facilities within the school include a gymnasium, a full-size track and football field, music rooms, computer and science labs, libraries, a large auditorium and a swimming pool. KHDA Inspection rating: Acceptable.

## Dubai American Academy
Int 4, Sheikh Zayed Rd Al Barsha 04 347 9222
www.gemsaa-dubai.com
Map 1 R6 Metro Mall of the Emirates
DAA offers the International Baccalaureate Diploma and an enriched American curriculum. It takes primary and secondary students, and has an after-school programme. Facilities include computer and science labs, gymnasium, library, swimming pool, athletics track and an auditorium. KHDA Inspection rating: Good.

## Dubai British School
Springs 3 Emirates Hills 04 361 9361
www.dubaibritishschool.ae
Map 1 K6 Metro Jumeirah Lakes Towers
Offering good facilities in the Emirates Hills area, DBS offers the English National Curriculum at primary and secondary levels, including a foundation year. Facilities at the school include a swimming pool, gymnasium and library. KHDA Inspection rating: Acceptable.

# Education

## Dubai College
**Nr Internet City** Al Sufouh **04 399 9111**
www.dubaicollege.org
Map **1 P4** Metro **Nakheel**
Offering the English National Curriculum and a
diverse range of facilities and activities, Dubai College
accepts students from Year 7 (around 11 years of age).
Sporting activities include athletics, rugby, football,
netball, tennis and swimming, in addition to non-
sporting activities such as music, public speaking and
drama. KHDA Inspection rating: Good.

## Dubai English Speaking College
**Academic City** Oud Metha **04 360 4866**
www.descdxb.com
This English curriculum secondary school opened
in 2005 offering Year 7 to Year 13 (12 and 13 are
equivalent to the sixth form in the UK). A dedication
to sport includes rugby, football, netball, basketball,
badminton, volleyball. KHDA Inspection rating: Good.

## Dubai English Speaking School
**Nr St. Mary's Church** Oud Metha **04 337 1457**
www.dessdxb.com
Map **2 L6** Metro **Oud Metha**
DESS first opened in a single room of a villa in
1963, and has since grown into a highly respected
school offering the English National Curriculum
from reception year to year 6. Facilities and activities
include computers, music, swimming, dance, a library
and various sports. KHDA Inspection rating: Good.

## Dubai International Academy
Emirates Hills **04 368 4111**
www.diadubai.com
Map **1 M6** Metro **Nakheel**
DIA follows the International Baccalaureate curriculum
including the primary years programme (PYP), the
middle years programme (MYP) and the diploma
programme (DP). The school has more than 80
classrooms, as well as music, art, dance and drama
rooms, science and computer labs, libraries, swimming
pools, playing fields, basketball and tennis courts.
KHDA Inspection rating: Acceptable.

## Emirates International School
**Jumeirah** > *p.161*
**Al Thanya Street** Jumeira **04 348 9804**
www.eischools.ae/jumeirah
Map **1 T5** Metro **First Gulf Bank**
EIS-Jumeirah was first opened in 1991 as a community
service of the Al Habtoor Group, and was the
first school in Dubai to be authorised to offer the
International Baccalaureate Diploma Programme.
They accept children at primary, middle school and
senior school levels and run an Alumni programme for
graduates. KHDA Inspection rating: Acceptable.

## Emirates International School
**Meadows** > *p.161*
**Meadows Drive** Emirates Hills **04 362 9009**
www.eischools.ae/meadows
Map **1 K5** Metro **Jumeirah Lakes Towers**
The Emirates International School Meadows' Campus
offers the International Baccalaureate curriculum to
primary and secondary students. Facilities include
large classrooms, computer and science labs, a library
and a theatre. KHDA Inspection rating: Acceptable.

## The English College
**Off Shk Zayed Rd** Al Safa **04 394 3465**
www.englishcollege.ac.ae
Map **2 B5** Metro **Business Bay**
EC offers the English National Curriculum and a varied
extra-curricular programme to primary and secondary
level students. The school has a long tradition of
academic and sporting excellence and a varied extra-
curricular programme offers activities such as chess,
rugby, tennis, trampolining, and even rock climbing.
KHDA Inspection rating: Good.

## Greenfield Community School
**Dubai Investment Park** Jebel Ali **04 885 6600**
www.gcschool.ae
Map **1 F11** Metro **Energy**
Located in Dubai Investments Park just beyond the
Green Community, Greenfield Community School
teaches the IB curriculum to primary and middle
years children, as well as to students in the diploma
programme. GCS has excellent facilities and a
progressive special needs policy. KHDA Inspection
rating: Good.

## Horizon English School
**Nr Park N Shop** Al Wasl **04 342 2891**
www.horizonschooldubai.com
Map **2 D4** Metro **Business Bay**
Horizon opened in 1992 with just 15 pupils, and
has expanded to a large complex complete with
top-class facilities offering the British Curriculum for
children from reception year to year six. They have
an additional campus at Safa Horizon School (04 394
7879). KHDA Inspection rating: Good.

## International School Of Choueifat
**Btn Jct no 4 & 5** Umm Suqeim **04 399 9444**
www.iscdxb-sabis.net
Map **1 P4** Metro **Dubai Internet City**
Choueifat offers the rigorous SABIS curriculum – a
unique method of education allowing students to learn
more in a shorter time. The school accepts primary
and secondary level children, including a foundation
year, and new students take placement tests to check
whether they have attained certain standards in English
and Mathematics. KHDA Inspection rating: Good.

# GIVING YOUNG MINDS
## THE RIGHT ENVIRONMENT
# TO GROW.

Opened in 1991, Emirates International School is a community service of the Al Habtoor Group. We offer Kindergarten through to Grade 13. Emirates International School was the first school in Dubai to offer the International Baccalaureate (IB) Diploma Programme having recieved authorisation as an "IB World School" in 1992.

Registration applications are accepted throughout the year.

Our two campuses are located in Jumierah and Meadows.

مـدرســة الإمــارات الــدوليــة
**Emirates International School**
JUMEIRAH

Telephone + 971 (0) 4-3489804

مـدرســة الإمــارات الــدوليــة
**Emirates International School**
MEADOWS

Telephone + 971 (0) 4-3629009

# Visit our website www.eischools.ae

# Education

## Jebel Ali Primary School

Jebel Ali **04 884 6485**
www.jebelalischool.org
Map **1 F5** Metro **Ibn Battuta**
Opened in 1977, JAPS teaches the English National
Curriculum as well as an excellent range of after-
school activities, with separate sites for infants and
juniors. Activities include football, netball, golf,
gymnastics, squash, drama, cooking, music and
computers. KHDA Inspection rating: Good.

## Jumeirah College

Off Al Wasl Rd, Opp Jumeirah Primary School, Nr
Park N Shop Al Safa **04 395 5524**
www.gemsjc.com
Map **2 C4** Metro **Business Bay**
JC offers the English National Curriculum, and as well
as all the regular sporting and cultural extra curricular
activities, the school has trampolining, ballet,
waterskiing, horse riding, rock climbing, and karate.
Accepts secondary level children. KHDA Inspection
rating: Outstanding.

## Jumeirah English Speaking School (JESS)

Nr Shk Zayed Rd Al Safa **04 394 5515**
www.jess.sch.ae
Map **2 C4** Metro **Business Bay**
JESS teaches the English National Curriculum from
Foundation Stage 1 up to Year 6 and it is one of the
most in-demand British schools and therefore has
a long waiting list. The campus has a gymnasium,
music rooms, two playing areas, a football pitch and a
swimming pool. KHDA Inspection rating: Outstanding.

## Jumeirah English Speaking School (JESS)

Arabian Ranches **04 361 9019**
www.jess.sch.ae
Map **1 R12**
A second branch of the successful JESS school, JESS
Arabian Ranches offers the English National Curriculum
to primary school students aged 3 and upwards with
a range of excellent facilities. Naturally, the majority
of the pupils live within the Arabian Ranches complex
making it a close-knit community of parents and pupils.
KHDA Inspection rating: Outstanding.

## Jumeirah Primary School

Nr Park N Shop, Jumeira Rd Al Safa **04 394 3500**
www.jumeirahprimaryschool.com
Map **2 C4** Metro **Business Bay**
JPS offers the English National Curriculum to primary
level students, including foundation year children.
Campus facilities include an active art department,
a specialist music department, a discovery centre,
modern computer facilities, gymnasium, swimming
pool, playing fields and a separate play area for the
foundation stage. KHDA Inspection rating: Good.

## Kings' Dubai

Off Al Wasl Rd (Street 17) Umm Suqeim
**04 348 3939**
www.kingsdubai.com
Map **1 S4** Metro **First Gulf Bank**
Kings' Dubai opened in 2004 and teaches the English
National Curriculum through an innovative, creative
approach; the school accepts primary age children
and offers a foundation year. The facilities include a
purpose-built auditorium, gymnasium, swimming
pool, games court and sports field. KHDA Inspection
rating: Outstanding.

## Raffles International School > p.163

Street 20 Umm Suqeim **04 427 1200**
www.rafflesis.com
Map **1 S4** Metro **First Gulf Bank**
Raffles International School offers the British/
International curriculums to children from nursery
age through to grade 9. The school has two main
campuses in Umm Suqeim, and six nurseries, in
Arabian Ranches, Emirates Hills, The Lakes, The Springs
and Old Town. All campuses have facilities to support
Raffles' Centres of Excellence in science, arts and
sports. KHDA Inspection rating: Good.

## Regent International School

The Greens **04 360 8830**
www.risdubai.com
Map **1 N5** Metro **Dubai Internet City**
Regent offers the English National Curriculum at
primary and secondary levels, including a foundation
year, on its campus in the Greens. Facilities include
state-of-the-art technology, multimedia zones, library,
computer, science and language labs, as well as a
football pitch, playing fields and gymnasium and a
swimming pool. KHDA Inspection rating: Acceptable.

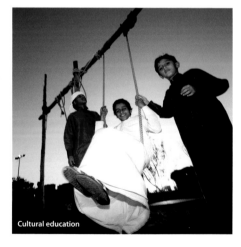
Cultural education

# MAKING OUR MARK
# IN THE WORLD

**RAFFLES**
INTERNATIONAL
SCHOOL

# Raffles International School

**Umm Suqeim West Campus** - IBPYP & Diploma Programme Candidate School*, CLSP and IGCSE
**Umm Suqeim South Campus** - KG Montessori, Cambridge International Primary, Lower Secondary and IGCSE

Competing on an international stage requires a foundation of global standards. Raffles International School provides students a platform for education and development that is recognised the world over. Providing young minds the finest holistic education for personal and professional success.

**RAFFLES PROVIDES STUDENTS FROM OVER 60 COUNTRIES:**
• State-of-the-art facilities • Effective student-teacher ratio • Centres of Excellence for Science, the Arts, and Sports Including FC Barcelona Soccer Academy • A wide variety of additional languages including French, German, Mandarin, and English Language Support.

\* Only schools authorized by the IB organization can offer any of its three academic programmes: The Primary Years Programme (PYP), the Middle Years Programme (MYP) , or the Diploma Programme. Candidate status gives no guarantee that authorization will be granted.

EMAAR
Education

For registration Call  800 723 3537, 800 RAFFLES (Toll Free) or +9714 427 1200 or visit www.rafflesis.com

# Education

Family & Education

## Repton School > p.165
Nad Al Sheba 3 & 4 Nad Al Sheba 04 426 9393
www.reptondubai.org
This prestigious school offers the English National
Curriculum to primary and secondary level students
and has premium facilities on its custom-built campus.
Repton is also the first school in Dubai to offer
boarding – students can board on a weekly or per-
term basis. KHDA Inspection rating: Good.

## Royal Dubai School
Off Airport Rd, Opp Arabian Center Mirdif
04 288 6499
www.royaldubaischool.com
Map 2 S12 Metro Rashidiya
Royal Dubai offers the English National Curriculum to
primary (from foundation year) and secondary level
students on its six-acre campus in Mizhar (near Mirdif).
School facilities are wide ranging and include music
and drama studios, art and science rooms, ICT suites
and a library. A large, multi-purpose sports hall has
been built along with a sports field, a 25m swimming
pool and covered play areas. KHDA Inspection rating:
Acceptable.

## The Sheffield Private School
Al Qusais 04 267 8444
www.sheffieldprivateschool.com
Map 2 T6 Metro Al Nadha
Currently accepting primary school students,
including foundation year, Sheffield Private School
offers the English National Curriculum. Facilities
include music and art studios, an ICT lab, covered play
areas, plus pools for swimming and wading. There
are plans to eventually offer schooling up to Year 13.
KHDA Inspection rating: Acceptable.

## St Andrews International School
Villa # 19, St 43 A Al Safa
04 394 5907
www.british-ild.com
Map 2 B4 Metro Business Bay
St Andrews follows the International Primary
Curriculum and a neuro-developmental programme,
based on the belief that children learn better when
they have personal coaching to help develop the main
senses. Its staff includes occupational, play, speech
and educational therapists as well as teachers.

## St. Mary's Catholic High School
Opp Iranian Club Oud Metha 04 337 0252
www.stmarysdubai.com
Map 2 L6 Metro Oud Metha
Founded in 1968, St Mary's retains the discipline
of a convent education but welcomes all religions.
The school teaches the English National Curriculum
to primary and secondary students. In addition to

various sports activities, other activities include
drama, music, debating, cookery and chess. KHDA
Inspection rating: Good.

## Star International School
Nr New Airport Terml Al Twar 04 263 8999
www.semsintl.com/altwar
Map 2 R8 Metro Al Qusais 1
Star International School Al Twar offers the English
National Curriculum and a day boarding facility, so
that you can leave your child at the school under full
supervision until 16:30. Primary and Secondary levels.

## Star International School Mirdif
Uptown Mirdif Mirdif 04 288 4644
www.starschoolmirdiff.com
Map 2 R12 Metro Rashidiya
This new school offers the English National Curriculum
from foundation year to year six, and will phase in
secondary school levels over the next few years.
With a 700 seat auditorium the school aims to be an
important location for the promotion and teaching of
arts and culture in the community KHDA Inspection
rating: Good.

## Star International School Umm Sheif
Umm Al Sheif 04 348 3314
www.semsintl.com
Map 1 S5 Metro First Gulf Bank
One of three Star International schools in Dubai
teaching the International Curriculum. A bright and
modern campus with great facilities for primary years.
KHDA Inspection rating: Acceptable.

## Universal American School Dubai
Festival Centre Festival City 04 232 5222
www.uasdubai.ae
Map 2 M8 Metro Emirates Head Office
UASD follows a full American curriculum culminating
with the American high school diploma. The school
accepts primary and secondary level students. The
campus has a gymnasium, Olympic size track and
football field, music rooms, art rooms, computer
and science labs, libraries, a large auditorium and a
swimming pool. KHDA Inspection rating: Acceptable.

## Uptown High School
Off Amman Street, Muhaisnah
04 264 1818
www.taaleem.ae
Map 2 T9 Metro Etisalat
Uptown High offers the International Baccalaureate
Middle Years Programme (MYP) and Diploma
Programme (DP) for students aged 11 to 19, many
coming from Uptown Primary. A variety of extra-
curricular activities and overseas trips are organised
for students. KHDA Inspection rating: Acceptable.

www.reptondubai.org

I shall not personify King Lear for personal gain.
I shall not personify King Lear for personal gain.
I shall not personify King Lear for personal gain.
I shall not personify King Lear for personal gain.
I shall not personify King Lear for personal gain.
I shall not personify King Lear for personal gain.
I shall not personi

**The best of British education in the Middle East.**
Now accepting applications for the Day and Boarding School.

Repton School in Dubai is the first Boarding school for girls and boys in the UAE, a school with 450 years of tradition. A school proud to be the first of its kind in the region. Repton offers the National Curriculum for England and was granted IB World status in 2009.

Our Boarding houses represent the very pinnacle of educational facilities on a 1.3million sq. ft. campus in Nad Al Sheba, the largest in the region. Become part of our growing community – contact Repton School today and enquire about our Day School, Full Boarding and Weekly Boarding programmes or visit our website for more information.

To register, or for more information please contact:
**Mr. Neil Macfarlane Boarding Admissions**
+971(0)4 426 9315 +971(0)4 426 9393
neil.macfarlane@reptondubai.org

Repton
School
Founded UK 1557, Dubai 2007

# Education

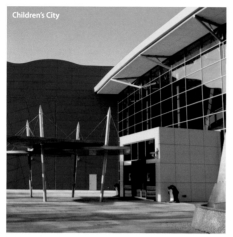
Children's City

## Uptown Primary School
**Cnr Algeria Rd and Rd 15** Mirdif **04 288 6270**
www.uptownprimary.ae
Map **2 Q12** Metro **Rashidiya**
Uptown Primary follows the International
Baccalaureate and accepts children from the age of
4 for its Primary Years Programme (PYP), and houses
an early learning centre developed specifically for
the under 6s. Facilities include a swimming pool,
gymnasium, library, computer labs, art studios, music
rooms, safe play areas and science labs. Students can
remain here into the Middle Years Programme (MYP).
KHDA Inspection rating: Good.

## Wellington International School
**Opp Mall of the Emirates** Al Sufouh **04 348 4999**
www.wellingtoninternationalschool.com
Map **1 Q4** Metro **Mall of the Emirates**
Wellington is renowned for its facilities (Prince Michael
of Kent is its patron), and offers the English National
Curriculum as well as the IB Diploma Programme.
Unique features in the school include an observatory,
TV station, creative garden and ICT, art and music
suites. It accepts students for primary and secondary
school. KHDA Inspection rating: Good.

## The Westminster School
Al Qusais **04 298 8333**
www.gemsws-ghusais.com
Map **2 S6** Metro **Stadium**
Westminster accepts children from Key Stage 1 (age 3)
up to Year 12 (age 16), and follows the English National
Curriculum. The school has 120 classrooms and a
multi-purpose auditorium. Laboratories for biology,
chemistry and physics are provided for the more
senior pupils along with three computer labs and
three libraries. KHDA Inspection rating: Acceptable.

## The Winchester School
**The Gardens** Jebel Ali **04 882 0444**
www.thewinchesterschool.com
Map **1 G5** Metro **Ibn Battuta**
Apart from a varied extra-curricular programme,
Winchester teaches the English National Curriculum
to primary school children. Facilities include a multi-
purpose auditorium, a sports field, music, art and
craft rooms, science and computer labs, a library and
audiovisual rooms. Foundation year is also available.
KHDA Inspection rating: Acceptable.

# University & Higher Education
Upon leaving school, children of expat families
have traditionally returned to their home country
to continue with higher education, but Dubai does
have a growing number of internationally recognised
universities and colleges offering degree and
diploma courses in the arts, sciences, business and
management, and engineering and technology. There
are also a number of opportunities for post-graduate
courses. Many institutions are based at Knowledge
Village near Media and Internet Cities – for more info
visit www.kv.ae. Dubai Academic City, on the outskirts
of Dubai, will house a number of tertiary institutions
and is due for completion by 2012.

Several business schools have also opened recently,
offering MBAs and other professional qualification
for those looking to advance their careers. A number
of UK institutions have shown enthusiasm in tapping
in to this potentially lucrative market. The London
Business School (www.london.edu/dubai-london) is
based in DIFC, as is Cass (www.cass.city.ac.uk/mba/
dubai, formerly known as City University Business
School). The latter specialises in energy and Islamic
finance. Warwick Business School (www.wbs.ac.uk) has
been offering MBAs in Dubai since 2003.

## Destination Education
Academic City (www.diacedu.ae) is a dedicated
tertiary development built to house a whole host
of international universities including American
University in the Emirates, Birla Institute of Technology
& Science Pilani, Cambridge College International
Dubai, Dubai English Speaking College, EHSAL, French
Fashion University Esmod, Hamdan Bin Mohamed
e-University (HBMeU), Heriot-Watt University Dubai
Campus, Hult International Business School, Institute
of Management Technology, Islamic Azad University,
JSS Education Foundation, Mahatma Gandhi
University, MAHE, Manipal-Dubai Campus, Manchester
Business School Worldwide, Michigan State University
Dubai, Middlesex University, Murdoch University
International Study Centre Dubai, PIM International
Center, S P Jain Center of Management, SAE Institute,
Saint-Petersburg State University of Engineering and
Economics, Shaheed Zulfikar Ali Bhutto Institute of

# Welcome to the
# Alliance Française of Dubai

## Our mission :

To promote contemporary arts and emerging artists as well as the French language and academic and intellectual exchanges

www.afdubai.com
info@afdubai.com
+ 971 (0)4 335 87 12

# Education

Science and Technology (SZABIST), Syrian Virtual University, The British University in Dubai, The University of Exeter, The University of Wollongong in Dubai (UOWD), Universitas 21 Global Pte Ltd, University of Bradford and University of Phoenix.

## Education UK Exhibition

Organised annually by the British Council, Education UK Exhibition (EDUKEK) is part of an innitiative to enhance educational relations between the UK and the UAE. Students from across the UAE can attend the event in order to gather information on UK universities, whether they have campuses here in the UAE or in the UK. The 2010 event was scheduled for 17-18 January in Dubai. For more information check out www.educationuk.org/me.

## Knowledge Village

Knowledge Village prides itself on creating an environment conducive to education, the business of education and networking. The operating rules and regulations are relatively straightforward and they simplify the application process for a one-year student's resident visa, too. Some of the tertiary institutions to be found here are: European University College Brussels, Institute of Management Technology, Islamic Azad University, Mahatma Ghandi University, UAE University, Royal College of Surgeons and the University of New Brunswick in Dubai. Find out more on www.kv.ae.

## Public Universities and Colleges

The Higher Colleges of Technology and Zayed University are the two most prominent local universities in Dubai. The HCT is the largest with around 16,000 students (all UAE national) studying at 16 campuses across the UAE offering diplomas, high diplomas, bachelors and masters across over 80 programmes. Previous to 2009, Zayed University also only offered programmes to UAE nationals, however they now invite UAE residents and international students to apply, see p.172.

## The American College Of Dubai

**Opp Dubai Festival City** Garhoud **04 282 9992**
www.centamed.com
Map **2 N7** Metro **Emirates**
The American College of Dubai offers courses that will provide students with university-level credits allowing them to transfer to institutions in the US, UK, UAE, Canada, Europe, India, or elsewhere around the world. Additionally, associate degrees in the liberal arts, business, and information technology are also available.

## American University In Dubai

**Sh Zayed Rd Int 5** Al Sufouh **04 399 9000**
www.aud.edu
Map **1 M4** Metro **Nakheel**
With its impressive main building that is something of a landmark along Sheikh Zayed Road, the American University in Dubai is a well-established institution with over 2,000 students of various nationalities. Courses offered include business, engineering, information technology, visual communication, interior design and liberal arts.

## American University Of Sharjah

**Sharjah Intl Airport St** Sharjah **06 515 5555**
www.aus.edu
Map **2 C2** Metro **Nakheel**
The American University of Sharjah offers a wide range of undergraduate programmes in areas such as language, literature, communications, business, finance, and various engineering degrees. Postgraduate courses are also offered from the schools of Arts and Sciences, Architecture and Design, Business and Management, and Engineering.

## Boston University Dental School

**Dubai Healthcare City** Umm Hurair **04 424 8777**
www.budubai.ae
Map **2 L6** Metro **Healthcare City**
The Boston University Institute for Dental Research and Education Dubai's faculty members are also Dental practitioners at the Dental Center housed in the same location in Healthcare city. The institute offers postdoctoral training with a three year combined Certificate of Advanced Studies (CAGS) and Master's of Science Degree (MSD).

## British University In Dubai

**Dubai Knowledge Village** Al Sufouh **04 391 3626**
www.buid.ac.ae
Map **1 N4** Metro **Dubai Internet City**
The British University In Dubai, established in 2004, is the region's first postgraduate research based university. BUID offers postgraduate degrees including MSC environmental design of buildings, MSC information technology and PhD programmes.

## Canadian University Of Dubai

**Sheikh Zayed Road** Sh. Zayed Rd. **04 321 8866**
www.cud.ac.ae
Map **2 G4** Metro **Financial Centre**
CUD strives to create an international academic experience for its students with credit transfer if you wish to continue your study in Canada. They offer various accredited degrees including business and marketing, human resource management, interior design and architecture, telecommunication engineering and health management.

KHDA, Academic City

Dubai International Academic City

Children's City

# Education

## Cass Business School

**Dubai International Financial Centre (DIFC)**
Trade Centre **04 401 9316**
www.cass.city.ac.uk
Map **2 H5** Metro **Emirates Towers**
Part of the City University London, the Cass Executive
MBA is targeted towards business executives in the
Middle East, with a focus on Islamic Finance or Energy,
and boasts elite status amongst EMBA programmes
around the world. It is a two year course (with lectures
over the weekends to avoid disruption to the working
week) and is accredited by both the Association of
MBAs (AMBA) and the European Quality Improvement
System (EQUIS). Students in Dubai can also have direct
access to the City of London contacts and can take
electives at the London campus.

## Dubai School of Government

**Dubai World Trade Centre** Trade Centre
**04 329 3290**
www.dsg.ae
Map **2 J5** Metro **Trade Centre**
Established under the patronage of His Highness
Sheikh Mohammed Bin Rashid Al Maktoum the DSG
is a research and teaching institution that focuses on
Arab world politics, public policy and administration,
economics, energy, history and operations
management. They offer two graduate programmes,
the Master of Public Administration (MPA), in
cooperation with Harvard Kennedy School, and the
Executive Diploma in Public Administration (EDPA),
which is awarded by the Lee Kuan Yew School of
Public Policy at the National University of Singapore.

## The Emirates Academy of Hospitality Management

Umm Suqeim **04 315 5555**
www.jumeirah.com
Map **1 S4** Metro **First Gulf Bank**
As part of the Jumeirah Group, the Emirates Academy
of Hospitality Management offers highly respected
hospitality management degree courses including
a BSc in International Hospitality Management,
Associate of Science Degree in International
Hospitality Operations or MSc in International
Hospitality Management. Students internships will be
in Dubai or a Jumeirah hotel overseas.

## Esmod French Fashion University

Academic City Blk 4 **04 429 1228**
www.french-fashion-university.com
The French Fashion University is the only University in
the Middle-East fully dedicated to fashion. Accredited
by the French Ministry of Education they carry

three year BA courses, fashion workshops of three
and six months, trend forecasting masterclasses,
merchandising training sessions for retailers and
individuals, and MBA in fashion management.

## European University College Brussels

**Dubai Knowledge Village** Al Sufouh
www.ehsal-dubai.net
Map **1 N4** Metro **Dubai Internet City**
EHSAL Dubai Campus was one of the first
international universities to offer an MBA programme
in Dubai. Their Bachelor in Business Administration
extends to a Masters and covers small and family
business management, marketing, finance and
risk management, human resources and business
information management. They share the campus
with the European Centre for Languages and
Communication Skills (ECLCS) which offers TOEFL
preparation (Test of English as a Foreign Language),
Arabic, French, German, Spanish and Dutch.

## Heriot-Watt University Dubai

Academic City **04 361 6999**
www.hw.ac.uk./dubai
One of the UK's oldest universities, Heriot-Watt has
now opened a campus at Academic City in Dubai
(with an office at Knowledge Village). The university
offers undergraduate and postgraduate courses in
business, management, finance, accounting, and IT.

## Manipal Academy of Higher Education

**Dubai Knowledge Village** Al Sufouh **04 429 1214**
www.mahedubai.com
Map **1 N4** Metro **Dubai Internet City**
Manipal Academy of Higher Education offers
certificate programmes, bachelors and masters
degree programmes in a range of subjects including
information systems, media and communications, and
fashion and interior design.

## Michigan State University in Dubai

Dubai International Academic City **04 436 1500**
www.dubai.msu.edu
This non-profit institution offers UAE and international
students Bachelor's and Master's degree programmes
in line with those at MSU in the US. Programmes
covered include business administration, computer
engineering, construction management, media
management, human resources and family
community services. The university encourages a
combination of teaching methods including lectures
and seminars, online classes, and internships/study
abroad options.

# GRADUATE ON PAR WITH INDUSTRY STANDARDS

## RAFFLES CAMPUS
## RESENTS HOSPITALITY MANAGEMENT COURSES IN DUBAI.

The hospitality industry in the UAE is set to grow exponentially in the next five years. It will usher in an enviable spread of career opportunities. However, qualification standards are stringent and you will be required to compete with the best in the industry. For years, Raffles Campus has been providing quality management education to students the world over. We now bring our expertise to our campus in Dubai with internationally recognised hospitality qualifications to suit every strata of experience, focusing on the hands-on training which provides real workplace skills at an operational and a supervisory level.

**PROGRAMMES OFFERED**
- BTEC National Diploma in Hospitality Management (Awarded by Edexcel)
- BTEC Higher National Diploma in Hospitality Management [Culinary Arts] (Awarded by Edexcel)
- Certificate IV in Hospitality (Awarded by Box Hill Institute, Australia)
- Advanced Diploma of Hospitality Management (Awarded by Box Hill Institute, Australia)

**SHORT TRAINING PROGRAMMES**
- Cooking programmes (Adult, Children, Family, or Corporate Teambuilding)
- Customised corporate training in customer service, telephone etiquettes, etc.

**EMAAR**
Education

 To Apply Call + 971 4 427 1427 | Fax: + 971 4 427 1428 | email: enquiries@rafflescampus.ae | website: www.rafflescampus.ae

# Education

## Middlesex University

**Dubai Knowledge Village** Al Sufouh **04 367 8100**
www.mdx.ac
Map **1 N4** Metro **Dubai Internet City**
The UK's Middlesex University recently opened a
campus at Knowledge Village. Students have the
option of studying for single or joint honours degrees,
in subjects including accountancy, business studies,
tourism, human resource management, marketing
and computing science.

## Murdoch University International Study Centre Dubai

Dubai International Academic City **04 435 5700**
www.murdochdubai.com
Murdoch University offers undergraduate degrees in
Business, Environmental Management, Information
Technology, Media and postgraduate degrees in
Business and Media. Their impressive campus houses
a fully professional HD TV studio, a sound recording
studio, two control rooms, an editing suite, a video
editing suite, an advanced editing suite and three radio
studios. Students can transfer all credits to Murdoch in
Australia if they wish to continue their studies there.

## NYU Abu Dhabi

**Behind the ADIA Tower** Abu Dhabi **02 406 9677**
www.nyuad.nyu.edu
Bringing NYU to the Emirates, this research university's
arts and science undergraduate programmes are
affiliated with the US campus. NYU Abu Dhabi opened
its doors in November in 2009 at 19 Washington
Square North, which will serve as New York
University's gateway to its new campus in Abu Dhabi.
The university's approach will be firmly set on campus
where students will learn and develop not just in
the lecture halls and libraries but also in residences,
clubs and campus events. Students across the Arts,
Humanities, Social Sciences, Science and Engineering
will choose from 18 majors and five multidisciplinary
concentrations in addition to the required classes in
their core curriculum.

## Paris-Sorbonne University Abu Dhabi (PSUAD)

Abu Dhabi **02 509 0609**
www.sorbonne.ae
This French-speaking university focuses on a
wide range of majors in Humanities and Law with
undergraduate degrees and masters in archaeology
and history of arts, economics and management,
French and comparative literature, geography and
urban planning, history, international business and
languages, law and political sciences, philosophy
and sociology. Classes are either in French (with
translation) or in English.

## Raffles Campus > p.171

**St 34** Umm Suqeim **04 427 1427**
www.emaareducation.ae
Map **1 U4** Metro **First Gulf Bank**
Raffles Campus runs a hospitality programme in
collaboration with Australia's Box Hill Institute. Courses
are offered on a full and part-time basis. Focus is
on vocational qualifications, including a BTEC in
hospitality, Certificate IV Hospitality (Supervision),
and Advanced Diploma of Hospitality Management.
International work attachment is a feature of the latter
two courses. The specialist campus has a training
centre which includes front office, housekeeping, and
food and beverage facilities for hands-on training.

## Rochester Institute Of Technology

**Dubai Silicon Oasis (DSO) 04 501 5566**
www.rit.edu/dubai/
Currently RIT Dubai mirrors the degree programmes of
RIT in the United States. Masters Degrees in Business
Administration (MBA), Engineering (electrical and
mechanical), Service Leadership and Innovation and
Networking and Systems Administrations. From 2010
an undergraduate programme will be offered.

## SAE Institute

**Dubai Knowledge Village** Al Sufouh **04 361 6173**
www.sae-dubai.com
Map **1 N4** Metro **Dubai Internet City**
This respected Australian film institute, which has
branches throughout the world, has an impressive
multimedia training facility. SAE offers courses
specialising in audio engineering, digital animation
and filmmaking.

## University Of Wollongong

**Dubai Knowledge Village** Al Sufouh **04 367 2400**
www.uowdubai.ac.ae
Map **1 N4** Metro **Dubai Internet City**
The University of Wollongong offers a number of
undergraduate and postgraduate programmes in
business and IT, in addition to certificates and awards
in accounting, banking and management. This
Australian university used to be situated along Beach
Road, but moved to Knowledge Village in 2005.

## Zayed University

Academic City **04 402 1111**
www.zu.ac.ae
While Zayed University has traditionally been a
UAE National only institution, their new campus in
Academic City and the South Campus in Abu Dhabi
now accept female students from all nationalities,
whether international or UAE residents. They offer
both Bachelors Degrees and Masters Programmes in
arts, sciences, business, communication and media,
education and IT.

**3,568 students from 108 countries
UOWD connects you to the world!**

Check **www.uowdubai.ac.ae**
Call **04 367-2400**
or visit us at Block 15, Dubai Knowledge Village

# UOWD

University of Wollongong in Dubai

An Academic Partner of
**DIAC**
**DUBAI**
INTERNATIONAL
ACADEMIC CITY
A member of
**TECOM** INVESTMENTS

Your Australian University in Dubai

# Special Needs & Learning Support

The UAE boasts an excellent private schooling system for expats, although children with special needs are often left sidelined when it comes to quality education.

If your child has physical or learning difficulties, there are several organisations that can help. In late 2009, it was announced by the Ministry of Education that private schools in the UAE would be required by law to provide adequate facilities for children with special needs. While it remains to be seen when or how this ruling will be implemented, recognising that less able children deserve the same quality of education as other children can surely be seen as a positive step, and one which is long overdue.

There are schools who seem to be leading the way in terms of opening doors to children with special needs. The American Community School in Sharjah boasts a state-of-the-art campus and actively addresses the needs of students with various different special needs. Certain other private schools in Dubai and Abu Dhabi will offer places to children with mild dyslexia, Down Syndrome or who are 'slow' learners.

Dr Lesley P Stagg, principal of Greenfield Community School, believes that as long as the school is able to meet the specific needs of a particular child in terms of facilities, curriculum and staff, then there is no reason to turn away a child with special needs. 'We assess each case individually, and our main decider is whether the child will benefit from being educated at our school' says Dr Stagg. 'In terms of special facilities and services, we offer in-class and withdrawal support, we have a therapy room where visiting therapists can work with students with special needs, and we request parents to employ personal assistants ('shadows') in cases where this helps the child remain focused in the classroom.'

Delice Scotto, principal at the Al Mizhar American Academy for Girls, implements a similarly broad-minded approach. 'All children who require learning support work in small groups and individually with learning support teachers according to Individualised Education Plans (IEPs),' she explains. 'With these support systems in place, learning support students at our school can be successfully integrated into mainstream school activities. 'Students are assessed at the admissions stage, and undergo a psycho-educational evaluation,' continues Scotto. 'Out of this assessment come recommendations that serve as a basis for that child's IEP, and as long as that child's needs are able to be met by our learning support department, they will be offered a place.'

There are currently three full-time learning support teachers at the Academy, all of who have Masters degrees in special education from the United States, as well as extensive experience in dealing with students with a variety of special needs, from dyslexia and ADHD to emotional disabilities and the Autism spectrum. At Greenfield Community School, there is a similarly progressive approach to ensuring staff can meet the needs of all children: 'several of our teachers have specialist training in all aspects of special educational needs, including gifted and talented children, and we offer ongoing professional development to raise skills further,' says Dr Stagg.

Dubai Dyslexia Support Group, a non-profit support group that holds regular meetings for families affected by dyslexia, are also a great resourse outside of the schooling system. The group is run by Anita Singhal, who

is well aware of the difficulties facing such families here: 'not all schools offer support,' she says. 'The main problem is finding a school with a learning support unit or specialist help, and unfortunately, awareness is lacking in many schools.'

However, it's not all bad news – according to Singhal, nearly all dyslexic children, bar those with severe dyslexia, can integrate fully into mainstream education with the correct support. And parents have a huge role to play in helping their children overcome learning challenges. 'One of the key things a parent can do is to develop a dyslexic child's self esteem' says Singhal. 'Never compare them with other siblings or their peers, and encourage their strengths rather than focusing on weaknesses'.

Unfortunately, the picture is not so bright for children with more severe learning difficulties or special needs. While in an ideal world it may be desirable for these children to attend 'normal' schools, the truth is that the majority of private schools in the UAE do not have sufficient facilities or support to cope with severe disabilities or meet the special needs of some children. While this may result in, for example, a child with a physical disability not being able to attend a mainstream school despite not having any cognitive impairment, some parents feel that there is little point pushing the issue.

Children with Down Syndrome are among those who find inclusion in mainstream schools a challenge. Although more and more schools are opening their doors to children with Down Syndrome, there are still many schools and nurseries that refuse to allocate places to these children, according to Ingeborg Kroese, co-ordinator 0-5 years, All 4 Down Syndrome Support Group. 'Even those children with Down Syndrome who are in mainstream schools require part-time or full-time learning support assistants who help them access the curriculum,' she says. 'These learning support assistants are funded by the parents, and so financial constraints are a very real problem.' One of the key mandates of the All 4 Down Syndrome group is to encourage early intervention activities (physiotherapy, speech and language therapy and occupational therapy), which can stimulate development of children with Down Syndrome under the age of 5. The group also holds regular talks with the Knowledge and Human Development Authority (KHDA) to discuss ways to increase inclusion of less able children in mainstream education organisations.

Organisations such as the British Institute for Learning Development aim to bridge a gap between private schools that may lack adequate facilities and more extreme solutions in the form of centres for children with severe disabilities. Although it focuses more on learning support and sensory therapy than on helping children with physical disabilities, the institute seeks to address children's learning and behavioural problems through occupational therapy and neuro-developmental therapy (Sensory Integration). Students are supported through work with speech therapists, psychologists and specially qualified teachers. With this approach, Dr Chris Reynolds, who established the institute in 2002, believes that both 'slow learners' and 'gifted learners' can make great progress.

See the list of Special Needs schools and groups on the following page.

# Special Needs Education

## Al Noor Training Centre For Children with Special Needs
Al Barsha **04 340 4844**
www.alnoorspneeds.ae
Map **1 R5** Metro **Mall of the Emirates**
This centre provides therapeutic support and educational and vocational training to 255 special needs children of all ages. A new facility is under construction which will allow the centre to expand its services to 300 children.

## All 4 Down Syndrome Support Group
Various Locations **050 880 9228**
www.downsyndromedubai.com
This support group is open to families whose lives have been affected by Down's Syndrome. The group is part of an awareness raising campaign, and offers advice on health, education and care for people with Down's. Social mornings are held every Sunday.

## American Community School of Sharjah
Sharjah **06 522 7583**
www.acssharjah.org
The POLARIS programme at the American Community School caters for children with special learning needs offering diagnostic testing, extra curricula services and specialist teaching support.

## British Institute For Learning Development
Opp Al Hanna Centre, Nr Rydges Plaza Al Mankool **04 394 5907**
www.british-ild.com
Map **2 B4** Metro **Al Quoz**
This centre focuses on learning support, occupational therapy and neuro-developmental therapy (sensory integration) to address children's learning and behavioural problems. Students are supported through work with speech therapists, psychologists and specially qualified teachers.

## Dubai Autism Center
Satwa **04 398 6862**
www.dubaiautismcenter.ae
Map **2 J3** Metro **Al Jafiliya**
This educational centre offers diagnostic, intervention, family support, training and school services for children with autism.

## Dubai Centre For Special Needs
Al Wasl **04 344 0966**
www.dcsneeds.ae
Map **2 B4** Metro **Business Bay**
A learning institution offering individualised therapeutic and educational programmes to its 130 students. A pre-vocational programme is offered for older students, which includes arranging work placements.

## Rashid Paediatric Therapy Centre
Al Barsha **04 340 0005**
www.rashidc.ae
Map **1 R5** Metro **Mall of the Emirates**
An educational centre offering classes for students with learning difficulties aged between 3 and 15, and a senior school offering functional academic and practical, life skills education for 13 to 17 year olds. Classes are taught in both Arabic and English.

## Riding For The Disabled
Desert Palms Polo & Country Club
www.rdad.ae
A therapeutic horse riding programme for children with special needs.

## Special Needs Families Centre
Karama **04 334 9818**
www.snfgroup.com
Map **2 K4** Metro **Karama**
An educational and vocational training centre for children with special needs.

# Language Courses
**Alliance Française** > *p.167* Umm Hurair, 04 335 8712, *www.afdubai.com*
**Arabic Language Centre** Trade Centre, 04 308 6036, *www.arabiclanguagecentre.com*
**Berlitz** Jumeira, 04 344 0034, *www.berlitz.ae*
**British Council**, 04 337 0109, *www.britishcouncil.org/uae*
**Dar El Ilm School Of Languages** Trade Centre, 04 330 0221, *www.dar-el-ilm.com*
**ELS Language Center** > *p.177* Deira, 04 294 0740, *www.elsmea.com*
**Eton Institute Of Languages** Al Sufouh, 04 433 2423, *www.eton.ac*
**Goethe-Institut German Language Center** Al Sufouh, 04 325 9865, *www.goethe.de/dubai*
**Inlingua** Oud Metha, 04 334 0004, *www.inlingua.com*
**Polyglot Language Institute** Deira, 04 222 3429, *www.polyglot.ae*

# Libraries
**Alliance Française** > *p.167* Umm Hurair, 04 335 8712, *www.afdubai.com*
**Archie's Library** Karama, 04 396 7924
**Dubai Municipality Public Libraries** Various Locations, *www.libraries.ae*
**Juma Al Majid Center For Cultural & Heritage** Deira, 04 262 4999, *www.almajidcenter.org*
**The Old Library** Al Barsha, 04 341 4777, *www.theoldlibrary.ae*

# ELS Language Centers
## The trusted way to learn English

Improve your Skills          Achieve your dreams

## TOEFL & IELTS Test preparation
Essential for achieving the required results

## General English
Improve speaking, reading & writing skills

## Professional Business Communication
Develop your English to enhance your career

### Sessions start every four weeks
### Tailor made business courses available

---

## Children's Sessions
**Build essential English skills - Prepare for IELTS - Improve skills for school**

---

Licensed Training Centers
Qualified native English-speaking Teachers . 100% instructor - led

**Abu Dhabi : 02 6426640**  |  **Al Ain   : 03 7623468**

**Dubai      : 04 2940740**  |  **Fujairah : 09 2244731**

e-mail : info@elsmea.com
www.elsmea.com

Study English | Explore | Succeed

Abu Dhabi 1994/19 Dubai 1995/41 Al Ain 1995/10 Fujairah 15042

Name:
Carmen Soto

Occupation:
MSF Doctor

Dependants:
2800

**MSF volunteer doctors and nurses provide unconditional medical aid wherever, whenever.** Help us help the helpless. **Call (02) 631 7645 or visit www.msfuae.ae or www.msf.org**

MEDECINS SANS FRONTIERES
أطبـاء بـلا حـدود

# Health, Fitness
# & Well-Being

# HEALTH

Both private and public healthcare services are available in the UAE. General standards are high, with English speaking staff and internationally trained medical staff in most facilities but, as in most countries, private healthcare is seen as preferable as you are likely to experience shorter waiting times and more comfortable inpatient facilities.

Under UAE labour law, an employer must provide access to healthcare for its employees. This can take two forms: either the employer pays for a private medical insurance policy, or it pays contributions towards government healthcare and covers the costs of obtaining a health card for each employee (p.181).

## Government Healthcare

In Dubai, the Department of Health & Medical Services (www.dohms.gov.ae) runs the following hospitals: Dubai, Rashid, Al Baraha (aka Kuwaiti), Maktoum and Al Wasl. Dubai Hospital is renowned as one of the best medical centres in the Middle East, while Al Wasl is a specialised maternity and paediatric hospital. DOHMS also operates a number of outpatient clinics. The Iranian Hospital, while not a government hospital, provides healthcare subsidised by the Iranian Red Crescent Society. With the exception of emergency care, you will need a health card to access government health services (see p.181). When you get your health card it will list a clinic or hospital to which you are assigned, although you're not obliged to use this one. In order to see a doctor, you will need to present your health card and a form of ID (ID card, labour card, driving licence or passport) and will be charged a nominal fee for a consultation. Additional charges may apply for further tests, treatment and medication.

## Accidents & Emergencies

Anyone can receive emergency treatment in government hospitals but charges apply to those without health cards. Some private hospitals have accident and emergency (A&E) departments but unless you have private medical insurance, you'll be landed with a large bill. Your best bet is to check with your insurer that you are covered for treatment in a particular hospital before heading there. The table on the inside back cover shows which hospitals have A&E units. Of the government hospitals, Rashid Hospital deals with most emergency cases as it has a well-equipped A&E department. This is the hospital that you're most likely to be taken to if you have an accident on the road. Dubai Hospital also has an emergency unit. Al Wasl Hospital offers emergency services to children under the age of 12 and women with maternity or gynaecological emergencies; they do not deal with trauma cases. The Iranian Hospital has a busy A&E. While finding a place to get emergency treatment is easy, getting there is more problematic as Dubai's paramedic services are somewhat under-developed. Ambulance response times below those in most western cities but the Dubai Health Authority (www.dohms.gov.ae), the Centre of Ambulance Services and Dubai Police, who receive all 999 calls, have been making concerted efforts over the last few years to improve upon these. In 2009, 35 new ambulances were added to the fleet bringing the total up to 135 well-equipped response vehicles. If you witness an accident or need an ambulance in an emergency situation, the number to call is 999. An ambulance will be dispatched to take the patient to the relevant hospital depending on the type of medical emergency. Rashid hospital receives all trauma patients; all other medical emergencies are transported to Dubai hospital with the exception of cardiac, neurological and gastrointestinal patients who are taken to Rashid or a specialty hospital.

## General Medical Care

For general non-emergency medical care, there are a few different options available. Most hospitals have a walk-in clinic where you can simply turn up, present your health or insurance card, register and queue to see a general practitioner. It's commonplace to be seen by a triage nurse who will take down the details of your medical history and ailment before you see a doctor. These departments usually operate on a first come, first served basis. It's advisable to call the hospital prior to visiting to make sure that they operate a walk-in service and to check opening times. If you are on a private healthcare plan, make sure in advance that the hospital is on your insurer's network.

### Health Call

European or North American certified doctors will visit your home, work or business 24 hours a day. It's a good idea to keep the number to hand for emergencies. A house call will cost upwards of Dhs.600 but when you're feeling really unwell, it'll be worth the expense. A Health Call clinic operates in Healthcare City. 04 363 5343, www.health-call.com

Many hospitals and smaller clinics offer family medicine as part of their outpatient services. You can usually call to make an appointment, but there's no guarantee that you'll get an appointment on the same day. If your usual family medicine department has no available appointments but you need immediate non-emergency medical care, they may admit you through the A&E department, but they will advise you of this when you call. American Hospital (p.186) offers a fast-track service through its A&E department for people needing immediate medical attention.

## Finding A General Practitioner

While some people prefer the convenience of walk-in clinics, others prefer to register with a practice where they are familiar with the administrative procedures and can see the same doctor on return visits. There are a number of clinics in Dubai which offer general practice and family medicine and it's worth asking friends and colleagues for recommendations. Most areas of the city have a local medical centre, so if proximity to your home or place of work is important, you should be able to find something nearby.

### Medical History

It's worth requesting a copy of your medical history from your GP practice at home and giving it to your new clinic to ensure your medical background is taken into consideration when you seek medical advice. Most insurance policies don't cover holiday vaccinations, so if you plan to travel beyond the UAE, you can save yourself a lot of money and needles if you have a record of which jabs you've already had.

### General Practice Clinics

**Al Diyafa Modern Medical Centre** Al Diyafah St, 04 345 4945
**Al Mousa Medical Centre** Jumeira, 04 345 2999, www.almousamedical.com
**Al Noor Polyclinic** Naif, 04 223 3324, www.alnoorpolyclinic.ae
**Belgium Medical Services** Umm Hurair, 04 362 4711
**Belhoul European Hospital** Satwa, 04 345 4000, www.belhouleuropean.com
**Dr Akel's General Medical Clinic (GMC)** Jumeira, 04 349 4880, www.groupgmc.net
**Drs Nicolas & Asp Clinic** Marsa Dubai, 04 360 9977, www.nicolasandasp.com
**Dubai London Clinic** Jumeira, 04 344 6663, www.dubailondonclinic.com
**The Dubai Mall Medical Centre** Downtown Burj Dubai, 04 449 5111, www.tdmmc.com
**General Medical Centre** Jumeira, 04 349 5020, www.groupgmc.net
**Green Community Medical Centre** Jebel Ali, 04 885 3225, www.groupgmc.net
**Health Call** Umm Hurair, 04 363 5343, www.health-call.com
**Manchester Clinic** Jumeira, 04 344 0300, www.manchester-clinic.com
**Mercato Family Clinic** Jumeira, 04 344 8844,
**NMC Family Clinic** Al Safa, 04 395 6660, www.nmcgroup.net
**Rosary Medical Centre** Springs Town Centre Emirates Hills, 04 363 8080

## Health Cards

Employers in the UAE must pay for health cover for all of their employees. An employer can decide whether to provide health cards for its staff or pay for a private insurance policy. If your employer provides you with a health card, you are entitled to subsidised healthcare at government-run hospitals and clinics. The health card must be renewed each year, but you only need to take a new medical test when your visa is up for renewal. Your employer should start the process for you, by telling you which hospital to go to. The two common options are Maktoum Hospital and Al Baraha (Kuwaiti) Hospital. Your health card costs Dhs.310.

## Private Health Insurance

If you have private health insurance, you will have access to a network of private hospitals and clinics. Levels of cover vary depending on the policy, so check what you're entitled to. Dental care, maternity and screening tests aren't usually covered as standard, and you may need to have been on the policy for a year before you can receive maternity cover. Before making an appointment to see a healthcare professional, always check whether the clinic or hospital is part of your insurer's network to avoid being landed with the full costs yourself. Your insurer will also provide details about its payment policy; some companies offer direct billing, which means the insurer pays the hospital or clinic directly and you only pay a nominal fee each time you access medical services, while others require you to pay the cost of the consultation, treatment and medication up front and then file a claim to the insurer.

If your employer is paying for your medical insurance, your employment contract will state whether your spouse and dependents are included in the policy. If you plan to cover the cost of insuring your family yourself, you may need to purchase a separate policy for them as it's not always possible to extend existing policies.

### Medical Insurance Companies

**Alliance Insurance** 04 605 1111, www.alliance-uae.com
**Allianz Worldwide** 04 702 6666, www.allianz.com
**American Life Insurance Company (ALICO)** 04 360 0555, www.alico-measa.com
**AXA Insurance – UAE** > p.35 04 324 3434, www.axa-gulf.com
**BUPA International** 04 331 8688, www.bupa-intl.com
**Greenshield Insurance** 04 397 4464, www.greenshield.ae
**Lifecare International** 04 331 8688, www.lifecareinternational.com
**Mednet** 800 4882, www.mednet-uae.com
**Nasco Karaoglan** 04 352 3133, www.nascodubai.com
**National General Insurance** 04 222 2772, www.ngi.ae
**Nextcare** 04 605 6800, www.nextcare.ae
**Oman Insurance** 800 4746, www.tameen.ae

# To Your Health

## Putting On The Pounds

While many people in Dubai spend the greater portion of their time in outdoor pursuits during the winter months, the heat of the summer means that for four months of the year it's easy to fall into lazy ways. In general, people have a more sedentary lifestyle here, and the city's car culture, all-you-can-eat-and-drink brunches and fast-food outlets at every turn see many new expats gaining the infamous 'Dubai stone'. Fortunately there are a number of weight loss groups and nutritionists on hand to help (p.202), as well as ample fitness centres and gyms (p.207) and opportunities to take part in sports (see Activity Finder, p.308) to keep you active and help shift the extra weight.

## Diabetes

Obesity is also a major contributing factor to the UAE's high incidence of diabetes. Recent figures from the Imperial College London Diabetes Centre in Abu Dhabi (www.icldc.ae) show that nearly 20% of the UAE's population suffer from diabetes, with the majority of them being Type 2, a preventable form of diabetes which is strongly linked to lifestyle and eating habits. The government is aggressively promoting awareness campaigns headed up by organisations, such as the Juvenile Diabetes Research Foundation (www.jdrf.org), to educate the population about preventative measures, healthy eating and the benefits of an active lifestyle. If you suffer from diabetes or think you may be at risk, you can speak to your doctor or contact a specialist diabetes clinic such as The Diabetes Endocrine Center (p.190) or the diabetes clinic at Welcare Hospital (p.188). There are also a number of nutritionists who can help you manage your condition through your diet (see Nutritionists & Weight Loss, p.202).

## New Germs

The UAE is a transitory place and with so many people coming and going and bringing new germs with them, you may find that bugs and colds are more common. With the stresses involved in moving to a new place, you may also find that your immune system is impaired for a while and you are not as resilient to germs as you normally are. Generally speaking, though, if you maintain an active lifestyle and a good diet, your immune system will fight off any unwanted lergies before you even know about it. It's worth keeping a closer eye on your kids and if any strange symptoms appear, a trip to the doctors is best, even if it's just to put your mind at rest.

While you're likely to enjoy a generous slice of the good life in Dubai, all-you-can-eat brunches and the party lifestyle will eventually take their toll. Living in hot, dry, dusty conditions can also have an effect on your well-being. Here are some of the common health complaints you should be aware of.

## Sun Safety

It goes without saying that extra sun care needs to be taken when out and about in the UAE. The hot sun and high temperatures are recipes for sunburn and heat stroke if you are not prepared. Sun block is widely available in supermarkets and pharmacies. Sun hats, light, loose clothing that covers your limbs, sun glasses and seeking shade are recommended when out and about in the hotter parts of the day and during the summer months. With high temperatures throughout the year, you should also ensure that you drink enough water to remain hydrated; this is particularly important when you exercise and during the summer months. It's wise to keep a couple of bottles of water in the car in case of emergencies. If you have a breakdown in busy traffic during the summer, you may be faced with an uncomfortable wait while the police or recovery truck comes to the rescue. You should also be aware of any changes to your skin, such as new moles or ones that change shape, colour or bleed. Contact your doctor or a dermatologist if you have any concerns.

## Other Ailments

If you suffer from asthma, you may find that the dusty outdoor environment and the dry, conditioned air indoors aggravate your symptoms and you may need to rely on your inhaler more often than you would at home. A number of medical practices offer asthma clinics, including GMC (p.181).

Sinusitis can also be triggered by the dust, although this is more common among people who have lived in the city for a number of years. Ear, nose and throat (ENT) specialists can advise the best course of treatment and arrange surgery if necessary.

The average working week in the UAE is longer than in many other countries. Spending longer hours in the office can take its toll on your body, making you more susceptible to bugs and colds; it can also make you prone to suffering from stress injuries such as repetitive strain syndrome.

## Mosquito Prevention

Finally, while the WHO declared the UAE malaria free in 2007, mosquitoes are common at the beginning and end of winter, particularly around the water, and the perfect al fresco evening can be ruined by bites from these tiny critters. Mild mosquito repellent sprays and lotions are usually effective enough to keep the mozzies at bay, so you shouldn't need to resort to DEET-based or tropical strength products. If you prefer natural remedies, citronella oil is reportedly an effective mosquito repellant and is available in health food stores such as Nutrition Zone (see Health Food & Special Dietary Requirements, p.375) and Neal's Yard (Wafi, 04 324 5141). To save yourself from being bitten while you sleep, plug-in mosquito repellers are available from most supermarkets and pharmacies.

### Prevention Is Better Than Cure

Well Woman, Well Man and Well Child packages are available at a number of clinics and hospitals including Welcare, American and Al Zahra Hospitals. These care packages involve thorough medical examinations, screenings for common diseases, and routine tests and offer wellbeing advice. You can even get your holiday vaccinations topped up as part of some packages.

Health, Fitness & Well-Being

# Pharmacies & Medication

The UAE has a more relaxed policy on prescription drugs than many other countries and most can be bought over the counter. If you know what you need it cuts out the hassle of having to see a doctor just so that you can get a prescription. Pharmacists are willing to offer advice, but bear in mind that they don't know your medical history. Always tell the pharmacist if you have any pre-existing conditions and allergies or are taking other medication, and make sure that you understand the administration instructions in case these aren't available in English.

You might find it frustrating that certain common medications from your home country are not available here (such as Gaviscon for infants and Pepto Bismol); you can however bring these into the country for your own personal use and often you can find a locally available equivalent. You may find that there are similar products (such as Infacol instead of infant Gaviscon) so it is worth take the medications to the pharmacy and asking if they have something that does the same thing. You may get the impression that your pharmacist is on commission as no doubt he or she will try and sell you accompanying products. There are pharmacies all over the city and a number are open 24 hours a day, such as Life Pharmacy on Al Wasl Road in Jumeira (04 344 1122). Supermarkets and petrol station convenience stores sell basic medications and first aid equipment.

## Prohibited Medications

Certain medications do require a prescription, and some medications (such as codeine, diazepam and temazepam) are banned here even though they are widely available over the counter in other countries. It's a crime to have these medicines in your possession or to take them, unless you can produce an official prescription from your doctor in your home country (but even then you might end up at the police station while it is translated into Arabic). So unless it is absolutely necessary and there's no alternative, avoid medications that are banned in the UAE.

The list of banned drugs changes regularly, so it's best to check with the Registration & Drug Control Department at the Ministry of Health (www.moh.gov. ae) before traveling with any medication.

# Main Hospitals

In general, both private and government hospitals deliver high standards of care in Dubai. Most hospitals offer a comprehensive range of inpatient and outpatient facilities, so if you like a particular hospital but need to see a specific specialist, the chances are the hospital will be able to cater to your needs. Once you have registered with one hospital it is easier to return there for further treatment.

For very specialist treatment, you'll be referred to somewhere else in the city. Many of the services offered in hospitals are also offered in clinics and small practices, so if you have a hospital phobia, then this might be a better option for non-emergency treatment. See Specialist Clinics & Practitioners, p.190. It is worth having a look around the main hospitals before deciding which one suits you – especially if you are intending to have a baby in Dubai. For more information on Having a Baby in Dubai see p.141.

### Al Baraha Hospital

**Nr Naif Rd, Al Baraha** Deira **04 271 0000**
Map **2 P3** Metro **Palm Deira**
One of the older medical facilities in Dubai, this government hospital is commonly referred to as the Kuwaiti Hospital and is situated on the Deira side of the Shindagha Tunnel, on the right-hand side. You're unlikely to use this hospital for treatment, but you might need to come here for your blood test when processing your residency or for a birth or death certificate.

### Al Maktoum Hospital

**Nr Fish Roundabout** Deira **04 222 1211**
www.dohms.gov.ae
Map **2 N4** Metro **Union**
Opened in 1949, this government hospital was the first modern healthcare facility in the region. The place is showing its age, but the facilities are adequate. Today however, the only reason you're likely to visit Maktoum Hospital is to go for the health test for your medical card (there are no emergency or surgical departments). For more information on the medical test, see p.38. Maktoum Hospital also has a department that carries out embalming.

**GOOD HEALTH** Ken Petersen, 32

*I fell ill shortly after arriving in Dubai and before my company had arranged my private medical insurance. Because I didn't have a health card either my only choice was to go to the Iranian Hospital. I visited the General Medical Care department which had a walk-in clinic. I went to the hospital during the middle of the day, when it was pretty quiet and I only had to wait about 15 minutes to see a triage nurse and doctor. I was sent for some investigations and asked to return two hours later for results. The doctor saw me straight away on my return and dispatched me to the pharmacy with a list of drugs, none of which I was charged for. All together I was charged under Dhs.200 and received excellent levels of care.*

Your Healthcare Partner for Life...

MOH 2510/2/1/31/10

The circle of life revolves around those relationships we have with our nearest and dearest. Friends and family provide love and support through all that life throws at us.

It is with this kind of unbreakable bond that Medcare Hospital is one of the leading provider of clinical care in the region.

Just like your loved ones, you can always turn to Medcare Hospital to receive safe, affordable and accessible healthcare to all.

Anaesthesiology • Audiology • Cardiology • Dentistry • Dermatology • Emergency • ENT Endocrinology • General Medicine • Gynaec-Laparoscopic Surgeries • Laboratory and Diagnostic • Neonatology • Nephrology & Dialysis • Obstetrics & Gynaecology • Oral & Maxillofacial Surgery • Orthopaedics • Internal Medicine • Paediatrics • Physiotherapy Plastic Surgery • Psychiatry • Radiology • Skin Care & Cosmetology • Surgery • Urology

Accredited by

| FOR **EMERGENCIES** PLEASE CALL : **04 4079111**
| All major medical insurance companies are accepted.

Sheikh Zayed road, intersection 2, Opp. Safa Park, Gate No. 1, Jumeirah, Dubai

Tel. +971 4 4079100    info@medcarehospital.com    www.medcarehospital.com

MED CARE
HOSPITAL
health first...

# Health

## Al Wasl Hospital
Oud Metha Rd Bur Dubai 04 219 3000
www.dohms.gov.ae
Map 2 K6 Metro Healthcare Cuty
Al Wasl government hospital specialises in obstetrics, gynaecology, paediatrics and paediatric surgery. It has an emergency department that provides 24 hour care, seven days a week to children up to the age of 12 years for medical, surgical and non-trauma cases; women with serious problems relating to pregnancy and gynaecology can also attend the walk-in emergency department. Al Wasl is the only hospital which deals with emergency pregnancies and it has a special baby care unit for premature and sick neonates. For expat residents admitted in an emergency without a valid health card, the charge is Dhs.100 a day as well as your medication bill on top.

## Al Zahra Hospital
Al Zahra Sq Sharjah 06 561 9999
www.alzahra.com
Al Zahra Hospital is the one of the main hospitals in Sharjah. It is a private facility and operates a 24 hour GP clinic and emergency unit, with consultants on call around the clock. Its ENT department has a good reputation and the hospital's special cardiac care ambulance is equipt to respond to cardiac emergencies. Al Zahra Private Medical Centre (p.190) is situated in Al Safa Tower on Sheikh Zayed Road in Dubai, offering a wide range of outpatient services with excellent levels of care.

## American Hospital > p.187
Oud Metha Rd, Opp Mövenpick Hotel Oud Metha
04 336 7777
www.ahdubai.com
Map 2 L5 Metro Oud Metha
With excellent in and outpatient facilities and an A&E unit with a fast-track system, American Hospital is usually pretty busy. Recently expanded, it has top-of-the-range diagnostic equipment and a number of dedicated units including The Heart Center and Cancer Care Center. Its maternity unit is a popular choice among expectant mums with packages for prenatal care and delivery, and private rooms on the labour ward. The medical staff hail from all corners of the globe. You can book appointments online.

## Belhoul Speciality Hospital
Al Khaleej Rd Deira 04 273 3333
www.belhoulspeciality.com
Map 2 P3 Metro Palm Deira
Belhoul Speciality Hospital's nephrology department offers state-of-the-art dialysis machines for kidney disorders. They also have advanced diagnostic technology and health check packages. They also has an emergency room and its own ambulance (04

---

## Dubai Healthcare City

The aim of this new development is to create a global hub for medical treatment, prevention, education and research by the world's most renowned names in healthcare and medicine. City Hospital (p.186) is already open, alongside a range of private clinics and research institutes including Boston University Institute for Dental Research & Education Dubai, American Academy of Cosmetic Surgery Hospital (p.205), Dubai Gynaecology and Fertility Center (p.192), Dubai Bone & Joint Center (p.202), Imperial Healthcare Institute, Moorfields Eye Hospital Dubai (p.198), The Diabetes Endocrine Center (p.190), Dubai Harvard Foundation for Medical Research and Harvard Medical School Dubai Center. For the full list visit www.dhcc.ae.

---

214 0333) and a range of in and outpatient services. Services are efficient with good customer service.

## Cedars Jebel Ali International Hospital
Off Jct 6 Sheikh Zayed Rd Jebel Ali 04 881 4000
www.cedars-jaih.com
Map 1 D4 Metro Energy
Cedars Jebel Ali International Hospital is a private healthcare facility situated near to the Jebel Ali Free Zone. Services include a 24 hour emergency clinic and dedicated ambulance (04 881 4000 and 04 881 8816). It specialises in trauma and occupational medicine. A hospital extension is currently under construction.

## The City Hospital
Dubai Healthcare City Umm Hurair 04 435 9999
www.thecityhospital.com
Map 2 L6 Metro Healthcare City
The first hospital to open in Dubai's flagship Healthcare City, it delivers private healthcare in state-of-the-art facilities. It's maternity unit has a good reputation and is becoming an increasingly popular choice. If you feel deserving of a different class of treatment to the rest of the hospital's patients (and have the wallet to match), you can take advantage of the VIP (very important patient) floor, which boasts a swimming pool, spa, gymnasium and butler service.

## Dubai Hospital
Nr Baraha Hospital Al Baraha 04 219 5000
www.dohms.gov.ae
Map 2 P3 Metro Palm Deira
One of the best government hospitals, Dubai Hospital opened in 1983 but is clean and well maintained. It offers a full range of medical, dentistry and general surgical services. It is large and usually busy but has a very efficient emergency department.

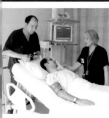

*Feel better . Heal better*

# THE HOSPITAL
## WHERE QUALITY AND TRUST MATTER

### Medical Specialities

· Cardiac Surgery / Cardiac Catheterization · Cardiology
· Cardiopulmonary · Diabetes / Endocrinology · Dietary Counseling
· Endoscopy · ENT Surgery · Primary Care
· Gastroenterology / Hepatology · Hematology · General Surgery
· Internal Medicine · Medical Imaging · Nephrology / Dialysis
· Neurology · Neurosurgery · Obstetrics / Gynecology
· Oncology / Chemotherapy · Ophthalmology · Orthopedics
· Pathology & Laboratory · Pediatrics (Children) · Dermatology
· Plastic, Cosmetic, Reconstructive and Maxillofacial Surgery
· Rheumatology · Sports Medicine & Physical Therapy
· Urology / Lithotripsy (Kidney Stones) · 24 Hour Emergency Service

P . O . B o x :  55 66  Dubai  -  United Arab Emirates
Tel: +971-4-336-7777    Fax: +971-4-336-5176
Website: www.ahdubai.com

The first hospital in the Middle East to be awarded Joint Commission International Accreditation (JCIA).
The first private laboratory to be certified by the College of American Pathologists (CAP)

MOH 1577/2/9/31/8/10

المستشفى الأمريكي
AMERICAN HOSPITAL
DUBAI دبي

Delivering better health in the Middle East

# Health

## Emirates Hospital

**Jumeira Beach Rd** Jumeira **04 349 6666**
www.emirateshospital.ae
Map **2 D3** Metro **Business Bay**
This small private hospital on Jumeira Road may not be the newest of Dubai's private medical facilities but it delivers a high standard of care. Primarily a surgical hospital, it also runs a number of out-patient clinics including a 24 hour walk-in clinic.

## Iranian Hospital

**Al Wasl Rd** Jumeira **04 344 0250**
www.ihd.ae
Map **2 H3** Metro **Al Jafiliya**
The mosaic-fronted Iranian Hospital sits opposite the Iranian Mosque at the Satwa end of Al Wasl Road. The hospital is affiliated to the Red Crescent Society of Iran and therefore isn't strictly a UAE government hospital. It offers its own health card and the fees are very reasonable. There are two cards: one for Dhs.100 and one for Dhs.250 which offer 20% and 40% discounts respectively for in-patient and out-patient services, but even without a card, the prices are very reasonable. In addition, some of the medicines which they prescribe are free. On the downside the hospital is rather busy, particularly at the walk-in clinic during peak hours.

## Medcare Hospital > p.185

**Opp Safa Park Gate 1** Jumeira **04 407 9101**
www.medcarehospital.com
Map **2 D4** Metro **Business Bay**
One of the newest and most modern hospitals in Dubai, the 60 bed private Medcare Hospital offers advanced medical care and emergency services, with a particularly strong maternity department. Staff are qualified to international standards. A satellite clinic Medcare Medical Centre, recently opened in Uptown Mirdif and takes walk-ins.

### H1N1

In 2009, a number of cases of swine flu were reported in the UAE. Although a handful of swine flu cases resulted in death, figures were minimal compared to other affected countries. The Ministry of Health has set up the Technical Health Committee for Combating H1N1 Virus to educate the population on the symptoms and work out a contingency plan should a mass outbreak occur. By the end of 2009, the UAE had stockpiled the vaccine should an outbreak occur. Travellers arriving in the country must pass through thermal scanners at the airport and may be detained and tested for H1N1 if they show symptoms. Tamiflu, the main drug recommended for treating the virus is available on prescription in pharmacies.

## Neuro Spinal Hospital

**Jumeira Beach Rd** Jumeira **04 342 0000**
www.nshdubai.com
Map **2 D3** Metro **Business Bay**
The Neuro Spinal Hospital has an emergency room that is open around the clock. The unit is prepared for all kinds of spinal, neurosurgical and neurological emergencies. The hospital has 40 beds and a multi-national team of specialists, doctors and nurses. As well as spinal treatment facilities, the hospital has a stroke centre for treatment of acute cerebro-vascular accidents and its own ambulance which can be dispatched by calling 04 315 7777.

## NMC Hospital

**Salahudeen Rd** Abu Hail **04 268 9800**
www.nmcgroup.net
Map **2 P5** Metro **Abu Baker Al Sidique**
NMC Private Hospital in Deira has a 24 hour walk-in general practice clinic so advance appointments are not necessary. The levels of service are high and the staff are generally efficient. The hospital has an emergency room and it's own ambulance with attendant doctors.

## Rashid Hospital

**Nr Maktoum Bridge** Oud Metha **04 219 2000**
www.dohms.gov.ae
Map **2 M5** Metro **Oud Metha**
Rashid Hospital is the main government hospital for accident and emergency, trauma, intensive care and paramedic services in Dubai. It's likely that you'll be brought here if you have an accident on Dubai's roads; it's also where most construction site accidents are dealt with and so is always busy. In addition to A&E, it offers diagnostics, surgery, maternity, paediatrics, physiotherapy and a social affairs unit. It also has the only psychiatric ward in Dubai. It delivers a good standard of care but because of its high demand you may be better off seeking non-emergency treatment in another government hospital.

## Welcare Hospital

**Nr Aviation Club** Al Garhoud **04 282 7788**
www.welcarehospital.com
Map **2 N6** Metro **GGICO**
Welcare Hospital's special services include a contact lens clinic, diabetic clinic, holiday dialysis and home call consultations (specialist and GP). Its prenatal and delivery care is considered to be among the best in Dubai. Welcare does postnatal packages for parents and their new baby, which is a nice way to meet other new mums. Welcare also operates primary healthcare clinics in Mirdif (04 288 1302) and Al Qusais (04 258 6466) and an ambulatory care unit in Knowledge Village (04 366 1030) that comes highly recommended. Appointments can be booked online.

# Serious Medical Conditions

Medical facilities for chronic medical conditions are continually improving in Dubai. Here's the lowdown on the most prevalent serious illnesses in the UAE and where to go to receive treatment for them.

If you suffer from a serious medical condition, you'll find a good range of services available in Dubai, and most clinics will help you seek treatment overseas or in your home country if services aren't available here.

Heart disease is the highest cause of death in the UAE with over 40% of UAE fatalities linked to heart problems, according to Ministry of Health figures. The MoH promotes heart disease awareness with regular campaigns to educate people about contributing factors such as smoking, obesity, stress, high blood pressure, diabetes and sedentary lifestyles, most of which have an above average prevalence in the UAE. Care for heart disease patients has improved dramatically in recent years with the opening of the German Heart Centre Bremen (p.191) and the Mayo Clinic (p.191) in Healthcare City and specialist heart units in hospitals such as American Hospital (p.186). Stroke is the third biggest killer in the UAE, after heart disease and accidents and, worldwide, is the most common cause of lifelong disability. Most major hospitals have a neurosciences department offering neurological screening, treatment, rehabilitation; the Neuro Spinal Hospital (p.188) has a dedicated stroke unit.

American Hospital has both a cancer care centre and a paediatric oncology unit. Tawam Hospital in Al Ain has a full oncology department, offering radiotherapy, chemotherapy, haematology, counselling and diagnostics. In the last few years, there has been a concerted breast cancer awareness campaign, much of it driven by the Safe & Sound programme based at BurJuman Shopping Centre, where many outreach initiatives take place. The campaign's website (www.safeandsound. ae) is packed with information on the disease, self examination and fundraising activities. Emirates Hospital (p.188), among others, has a dedicated breast cancer clinic.

With all chronic disease or serious illness it is imperative to seek medical attention as early as possible to improve the chances of survival and minimise any lasting effects. Some insurance policies do not cover pre-existing or chronic medical conditions, so check your paperwork carefully and consider taking out additional cover if you have a family history of disease or are particularly at risk through contributing factors. Well woman, well man and well child packages are available at a number of hospitals and clinics throughout Dubai, including Welcare, American and Al Zahra Hospitals (see Main Hospitals, p.184). These packages are a good way to get an overall health check and assessment of any potential illness to which you may be particularly susceptible. A good package should involve a thorough medical examination, screenings for common diseases, routine tests (such as cervical smears for women) and offer wellbeing advice based on your lifestyle. You can even get your holiday vaccinations topped up as part of some packages.

## Zulekha Hospital

**Nr Dubai Women's College** Al Qusais **04 267 8866**
www.zulekhahospitals.com
Map **2 T7**
The Zulekha Hospital and diagnostic centre contains both outpatient and inpatient facilities, including a 24 hour emergency department and a fully equipped intensive care unit. It is usually very busy so waiting times can be long and the service rushed.

# Specialist Clinics & Practitioners

Whatever your ailment, the chances are you'll find a relevant specialist in Dubai. You don't need a referral to be seen by a specialist, so you are free to seek whatever medical advice is relevant to your condition. If you are not sure what is wrong with you, or which kind of specialist you should consult, you can ask your doctor or ask advice from a hospital. Most places will advise you over the phone to save you the hassle of getting an appointment.

The majority of hospitals also offer a range of outpatient medical specialties (see Main Hospitals, p.184), although many people prefer the more personalised environment of smaller practices for long term medical care. In addition, many general practice clinics offer a range of medical services so its worth checking at your local clinic before seeking specialist services elsewhere (see General Medical Care, p.180).

## Al Borj Medical Centre

**Mazaya Centre** Al Wasl **04 321 2220**
Map **2 F5** Metro **Burj Dubai**
Specialises in endocrinology, dermatology, plastic surgery, gynaecology, paediatrics and general surgery.

## Al Shifa Al Khaleeji Medical Center

**Next to Clock Tower** Deira **04 294 0786**
Map **2 N5** Metro **Al Rigga**
This clinic offers paediatrics, gynaecology, dentistry, internal medicine and orthopaedic medical services.

## Al Zahra Private Medical Centre > p.xv

**Al Safa Tower, Shk Zayed Rd** Trade Centre
**04 331 5000**
www.alzahra.com
Map **2 H4** Metro **Emirates**
A large medical facility offering wellness packages, maternity care and diagnostics in addition to a full range of outpatient services.

## Allied Diagnostic Centre

**Al Diyafah St, Satwa R/A** Satwa **04 332 8111**
Map **2 J4** Metro **Al Jafiliya**
Provides diagnostic services for clinics that do not have on-site facilities. You may be referred here for investigative procedures.

## Atlas Star Medical Centre

**Nr Royal Ascot Hotel** Bur Dubai **04 359 6662**
www.atlasstarcentre.com
Map **2 L3** Metro **Al Fahidi**
Offers general practice, general surgery, ENT, gynaecology and dental services.

## British Medical Consulting Centre

**Jumeira Rd, Opp Mercato Mall** Jumeira
**04 344 2633**
Map **2 F3** Metro **Business Bay**
Western-trained medical staff specialising in cosmetic surgery, psychotherapy, psychology, dentistry, hair transplantation and marriage counselling.

## The Diabetes Endocrine Center

**Dubai Healthcare City** Umm Hurair **04 375 2344**
Map **2 L6** Metro **Healthcare City**
Screening and treatment clinic for diabetes and thyroid problems.

## Dr Al Rustom's Medical & Day Care Surgery Centre

**Nr Jumeira Plaza** Jumeira **04 349 8800**
www.skin-and-laser.com
Map **2 H3** Metro **Al Jafiliya**
A specialist dermatology clinic offering cancer services, laser surgery and cosmetic procedures.

## Dr Mahaveer Mehta Skin Medical

**Rigga St, Al Ghurair City** Deira **04 221 9300**
www.skinlaserdubai.com
Map **2 N4** Metro **Union**
Laser surgery clinic offering treatment for dermatological conditions and cosmetic procedures.

## Dr Mohamed Al Zubaidy Clinic

**Rigga St, Burger King Bldg.** Deira **04 227 7533**
Map **2 N4** Metro **Union**
Dr Al Zubaidy offers dermatology and venereology investigations and treatments.

## Dr Ray's Medical Centre

**Khalid Al Attar Bldg, Nr BurJuman Ctr** Karama **04 397 3665**
www.drmc.all.ae
Map **2 L4** Metro **Khalid Bin Al Waleed**
Offers obstetrics, gynaecology, homeopathy, dentistry and ophthalmology.

## Dr Simin Medical Center

**Villa 155, Nxt to Mercato** Jumeira **04 344 4117**
www.drsimin.com
Map **2 F3** Metro **Financial Centre**
Dermatology, orthopaedics and sports injuries are the main focuses of this clinic.

Health, Fitness & Well-Being

## Dr Taher H Khalil Clinic
**Zarouni Bld, Al Rigga St** Deira **04 268 7655**
Map **2 N4** Metro **Union**
A general medical clinic specialising in hormone therapy including treatment for low fertility, diabetes and thyroid irregularities.

## Dubai London Clinic
**Jumeira Rd** Umm Suqeim **04 344 6663**
www.dubailondonclinic.com
Map **1 T3** Metro **First Gulf Bank**
A long-established clinic with brand new medical and surgical premises in Umm Suqeim. Another branch is located at Festival City (04 232 5751) and Dubai London Dental Clinic is on Al Wasl Road (p.196).

## German Heart Centre Bremen
**Dubai Healthcare City, Bldg.39** Umm Hurair
**04 362 4797**
www.german-heart-centre.com
Map **2 L6** Metro **Healthcare City**
Cardiac treatment, investigation and intervention services, and after treatment care from Germany's most renowned cardiology clinic.

## German Medical Center
**Dubai Healthcare City** Umm Hurair **04 362 2929**
www.germanmedicalcenterdhcc.com
Map **2 L6** Metro **Healthcare City**
Offering medical specialties including urology, andrology, infertility, gynaecology, obstetrics, internal medicine, general and orthopedic surgeries and ENT.

## Health Care Medical Centre
**Jumeira Centre, First Floor** Jumeira **04 344 5550**
Map **2 H3** Metro **Al Jafiliya**
A small practice offering ENT, dentistry and ophthalmology.

## Jebel Ali Hospital
**Nxt to Jebel Ali Primary School** Jebel Ali
**04 884 5666**
www.jebelalihospital.com
A boutique hospital offering luxury healthcare with chauffeur-driven transfers and private suites. They also have an excellent maternity wing

## Skin Sense
The strong sun in Dubai means you should be especially wary of any new moles or irregular marks that appear on your skin, or if existing moles change or grow in size. A number of clinics specialise in looking after your skin, including Mahaveer Mehta Skin Medical Centre (p.190) and Dr Al Rustom's clinic (p.190).

## Mayo Clinic
**Dubai Healthcare City** Umm Hurair **04 362 2900**
www.mayoclinic.org
Map **2 L6** Metro **Healthcare City**
This clinic offers diagnostic and evaluative services, and surgical aftercare. Patients are referred to the Mayo Clinic in the US for treatment.

## Medic Polyclinic
**Khoory Bld, Bank St** Bur Dubai **04 355 4111**
Map **2 L4** Metro **Khalid Bin Al Waleed**
A medical clinic and a diagnostics centre.

## NMC Specialty Hospital
**Nr Dubai Women's College** Al Nahda **04 267 9999**
www.nmc.ae
Map **2 S6** Metro **Stadium**
Facilities including an excellent cardiac care and surgery department, a maternity ward, an allergy department and a sleep lab treating sleep-related problems from snoring to narcolepsy.

## Prime Medical Center
Various Locations **04 349 4545**
www.pmcdubai.com
The Prime healthcare group runs six clinics in Dubai offering a wide range of outpatient services, plus a diagnostics centre in Deira (04 272 0720).

## Wellness Medical Centre
**Jumeira Road** Umm Suqeim **04 395 3115**
www.wellnessmedicalcentre.com
Map **2 A3** Metro **Al Quoz**
Offering primary, secondary and tertiary medical services including surgery, dentistry, family medicine, rheumatology, diagnostics, psychiatry, endocrinology, urology and paediatrics.

# Obstetrics & Gynaecology
Most hospitals and general practice clinics in Dubai offer gynaecologic and obstetric medical services. In your home country you may be used to receiving reminders from your doctor when you are due for a smear test or mammogram; in the UAE you will need to be more proactive, and while a gynaecologist can advise you on how frequently you should have check-ups, it will be up to you remember when you're due and schedule an appointment. If you are looking for a long-term gynaecologist then its worth checking out some of the specialist clinics listed below. Well woman check-ups can be done on a regular basis (usually annually) and offer the chance to get your regular check-ups out of the way in one go, at the same time as giving you a general health check.

The majority of contraceptives are available in Dubai (although the morning after pill is not) and a gynaecologist will be able to advise you on the most suitable form of contraception for you. If you take oral contraceptives, a variety of brands are available over the counter in pharmacies without prescription. Because of the risk of thrombosis, you should make a point of going to your doctor to have your blood pressure checked every six months, just to make sure everything is ok. It's worth noting that while rarely enforced, the law is that you should be married in order to be prescribed or purchase contraceptives.

## Maternity Care

If you are having a baby, the level of maternity care in Dubai is excellent. Among expats, the most popular maternity hospitals are Welcare, American and Al Wasl hospitals (see Main Hospitals, p.184). Al Wasl Hospital may lack some of the private hospital frills but it has an excellent reputation for maternity care and paediatrics. Before you decide on a government hospital, check its policy regarding husbands and family members in the labour ward. Certain hospitals may not allow husbands in the labour ward (although they can be present at delivery and often, if you are persuasive and there are no local ladies admitted, they will allow access).

All government hospitals now charge expats for maternity services and delivery, and costs vary depending on the package you choose. Private hospitals will be more expensive, although if you shop around you may be surprised to find that in some cases the difference between government and private is not as great as you might think.

No matter which you choose, if you have medical insurance check that it covers maternity costs – some have a limitation clause (you normally need to have been with the insurer for at least 12 months before conception) and some may not cover any costs at all.

---

### Breastfeeding Support

A support group for mothers who do, or who want to, breastfeed, Breastfeeding Q&A was established in Dubai in 2006. It provides encouragement and evidence-based information to members, predominantly online, but also during regular get-togethers. Visit http://groups.yahoo.com/group/breastfeedingqa.

---

Private hospitals offer maternity packages that include prenatal care, delivery and postnatal care for you and the baby. But remember that the price you are quoted by the hospital is for the basic 'best case scenario' delivery, and if you have additional requirements, such as an epidural (when the anaesthetist must be present) or an assisted delivery (when the paediatrician must be present), you will be charged extra. If you give birth by caesarean section, the cost is usually significantly higher and the hospital

stay is longer (five days, compared to two days for standard delivery).

If you go to an independent gynaecologist for your prenatal care, you will usually be offered a choice of hospitals and delivery packages, where your doctor can attend you for the birth.

## Obstetric & Gynaecology Clinics

Prenatal care and maternity services are offered at many main hospitals (p.184) and specialist clinics (p.190); the medical facilities and practitioners listed below are those which exclusively offer or specialise in obstetrics, gynaecology and pre and post-natal care. A number of gynaecology clinics offer fertility testing, but only a few clinics offer assisted reproductive technology and IVF treatment.

### Dr Fakih Gynaecology & Obstetrics Center

**Emirates Hospital, Jumeira Rd** Jumeira
**04 349 2100**
www.firstivf.com
Map **2 D3** Metro **Business Bay**
Dr Fakih specialises in IVF and assisted reproductive technology. His clinic is one of the few places in Dubai that offers these services. Gynaecology and obstetric care of non-IVF pregnancies is catered for by Dr Fakih's team of clinicians.

### Dr Leila Soudah Clinic

**Villa 467B** Jumeira **04 395 5591**
www.drleilasoudah.com
Map **2 C3** Metro **Business Bay**
An independent gynaecology clinic offering pre and post-natal care. Dr Leila is affiliated with American Hospital, so most of her patients deliver there.

### Dubai Gynaecology & Fertility Centre

**Dubai Healthcare City, Al Razi Bldg.** Umm Hurair
**04 439 3800**
www.dgfc.ae
Map **2 L6** Metro **Healthcare City**
This clinic is located within the grounds of Rashid Hospital and specialises in assisted reproductive technology. It is the one of the few facilities in Dubai which offers IVF treatment. A range of gynaecological services are also available.

### German Clinic

**Dubai Healthcare City, Al Razi Bldg, 2nd floor 2008** Umm Hurair **04 429 8346**
www.germanclinic-dubai.com
Map **2 L6** Metro **Healthcare City**
A specialist gynaecology, obstetrics and paediatrics clinic designed to meet German standards of healthcare, based in Dubai Healthcare City. Wellness, fertility and antenatal packages are also available.

## Mitera Clinic

**Dubai Healthcare City** Umm Hurair **04 363 5464**
www.miteraclinic.com
Map **2 L6** Metro **Healthcare City**
Dr Rihab Awad has a number of long term patients who have followed her from American Hospital to her new clinic in Healthcare City. She is progressive in terms of stem cell technology and also teaches breast examinations when you have a check up. If you're looking for a long-term gynaecologist and obstetrician then it's worth getting on her patient list, but for a quick check-up you may be better looking elsewhere.

## Primavera Medical Centre

**Dubai Healthcare City** Umm Hurair **04 375 4669**
www.dhcc.ae
Map **2 L6** Metro **Healthcare City**
This clinic is run by obstetrician, gynaecologist and fertility specialist, Dr Rosalie Sant, who comes highly recommended.

┌─ **Working Mums** ─────────────────

Mums that have been in a private sector job for more than one year can claim up to 45 days maternity leave on full pay. This can only be used directly before and after the birth. See Having a Baby p.141, for more.

└────────────────────────────────────

# Paediatrics

Most public and private hospitals and medical centres in Dubai have full time paediatricians on staff, with a growing number having devoted paediatric departments. American Hospital and Welcare Hospital (both private) have teams of specialist paediatric doctors, while Al Wasl Hospital (government) has dedicated paediatric surgeons and neurodevelopment therapists who care for children with special needs and learning difficulties. Dr Anil Gupta at American Hospital, Dr Zuhair Mahmandar at Emirates Hospital and Dr Loubser at Infinity Clinic (04 394 8994) are popular paediatricians among expat parents. The GMC clinic in Jumeira has friendly paediatricians who will take the trauma out of doctor's appointments for your child and who specialise in allergies (04 3494 880). Health Call sends doctors for home visits 24 hours a day and is a handy service if your child is too sick to take to a surgery or hospital (04 363 5343, www. health-call.com). The clinics listed below specifically focus on paediatric care. For a full listing of clinics and hospitals that offer paediatric services, visit www. liveworkexplore.com.

## Cooper Health Clinic

**Al Wasl Road** Umm Suqeim **04 348 6344**
www.cooperhealthclinic.com
Map **1 T4** Metro **Al Quoz**
This family medicine clinic offers paediatric, obstetric and gynaecology specialties as well as antenatal classes and infant massage. Dr Khan at the clinic is a popular paediatrician.

## Dr Keith Nicholl

**Keith Nicholl Medical Centre** Umm Suqeim **04 394 1000**
www.keithnicholl.com
Map **2 B3** Metro **Al Quoz**
A child-friendly practice staffed by a paediatrician, paediatric nurses and a parent counsellor and educator. In addition to standard paediatric services, it offers well baby check-ups, immunisations, development checks and first aid courses for parents, nannies and other caregivers.

## Health Bay Polyclinic

**Villa 977, Al Wasl Road** Umm Suqeim **04 348 7140**
www.healthbayclinic.com
Map **1 U4** Metro **Al Quoz**
A family clinic with excellent neonatal and paediatric services. Antenatal care, wellbeing clinics and gynaecological services are also available. Friendly, western trained midwives are on hand to offer advice for new parents, and provide Well Baby check-ups and baby massage and yoga classes.

**P A E D I A T R I C   C A R E**   Dr Rita Kovesdi, paediatrician, **Dru Campbell,** head midwife, Health Bay Polyclinic

*In Dubai, the first routine check-up with a paediatrician would be at six weeks of age. It involves a detailed developmental check which includes a review of your baby's heart and respiratory system, sight, hearing and also rules out any hip joint concerns. Follow up developmental checks are usually scheduled at 3, 6, 12 and 18 months of age. Vaccinations in the UAE are primarily on the US schedule, although some clinics (including Health Bay) will administer vaccine brands which are given also in Australia and the UK. The major difference here to other parts of the world is the administering of the BCG vaccine to protect against tuberculosis, which is given to all babies born in the UAE and also recommended by the Department of Health for all children living in the country.*
*The most common health problems for children in the UAE are allergic conditions, which are directly related to the humid, dusty weather and the use of air conditioning. Asthma is common in children here, as well as allergic rhinitis (the irritation or inflammation of the nose and eyes).*

# Health

## Troubled Minds

If your child is having trouble adjusting to life in Dubai, finding it hard to fit in at a new school or missing friends and family back home, an outside perspective can sometimes help. The Dubai Community Health Centre (p.205) offers child counselling and psychology services which are useful for children with emotional difficulties and those whose parents are going through divorce. The Counselling & Development Clinic (p.205) deals with psychiatric disorders in children and offers a range of therapies including counselling and family therapy. Rashid Hospital also has a mental health unit.

### Isis – The French Pediatric Clinic
**Dubai Healthcare City** Umm Hurair **04 429 8450**
www.isisclinicdubai.com
Map **2 L6** Metro **Healthcare City**
Located close to the Alliance Francaise (p.176) and the Ecole George Pompidou (p.176) this practice offers specialist paediatric pulmonary care in addition to asthma, allergies, paediatric general practice and neonatal clinics. Standards are monitored by Dubai Healthcare City and the Harvard Medical School.

### kidsFIRST Medical Center
**Al Wasl Rd** Umm Suqeim **04 348 5437**
www.kidsfirst.ae
Map **1 S4** Metro **First Gulf Bank**
In addition to paediatric medicine, Kids First offers occupational therapy, speech therapy and physiotherapy for kids.

## Dentists & Orthodontists

Dentistry in Dubai is, like most other medical services, of a high standard with prices to match. Standard health insurance packages generally don't cover dentistry, unless it's for emergency treatment brought about by an accident. You may be able to pay an additional premium to cover dentistry, but the insurer may first want proof that you've had regular, six-monthly check-ups for the previous two or three years.

If you have a health card, you're entitled to dentistry at your assigned hospital, and if your hospital doesn't have a dental section, they'll refer you to another public hospital that does, such as Rashid Hospital. You will be charged Dhs.100 for the visit, as well as for any other services that are performed, such as cleaning and filling. Service is generally good, but the rates may not be any lower than at a private dental clinic.

For a standard filling you could be looking at paying anywhere between Dhs.50 and Dhs.1,000. If it is root canal treatment that you need, expect to part with anything from Dhs.600 to Dhs.3,000.

As well as routine and surgical dental treatment, cosmetic dentistry is also big business in Dubai, so if you're looking for a smile make-over, there is plenty of choice.

The clinics listed below are specialist dental clinics. Many primary healthcare clinics and hospitals also offer dental services. For a full listing of dental practices and surgeons in Dubai, log on to www.liveworkexplore.com.

### American Dental Clinic
**Jumeira Rd, Nr Dubai Zoo** Jumeira
**04 344 0668**
www.american-dental-clinic.com
Map **2 G3** Metro **Al Jafiliya**
Among a wide range of dental services available, this surgery specialises in neuromuscular dentistry. It offers a special service for patients with disabilities and those who suffer from dental phobia and anxiety attacks when visiting the dentist.

### British Dental Clinic
**Al Wasl Rd, Opp Emirates Bank International** Jumeira **04 342 1318**
www.britishdentalclinic.com
Map **2 F3** Metro **Financial Centre**
This clinic delivers a wide range of dental services in comfortable surrounds. Evening appointments are only available on request.

### Charly Polyclinic
**Sana Fashions Bldg** Karama **04 337 9191**
www.charlypolyclinic.com
Map **2 K4** Metro **Karama**
This practice offers a range in dental services including cosmetic, laser, implant and general dentistry, orthodontics and oral surgery. Also based at the clinic are an ophthalmologist, gynaecologist and two homeopaths.

### The Dental Center
**Dubai Healthcare City** Umm Hurair **04 375 2175**
www.the-dental-center.com
Map **2 L6** Metro **Healthcare City**
This bright and modern clinic in Healthcare City offers cutting edge dentistry including Virtual Consultations with overseas specialists. Routine dentistry and cosmetic procedures including dental make-overs are available.

### The Dental SPA Family & Cosmetic Dentistry
**Jumeira Road** Jumeira **04 395 2005**
www.thedentalspa.org
Map **2 B3** Metro **Al Quoz**
Bringing a pampering touch to dentistry, this clinic offers spa-like surrounding with calming mood

## GENERAL DENTISTRY
Dr E Nicolas, USA
Dr Sven Asp, Sweden
Dr Joan Asp, Sweden
Dr Tomas Von Post, Sweden
Dr E. Izabela Jaroszewicz, Poland
Dr Chris Johansson, Sweden
Dr Helen Khatib, UK
Dr Catarina Faerbom, Sweden
Dr Ruby Ghaffari, USA
Dr Farman Pour, Sweden
Dr Gavin Van Vledder, South Africa
Dr Flora Rissler, Sweden
Dr Samuel Hyatt, Denmark
Dr Thomas Peters, Germany
Dr Peter Silver, UK
Dr Bijan Barfaraz, Germany
Dr Rita Hyysalo, Finland

## ORTHODONTICS (BRACES)
Dr Salam Al - Khayyat, Turkey
Dr Brittany Nicol, Australia
Dr Tanja Nakovics, Germany
Dr Ahmad Ismail, France

## CLEFT LIP & PALATE
Dr Salam Al - Khayyat, Turkey

## ORAL SURGERY & IMPLANTS
Dr David Roze, France
Dr Samuel Hyatt, Denmark

## ENDODONTICS (ROOT CANAL)
Dr Diane Farhang, France
Dr Maria Morales, Venezuela

## PAEDIATRIC DENTISTRY
Dr Agnes Roze, France
Dr Chantal Kengo, France

## ORAL MAXILLOFACIAL SURGERY
Dr Christer Dahlin, Sweden
Dr Dirk Nolte, Germany

## DENTAL HYGIENE
Kate Paszkowska, Poland
Rahleh Mahtabpour, Iran
Marilyn Lopez, Canada
Ieva Odzala, Canada

CARING IS OUR CONCERN

دكـتــور نيــقــولا وآسـب
## DRS. NICOLAS & ASP

| JUMEIRAH | GREEN COMMUNITY | MARINA WALK | JBR MURJAN | JBR RIMAL | MIRDIF | DHCC |
|----------|-----------------|-------------|------------|-----------|--------|------|
| Dental | Dental | Dental & Medical | Dental | Medical | Dental | Dental |
| 04 394 7777 | 04 885 4440 | 04 360 9977 | 04 434 3077 | 04 436 4077 | 04 288 4411 | 04 362 4788 |

24/7 EMERGENCY HOTLINE  050 551 7177
www.nicolasandasp.com   enquiries@nicolasandasp.com
Healthcare provider for all major insurers
Financing Available
## CARING IS OUR CONCERN

MOH: 1885/2/9/31/9/09

music and aromatherapy pillows for your general or cosmetic dental treatment. You can also opt for foot and hand massages during your check-up.

### Dr Akel's Dental Clinic
**Magrudy's Shopping Complex** Jumeira **04 344 9150**
www.groupgmc.net
Map **2 H3** Metro **Al Jafiliya**
Using the latest laser dental technology, Dr Akel's promises painless treatment without the use of drills and anesthetics, making it a good option for people with dental phobias.

### Dr Michaels Dental Clinic
**Al Wasl Rd, Villa No. 418** Jumeira
**04 349 5900**
www.drmichaels.com
Map **2 F4** Metro **Financial Centre**
This clinic prides itself on its personalised service, high safety standards, state-of-the-art dental equipment and an international team of dentists who deliver a full range of dental services at its two branches in Jumeira and Umm Suqeim (04 394 9433).

### Drs Nicolas & Asp Clinic > *p.195*
Jumeira **04 394 7777**
www.nicolasandasp.com
Map **2 D3** Metro **Business Bay**
In addition to general practice (see listing on p.180), Drs Nicolas & Asp offers comprehensive dental services with resident dentists and dental surgeons, plus a state-of-the-art dental lab for creating implants, veneers and crowns on site. Cosmetic dentistry, advanced brace fitting and oral maxillofacial surgery are also available at its various dental clinics. The practice also runs a postgraduate dental college in Healthcare City.

Medcare Hospital

### Dubai London Clinic
**Al Wasl Rd** Jumeira **04 344 4359**
www.dubailondonclinic.com
Map **1 T3** Metro **First Gulf Bank**
Dubai London Clinic runs a dedicated dental surgery for routine dental care and cosmetic treatment.

### Dubai Sky Clinic
**Bur Juman Business Tower, Level 21** Bur Dubai
**04 355 8808**
www.dubaiskyclinic.com
Map **2 L4** Metro **Khalid Bin Al Waleed**
Dubai Sky Clinic offers a full range of dental services from its high-tech clinic on the 21st floor of Bur Juman Business Tower.

### Modern Dental Clinic
**Knowledge Village Blk 18** Al Sufouh **04 369 3625**
www.clinickv.com
Map **1 N4** Metro **Dubai Internet City**
A full range of routine, surgical and cosmetic dental procedures are available. In true Dubai bling-style, Modern Dental Clinic also offer dental jewellery. There is another branch at Uptown Mirdiff (04 284 7888). Top Modern Dental Clinic in Dubai Marina offers special children-friendly rooms with colourful cartoons painted on the walls, and luxury treatment rooms with five-star touches and Marina views to soothe the most nervous dental patient.

### Seven Dental Centre > *p.197*
**Jumeira Rd** Jumeira **04 395 2177**
www.sevendentalcentre.com
Map **2 C3** Metro **Business Bay**
A french dental practice with all french dental staff, offering a no pain policy. Cosmetic, prosthetic and orthodontic procedures are available in addition to routine and children's dentistry.

### Swedish Dental Clinic
**United Insurance Bldg, Al Maktoum St** Deira
**04 223 1297**
www.swedishdentalclinic.net
Map **2 N4** Metro **Union**
This practice, established in Deira in 1985, offers dental and orthodontic care for patients of all ages.

### Swiss Dental Clinic
**Crowne Plaza** Shk Zayed Rd. **04 332 1444**
www.swissdentalclinic.com
Map **2 H4** Metro **Emirates Towers**
Dr Fedele at Swiss Dental Clinic offers a personable service and seeks to put patient's treatment anxieties to rest. General and aesthetic dentistry are available and Dr Fedele will explain procedures to his patients thoroughly before undertaking any treatment. He speaks English, French, German, Italian and Spanish.

# 7 SEVEN DENTAL CENTRE

| | |
|---|---|
| **Dr. Roland Ceyte** <br> **Dr. Joanna Fadel** | Cosmetic and General Dentistry |
| **Dr. Michel Brunel** <br> **Dr. Pascal Paldino** | Implants and Gum Surgery |
| **Dr. Firas Haj Ibrahim** | Orthodontist |

**Welcome to a french dental clinic in Dubai whose goal is simply the best for you!**

DOH 2947/2/131109

**Jumeirah 3 Beach Road • Tel : 04 3952177 - 3955660**
**Fax : 04-3952377 • www.sevendentalcentre.com**

### Talass Orthodontic & Dental Center
Jumeira Rd, Opp Dubai Zoo Jumeira
**04 349 2220**
Map **2 G3** Metro **Al Jafiliya**
Talass specialises in cosmetic dentistry including crowns, veneers and teeth whitening procedures.

### Tower Clinic
Dubai Healthcare City, Ibn Sina Bldg No.27
Umm Hurair 2 **04 362 2939**
www.towerclinic.com
Map **2 L6** Metro **Healthcare City**
This dental surgery offers general dentistry and orthodontics plus oral surgery. Tooth replacements and inlays come with a six year guarantee.

## Opticians & Ophthalmologists
You're never far from an optician in Dubai, with most of the malls and shopping centres having at least one outlet.

The dry, dusty environment in Dubai can cause problems for eyes, even if you've had no trouble in the past. Natural tear or refresher eye drops can increase eye comfort and are available in most opticians and pharmacies. Spending lengthy periods in air-conditioned environments can cause problems for contact lens wearers. Opticians can advise on the most suitable lenses. Sunglasses are an essential accessory in Dubai and prescription lenses are widely available.

For eye problems requiring specialist treatment, many hospitals and clinics, including Moorfields Eye Hospital and American Hospital, have well-equipped ophthalmology departments. If you want to ditch the glasses, a number of clinics and medical centres offer laser eye surgery. Prices start from around Dhs.4,000 per eye rising to around Dhs.7,500. All good laser surgery packages should include a complete year's follow-up care.

Even if you've never had an eye test in your life, you will need to undergo one in order to get a driving licence (see Driving Licence, p.40). This test can be carried out at most opticians for a minimal fee, sometimes free of charge.

## Ophthalmology & Vision Correction Clinics

### The Atlanta Vision Clinic
Jumeira Rd, Opp Jumeirah Beach Hotel
Umm Suqeim **04 348 6233**
www.dubailasik.com
Map **1 S4** Metro **First Gulf Bank**
This clinic specialises in Bausch & Lomb Z100 Zyoptix (TM) System vision correction promising over 90% success rate for improved vision and in many cases to a 20/20 level. Patients can have a consultation to asses whether they are a candidate for LASIK.

### Gulf Eye Centre
Fairmont Dubai Trade Centre **04 329 1977**
www.gulfeyecenter.com
Map **2 J4** Metro **Trade Centre**
Specialises in laser vision correction and surgery. Other ophthalmological services and eye-related cosmetic procedures are available.

### Moorfields Eye Hospital Dubai > p.199
Dubai Healthcare City Umm Hurair **04 429 7888**
www.moorfields.ae
Map **2 L6** Metro **Healthcare City**
The Dubai branch of this long-established and well-respected London eye hospital opened in 2006, providing high quality optometric, ophthalmic and orthoptic (relating to eye movement disorders) care. The services available range from simple eye tests to complex surgical procedures and ongoing non-surgical corrective treatment, with a special service for children's eyecare and assessment.

### Sharif Eye Center
Dubai Healthcare City Umm Hurair **04 423 3664**
www.sharifeyecenter.com
Map **2 L6** Metro **Healthcare City**
An eye surgery clinic specialising in vision correction.

## Opticians
**Al Jaber Optical Centre** Various locations, 04 341 1322, *www.aljaber.ae*
**Barakat Optical** For locations, see www.barakatoptical.com
**City Optic** Deira, 04 295 1400,
**Dubai Opticals** For locations, see *www.dubaioptical.com*
**Fashion Optics** Jumeira, 04 346 1931,
**Grand Optics** For locations, see *www.grandoptics.com*
**Lunettes** Jumeira, 04 349 2270
**Lutfi Opticals Centre** Umm Hurair, 04 324 1865, *www.lutfioptical.com*
**Magrabi Optical** For locations, see *www.magrabioptical.com*
**Optic Center** Mirdif, 04 284 5550
**Optivision** Bur Dubai, 04 352 8171
**Pearle Opticians** Jebel Ali, 04 368 5926
**Top Visions Optics** Satwa, 04 398 4888
**Yateem Optician** For locations, see p.426
*www.yateemgroup.com*

## Alternative Therapies
The UAE Ministry of Health grants licences to and administrates qualified practitioners of alternative medicine through its dedicated department for Traditional, Complementary & Alternative Medicine. Natural medicine can be very specialised, so when consulting with someone make sure that you ask questions and explain your needs and expectations

www.moorfields.ae

# Bringing over 200 years of UK specialist eye care to Dubai.

Long recognised as one of the leading eye hospitals we have replicated the exceptional standards of our London hospital here in Dubai. Our brand new, state-of-the-art facility in Dubai Healthcare City is fully equipped and staffed by highly qualified consultants.

If you have any concerns about your, or your family's vision (under performance at school can be caused by poor vision), please contact us.

**Call 04 429 7888 or visit www.moorfields.ae today for more information.**

## Moorfields
### Eye Hospital Dubai
A BRANCH OF MOORFIELDS LONDON

LASIK | CATARACT | COSMETIC | RETINA | CORNEA | GLAUCOMA

2320/2/12/28/2/10

# Health

to ensure practitioners can help with your situation. Prices vary but are generally comparable to western medicine, and most insurance companies will not cover the costs. As always, word of mouth is the best way of establishing who might offer the most appropriate treatment.

Yoga and Pilates are available at a number of studios and health clubs. Both fitness-focussed and classic, meditative forms of yoga are available. See Yoga & Pilates, p.204. There is also a range of clinics providing 'well-being' services, such as U Concept (p.204), which combine personal fitness, balanced diet and relaxation techniques to help you achieve a healthy lifestyle.

## Al Karama Ayurvedic & Yoga Centre
Karama Centre Karama **04 335 5288**
Map **2 L4** Metro **Karama**
Operating for over 12 years, this centre is run by qualified professionals with expertise in the traditional systems of Ayurveda, herbal beauty care, yoga and meditation. They have all the necessary facilities to take care of healing, rejuvenation and beauty care. Separate areas are available for men and women.

## Art Of Living
**Nr New Gold Souk** Bur Dubai
www.artoflivingme.org
Map **2 K3** Metro **Karama**
Under the guidance of Sri Sri Ravi Shankar, this worldwide, non-profit NGO seeks social change through peaceful, individual empowerment. In Dubai, individual courses and corporate packages are available which teach the principles and practice of yoga, meditation and breathing techniques to bring inner peace and stress relief.

## Dubai Herbal & Treatment Centre
Umm Hurair **04 335 1200**
www.dubaihtc.com
Map **2 J6** Metro **Healthcare City**
The Dubai Herbal & Treatment Centre offers a full range of Chinese, Indian and Arabic herbal medicines. The facility, which is unique in the GCC region, currently caters to outpatients only, but there are plans to expand the facility to offer inpatient services.

## Feet First
**Town Centre Jumeirah** Jumeira **04 349 4334**
www.feet1st.com
Map **2 F3** Metro **Financial Centre**
Alongside manicure and pedicure services, Feet First offers Oriental reflexology, shiatsu massage and acupressure massage in relaxing spa surrounds. A Chinese medicine slimming programme is also available. Branches are located around Dubai, with a men's studio at the Town Centre Jumeirah clinic (04 349 4553).

## GMCKS Pranic Energy Healing Centre
Trade Centre Rd **04 336 0885**
www.pranichealingmea.com
Intended as a complementary therapy to orthodox medicine, pranic healing is a method of rebalancing the body's energy field or aura and transferring life energy from the healer to the patient. As well as giving physical pain relief, it is said to help alleviate emotional, mental and spiritual problems.

## Healing Zone
**050 654 2998**
anne@thehealingzone.net
www.thehealingzone.net
This complementary therapy practice offers treatments including allergy testing, ear candling, and crystal therapy. Reiki training classes and other therapy workshops are held regularly.

## Holistic Healing Medical Centre
**Villa #783, Jumeirah Beach Road** Umm Suqeim
**04 348 7172**
www.healthholistic.com
Map **1 T3** Metro **First Gulf Bank**
In addition to more common forms of alternative medicine such as Chinese medicine and homeopathy, this centre offers iridology (medical diagnosis through the study of the iris), Etiopathy (a form of diagnosis and painless manipulation of the joints and bones), colon hydrotherapy and yoga therapy.

## House Of Chi & House Of Healing
**Musalla Towers, Khalid bin Al Walid St** Bur Dubai
**04 397 4446**
www.hofchi.com
Map **2 L4** Metro **Khalid Bin Al Waleed**
The two 'houses' offer training in martial and meditative arts, including Tai Chi, yoga and Pilates, and therapeutic treatments including Chinese medicine, weightloss solutions, massage and beauty therapy.

# Sports Injuries

Many Dubai residents lead an active lifestyle, working hard and then playing harder. But accidents and injuries do happen, so whether you got roughed up playing rugby, pulled something in the gym or put your back out moving a wardrobe you'll be pleased to hear that the city has some excellent facilities with specialists from all around the world to help you on the road to recovery.

Chiropractic and osteopathic treatments are non-invasive and aim to improve the functioning of the nervous system or blood supply to the body through manipulation of the skeleton. Chiropractic therapy focuses on realigning the joints, especially those of the spinal column, while osteopathy combines skeletal manipulation with muscular massage.

Healthcare City

Orthopaedics concerns the repair of damaged bones and joints, whether sustained through injury, disease or genetics. Pilates is said to be the safest form of neuromuscular reconditioning and back strengthening available. Classes are offered by a number of gyms as part of their group exercise schedules. For specialist Pilates studios, see p.333.

In addition to the clinics listed below which specialise in various kinds of musculoskeletal assessment and treatment Drs Nicolas & Asp (p.181) offers sports medicine and physiotherapy, and House of Chi & House of Healing (p.200) offers tai chi, Pilates and a range of other exercises which can help prevent future sports injuries.

## Canadian Chiropractic & Natural Health Centre
Al Wasl Rd, Nr Jumeira Post Office, Jumeira, 04 342 0900
Map 2 E4 Metro Business Bay
This clinic offers chiropractic treatments and accupuncture as well as reflexology. They also treat sports injuries and give advice for people with long term back problems.

## Chiropractic Health & Medical Centre
Villa # 967, Al Wasl Rd Umm Suqeim 04 348 8262
www.dubaichiropractor.net
Map 1 T4 Metro First Gulf Bank
This health clinic treats a range of health problems and sports injuries including ADHD, headaches, stress, scoliosis, neck pain, asthma and pain following accidents. A number of physiotherapists and a nutritionist are also based at the clinic.

## Dubai Bone & Joint Center
Dubai Healthcare City Umm Hurair 04 423 1400
www.dbaj.ae
Map 2 L6 Metro Healthcare City
This medical facility focuses on research into and treatment of musculoskeletal problems. Well equipped with diagnostic technologies, the centre offers rehabilitative services including physiotherapy and sports medicine, and has a very high standard of facilities for joint replacements, orthopaedic, and back and neck surgeries.

## Dubai Physiotherapy Clinic
Town Centre Jumeirah Jumeira 04 349 6333
www.dubaiphysio.com
Map 2 F3 Metro Burj Dubai
This clinic offers physiotherapy for the full spectrum of musculoskeletal disorders and sports injuries. Many of the patients are regular and also have access to the services of a general practitioner, nutritionist, speech therapist and osteopath.

## Gulf American Clinic
The Village Jumeira Beach Rd 04 344 2050
www.groupgmc.net
Map 2 H3 Metro Financial Centre
Specialising in musculoskeletal medicine, Gulf American Clinic offers chiropractic, orthopaedics, physiotherapy, Chinese medicine and acupuncture, for a range of joint, bone and muscle conditions including sports injuries, neck and back pain, arthritis and rheumatology. It also has an on-site gym which offers annual memberships.

## OrthoSports Medical Center > p.203
Jumeira Rd Jumeira 04 345 0601
www.orthosp.com
Map 2 H3 Metro Al Jafiliya
OrthoSports Medical Center in Jumeira specialises in orthopaedics and sports medicine, offering physiotherapy, hydrotherapy and orthopaedic surgery to international standards. Sports therapy for fitness and injury rehabilitation and hydrotherapy for a range of conditions including obesity, arthritis, back pain and joint replacements are also available.

## Osteopathic Health Centre
Al Wasl Rd, Opp Jumeira Beach Park Umm Suqeim 04 348 7366
www.osteopathydubai.com
Map 1 T4 Metro First Gulf Bank
This practice has a number of therapists practising osteopathy in addition to physiotherapists, exercise therapists, a kinesiologist and massage and orthotics specialists. The centre also offers ante-natal classes and hosts a number of support and discussion groups.

## Specialist Orthopaedic Surgery Centre
Al Wasl Rd Jumeira 04 349 5528
Map 2 D3 Metro Business Bay
This clinic offers othopaedic surgery and therapeutic (non-medical) massage including anti-stress, deep tissue and hot stone massage.

# Nutritionists & Slimming
With such a variety of dining options in Dubai, and with the emphasis very much on lounging and relaxing, it's easy to let your diet suffer and pile on the pounds. Thankfully, a number of slimming clubs and nutritionists are on hand to help. In addition, plenty of clinics and hospitals offer nutritional advice for conditions and weight loss surgeries. Dietary advice for diabetes, allergies, menopause, pregnancy and digestive disorders such as Reflux, IBS and coeliacs, is also available.

Of the hospitals, Welcare Hospital (p.188) provides a dietary counselling service, where a team of dieticians and nutritionists will educate and evaluate the patient's eating habits, and then point

...be fit

● orthopedic surgery   ●   sports medicine   ●   physiotherapy   ●   hydrotherapy   ●

www.orthosp.com

# ORTHOSPORTS
## MEDICAL CENTER
### THE SPORTS MEDICINE SPECIALISTS

BEACH ROAD  JUMEIRA
TEL: 04-345 0601  FAX: 04-345 0028

them in the right direction with a unique diet plan. The American Hospital (p.186) offers a food and nutrition service managed and provided by ADNH Compass. The hospital also runs a Diabetic Centre of Excellence. Emirates Hospital (p.188) has a weight reduction programme that uses liquid supplements and a very low calorie diet. The hospital has dietician and nutrition experts who specialise in medically supervised weight reduction programmes, obesity in children, obesity in diabetic patients and patients with high blood pressure or cholesterol. It also offers weight loss programmes through gastric band fitting. For a more holistic approach to nutrition, the Osteopathic Health Centre offers a complete nutritionist service (p.202). Many small clinics and family practices have dieticians on staff including Cooper Health Clinic (p.193), Dubai London Clinic (p.181) and Drs Nicolas & Asp (p.181).

## Eternal MedSpa Dubai

Opp Jumeirah Beach Park, Jumeira, **04 344 0008**
www.eternalmedspa.com
Map **2 D3** Metro **Business Bay**
Offers mesotherapy for cellulite treatment, botox, laser hair removal, slimming treatments as well as general wellness coaching.

## Good Habits

Various Locations **04 344 9692**
www.goodhabitsuae.com
Good Habits helps people lose weight through healthy eating. Meetings are held every week at various locations all over Dubai, and often include food tasting and cookery demos. Exercise classes are also organised and individual programmes are offered over six week periods. They also have a cookery book available on the website with 90 recipes to keep you on the straight and narrow.

## Hypoxi @ Hayya!

**Hayya** Emirates Hills **04 363 8318**
www.hypoxitherapy.com
Map **2 N7** Metro **Nakheel**
Relatively new to the Dubai weight loss scene, Hypoxi combines cardiovascular exercise with applied pressure to increase the blood flow to fatty problem areas. Improvements can be noticed within four weeks and most results can be achieved within 12 weeks with three sessions a week. As a non-chemical, non-surgical therapy there are few side effects. Basically you wear what feels like a wet suit and speed walk on a treadmill or cycle inside a vacuum pod. For most people results are felt in reduced inches (and each session the trainer will measure your chest, waist and hips), although weight loss can also occur. There is also a Hypoxi studio at the Aviation Club (2824122).

## Lifestyle UAE

**Cooper Health Clinic** Umm Suqeim **04 348 6344**
www.lifestyle-uae.com
Map **1 T4** Metro **First Gulf Bank**
Belinda Rennie is based at Cooper Health Clinic. She promotes a mind, body and spirit balance through healthy eating. Her nutritional advice focuses on meal planning based on lifestyle and finding the right balance of food, homeopathic mineral salts, and probiotic and wholefood supplements to achieve well being. Her approach is suitable for pregnancy, stress management, weight loss and a digestive disorders.

## Perfect Figure Studio

Various Locations **800 49 7694**
www.allbodysolutions.com
This studio creates personal weight loss and toning programmes, which combine exercise using Hypoxi and Vacunaut machines, with nutritional advice.

## Right Bite

Various Locations **04 338 8763**
www.right-bite.com
Right Bite offers a tailor-made healthy eating service. Tasty, low calorie, low fat and low cholesterol meals, devised by their own dieticians, are freshly prepared and delivered to your door.

## Time For Change

Umm Hurair, **04 336 0455**
www.tfchange.com
Map **2 J6** Metro **Healthcare City**
Through nutritional advice, exercise and dietary supplements the TFC team offer weight loss and diabetes management programmes.

## U Concept

**The Village** Jumeira **04 344 9060**
www.uconcept6.com
Map **2 H3** Metro **Al Jafiliya**
U Concept offers a 'unique lifestyle service', combining personal training, nutritional advice, and a range of relaxation treatments. A consultant will help you design a 12 week programme to allow you to meet your personal health and fitness goals, lose weight and cope with stress and advises on nutrition.

## VLCC

Various Locations **800 8522**
www.vlccinternational.com
VLCC offers hair removal, beauty services and customised weight loss programmes which combines dietary advice, exercise and toning and detox therapies. There are women-only centres at Jumeirah Centre (04 3429 986) and Uptown Mirdiff (04 288 4880) and mixed centres including Deira (04 234 7870) and Bur Dubai (04 3599 552).

# Cosmetic Treatment & Surgery

Dubai is becoming established as a luxury healthcare destination. This is in part due to a concerted marketing effort by Dubai Governmentto attract the most renowned names in the medical industry to centres like Dubai Healthcare City. Cosmetic surgery is at the heart of this growing industry and the city now boasts a mass of clinics that specialise in reducing, reshaping, removing and enlarging various parts of your anatomy. The clinics listed below are exclusively cosmetic practices, but many of the private hospitals (p.180) and independent clinics (p.180) offer cosmetic services including aesthetic and reconstructive surgery. As with all medical facilities, standards are generally high, but it's worth checking out a few different clinics before you go under the knife. If you want a bit of sprucing and don't fancy slicing, a lot of the cosmetic clinics will do botox and other non-surgical treatments.

## Cosmetic Surgery Clinics

**Aesthetica Clinic** 04 339 1700,
*www.aestheticaclinic.com*
**American Academy of Cosmetic Surgery Hospital**
Umm Hurair, 04 423 7600, *www.aacsh.com*
**Cosmesurge** Jumeira, 04 344 5915,
*www.cosmesurge.com*
**Dubai Cosmetic Surgery** Umm Suqeim, 04 348 5575,
*www.dubaicosmeticsurgery.com*
**Dubai Medical Village** Jumeira, 04 395 6200
**General Medical Center** Trade Centre, 04 331 3544,
*www.groupgmc.net*
**Gulf Specialty Hospital** Deira, 04 269 9717,
*www.gshdubai.net*
**Imperial Healthcare Institute** Umm Hurair,
04 439 3737, *www.imperialhealth.org*
**London Centre For Aesthetic Surgery** Umm Hurair,
04 375 2393, *www.dubaiplasticsurgery.ae*

# Counselling & Therapy

Starting a new life in a different country can be a stressful process, and whether you are new to the city or not, sometimes it can help just to talk through whatever issues and anxieties you are facing. Mental health services in the UAE are not as developed as in some countries; at present only Rashid Hospital (p.188) has a dedicated psychiatric ward, although levels of care here are generally high. There are however a number of well-regarded therapy centres offering services including counselling, psychodynamic therapy, family and couple therapy, paediatric psychiatry, treatment of mental health disorders and learning difficulties support. Dubai Community Health Centre offers a range of counselling and psychiatry services and provides space for support group meetings; it comes highly recommended, as does the Counselling &

Development Clinic. In addition to the clinics and centres listed below, the British Medical Consulting Centre (p.190) and Drs Nicolas & Asp (p.181) are medical practices that have counsellors, family therapists and psychiatrists on staff. Dubai Herbal & Treatment Centre has a psychodynamic counsellor, a psychologist and a learning specialist, and is recommended for child counselling services (p.200).

## Counselling & Development Clinic

**Villa 4158, Opp Jumeirah Beach Park** Jumeira
**04 394 6122**
*www.drmccarthypsychologyclinic.com*
Map **2 D3** Metro **Business Bay**
This centre offers psychology services for adults and children. As well as assessing and treating psychological disorders, the clinic offers counselling, family therapy and couples' clinics. It is particularly well regarded for the treatment and management of bipolar disorder (manic depression), Asperger's syndrome and narcissism.

## Dubai Community Health Centre

**Jumeira Road** Jumeira **04 395 3939**
*www.dubaicommunityhealthcentre.org*
Map **2 C3** Metro **Business Bay**
This private, non-profit facility provides an extensive range of mental health and developmental care services in a friendly, caring environment. In addition to counselling, family and marriage therapy, speech and language therapy, psychology and parenting courses, it offers occupational therapy, dietetics, special needs education, homeopathy and yoga. Attendance is by appointment only.

## Health Psychology UAE

**Well Woman Clinic** Al Diyafah Rd **04 332 7117**
*www.healthpsychuae.com*
Map **2 J3** Metro **Al Jafiliya**
Dr Melanie C Schlatter is a health psychologist helping people manage the psychological impact of illnesses and medical conditions which they have. She also offers preventative health psychology in the form of stress management and coping with anxiety, phobias (particularly medical related such as the fear of injection needles), depression, grief and anger.

## Human Relations Institute

**Knowledge Village** Al Sufouh **04 331 4777**
*www.hridubai.com*
Map **1 N4** Metro **Dubai Internet City**
The HRI's services including clinical, forensic, organizational, educational and domestic psychology. It offers counselling, life coaching, psychotherapy and workshops for conditions including anxiety, phobias, addiction, behavioural and eating disorders, stress, low self-confidence and depression.

**Health, Fitness & Well-Being**

### Pastoral Counselling
**050 297 3221 or 050 422 0251**
Neil Obeyesekere has over 15 years' counselling experience. His support service is available whatever the problem, with the aim of restoring the joy and significance of living.

# WELL-BEING

Whether it's shifting the Dubai stone, hitting the beach bootcamp-style, being pampered at a health spa, receiving meditation advice from a guru, or limbering up with a body massage: whatever you definition of well-being there's a good chance that someone, somewhere in Dubai will have the necessary facilities and skills to have you feeling better in no time.

## Personal Grooming

Beauty is big business in Dubai. Salons are everywhere and with certain services such as manicures, pedicures and waxing costing less than in many other international cities, you may find that a trip to the beauticians becomes a more regular diary fixture than at home. Fridays are usually the busiest day so make sure you book ahead; on other days many places accept walk-ins or bookings at short notice. In the lead up to big social events, such as Ladies Day at the Dubai World Cup (p.261), appointments at the best salons are like gold dust so make sure you book in plenty of time.

In hotels you'll find both male and female stylists working alongside each other, but in establishments located outside hotels, only female stylists are permitted to work in ladies' salons. These salons are very private and men are not permitted inside – even the windows are covered.

There are also numerous salons aimed primarily at Arabic ladies, which specialise in henna designs, so look out for a decorated hand poster in salon windows. The traditional practice of painting henna on the hands and feet, especially for weddings or special occasions, is still very popular with UAE Nationals. For tourists, a design on the hand, ankle or shoulder can make a great memento – it will cost about Dhs.40 and the intricate brown patterns fade after two to three weeks.

There are plenty of options for male grooming as well, with barbershops and salons to suit all budgets, and a growing number of specialist men's spas. So whether you're after a short back and sides, a traditional shave, a chest wax or a facial, there's something for all.

Many hair salons and nail bars offer a combination of services, but as the quality, prices and service vary greatly, trial and error and word of mouth are the best ways to find a dependable salon. The listings below are a good starting place if you're new to the city. For a full listing of hairdressers, beauty salons and nail bars, visit www.liveworkexplore.com.

## Beauty Salons & Nail Bars

Beauty salons and nail bars are dotted all over Dubai, so whether you need plucking, waxing, polishing or buffing, there is plenty of choice. Dubai Mall (p.402) houses a number of flagship stores for international beauty and cosmetic brands, many offering in-store makeovers and skin consultations. Spaces (p.207) has special offers on Mondays, with the discounted treatment changing weekly. Nivea Haus (p.207) offers skin and hair consultations and treatments, and a range of reasonably priced pampering treatments for both men and women. Many spas and hairdressers offer a side-line in beauty treatments. Elche (p.213) offers skin consultations and treatments using 100% organic products.

### ┌─ Mobile Beauty ─

If you're too busy to get to a salon, or simply prefer the comfort of your own home, a number of companies will send out therapists to attend you at your leisure. Chez Toi and Nails-At-Home can send therapists to your door for a range of beauty treatments. If you're looking for a special twist to a baby shower or hen party a whole army of therapists can be rallied for all your beauty needs.

With all-year round sunshine holding endless possibilities for strappy shoes, flip-flops, sandals and summery wedges, there's not excuse for having less than perfect pinkies. It's worth trying out a few different nail bars to find one that you really like because the chances are you'll be making regular appearances there. N.Bar (p.207), The Nail Spa (p.207) and NStyle (p.207) are all popular chains with numerous branches around Dubai. Gloss Nail Spa offers a 'Little Miss Sparkle' treatment for little girls aged 10 and under who can have their nails painted in pretty colours and decorated with stars and flowers – a great idea for some special mother and daughter time. Tips & Toes Nail Haven (p.207) offers slimming treatments in addition to a full range of nail, beauty and massage services.

**Aroushi Beauty Salon** Oud Metha, 04 336 2794
**Chez Toi** 04 339 7117,
*www.cheztoibeauty.com*
**Clarins Boutique** Downtown Burj Dubai,
04 434 0522, *www.clarins.com*
**Dermalogica On Burj** Downtown Burj Dubai,
04 339 8250, *www.dermalogicaonburj.com*
**Essentials Beauty Salon** Al Wasl, 04 395 5909,
*www.essentialsdubai.com*

**Finola's Beauty Salon** Jumeira, 04 344 4757
**Gloss Nail Spa** Mirdif, 04 284 7111,
**N.Bar** Jumeira, 04 346 1100, *www.thegroomingco.com*
**Nail Moda** Wafi, 04 327 9088,
*www.nailmoda.com*
**The Nail Spa** Downtown Burj Dubai, 04 339 9078,
*www.thenailspa.com*
**Nail Zone** Jumeira, 04 344 6969
**Nails At Home** Garhoud, 04 208 7667
**Nailstation** Jumeira, 04 349 0123
**Nivea Haus** Downtown Burj Dubai, 04 434 0777,
*www.niveahaus.ae*
**NStyle Nail Lounge** Al Barsha, 04 341 3300,
*www.nstyleintl.com*
**Spaces Ladies Salon & Spa** Mirdif, 04 284 5673,
*www.arabiancenter.ae*
**Tilia & Finn** Dubai Marina, 04 438 0636,
*www.tiliaandfinn.ae*
**Tips & Toes Nail Haven** Dubai Marina, 04 429 3477,
*www.tipsntoeshaven.com*

# Hairdressers

If you're just looking for a trim and tidy-up, most malls have salons which take walk-ins. Usually you'll need an appointment for a hairdresser, although you rarely need to book very far in advance. Salons normally charge separately for cutting and blow drying hair. Average prices for ladies are around Dhs.150 for a cut and Dhs.100 for a blow dry, and Dhs.70 for a men's wash and cut, although there's something for all budgets. There are a number of small barber shops and salons around Karama, Satwa, Bur Dubai and Deira. Gents can get a haircut (and relaxing head massage) for as little as Dhs.15, with the option of a shave with a cut-throat razor for a few extra dirhams. Ladies should be able to find salons where a basic haircut starts at around Dhs.60.

Many beauty salons and some spas offer hairdressing, so check the listings on p. 206 and p.211 for additional recommendations. Nivea Haus offers specialist hair advice and treatments for both men and women (p.207).

**Alain & Milad** Al Sufouh, 04 390 2815,
*www.alainmilad.com*
**Bare Gents Salon** Jebel Ali, 04 368 5111
**Carla K Styling Centre** Trade Centre, 04 343 8544
**Cut & Shape** Satwa, 04 398 6008,
**The Edge Hair & Beauty** Umm Hurair, 04 324 0024
**Elyazia Beauty Center** International City,
04 422 6149, *www.nbeautywoman.com*
**Franck Provost** Mall of the Emirates, 04 341 3245,
*www.franckprovostdubai.com*
**The Gold Salon** Trade Centre, 04 321 1425,
*www.goldsalondubai.com*
**Hair Corridor** Al Wasl, 04 394 5622

**The Hair Shop** Trade Centre, 04 332 6616,
*www.hairshop-uae.com*
**Hair Spa** Jumeira, 04 346 1111
**Hair Station** Mirdif, 04 288 2265
**Hair@Pyramids** Umm Hurair, 04 324 1490,
*www.wafi-health-leisure.com*
**Hairworks** Umm Suqeim, 04 394 0777
**Jen's Hair Studio** Dubai Marina, 800 5367,
*www.jenshairstudio.com*
**Lamcy Hair & Beauty Centre** Oud Metha,
04 335 1101,
**MariaDowling** Bur Dubai, 04 345 4225,
*www.mariadowling.com*
**Pace e Luce** Downtown Burj Dubai, 04 420 1165,
*www.paceeluce.com*
**Pastels** Jumeira, 04 394 7393, *www.pastels-salon.com*
**Patsi Collins Hair Beauty Nails** Garhoud,
04 286 9923, *www.dubaibeautysalon.com*
**Reflection Hair & Beauty Care** Al Wasl, 04 394 4595,
**Roots Salon** Jumeira, 04 344 4040,
**Saks Hair Salon** Downtown Burj Dubai, 04 430 8572,
*www.saks.co.uk*
**Sisters Beauty Lounge** Jumeira, 04 342 0787,
*www.sistersbeautylounge.com*
**SOS Beauty Salon** Jumeira, 04 349 1144
**Ted Morgan** Palm Jumeirah, 04 430 8190,
*www.tedmorganhair.com*
**Toni & Guy** Trade Centre, 04 330 3345,
*www.toniandguy.com*
**Top Style Salon** Garhoud, 04 282 9663,
*www.topstylesalon.com*
**Zouari** Al Sufouh, 04 399 9999,
*www.oneandonlyroyalmirage.com*

## Unbeweavable

You can find a few salons specialising in afro hair, braiding and extensions near the fish roundabout in Deira, although standards vary. Elyazia Beauty Center (p.207) in International City specialises in relaxing, weaving, dreadlocks and afro hair treatments.

# Gyms & Fitness Clubs

It's not uncommon to have access to fitness facilities in your accommodation whether you live in an apartment block, community setting or independent villa. Some of the newer apartment towers have excellent facilities with swimming pools, squash courts and gymnasiums available for residents' use. Other places have a pool and some have sports courts. See Housing p.71 for an overview of accommodation facilities.

There are a number of independent gyms and fitness centres. Most charge a monthly or yearly membership fee for access to facilities – look out in the local press for joining discounts and special offers.

# Well-Being

Most gyms offer a daily rate or visitor pass at around Dhs.100 – Dhs.250. Most gyms also run aerobics classes, which may be included in the membership fees or paid for on a class-by-class basis.

In addition many hotels offer memberships to their fitness facilities. Although usually more expensive, these gyms are often quieter and sometimes include access to spa facilities, so it's worth ringing around to compare quotes before you sign up. Some of the more popular ones are Le Meridien Mina Seyahi, the Grand Hyatt and Jebel Ali Golf Resort & Spa (see Dubai Hotels, p.228).

If losing weight is your goal, companies such as U Concept (p.204) and Time For Change (p.204) can create a personal programme combining exercise and diet. If your motivation is your biggest exercise hurdle, there are options ranging from personal trainers to group fitness classes, and if you're serious about getting fit, military-style bootcamps, held in the early morning or evening on Dubai's beaches, are intensive training sessions aimed at increasing fitness levels in a short time frame. For more information on slimming and nutrition see p.202.

For the more sociable types, all kinds of sports are on offer in Dubai and for most of them you can find like-minded people to play with. See Activities p.308 for more details.

## The Aviation Club
**Nr Tennis Stadium** Al Garhoud **04 282 4122**
www.aviationclub.ae
Map **2 N7** Metro **GGICO**
The fitness club at The Aviation Club has excellent facilities including tennis courts, swimming and plunge pools, a sauna, a gymnasium, a physiotherapy clinic and a hypoxi studio. Swimming and tennis coaching and group exercise classes are also available. Classes are open to non-members. The Aviation Club also runs a rare indoor-outdoor boot camp, which combines indoor circuit training with outdoor exercise.

## The Big Apple
**Boulevard at Emirates Towers** Trade Centre **04 319 8660**
www.jumeirahemiratestowers.com
Map **2 H5** Metro **Emirates Towers**
Located in the Emirates Towers, Big Apple caters to professionals that work in the DIFC, although memberships are open to all. Both single and couple's memberships are available for one, three and six months or one year. Prices range from Dhs.7,350 for a yearly couple's membership to Dhs.675 for a one month single membership. Classes are available at Dhs.30 for members and Dhs.40 for non-members. The gym's equipment is all branded and there are plenty of cardio machines, so waiting is rarely a problem.

## Bodylines Leisure & Fitness Club
**Towers Rotana** Trade Centre **04 343 8000**
www.rotana.com
Map **2 G5** Metro **Financial Centre**
Located in Rotana hotels throughout the city, Bodylines provides its clients with an upscale workout environment that caters more towards older adults. Each gym has a full set of branded cardio equipment as well as free weights and weight machines. Fitness classes are available, as are personal trainers.

## Chevrolet Insportz Club
**Cnr Street 17, Beh Garden Centre** Al Quoz **04 347 5833**
www.insportzclub.com
Map **1 S5** Metro **First Gulf Bank**
Insportz is an indoor sports centre and features five multi-purpose courts, a cricket coaching net and cafeteria, all within the comfort of air-conditioned surrounding. Sports available include table tennis, cricket, football, basketball and hockey, and prices (inclusive of equipment) start from Dhs.30 for children and Dhs.35 for adults. There's a coaching programme and a summer camp for juniors too. The club can also be booked for functions such as kids' parties and corporate team building.

## Core Studio
**Damac Waves Tower** Dubai Marina **04 362 6385**
www.corestudiome.com
Map **1 K4** Metro **Jumeirah Lakes Towers**
This fitness centre offers over 200 scheduled fitness classes. Each class is a signature brand of fitness aimed at making the experience of exercising as enjoyable as possible, to boost your motivation. Popular classes include the yoga and Pilates blend 'yogilates' class (which is also held in Safa Park during the winter), spinning, dance fitness classes and boot camps. Personal training is also available and memberships start from Dhs.300 per month.

## Dubai Fit Camp
**Safa Park** Al Wasl **050198 0663**
www.dubaifitcamp.com
Map **2 D4** Metro **Business Bay**
Dubai Fit runs bootcamps at Dubai Offshore Sailing Club, Safa Park and Jumeirah Beach Residences. Personal training and nutritional advice are also offered.

## Dubai Ladies Club
**Jumeira Rd** Jumeira, **04 349 9922**
www.dubailadiesclub.com
Map **2 D3** Metro **Business Bay**
Aquaerobics classes are held in the club pool on Sundays, Tuesdays and Thursdays at 09:30, on Sundays and Mondays at 18:30, and on Wednesdays at 19:00.

# Your guide to living in and loving the UAE

**Liveworkexplore**

The one-stop magazine for expats in the UAE, from the publishers of the No.1 best selling Dubai Explorer - Live Work Explore.

www.liveworkexplore.com

## Slimming Made Easy

If you can't stand the thought of going to the gym, try Hypoxi therapy. The training system is said to maximise cellulite and fat burn by combining exercise with vacuum suction. The method is non-invasive and painless and can be directed at those problem areas where you find it hard to lose weight. Visible results can be noticed after a couple of sessions and most results can be achieved in around 12 weeks. The treatment is gaining in popularity and you can try it at The Aviation Club (04 282 4122), at Hayyaa Health Club (Meadows Town Centre, 3638318), Perfect Figure Studio (800 497 694) and Club Active Plus (04 336 0001) in Oud Metha. Find out more at www.hypoxi.net.

### Exhale Fitness Studio

**Jumeirah Beach Residence 04 424 3777**
www.exhaledubai.com
Map **1 K3** Metro **Jumeirah Lakes Towers**
This ladies-only fitness centre is mainly a yoga and Pilates studio but it also offers some of the most innovative dance fitness classes in the city. Girls can get fit through belly dancing, hulaerobics, African dance, street dance and Latino cardio classes. Specific programmes aimed at weight loss are available, making the studio popular with women of all nationalities. There are also kids' dance fitness classes.

### Fitness First

**Dubai International Financial Centre (DIFC)**
Trade Centre **04 363 7444**
www.fitnessfirst.ae
Map **2 G5** Metro **Financial Centre**
With nine branches located across the city, Fitness First is quickly taking over the Dubai health club scene. Compared to other health clubs of the same caliber, the memberships here are less expensive, with classes included in the membership price. All of the branches are large and some have pools. Most of the locations tend to get crowded after work and at the weekends, so if you don't like the 'social gym' atmosphere, you might want to look elsewhere. But if you wanna hang out for coffee after your workout, borrow DVDs and check your emails then find the nearest branch to you. Promotions are common, so check the website for your nearest branch and current deal. Locations include: Ibn Battuta Mall (04 366 9933), Uptown Mirdiff (04 288 2311), Burjuman Centre (04 351 0044), Dubai Festival City (04 375 0177), Al Mussalla Towers (04 397 4117), Al Hana Centre (Ladies Gym, 04 398 1866; Mixed, 04 398 9030), Dubai Media City (04 424 3999), Oasis Centre (ladies only, 04 330 7736) and DIFC (04 363 7444).

### Fitness O2

**Nxt to Mall of the Emirates** Al Barsha **04 395 2922**
www.fitness02.com
Map **1 R5** Metro **Mall of the Emirates**
Fitness O2 offers a variety of different bootcamps, personal training, and corporate health solutions and events. It also runs a children's football academy and Fat Fighters weight loss club.

### Goal Attained

Various Locations **056 693 9258**
www.goalattained.com
Goal Attained offers personal training and a variety of group fitness programmes including a circuit training-style bootcamp combining kayaking, cycling and running in outdoor locations. Led by former military instructor Bruce King, sessions start at Dhs.100.

### Hayya!

**The Lakes** Emirates Hills **04 362 7790**
www.hayya.ae
Map **1 K6** Metro **Jumeirah Lakes Towers**
Hayya! has four health clubs located in the Springs, the Meadows, the Lakes and Old Town. All have a pleasant environment and good facilities. Each branch has a pool and gym, and some include squash courts, restaurants, creches, cafes and children's pools. The clubs frequently offer promotions for couples and families.

### India Club

**Nxt to Indian High School** Oud Metha **04 337 1112**
www.indiaclubdubai.com
Map **2 L5** Metro **Oud Metha**
Opened in 1964, this club has served over 6,500 members. It provides facilities for sports, entertainment and recreation, and to promote business. Facilities include a library, gym, separate steam rooms and saunas for men and women, badminton, squash and tennis courts, table tennis, basketball hoops, a bowling alley, a swimming pool and a variety of indoor games. Yoga classes and sports coaching are also available.

### Original Fitness Co

**Boulevard at Emirates Towers** Trade Centre
**04 313 2081**
www.originalfitnessco.com
Map **2 H5** Metro **Emirates Towers**
Original Fitness Co offers a new series of programmes from boot camp expert Corey Oliver, including four-week fitness camps, women only and kids classes, as well as personal training. They also offer special bespoke programmes for corporate groups to encourage teamwork as well as improved fitness levels. Alternatively if you want to get rid of your work stress try their Punch Fitness classes.

## Pharaohs' Club
**Pyramids** Wafi **04 324 0000**
www.wafi-health-leisure.com
Map **2 P6** Metro **Healthcare City**
Pharaohs' Club features an indoor climbing wall, a fitness centre and swimming pool and offers group classes which are open to members and non-members.

## Physical Advantage
Various Location **04 311 6570**
www.physicaladvantage.ae
Physical Advantage specialises in military-style bootcamps at various locations around Dubai. Personal training and group exercise classes are also available.

## Sharjah Wanderers Sports Club
**Nr Sharjah English School** Sharjah **06 566 2105**
www.sharjahwanderers.com
This is a popular club supported by the expat community in Sharjah, Dubai and the Northern Emirates. Facilities include floodlit tennis courts, football, rugby and hockey fields, squash courts, swimming pool, gym, library, snooker, darts, aerobic classes, yoga, dancing for kids, netball and a kids' play area. Memberships are available and this is one of the only places in Sharjah were people can enjoy a post workout drink.

## Spring Dubai
Various Locations **050 378 7367**
www.springdubai.com
Peter Sullivan at Spring Dubai offers kettle bell classes – the latest celebrity fitness craze. Kettle bells classes help to sculpt and tone the body through strengthening exercises. Personal training and functional biomechanics for optimising performance are also available.

## Surf Fit
**Umm Suqeim Beach** Umm Suqeim **050 459 2672**
www.surfingdubai.com
This innovative fitness regime combines beach boot camp training with surf moves such as paddling and beach board work on the sand. Dhs.1,200 for eight classes.

## Top Sport
**Nr Grand City Mall** Al Quoz **04 340 7688**
Map **1 T6** Metro **Al Quoz**
Best known for its boxing gym, this surprisingly clean club in Al Quoz has a five-a-side football pitch, basketball courts, weight room and indoor tennis courts. Memberships are available on a monthly basis and cost Dhs.500. Members have free access to all of the facilities. Non-members can also use the facilities but need to book at least one week in advance.

# Health Spas & Massage

Soothing for the body, mind and soul, a massage could be a weekly treat, a gift to someone special, or a relaxing way to get you through a trying time at work. All sorts of unusual treatments are available in Dubai. See p.200 for some of the most unique ones. Numerous massage and relaxation techniques are available, but prices and standards vary, so it's worth doing your research into what's on offer. Spas range from those at opulent 'seven-star' hotels where every detail is customised for a blissful experience, to comfortable independent places which offer fewer facilities but better value for money if you just want someone to loosen your knots.

## 1847
**Grosvenor House** Dubai Marina **04 399 8888**
www.grosvenorhouse-dubai.com
Map **1 L4** Metro **Dubai Marina**
Men are the centre of attention at 1847, the first dedicated 'grooming lounge' for men in the Middle East. Skilled therapists offer traditional shaves, beard styling, facials, massages, manicures and pedicures, so whether you're looking for relaxation, invigoration or a regular spruce-up there's something on the menu for you. Other branches are located on The Walk at Jumeirah Beach Residences (04 437 0252) and Emirates Towers Boulevard (04 330 1847).

## Akaru Spa
**The Aviation Club** Garhoud **04 282 8578**
www.akaruspa.com
Map **2 N7** Metro **GGICO**
The Akaru Spa's autumnal colours and natural decor create a truly tranquil effect. Exotic treatments range from specialised facials and wraps to Oxyspa and Hydrodermie treatments. During the cooler months, a selection of Sky Therapies are administered on the rooftop terrace. A Turkish room with sauna is also available.

## Amara Spa
**Park Hyatt Dubai** Port Saeed **04 602 1234**
www.dubai.park.hyatt.com
Map **2 M6** Metro **GGICO**
Amara spa is something of a breath of fresh air in Dubai's spa world which, while sublime, tends to follow the same formula. That's not to say that dimmed lighting, rose petals, candles and hypnotic music don't make for a heavenly experience, but what sets Amara apart are the treatment rooms. After arriving at the grand spa entrance, guests are escorted directly to the treatment room which acts as a personal spa. Here you have all the facilities of a changing room as well as a relaxation corner. After your treatment, or during if you are having a scrub

or wrap, you can treat yourself to a shower under the sun in your very own private outdoor shower (very liberating) with a relaxation area for you to dry off under the warm rays.

## Angsana Spa Arabian Ranches

**Dubai Polo & Equestrian Club** Arabian Ranches
**04 361 8251**
www.angsanaspa.com
Map **1 N12**

The minimalist Asian surroundings feature rich, dark wood, while incense, exotic oils, low light and soft music set the tone for relaxation. The impeccably trained staff work wonders on stressed, aching bodies, turning tight muscles into putty and sending overworked minds to cloud nine. Unique massages, ranging from Balinese to Hawaiian to Thai, are certainly at the higher end of the scale in terms of price, but the quality of treatment ensures value for money. This Singaporean and Thai affiliate brand of Banyan Tree has certainly brought its highly reputed standards to Dubai. Other locations include Dubai Marina (04 368 4356), Emirates Hills (04 368 2222) and The Address Montgomerie Dubai (04 360 9322).

## Armonia Spa

**Sheraton Jumeirah Beach** Dubai Marina
**04 399 5533**
www.starwoodhotels.com
Map **1 J3** Metro **Jumeirah Lakes Towers**

After a refreshing beverage, you'll begin with a welcome ritual, involving a warm herbal aromatic foot massage in a wood-themed, candle-lit treatment room. Pampering options on offer include facials, full-body massages and luxurious body wraps for both men and women. The massage may be a little too gentle for some, so don't be afraid to tell your therapist to increase the pressure if required. A sauna and steam room are available should you wish to arrive a little early.The spa is on the small side, and facilities not as comprehensive as some other spas in town, but this remains a good place to come for facials and massages.

## Assawan Spa & Health Club

**Burj Al Arab** Umm Suqeim **04 301 7338**
www.jumeirah.com
Map **1 S3** Metro **Mall of the Emirates**

Situated on the 18th floor of the breathtaking Burj Al Arab, unsurprisingly, Assawan is an elaborate affair. There are female only and mixed environments, including a state of the art gym with studios for exercise classes, saunas, steam rooms, plunge pools and two wonderfully relaxing infinity pools decorated in mosaic and gold leaf tiles. You can literally swim up to the edge of the pool, put your nose to the window, and enjoy the amazing views of the Palm and the

World islands. The personal service here is excellent; you are pampered from the minute you walk through the door. For pure unadulterated indulgence, try the caviar body treatment. Also on offer is a 'men only' range including massage, facial, manicure, pedicure and more. If you really want to feel like royalty then this seriously sublime spa is a dream come true.

## Bliss Relaxology

**Emirates Bld, Beh Welcare Hospital** Garhoud
**04 286 9444**
Map **2 N6** Metro **GGICO**

This small relaxation centre offers aromatherapy oil massage, reflexology and Thai massage. Appointments can usually be made 30 minutes in advance, so it's perfect for easing the strain after a busy day at the office. A one hour Thai massage costs Dhs.150 and it's Dhs.210 for an aromatherapy rub down.

## Cleopatra's Spa

**Pyramids** Wafi **04 324 7700**
www.wafi-health-leisure.com
Map **2 P6** Metro **Healthcare City**

Don't be put off by first impressions at Cleopatra's Spa. The entrance and changing facilities may lack the opulence of some hotel spas, but what it lacks in ostentation it makes up for in occasion. The relaxation area is an ancient Egyptian affair with drapes, silk cushions and majlis-style seats. There is also a small plunge pool with Jacuzzi and sauna. The treatment rooms are comfortable, softly lit and with luxurious touches and the obligatory hypnotic tunes. The spa menu should satisfy all, with everything from massages (including pregnancy) and facials to body wraps and anti-ageing miracles. The big bonus is that if you book a package you get a pool pass which allows you to float round the lazy river at the Pharaohs' Club's idyllic tree-shaded pool area. There is also a separate spa for men.

## Dragonfly Spa

**BurJuman** Bur Dubai **04 351 1120**
www.dragonfly.ae
Map **2 L4** Metro **Khalid Bin Al Waleed**

Set amid the hustle of Fitness First at BurJuman shopping mall, Dragonfly is a haven for shoppers and gym bunnies alike. The three flights of stairs to reception really do lead guests to believe they are escaping the outside world, and your arrival is announced by a large gong at reception. Dark woods and traditional ornaments complement the treatment menu which focuses on Chinese and Japanese shiatsu styles. Guests can relax in a chill-out space after their treatment with some soothing green tea. For a real treat, book in to the Crystal Suite, a massive crystal-adorned treatment room with a private bathroom and relaxation space.

### Dubai Marine Spa

**Dubai Marine Beach** Jumeira **04 304 8081**
www.dxbmarine.com
Map **2 H3** Metro **Al Jafiliya**
A compact spa offering an excellent array of treatments with branded products from Guinot, Payot and Ionithermie. Particularly pleasurable is the hot stone massage that can also be combined with a facial, manicure and pedicure. Also on offer are full and half-day packages and a limited range of treatments for men.

### Elche

**Beh Jumeirah Plaza, St 10, Villa 42** Jumeira
**04 349 4942**
www.elche.ae
Map **2 H3** Metro **Al Jafiliya**
Elche uses 100% organic herbs, flowers, vegetables and fruit in its treatment products. Traditional know-how and contemporary scientific techniques combine to give Elche a unique advantage in Dubai's spa landscape. Warm tones decorate the interior of the villa, and are accented by sensuous music and a delicious aroma of fresh ingredients. The certified Hungarian beauty and massage therapists are specially trained in using Elche products, some of which have been specially developed to cope with Dubai's harsh climate. Your skin type will be assessed

before a treatment is recommended. The two-hour cleansing facial with a unique paprika mask is fiercely popular so book in advance.

### Elixir Spa

**Metropolitan Resort** Dubai Marina **04 399 5000**
www.habtoorhotels.com
Map **1 L3** Metro **Dubai Marina**
Don't be fooled by the first impressions of this spa's busy reception location, the six large treatment rooms are the height of relaxation and luxury. There is also a dry float room, rasul mud chamber, a nail station, wet spa facilities and a recovery area stocked with herbal teas. Treatment offerings include Karin 02 Herzog skincare treatments from Switzerland and the therapist will spend time explaining your treatment to ensure it results, with you emerging feeling pampered and relaxed.

### Eternal MedSpa Dubai

**Jumeira Rd, Villa 397, Opp Jumeirah Beach Park**
Jumeira **04 344 0008**
www.eternalmedspa.com
Map **2 E3** Metro **Business Bay**
The medspa concept combines the pampering and decor of a spa with treatments performed by medical professionals. Eternal Medspa offers the same non-surgical treatments that are usually performed at

Angsana Spa

# Well-Being

**Health, Fitness & Well-Being**

cosmetic surgery and dermatology clinics. Several options are available, including fillers, thermage treatments and health coaching. The spa regularly promotes treatments through special offers, and patients can book treatment packages to suit their specific needs.

## Express Unwind
**Trafalgar Bld, CBD 7, International City 04 430 8304**
www.expressunwind.com
The Thai staff at this small spa in International City are experts at their native form of massage, which combines firm stretching and body contortion in a forceful body workout. Don't go expecting a gloriously relaxing hour of soft touches and little whispers in your ear. Instead, all of your aches and knots will be pulled out of you by well-trained hands. The simple decor is identical to something you'd find in Thailand, and the tiny treatment rooms are only a bit bigger than the floor mat you'll be kneaded on. This is the type of massage you could get every two weeks without leaving a gapping hole in your wallet.

## The Grand Spa
**Grand Hyatt Dubai Umm Hurair 04 317 1234**
www.dubai.grand.hyatt.com
Map **2 L7** Metro **Healthcare City**
Contrary to its name, this petite spa wins on atmosphere and attention to detail. The changing room and adjacent relaxation area have dark wooden floors and walls and are lit by rows of candles. The wet area is drizzled with rose petals and houses a Jacuzzi, plunge pool, sauna and steam room as well as spacious showers. The treatments on offer range from facials, all designed with preservation and attainment of youth in mind, to massages with specialist 'aromasoul' treatments using essential oils. Fusion packages allow you to combine a treatment, facial and an activity class for top-to-toe indulgence.

## H2O The Male Spa
**Boulevard at Emirates Towers** Trade Centre
**04 319 8181**
www.jumeirahemiratestowers.com
Map **2 H5** Metro **Emirates Towers**
Tucked away on the lower floor of the Emirates Towers, H2O is a compact, sophisticated men-only spa. The dim lighting and dark wood panelling induces a calming, tranquil atmosphere that lowers the stress levels at once. The hour-long H2O signature treatment uses a combination of aromatherapy oils and massage techniques to de-stress and revitalise the weary, while other options cater to specific requirements. There's also a flotation pool, oxygen bar and a range of Aromatherapy Associates oils and products available to purchase on your way out.

## The Health Club
**Emirates Towers** Trade Centre **04 319 8888**
www.jumeirahemiratestowers.com
Map **2 H5** Metro **Emirates Towers**
As well as unisex gym facilities, a refreshing outdoor swimming pool and a sun terrace, The Health Club offers a range of spa treatments for ladies only. Personally tailored treatments include aromatherapy, Swedish and Shiatsu massage, facials, and manicures and pedicures. The signature Pure Indulgence Exclusive 4 U full body massage is relaxation heaven, employing varied techniques and oils to perfectly match your state of mind and body. Tanning sessions can be booked to give you a pre, post or mid-holiday boost, while steam and sauna rooms are situated in the luxurious locker rooms to help round off the cleansing rituals.

## Heavenly Spa
**The Westin Dubai Mina Seyahi Beach Resort & Marina** Al Sufouh **04 399 4141**
www.starwoodhotels.com
Map **1 M3** Metro **Nakheel**
The Heavenly Spa leaves nothing to be desired: the therapists are neither neglectful nor intrusive, making you feel instantly comfortable. The clean, contemporary decor manages to feel warm and inviting, helping to clear your mind for the gorgeous treatments that await. The spa's signature treatment is the Heavenly Massage, which uses four hands moving in syncronization. The effect is unlike anything you're likely to experience again, unless you make this a regular occurrence.

## A Touch Of Arabia

For a typically Arabian pampering experience, opt for an Oriental Hammam. This treatment is traditional in the Middle East region and shares similarities with Turkish baths. The name refers to the bath (the room) in which the treatment takes place – typically an elaborate affair in Dubai's five-star spa scene. A hammam involves a variety of different experiences, including being bathed, steamed, washed with black soap, scrubbed with a loofah and massaged on a hot marble table; some treatments also involve mud masks and henna. While this may sound a little invasive, and more than a tad vigorous, it's a wonderfully invigorating experience which leaves your skin feeling as soft as cream. An absolute must-do while in Dubai, the hammams at The Spa at Jebel Ali Golf Resort & Spa(p.216), The Oriental Hammam (p.215) and The Spa at The Palace (p.218) are highly recommended.

## Lily Pond Massage & Retreat

**Yansoon Building 9, Old Town Souk 23**
Downtown Burj Dubai **04 420 5230**
Map **2 F5** Metro **Burj Dubai**
Lily Pond has quickly established itself as a favourite retreat for those in the know. It may not be as polished as some other nail bars and massage centres but if you are looking for an authentic experience then you're in for a treat. Head and shoulder massages during manicures and pedicures aren't tokenistic but the real de-stressing deal, administered by tiny but incredibly strong therapists. Prices for waxing, threading, nail treatments and massages are very competitive and service is always friendly. The Jumeirah Beach Residences (04 423 3722) branch offers rain shower massages.

## Lime Spa

**Desert Palm Dubai 04 323 8888**
www.limespas.com
Lime is more of a retreat than a spa, and with any treatment you get use of the facilities for the day, so you can linger in the relaxation rooms or lounge around the pool. The spa itself is one of the most beautiful in the city and has six treatment rooms, all naturally lit by large windows overlooking the polo fields. The couples' treatment room has its own plunge pool and private relaxation area. The communal relaxation area is a sublime place to enjoy a cup of herbal tea after your treatment – the heated beds are heavenly. A range of massages and facials are available at the spa, all drawing on colour therapy to tailor each treatment to the needs of each individual. Highly recommended, not just for a specific treatment, but for a full-on, girly spa day out.

## Man/Age

**The Walk, Jumeirah Beach Residence** Dubai Marina
**04 435 5780**
www.managespa.com
Map **1 K3** Metro **Jumeirah Lakes Towers**
This luxury men's spa offers male grooming including haircuts and shaving, manicures, massages and facials. It also has a Moroccan bath. 6 month and yearly memberships are available. A second branch is located in Media City (04 437 0868).

## Natural Elements Spa & Fitness

**Le Meridien Dubai** Garhoud **04 702 2430**
www.starwoodhotels.com
Map **2 N7** Metro **GGICO**
The most unique touch of Natural Elements Spa is the the Aroma Heat Cave. This beautiful cocoon of relaxation has a (faux) starlit sky, large comfortable loungers and special aromatherapy fragrances throughout. Beforehand, there's the matter of your

treatment and the spa offers a huge range of services. Choose from hot stone massages and luxury hand and foot treatments, to facials and grooming rituals. Products used are from Pevonia Botanica, renowned for their natural, holistic treatment properties.

## One&Only Spa > p.451

**One&Only Royal Mirage** Al Sufouh **04 315 2140**
www.oneandonlyresorts.com
Map **1 M3** Metro **Nakheel**
Understated decor, neutral colours, natural light and soft music create a serene effect in the treatment rooms. While this spa offers a variety of facials and Swedish, lymphatic drainage, slimming and sports massages, its speciality is the Canyon Love Stone Therapy, an energy-balancing massage using warm and cool stones. The volcanic stones have been specially selected, are 'charged' in the moonlight and cleansed with salt. The stones are placed on specific points around the body, and then used to massage the skin. For high-level pampering, opt for a peel, wrap or oil bath, exclusively with Espa products.

## The Oriental Hammam

**One&Only Royal Mirage** Al Sufouh **04 315 2130**
www.oneandonlyresorts.com
Map **1 M3** Metro **Nakheel**
Welcomed by the attentive staff, you'll be put at ease as the Oriental Hammam Experience is explained. Like the Royal Mirage hotel itself, the spa surroundings are elegant but not overly opulent, with a warm traditional feel. The hammam and spa is an impressive area with mosaic arches and intricate carvings on the high domes. Hammam users also have access to the spa's Jacuzzi, plunge pools and the sensually sleep-inducing relaxation room.

## Raffles Amrita Spa

**Raffles Dubai** Umm Hurair **04 324 8888**
www.dubai.raffles.com
Map **2 K6** Metro **Healthcare City**
As you might expect from Raffles Hotel, the Amrita Spa offers the height of decadent indulgence. Treatment rooms have private changing rooms, complete with power shower, fluffy towels and luxury toiletries. Atmospheric lighting, relaxing music, a heated treatment bench with warmed towels await you whichever treatment you chose. For the ultimate spa experience try Dubai Decadence – a full six hours of head-to-toe pampering including a steam bath, body scrub, hot stone massage, facial, manicure and pedicure. Male and female hair and beauty salons, a gym, pool, sauna, steam bath and whirlpool are also available, should you wish to delay your departure further. Couples packages are also on offer.

### Royal Waters Health Spa

**Al Mamzar Centre** Deira **04 297 2053**
Map **2 R5** Metro **Al Quiadah**
A warm welcome awaits from friendly, knowledgeable staff who will advise you on the vast range of treatments available here for health, relaxation and beauty. The spa has simple tiled decor with soft lighting and tranquil music. Walk through the well-equipped gym and up on the roof you'll find the swimming pool with views of the bustling area below. The spa offers treatments for cellulite and stretch marks, and they have a wonderful hydrotherapy circuit designed to leave you refreshed after a hard day. A sauna and steam room are also available.

### Satori Spa

**Bab Al Shams Desert Resort & Spa 04 809 6232**
www.jumeirah.com
The spa's location in the middle of the desert adds to the all natural feeling that you immediately get when you walk through the doors. Satori's treatments are worth every penny. Aromatherapy Associates is the oil of choice here, and a beguiling scent surrounds you as you are kneaded and massaged into a state of semi-conscious bliss. The treatment rooms feature a window with a wooden blind, which is quite unusual for spas in Dubai which are usually cosseted away in the deep innards of a hotel. Here, the sense of being close to the desert in its natural state seeps into the gently lit room, and the quiet tinkle of spa music empties your mind of everything but the rhythmic strokes of the therapist.

### SensAsia Urban Spa

**The Village** Jumeira **04 349 8850**
www.sensasiaspas.com
Map **2 H3** Metro **Al Jafiliya**
SensAsia may not have all the trimmings of some five-star spas, but what it lacks in the way of plunge pools and Jacuzzis it makes up for in the 60+ minutes you spend in a heightened state of bliss. The hot stone massage is particularly sensational, with your choice of aroma, strength of massage and the temperature control of the stones. With treatments from Bali, Thailand and Japan, and prices that undercut the big spas, you'll want to make space in your diary every month. Plus, regardless of the lack of hotel opulence the relax areas, showers and treatment rooms are still of a very high standard.

### The Spa at Jebel Ali Golf Resort & Spa

**Jebel Ali Golf Resort & Spa** Jebel Ali **04 883 6000**
www.jebelali-international.com
An excellent level of service is offered for both men and women, in intimate and well-presented surroundings. The communal area has an invigorating shower, sauna, Jacuzzi and steam room. While the changing areas are a little small, they are equipped with Elemis goodies, and the tranquil after-treatment area overlooks the beach. Recommended is the 90 minute Royal Hammam Ritual which involves black soap, a henna mask, some exuberant exfoliating and a rasul mud mask before a darn good wash down. This style of pampering is literally from head to toe. Just leave any shyness at the marble door – but not your partner, if you're brave enough to try the couple's option.

### The Spa At Shangri-La

**Shangri-La Hotel** Trade Centre **04 343 8888**
www.shangri-la.com
Map **2 G5** Metro **Financial Centre**
Both the health club and spa have all of the facilities you would expect from a five-star location, and a salon and barber, juice bar and boutique complete the package. Surroundings are minimalist and the treatment rooms are a little on the clinical side, while the communal areas lean more towards fitness club than spa, with too many open spaces and not enough privacy. That said, it's ideal for a healthy break for those working on the Sheikh Zayed Road strip.

### The Spa At The Address Downtown Burj Dubai

**The Address Downtown Burj Dubai**
Downtown Burj Dubai **04 436 8751**
www.theaddress.com
Map **2 F6** Metro **Burj Dubai**
Step into total relaxation from the moment you arrive at The Spa at The Address, thanks to muted decor, ambient music, and a cold towel and refreshing cucumber and mint drink handed to you. The Spa has male and female treatment rooms, a couple's room, and a range of treatments including facials, massages and wraps using ESPA products. Lie back and relax on heated beds while the therapist performs your treatment after a skin analysis, and then take some time to enjoy the beautiful views over the Downtown area. The Spa At The Address Dubai Mall (04 423 8888) and Spa At The Address Dubai Marina (04 436 7777) opened in late 2009.

### The Spa At The Atlantis > p.217

**Atlantis The Palm** Palm Jumeira **04 426 1020**
www.atlantisthepalm.com
Map **1 N0** Metro **Nakheel**
You'll enter this spectacular spa with the highest of expectations and disappointment is definitely not on the menu here: from the minute you walk into the boutique area (where you can sample a wide range of products used in the spa, and load up on girly goodies) up until the end of your treatment, when you're sipping green tea in the relaxation lounge, it's a heavenly experience. Even though it has 27 treatment

# The Atlantis Spa

The Atlantis Spa presents a memorable experience, awakening your senses within awe inspiring and serene water surroundings. Set over two magnificent floors, the 27 treatment rooms provide the ultimate privacy for both his and her relaxation time. Exclusive therapies with manicures and pedicures by Bastien Gonzalez and glamorous products all available for your pure indulgence.

For more information and bookings call +971 4 426 1020
or email spa@atlantisthepalm.com
atlantisthepalm.com

## ATLANTIS
THE PALM, DUBAI

# Well-Being

rooms, set over two floors, it doesn't feel like a big spa; perhaps because of the personal touch you will treated to. Whether you choose a massage, a facial, a Bastien Gonzalez manicure or pedicure, or one of the delectable Spa Journeys, your therapist has one clear focus: you. For the ultimate in indulgence book yourself in for the whole day.

## The Spa At The Palace

**The Palace – The Old Town** Downtown Burj Dubai
**04 428 7888**
www.thepalace-dubai.com
Map **2 F6** Metro **Burj Dubai**
You couldn't find a more suitable address for the Spa at the Palace; a treatment here will leave you feeling like royalty. The facilities are wonderful and include two Oriental bath houses, monsoon showers and two Hydrospa bath tubs with therapy jets. Beautifully decorated with mosaic designs on the walls, it is a haven of tranquility. Sink in to a welcoming Hydrospa bath tub or unwind in the steam room until you are called for your treatment – there is a huge range on offer, but for a unique regional experience, you really should try the Hammam.

## Spa At The Ritz-Carlton, Dubai

**The Ritz-Carlton, Dubai** Dubai Marina **04 318 6184**
www.ritz-carlton.com
Map **1 L3** Metro **Dubai Marina**
The opulence of the Ritz-Carlton quietly asserts itself amidst the brash and trendy spots that dominate Dubai's beachfront. The Ritz-Carlton's spa, a tranquil retreat, is very much in keeping with the hotel's character. The treatment rooms are lit by candles, showing flickers of the muted tones with wood and natural stone finishes. Guests are encouraged to arrive early for their appointments to enjoy the spa's facilities – a dry sauna, eucalyptus steam room, whirlpool and relaxation room – to ready themselves for a massage, facial or body ritual from the extensive menu.

## Taj Spa

**Taj Palace Hotel** Deira **04 211 3101**
www.tajhotels.com
Map **2 N5** Metro **Al Rigga**
This tranquil spa has a mystical, romantic atmosphere. It offers modern Ayurvedic treatments as well as popular European and far eastern ranges and natural therapies. Massage techniques, movements, herbal selection and products used are tailored to the individual guest, supporting the holistic principle that each individual has a unique body type and will therefore have different balancing needs. The changing rooms are welcoming and have a sauna and steam room, while the relaxation area is hard to tear yourself away from.

## Talise Spa

**Madinat Jumeirah** Umm Suqeim **04 366 6818**
www.jumeirah.com/talise
Map **1 R4** Metro **Mall of the Emirates**
This regal spa is made up of luxurious lounges and treatment rooms connected by garden walkways. The rooms themselves are exotic and well-appointed with warm shades and ambient music. The welcoming staff truly set this spot apart, advising on products and technique before your individually designed treatment. The range of therapies is extensive but not overwhelming, with a focus on body treatments using natural oils. A true destination spa, take advantage of the steam room, sauna and plunge pools before or after your appointment, or read a magazine while sipping on ginger tea sweetened with honey in one of the chill out rooms. Yoga, including the popular classes held under the stars, is also available.

## Timeless Spa

**Dubai Marriott Harbour Hotel & Suites** Dubai Marina **04 319 4000**
www.marriott.com
Map **1 L4** Metro **Dubai Marina**
Once inside this Asian-inspired spa, you can delve straight into your treatments or spend a few minutes using the sauna, steam room and Jacuzzi – your therapist will explain which will complement your treatments best. There are separate areas for men and women and each treatment room has soft lighting, ambient music, and a bed in the centre of the room. You'll find a comprehensive range of treatments here (sports massages, facials and even a massage used for Hawaiian royalty), which use products like Sodashi and Babor.

## Willow Stream Spa

**Fairmont Dubai** Trade Centre **04 311 8800**
www.fairmont.com
Map **2 J4** Metro **Trade Centre**
In keeping with the eclectic decor of The Fairmont Dubai, Willow Stream is decorated in a luxurious Greco-Roman style, with beautiful mosaics and sleek white pillars. Soft, white towels and subtle candlelight create a wonderful sense of calm. There is a comprehensive selection of top-to-toe spa and beauty treatments using Phytomer and Aromatherapy Associates product lines. Before or after your treatment you can use the steam room, sauna, Jacuzzi, fitness centre, the outdoor swimming pools or simply relax with a herbal tea or fresh juice. They also have healing mineral pools and an excellent gym, and after you have worked out or spaced out you can enjoy a stroll around the lush gardens. Check out www.willowstream.com and get inspired by the Willow Stream magazine.

Raffles Amrita Spa

Willow Stream Spa

The Oriental Hammam

Akaru Spa

Talise Spa

# FUN-FILLED ACTIVITIES ONLY AT ATLANTIS DUBAI

## AQUAVENTURE WATERPARK
### LARGEST WATERPARK WITH OVER 10 SLIDES AND RIDES

Splash right in to the largest and most exciting waterpark in the Middle East. Aquaventure is overflowing with 42 fun-filled acres, Master Blasters, a speedslide, rivers, rapids, lush tropical landscapes and access to a private beach.

**Open daily: 10:00am - Sunset**

**No bookings necessary.**

## THE LOST CHAMBERS
### OVER 20 MARINE EXHIBITS

Walk through The Lost Chambers with over 20 fresh and seawater marine exhibits including sharks, rays, piranha, giant arapaima, giant grouper, lionfish, lookdowns and much more.

**Open daily: 11:00am - 1:00am**

**No bookings necessary.**

## FEED THE COWNOSE RAYS
### AT AQUAVENTURE

Wade in waist-high water surrounded by our friendly rays as they eagerly wait to be fed from your hand. Book early! Limited spaces available! AED 175 per person

**3 Sessions a day at 10:40am, 1:10pm and 2:10pm**

**For bookings please call +971 4 426 1030**

# ATLANTIS
## THE PALM, DUBAI

atlantisthepalm.com

# Discover Dubai

# DISCOVER DUBAI

Dubai has put itself well and truly on the global map over the past decade as one of the top places to visit. Its desire to build the biggest and best of everything has, as planned, caught much of the world's attention. Its ever-growing skyline, audacious man-made islands, mega-malls, seven-star service and permanently sunny weather have combined with its position as a major airline hub to transform it into an international holiday destination, a regional shopping magnet, and the Middle East's most ostentatious, glamorous party capital.

All this is good news for the leisure time of expats lucky enough to have relocated to this headline-grabbing emirate – but there's more to Dubai than just the high-living holiday highlights. Scratch the surface and you'll discover plenty of cultural delights, multicultural attractions, traditional gems and even simple, sedate everyday leisure activities.

As an adopted Dubai local, there are plenty of ways to fill your leisure time. Start by exploring the city. There's a definite divide between the old and the new parts of town. Head to the creek and its surrounding areas of Deira and Bur Dubai for a flavour of what Dubai used to be like before the economic boom turned it into a modern, international metropolis. Souks, narrow side streets, heritage sites, local restaurants and a bustling waterway make this a great part of town to investigate. In contrast, the mind-boggling modern developments that make up New Dubai – Downtown Burj Dubai, Palm Jumeirah and Dubai Marina – accommodate spectacular buildings, high-living hotels and shopping delights, and more besides.

The city's art scene is starting to bubble up into something interesting too, with more and more modern galleries popping up in the industrial area of Al Quoz (see p.242), and there's a full calendar of international events to keep sports fans happy (p.25).

During the cooler months, there are some excellent outdoor options for get-togethers with family and friends; Dubai's green parks are superbly maintained, while the beaches draw crowds of sunbathers and swimmers at the weekends (p.246 and p.248). There's family fun to be had too at the various waterparks, aquariums and amusement centres scattered around town (p.252).

You're not likely to tire of enjoying the urban attractions anytime soon, but even if you do, there's a huge adventure playground just beyond the city limits that's waiting to be explored. Head off-road to make the most of the awe-inspiring desert sands and wadi beds, hike in the mountain peaks, go camping or take to the sea for some excellent diving, snorkelling and sailing (p.255). And that's just Dubai – there are six other emirates to get to know too (see Out Of The City, p.274).

# PLACES OF INTEREST

## Deira & The Creek

Once the central residential hub of Dubai, Deira remains an incredibly atmospheric area. Narrow convoluted streets bustle with activity while gold, spices, perfumes and general goods are touted in its numerous souks. Likewise, Dubai Creek, beside which Deira sits, was the original centre of Dubai commerce, and today it still buzzes with boats plying their transport and cargo trades. Both sides of the creek are lined by corniches that come alive in the evenings as residents head out for a stroll and traders take stock. Take the time to meander along the Deira side,

Deira creekside

## WATER TAXIS

The water taxi system on the creek will provide a new form of public transport when it comes into operation in 2010. Like land taxis, the vessels will be available for private hire. Passengers will be able to call the RTA and have a craft pick them up from one of 10 purpose-built piers to take to them to their waterfront destination of choice, or simply for their own private boat tour of the creek.

where men in traditional south Asian garb unload wooden dhows docked by the water's edge, tightly packed with everything from fruit and vegetables to televisions and maybe even a car or two, often traded between Iran, the UAE's neighbour across the Gulf.

No resident should miss the chance to experience a trip across the water on a commuter abra (p.55) for Dhs.1, or you can hire your own (plus driver) for an hour-long tour for Dhs.100.

For a full creek experience, start at Bastakiya (p.223), wander through the Textile Souk (p.397) on the Bur Dubai side before taking an abra towards Deira. Once on the Deira side, cross the corniche and head towards the souk district. First stop is the Spice Souk (p.239), where the aroma of saffron and cumin fills the air. Nearby, the streets in and around the Gold Souk (p.396) are crammed with shops shimmering with gold and platinum.

### Creek Tours

A cruise on Dubai Creek is a wonderful way to enjoy views of new and old parts of the city side by side. Many of the tours are in traditional wooden dhows, but even these often have air conditioning inside to avoid the summer heat and humidity. In the cooler months, the top deck is the place to be. Prices per adult range from about Dhs.45 for a daytime trip to Dhs.150 for a bargain dinner cruise and up to Dhs.325 for a top-class evening cruise with fine food. For more information see Boat Tours, p.266.

Take a wander around the area behind the souks to discover alleyways and narrow one-way streets that deal in almost any kind of goods imaginable. Tiny cafeterias, old barbershops and odd knick-knack stores appear around almost every corner, and life in general seems to move at its own energetic pace.

If it's rugs you want, then Deira Tower on Al Nasr Square is worth a visit. Around 40 shops offer a colourful profusion of carpets from Iran, Pakistan, Turkey and Afghanistan to suit most people's taste and pocket. For dinner with a view, head to the top of the Hyatt Regency where Al Dawaar (p.450) hosts

an incredible buffet within its rotating dining room. Afterwards, you can burn off the buffet belly by strolling along the gulf-side Deira corniche, which is where you'll find both the atmospheric Fish Market (p.395) and Al Mamzar Beach Park (p.246), a great spot for a day out by the sea.

Further up the creek, on the other side of the souks, are some fascinating buildings that seemed years ahead of their time when they were built. The large golf ball that sits atop the Etisalat building is testimony to the unique imagination of Dubai's modern architecture. The sparkling glass building housing the National Bank of Dubai (known fondly as the 'pregnant lady') is a sculptural vision, standing tall like a magnificent convex mirror that reflects the bustling activity of the creek.

### Good As Gold

The Gold Souk is an Aladdin's cave of gold shopping. Bargaining is expected, and discounts depend on the season and the international gold rate. Dubai Shopping Festival and Dubai Summer Surprises are the main periods for low prices, when huge discounts attract gold lovers from around the world. Individual pieces can be made, or copies done to your own specifications, within a few days. Even if you aren't buying, an evening stroll through the Gold Souk, when it's glistening, is worth the experience.

It is also in this area that you can find three of Dubai's original five-star hotels: Hilton Dubai Creek, Sheraton Dubai Creek, and the Radisson Blu, Dubai Deira Creek (formerly the InterContinental), which recently celebrated its 30th anniversary. Nearby is the dhow wharfage, where more of the large wooden trading boats dock.

Inland is Deira City Centre, one of Dubai's first mega malls, while bordering the creek for about 1.5km between Maktoum and Garhoud bridges is an enticing stretch of carefully manicured greenery, home to the Dubai Creek Golf & Yacht Club (p.324). The impressive golf clubhouse is based on the shape of dhow sails (the image of this famous building is found on the Dhs.20 note), while the yacht club is aptly in the shape of a yacht. This is also the site of one of the city's top five-star hotels, the Park Hyatt Dubai, which features Mediterranean-style low buildings offering creek views and some great restaurants.

## Bastakiya: Old Dubai

For a dose of tradition, step out of the modern world and into a pocket of the city that harks back to a bygone era. The Bastakiya area, which is in Bur Dubai by the creek, is one of the oldest heritage sites in Dubai and certainly the most atmospheric. The

# Places Of Interest

## Port & Leisure

To the south-west of Bur Dubai is Port Rashid, where you'll find the Dubai Ports Authority building. A large glass and chrome construction imaginatively designed like a paddle steamer, all the paraphernalia of a port can be glimpsed over the surrounding fence.

neighbourhood dates from the early 1900s when traders from the Bastak area of southern Iran were encouraged to settle there by tax concessions granted by Sheikh Maktoum bin Hashar, the ruler of Dubai at the time. The area is characterised by traditional windtower houses, built around courtyards and clustered together along a winding maze of alleyways. The distinctive four-sided windtowers (barjeel), seen on top of the traditional flat-roofed buildings, were an early form of air conditioning. There are some excellent cultural establishments in and around Bastakiya, including Dubai Museum (p.240), XVA Gallery (p.245) and The Majlis Gallery (p.244), while a short stroll along the creek will bring you to the Textile Souk and abra station, from where you can cross the water to explore the souks on the Deira side (see p.222). You can make a single crossing on a communal abra for Dhs.1 (see p.55), or take a private tour up and down between

### BUR DUBAI

Up until only a few years ago, Bur Dubai, and Deira across the creek, were the business districts of the city. Today, the business hubs may have shifted to other, newer areas, but Bur Dubai remains an atmospheric, bustling part of the city. Here you'll find a multitude of nationalities living in squeezed-together multi-storey apartment blocks, busy shopping streets, seedy bars in older hotels, and some of the best historical and cultural attractions in Dubai. A walk along the corniche between Bastakiya and Shindagha (see above) will take you through crowds of people buying and selling fabrics from the Textile Souk, jostling to board an abra, or heading for prayers at one of the mosques or the atmospheric Hindu temple. From Bastakiya it is possible to follow the corniche up along the creekside where a number of luxury cruise boats moor (you can board one of these for a dinner cruise. The relaxed atmosphere of this stretch, with its grassy areas often full of people, makes it a great place to view the flashy buildings on the Deira side of the creek and watch the water traffic. Numerous embassies are located in this area, while further inland from the creek is the popular BurJuman shopping centre (p.398).

Maktoum Bridge and Shindagha (the official RTA rate is Dhs.100 for an hour). Beyond the Textile Souk is Shindagha, another interesting old area where you'll find Sheikh Saeed Al Maktoum's House (see p.241) and the Heritage & Diving Villages (p.240).

## Take Your Time

While in the area, take time to linger and absorb the unique sights, sounds and smells of Bur Dubai over a meal at Kan Zaman (p.477).

## Jumeira

Jumeira might not have the exotic atmosphere or history of Deira, but its beaches, shopping centres and pleasant, wide streets make up for it. The area is traditionally one of the most desirable addresses for well-off expats, and the origin of the infamous 'Jumeira Jane' caricature – well-off expat women who can often be found shopping or dining with fellow Janes in the establishments along Beach Road. The area is home to a range of stylish boutiques, Mercato Mall (p.406), and excellent cafes such as Limetree and THE One Restaurant (p.487).

### Just Outside Jumeira

Several places of interest surround the Jumeira area. To the south is Umm Suqeim, where the ultimate attraction has to be the iconic Burj Al Arab hotel (p.230) – be sure to visit its restaurants or spa at least once while you live here. If you prefer your leisure to be free of charge, there's plenty of public beach to enjoy – just turn up, pop your towel down and relax at Umm Suqeim beach (p.248), while for some more energetic aquatic fun there's Wild Wadi Water Park (p.250). Just behind Jumeira is the family friendly Safa Park (p.248), which is one of the main highlights on the villa and shop-lined Al Wasl Road.

It's a great part of town for hitting the beach too; the popular Jumeira Open Beach has showers and lifeguards, but unfortunately attracts a few voyeurs, so you may prefer to try the more private Jumeira Beach Park (p.246).

That's not to say Jumeira is all sun, sea and shopping – there are some interesting cultural spots here too. Jumeira Mosque (p.240) is one of the most recognisable places of worship in the city and welcomes visitors with tours and educational programmes, while the many galleries will keep art enthusiasts happy.

Just outside Jumeira, on the border with Satwa, lies Al Diyafah Street. It offers a completely different vibe to the sedate Jumeira suburbs; it's a hectic thoroughfare lined with shops and restaurants, and is the main destination for anyone needing to feed

Emirates Towers

Rising skyline

Dubai Marina

Bur Dubai

Bastakiya

# Streetlife: Karama & Satwa

They may not offer too much in the way of spectacular modern developments or five star luxury, but for a dose of interesting street life, plus a real flavour of the subcontinent and the Philippines, Karama and Satwa are well worth a visit.

Karama mainly consists of low-rise apartment buildings, but is also home to a range of shops selling all kinds of cheap clothing and goods – some not always the genuine article. Karama's merchants are a far cry from their mall counterparts, and you can expect to have to haggle to get your bargain. The other big draw for Karama is the range of excellent, low budget south Asian restaurants, serving firey Indian, Sri Lankan and Pakistani fare. Highlights include Saravana Bhavan (p.492) and Karachi Darbar (p.477).

Satwa is a mix of villas and apartments, but the real character of the area shines through on its main busy thoroughfares, Al Diyafah Street and Satwa Road. Al Diyafah is the heartbeat of the area, where people go to eat, socialise and be seen. Satwa Road branches off Al Diyafah, and around this one-way loop you'll find pots and plants, pet shops, fabric shops and hardware outlets, and a small area full of car repair shops. It's also a great spot to find a bargain tailor (see Shopping, p.438). Head here on a Saturday evening to soak up the atmosphere, but women are advised to cover up to avoid being stared at.

their post-club hunger, show off their expensive customised cars, or watch the city pass by as they enjoy some street-side Lebanese fare. If you're out past midnight, don't miss having a bite at either Al Mallah (p.452) or Ravi's (p.490).

## Jumeira or Jumeirah?

According to the 'official' spelling used by Dubai Municipality, it's Jumeira, so that's what we use when referring to this area. However, many hotels, parks, clubs, schools, and residential developments have added an 'h' to the end, so don't be surprised if you see the two different spellings side by side throughout the book.

## Downtown Burj Dubai

The newest place in town to explore, Downtown Burj Dubai is a spectacular mix of shops, restaurants, entertainment and architecture, while nearby is a stretch of Dubai's original stunning skyscraper strip, which lines Sheikh Zayed Road and features some of the city's top hotels and building design.

At the heart of Downtown is the world's tallest tower, the shimmering Burj Dubai, which points like a needle more than 800m skywards and, when fully open in 2010, will contain apartments, hotels, shops and entertainment facilities. By its base are Dubai Mall and Old Town, while the centrepiece is the spectacular Dubai Fountain, which draws crowds to witness the regular evening shows where jets of water shoot 150m into the air along the length of the Burj lake in synchronisation with classical and Arabic music. Take a seat at any of the restaurant terraces that line the lake for a perfect view. Dubai Mall (p.402) is a huge shopping centre full of top-end retail brands, an array of excellent eateries and some fantastic entertainment options such as Dubai Aquarium (p.250) and SEGA Republic (p.254).

There are two Address hotels in the area (p.230), with the views from the 63rd floor Neos bar (p.513) at the Downtown Address well worth taking in. Old Town, which is home to the atmospheric Souk Al Bahar (p.396), takes strong influences from traditional Arabia, with windtowers, mosaics, courtyards, passageways and fortress-like finishes, all of which are beautifully lit at night. Other hotels in the Downtown area include The Palace Hotel and Al Manzil, which are home to Asado steakhouse (p.457) and upmarket sports bar Nezesaussi (p.513) respectively.

Just behind Downtown, the buzzing strip over on Sheikh Zayed Road is known for the striking architecture of its high-rise residential buildings, office towers and top-class hotels including Emirates Towers (p.232) and the Shangri-La. From the Dubai World Trade Centre to Interchange One (known as Defence Roundabout), the wide, skyscraping 3.5km stretch is the subject of many a photo, as well as after-hours hook ups in the various happening hotspots. With so many residents, tourists and business people around, this area really comes to life at night, as the crowds flit from restaurants to bars to clubs.

### HEAD FOR HEIGHTS

After growing like a beanstalk before the eyes of residents over the last few years, the Burj Dubai has finally reached its zenith, and at over 800m in height, is now officially the world's tallest building. After its doors open at the beginning of 2010, members of the public will be able to ride the elevators all the way to the 124th floor to take in the staggering views from the observation deck, At The Top. Visitors will be able to get 360° views of the city, plus step out onto and outdoor deck, and there will be interactive displays too to enhance the experience. Check out www.liveworkexplore.com for more details.

## The Palm Jumeirah & Al Sufouh

This stretch of coastline, between Dubai Marina and Umm Suqeim, is home to some of the most prestigious and popular resorts in Dubai. From the exclusive, iconic Burj Al Arab and Jumeirah Beach Hotel at one end, along Beach Road past the One&Only Royal Mirage, The Westin and finally, at the other end, Le Meridien Mina Seyahi (with everyone's favourite beach party bar, Barasti (p.507), this section of the Gulf contains more pricey hotels than a Monopoly set.

In the middle of all this, stretching several kilometres out to sea, is The Palm, Dubai's original mind-boggling man-made island, with its countless luxury villas and apartments, and the Disney-esque Atlantis hotel as its crowning showpiece. As the name suggests, the water theme is an important part of the Atlantis set-up. Aquaventure is the resort's thrilling water park (p.248), and you get up close to the marine life at Dolphin Bay and the Lost Chambers aquarium (p.252). Atlantis is also home to several top restaurants, including Nobu (p.486) and Rostang (p.491). You can drive the length of The Palm and around its perimeter for great views back to the shore, or you can take a ride on the monorail for an elevated view of the luxury-villa-lined fronds (p.226).

Within all of the resorts in Al Sufouh are dozens of excellent eating and drinking choices, open to all, while Souk Madinat Jumeirah (p.408) and, just back from the coast, Mall of the Emirates (p.405) are great spots for shopping, dining and entertainment.

Sun and water lovers are well catered for here too, with a great public beach (p.248) and another excellent water park, Wild Wadi (p.250).

## Dubai Marina & JBR

Previously home to just a handful of waterfront hotels, the Marina is the epitome of new Dubai's rise to modern prominence. Apartment buildings (finished or still under construction) have sprouted up along every inch of the man-made waterway, while between the marina and the shore is the massive Jumeirah Beach Residence (JBR) development, which now dwarfs the five-star beach resorts such as the Hilton and Ritz-Carlton.

The pedestrianised walkways that run around the marina and parallel to the coast have evolved into lively strips of cafes and restaurants, which throng with people in the evenings when the lit-up skyscrapers are at their most impressive. Marina Walk boulevard, when completed, will provide continuous pedestrian access around the 11km perimeter of the water. The popular area by Dubai Marina Towers was the first to be developed, and is home to several independent eateries, such as popular Lebanese restaurant and shisha spot Chandelier (p.466). It is a great place for a stroll any time but it really comes to

Burj Al Arab

life in the evenings and cooler months when you can sit and gaze out across the rows of gleaming yachts and flashing lights of high-rise hotels and apartments. Further along the walkway, on the same side of the water, is the new Dubai Marina Mall (p.411).

Nearby, The Walk at JBR is an outdoor parade of shops, restaurants and hotels parallel to the beach that has become a huge leisure-time draw for Dubai residents. Strolling from one end to the other of this 1.7km promenade will take you past a whole host of retail and eating options, with the scores of alfresco diners and Saturday strollers creating a lively atmosphere and providing some excellent people watching opportunities. From Wednesday to Saturday the outdoor Covent Garden Market by Rimal court is an added attraction, with street entertainers and craft stalls creating a colourful atmosphere (see p.395).

There's also an excellent beach here, which is massively popular during the cooler months. The spaces in front of the hotels are reserved for guests, but there are plenty of areas in between that fill with crowds of families and groups of friends at weekends. The waters are fairly calm here and the shallow areas are scattered with bathers, while the hotels offer a variety of watersports such as parasailing and boat rides that anyone can sign up for. There is a big carpark near the Rimal JBR block for beach goers, but access to this gets fairly congested at peak times.

# DUBAI HOTELS

One thing you'll soon discover once you get to know Dubai is that much of the social scene revolves around the city's many hotels. Whereas in, say, Europe, where generally a city hotel's main purpose is to provide accommodation and host the odd corporate function, in Dubai hotels also act as places for residents to go for a drink, for dinner, to a nightclub, for a workout and to relax at the weekend.

There are dozens of the world's leading hotel brands to be found here, many of them housed in some of the city's most iconic buildings. Your first encounter with them may be when you come to Dubai on a reconnaissance mission before you make the decision to move permanently. You might also find yourself staying in one when you first move out, often hosted by your new company, while you find your feet and look for some accommodation of your own.

Once you're settled in, you'll soon become familiar with many of the places listed in this section. Whether you're going out for Friday brunch, after-work drinks or a romantic dinner, the UAE's licensing laws – alcohol can only be served in hotels or sports clubs – mean that it's likely to be in a hotel.

## New Addresses

The Address is a relatively new entrant to the Dubai hotel scene, but already it has five impressive properties on its books: The Address Downtown Burj Dubai (p.230), The Address Dubai Marina (p.230), The Address Dubai Mall, The Address Montgomerie Dubai and The Palace – The Old Town (p.236). See www.theaddress.com for full property details.

Putting your visitors up in a hotel (should lack of space dictate and budget allow) is also something you may need to do; Dubai's popularity as a tourist destination means that most hotels are excellently geared up for holidaymakers, with many located on the beach or near to some of the main attractions.

And, if you're a big fan of hotel life, you can always choose to live in one – serviced hotel apartments can be found throughout town, and prices have fallen enough recently for this to become a potential alternative to renting an apartment. See Housing, p.69, for more details.

There are a vast array of hotels, ranging from one of the most superlative and opulent in the world, the Burj Al Arab (p.230), with a rack rate in the region of Dhs.11,000 for a night in a standard suite, right down to the cheapest digs in areas such as Deira costing under Dhs.200 a night. While the hotels at the higher end of the market offer superb surroundings and

facilities, those at the cheaper end vary – and you certainly get what you pay for.

For people arriving in Dubai on a holiday package, hotels are normally five or four star, but if you are looking for cheaper accommodation at the lower end of the market, make sure you check out the hotel and have a look at one of the rooms before checking in.

## New Hotels

Despite the economic slowdown, new hotels are still springing up all the time across the city. Establishments expected to open their doors in 2010 include Armani Hotel in the Burj Dubai (www.armanihotels.com), The Taj Exotica Resort & Spa (www.tajhotels.com), Fairmont Palm Jumeirah (www.fairmont.com) and The Royal Amwaj (www.moevenpick-hotels.com) on the Palm Jumeirah, and a Sofitel (www.sofitel.com), Mövenpick (www.moevenpick-hotels.com) and Rotana (www.rotana.com) on The Walk at JBR. Keep an eye on www.liveworkexplore.com for the latest information on new openings.

Remember that, as with anywhere else in the world, you can usually get a discount on the rack rate or published price if you negotiate.

Many hotels also offer seasonal discounts to GCC residents, particularly in the hot summer months when prices can be 50% lower than at peak times, providing a great opportunity for a bargain break.

The Dubai Department of Tourism & Commerce Marketing (DTCM) oversees a hotel classification system that gives an internationally recognised star rating to hotels and hotel apartments so that visitors can judge more easily the standard of accommodation they will receive.

The DTCM also operates an internet reservation system for Dubai's hotels on its website (www.dubaitourism.com). This enables guests to reserve rooms online and allows them to take a virtual tour of the hotel before they book. Alternatively, the DTCM Welcome Bureau at the airport offers instant hotel reservations, often at greatly discounted rates.

For restaurants and bars that operate in Dubai's hotels, refer to the index at the back of the book. Just look up the hotel name, and all of its outlets that are featured in the book will be listed underneath.

## Get Away

If you'd like to escape the city for a day or two, there are a number of excellent desert, beach and mountain resorts within Dubai emirate that are worth checking out – see Discover, p.254, for full details.

# *Bonnington*

## JUMEIRAH LAKES TOWERS
### DUBAI

A new level of quality, charm and service has arrived in Dubai. In the heart of New Dubai, Bonnington brings to you a stunning property. Bonnington is a landmark of heritage and style, towering gracefully in the midst of Jumeirah Lakes Towers, providing a chic five star residential address to all who walk through her doors.

## A CENTURY OF HOSPITALITY

Bonnington has welcomed guests for over 100 years and with each year, like a fine vintage, Bonnington improves with age. Since the turn of the century, Bonnington has refined the true meaning of British Hospitality.

Bonnington, Jumeirah Lakes Towers, Dubai is a five star deluxe hotel with serviced apartments, several restaurants, bars and lounges, meetings and events facilities and a leisure deck on the 12th floor with infinity pool and a state of the art gym, saunas and steam rooms.

### it's all about you

Tel: +971 (4) 356 0000
Fax: + 971 (4) 356 0400
Email: info@bonningtontower.com
www. bonningtontontower.com

# Dubai Hotels

### The Address Downtown Burj Dubai

Burj Dubai Blvd Downtown Burj Dubai
04 436 8888
www.theaddress.com
Map 2 F6 Metro Burj Dubai

Even at over 300 metres in height, The Address is dwarfed by its neighbour, the Burj Dubai – but breathtaking views, beautiful interiors and eight dining outlets (including Neos, the panoramic bar on the 63rd floor) make this one of the most popular addresses in town.

### The Address Dubai Marina

Dubai Marina 04 436 7777
www.theaddress.com
Map 1 L4 Metro Dubai Marina

This stylish new building next to Dubai Marina Mall dominates the marina skyline, and is home to some impressive facilities. With nearly 150 guestrooms, and restaurants including French Rive Gauche as well as a bar, Blends, overlooking the water, this is a handy spot for Marina residents to come to relax or put their visitors up for a short stay.

### Al Bustan Rotana Hotel

Casablanca Rd Garhoud 04 282 0000
www.rotana.com
Map 2 N7 Metro GGICO

A central location near the airport, Deira City Centre and the Dubai Creek makes this hotel accessible for tourists and business visitors. Renowned for its good restaurants, particularly Benihana (Japanese) and Blue Elephant (Thai).

### Al Manzil Hotel

Burj Dubai Blvd Downtown Burj Dubai
04 428 5888
www.southernsunme.com
Map 2 F6 Metro Burj Dubai

In the heart of Old Town, this four-star hotel is conveniently located for business and leisure trips. It also houses Nezesaussi, the popular antipodean sports bar.

### Atlantis The Palm > p.231

Crescent Rd Palm Jumeirah 04 426 1000
www.atlantisthepalm.com
Map 1 N0 Metro Nakheel

With a staggering 1,539 rooms and suites, all with views of the sea or the Palm Jumeirah, Atlantis is certainly one of Dubai's grandest hotels. It has no less than four restaurants featuring the cuisine of Michelin-starred chefs, including a branch of Nobu. It is also home to Aquaventure, the biggest water park in the Middle East.

### Bonnington, Jumeirah Lakes Towers > p.229

Jumeirah Lakes Towers 04 361 9044
www.bonningtontower.com
Map 1 K4 Metro Jumeirah Lakes Towers

This British five-star institution makes its Dubai debut in Jumeirah Lakes Towers. Containing both hotel suites and serviced apartments, as well as six restaurants and bars and a leisure deck with infinity pool, it has great connections to Dubai Marina, as well as the rest of the city via the nearby Metro stop.

### Burj Al Arab

Jumeira Rd Umm Suqeim 04 301 7777
www.jumeirah.com
Map 1 S3 Metro Mall of the Emirates

Standing on its own man-made island, this dramatic Dubai icon's unique architecture is recognised around the world. Suites have two floors and are serviced by a team of butlers. To get into the hotel as a non-guest, you will need a restaurant reservation.

### City Centre Hotel & Residence

Nr Deira City Centre Port Saeed 04 294 1222
www.accorhotels.com
Map 2 N6 Metro Deira City Centre

A good location adjoining Deira City Centre and views over the greens of Dubai Creek Golf & Yacht Club make this a great place to stay for shoppers and golfers. The hotel also has a collection of serviced apartments.

### Crowne Plaza

Sheikh Zayed Rd Trade Centre 04 331 1111
www.ichotelsgroup.com
Map 2 H4 Metro Emirates Towers

One of Dubai's older five-star hotels, with an excellent collection of food and beverage outlets including Trader Vic's, Wagamama and Oscar's Vine Society.

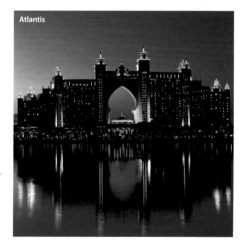
Atlantis

# Where Water Meets Wonder

Atlantis is the majestical focal point of Palm Jumeirah, a man-made island that has captured the world's imagination with its magnificent scale and ingenuity. The resort offers relaxation and thrills for couples and families alike, including Aquaventure the largest water-themed attraction in the Middle East, over 20 marine exhibits in Lost Chambers, 17 bars & restaurants, a private 2km beach, an indulgent spa and over 30 cosmopolitan boutiques.

For room bookings call +971 4 426 1000
atlantisthepalm.com

## ATLANTIS
### THE PALM, DUBAI

# Dubai Hotels

### Crowne Plaza Festival City

Festival City 04 701 2222
www.crowneplaza.com/dfc
Map 2 M8 Metro Emirates Head Office

On the banks of the creek, this Crowne Plaza is excellently positioned within the Festival City complex. One of its highlights is Belgian Beer Café, an atmospheric bar that serves a great selection of European beers and is extremely popular with Dubai expats.

### Dubai Marine Beach Resort & Spa

Off Jumeira Rd Jumeira
04 346 1111
www.dxbmarine.com
Map 2 H3 Metro Al Jafiliya

This beachside hotel has 195 villa-style rooms nestled among lush, green landscaped gardens, waterfalls and streams. The grounds offer three swimming pools, a spa, a health club and a small private beach. The restaurants and bars are perennially popular, especially the Ibiza-esque Sho Cho and beautiful hangout, Boudoir.

### Dubai Marriott Harbour Hotel & Suites

Al Sufouh Rd Dubai Marina 04 319 4000
www.marriott.com
Map 1 L4 Metro Dubai Marina

With 261 spacious suites, each with its own fitted kitchen, staying in The Harbour is like having your very own luxury apartment. The hotel is home to a range of dining options including The Observatory (great views from the 52nd floor) and 24 hour deli Counter Culture. Formerly managed by Emirates, it switched hands to Marriott in 2009.

### Dusit Thani Dubai

Nr Int 1, Shk Zayed Rd Trade Centre
04 343 3333 www.dusit.com
Map 2 G5 Metro Financial Centre

This member of the upmarket Thai hotel chain is situated in the 'clasped hands' (or 'pair of trousers') building on the main stretch of Sheikh Zayed Road. It features 321 rooms, and several food and beverage outlets including Benjarong, which serves 'royal Thai cuisine'.

### Emirates Towers Hotel

Shk Zayed Rd Trade Centre 04 330 0000
www.jumeirah.com
Map 2 H5 Metro Emirates Towers

Sophisticated and elegant, this award-winning hotel forms one part of Dubai's original iconic twin skyscrapers. It has 400 rooms, some excellent restaurants and bars (including Harry Ghatto's for hilarious karaoke nights), as well as an exclusive shopping mall.

### Fairmont Dubai

Shk Zayed Rd Trade Centre 04 332 5555
www.fairmont.com/dubai
Map 2 J4 Metro Trade Centre

Home to the legendary Spectrum on One restaurant, a beautiful rooftop pool, and the renowned Willow Stream spa, Fairmont Dubai is as notable for its modern interior as it is for its striking architecture, which is based on traditional Arabian windtowers and stands tall over the busy Sheikh Zayed Road strip.

### Grand Hyatt Dubai

Nr Garhoud Bridge Umm Hurair 04 317 1234
www.dubai.grand.hyatt.com
Map 2 L7 Metro Healthcare City

The eye-catching design of this huge hotel near the Garhoud Bridge is not random: from the air the shape of the building spells out the word 'Dubai' in Arabic. It has excellent leisure facilities, a great selection of restaurants, and one of the most impressive lobbies in Dubai.

### Grosvenor House

Dubai Marina 04 399 8888
www.grosvenorhouse.lemeridien.com
Map 1 L4 Metro Dubai Marina

This neon-blue skyscraper at the mouth of Dubai Marina is run by Le Meridien group, and features 422 guest rooms and serviced apartments, as well as some iconic nightlife venues: Buddha Bar, Gary Rhodes' Mezzanine and the crow's nest Bar 44 are all here and well worth a visit. There's also a branch of luxury male-only spa 1847 here.

### Habtoor Grand Resort & Spa

Dubai Marina 04 399 5000
www.grandjumeirah.habtoorhotels.com
Map 1 L3 Metro Dubai Marina

The twin-towered Habtoor Grand, on the beach at the northern end of Dubai Marina, offers 442 spacious rooms and suites with garden or sea views. Pools, restaurants and bars are set amid the hotel's tropical gardens bordering the Arabian Gulf, while The Underground bar draws in the expat football fan crowd for its multiple screens.

### Hilton Dubai Creek

Baniyas Road, Deira 04 227 1111
www.hilton.com
Map 2 N5 Metro Union

With very flash yet understated elegance, this ultra-minimalist hotel features interiors of wood, glass and chrome. Centrally located and overlooking the creek with splendid views of the Arabian dhow trading posts, the hotel has two renowned restaurants in Glasshouse and Gordon Ramsay's Verre.

The Address Downtown Burj Dubai

Burj Al Arab

The Palace – The Old Town

Raffles Dubai

Grosvenor House

# Dubai Hotels

## Hilton Dubai Jumeirah

Jumeirah Beach Residence Dubai Marina
04 399 1111
www.hilton.com
Map 1 K3 Metro Dubai Marina

Situated between The Walk and the JBR beach, the Hilton Dubai Jumeirah features excellent restaurants, including Italian BiCE and the Latin American Pachanga, as well as a sports bar, Studio One. There's a beach bar too – Wavebreaker – which is a great spot for sundowners. Dubai Marina is within walking distance.

## Hyatt Regency Dubai

Nr Galleria Mall Deira 04 209 1234
www.dubai.regency.hyatt.com
Map 2 N3 Metro Palm Deira

The restaurants alone in this hotel are well worth fighting the Deira traffic for – particularly Al Dawaar, Dubai's only revolving restaurant which boasts amazing views of the creek and coast. All 400 rooms have creek views too.

## InterContinental Dubai Festival City

Festival City 04 701 1111
www.intercontinental.com/dubai
Map 2 M8 Metro Creek

Worth a visit if only to taste fine fare served up in Michelin-starred chef Pierre Gagnaire's excellent restaurant, or to enjoy the panoramic views from the Eclipse bar. The hotel also features an excellent spa, 498 rooms and suites, and access to the Festival Waterfront Centre.

## Jumeirah Beach Hotel

Jumeira Rd Umm Suqeim
04 348 0000
www.jumeirah.com
Map 1 S3 Metro Mall of the Emirates

Built in the shape of an ocean wave with a dynamic and colourful interior, the hotel has 618 rooms, all with a sea view. It is also home to some excellent food and beverage outlets, including Uptown for happy hour cocktails and a great view of the Burj Al Arab. Kids and families will love Wild Wadi Water Park, which is located here.

## JW Marriott Hotel

Abu Baker Al Siddique Rd Deira 04 262 4444
www.marriott.com
Map 2 P5 Metro Abu Baker Al Siddique

Set in the bustling heart of Deira, the Marriott is best known for its theme nights and legendary brunches in Bamboo Lagoon, the Market Place and Hofbrauhaus, three restaurants situated around a grand staircase that snakes up from the lobby.

## Kempinski Hotel Mall of the Emirates

Mall of the Emirates Al Barsha 04 341 0000
www.kempinski-dubai.com
Map 1 R5 Metro Mall of the Emirates

Part of the Middle East's first indoor ski resort, the hotel has 395 deluxe rooms and 15 unique ski chalets overlooking the slopes. It houses a spa, an infinity pool, a fitness centre, a tennis court and, of course, access to the ski slope.

## Le Meridien Dubai

Airport Rd Garhoud 04 217 0000
www.lemeridien-dubai.com
Map 2 N7 Metro GGICO

Le Meridien has 383 rooms in an ultra convenient location, just across from the Dubai airport and a stone's throw from the Aviation Club. Hotel guests and visitors can enjoy the Natural Elements spa and the many excellent restaurants inside the hotel – most notably Yalumba, which offers a famous Friday brunch.

## Le Meridien Mina Seyahi Beach Resort & Marina

Al Sufouh Rd Al Sufouh 04 399 3333
www.lemeridien-minaseyahi.com
Map 1 M3 Metro Dubai Marina

This hotel has one of the longest stretches of private beach in Dubai, its own marina and a variety of water activities such as sailing and waterskiing. The 211 rooms come with views of the sea or the landscaped grounds and the clincher for families is the Penguin Club, which entertains kids. It's also home to the legendary beach bar, Barasti.

## Le Royal Meridien Beach Resort & Spa

Dubai Marina 04 399 5555
www.leroyalmeridien-dubai.com
Map 1 L4 Metro Dubai Marina

Large-scale beach resort at Dubai Marina. Good leisure facilities and a big selection of bars and restaurants including Mexican Maya and seafood outlet Me Vida. A shuttle bus transfers guests through the Marina's construction and traffic hazards to use access the facilities of the near-neighbour Grosvenor House.

## Madinat Jumeirah

Jumeira Rd Umm Suqeim 04 366 8888
www.jumeirah.com
Map 1 R4 Metro Mall of the Emirates

This extravagant resort has two hotels, Al Qasr and Mina A'Salam, with 940 luxurious rooms and suites, and the exclusive Dar Al Masyaf summer houses, all linked by man-made waterways navigated by abras. Nestled between the two hotels is the Souk Madinat, which has over 75 shops within its labyrinth network of passageways. There is also a total of 45 bars, restaurants and cafes.

Fairmont Dubai

# Dubai Hotels

## The Monarch Dubai

1 Shk Zayed Rd Trade Centre
04 501 8888
www.themonarchdubai.com
Map 2 J4 Metro Trade Centre

The Monarch has one of the most desirable
addresses in Dubai: One Sheikh Zayed Road. The
hotel has 236 rooms and suits, including 53 serviced
residential apartments, but for a night (and bill) to
remember book The Monarch Suite, which is located
on the 32nd and 33rd floor and features a private
outdoor pool.

## Mövenpick Hotel Bur Dubai

Opp American Hospital Oud Metha 04 336 6000
www.moevenpick-hotels.com
Map 2 K5 Metro Oud Metha

Located near Lamcy Plaza and Wafi, this hotel offers
a high standard of service in keeping with the chain's
Swiss background. Home to some good food and
beverage outlets.

## Oasis Beach Tower > p.237

The Walk, JBR Dubai Marina 04 399 4444
www.jebelali-international.com
Map 1 K4 Metro Jumeirah Lakes Towers

Situated in prime position in the middle of The Walk
at JBR, this gleaming glass tower houses a range
of two, three and four bedroom hotel apartments
for holiday or long-term use. At the foot of the twin
tower complex (the other tower contains residential
apartments) are the popular prime eating and
drinking spots Wagamama, Frankie's and Trader Vic's
Mai Tai Lounge.

## One&Only Royal Mirage > p.451

Jumeira Rd Al Sufouh 04 399 9999
www.oneandonlyresorts.com
Map 1 M3 Metro Nakheel

This resort is home to three different properties;
The Palace, Arabian Court and Residence & Spa. The
hotel features unparalleled service and dining (try
delectable Moroccan cuisine in the opulent Tagine,
or enjoy cocktails with a view in the Rooftop Lounge
& Terrace), and a luxury spa treatment here is the
ultimate indulgence.

## The Palace – The Old Town

Burj Dubai Blvd Downtown Burj Dubai
04 428 7888
www.thepalace-dubai.com
Map 2 F6 Metro Burj Dubai

Palatial indeed, The Palace is right near the mighty
Burj Dubai, and boasts 242 luxurious rooms and suites,
a beautiful spa and some excellent restaurants.

## Other Options

Aside from the headline hotels listed in this
section, there are plenty of alternative options
available for visitors to rest their heads in.
Radisson Blu (www.radissonblu.com), Rotana
(www.rotana.com) and Holiday Inn all have
several outlets in Dubai (www.holidayinn.com).
Al Barsha is home to a number of decent, less
spectacular hotels, while in Bur Dubai and Deira
you'll find a number of places that offer good
facilities and a central location, such as the Dhow
Palace Hotel (www.dhowpalacedubai.com).

Guest houses are also becoming more
popular in Dubai. While smaller in size, B&Bs
offer a homely feel and are ideal for guests who
want to see more of the 'real Dubai'. Located
in residential areas, they won't have access
to private beaches, but there is no shortage
of good public beaches to enjoy. Some will
have their own pool and benefit from intimate
surroundings, while owners will be only too
happy to give personal recommendations on
what to see and do. Fusion B&B (050 478 7539,
www.fusionhotels.com), located in Jumeira 3,
has a large swimming pool and modern decor.
Villa 47 (04 286 8239, www.villa47.com) has
only two guest rooms, but is located close to
the airport in Garhoud. La Maison d'Hôtes (04
344 1838, www.lamaisondhotesdubai.com)
has 20 guest rooms and a continental-inspired
restaurant. The hotel does not have an alcohol
licence, but is within minutes of the bigger
resorts. Another establishment getting good
notices is The Jumeirah Garden Guesthouse (050
956 2854, www.lamaisondhotesdubai.com), a
villa that features 10 rooms, peaceful gardens
and a good restaurant.

## Park Hyatt Dubai

Nxt to Dubai Creek Golf & Yacht Club Port Saeed
04 602 1234
www.dubai.park.hyatt.com
Map 2 M6 Metro GGICO

Enjoying a prime waterfront location within the
grounds of Dubai Creek Golf & Yacht Club, the
Park Hyatt is Mediterranean in style with low-rise
buildings, natural colours and stylish decor. The hotel
has 225 rooms and suites, all with beautiful views,
as well as some great dining outlets and one of the
city's best spas, which features a luxury couples
massage option. Excellent restaurants include The
Thai Kitchen and Traiteur.

# Stay in Dubai's only
luxury seaside apartments.

Location, location, location. There is nothing quite like living in the heart of Dubai Marina, just steps from the beach overlooking the Arabian Gulf. Add to that an enviable location on Dubai's only outdoor seaside shopping promenade 'The Walk at Jumeirah Beach Residence', filled with boutique shops, restaurants and sidewalk cafes. With its spacious 2, 3 and 4-bedroom luxury serviced apartments offering breathtaking views over new Dubai, Oasis Beach Tower is the perfect place to start your own Dubai story.

**Seeing is believing:** for your personal showaround please call +971 4 399 4444 or visit www.oasisbeachtower.com for reservations

A MEMBER OF

**BEL ALI INTERNATIONAL**
HOTELS

OASIS
BEACH TOWER

Luxury Hotel Apartments by the Sea

# Dubai Hotels

Discover Dubai

### Radisson Blu Hotel, Dubai Deira Creek > p.239

Baniyas Rd Al Rigga 04 222 7171
www.radissonblu.com
Map 2 N4 Metro Union

Proving that sometimes the oldies are the goodies, this classic hotel on the banks of the creek features some popular restaurants and a great 'Old Dubai' location, particularly for business visitors.

### Radisson Blu Hotel, Dubai Media City

Dubai Media City Al Sufouh 04 366 9111
www.radissonblu.com
Map 1 M4 Metro Nakheel

A busy hotel in the heart of Media City. Convenient for business travellers, and also popular with local workers who make a beeline for Italian restaurant Certo and rooftop bar Tamanya Terrace after office hours.

### Raffles Dubai

Wafi Umm Hurair 04 324 8888
www.raffles.com
Map 2 L6 Metro Healthcare City

With 248 stunning suites, the renowned Raffles Amrita Spa and a unique Botanical Sky Garden, this is one of Dubai's most noteworthy city hotels. Nine food and beverage outlets offer a mix of international and far eastern cuisine.

### Renaissance Dubai

Salahuddin Rd Deira 04 262 5555
www.renaissancehotels.com
Map 2 P4 Metro Abu Baker Al Siddique

It may be slightly off the beaten track in the heart of Deira, but it pulls the crowds thanks to legendary buffet restaurant Spice Island; an all-you-can-eat-and-drink night here is a Dubai rite of passage.

### The Ritz-Carlton, Dubai

The Walk, JBR Dubai Marina 04 399 4000
www.ritzcarlton.com
Map 1 L3 Metro Dubai Marina

Even though it is the only low-rise building amid the sea of Marina towers behind it, all 138 rooms have beautiful views of the Gulf. Afternoon tea in the Lobby Lounge is a must, and there are several other excellent restaurants onsite.

### Shangri-La Hotel

Shk Zayed Rd Trade Centre 04 343 8888
www.shangri-la.com
Map 2 G5 Metro Financial Centre

Featuring great views of the coast and the city from Sheikh Zayed Road, this hotel has 301 guest rooms and suites, 126 serviced apartments, a health club and spa, two swimming pools and a variety of restaurants and bars including majestic Moroccan Marrakesh and seafood specialist Amwaj.

### Sheraton Dubai Creek Hotel & Towers

Baniyas St Deira 04 228 1111
www.sheraton.com/dubai
Map 2 M4 Metro Union

This hotel's location on the Deira bank of the creek means that most of the 255 rooms have beautiful waterway views. There are some great eateries too; Ashiana is renowned as one of the best traditional Indian restaurants in Dubai, Creekside is a favoured Japanese diner and Vivaldi shines as a wonderful Italian venue with great views.

### Sheraton Jumeirah Beach Resort & Towers

The Walk, JBR Dubai Marina 04 399 5533
www.sheraton.com/jumeirahbeach
Map 1 J3 Metro Jumeirah Lakes Towers

An older waterfront resort right at the southern end of JBR beach, this hotel has a secluded stretch of the golden sands to itself, plus green gardens and a couple of decent restaurants, including Peacock Chinese Restaurant and The Grill Room. Hosts a chill-out evening on Fridays, Ocean Club, which is popular with local residents.

### The Westin Dubai Mina Seyahi Beach Resort & Marina

Al Sufouh Rd Al Sufouh 04 399 4141
www.westin.com/dubaiminaseyahi
Map 1 M3 Metro Nakheel

Set on 1,200 metres of private beach, The Westin has 294 spacious rooms and suites with all the luxury amenities you would expect of a five-star hotel, including the aptly named Heavenly Spa. There are plenty of dining venues, including perennially popular Italian Bussola, Senyar for cocktails and tapas, and wine and cheese bar Oeno.

The Ritz-Carlton, Dubai

# Your favourite restaurants & bars under one roof !

**boulvar** — International Restaurant

**yum!** — Noodle Bar

**THE CHINA CLUB** — Trendy Chinese

**炭火屋 Sumibiya** — Japanese Barbeque

**FISH MARKET** — Award-Winning Seafood Restaurant

Authentic Persian

**minato** — Indisputable Japanese

**PALM GRILL** — Contemporary Steakhouse

**LA MODA** — Fashionable Italian

**THE PUB** — Traditional English

Jazz Bar

**MARBLES** — Lobby Bar

**ku-bu** — Tattoo Themed Bar

**Pool Bar** — Pool Bar

**al mansour dhow** — Traditional Dhow Cruise

**Boulevard Gourmet** — Cake Shop

Whether you are looking for a tastefully grilled steak, just the right touch of Chinese, authentic Persian, trendy Italian, fresh Seafood or a drink while enjoying the great views, there's a choice for everyone at the Radisson Blu Hotel, Dubai Deira Creek.

Visit one of our 10 restaurants, 5 bars, dhow and cake shop to embark on an ultimate gourmet journey.

**Radisson Blu Hotel, Dubai Deira Creek**
Baniyas Road, P.O. Box 476, Dubai UAE
For Bookings, please call 04-205 7333
Infocenter.Dxbza@radissonblu.com
radissonblu.com/hotel-dubaideiracreek

*Radisson* **BLU**
HOTEL, DUBAI DEIRA CREEK

# ART & CULTURE

## Heritage & Cultural Sites

Old Dubai features many fascinating places to visit, offering glimpses into a time when the city was nothing more than a small fishing and trading port. Many of the pre-oil heritage sites have been carefully restored, paying close attention to traditional design and using original building materials. Stroll through the Bastakiya area, with its many distinctive windtowers, and marvel at how people coped in Dubai before air-conditioning. Dubai Museum and Jumeira Mosque both offer interesting insights into local culture.

### Ramadan Timings

During Ramadan, timings for many companies in Dubai change significantly. Museums and heritage sites usually open slightly later in the morning than usual, and close earlier in the afternoon. Check before you go.

### Al Ahmadiya School & Heritage House

Al Khor St Al Ras Deira 04 226 0286
www.dubaitourism.ae
Map 2 M3 Metro Al Ras

Al Ahmadiya School was the earliest regular school in the city and a visit is an excellent opportunity to see the history of education in Dubai. Established in 1912 for Dubai's elite, this building was closed in 1963 when the school relocated to larger premises. Situated in what is becoming a small centre for heritage in Deira (Al Souk Al Khabeer), it sits just behind the Heritage House, an interesting example of a traditional Emirati family house and the former home of the school's founder, Mr Ahmadiya, dating back to 1890. Both buildings have been renovated and are great places for a glimpse of how life used to be. Admission to both is free. Open Saturday to Thursday 08:00 to 19:30 and 15:00 to 19:30 on Friday.

### Dubai Museum

Al Fahidi Fort Bur Dubai 04 353 1862
www.dubaitourism.ae
Map 2 M3 Metro Al Fahidi

Located in and under Al Fahidi Fort, which dates back to 1787, this museum is creative and well thought-out and interesting for all the family. The fort was originally built as the residence of the ruler of Dubai and for sea defence, then renovated in 1970 to house the museum. All parts of life from Dubai's past are represented in an attractive and interesting way; walk through a souk from the 1950s, stroll through an oasis, see into a traditional house, get up close to

local wildlife, learn about the archaeological finds or go 'underwater' to discover pearl diving and fishing industries. There are some entertaining mannequins to pose with too. Entry costs Dhs.3 for adults and Dhs.1 for children under 6 years old. Open daily 08:30 to 20:30 (14:30 to 20:30 on Fridays).

### Heritage & Diving Village

Nr Al Shindagha Tunnel Al Shindagha 04 393 7139
www.dubaitourism.ae
Map 2 M3 Metro Al Ghubaiba

Located near the mouth of Dubai Creek, the Heritage & Diving Village focuses on Dubai's maritime past, pearl diving traditions and architecture. Visitors can observe traditional potters and weavers practising their craft the way it has been done for centuries. Local women serve traditionally cooked snacks – one of the rare opportunities you'll have to sample genuine Emirati cuisine. Camel rides are also available most afternoons and evenings. The village is very close to Sheikh Saeed Al Maktoum's House (see opposite page), and is part of the area of Shindagha currently being developed into a cultural centre. It is particularly lively during the Dubai Shopping Festival (p.25) and Eid celebrations, with performances including traditional sword dancing. Open daily 09:00 to 21:00 (Fridays 15:00-22:00).

### Jumeira Mosque

Jumeira Beach Rd Jumeira 04 353 6666
www.cultures.ae
Map 2 H3 Metro Al Jafiliya

This is the most beautiful mosque in the city and perhaps the best known – its image features on the Dhs.500 banknote. Non-Muslims are not usually permitted entry to a mosque, but the Sheikh Mohammed Centre for Cultural Understanding (see

Bastakiya

below) organises weekly tours (Saturday, Sunday, Tuesday and Thursday mornings at 10:00). Visitors are guided around the mosque and told all about the building, and then the hosts give a talk on Islam and the prayer ritual. The tour offers a fascinating insight into the culture and beliefs of the local population, and is thoroughly recommended during your time in Dubai. You must dress conservatively – no shorts and no sleeveless tops. Women must also cover their hair with a head scarf or shawl, and all visitors will be asked to remove their shoes. Cameras are allowed and large groups can book private tours. There is a registration fee of Dhs.10 per person. The Lime Tree Café (p.480) is just next door for post-tour refreshments.

## Majlis Ghorfat Um Al Sheef

Jumeira Beach Rd Jumeira 04 394 6343
www.dubaitourism.ae
Map 2 D3 Metro Business Bay

Constructed in 1955 from coral stone and gypsum, this simple building was used by the late Sheikh Rashid bin Saeed Al Maktoum as a summer residence. The ground floor is an open veranda (known as a leewan or rewaaq), while upstairs the majlis (the Arabic term for meeting place) is decorated with carpets, cushions, lanterns and rifles. The roof terrace was used for drying dates and even sleeping and it originally offered an uninterrupted view of the sea, although all you can see now are villa rooftops. The site has a garden with a pond and traditional falaj irrigation system. In another corner there's a barasti shelter constructed from palm branches and leaves. The Majlis is located just inland from Beach Road on Street 17, beside HSBC bank and Reem Al Bawardi Restaurant – look for the brown Municipality signs. Entry is Dhs.1 for adults and free for children under 6 years. Closed Friday mornings.

## Sheikh Mohammed Centre For Cultural Understanding

Bastakiya Bur Dubai 04 353 6666
www.cultures.ae
Map 2 M3 Metro Al Fahidi

Located in the Bastakiya area of the city (see p.223), this centre was established to help visitors and residents understand the customs and traditions of the UAE through various activities and programmes. These include fascinating guided tours of Jumeira Mosque (see previous page), a walking tour around Bastakiya, Arabic language courses, cultural awareness programmes and weekly coffee mornings where UAE nationals explain the Emirati way of life. The building that houses the centre is also worth a look for the majlis-style rooms located around the courtyard and great views through the palm trees and windtowers. Open Sunday to Thursday 08:00 to 15:00, Saturdays 09:00 to 13:00.

## Sheikh Saeed Al Maktoum's House

Nr Heritage & Diving Village Al Shindagha
04 393 7139 www.dubaitourism.ae
Map 2 M3 Metro Al Ghubaiba

The modest home of Dubai's much-loved former ruler was once strategically located at the mouth of Dubai Creek but now lies close to the Bur Dubai entrance to Al Shindagha Tunnel. Dating from 1896, this carefully restored house-turned-museum is built in the traditional manner of the Gulf coast, using coral covered in lime and sand-coloured plaster. The interesting displays in many rooms show rare and wonderful photographs of all aspects of life in Dubai pre-oil. There is also an old currency and stamp collection and great views over the creek from the upper floor. Entry is Dhs.2 for adults, Dhs.1 for children and free for under 6s.

## Art Galleries

While there's nothing like the Tate or the Louvre in Dubai yet, there are a number of galleries that have interesting exhibitions of art and traditional Arabic artefacts, and more are springing up, particularly in the Al Quoz area. Most operate as a shop and a gallery, but some also provide studios for artists and are involved in the promotion of art within the emirates. The Majlis Gallery, The Courtyard and the XVA Gallery are all worth visiting for their architecture alone. They provide striking locations in which you can enjoy a wide range of art, both local and international. Many art shops also have galleries as well – see Shopping, p.356. Visit www.liveworkexplore.com for up-to-date listings on new exhibitions throughout the year.

## Artsawa

Hasa Rd Al Quoz 04 340 8660
www.artsawa.com
Map 1 U6 Metro Al Quoz

Artsawa opened in 2008 in the burgeoning art area of industrial Al Quoz. It hosts up to 15 exhibitions annually, and focuses on the promotion of contemporary Arab art in a variety of mediums including collage, etching, installation, painting, photography, sculpture and video. Artsawa also holds educational events aimed at engaging the local and international communities.

## Ayyam Gallery

Exit 43, Sheikh Zayed Rd Al Quoz 04 323 6242
www.ayyamgallery.com
Map 1 U5 Metro Al Quoz

Leading purveyor of Syrian art in Damascus which has now opened a branch in Al Quoz. As well as hosting a range of regional exhibitions, it also runs the Shabab Ayyam Project, a programme that encourages the development of 'young and experimental' talent in the region.

# Al Quoz –
# The Art District

Meem Gallery

When it comes to exploring Dubai's neighbourhoods, Al Quoz is probably the last place you'd put on your 'must see' list. For the large part it's a dirty, dusty industrial zone, where polluting factories, box-kit warehouses and depressing-looking labour accommodation line the gridded network of roads. For the majority of tourists, and indeed most residents, it's a place to ignore. To do so though would be to miss out on what may be the country's most hopeful and expressive arts community. Tucked away in massive warehouses, often out of sight, are a collection of galleries and impressive interior design shops that are some of Dubai's best bets in truly joining the global arts landscape. Add to that an endless selection of cheap south Asian cafeterias, the Gold and Diamond Park, Times Square Center and a few less-ambitious shopping centres, and Al Quoz quickly becomes a destination worth exploring.

The Al Quoz art scene, though less-publicised than massive state-sponsored cultural projects in Abu Dhabi or Doha, is the heart of Arab arts in the gulf. It is here that lesser-known artists can find exhibition space, and the galleries are working to promote Arab art on the international scene.

At one end of the spectrum sit smaller Al Quoz galleries such as **4walls** (04 338 8892, www.4walls-dubai.com) and **B21** (04 340 3965, www.b21gallery.com), which tend to exhibit works from up and coming artists, providing an outlet for the region's otherwise voiceless creatives.

At the other end are the well-known, relatively long-established galleries that have experienced art collectors as their main clients. One of the best recognised is **The Third Line** (p.245). The gallery itself is impressive and the art it contains is some of the most innovative in the city. In addition to monthly exhibitions, the gallery hosts alternative programmes which include film screenings, debates and international multimedia forums, all with the intention of promoting interaction between regional artists and the public.

Equally impressive is **Ayyam Gallery** (p.241), which had already established itself as a leading purveyor of Syrian art in Damascus before opening its warehouse gallery here. In 2008, **Art Sawa** (p.241) opened its doors and has since been combining fascinating exhibitions with grass roots educational programmes as a way of extending the reach of Dubai's art scene. Less than a five minute drive from Art Sawa sits The Courtyard, home to the **Total Arts Gallery** (p.245), which has long showcased Middle Eastern art with an emphasis on Iranian artists. The Courtyard also stands out as being a little different as it frequently exhibits traditional handicrafts and antique furniture.

Some of Dubai's most significant culture is hidden away among the sand-covered warehouses, factories and labour camps of Al Quoz.

Another of the more prominent Al Quoz galleries is **Meem** (p.245), which prides itself on exclusively representing leading Middle Eastern artists such as Ali Omar Ermes and Nja Majdaoui. Much like Art Sawa, Meem promotes education oriented programmes for teens and university students, often devoting gallery space to university exhibitions.

Along with the promotion and exhibition of regional art, Al Quoz has also become a centre for the creative process. **The Jam Jar** (p.244) offers an extensive schedule of workshops and open studio sessions geared towards amateur artists looking for a welcoming outlet. Workshops range from advanced painting skills to the basics of lomography. The Jam Jar also hosts several exhibitions each year in its gallery space.

For professional creatives, **Shelter** (04 434 5655, www.shelter.ae) promotes regional creatives with a host of entrepreneurial services including office space, business setup assistance and an environment to nurture contacts. Along with its office spaces and meeting rooms, Shelter includes a brasserie run by More Café and a boutique shop selling design-centric gifts and clothing produced by its members.

Ayyam Gallery

# Art & Culture

## Carbon 12 Dubai

Marina View Towers Dubai Marina 050 464 4392
www.carbon12dubai.com
Map 1 L4 Metro Dubai Marina

A new gallery in the heart of Dubai Marina, Carbon 12 hosts 10 exhibitions a year, and states its mission as bringing together a colourful variety of international movements with one common point: contemporary art at its best.

## Creative Art Centre

Beh Jumeira Rd Jumeira 04 344 4394
Map 2 F3 Metro Burj Dubai

A large gallery and shop with eight showrooms set in two villas, Creative Art Centre has a wide range of original art, framed maps, and Arabian antiques and gifts. The selection includes Omani chests and old doors, and there's also a good selection of old weapons and silver. The gallery offers a picture-framing service, and specialises in the restoration of antiques and furniture. It is set back from Beach Road – take the turning inland between Choithram and Town Centre shopping mall.

## The Empty Quarter

Gate Village, Bldg 02 Trade Centre 04 323 1210
www.theemptyquarter.com
Map 2 H5 Metro Trade Centre

This gallery deals exclusively in fine art photography, staging exhibitions from both emerging and established artists. Work displayed comes from across the globe and features a range of material from art to abstract to photojournalism. The gallery also features books, and audio and visual presentations on photographers.

## The Flying House

Al Quoz 04 265 3365
www.the-flyinghouse.com
Map 2 C5 Metro Al Quoz

Al Quoz space dedicated to contemporary Emirati artists. The Flying House is a non-profit organisation that holds a collection of important Emirati works that have been assembled over a period of 30 years.

## Green Art Gallery

Villa 23, 51st Street, Nr Dubai Zoo Jumeira
04 344 9888
www.gagallery.com
Map 2 G3 Metro Financial Centre

Since its founding in 1995, Green Art Gallery has focused on art from the Arab world. It has acted as a catalyst for many internationally recognised artists from the Levant and continues to stay relevant in the growing contemporary Arabic art scene. With large white minimalist walls and lots of floor space, Green Art makes a great stop-off if you fancy some peace and quiet and some incredible culture. Seasonal exhibitions are held throughout the year.

## Hunar Art Gallery

Villa 6, St 49a Al Rashidiya 04 286 2224
www.hunargallery.com
Map 2 C3 Metro Business Bay

This gallery exhibits international fine art. Beautifully decorated Japanese tiles, Belgian pewter and glass pieces fill the spaces between ever-changing, contemporary local and world art. Some artists receive more regular showings, but typically there is a diverse array of artists shown. Exhibitions last for around a month. The gallery will also, on occasion, display the works of talented local scholars. Many of the pieces in the gallery can be purchased.

## The Jam Jar

Exit 39 from Sheikh Zayed Rd, St 17a, Beh Dubai Garden Ctr Al Quoz 04 341 7303
www.thejamjardubai.com
Map 1 S6 Metro First Gulf Bank

A studio and workshop space for creatives, Jam Jar also hosts several exhibitions each year in its gallery, as well as hosting other arts events such as film screenings.

---

### Abu Dhabi Art Scene

Establishing itself as a major centre for arts and culture is high on the agenda for Abu Dhabi, which promises to be great news for art lovers in the UAE. Top of the bill of forthcoming attractions will be branches of the Louvre and the Guggenheim in the new Saadiyat Island Cultural District, while Emirates Palace regularly plays host to some excellent international exhibitions in association with some of the world's leading institutions – notable recent exhibits include a selection of works on loan from the Musée National Picasso in Paris. There's an increasingly important annual event on the calendar too, the Abu Dhabi Art fair (www.abudhabiartfair.ae), which is staged in November.

---

## The Majlis Gallery

Bastakiya Bur Dubai 04 353 6233
www.themajlisgallery.com
Map 2 M3 Metro Al Fahidi

Set in traditional surroundings in the old Bastakiya area (see p.223), The Majlis Gallery is a converted Arabic house, complete with windtowers. Small whitewashed rooms lead off the central courtyard and host a variety of exhibitions by contemporary artists. In addition to the fine art collection, there's an extensive range of handmade glass, pottery, fabrics, frames, unusual pieces of furniture and other bits and bobs. The gallery hosts exhibitions throughout the year, but is worth visiting at any time. Open Saturday to Thursday.

## Meem Gallery

Umm Suqeim Road Al Quoz 04 347 7883
www.meem.ae
Map 1 S6 Metro Mall of the Emirates

Launched in 2007, Meem features work from modern and contemporary Middle Eastern artists. It's also home to The Noor Library of Islamic Art, which houses a comprehensive collection of books, journals and catalogues on regional and Islamic art. Closed on Fridays.

## Miraj Islamic Art Centre

582 Jumeira Beach Rd Jumeira 04 394 1084
www.mirajislamicartcentre.com
Map 2 B3 Metro Al Quoz

Miraj holds a fantastic collection of Islamic art objects from silver, metalware and marble, to intricate astrolabes, painstakingly crafted carpets and textiles, and displays of calligraphy and engraving. Just up the road is Saga World (04 395 9071), a souk-style, high-end department store, where you can buy a range of Middle Eastern and Indian handcraft products similar to those on display in the gallery.

## Mojo

Al Quoz 04 323 6367
www.themojogallery.com
Map 1 U5 Metro Al Quoz

Mojo is one of Dubai's newest galleries. Opened in Al Quoz in late 2009, it promises to stage a range of exhibitions featuring contemporary themes in multiple formats.

## Opera Gallery

Dubai International Financial Centre (DIFC)
Trade Centre 04 323 0909
www.operagallery.com
Map 2 G5 Metro Financial Centre

Part of an international chain, Opera Gallery opened in 2008 in Dubai International Financial Centre. It has a permanent collection of art on display and for sale, mainly European and Chinese, with visiting exhibitions changing throughout the year. The permanent collection also includes several masterpieces, so look out for the odd Dali or Picasso.

## The Third Line

Beh Times Square Al Quoz 04 341 1367
www.thethirdline.com
Map 1 T5 Metro Al Quoz

One of the leading lights of the Dubai art scene, The Third Line gallery in Al Quoz hosts exhibitions by artists originating from or working in the Middle

East. There are indoor and outdoor spaces for shows, many of which have caught the eye of both local and international collectors. Open Monday to Thursday 10:00 to 12:30 and 16:30 to 21:00. On Fridays the gallery opens at 17:00 and closes at 22:00.

## Total Arts Gallery

The Courtyard Al Quoz 04 347 5050
www.courtyard-uae.com
Map 1 U5 Metro Al Quoz

Dubai's biggest gallery occupies two floors of The Courtyard in Al Quoz. It usually exhibits works of art from a variety of cultures and continents, although there is a leaning towards regional talent (particularly Iranian). There are over 300 paintings on permanent display, and regular shows of traditional handicrafts and antique furniture. One of the main attractions is the beautiful cobbled courtyard itself, surrounded by different facades combining a variety of building styles from around the world.

## Traffic

Saratoga Bldg Al Barsha 04 341 8494
www.viatraffic.org
Map 1 Q5 Metro Sharaf DG

A stylish multi-disciplinary art and design practice, which features a gallery, store and studio. Work is displayed from established designers as well as up and coming talents in the field, while the store sells a wide range of aesthetically pleasing items, from small items such as cutlery through to inspirational furniture.

## XVA Gallery

Bastakiya Bur Dubai 04 353 5383
www.xvagallery.com
Map 2 M3 Metro Al Fahidi

Located in the centre of Bastakiya, this is one of Dubai's most interesting galleries. Originally a windtower house, it is now fully restored and worth a visit for its architecture and displays of local and international art. The gallery focuses on paintings and hosts many different exhibitions throughout the year, as well as free film screenings on Wednesday evenings throughout the winter. XVA can also lay claim to the title of Dubai's hippest hotel, with eight guest rooms located on the upper floors.

### Art Dubai

Art Dubai is an annual get-together of industry people from across the Middle East and Asian art world. Held in March at Madinat Jumeirah, one of the main events is the Global Art Forum, which attracts artists, curators, museum groups and international media representatives. Several exhibitions and events also run alongside the forum, drawing thousands of visitors.

# PARKS, BEACHES & ATTRACTIONS

## Parks

Dubai has a number of excellent parks, with lush green lawns and a variety of trees and shrubs creating the perfect escape from the concrete jungle of the city. In winter months, the more popular parks can be very busy at weekends. Most have a kiosk or cafe selling snacks and drinks, and some have barbecue pits (remember to take your own wood or charcoal).

Regulations among the parks vary, with some banning bikes and rollerblades, or limiting ball games to specific areas. Pets are not permitted and you should not take plant cuttings. Some parks have a ladies' day when entry is restricted to women, girls and young boys, and certain smaller ones actually ban anyone other than ladies through the week, while allowing families only at the weekends. Entrance to the smaller parks is generally free, while the larger ones charge up to Dhs.5 per person. The Al Mamzar and Jumeira beach parks have the added bonus of sand and sea to accompany their green spaces. Opening hours of most parks change during Ramadan.

### Community Parks

Besides the parks listed here, many residential areas have smaller, community parks that are great places to escape to. Rashidiya Park, close to Mirdif, features large grassy areas and play sections for kids (it's women and children only during the week though). A similar smaller park is located in the Safa residential area (Safa 2 Park), and while it may not have the attractions of the main Safa Park, it's a perfect spot to take the younger kids to let off steam. There's a great local park at Nad Al Sheba, while Emirates Hills has several small green spaces and playing areas, and, like other gated communities, has communal pool and sports courts areas. Check out your local area for any hidden recreational gems.

### Al Mamzar Beach Park

Nr Hamriya Port Al Hamriya 04 296 6201
Map 2 T3 Metro Al Quladah

With its four clean beaches, open spaces and plenty of greenery, Al Mamzar is a popular spot – although the previously clear sea views have become a little obstructed by the work on the Palm Deira. The well-maintained beaches have sheltered areas for swimming and changing rooms with showers. Air-conditioned chalets, with barbecues, can be rented, costing from Dhs.150 to Dhs.200. There are two pools with lifeguards on duty. Bike hire is also available. Entrance is Dhs.5 per person or Dhs.30 per car.

### Creekside Park

Nr Wonderland Umm Hurair 04 336 7633
Map 2 M6 Metro Healthcare City

Situated in the heart of the city but blessed with acres of gardens, fishing piers, jogging tracks, barbecue sites, children's play areas, mini-golf, restaurants and kiosks, this is the ultimate in park life. There's also a mini falaj and a large amphitheatre. Running along the park's 2.5km stretch of creek frontage is a cable car system which allows visitors an unrestricted view from 30 metres in the air. From Gate Two, four-wheel cycles can be hired for Dhs.20 per hour (you can't use your own bike in the park). Rollerblading is permitted, and there are no ladies-only days. The park is also home to Dubai Dolphinarium (p.250) and the enjoyable Children's City (p.252). Entrance fee: Dhs.5. Cable car: adults Dhs.25; children Dhs.15. Children's City: adults Dhs.15; children Dhs.10.

### Jumeira Beach Park

Nr Jumeirah Beach Club Jumeira 04 349 2111
www.dm.gov.ae
Map 2 D3 Metro Business Bay

You get the best of both worlds here with plenty of grassy areas and vast expanses of beach. The facilities include sunbed and parasol hire (Dhs.20 – get there early to ensure they haven't run out), lifeguards, toilets, showers, snack bar, play park and barbecue pits. Away from the beach there are plenty of grassy areas and landscaped gardens, children's play areas, and barbecue pits available for public use. Cycling is not allowed (except for small children) and neither is rollerblading. Entry is Dhs.5 per person or Dhs.20 per car, including all occupants. Mondays are for women and children only. Open daily from 07:30, closing at 22:00 Sunday to Wednesday, and at 23:00 Thursday to Saturday and on holidays.

### Mushrif Park

Al Khawaneej Rd Mushrif 04 288 3624
www.dm.gov.ae

The grounds of Mushrif Park, close to Mirdif, are extensive, and although it is a 'desert park', there are many large stretches of beautiful green lawn. There are two large pools (one for men, one for women), and a smaller pool for young children. Numerous playgrounds are dotted around the park, and a central plaza features fairground rides and trampolines. You can get close to horses, camels, goats and even a turkey at the animal enclosure, while pony and camel rides are available from Dhs.5 for a short ride. There is also a mini-town, where you can wander around miniature houses themed on different building styles from around the world, and a train that tours the park in the afternoons (Dhs.2 per ride). Entry is Dhs.3 per person or Dhs.10 per car. Swimming pool entrance is Dhs.10 per adult and Dhs.5 per child.

# The No.1 off-road guides to the UAE & Oman

The ultimate accessory for any 4WD, the *UAE & Oman Off-Road Explorers* help drivers to discover the region's 'outback'. Just remember your 4WD was made for more than just the school run.

**Off-Road Explorer**
What your 4WD was made for

www.explorerpublishing.com

**EXPLORER**

## Parks, Beaches & Attractions

### Safa Park

Al Wasl Rd Al Wasl 04 349 2111 www.dm.gov.ae
Map 2 D4 Metro Business Bay

This huge, artistically landscaped park is a great place to escape the commotion of nearby Sheikh Zayed Road. Its many sports fields, barbecue sites, play areas and fun fairground rides make it one of the best places in the city for the coming together of locals and expats. There's a large boating lake in the centre of the park, tennis and basketball courts for the public, and a flea market (p.395) held on the first Saturday of every month. Various informal football and cricket games take place on the large areas of grass. Tuesday is ladies' day, but there is also a permanent ladies' garden within the park. Bikes are available for hire. Entry costs Dhs.3 (free for children under 3 years old). There's a great running track around the park's perimeter.

### Umm Suqeim Park

Nr Jumeirah Beach Hotel Umm Suqeim 04 348 4554
Map 1 T3 Metro First Gulf Bank

This ladies' park is closed to men except for weekends. It is fairly large and has three big playgrounds with some great equipment. There are also plenty of shady, grassy areas so that mums can sit and rest while the kids let off steam. In the middle of the park there is a popular coffee shop. Entrance is free.

### Zabeel Park

Nr Trade Centre R/A Zabeel
Map 2 J5 Metro Al Jafiliya

Zabeel Park is divided into three zones – alternative energy, communications and technology – and is also home to Stargate (see p.254). There are recreational areas, a jogging track, a mini cricket pitch, a football field, boating lake and an amphitheatre, plus a number of restaurants and cafes. Mondays are ladies only. Entry costs Dhs.5. The park is open from 08:00 weekly, closing at 23:00 Sunday to Wednesday, and at 23:30 Thursday to Saturday.

## Beaches

Blessed with warm weather, calm ocean waters and long stretches of sand, Dubai offers its residents the choice of several beautiful beaches. There are three types of beach to choose from: public beaches (limited facilities but no entry fee), beach parks (good facilities and a nominal entrance fee), and private beaches (normally part of a hotel or resort).

Options for public beaches include the area around Al Mamzar Beach Park (p.246), which has a cordoned-off swimming area, chalets, jet skis for hire and free beaches along the lagoon to the south. South of Dubai Creek, you'll come to Jumeira Open Beach, which is great for soaking up the sun, swimming and people watching. Moving down the coast past Jumeira Beach Park (p.246) brings you to the small beaches between Dubai Offshore Sailing Club and Jumeirah Beach Hotel. One of these, Umm Suqeim beach, is close to the Burj Al Arab and is one of the busiest public beaches at the weekends. Another section of public beach, known unofficially as Palace Beach, is to be found on Beach Road in a gap amid the grand palaces between Madinat and The Palm, opposite the Barsha road. A sign says 'no unauthorised vehicles', but despite this it remains a popular location.

The long stretch of sand at JBR contains some beach hotels, but it's also accessible to the public and is extremely popular with Marina residents in the cooler season. Those looking for more natural beaches used to go to Jebel Ali, but this previously quiet area is now also being developed with the construction of Palm Jebel Ali and Dubai Waterfront, which means that all but the smallest, scrappiest bit of beach has been closed to the public. For new options only a little further from town, and great for kitesurfing, drive south of Jebel Ali and turn right at the first major junction, actually in Abu Dhabi emirate, where the beaches are still quiet and, as yet, undeveloped.

> **Swim Safely**
>
> Although the waters off the coast generally look calm and unchallenging, very strong rip tides can carry the most confident swimmer away from the shore very quickly and drownings have occurred in the past. Take extra care when swimming off the public beaches where there are no lifeguards.

Regulations for public beaches are quite strict. Dogs are banned and so is driving. Officially, other off-limit activities include barbecues, camping without a permit and holding large parties. Contact the Public Parks & Recreation Section (04 336 7633) for clarification. It is fine to wear swimming costumes and bikinis on the beach, as long as you keep both parts on.

## Waterparks

### Aquaventure > p.220

Atlantis The Palm Palm Jumeirah 04 426 1000
www.atlantisthepalm.com
Map 1 N0 Metro Nakheel

Aquaventure is the ultimate destination for thrill seekers: to get the adrenaline pumping try the Leap of Faith, a 27 metre near-vertical drop that shoots you through a tunnel surrounded by shark-infested waters. The Rapids will take you on a tumultuous journey down a 2.3km river, complete with waterfalls and wave surges. For the little ones, there is Splashers, a water playground. Open daily from 10:00 until sunset. Entrance for those over 1.2m is Dhs.200, and Dhs.165 for those under that height. Children younger than 2 years old and Atlantis hotel guests get in for free.

# Play With Dolphins

Wade into crystal clear waters and enjoy a 90 minute shallow water experience, bringing you closer to our fun-loving family and providing an experience which is intimate, exciting, entertaining, educational and conservation minded.

Open daily: 10:00am - Sunset
To book please call +971 4 426 1030
atlantisthepalm.com

**ATLANTIS**
THE PALM, DUBAI

# Parks, Beaches & Attractions

---

### Water, Water Everywhere

When you've ridden the Jumeirah Sceirah so many times that you've screamed yourself hoarse and taken the Leap Of Faith that often you're on first-name terms with the sharks, head to Umm Al Quwain for a new water challenge at Dreamland Aqua Park (p.289), a great family-friendly waterland with 25 rides and even camping facilities.

---

## SplashLand
**WonderLand** Umm Hurair **04 324 1222**
www.wonderlanduae.com
Map **2 L7** Metro **Healthcare City**

It may feel at times like a bit of a ghost town, but the waterpark within WonderLand offers fun for kids or adults with nine rides including slides and twisters, a lazy river, an adults' pool and a children's activity pool with slides, bridges and water cannons. Alternatively, you can just relax by the pool and sunbathe. Lockers and changing rooms are available.

## Wild Wadi Water Park > *p.251*
**Jumeirah Beach Hotel** Umm Suqeim
**04 348 4444**
www.wildwadi.com
Map **1 S3** Metro **Mall of the Emirates**

Spread over 12 acres beside Jumeirah Beach Hotel, this water park has a host of aquatic rides and attractions to suit all ages and bravery levels. Depending on how busy it is you may have to queue for some of the rides, but the wait is worth it. After paying the entrance fee there is no limit to the number of times you can ride. Highlights include Wipeout, a permanently rolling wave that is perfect for showing off your body-boarding skills, and the white-knuckle Jumeirah Sceirah. The park opens at 11:00 and the closing time depends on the time of year. Admission is Dhs.195 for adults and Dhs.165 for children. There is also a 'sundowner' rate (for the last three hours of opening), when adults and children pay Dhs.100.

## Wildlife

## Dolphin Bay > *p.249*
**Atlantis The Palm** Palm Jumeirah **04 4426 1030**
www.atlantisthepalm.com
Map **1 N0** Metro **Nakheel**

Playing with a bottlenose dolphin on the Shallow Water Interaction package at Dolphin Bay is an unforgettable experience. Touching, hugging, holding 'hands', playing ball and feeding are all encouraged, under supervision of the marine specialists. A 90 minute session will set you back Dhs.790 per person (with discounts for hotel guests)

and is open to all ages. Your family and friends can watch and take photos from the beach for Dhs.300, but this also grants them access to Aquaventure, Lost Chambers and the private beach. There's also a deep water experience, where visitors can swim and snorkel alongside the mammals with the aid of an underwater scooter.

## Dubai Aquarium
**Dubai Mall** Downtown Burj Dubai **04 448 5200**
www.thedubaiaquarium.com
Map **2 F6** Metro **Burj Dubai**

The Dubai Aquarium is a sight to behold in the middle of Dubai Mall; through its three storey main viewing panel the bewildering variety of tropical fish (over 33,000 in total) is displayed to fish fans and passing shoppers free of charge. For a closer view of the main tank's inhabitants, which include fearsome looking but generally friendly sand tiger sharks, you can pay to walk through the 270° viewing tunnel. Also well worth a look is the Underwater Zoo, which has exhibits from the world's waters, and includes residents such as penguins, piranhas and an octopus. If you're feeling adventurous, you can even go for a scuba dive in the tank (call ahead to book). A ticket to the interactive Underwater Zoo and Tunnel Experience costs Dhs.50 (or Dhs.25 for just the tunnel).

## Dubai Dolphinarium > *p.253*
**Creekside Park** Umm Hurair **04 336 9773**
www.dubaidolphinarium.ae
Map **2 L6** Metro **Healthcare City**

Despite the controversy surrounding its opening, the Dolphinarium has proved to be a popular addition to Creekside Park (p.246). The main attraction is the seal and dolphin show which runs twice a day during the week, and three times daily at weekends. During the show you will meet the three resident black sea bottlenose dolphins and the four northern fur seals, and afterwards you can have your picture taken with them, or even get up close and personal with them in the water. Prices start from Dhs.100 for an adult and Dhs.50 for a child, but a whole range of group and family discounts are available.

## Dubai Zoo
**Jumeira Rd** Jumeira **04 349 6444**
www.dubaitourism.ae
Map **2 G3** Metro **Financial Centre**

This is an old-fashioned zoo, with lions, tigers, giraffes, monkeys, deer, snakes, bears, flamingos, giant tortoises and other animals housed behind bars in small cages. The curator and his staff do their best, with the woefully inadequate space and resources, to look after the animals, but it's not a place that animal lovers will enjoy visiting. Entry costs Dhs.2 per person, while under 2s go free. Closed on Tuesdays.

# CAN YOU CAPTURE THE EXPERIENCE??

Ride the wave and let the fun flow. Email your Wild Wadi snapshots and memories and share them with the world at www.wildwadi.com

WATERPARK

Master Blaster | Tunnel of Doom | Jumeirah Sceirah | Flowriders | Lazy River | Wave Pool | Flood River | Children's Play Structure

**Shops. Restaurants. Parking. Cashless Payment. Sun Beds. Available for Birthday Packages, Corporate and Group Outings. For more information call +971-4-348 4444 or log on to www.wildwadi.com**

## WILD TIMES ARE CALLING

While Dubai Zoo may not be the best facility in the world, there are several higher quality places beyond the city limits that are well worth a visit for animal lovers. Al Ain Wildlife Park & Resort (p.280) has tie-ins with the world-renowned San Diego Zoo, and contains excellent facilities for a big range of animals from around the globe. Sharjah also has several places to get up close to birds, beasts and fish: it has its own aquarium (p.286), plus the Arabian Wildlife Centre and Children's Farm (both part of the Sharjah Desert Park, p.286). Closer to Dubai, on the edge of town, is Ras Al Khor Wildlife Sanctuary, which is a stopping off point for thousands of migrating birds each year, including about 1,500 flamingos. There are a number of hides to view the action from: one beside Ras Al Khor Road, and two off Oud Metha Road (www.wildlife.ae, 04 206 4240).

### Lost Chambers > p.220

Atlantis The Palm Palm Jumeirah 04 426 0000
www.atlantisthepalm.com
Map 1 N0 Metro Nakheel

The ruins of the mysterious lost city provide the theme for the aquarium at Atlantis. The maze of underwater halls and tunnels provide ample opportunity to get up close to the aquarium's 65,000 inhabitants, ranging from sharks and eels to rays and piranhas, as well as multitudes of exotic fish. The entrance fee is Dhs.100 for adults and Dhs.70 for 7 to 11 year olds. Hotel guests get in for free, and while you can see quite a lot from the windows in the hotel, it is worth splashing out for the views inside.

## Amusement Centres

### Children's City

Creekside Park Umm Hurair 04 334 0808
www.childrencity.ae
Map 2 M6 Metro Healthcare City

Children's City is an educational project that offers kids their own learning zone and amusement facilities, by providing hands-on experiences relating to theory they have been taught at school. There's a planetarium focusing on the solar system and space exploration, a nature centre for information on land and sea environments, and the Discovery Space, which reveals the miracles and mysteries of the human body. It is aimed at 5 to 12 year olds, although items of interest are included for toddlers and teenagers. The centre opens daily from 09:00 to 20:30, except on Fridays when it opens at 15:00. Entrance costs Dhs.10 for children under 16 and Dhs.15 for anyone over 16.

### Encounter Zone

Wafi Umm Hurair 04 324 7747
www.waficity.com
Map 2 L6 Metro Healthcare City

With a range of activities for all ages, Encounter Zone is a great stop-off if you want to reward your kids for being good while you have shopped up a storm in Wafi's many boutiques. Galactica is for teenagers and adults and features an inline skating and skateboarding park. Lunarland is for kids aged 1 to 8, and is packed with activities designed especially for younger children, including a small soft-play area for little ones. Prices range from Dhs.3 to Dhs.27, or you can buy a five-hour pass for Dhs.45. Open from 10:00 to 22:00 Sunday to Wednesday and from 10:00 to midnight on Thursday and Friday.

### Fantasy Kingdom

Al Bustan Centre Al Qusais 04 263 0000
www.al-bustan.com
Map 2 R7 Metro Al Nahda

Themed as a medieval castle, Fantasy Kingdom offers adventure and excitement for the little ones. The centre has a 24,000 square foot indoor play area, which is divided into sections for different age groups. Younger children can enjoy the merry-go-round, cars to ride and the soft-play area, while older kids can play interactive games, video games, bumper cars, pool and air hockey. There is also a children's cafeteria.

### KidZania

Dubai Mall Downtown Burj Dubai
www.kidzania.com
Map 2 F6 Metro Burj Dubai

This new addition to Dubai Mall offers kids the chance to become adults for the day. Billed as a 'real-life city' for children, youngsters can dress up and act out more than 75 different roles, from policeman to pilot and doctor to designer. The KidZania city even has its own currency, which children can earn and spend. It's intended to be both fun and educational.

### Magic Planet

Deira City Centre Deira 04 295 4333
www.deiracitycentre.com
Map 2 N6 Metro Deira City Centre

These blaring, boisterous play areas are located in Deira City Centre and Mall of the Emirates (04 341 4000), and are hugely popular for kids accompanying their mums and dads on long shopping trips. There are various rides, including merry-go-rounds, a train, bumper cars and the latest video games. For tinier tots there is a large activity play gym and a small soft-play area. Entrance is free, and you use the facilities on a 'pay as you play' basis, or buy a Dhs.50 special pass for unlimited fun and entertainment.

GOVERNMENT OF DUBAI

DUBAI MUNICIPALITY

*If you love dolphins,*
*a visit to*
*Dubai Dolphinarium*
*is a MUST!!!*

## Dream... Feel... Enjoy...
## A true connection with dolphins

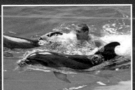

*Swimming with Dolphins (Daily)*

### SHOW TIME:
**MON, TUE, WED & THU** 11 am | 5 pm    **FRI & SAT** 11 am | 3 pm | 6 pm

**FOR RESERVATIONS**
Call: +971 4 336 9773  Fax: +971 4 336 9774
Email: smo@dubaidolphinarium.ae
Online Booking: www.dubaidolphinarium.ae

DUBAI
DOLPHINARIUM
CREEK PARK, GATE 1

# Parks, Beaches & Attractions

## SEGA Republic

Dubai Mall Downtown Burj Dubai 04 448 8484
www.segarepublic.com
Map 2 F6 Metro Burj Dubai

This indoor theme park located in Dubai Mall offers a range of indoor thrills and spills, courtesy of the nine main attractions and the 150 arcade games. A Power Pass (Dhs.125) gets you all-day access to the big attractions, which include stomach-flipping rides like the Sonic Hopper, the SpinGear and the Halfpipe Canyon. Unlike many other shopping mall amusement centres, SEGA Republic is for all ages, and features some truly unique thrills.

## Stargate

Zabeel Park Zabeel 800 9977
www.stargatedubai.com
Map 2 J5 Metro Al Jafiliya

Kids will love Stargate; this massive complex, located in Zabeel Park, is free to enter, with access to the five giant play domes paid for by a rechargeable card. Each area contains a different adventure; there's a multi-storey soft-play area, two go-kart tracks, an ice rink, an indoor rollercoaster and a 3D fun zone. The walkways connecting the play domes house plenty of food venues and retail outlets, and there are enough arcade games dotted throughout to keep everyone happy.

## Desert Resorts & Getaways

Out of the city limits but still within Dubai emirate there are several resorts that offer luxurious getaways and both day and night time activities for Dubai residents. You can make a short break or holiday of it by checking in for a few nights, or you can use most of the sports, leisure and dining facilities as a paying day visitor at most of the resorts.

The perfect desert break can be had at either Al Maha Desert Resort & Spa or Bab Al Shams. Al Maha is the more exclusive, with the resort's facilities, located in a desert conservation area, reserved for staying guests, while the upmarket Bab Al Shams, operated by Jumeirah, opens its stylish facilities and restaurants to day visitors. Hatta Fort Hotel makes for a great day trip or break to the Hajar Mountains (see Out Of The City, p.289), Jebel Ali Resort offers beach, spa, golf and dining facilities, and Desert Palm provides respite just past the city limits.

## Al Maha Desert Resort & Spa

Dubai- Al Ain Rd 04 832 9900
www.al-maha.com

Set within the 225 square kilometre Dubai Desert Conservation Reserve, with breathtaking views of picturesque dunes and rare wildlife, this luxury getaway describes itself as 'the world's first Arabian ecotourism resort' and was named as one of the best ecotourism models by *National Geographic* in 2008. Al Maha is designed to resemble a typical Bedouin camp, but conditions are anything but basic. Each suite is beautifully crafted and has its own private pool. Guests are welcome to dine on their own veranda, with impeccable, yet discreet, butler service, or in the elegant restaurant. Activities include horse riding, camel trekking and falconry. There is also a superb spa.

## Bab Al Shams Desert Resort & Spa

Nxt to Endurance Village 04 809 6100
www.jumeirah.com

Bab Al Shams ('The Gateway to the Sun') is a beautiful desert resort built in the style of a traditional Arabic Fort. Each of its 115 rooms is decorated with subtle yet stunning Arabian touches, and pristine desert dunes form the backdrop. Al Hadheerah (p.452), an authentic, open-air, Arabic desert restaurant, is highly recommended. There is a kids' club, a large swimming pool (complete with swim-up bar), lawn games and the luxurious Satori Spa (p.216).

## Desert Palm Dubai

Al Awir Rd Al Awir 04 323 8888
www.desertpalm.ae

Located just outside the city, Desert Palm is so tranquil you'll never want to leave. Overlooking polo fields, guests can chose from suites, or private villas with a pool. The extensive spa menu features massage and holistic therapies including reiki. Signature restaurant Rare is a must for meat lovers, while Epicure is a lovely gourmet deli and a great breakfast venue.

## Jebel Ali Golf Resort & Spa

Nr Palm Jebel Ali Jebel Ali 04 814 5555
www.jebelali-international.com

Just far enough out of Dubai to escape the hustle and bustle, this resort offers 392 luxurious rooms in resplendent surroundings, with a peaceful atmosphere – the perfect place for a weekend break. The two distinct properties, the Jebel Ali Hotel and The Palm Tree Court & Spa, are set in 128 acres of lush, landscaped gardens, with an 800 metre private beach, a marina and a golf course. Guests can also enjoy horse riding, shooting and a variety of watersports. Although the trunk of Palm Jebel Ali (still under construction) is only 400 metres away, it doesn't detract from the tranquility.

### Weekend Breaks

If you want more ideas on the best places to head for a city escape, get hold of *Weekend Breaks Oman & UAE*. The book features detailed reviews of some of the region's top hotels, as well as sightseeing highlights. See www.explorerpublishing.com/shop.

# OUT & ABOUT

The UAE has much more to offer than its headline-grabbing, metropolis-based attractions. Beyond the city limits, in all directions, is a varied and fascinating landscape that has great potential for exploring and leisure-time activities. Getting out into the deserts and wadis by 4WD is a must-do while you're a Dubai resident, and once you're out there there are some super hiking and camping spots to take advantage of too. The sea that surrounds the country is also a great adventure playground, and the warm Gulf waters provide a wonderful opportunity to try snorkelling, diving and sailing.

## Off-Roading

With the vast areas of virtually untouched wilderness in the UAE, wadi and dune bashing are very popular pastimes. Every other vehicle on the road in Dubai seems to be a four wheel drive, but unlike in many countries, in the UAE there's ample opportunity to truly put them to the test in an off-road environment. Dune bashing, or desert driving, is one of the toughest challenges for both car and driver, but once you have mastered it, it's also the most fun. Driving in the wadis is a bit more straightforward. Wadis are (usually) dry gullies, carved through the rock by rushing floodwaters, following the course of seasonal rivers.

## Water Choice

As well as boating, diving and snorkelling, there are plenty of other waterborne activities you can fill your leisure time with. Kitesurfing (p.328) is a growing pastime worldwide, and there are a couple of good spots in town. Regular surfing is possible in Dubai, although the waves are more Clacton than California. Nonetheless there is a local group, Surfing Dubai, that is open to beginners and die-hards alike (p.340). Windsurfing, jetskiing and waterskiing are all available from various beachfront hotels and sports clubs (p.342), while canoeists and kayakers can take advantage of the mangroves and lagoons on both of the country's coastlines for some first-class exploring (see p.311).

# ADRENALINE SPORTS

Thrill-seekers don't need to head out to sea or to distant shores to get a taste of extreme adventure; you can spend the morning diving with sharks, the afternoon driving like an F1 racer, and the evening catching air on a snowboard, all without leaving the city limits.

Dubai Aquarium (p.250) offers the chance to climb inside its 10 million litre tank and get up close to some of the 33,000 aquatic inhabitants. Whether you're an experienced diver or have never strapped on a tank before, the highly qualified instructors from Al Boom Diving can guide you through the waters, allowing you to mingle with some of the exotic residents, including sand tiger sharks, stingrays and giant groupers, and be part of the attraction yourself.

At Dubai Autodrome (p.327) speed junkies can climb inside a racing car and tear up the track as part of the F1 Style Single Seater Experience package. You'll be fully briefed and supervised as you roar out of the pits and follow a leader car around the hair-pins and straights. If you get the bug, come back for more to crank it up a notch and be a bit more adventurous with your driving.

Finally, if you've moved to Dubai from cooler climes and are missing your fix of powder and mountains, head to Ski Dubai (p.338) – the indoor piste in the heart of the city, complete with its very own 'black run'. Lessons for beginners are available, while experienced downhillers can go on Freestyle Night to get some serious air on the jumps, kickers and rails.

Some of the UAE's regional highlights include:

**Northern Emirates:** For a full day out, with some of the best driving in the emirates, combine the mountains around Wadi Bih, near Ras Al Khaimah, with one of the interesting wadi routes on the east coast.

**East Coast**: From Dubai, the east coast can be reached in about two hours. The mountains and beaches are fantastic spots for camping, barbecues and weekend breaks, as well as various other activities. There are some great wadi and mountain routes here, and the area is also renowned for its diving and snorkelling opportunities, particularly around Snoopy Island.

**Hatta**: The Hatta region is home to the popular Big Red sand dune, a huge draw and a must-do challenge for off-roaders and quad bikers, as well as the Hatta Pools, a great swimming spot in the Hajar Mountains.

**Al Ain**: The oasis town of Al Ain is worthy of a visit in its own right, while nearby are the imposing Jebel Hafeet and Hanging Gardens, a great trekking spot.

**Liwa**: A trip to Liwa is one you'll never forget – it's one of the few remaining chances to experience unspoiled dunes. The drive from Abu Dhabi or Dubai is long, more suitable for a two or three day camping trip, but the journey is worth it. Prepare for the most adventurous off-road driving the UAE has to offer, and some of its most incredible scenery.

For further information and tips on driving off-road check out both the *UAE Off-Road Explorer* and *Oman Off-Road Explorer*. These books feature a multitude of detailed routes, and gives advice on how to stay safe, where to camp and things to do along the way.

# Beginners' Guide To Desert Driving

Off-road driving is exciting and adventurous, but it shouldn't be undertaken lightly; it requires skill, the correct equipment, and a little planning before venturing out for the first time.

The key to driving on sand is maintaining controlled momentum and always looking ahead so you can plan for obstacles before you reach them. Most of the tracks on routes such as Fossil Rock (see the feature in Out Of The City, p.295) shouldn't present any problems, but they will get you used to how your car handles on sand and the different style needed to driving on hard surfaces.

Before you start driving, deflate your tyres to 15-18psi. This increases the surface area of the tyre in contact with the sand, providing added traction for the soft conditions and saving your engine from being overworked.

Make sure you are in 4WD (high range), and use the lower gears at higher than normal revs. You will find you use first and second a lot, but on more open and flatter tracks, you will get into third and even fourth, and at times it will feel very similar to driving on the road.

When the track becomes undulating or you head into the dunes, slow down, keep a steady pace and stay alert for obstacles. You should try to use the accelerator more than anything else, barely touching the brakes or clutch. If you do brake, do so lightly and smoothly to avoid sinking into the sand.

At first even small dunes can seem quite extreme, so take things cautiously. Plan your ascents to take the smoothest route and try to reduce your speed so that you coast over the top of a rise or a dune at close to walking pace so you will be in control for the descent. Go easy on the gas – it is far better to fail to make a climb because you were going too slow than to end up jumping over the top of a dune.

When you get over the top, brake gently and stop just on the downward slope. This will allow you to start going again easily. You will often not know what the slope is like until you are right on it; point your car straight down the dune and let your engine do most of the controlling of your speed.

Drivers of automatic cars can do the same using the accelerator; pressing down hard will change down gears, but you may need to use the gear stick to ensure the car doesn't change back up before you want it to, robbing you of the momentum and power you need to climb dunes. Descending, you will need to change into first or second so the car doesn't race away from you.

Don't worry too much about getting stuck, it happens to everyone. If you do, don't keep revving the engine – chances are it will just dig you in further. Get out of your car to assess the situation, and try to work out how it happened so you can learn for next time. Usually clearing a little sand from around the wheels and a few people pushing will get most cars out of minor problems. If you are in deeper, you may need to dig the car free, lower the tyre pressures more or get someone to tow you out.

> Don't worry too much about getting stuck – it happens to everyone. Clearing a little sand from around the wheels and a few people pushing will get most cars out of minor problems.

## Essential Equipment

There are some basic technical requirements for anyone driving in the desert. A well-maintained and fully serviced vehicle, a spare tyre in good condition, a jack, a tool kit including everything to change a tyre, a sturdy plank or block of wood in case you need to change wheels in sand, a tow rope and shackles, a pressure gauge, and a shovel are all essential. And as with any other time you venture out into the desert, you should always have at least one other car with you – even on the simplest routes you might get stuck deep enough to need towing out. Remember to make sure you have plenty of fuel in the tank too.

Other things that can help get you out of sticky situations include sand mats or trays (or your floor mats if you are not too attached to them), a compressor to re-inflate tyres, heavy duty gloves, jump leads, a fully charged mobile phone, and a GPS, which can help take the guesswork out of navigation. Also make sure everyone in your car has plenty of water, sun cream and a hat, and shoes rather than sandals, as the sand can still get very hot.

**Discover Dubai**

If you want a wilderness adventure but don't know where to start, contact any of the major tour companies (see Tour Operators, p.268). All offer a range of desert and mountain safaris.

If you're really keen to learn, OffRoad-Zone (p.316) runs a driving centre at the Jebel Ali Shooting Club where you can practise tackling various obstacles that you might find while off-roading, including deep water, loose rocks and steep descents.

### DRIVE WITH CARE

To protect the environment from damage, you should try to stick to existing tracks rather than create new tracks across virgin countryside. While it may be hard to deviate from the track when wadi bashing, dunes are ever changing so obvious paths are less common. Although the sandy dunes may look devoid of life, there is a surprising variety of flora and fauna that exists. The main safety precaution to take when wadi bashing is to keep your eyes open for developing rare, but not impossible, thunderstorms – the wadis can fill up quickly and you will need to make your way to higher ground pretty quickly to avoid flash floods.

### Camping

Constant sunshine and an awe-inspiring array of locations make camping a much-loved activity in Dubai and the UAE. In general, warm temperatures and next to no rain means you can camp with much less equipment and preparation than in other countries, and many first-timers or families with children find that camping becomes their favourite weekend break. For most, the best time to go is between October and April, as in the summer it can get unbearably hot sleeping outside.

Choose between the peace and tranquility of the desert, or camp among the wadis and mountains next to trickling streams in picturesque oases. Many good campsites are easily accessible from tarmac roads so a 4WD is not always required. You can camp just about anywhere, but there are some stand-out spots that are super places to pitch up. Jebel Yibir is the UAE's highest peak, and as such camping out on the mountain (there's a road up to the summit) is a good option for the warmer months as the temperatures up there are much cooler than down below. The Wadi Sidr off-road route leads to a plateau that offers some good places to camp, with great views, while both Fossil Rock and the drive from Madam to Madah provide terrific, accessible dune driving and camping spots. The ultimate camping experience however is to be had in the sea of dunes at Liwa, where you can go to sleep beneath a perfect starry sky and then wake

up completely surrounded by one of the world's most mesmerising dunescapes (see Out Of The City, p.273). For more information on off-road adventuring and places to camp, refer to the *UAE Off-Road Explorer*.

### Hiking

Despite Dubai's flat terrain, spectacular hiking locations can be found just an hour outside the city limits. To the north, the Ru'us Al Jibal Mountains contain the highest peaks in the area and stand proud at over 2,000 metres. To the east, the impressive Hajar Mountains form the border between the UAE and Oman, stretching from Musandam to the Empty Quarter desert, hundreds of kilometres to the south.

Most of the terrain is heavily eroded due to the harsh climate, but there are still places where you can walk through shady palm plantations and lush oases. Routes range from short, easy walks leading to spectacular viewpoints, to all-day treks over difficult terrain, and can include major mountaineering. Some hikes follow centuries old Bedouin and Shihuh mountain paths, a few of which are still being used.

One of the nearest and easiest places to reach is the foothills of the Hajar Mountains on the Hatta Road, near the Oman border. After passing through the desert, the

# Carry When Camping

Although the UAE has low rainfall, care should be taken in and near wadis as flash floods can and do occur (remember, it may be raining in the mountains miles from where you are).
You should consider taking the following equipment:
- Tent
- Lightweight sleeping bag (or light blankets and sheets)
- Thin mattress (or air bed)
- Torches and spare batteries
- Cool box for food
- Water (always take too much)
- Camping stove, or BBQ and charcoal if preferred
- Firewood and matches
- Insect repellent and antihistamine cream
- First aid kit (including any personal medication)
- Sun protection (hats, sunglasses, sunscreen)
- Jumper/warm clothing for cooler evenings
- Spade
- Toilet rolls
- Rubbish bags (ensure you leave nothing behind)
- Navigation equipment (maps, compass, Global Positioning System (GPS)
- Mobile phone (fully-charged)

flat stark, rugged outcrops transform the landscape. Explore any turning you like, or take the road to Mahdah, along which you'll find several options.

Other great areas for hiking and exploring include Al Ain and its surroundings, many places in the mountains in and around Musandam, and the mountains near the east coast. The mountains in the UAE don't generally disappoint, and the further off the beaten track you get, the more likely you are to find interesting villages where residents live much the same way as they did centuries ago.

For somewhere a bit further afield see *Oman Trekking*, a guide book from Explorer Publishing with pull-out maps covering major signed routes in Oman.

As with any trip into the UAE 'outback', take sensible precautions. Tell someone where you are going and when you should be back and don't forget to take a map, compass, GPS equipment and robust hiking boots. Don't underestimate the strength of the sun – take sunscreen and, most importantly, loads of water.

For most people, the cooler and less humid winter months are the best season for serious mountain hiking. Be particularly careful in wadis (dry riverbeds) during the wet season as flash floods can immerse a wadi in seconds. Also note that there are no mountain rescue services in the UAE, so anyone venturing out should be reasonably experienced or accompanied by someone who knows the area.

See Activities, p.325, for companies that offer organised hikes.

**Diving in Dubai Aquarium**

## Diving

The UAE offers diving that's really very special; the lower Arabian Gulf and the Gulf of Oman will satisfy all tastes and levels of experience for divers and snorkellers alike. You can choose from over 30 wrecks in relatively shallow water, tropical coral reefs and dramatic coastlines that are virtually undived. And these are bathed in warm water all year round.

Water temperatures range from a cooler 20°C in January to a warmer 35°C in July and August. Although the land temperatures can be in the high 40s in the summer months, it is rarely too hot when out at sea or dipping into the water.

The UAE's coastal waters are home to a variety of marine species, coral life and even shipwrecks. You'll see some exotic fish, like clownfish and seahorses, and possibly even spotted eagle rays, moray eels, small sharks, barracuda, sea snakes and stingrays. Most of the wrecks are on the west coast, while the beautiful flora and fauna of coral reefs can be seen on the east coast.

There are many dive sites on the west coast that are easily accessible from Dubai. Cement Barge, Mariam Express and the MV Dara wrecks are some of the more popular dive sites. Off the east coast, a well-known dive site is Martini Rock, a small, underwater mountain covered with colourful soft coral, with a depth range of three to 19 metres. North of Khor Fakkan is the Car Cemetery, a reef that has thrived around a number of cars placed 16 metres below water. Visibility off both coasts ranges from five to 20 metres.

Another option for diving enthusiasts is to take a trip to Musandam (p.296). This area, which is part of the Sultanate of Oman, is often described as the 'Norway of the Middle East' due to the many inlets and the way the sheer cliffs plunge directly into the sea. It offers some spectacular dive sites. Sheer wall dives with strong currents and clear waters are more suitable for advanced divers, while the huge bays, with their calm waters and shallow reefs, are ideal for the less experienced. Visibility here is between 10 and 35 metres. If you plan to travel to Khasab, the capital of the Musandam, you may not be able to take your own air tanks across the border and will have to rent from one of the dive centres there. You may also require an Omani visa. Alternatively, from Dibba on the UAE east coast, you can hire a fast dive boat to take you anywhere from five to 75 kilometres up the coast. The cost ranges between Dhs.150 and Dhs.500, for what is usually a two-dive trip.

There are plenty of dive companies in the UAE where you can try diving for the first time, or improve on your existing diving skills (see Activities, p.316). Most companies offer both tuition and straight forward dive outings, with equipment.

# Spectator Sports

## Snorkelling

Snorkelling is a great hobby and with the conditions in the UAE consisting of relatively calm waters for most of the year, this is the perfect place to get into it. Whatever your age or fitness levels snorkelling will get you into the sea, and the minute you get your first glimpse of bright reef life, you'll be hooked.

Snorkelling offers a different experience to diving, with many interesting creatures such as turtles, rays and even sharks all frequently seen near the surface. It's a great way for the family to enjoy an activity together, and all you need is some basic equipment and you're ready to go.

You can pretty much snorkel anywhere off a boat – all you need is a mask and fins, and you'll likely see something swimming around – but there are certain areas where you're guaranteed to enjoy great marine action.

The east coast is a great area for snorkelling and has the most diverse marine life. Most dive centres take snorkellers out on their boats (along with divers, and the trip lasts for about two hours in total). Some centres can make arrangements to take you to Shark Island (also called Khor Fakkan Island) where you can spend the day. They'll come and collect you at the time you agree on. If that's what you'd like to do, it's best to arrange this with your dive centre in advance. Depending on your swimming ability and the water conditions, you can go to Sandy Beach Hotel and spend the day on the beach and swim out to Snoopy Island, just a short distance from shore. In winter time the water recedes a long way and the distance you have to swim is even less – but the water temperature will be considerably cooler too.

The west coast is not so great, with the best places for seeing fish mainly the waters by harbour walls, but take care: on the outside harbour walls the waves tend to bash against the rocks and you may get caught off guard by a rogue wave (created by boats in the construction areas). You can snorkel on the inside of the harbour walls, but the water there is rather still and tends to silt up. The fish also prefer the outside walls.

Musandam offers good snorkelling too, but the waters there can have strong currents so it's a good idea to go with a tour company and have a guide to point out the best sites. The best fish life is to be found between the surface and 10 metres below, so try to snorkel along the side of rocks and islands. There are a number of tour companies that offer dhow trips for dolphin watching and snorkelling, and the boats usually moor in areas that are safe to snorkel in (see p.268).

Check out the *UAE Underwater Explorer* for further information on where to go snorkelling. Go to www.explorerpublishing.com/shop to purchase a copy.

## Boating

With calm waters and year-round sunshine, the UAE offers ideal conditions for those wishing to sample life on the ocean waves. A number of companies provide boat charters, offering everything from sundowner cruises of a couple of hours and overnight trips with snorkelling stopovers, to scuba diving excursions to remote destinations such as Musandam. Large sailing yachts, speedboats and other motorboats can be hired for private charter and corporate events; other companies offer outings on dhows and also cater to weddings and birthday parties. Fishing trips and watersports packages are also available. If you're on the east coast and fancy a traditional boating experience, large independent groups can charter a dhow from the fishermen at Dibba. If you haggle you can usually knock the price down substantially. Respected UAE charter companies include ART Marine (www.artmarine.net), Bristol Middle East Yacht Solution (www.bristol-middleeast.com), Leisure Marine (www.leisuremarinecharters.com), Marine Concept (www.marine-charter-concept.com) and Ocean Active (www.oceanactive.com). See Activities, p.319, for more details.

*Dubai Yachting & Boating* has advice on buying and mooring a boat, details of local marinas, local rules and regulations, handy maps, suggested cruising areas and a comprehensive contacts directory. With so much invaluable information, this is the ultimate resource for boaters old and new.

# SPECTATOR SPORTS

For eight months of the year, Dubai residents can enjoy a packed calendar of sporting events. The UAE's sunny winter climate, its location within easy reach of Europe and Asia, and its development of some excellent sporting facilities means the country is growing ever more attractive as a venue for international sporting associations to include on their schedules. All of this is great news for sports fans; from big headline events such as the Grand Prix and FIFA Club World Cup, to regular tennis and golf tournaments and even local horse and camel racing meets, there's an awful lot going on.

## Camel Racing

This is a chance to see a truly traditional local sport up close. Apart from great photo opportunities and the excitement of the races, you can also have a browse around the shops; most race tracks have camel markets alongside (they are dark and dusty but should not be missed). The best buys are the large cotton blankets (used as camel blankets), which make excellent bedspreads, throws and picnic blankets, and only cost around Dhs.40. It is also interesting to see the old traders sitting on the floor of their shop, hand weaving camel halters and lead-ropes.

Races take place during the winter months, usually on Thursday and Friday mornings, at tracks in Dubai, Ras Al Khaimah, Umm Al Quwain, Al Ain and Abu Dhabi. Often, additional races are held on National Day and certain other public holidays. Races start early (about 07:30) and are usually over by 08:30. Admission is free.

Ras Al Khaimah has one of the best racetracks in the country at Digdagga, situated on a plain between the dunes and the mountains, about 10km south of the town.

The camel racetrack in Dubai used to be near Nad Al Sheba, but it has now been moved to make way for the Meydan development. To find the new location (it's always a good place to take visitors), head up the Al Ain Road, past the Dubai Outlet Mall, until you reach the Al Lisali exit. Turn right off this exit and you will see the big track on your right. Races are usually early on a Friday morning, but you should see plenty of camels being exercised throughout the day in the cooler months.

### Robotic Jockeys

Racing camels used to be ridden by children, but this practice has since been outlawed – and robotic jockeys have taken over. The operators follow the race in 4WDs while directing the jockeys by remote control – quite a bizarre sight.

## Cricket

Dubai has a large population from the subcontinent, so naturally cricket is a favourite sport of many residents. Although there isn't much on offer in the way of professional domestic leagues, Dubai now boasts a world-class cricket venue: Dubai Sports City's Cricket Stadium. The opening of this arena, coupled with the fact that the International Cricket Council has its headquarters in the city, looks set to ensure that Dubai hosts its fair share of major international matches in the future. The likes of Pakistan, Australia and New Zealand all played here in 2009, the stadium's inaugural year. Keep an eye on local media and www.dubaisportscity.ae for news of upcoming fixtures.

## Football

Football is as popular in the UAE as it is the world over, and in recent years there has been plenty of action for fans of the game to watch. Abu Dhabi was awarded the honour of hosting the FIFA World Club Cup in 2009 and 2010, a tournament which sees the champions of each continent competing in a one-off knock-out competition. In 2009 Dubai hosted the FIFA Beach Soccer World Cup, and it regularly plays host to winter friendly matches between big European teams.

There's a strong domestic competition too, the UAE Football League, and attending one of these games makes for a really colourful experience – Emirati supporters are fanatical about their teams, and there are some strong local rivalries. Dubai's Al Ahli were the 2008-09 champions, while other traditionally strong teams include Al Ain and Al Wasl. There are also several opportunities to see the UAE national team play in qualifying matches for the major international tournaments. See www.uefa.ae for fixture details.

## Golf

Dubai has become a major destination on the world golf circuit. Its first-class courses are a magnet for not only keen amateurs, but also for some of the game's top professional players. Each February, the Dubai Desert Classic is staged at Emirates Golf Club. Part of the European PGA Tour, previous winners include Tiger Woods, Henrik Stenson and Rory McIlroy. The competition lasts for four days, and is a popular event with spectators who can follow their favourite players round the course, or take a seat in one of the grandstands and watch the whole cast of golfers play past. See www.dubaidesertclassic.com for ticket details.

In November 2009, a new tournament made its debut – the Dubai World Championship, staged at the new Jumeirah Golf Estates, is the culmination of the European Tour's Race To Dubai, and is set to be staged again in 2010 (www.dubaiworldchampionship.com). Golf fans also have another major international tournament to look forward to: the Abu Dhabi Golf Championship (www.abudhabigolfchampionship.com), staged at Abu Dhabi Golf Course each January.

## Horse Racing

A trip to the races is an essential experience for anyone living in Dubai. Previously the main course, Nad Al Sheba, held exciting race nights and the world's richest horse race, the Dubai World Cup (see p.26). It was one of the top international racing facilities, with top jockeys from Australia, Europe and the USA regularly competing throughout the season (October-April), as well as home to the successful Godolphin racing stables. It closed for good, however, in 2009, to make way for a brand new development, Meydan which opened for the 2009-10 season and takes over the hosting of both the race nights and Dubai World Cup. Race nights under the floodlights are an atmospheric affair. There is officially no gambling, in line with the country's rules, but everyone can take part in various free competitions to select the winning horses, with the ultimate aim of taking home prizes or cash. You can also catch a slightly more raw form of horse racing at Jebel Ali racecourse, near the Greens, every other Friday afternoon during the season. See www.dubairacingclub.com for the season's full schedule.

For horse excitement of a different kind, the Dubai Polo & Equestrian Club (p.326) stages Friday chukka events during the season. For Dhs.50 you can drive pitchside and pitch up your picnic chairs, blanket and cool box full of Spinneys' finest. For a more extravagant option order a bespoke Polo Picnic Box from the Clubhouse and then mingle with the players for the polo after party from 18:00 to midnight. Polo matches start around 15:00 but arrive from 13:30 to get the pick of the parking spots. 04 3618111, www.poloclubdubai.com.

## Motorsports

The Grand Prix is the UAE's new headline motor racing event, and was a roaring success when it debuted at the Yas Marina Circuit in 2009. It is set to be held again towards the end of 2010, but motorsports fans don't need to wait that long to get their fix. Dubai Autodrome hosts events of various categories year round, from GT to speedcar to endurance races. See www.dubaiautodrome.com for a full calendar of meetings. The annual Abu Dhabi Desert Challenge, held in March, is a great spectator event for rally fans (www.uaedesertchallenge.com).

## Rugby

Although amateur club matches take place in Dubai, Abu Dhabi and Al Ain throughout the year, the big rugby event takes place every December, when fans of the oval ball from around the country and beyond head to the The Sevens stadium on the Al Ain road for the Emirates Airline Dubai Rugby Sevens – three days of rugby and revelry. This 'light' version of the sport is fast paced and competitive, with young, up-and-coming international stars taking centre stage in this knock-out format. Just as much about the atmosphere as the sport, it's a great day out for groups of friends. www.dubairugby7s.com.

## Tennis

One of the highlights of Dubai's sporting calendar is the Barclays Dubai Tennis Championships, which is held at the Aviation Club every February. It is a great opportunity to catch some of the top players in the game at close quarters, and features both men's and ladies' tournaments. Tickets for the later stages sell out in advance so keep an eye out for sale details, although entrance to some of the earlier rounds can be bought on the day. See www. barclaysdubaitennischampionships.com.

## Watersports

Sailing is an important part of Dubai's heritage, and this is reflected in the number of water-based sporting events that take place. The emirate's waters are a major venue on the Class 1 World Power Boating

Championship (www.class-1.com). These stylish heavyweights of the powerboating world race around a grand prix circuit through Mina Seyahi lagoon at speeds of up to 160mph, just metres from the beach. Held at the end of November and beginning of December, the twin Dubai competitions are the finale in the European circuit, which has seen Dubai's Victory Team win the series an impressive eight times. For a quieter but still vigorous display of boating prowess, look out for the various dragon boat events held throughout the year (www.dubaiflyingdragons.com), and keep an eye out for the many sailing and dhow racing events that take place off Dubai's shoreline, including the 10 day Maktoum Sailing Trophy, which takes place each February (www.dimc.ae).

# TOURS & SIGHTSEEING

As befits a leading international tourist destination, Dubai is well geared up for taking people on tours of its attractions and highlights. While many of these are primarily aimed at visitors, there's nothing to stop residents getting to know – and simply enjoying – the various leisure pursuits on offer to holidaymakers.

Some tours are offered by most operators, particularly desert experiences and dhow cruises; both of these are great options for when you have guests in town. Other companies run memorable, specialised tours, such as diving trips, aerial sightseeing and trekking, while almost all the firms listed here will tailor programmes to suit individual needs.

The classic option is the desert safari. Expert drivers blast four wheel drives up, down and around massive dunes while passing old Bedouin villages and pointing out incredible natural attractions. Mountain safaris lead passengers through the narrow wadis and steep passes of the Hajar Mountains. Most driving safaris include pickup from your place of residence and lunch. Some end the day of daredevil driving at a replica Bedouin camp where passengers can watch a belly dancer, eat Arabic delicacies and smoke shisha. Some operators even run overnight safaris that combine half-day treks with some sort of driving adventure.

When booking your tour, it is useful to reserve a place three or four days in advance.

## Bus Tours

If you've got visitors here on a short visit or on a whirlwind stopover in Dubai before they jet off elsewhere, a bus tour of the city is a great way to take in all the highlights in one go. It's also a good way to get acquainted with what's where when you first move to Dubai.

# Experience the difference

Whether it's the excitement of learning to play camel polo, the thrill of desert off-road action or the challenge of Dubai's world class golf courses, Gulf Ventures will ensure your experience of Arabia is truly magical.

**GULF VENTURES**

Call: (+971 4) 404 5880
Email: enquiries@gulfventures.ae
Visit: gulfventures.ae

Destination Management Specialists

# Tours & Sightseeing

## Art Bus
04 341 7303
www.artinthecity.com
Bus service that runs from The Jam Jar (p.244) to galleries across town during major art festivals and exhibitions.

## The Big Bus Company
Wafi Umm Hurair 04 340 7709
www.bigbustours.com
Map 2 L6 Metro Healthcare City
A fleet of London double decker buses that provide a hop-on hop-off service, with commentary, to attractions across town. Tickets are valid for either 24 or 48 hours.

## Wonder Bus Tours
BurJuman Bur Dubai 04 359 5656
www.wonderbusdubai.net
Map 2 L4 Metro Khalid Bin Al Waleed
Two-hour mini tours by, and on, the creek, in an amphibious bus, covering Creekside Park and Dubai Creek Golf & Yacht Club, under Maktoum Bridge towards Garhoud Bridge, then back to BurJuman.

# Desert & Mountain Tours
Desert safaris are by far the most popular tour available, perhaps because a good safari offers many activities in one day. Starting with an exciting ride up and down some of the desert's biggest dunes, you can try sand skiing before watching the sun set over the desert. After driving a short distance further to a permanent Bedouin-style camp, you are treated to a sumptuous barbecue, followed by shisha, belly dancing, camel rides and henna painting.

You can vary the length of your safari, choosing to stay overnight or combine it with a trip into the mountains, if desired. However, a safari to the mountains is highly recommended, if only to see how the landscape changes from orange sand dunes to craggy mountains within the space of a few kilometres.

The approximate cost for a desert safari is Dhs.150-Dhs.300 (overnight up to Dhs.500). Many companies offer these types of tour (see Main Tour Operators, p.268); below is a selection of typical itineraries you can choose from.

## Dune Dinners
Enjoy some thrilling off-road desert driving before settling down to watch the sun set behind the dunes. Starting around 16:00, tours typically pass camel farms and fascinating scenery that provide great photo opportunities. At an Arabian campsite, enjoy a delicious dinner and the calm of a starlit desert night, returning around 22:00.

## Full-Day Safari
This day-long tour usually passes through traditional Bedouin villages and camel farms in the desert, with a drive through sand dunes of varying colours and heights. Tours often visit either Fossil Rock or the Hajar Mountains. A cold buffet lunch may be provided in the mountains before the drive home.

## Hatta Pools Safari
Hatta is a quiet, old-fashioned town nestled in the foothills of the Hajar Mountains, famed for its fresh water rock pools that you can swim in. The full-day trip usually includes a stop at the Hatta Fort Hotel, where you can enjoy the pool, landscaped gardens, archery, and nine-hole golf course. Lunch is served either in the hotel, or alfresco in the mountains. The trip costs Dhs.260-Dhs.350.

## Mountain Safari
Normally a full-day tour takes you to the east coast, heading inland at Dibba and entering the spectacular Hajar Mountains. You will travel through rugged

### DHOW & OUT
An option for large independent groups is to charter a dhow from the fishermen at Dibba on the east coast to travel up the coast to Musandam (p.296). If you're prepared to haggle you can usually knock the price down substantially, especially if you know a bit of Arabic. Expect to pay around Dhs.2,500 per day for a dhow large enough to take 20-25 people, or Dhs.100 per hour for a smaller one.

You'll need to take your own food and water, as nothing is supplied onboard except for ice lockers suitable for storing supplies. Conditions are basic, but you'll have the freedom to plan your own route and to see the beautiful fjord-like scenery of the Musandam from a traditional wooden dhow.

The waters in the area are beautifully clear and turtles and dolphins can often be seen from the boat, although sometimes unfavourable weather conditions can seriously reduce visibility for divers. If you leave from Dibba (or Daba), Omani visas are not required, even though you enter Omani waters.

It is also possible to arrange stops along the coast and it's worth taking camping equipment for the night, although you can sleep on board. This kind of trip is ideal for diving but you should hire any equipment you may need before you get to Dibba (see Diving, p.316). If diving is not your thing, you can just spend the day swimming, snorkelling and soaking up the sun.

👍 Proud to be SAFARI LEADERS

Enjoy the thrill and fun of

# DESERT SAFARI

*Promise of Excellence*

**Programe Includes:**
Dune Bashing - Sand Boarding & Camel Riding
BBQ Dinner - Arabic Tea & Coffee - Soft Drinks & Refreshments
Photograph in Local Dresses - Henna Painting & Tattos
Enchanting Belly Dancing Show - Sheesha (Hubbly-Bubbly)
& a lots more entertainment troughout the evening

**Dhs. 200/-** Per Person

Pick up: 3:00 - 3:30pm - Drop off: 9:00 - 9:30pm
Pick-up & Drop-back facility from Dubai & Sharjah

## DHOW CRUISE DINNER
**A memorable evening in Dubai**

- 2 Hours Cruising
- Welcome Drinks
- Entertainment
- Candle light dinner with music
- Continental and Arabic Buffet

Timing: 8:30pm to 10:30pm - Pick & Drop off from Dubai & Sharjah

**Dhs. 150/-** Per Person

## HATTA MOUNTAIN SAFARI

- Red Dunes Safari & Sand Boarding
- Sight Seeing to various scenic locations
- Chance to Dip n Dive in fresh water pools
- Lunch at 5 Star Hatta Fort Hotel
- Visit to Carpet Market
- Heritage Village
- Hatta Mountain Safari

Timing: 8:00am to 2:30pm - Pick-up & Drop-back facility from Dubai & Sharjah

**Dhs. 300/-** Per Person

**Oasis Palm**
TOURISM L.L.C.

**24 Hrs. Reservation**
**Tel: 04-2686826   Mob: 050-2531138**
E-mail: optdubai@emirates.net.ae   Web: www.opdubai.com

QRG CERT
ISO 9001:2008 Certified

# Tours & Sightseeing

canyons onto steep winding tracks, past terraced mountainsides and old stone houses. It returns via Dibba, where the journey homewards stops off at Masafi Market on the way.

## Overnight Safari

This 24 hour tour starts at about 15:00 with a drive through the dunes to a Bedouin-style campsite. Dine under the stars, sleep in the fresh air and wake to the smell of freshly brewed coffee, before heading for the mountains. The drive takes you through spectacular rugged scenery, past dunes and along wadis, before stopping for a buffet lunch and returning to Dubai.

## Boat Tours

An evening aboard a dhow, either on Dubai Creek or sailing along the coast, is a wonderfully atmospheric and memorable experience. Some companies run regular, scheduled trips, while others will charter out boats to private parties. Many boats also offer dinner cruises from the Bur Dubai side of the creek. Charters of luxury yachts, catamarans and fishing boats are available from several operators, and many firms will consider letting out their tour boats for the right price.

### Al Boom Tourist Village

Nr Garhoud Bridge Umm Hurair 04 324 3000
www.alboom.ae
Map 2 L7 Metro Healthcare City

Operates several dhows on the creek, with capacities ranging from 20 up to 350 passengers. Various packages are available.

### Al Marsa Musandam

Salahuddin Rd Sharjah 06 544 1232
www.musandamdiving.com

Runs dhow voyages off Musandam for divers, snorkellers and sightseers.

### Al Wasl Cruising & Fishing > p.267

Nr United Hypermarket Hor Al Anz
04 268 1468
www.cruiseindubai.com
Map 2 Q5 Metro Abu Hail

Specialises in a variety of deep sea fishing, yacht, and dhow trips and charters.

### Bateaux Dubai > p.461

Nr British Embassy Al Hamriya 04 399 4994
www.bateauxdubai.com
Map 2 M4 Metro Khalid Bin Al Waleed

Sleek sightseeing vessel that offers daily tours and dinner cruises, and can also be chartered for parties of up to 300 people.

### Bristol Middle East Yacht Solution

Marina Walk Dubai Marina 04 366 3538
www.bristol-middleeast.com
Map 1 L4 Metro Dubai Marina

Marina-based company that offers charters and packages on boats of all shapes and sizes, from luxury yachts to its old wooden dhow, Captain Jack, which regularly takes one-hour pleasure cruises along the coast from the Marina. The firm puts together land and air tours.

### Charlotte Anne Charters

Fujairah International Marine Club Fujairah
09 222 3508
www.charlotteannecharters.com

Operates live-aboard diving charters around Musandam in a classic oak vessel built in Denmark in 1949.

### Dusail

Mina Seyahi Dubai Al Sufouh 04 398 9146
www.dusail.com
Map 1 L3 Metro Dubai Marina

Provides coastline tours aboard a 50 foot flagship luxury yacht, Andorra, as well as deep sea, reef or fly fishing packages, and rentals of motor and rigid inflatable boats.

### El Mundo

Dubai International Marine Club Al Sufouh
050 452 3202
www.elmundodubai.com
Map 1 M3 Metro Dubai Marina

El Mundo is a 60 foot catamaran that can be chartered for all manner of occasions. Other vessels available include luxury yachts, and the smaller Nina Marina II.

### ENJOY Yachting

050 465 0425
www.uaeyachting.com

Offers a variety of scheduled and bespoke trips, plus a powerboat taxi service between the creek and Marina.

### Jebel Ali Golf Resort & Spa

Nr Palm Jebel Ali Jebel Ali 04 804 8058
www.jebelali-international.com

One or two-hour boat trips for up to seven people on Club Joumana's 36ft fishing boat.

### Khasab Travel & Tours

Warba Centre Deira 04 266 9950
www.khasabtours.com
Map 1 P5 Metro Abu Baker Al Siddique

Dhow cruise from Dibba that includes lunch, refreshments and snorkelling.

👍 Proud to be Fishing & Cruising Pioneers

*turning moments...
into memories.*

Experience the ultimate Thrill & Fun of

# DEEP SEA FISHING
# & CRUISING *Daily*

Cruise around the Iconic Burj Al Arab,
The Palm & The World Islands

### Onboard Facilities:

Fishing Boats and luxury Yachts are fully equipped and insured.
Refreshments - Soft drinks - Chips - Nuts & Fishing equipment available on board.
Pick-up & Drop-back facility included
Call for tailor made packages to suit your requirements.

Daily Fishing trip 4 hours **AED 2800/-** Exclusive up to 8 Pax

Daily Fishing trip 4 hours **AED 600/-** Per Person. Min. 2 Pax.

## Amazing Mussandam DIBBA & KHASAB

Wholesome fun filled family and friends day out, ideal for Sea & Nature lovers

**Package Includes:**
Scenic Drive - Dhow Cruise - Diving - Snorkeling - Swimming - Fishing -
Refreshments & Continental Buffet Lunch
Round trip transfers - Pick-up 07:30AM - Drop-off 7:30PM

Per Person (For Dibba) **AED 380/-**

Al Wasl
Cruising & Fishing

Asia Pacific
TRAVELS & TOURISM

### 24 Hrs. Reservation
## Tel: 04 2681468 Mob: 050 9266209
Email: alwasl@cruiseindubai.com   www.cruiseindubai.com

QRG
CERT
ISO 9001:2008 Certified

## Tours & Sightseeing

### Le Meridien Mina Seyahi Beach Resort & Marina

Al Sufouh Rd Al Sufouh 04 399 3333
www.lemeridien-minaseyahi.com
Map 1 M3 Metro Dubai Marina

Le Meridien operates a variety of charter cruises from its marina, including for deep-sea fishing, trawling and sightseeing.

### Ocean Group

Wafi Residence Umm Hurair 04 324 3327
www.oceanindependence.com
Map 2 L6 Metro Healthcare City

Provides a range of luxury yacht charters from short trips to overnight stays and holidays on the water. Also sells vessels and runs charters internationally.

### Tour Dubai > p.499

Nr Lamcy Plaza Oud Metha 04 336 8409
www.tour-dubai.com
Map 2 L5 Metro Oud Metha

Offers a variety of creek dhow tours and charter packages that range from romantic dinners for two to corporate hospitality for up to 200 guests.

## Aerial Tours

With its soaring skyscrapers, rolling sand dunes and spectacular man-made islands, Dubai from the air is an impressive sight. Swoop over the cityscape in a helicopter, fly along the coast in a seaplane, or take in the serenity of the desert from a graceful hot air balloon flight – any one of these experiences will live long in the memory. As with boat tours, most aerial tour companies offer a seat on a set tour as well as charter options.

### Aerogulf Services Company

Dubai International Airport Garhoud
04 220 0331
www.aerogulfservices.com
Map 2 P6 Metro Airport Terminal 1

Helicopter tours over the city. A half-hour tour for four people costs Dhs.3,200, or charter a chopper by the hour and choose your route.

### Shopping Tours

Dubai has a well-deserved reputation as the shopping capital of the Middle East. From designer clothes, shoes and jewellery in the malls, to electronics, spices and textiles in the souks, everything is available. This half-day tour (available with most of the main tour operators) takes you round some of the hottest shopping spots in Dubai. Whether or not you walk away with some bargains depends on your haggling skills.

### Balloon Adventures Emirates > p.271

Nr Bin Sougat Centre Al Rashidiya 04 285 4949
www.ballooning.ae
Map 2 P10 Metro Rashidiya Station

Tours for individuals and groups in four large, advanced balloons. Flights depart before sunrise between October and May, and are followed by dune driving.

### Fujairah Aviation Academy

Fujairah Intl Airport Fujairah 09 222 4747
www.fujaa.ae

An enthralling bird's-eye view of Fujairah's coastline, rugged mountains, villages and date plantations. Flights can accommodate one to three people.

### Seawings

Jebel Ali Hotel, Jebel Al Golf Resort & Spa Jebel Ali
04 807 0708 www.seawings.ae

Take off from the water in a seaplane from Jebel Ali or Dubai Creek for spectacular flights over the Gulf and city. Various package options are available.

## Main Tour Operators

Almost all operators offer variations on the main types of excursions: city tours, desert safaris and mountain safaris. Some, however, offer more unique activities, such as fishing or diving trips, expeditions to see the Empty Quarter in Liwa, helicopter tours and desert driving courses. The main tour companies and those that offer something a little bit different are listed in this section, along with some of their highlights – contact them directly for their full programmes.

### Alpha Tours

Beh Nissan Showroom, Al Hai Bld Port Saeed
04 294 9888
www.alphatoursdubai.com
Map N5 Metro Deira City Centre

Provides a full range of tours including shopping trips, desert safaris, flights and cruises.

### Arabian Adventures

Emirates Holiday Bldg, Shk Zayed Rd
Trade Centre 04 303 4888
www.arabian-adventures.com
Map 2 E5 Metro Business Bay

Offers a range of tours and itineraries including desert safaris, city tours, sand skiing, dhow cruises, camel riding, and wadi and dune bashing.

### Desert Adventures Tourism

Al Maktoum St Deira 04 224 2800
www.desertadventures.com
Map 2 N5 Metro Al Rigga

Offers a full range of city and desert tours throughout the emirates.

### Desert Rangers

Oud Metha 04 357 2233
www.desertrangers.com
Map **2 L5** Metro **Oud Metha**
Runs a wide variety of standard and specialist desert
and mountain tours, including activities such as
rock climbing, helicopter tours and kayaking. Also
organises corporate events.

### Desert Rose Tourism

Green Community Jebel Ali 04 335 0950
www.holidayindubai.com
Map **1 G8**
Offers city discovery tours with a personal guide/
driver, plus various trips that showcase the best of the
UAE and Oman, including desert and camel safaris and
dhow dinner cruises.

### Dream Explorer

Saeed Tower, Shk Zayed Rd Trade Centre 1
04 331 9880
www.dreamexplorerdubai.com
Map **2 J4** Metro **Al Jafiliya**
Desert and mountain tours, dune buggying, plus
specialist white-knuckle jet boat rides. A luxury desert
option combines dune driving with a visit to Bab Al
Shams Desert Resort.

### Dubai Tourist & Travel Services

Nr Splash Al Abbar Bld Bur Dubai
04 336 7727
www.dxbtravels.com
Map **2 M5** Metro **Oud Metha**
City shopping tours, creek dinner cruises, cultural
tours to Sharjah and Ajman, plus desert, mountain and
east coast excursions.

### Gulf Ventures > p.263

Nr Gold Souk Deira 04 404 5880
www.gulfventures.ae
Map **2 M3** Metro **Al Ras**
Options include Bedouin camps, creek cruises, tours
around the east coast, plus activities such as fishing,
polo and ballooning, and a range of city tours.

#### Tour Tips

If you are booking a tour, make sure you ring
around to get the best price. Dubai is dedicated
to discounts, particularly at the moment, and
you can often get a better rate as a resident. Just
remember it is all about putting on the charm –
not being a cheeky customer. Also keep an eye on
www.liveworkexplore.com/members throughout
the year for some great sightseeing discounts.

Dubai Creek from the air

# Tours & Sightseeing

### Knight Tours & Services
Al Wadi Bldg, Shk Zayed Road Al Wasl
04 343 7725
www.knighttours.ae
Map 2 F4 Metro Burj Dubai
Desert and city tours, trekking, boat trips, plus private camping options.

### Lama Desert Tours
Al Sayegh Bldg, Oud Metha Rd Oud Metha
04 334 4330
www.lama.ae
Map 2 L5 Metro Oud Metha
Tours include desert safaris, dhow cruises, city excursions and fishing tours.

### Net Tours
Al Bakhit Centre Al Buteen 04 266 6655
www.nettoursdubai.com
Map 2 N5 Metro Abu Baker Al Siddique
Full spectrum of options includes mountain tours, theme parks, dhow cruises and desert safaris, plus Bedouin experience desert campsites.

### Oasis Palm Tourism> p.265
Royal Plaza Bldg Al Rigga Rd 04 262 8889
www.opdubai.com
Map 2 M4 Metro Khalid Bin Al Waleed
Offers desert safaris, dhow dinner cruises and wadi trips, plus east coast tours and diving and deep sea fishing trips.

### Off-Road Adventures
Shangri-La Hotel Trade Centre 050 628 9667
www.arabiantours.com
Map 2 G5 Metro Financial Centre
Runs a range of off-road excursions, including overnight camping, and expeditions to Liwa and the Empty Quarter. Also arranges watersports and airborne activities.

### Orient Tours
Nr Le Meridien Garhoud 04 282 8238
www.orienttours.ae
Map 2 N6 Metro GGICO
City tours, including trips to the horse and camel races, desert safaris, sea safaris around Musandam, off-road trips to Hatta and day tours of the Empty Quarter in Liwa.

### Planet Travel Tours & Safaris
Airport Rd Garhoud 04 282 2199
www.planetgrouponline.com
Map 2 N6 Metro GGICO
Coach, heritage and shopping tours within Dubai, plus safari and desert tours.

### Sunflower Tours
Zabeel Rd Karama 04 334 5554
www.sunflowerdubai.com
Map 2 L5 Metro Oud Metha
Desert and city tours, as well as camel safaris, crab hunting, diving, fishing and helicopter tours.

---

**Up And Away**   Peter Kollar owner and pilot, Balloon Adventures Emirates

*Flying in a hot-air balloon feels like the proverbial 'magic carpet ride' as we float above red sand dunes, green oases, elegant gazelles and the nonchalant camels below. We start early every morning, at sunrise, when it is cool, calm and quiet in the desert, and we take off in the heart of the sands from an oasis located just north of Al Ain.*

*For me, the early start is part of the thrill and the excitement. Flying a hot air balloon is not just a ride, it's a unique experience. Watching the sun rise above the Hajar Mountains from high in the sky is breathtaking, and every time I am up there I marvel at how majestic and peaceful it is.*

*I still love my job, even after 17 years of professional flying, as every flight is different. You never really know where you will land and who you will meet at the landing place. There is a fair amount of uncertainty in ballooning and this is exactly what makes it the very definition of an adventure.*

*The wind on the day determines our direction and the landing area, so our ground crew has a new challenge every day to make sure that they get to the spot where the balloon landed. The remoteness of the area, and the lack of sealed roads means that retrieving the balloon can often turn into an expedition, so we have specialised desert vehicles that are well equipped for such a task.*

*Entertaining my passengers is as much part of the job as flying the balloon, as I explain the navigational and safety aspects to them throughout the journey. It's the balance between the skill of flying and interacting with the passengers that makes hot air ballooning such a perfect profession for me.*

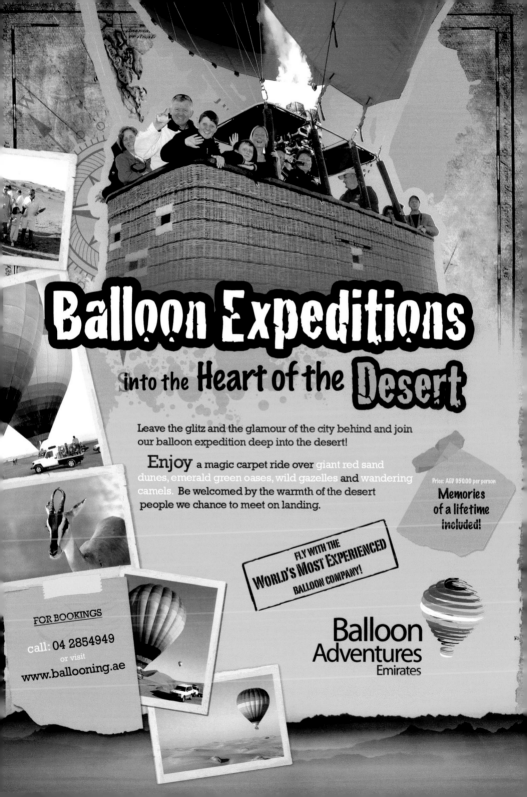

## MICE facilities of Abu Dhabi Falcon Hospital the unique MICE venue in Abu Dhabi

## Falcon World Tour Your Exclusive Tourist Destination Abu Dhabi Falcon Hospital

To make a booking
or for more information
call Mr. Amer Abu Aabed,
mobile 050-6660739
P.O.Box 45553, Abu Dhabi,
United Arab Emirates
Phone: +971-2-5755155
Fax: +971-2-5755001
Email: info@falconhospital.com
Web: www.falconhospital.com

مستشفى أبوظبي للصقور
ABU DHABI FALCON HOSPITAL

# Out Of The City

# OUT OF THE CITY

Dubai may have everything from ski slopes and souks to boutiques and beaches, but there are a number of interesting and varied areas outside the city and country that deserve a place in your weekend plans. There are six other emirates in the UAE and five other countries in the GCC, all of which warrant exploration.

All six of the other emirates in the UAE – Abu Dhabi, Sharjah, Ras Al Khaimah, Umm Al Quwain, Fujairah and Ajman – are within a two-hour drive from the centre of Dubai. From the sleepy streets of Umm Al Quwain and the rugged mountains of Ras Al Khaimah to the cultural grandiose of Sharjah, each emirate has something different to offer, and each can be explored, at least in part, over a weekend. The country's vast deserts and harsh-looking mountains are equally accessible with a copy of the *UAE Off-Road Explorer* and can be reached within a 45 minute drive from Dubai, if you need to avoid civilisation for a while.

Dubai's status as an international hub means it's easy to find quick, cheap flights to the neighbouring GCC countries of Oman, Saudi Arabia, Qatar, Bahrain and Kuwait, none of which are more than an hour and a half flight away. Oman is considered by many to be one of the most beautiful and culturally interesting countries in the region and it can easily be reached and explored by car – Muscat is only a four hour drive from Dubai.

Like the UAE, the countries in the GCC are growing at a phenomenal rate and are trying to attract more tourism. Many hotels in the GCC, including in the UAE, regularly offering hold promotions discounted rooms, especially in the summer months. It's a good idea to sign up for the mailing lists of regional travel agencies, such as Dnata (www.dnata.ae), to find out about any weekend getaway packages they offer.

# UAE – THE OTHER EMIRATES

## Abu Dhabi

Dubai may be the UAE's bold and brash member, but Abu Dhabi remains both the nation's capital and the richest of all the emirates, with a blossoming, burgeoning city to prove it. In recent years there has been a greater commitment to tourism, and projects such as Yas Island with its Grand Prix racetrack (p.278) and the development of the Desert Islands are proof of that. While there isn't much you can get in Abu Dhabi that you can't find in Dubai, its slightly slower pace makes for a refreshing change. The city itself lies on an island shaped liked a scorpion and is connected to the mainland by causeways. It is home to numerous internationally renowned hotels, a selection of shiny shopping malls and a sprinkling of culture in the form of heritage sites and souks. There are often good deals to be had on hotel breaks.

Abu Dhabi is marketed as the cultural capital of the UAE and is home to an annual jazz festival, a film festival, and a music and arts festival, and hosts numerous art exhibitions throughout the year. Find out more from the Authority for Culture & Heritage (www.adach.ae).

---

### Abu Dhabi Boating

Abu Dhabi City and its surrounding islands are popular with the UAE's boating community. The city island has several marinas and more adventurous boaters can take an overnight trip to Sir Bu Naair island, 50 kilometres from the coast. *Dubai Yachting & Boating* is the go-to guide for the city's yacht-crowd.

---

In the cooler months, the newly renovated and extended corniche is a lovely spot for a stroll, and on weekend evenings the area comes alive with families meeting up to enjoy a barbecue and shisha.

The many islands just off the coast, west of the city, are popular with boating and watersports enthusiasts. Driving west past the city reveals kilometre upon kilometre of gorgeous, untouched sea and a few open beaches. The coast between Dubai and Abu Dhabi is home to a few beaches that are popular with watersports enthusiasts and provide a good, quick getaway from Dubai.

The emirate is also home to a large part of the Empty Quarter (Rub Al Khali), the largest sand desert in the world. The large Liwa Oasis crescent acts as a gateway to the endless dunes and is a popular weekend destination for adventure-hungry residents from Dubai.

## Abu Dhabi Attractions

### Al Bateen

This is one of Abu Dhabi's oldest districts and home to a dhow building yard, the Al Bateen Marina, a few historically accurate buildings and the future Al Bateen Wharf. It's a nice area to walk around, with plenty of open green spaces.

---

### Bird Watchers

The Abu Dhabi Falcon Hosptial > *p.274* (050 614 4024, www.falconhospital.com) specialises in treating the region's falcons and its various species of birds. The hospital is also dedicated to promoting awareness and preventing the spread of disease. The hospital offers two hour guided tours on weekdays that must be booked in advance.

---

# Liwa Oasis & Al Gharbia

Located way west of Abu Dhabi, further than most people usually venture, the Al Gharbia region actually makes up over two thirds of the UAE. Along its hundred kilometres of coastline can be found some stunning beaches, as well as a number of islands, which are being developed and promoted for visitors. But the main reason to make the drive is Liwa – a destination that will blow you away with massive expanses of awesome desert and the biggest dunes this side of the Sahara. The Liwa Oasis sits at the entrance to the Rub Al Khali, the largest sand desert in the world. Most of the Rub Al Khali (Empty Quarter) is uninhabitable, and Bedouin tribes occupy only the outer fringes of it. The Liwa Oasis is a fertile crescent, dotted with small villages, that stretches over 150 kilometres. It's a five-hour drive from Dubai, and a weekend of camping and incredible dune-bashing is a must for any Dubai resident. There are a few hotels in Liwa, including the luxurious Qasr Al Sarab (p.278) and the Liwa Hotel (p.278). Abu Dhabi's incredible coast stretches far beyond the island coast, nearly all the way to Qatar. Just off the coast lie the Desert Islands, including Sir Bani Yas Island (p.278). One of the more impressive is Delma Island, which has been populated for over 7,000 years and was once the centre of the region's pearl-diving trade. There's also the Al Mirfa Public Beach, which is 120 kilometres from Abu Dhabi. The beach is almost always empty and is the best place to enjoy a weekend of beachside camping. Pick up a copy of the *UAE Off-Road Explorer* to better understand the entire Al Gharbia region.

Exploring the Western Region

## The Corniche

**Off Corniche Rd, Central Abu Dhabi** Abu Dhabi
Corniche Road boasts six kilometres of parks that include children's play areas, separate cycle and pedestrian paths, cafes and restaurants, and a wonderful lifeguarded beach park. There is plenty of parking on the city side of Corniche Road, and underpasses at all the major intersections connect to the waterfront side. Bikes can also be rented from outside the Hiltonia Club for Dhs.20 per day, and can be dropped off at several points along the Corniche.

## Heritage Village

**Nr Marina Mall** Abu Dhabi **02 681 4455**
Located on the city's breakwater near the Marina Mall, the educational village offers an interesting glimpse into the country's past. Traditional aspects of Bedouin life are demonstrated and explained, and there are workshops where craftsmen demonstrate traditional skills.

## Qasr Al Hosn

**Electra St** Abu Dhabi **02 621 5300**
www.adach.ae
Qasr Al Hosn (also known as the Old Fort or the White Fort) is the oldest building in Abu Dhabi and dates back to 1793. Situated in the centre of Abu Dhabi, the fort has undergone a series of renovations over the years. Although there aren't any guides, you are encouraged to walk around the exterior of the building and marvel at the incredibly high walls. At the end of 2009 it was closed for renovation so make sure you call before visiting.

## Sheikh Zayed Grand Mosque

**Off Eastern Ring Rd** Abu Dhabi **02 444 0444**
www.visitabudhabi.ae
One of the largest mosques in the world, this architectural masterpiece can accommodate 40,000 worshippers. It features 80 domes and the world's largest hand-woven Persian carpet. It is open to non-Muslims every day except Friday.

## Emirates Palace Attractions

More than just a grand hotel, Emirates Palace (p.278) is also one of Abu Dhabi's top cultural and entertainment centres. It stages several international music concerts each year, ranging from the annual Abu Dhabi Classics season (www.abudhabiclassics.com) to world-renowned pop artists Coldplay, The Killers and Elton John. Emirates Palace also hosts major art exhibitions that have featured the likes of Pablo Picasso, as well as the yearly Abu Dhabi Art fair (www.abudhabiartfair.ae). Keep an eye on the Abu Dhabi Tourism website (www.abudhabitourism.ae) for details of upcoming events.

# LONG-WEEKEND TRIPS

Make the most of a long weekend by heading off to one of many great travel destinations within easy reach of the UAE.

Dubai's central location makes it an ideal base for exploring the region beyond the GCC countries. If you can't find a cheap flight from Dubai International Airport, don't hesitate to look for better deals departing from either Abu Dhabi or Sharjah. The country now has two low-cost carriers, Air Arabia at Sharjah Airport and Flydubai at Dubai Airport. Both offer some incredible deals. If you'd rather fly in style, both Emirates and Etihad fly to enough locations to keep you planning for years to come.

## Cyprus

It's hard to believe that this idyllic Mediterranean island is such a short flight from Dubai. Three main towns, Larnaca, Limassol and Paphos, each offer unique accommodation and leisure options, and capital city Nicosia is great for shopping and nightlife. Whether you choose to rent a self-catering apartment or stay in a luxurious hotel on full board, a holiday in Cyprus is a huge change from the Gulf. You can drive up mountains for crisp, cool air and some awesome views, and explore quiet local villages off the beaten track.

### Flights:
**Emirates** – Dubai to Larnaca, Dhs.2,000
**Air Liban** – Abu Dhabi to Larnaca, Dhs.2,600
**Etihad** – Abu Dhabi to Larnaca, Dhs.1,900

## Egypt

Egypt is an ideal trip for history fans. It's one of the oldest civilisations in the world and home to famous historical sites such as the Pyramids and Sphinx. It also has some amazing scenery: there is the moon-like White Desert and the isolated Siwa Oasis in the west, the Red Sea and the vast Sinai Peninsula in the east, and, of course, the Nile, which flows south to north through the country, past the incredible ruins between Aswan and Luxor. Cairo's chaotic streets are a constant adventure and the city has an active nightlife.

### Flights
**Air Arabia** – Sharjah to Luxor, Dhs.1,700
**Etihad** – Abu Dhabi to Cairo, Dhs.2,500
**Flydubai** – Dubai to Alexandria, Dhs.1,300

## India

India is a land of many guises, from the beautiful beaches of Goa to the vibrant city of Mumbai or the imposing mountains of Kashmir. It's best to avoid the summer monsoon, but if you do get caught in the rain, you can take advantage of good off-season deals. Some areas such as Ladakh in northern India and the desert state of Rajasthan receive very little, if any, rain all year.

### Flights
**Air Arabia** – Sharjah to Kochi, Dhs. 1,300
           Sharjah to Jaipur, Dhs.1,200
           Sharjah to Hyderabad, Dhs.1,400
**Jet Airways** – Dubai to Delhi, Dhs.1,100
**Jet Airways** – Abu Dhabi to Delhi, Dhs.1,500

## Jordan

Jordan is packed with religious and historical sites, incredible architecture, and friendly, welcoming people. The capital Amman offers enough dining and cultural attractions to fill up a few days, but to truly experience the country, you'll need to get out of

Petra

the city. Head south to feast your eyes on Petra, the ancient city built into solid rock canyons. On your way, don't miss the opportunity to float atop the waters of the Dead Sea. History and religious experts will be fascinated by the many holy sites that dot the country, and movie buffs shouldn't miss a trip to Wadi Rum, where Lawrence of Arabia was filmed.

### Flights
**Air Arabia** – Sharjah to Amman, Dhs.1,600
**Etihad** – Abu Dhabi to Amman, Dhs.2,300
**Flydubai** – Dubai to Amman, Dhs.1,200

## Lebanon
Lebanon's blossoming development as a vibrant tourist destination has suffered some knockbacks recently with conflicts both internally and externally. But never a nation to take things lying down, it is doing everything possible to rebuild itself. Beirut's nightlife is considered by many to be the best in the Middle East, and its culinary excellence is well known. Outside of Beirut is just as interesting; the massive Roman temples in Baalbek are not to be missed, and the many villages scattered throughout the country hold the key to Lebanon's incredible hospitality.

### Flights
**Air Arabia** – Sharjah to Beirut, Dhs.1,400
**Etihad** – Abu Dhabi to Beirut, Dhs.2,300
**Flydubai** – Dubai to Beirut, Dhs.1,000

## Sri Lanka
The beauty of Sri Lanka, apart from the short flight time and negligible time difference, is that you can either have a fantastic holiday on a small budget, or a luxurious holiday of a lifetime. Colombo has enough attractions to occupy travellers for at least a day, although most holidaymakers choose to spend their time in the lush mountains or at the untouched beaches.

### Flights
**Air Arabia** – Sharjah to Colombo, Dhs.1,600
**Emirates** – Dubai to Colombo, Dhs.2,600
**Qatar Airways** – Dubai to Colombo, Dhs.1,500

## Syria
With Damascus, the oldest continuously inhabited city in the world, Aleppo, the food capital of the world, and untouched countryside, Syria is a traveller's dream. The country has enough souks, restaurants, and ruins to please both the history buff and the modern culture geek. The old part of Damascus is a joy to explore on foot thanks to the many souks and unique architecture. The ancient city of Palmyra (known as Tadmor in Syria) is only a four-hour bus ride from Damascus and a must for anyone interested in the country's incredible past. Syria is a great choice for budget-minded travellers, as flights to and from the UAE are cheap and you could spend an entire week eating only the delicious street food.

### Flights
**Air Arabia** – Sharjah to Damascus, Dhs.1,400
**Etihad** – Abu Dhabi to Damascus, Dhs.2,900
**Flydubai** – Dubai to Damascus, Dhs.1,100

Turkey

## Turkey
Perfectly placed between contrasting cultures of east and west, Turkey is a popular holiday destination with beautiful landscapes, great weather, sun, sea and mountains. Istanbul is an amazing city – full of history, great food and a surprisingly vibrant nightlife. Alternatively, take a road trip to the capital, Ankara, for a taste of Turkish student life and a glimpse of the country's most modern city. If you need a break from big-city life, head south to the equally impressive Bursa, where you'll find the iconic Ulu Cami mosque and huge, communal thermal baths.

### Flights
**Air Arabia** – Sharjah to Istanbul, Dhs.1,100
**Emirates** – Dubai to Istanbul, Dhs.1,900
**Etihad** – Abu Dhabi to Istanbul, Dhs.2,800

### — DIRECTORY: —
**Air Arabia** – www.airarabia.com
**Emirates** – www.emirates.com
**Etihad** – www.etihadairways.com
**Flydubai** – www.flydubai.com
**Jet Airways** – www.jetairways.com
**Qatar Airways** – www.qatarairways.com

### Sir Bani Yas Island
Jebel Dhanna 02 801 5400
www.desertislands.anantara.com
Half nature reserve, half luxury resort and spa, Sir Bani Yas Island is the centrepiece of Abu Dhabi's Desert Islands development plan. Home to the Arabian Wildlife Park, and Desert Island Resort & Spa, the island is home to thousands of free-roaming animals. Hiking, mountain biking and 4WD safaris, as well as snorkelling and kayaking trips, are available and you can reach the island by a private seaplane.

### Yas Island
North-east of Abu Dhabi Abu Dhabi 02 696 4444
www.yasisland.ae
Already home to the Yas Marina Circuit and the Yas Hotel, Yas Island will eventually house Ferrari World Abu Dhabi, several seaside golf courses and six marinas. The beautifully modern Yas Hotel (02 656 0700, www.theyashotel) straddles the Grand Prix circuit and is worth a visit just to look around.

## Abu Dhabi Hotels

### Al Raha Beach Hotel
Al Raha Corniche, nr Airport Abu Dhabi 02 508 0555
www.ncth.com
Excellent service, gorgeous spa and unsurpassed comfort in an idyllic boutique beach setting.

### Beach Rotana Hotel & Towers
Abu Dhabi 02 697 9000
www.rotana.com
Plenty of popular dining options as well as a private beach, sports courts and the Zen spa.

### Danat Resort Jebel Dhanna
West of Abu Dhabi Jebel Dhanna 02 801 2222
www.ncth.com
Located 240 kilometres west of Abu Dhabi city, close to Sir Bani Yas Island, this resort features plenty of watersports, private beach and sand golf.

### Emirates Palace
Corniche Road West Abu Dhabi 02 690 9000
www.emiratespalace.com
Abu Dhabi's answer to the Burj Al Arab is the ultimate in luxury, and perhaps even more ostentatious. With 12 restaurants, 390 rooms and suites with butler service, an amazing collection of pools and a private beach, all set in 200 acres of lush gardens.

### Fairmont Abu Dhabi Creek
The Creek Abu Dhabi 02 654 3333
www.fairmont.com
Abu Dhabi's newest luxury hotel, located right between the two bridges on the mainland outside the city.

### Golden Tulip Al Jazira Hotel & Resort
Btn Dubai & Abu Dhabi Jazira 02 562 9100
www.goldentulipaljazira.com
Less than an hour's drive from Dubai, these luxury beachside bungalows are great for a quick getaway.

### Hilton Abu Dhabi
Corniche Rd West Abu Dhabi 02 681 1900
www.hilton.com
This 10 storey luxury hotel on Corniche Road has three swimming pools and a private beach, plus a wide range of watersports. Each room boasts enviable views, and the hotel houses some of the best restaurants in the city.

### InterContinental Abu Dhabi
Bainunah St Abu Dhabi 02 666 6888
www.intercontinental.com
Adjacent to the marina, the hotel is surrounded by lush parks and gardens. With five restaurants, four bars and 330 deluxe rooms offering views of the city and the Arabian Gulf, the hotel is popular with business travellers. Following the hotel's recent renovation, many of the restaurants and bars are worth a visit.

### Le Meridien Abu Dhabi
Abu Dhabi 02 644 6666
www.starwoodhotels.com/lemeridien
Famous for its health club and spa, private beach, and Culinary Village with 15 outlets, there is a children's swimming pool and activities including tennis, squash and volleyball.

### Liwa Hotel
Liwa 02 882 2000
www.ncth.com
The majestic Liwa Hotel overlooks the Rub Al Khali desert, one of the most stunning panoramas in the world. Facilities include a beautiful pool, a sauna, Jacuzzi and steam room, tennis and volleyball courts.

### Qasr Al Sarab Desert Resort
1 Qasr Al Sarab Road, Nr Hamim Liwa 02 886 2088
www.anantara.com
This hotel has a stunning location amid the giant dunes outside Liwa. Designed as an Arabic fort, guests can enjoy a wide range of desert activities before relaxing in oversized bathtubs, dining on gourmet dishes and being pampered in the spa.

### Shangri-La Hotel, Qaryat Al Beri
Qaryat Al Beri Abu Dhabi 02 509 8888
www.shangri-la.com
Overlooking the creek that separates Abu Dhabi island from the mainland, the 214 rooms and suites all have private terraces. There is also the Souk Qaryat Al Beri, with shops and restaurants connected by waterways.

Abu Dhabi Investment Authority

National Bank Of Abu Dhabi

Sheikh Zayed Grand Mosque

Emirates Palace

# Al Ain

Al Ain is the second city in Abu Dhabi emirate and of great historic significance in the UAE. Its location on ancient trading routes between Oman and the Arabian Gulf meant that the oasis was of strategic importance. Commonly known as 'The Garden City', Al Ain features oases and lovely patches of greenery. After a greening programme instigated by the late Sheikh Zayed, the seven natural oases are now set amid tree-lined streets and beautiful urban parks.

It's unique history means that Al Ain is home to a variety of interesting sights and attractions, including the Hili Archaeological Garden and the Al Ain Museum.

Just outside the city sits one of the largest mountains in the UAE, Jebel Hafeet. The rolling, grass-covered hills of Green Mubazzarah Park (03 783 9555) at the bottom of the mountain are great for picnics and mid afternoon naps.

## Al Ain Attractions

### Al Ain Camel Market

Nr Jebel Hafeet, Al Ain
The last of its kind in the UAE, the well known market sits east of Jebel Hafeet. The market provides and opportunity to view the gentle giants up close. Only open in the mornings, it is always busy and a great place to enjoy some local colour.

### Al Ain National Museum

Nr Al Ain Oasis Al Ain 03 764 1595
www.aam.gov.ae
Divided into three main sections – archaeology, ethnography and gifts – the presentations include photographs, Bedouin jewellery, musical instruments, weapons and a traditional majlis. Some of the artefacts date back over 2,000 years.

### Al Ain Oasis

Nr Al Ain Museum Al Ain
This impressive oasis in the heart of the city is filled with palm plantations, many of which are still working farms. The cool, shady walkways transport you from the heat and noise of the city to a tranquil haven. You are welcome to wander through the plantations, but it's best to stick to the paved areas which will take you on a relaxing meander through the trees. The farms have plenty of working examples of falaj, the traditional irrigation system which has been used for centuries to tap into underground wells. There are eight different entrances, some of which have arched gates, and there is no entry fee.

### Al Ain Wildlife Park & Resort > p.281

Nr Traffic Police Al Ain 03 782 8188
www.awpr.ae
Located at the foot of Jebel Hafeet, this 900 hectare wildlife park is one of the most progressive of its kind in the region and nearly 30% of its 180 species are endangered. Conditions for the animals are open and modern, and some of the highlights include zebras, rhinoceroses and large numbers of gazelle and Arabian oryx. The park is open daily 10:00 to 19:00. Entrance is Dhs.15 for adults, Dhs.5 for children and it's free for those under 6 years. Within the park there is a free train which transports visitors around.

### Al Jahili Fort & Park

Nr Public Garden Al Ain
Celebrated as the birthplace of the late Sheikh Zayed bin Sultan Al Nahyan, the picturesque fort was erected in 1891 to defend Al Ain's precious palm groves. It is set in beautifully landscaped gardens, and visitors are encouraged to explore the exterior.

Al Ain Palace Museum

Al Ain Wildlife Park & Resort

# FOR A DAY,
# A WEEK
# OR A LIFETIME.
## www.awpr.ae

متنزّه العين
للحياة البرية
**AL AIN WILDLIFE
PARK & RESORT**

أقرب إلى الطبيعة
In touch with nature

Experience and learn about wildlife, conservation and sustainable living at the Al Ain
Wildlife Park & Resort in its unique natural desert setting at the foothills of Jebel Hafeet.
Exciting animal safaris, luxury resort accommodation, themed retail outlets and tranquil
residential communities are all on the way at the Al Ain Wildlife Park & Resort.
For a day, a week or a lifetime - enjoy life in touch with nature.

In collaboration with
**SAN DIEGO ZOO**
CONSERVATION FIRST

### Hili Archaeological Garden

Mohammed Bin Khalifa St Al Ain
www.visitabudhabi.ae

Located 10 kilometres outside Al Ain on the Dubai-Al Ain highway, the gardens are home to a Bronze Age settlement (2500-2000BC), which was excavated and restored in 1995. Many of the artefacts found during the excavation are now in the Al Ain National Museum.

## Al Ain Hotels

### Al Ain Rotana Hotel

Sheikh Zayed Rd Al Ain **03 754 5111**
www.rotana.com
Map **1 E3**

Located in the centre of the city, the hotel's rooms, suites, and chalets are extremely spacious and the hotel is a nightlife hub with six dining venues.

### Hilton Al Ain

Khalid bin Sulthan St Al Ain **03 768 6666**
www.hilton.com

Located near the heart of Al Ain, this ageing hotel is a good base from which to explore the wildlife park (p.280), museum, Jebel Hafeet and the Hili Tombs. Accomodation overlooks landscaped gardens, and tennis and squash courts, health club and a nine-hole golf course are all on offer.

### InterContinental Al Ain Resort

Khalid bin Sulthan St Al Ain **03 768 6686**
www.intercontinental.com

One of the most impressive inland resorts in the UAE, this hotel has landscaped gardens, swimming pools, luxurious guestrooms, deluxe villas and a Royal Villa with a private Jacuzzi. Great family facilities, plus a delightful spa.

### Mercure Grand Jebel Hafeet

Jebel Hafeet **03 783 8888**
www.mercure.com

Situated spectacularly near the top of Jebel Hafeet (p.280), the Mercure offers incredible views of Al Ain from all of its simply decorated rooms, and terraced restaurants. There are also three swimming pools, plus a water slide. There is a pub, buffet restaurant and poolside cafe serving excellent evening barbecues.

---

### Camel Safaris

Al Ain Golden Sands Camel Safaris offer a selection of tours that include a camel ride over the dunes of Bida Bint Saud. The rides usually last one to two and a half hours, and all tours include transfers from Al Ain, Arabic coffee and dates, and soft drinks. Call 03 768 8006 for more information

# Hats Off To Hatta

Out of the city, but not strictly out of Dubai, is the mountain town of Hatta. It lies within Dubai emirate, about an hour's drive south-east of the city, but makes for a great overnight out-of-town trip. The Hatta Fort Hotel > *p.283* (04 852 3211, www.jebelali-international.com) is a perfectly secluded mountain retreat in tranquil gardens. The hotel is fully equipped with numerous facilities and activities, including two swimming pools, a children's pool, a bar and restaurant, the Senses Beauty Salon, a driving range and chipping green, floodlit tennis courts and archery. The 50 spacious chalet-style rooms and suites all come with patios overlooking the impressive Hajars.

There are several good off-road optons for those who want to do some 4WD exploring, including the nearby Hatta Pools, which you can swim in. They're fairly accessible from the town along an unpaved road, and there signs to guide you there. Pick up a copy of UAE Off-Road Explorer for other great routes in the area.

Back in town is the Hatta Heritage Village (www.dubaitourism.ae). It is constructed around an old settlement and was restored in the style of a traditional mountain village. Explore the tranquil oasis, the narrow alleyways and discover traditional life in the mud and barasti houses. Hatta's history goes back over 3,000 years and the area includes a 200 year-old mosque and the fortress built by Sheikh Maktoum bin Hasher Al Maktoum in 1896, which is now used as a weaponry museum. Entry is free.

**HATTA FORT HOTEL**
*Your Exclusive Mountain Retreat*

A MEMBER OF

JEBEL ALI INTERNATIONAL
HOTELS

# Picturesque Perfection

After a trip to the wadis, deserts and mountains, unwind in a retreat where you can reflect at leisure on your discovery of uncharted nature. Stay in a deluxe chalet-style room overlooking the majestic Hajar Mountains or discover 80 acres of lush gardens and walking trails. Refresh in the temperature-controlled swimming pool, relax with a massage or choose from a range of leisure activities before you enjoy sundowners and gourmet cuisine. A children's pool and playground are also available for the fun and enjoyment of the younger guests at the Hatta Fort Hotel – all just an hour's drive from Dubai.

For more information please call +971 4 852 3211
E-mail: hfh@jaihotels.com ☻ www.hattaforthotel.com

# Sharjah

Despite being eclipsed by Dubai in the international spotlight, Sharjah has substantially more culture and heritage to offer visitors. So much so, that it was named the cultural capital of the Arab world in 1998, by Unesco, thanks to its eclectic mix of museums, heritage preservation and traditional souks. Sharjah is a direct neighbour to Dubai and the border between the two cities is barely noticeable when driving from one to the other. This means it's easy to visit and explore Sharjah without having to check into a hotel.

Sharjah is built around Khalid Lagoon, also known as the creek, and the surrounding Buheirah Corniche is a popular spot for an evening stroll. From various points on the lagoon, small dhows can be hired to see the city lights from the water. Joining Khalid Lagoon to Al Khan Lagoon, Al Qasba (p.284) is home to a variety of cultural events, exhibitions, theatre and music – all held on the canal-side walkways or at dedicated venues.

The city's main cultural centres, The Heritage Area (p.287) and The Arts Area, are two of the most impressive collections of museums and heritage sites in the country. The ruling Al Qassimi family are renowned collectors of historical artefacts and art, and in an emirate known for its conservatism, many of the works held within the Arts Area are surprising in their modernity. Sharjah's cultural worth is so great that visitors should avoid trying to absorb it all in one trip.

Shoppers will have a blast as well, searching for gifts through Sharjah's souks. Souk Al Arsah (p.396) has recently been renovated and is the oldest souk in the emirate, while the Central Souk is known for its well-respected upstairs carpet shops. There's also high-street shopping at Sharjah Mega Mall (www.sharjahmegamall.com, 06 574 2574) for days when culture and curiosities aren't on the agenda.

Majarra

# Sharjah Attractions

### Al Hisn Kalba

Nr Al Hisn Fort Kalba East Coast Kalba 09 277 4442
www.sharjahtourism.ae
Located in the East Coast town of Kalba, this complex consists of the restored residence of Sheikh Sayed Al Qassimi and Al Hisn Fort, which houses the town's museum and contains a limited display of weapons. It won't take long to get round but luckily there's also a collection of rides for children. Entrance is Dhs.3 for individuals and Dhs.6 for families.

### Al Mahatta Museum

Nr Dept of Immigration Sharjah 06 573 3079
www.sharjahmuseums.ae
Home to the first airfield in the Gulf in 1932, Sharjah played an important role as a primary stop-off point for the first commercial flights from Britain to India, and the museum looks at the impact this had on the traditional way of life in Sharjah. Four of the original propeller planes have been fully restored and are on display. Located behind Al Estiqlal Street, entry is Dhs.5 for adults and Dhs.10 for families.

### Al Qasba

Btn Al Khan & Khalid Lagoons Sharjah 06 556 0777
www.qaq.ae
With an ever-changing events calendar that includes Arabian poetry readings, film viewings and musical events, the emphasis at Al Qasba is clearly on culture. The complex's shops, event spaces and restaurants are laid out between Sharjah's two lagoons and are packed on cooler evenings with window shoppers, diners and families. Motorised abras provide boat tours up and down the canal, but perhaps the biggest draw, and certainly the most visible, is the Eye of the Emirates – a 60 metre high observation wheel with air-conditioned pods offering amazing views over Sharjah and across to Dubai.

### Discovery Centre

Opp Sharjah Airport Al Dhaid Rd Sharjah
06 558 6577
www.discoverycentre.ae
The Discovery Centre is a great family day out and children of all ages, including toddlers, can explore the many themed areas and experiment and interact with the exhibits. The underlying aim is to teach youngsters about the biological, physical and technological worlds in a practical way. There is good pushchair access, an in-house cafe serving a light menu and ample parking. Entrance is Dhs.5 for children and Dhs.10 for adults. Open from 08:00 to 14:00 Sunday to Thursday, and 16:00 to 20:00 Friday and Saturday. Be aware it can get busy on the weekends.

# Something
## for the
# Weekend...

From idyllic beach
getaways to activity-
packed city breaks, this
guide is the ultimate
resource for pepping
up your downtime.

Supported by:

**The Wave**
MUSCAT

www.explorerpublishing.com

**EXPLORER**

## Sharjah Aquarium

Al Khan Sharjah **06 556 6002**
www.sharjahaquarium.ae

Although eclipsed by the two aquariums that opened in Dubai in 2008, Sharjah Aquarium is the city's newest attraction and draws big crowds, especially at the weekends. Situated next door to Sharjah Maritime Museum at the mouth of Al Khan Lagoon, its location allows visitors to view the Gulf's natural underwater life. There are over 250 species in the aquarium, as well as many interactive displays to educate visitors. Opening hours are 08:00 to 20:00 Saturday to Thursday, 16:00 to 20:00 on Fridays and closed Sundays. Admission is Dhs.20 for adults, Dhs.10 for children and Dhs.50 for families.

## Sharjah Archaeological Museum

Nr Cultural R/A Sharjah **06 566 5466**
www.sharjahmuseums.ae

This hi-tech museum offers an interesting display of antiquities from the region. Using well-designed displays and documentary film, the museum traces man's first steps and progress across the Arabian Peninsula through the ages, and one area features the latest discoveries from excavation sites in the UAE. The museum is closed on Sunday, and for part of the afternoon on other days, so it is best to call before you visit to check times.

## Sharjah Art Museum

Sharjah Arts Area Sharjah **06 568 8222**
www.sharjahmuseums.ae

The centrepiece of the Arts Area, the Art Museum was originally built to house the personal collection of over 300 paintings and maps belonging to the ruler, HH Dr Sheikh Sultan bin Mohammed Al Qassimi. Permanent displays include the work of 18th century artists, with oil paintings and watercolours depicting life from all over the Arab world, while other exhibits change frequently. There's also an art reference library, bookshop and coffee shop, and the museum hosts various cultural activities. The museum is closed on Mondays and Friday mornings, while Wednesday afternoons are for ladies only. Adult entry costs Dhs.5 and Dhs.10 for families.

## Sharjah Desert Park

Sharjah Natural History & Botanical Museum
Sharjah **06 531 1999**
www.sharjahtourism.ae

Located 25 kilometres outside the city, Sharjah Desert Park is comprised of the Natural History Museum, the Arabian Wildlife Centre, the Childrens' Farm and the recently opened Sharjah Botanical Museum. The Natural History and Botanical Museums feature interactive displays about the relationships between man and the natural world in the emirate and beyond,

Sharjah Corniche (image courtesy SCTDA)

while at the Arabian Wildlife Centre you get the chance to see many reptiles, birds, mammals and creepy crawlies, including the rare Arabian leopard. The facilities are excellent and the animals are treated well. There is also a Children's Farm with farm animals that can be fed and petted. Picnic areas are available, plus cafes and shops. Closed on Tuesdays, entry costs Dhs.5 for children, Dhs.15 for adults, Dhs.30 for families, and includes access to everything.

### Sharjah Heritage Area
Nr Arts Area Sharjah 06 568 1738
www.sharjahmuseums.ae
The beautifully restored heritage area includes a number of old buildings including Al Hisn Fort (Sharjah Fort), Sharjah Islamic Museum, Sharjah Heritage Museum (Bait Al Naboodah), the Maritime Museum, the Majlis of Ibrahim Mohammed Al Midfa and the Old Souk (Souk Al Arsah). Traditional local architecture and life from the past 150 years is described, depicted and displayed throughout. Toilets can be found at each venue and there's an Arabic coffee shop in the shady courtyard of Souk Al Arsah.

### Sharjah Heritage Museum
Sharjah Heritage Area Sharjah 06 568 0006
www.sharjahmuseums.ae
Also known as Bait Al Naboodah, this two-storey

building was once owned by the late Obaid bin Eesa Al Shamsi (nicknamed Al Naboodah), and is a reconstruction of a family home (bait) as it would have been around 150 years ago. The home is built around a large courtyard, as were many traditional Arabic houses at the time. Each room shows various historical artefacts including clothing, weapons, cooking pots and goatskin water bags. Entry costs Dhs.5 for adults and Dhs.10 for families.

### Sharjah Islamic Museum
Sharjah Heritage Area Sharjah 06 568 3334
www.sharjahtourism.ae
Housed in a 200 year old building, the Islamic masterpieces and manuscripts represent the cultural history of Muslims spanning 1,400 years. Plucked from HH Dr Sheikh Sultan bin Mohammed Al Qassimi's private collection, the works include examples of ceramics, manuscripts, jewellery, textiles and an impressive collection of gold-plated Qurans. There is also a Science Hall, particularly fascinating for its map of the globe, the first of its kind, made by Al Shareef Al Idrisi (born 1099AD), which appears upside down compared to modern maps. The museum is open during holy days and public holidays. Wednesday afternoons are for ladies and children under 12 only. Closed on Mondays and Friday mornings. Entrance is Dhs.5 for adults and Dhs.10 for families.

## Sharjah Maritime Museum

**Sharjah Heritage Area** Sharjah 06 556 6002
www.sharjahmuseums.ae

With the goal of documenting the development of seafaring in the Middle East, the museum's displays feature fishing, trading, pearl diving and boat construction methods native to the UAE. Each room in the museum informs visitors about a different aspect of marine industry. The museum also houses several real examples of traditional seafaring boats.

## Sharjah Museum of Islamic Civilization

**Corniche St – Al Majarrah Area** Sharjah 06 565 5455
www.islamicmuseum.ae

With vaulted rooms, and impressive galleries and halls, the architecture of this new museum alone makes a visit worthwhile, but with over 5,000 Islamic artefacts, and reams of information, this is one of the best places to learn about Islam and Islamic culture. The museum is organised according to five themes: the Islamic religion, Islamic art, artefacts, craftsmen and weaponry, each in it's own gallery; the Temporary Exhibition Gallery hosts a programme of visiting exhibitions. Entry for adults is Dhs.5; children are free.

## Sharjah Science Museum

**Nr TV Station** Sharjah 06 566 8777
www.sharjahmuseums.ae

The interactive museum's exhibits and demonstrations cover subjects such as aerodynamics, cryogenics, electricity and colour. There's also a planetarium and children's area where the under 5s and their parents can learn together. The Learning Centre offers more in-depth programmes on many of the subjects covered in the museum. Entry costs Dhs.5 for children aged 3 to 17 years; and Dhs.10 for adults.

## Sharjah Hotels

### Lou Lou'a Beach Resort

**Sheikh Sultan Al Awal Road** Sharjah 06 528 5000
www.louloubeach.com

Beach resort situated on the Sharjah coast. Offers watersports and spa facilities.

### Millennium Hotel Sharjah

Sharjah 06 519 2222
www.millenniumhotels.com

This gorgeous new resort is located on the corniche and boasts some of the best facilities in the emirate.

### Radisson Blu Resort Sharjah

Sharjah 06 565 7777
www.radissonblu.com

Located on the Sharjah Corniche, close to the city's main cultural attractions, the hotel has several watersports and its own beach.

### Sharjah Rotana

Sharjah 06 563 7777
www.rotana.com

Located in the centre of the city, within walking distance of the heritage and art areas, the Rotana caters mostly for business travellers.

## Ajman

The smallest of the emirates, Ajman is situated around 10 kilometres from the Sharjah city centre, and the two cities merge with each other along the coast. There is a nice stretch of beach and a pleasant corniche to walk along. Ajman Kempinksi Hotel & Resort is a grand offering for those who want a luxurious stay, while there are some other cheaper options along the beach. Ajman Museum (p.288) houses a variety of interesting displays in a restored fort that is worth visiting as much for the building itself as for the exhibits. The tiny emirate is known for being one of the largest boat building centres in the region, and while it is mainly modern boats that emerge from the yards these days, you may still catch a glimpse of a traditionally built wooden dhow sailing out to sea. The emirate's main souk is a reminder of a slower pace of life, while Ajman City Centre (06 743 2888) holds plenty of shops and a cinema.

## Ajman Attractions

### Ajman Museum

**Opp Etisalat** Ajman 06 742 3824
www.am.gov.ae

Ajman Museum's interesting and well arranged displays have descriptions in both English and Arabic. The museum has a variety of exhibits, including a collection of Ajman-issued passports and dioramas of ancient life, but it's the building itself that will most impress visitors. Housed in a fortress dating back to around 1775, the museum is a fascinating example of traditional architecture, with imposing watchtowers and traditional windtowers. Entry is Dhs.5 for adults. Morning opening times are 09:00 to 13:00 then 16:00 to 19:00 in the evening. Closed on Fridays.

## Ajman Hotels

### Kempinski Hotel Ajman

**The Corniche** Ajman 06 714 5555
www.ajmankempinski.com

Visitors to Ajman can relax on half a kilometre of the Kempinski's private beach or around its superb pool facilities. The hotel has 185 seaview rooms and a diverse range of international restaurants, cafes and bars, as well as a grand ballroom. The Laguna Spa offers a comprehensive spa menu, including an outdoor Balinese massage.

# Umm Al Quwain

Nestled on the coast between Ajman and Ras Al Khaimah, not much has changed over the years in Umm Al Quwain. The main industries are still fishing and date cultivation. The emirate has six forts, and a few old watchtowers surround the town. With plenty of mangroves and birdlife, the emirate's lagoon is a popular weekend spot for boat trips, windsurfing and other watersports.

The area north of the lagoon is known for being a regional activity centre. Umm Al Quwain Aeroclub (p.338) offers flying, skydiving, paramotoring and microlighting, and can also arrange 10 minute air tours, either in a Cessna or a microlight, at reasonable prices. Emirates Motorplex (www.motorplex.ae) hosts all types of motorsport events, including the Emirates Motocross Championship which takes place here on a specially built track. One of the Emirate's most popular attractions is Dreamland Aqua Park (p.289). Another favourite destination for Dubai residents is the adjacent Barracuda Beach Resort (below), which is particularly popular thanks to its well-stocked duty-free liquor store.

The emirate has not escaped the attention of the developers though, and a project currently underway will see over 9,000 homes and a marina emerge on the shore of the Khor Al Beidah wildlife area. What impact this will have on the delicate ecosystem and abundant plant and animal life remains to be seen.

## Umm Al Quwain Attractions

### Dreamland Aqua Park > *p.xiii*
**North of UAQ on the RAK Rd** Umm Al Quwain
06 768 1888
www.dreamlanduae.com
With over 25 water rides, including four 'twisting dragons', Dreamland Aqua Park is massive. If extreme slides aren't your thing, there's the lazy river, a wave pool, an aqua play area, and a high-salinity pool for floating about. If you prefer not to get wet there's also a 400 metre go-kart track. Overnight accommodation in provided tents or cabana huts is also available. Admission costs Dhs.100 for adults and Dhs.70 for children under 12, while children under 4 go free. The park is open all-year-round, and Fridays, Saturdays and holidays are reserved for families only.

## Umm Al Quwain Hotels

### Barracuda Beach Resort
**Nr Dreamland Aqua Park** Umm Al Quwain
06 768 1555
www.barracuda.ae
Known in Dubai for its popular tax-free booze emporium, Barracuda is also a pleasant resort for quick weekend getaways. Aside from the main hotel, the resort offers several lagoon-side one-bedroom chalets that can accommodate up to five people each. The chalets come with kitchenettes and barbecues – perfect for private overnight parties. There's also a large temperature-controlled pool and Jacuzzi.

### Flamingo Beach Resort
**After UAQ Hospital R/A** Umm Al Quwain
06 765 0000
www.flamingoresort.ae
Cheap and cheerful, this resort is surrounded by an unpolluted, shallow lagoon interspersed with many green islands that attract a variety of birdlife, including migrating flamingos. Evening crab hunting adventures around the mangrove islands are available for non-guests.

### Imar Spa
**Nr Palma Beach Hotel** Umm Al Quwain **06 766 4440**
www.imarspa.com
This five-star ladies-only spa haven is in the heart of Umm Al Quwain, in a peaceful, seaside setting. The hotel has a small private beach and terrace, a fabulous temperature-controlled pool and a saltwater aqua therapy pool. Accommodation is limited (with only two twin rooms and three singles) so booking in advance is advised.

# Ras Al Khaimah

Ras Al Khaimah contains several archaeological sites, some dating back to 3000BC. Take the Al Ram road out of the Al Nakheel district towards the Hajar Mountains to discover some of the area's history, including the Dhayah Fort, Shimal Archaeological Site and Sheba's Palace. The bare ruins of the Dhayah Fort can be spotted from the road, but you might need a 4WD to access it. Further inland is the Shimal archaeological site and Sheba's Palace. Both are a little obscure, but worth the difficulty of finding them. Shimal includes a tomb from the Umm An Nar period, roughly 5,000 years ago. It was built as a communal burial place and the remains of more than 400 bodies have been found there. Further down the same road is another tomb, which dates back to the Wadi Suq period (2000BC). Many of the artefacts from these locations can be found at the National Museum at Ras Al Khaimah (p.290).

With the majestic Hajar Mountains rising just behind the city, the Arabian Gulf stretching out from the shore and the desert starting just to the south near the farms and ghaf forests of Digdagga, Ras Al Khaimah (RAK) has possibly the best scenery of any emirate in the UAE. The northern-most emirate in the country, a creek divides the main city into the old town and the newer Al Nakheel district.

The past couple of years have witnessed RAK's transformation into a prominent weekend destination, and several new resorts have opened for the overworked residents of Dubai and Abu Dhabi. The Tower Links Golf Course (07 227 9939, www.towerlinks.com) is also popular at weekends and is laid out among the mangroves around the creek.

If you're visiting for the day you should make time to visit the souk in the old town and the National Museum of Ras Al Khaimah (p.290), which is housed in an old fort. Manar Mall is a large shopping and leisure facility, housing a cinema complex, family entertainment centre, a watersports area and dining options overlooking the creek and mangroves. The town is quiet and relaxing, and is a good starting point for exploring the surrounding mountains, visiting the ancient sites of Ghalilah and Shimal (p.289), the hot springs at Khatt and the camel racetrack at Digdagga. There are also several chances to get into the mountains up the coast north of the city, as well as south of RAK in places like Jebel Yibir – the tallest mountain in the country, where a new track takes you nearly to the top for spectacular views.

## Ras Al Khaimah Attractions

### National Museum of Ras Al Khaimah
Nr Police HQ Ras Al Khaimah 07 233 3411
www.rakmuseum.gov.ae
Housed in an impressive fort that was once the home of the present ruler of Ras Al Khaimah, this museum focuses on local natural history and archaeological displays, including a variety of paraphernalia from pre-oil, Bedouin life. Look out for fossils set in the rock strata of the walls of the fort – these date back 190 million years. The building has battlements, a working windtower, and ornate, carved wooden doors. Entrance is only Dhs.2 for adults and Dhs.1 for children, and directions can be found on the museum website. Open September to May from 10:00 to 17:00, and from June to August from 08:00 to 12:00 and 16:00 to 19:00.

## Ras Al Khaimah Hotels

### Al Hamra Fort Hotel > p.323
Off the E11, South of RAK Ras Al Khaimah
07 244 6666
www.alhamrafort.com
With traditional Arabic architecture set amongst acres of lush gardens along a strip of sandy beach, this hotel offers a peaceful get-away. A range of watersports and activities, including two floodlit golf courses and an onsite dive centre, will keep you entertained, and the eight themed eateries offer a wide variety of cuisine and atmosphere. There is also a kid's club and babysitting service, making it ideal for families.

### Banyan Tree Al Wadi
Ras Al Khaimah 07 206 7777
www.banyantree.com
Banyan Tree Al Wadi combines superior luxury with exclusive spa facilities, desert activities and a wildlife conservation area. Set within Wadi Khadeja, the resort's individual villas are designed for optimum relaxation.

### The Cove Rotana Resort
Ras Al Khaimah 07 206 6000
www.rotana.com
Built into the hills overlooking the Arabian Gulf, The Cove's sprawling layout of 204 rooms, 72 private villas and winding pathways is reminiscent of an old Mediterranean hill town. The resort revolves around an immaculate lagoon, protected from the sea by 600 metres of pristine beach. A Bodylines spa and several impressive restaurants round out the package.

### Hilton Ras Al Khaimah Resort & Spa
Hilton Beach Club Rd Ras Al Khaimah 07 228 8888
www.hiltonworldresorts.com
Tucked away on an exclusive bay, out of sight of the city, the resort's many guest rooms and villas are perfect for a beach break. The pool bar, spa and laid-back dining options make this one of the most relaxing destinations in the region. Guests of the older Hilton Ras Al Khaimah (07 288 8888, www.hilton.com), located in the city, can use the facilities.

### Khatt Springs Hotel & Spa
Ras Al Khaimah 07 244 8777
www.khatthotel.com
Simple and subdued, Khatt Springs Hotel & Spa relies on mountain views, uninterrupted tranquillity and incredible spa packages to attract weekend visitors. Next door to the hotel, you can take a dip in the public Khatt Hot Springs – piping hot water which, it is claimed, has curative powers. Men and Women have separate pools and a variety of massages are also available including Ayurveda. It is a good idea to visit the hot springs in the morning and avoid Fridays as it can get very busy with lots of families.

### Stellar Cellar
The Al Hamra Cellar, although owned by MMI (www.mmidubai.com), is a tax-free liquor store that is well worth the trip. You won't find dodgy booze past its sell-by date; instead, you can browse a wide range of fine wines, spirits and beers in a pleasant environment at tax-free (and very competitive) prices. Their loyalty programme means the more you buy the better deal you'll get on your next visit. Call 07 244 7403 for more info.

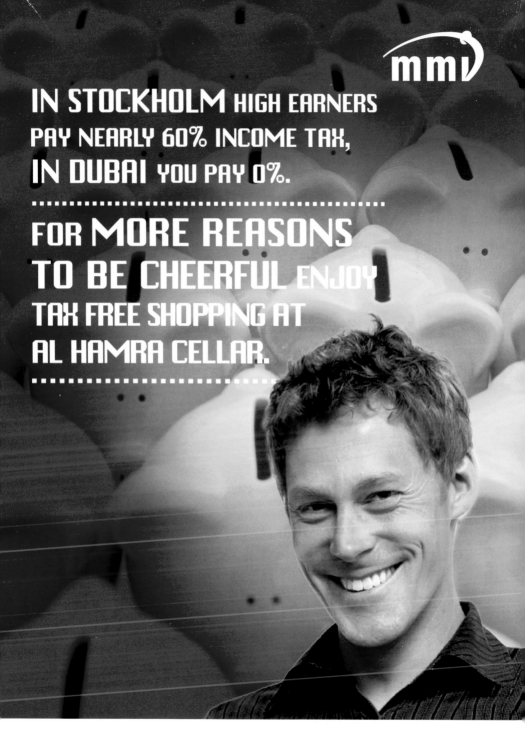

IN STOCKHOLM HIGH EARNERS
PAY NEARLY 60% INCOME TAX,
IN DUBAI YOU PAY 0%.

FOR MORE REASONS
TO BE CHEERFUL ENJOY
TAX FREE SHOPPING AT
AL HAMRA CELLAR.

**VISIT OUR SHOPS AT** TRADE CENTRE RD • AL WASL • IBN BATTUTA MALL • BUR DUBAI • GREEN COMMUNITY • DEIRA
MALL OF THE EMIRATES • KARAMA • SHEIKH ZAYED ROAD • DUBAI SILICON OASIS • FESTIVAL CITY **Shop finder** www.mmidubai.com

# Fujairah

A trip to the east coast is a must for any Dubai resident. Made up of the emirate of Fujairah and several enclaves belonging to Sharjah, the villages along the east coast sit between the rugged Hajar Mountains and the gorgeous Gulf of Oman. The two-hour drive to the east coast from Dubai passes through some of the country's most scenic mountain passes. Fujairah city has seen little development compared to cities on the west coast, but the real draw here is the landscape. The mountains and wadis that stretch west of the coast contain some of the country's best and most accessible camping spots and the beaches, reefs and villages that line the coast attract visitors from Dubai throughout the year.

## Bidiyah

The site of the oldest mosque in the UAE, Bidiyah is one of the oldest settlements on the east coast and is believed to have been inhabited since 3000BC. The mosque is made from gypsum, stone and mud bricks finished off with plaster, and its original design of four domes supported by a central pillar was considered unique, but the shape was changed to stepped domes during the recent renovation. The building is believed to date back to the middle of the 15th century. The mosque is still used for prayer, so non-Muslim visitors can't enter. Built next to a low hillside with several restored watchtowers on the ridge behind, the area is now lit up at night with coloured light.

## Dibba

Located at the northern-most point of the east coast, on the border with Musandam (p.296), Dibba is made up of three fishing villages. Unusually, each part comes under a different jurisdiction: Dibba al Hisn is part of Sharjah, Dibba Muhallab is Fujairah and Dibba Bayah is Oman. The three Dibbas share an attractive bay, fishing communities, and excellent diving locations – from here you can arrange dhow trips to take you to unspoilt dive locations in the Musandam. The Hajar Mountains provide a wonderful backdrop, rising in places to over 1,800 metres. There are some

good public beaches too, where your only company will be the crabs and seagulls, and where seashell collectors may find a few treasures.

## Fujairah

The town of Fujairah is a mix of old and new. The surrounding hillsides are dotted with ancient forts and watchtowers, which add an air of mystery and charm. Most of these appear to be undergoing restoration work. Fujairah is also a busy trading centre, with its modern container port and a thriving free zone attracting major companies from around the world.

Off the coast, the seas and coral reefs make a great spot for fishing, diving and watersports. It is a good place for birdwatching during the spring and autumn migrations it is on the route from Africa to Central Asia. Since Fujairah is close to the mountains and many areas of natural beauty, it makes an excellent base to explore the countryside and discover wadis, forts, waterfalls and even natural hot springs.

---

### Bull Butting

On Friday afternoons during winter, crowds gather between the Hilton Hotel and the Khor Kalba area to watch 'bull butting'. This ancient Portuguese sport consists of two huge bulls going head to head for several rounds, until after a few nudges and a bit of hoof bashing, a winner is determined. It's not as cruel or barbaric as other forms of bullfighting, but animal lovers may still want to avoid it.

---

## Kalba

Just to the south of Fujairah you'll find Kalba, which is renowned for its mangrove forest and golden beaches. It's a pretty fishing village that still manages to retain much of its historical charm. There is a road through the mountains linking Kalba to Hatta which makes for an interesting alternative for returning to Dubai.

## Khor Kalba

Set in a beautiful tidal estuary (khor is Arabic for creek), Khor Kalba is the oldest mangrove forest in Arabia and home to a variety of plant, marine and birdlife not found anywhere else in the UAE. The mangroves flourish in this area thanks to a mix of seawater and freshwater from the mountains, but are receding due to the excessive use of water from inland wells. For birdwatchers, the area is especially good during the spring and autumn migrations when special species of bird include the reef heron and the booted warbler. It is also home to a rare subspecies of white collared kingfisher, which breeds here and nowhere else in the world. A canoe tour by Desert Rangers (p.269) is an ideal opportunity to reach the heart of the reserve. There is also the possibility of seeing one of the region's endangered turtles.

---

### East Coast Made Easy

To reach the UAE's east coast from Dubai takes about an hour and a half by road. The most popular route is to pick up the E88 that runs from Sharjah to Masafi, and then turn left to Dibba or right to Fujairah. A quieter alternative is the S116, which heads south-east out of Sharjah, past Fossil Rock and through the Hajar Mountains, hitting the coast at Kalba. It's faster than the E88, it's smooth, it's got tunnels, great scenery, and is so quiet you'll wonder why no-one else seems to know about it yet.

---

# ESCAPE. EXPLORE. ENJOY.

Explore the endless opportunities to unwind and relax. And do it in style with
Le Méridien Al Aqah Beach Resort.

All Sea view rooms • One of the largest swimming pool in the UAE• Wide
unspoilt private beach • Professional dive centre (with easy access to the best
East Coast dive sites) • Water sports Centre (windsurfing, sailing, water-skiing)
• Room size starting from 48 sq meters • Choice of 9 restaurants & bars - Thai,
Seafood and Indian fine Dining • Three floodlit tennis courts • Gymnasium •
Squash court • Sauna and steam room • Penguin Club – children's recreational
area with pool • Jacuzzi • Spa Al Aqah with Ayurvedic centre • Safaris &
mountain excursions • Boat & dhow trips to Musandam • Chartered fishing
trips • Mountain, coastal and heritage discovery tours • Business, meeting &
conference facilities.

For more information or to make a reservation, please visit
lemeridien.com/fujairah or call + 971 4 244 9000 or email: reservations@lemeridien-alaqah.com

LE MERIDIEN
AL AQAH BEACH RESORT
N 25° 30′ E 56°21′

# Fujairah Attractions

## Dibba Castle
Dibba, Oman
Hidden away in the Omani part of Dibba (aka Daba), adjacent to the vast area of farms and plantations, Dibba Castle is an interesting place to have a poke around. Built over 180 years ago, it has been restored and while there aren't a lot of artefacts on show, you can access all the rooms, and climb up all towers, where you'll get great views over the castle and the area around it. It is signposted off the road past the UAE border check post.

## Fujairah Fort
Nr Fujairah Museum Fujairah
Part of the east coast's rich heritage, Fujairah Fort has undergone a major renovation programme. Although you cannot enter the fort itself, the surrounding heritage buildings are open for viewing. Carbon dating estimates the main part of the fort to be over 500 years old, with other sections being built about 150 years later. The museum next door is worth a look too and has commentaries translated into English.

## Fujairah Heritage Village
Nr Fujairah Fort Fujairah
Situated just outside Fujairah City, this collection of fishing boats, simple dhows, and tools depicts life in the UAE before oil was discovered. There are two spring-fed swimming pools for men and women and chalets can be hired by the day.

## Fujairah Museum
Opp Ruler's Palace Fujairah 09 222 9085
This interesting museum offers permanent exhibitions on traditional ways of life including the not-so-distant Bedouin culture. There are also artefacts which were found during archaeological excavations throughout the emirate. Some of the items include weapons from the bronze and iron ages, finely painted pottery, carved soapstone vessels and silver coins. The museum is closed on Saturdays. Entry fee is Dhs.5.

# Fujairah Hotels

## Fujairah Rotana Resort & Spa
Fujairah 09 244 9888
www.rotana.com
Each of the Rotana's 250 guest rooms and suites has its own balcony and view over the sea. The hotel offers some of the best dining options on the east coast, as well as an indulgent spa, a private beach, a huge pool with swim up bar, a kid's pool and a kid's club.

## Golden Tulip Resort Dibba
Dibba 09 26 836 654
www.goldentulipdibba.com
Simple, clean and with a great beach this is a good option for an affordable getaway. From the nearby Dibba Port you can take a Dhow cruise and the hotel is also in a great location for snorkelling.

## Hilton Fujairah Resort
Al Ghourfa Rd Fujairah 09 222 2411
www.hilton.com
The Hilton Fujairah, set on the north end of Fujairah corniche within sight of the grand Hajar Mountains, is a relaxing resort with all the facilities needed for a wonderful weekend away. If you get tired of lounging by the temperature-controlled swimming pool, or activities such as tennis, snooker, basketball or the watersports offered on the private beach, you could always explore the rugged splendour of the surrounding mountains. The hotel is great for families, and there is a safe play area for children.

## Hotel JAL Fujairah Resort & Spa
Dibba 04 262 5289
www.jalfujairahresort.ae
Its pastel exterior might be an acquired taste, but the modern, business-like interior and wonderful restaurants that lie inside are a treat to the senses. The whole place is reminiscent of a spa, with clean lines and wholesome colours. There's also a wonderful Japanese spa and plenty of private beach.

## Le Meridien Al Aqah Beach Resort > p.293
Al Aqah 09 244 9000
www.lemeridien-alaqah.com
All the rooms have views over the Indian Ocean, and the grounds are covered by lush foliage. It is particularly geared up for families, with a kids' pool and outdoor and indoor play areas. There's an extensive spa, a dive centre, and entertainment options include a cinema, bars and restaurants serving a range of Thai, Indian and European cuisine.

## Snoopy Island & Sandy Beach Hotel
Al Aqah 09 244 5555
www.sandybm.com
Snoopy Island is one of the best diving spots in the country and is right off the coast from the Sandy Beach Hotel, making it a firm favourite with UAE residents. Day trippers can purchase a day-pass to the hotel to access the temperature-controlled pool, watersports and beach bar services. There is also a Five-Star Padi Dive Centre within the hotel that rents diving and snorkelling gear for exploring the reefs around Snoopy Island.

# Exploring Fossil Rock

A brief guide to the perfect route for first-timers.

Fossil Rock is the UAE's easiest desert route to access, and to drive, with some superb and varied scenery along the way. Starting at Al Awir, off the E44 Hatta road only 20 minutes outside Dubai, it is the perfect drive for absolute beginners and novices to cut their teeth in the desert and gain some valuable lessons, but as with anywhere, it's definitely better to accompany an experienced driver the first couple of times you head out.

The route is pretty straightforward to navigate – the driving starts along a sandy track then graduates to rolling through some easy medium-sized dunes later on.

Making its way to the starting point in the fertile oasis town of Al Awir, the road weaves through a surprising amount of greenery, trees and farms, and many palaces and stately homes. Keep a look out for the estate that's home to herds of gazelle and deer, race horses that can often be spotted training, and the long wall of the summer palace belonging to the Maktoum family.

Existing tracks normally define the best path to take, especially on this route. They offer the easiest route, with only gentle inclines and descents, and limit damage to flora and fauna. However, when you start to get the hang of it, there are some places where you can climb up to the top of the dunes following alongside the track to weave your way along the ridges.

## Off-Road Expert

For more information on everything to do with driving off road and exploring all corners of the country, pick up a copy of the *UAE Off-Road Explorer*. Fossil Rock is one of 26 routes featured in full detail, with annotated satellite images and detailed descriptions of the route along with attractions and activities along the way.

The first half of the route finishes in sight of a main road, where it turns and follows the sandy river bed of Wadi Fayah along the bottom of the dunes. This fast and fun track weaves through bushes, trees, dunes and some rocky outcrops to a short gravely climb out onto the road.

After crossing the road, sticking with the main undulating sandy track heading up into the dunes will take you quite smoothly and easily towards Fossil Rock, clearly visible ahead. If you are feeling confident with your new skills, there is plenty of adventurous terrain just off the main track to test your driving among the dunes and bowls on either side, including in the area around the rock known as Camel Rock. The striking Fossil Rock is always there as a landmark to avoid getting lost, and whenever you have had enough, just pick up the track again and head towards the rock.

When you reach the hard track under the pylons with Fossil Rock directly in front of you, the quickest and easiest exit route is to turn right and head back past the village of Maleihah and the main road. It is possible to head straight on for even more challenging driving and the climb up to Fossil Rock (or Jebel Maleihah as it is officially called) itself, but this is more one for expert drivers.

If you do make it up to the top, whether on foot or behind the wheel, it is a fun place for a scramble, and for the views and a poke around to see if you can spot a fossil or two.

After leaving the desert, don't forget to re-inflate your tyres as soon as possible, as driving on tarmac with soft tyres can cause blowouts. To get to the nearest petrol station, when you meet the tarmac road turn left and it is roughly two kilometres along the road on the right. If you carry on a little further, you will reach the S116 – the fastest way back to civilisation.

# GCC

Over the past decade, the countries that make up the Gulf Cooperation Council (Kuwait, Bahrain, Qatar, Oman and Saudi Arabia) have been building their tourism industries in an effort to diversify their oil-based economies. Several international brands have opened hotels in the region and the respective governments have made a real effort to promote their heritage and culture. To learn more about the region's history, see the UAE chapter on p.274.

## Oman

The most accessible country in the GCC for residents of Dubai, Oman is a peaceful and breathtaking place, with history, culture and spectacular scenery. The capital, Muscat, has enough attractions to keep you busy for a good long weekend, including beautiful beaches, some great restaurants and cafes, the mesmerising old souk at Mutrah, and the Sultan Qaboos Mosque. Out of the capital you will find many historic old towns and forts, and some of the most stunning mountain and wadi scenery in the region. Salalah (p.296) in the south has the added bonus of being cool and wet in the summer.

### Visas

Visas for Oman are required whether entering by air or road, and different regulations apply depending on your nationality and how long you want to stay. Nationalities are split into two groups – check out the Royal Oman Police website, www. rop.gov.om, for full lists (click on 'Directorates', then 'DG of Passports'). People in group one can get a visit visa at the border – it's usually free for visitors but Dubai residents are likely to incur a Dhs.30 charge for single entry or Dhs.100 for multiple entry. Residents from group two, however, will need to get a visa from the Oman consulate or embassy in advance, which may take a few days to process. The charges are the same for both groups. Oman does have a common visa facility with Dubai, meaning people on a Dubai visit visa will not need a separate visa to visit Oman.

A flight from Dubai to Muscat takes 45 minutes, but when you factor in check-in times and clearing customs it's not much quicker than driving. There are daily flights from Dubai with Emirates and Oman Air, while Air Arabia (p.54) flies from Sharjah. Regular flights direct to Salalah from Dubai are also available. There is also a bus service from Dubai to both Muscat and Salalah, taking six and 16 hours respectively, and costing from Dhs.50 for Dubai to Muscat (www.ontcoman.com).

For further information on Oman check out the Oman Mini Visitors' Guide, Oman Off-Road

Explorer and the Oman Trekking Explorer – see www. explorerpublishing.com/shop.

### Musandam

The UAE's northern neighbour, Musandam is an isolated enclave belonging to Oman. The region is dominated by the same Hajar Mountains that run through the eastern UAE. As the peninsula juts into the Strait of Hormuz, it breaks up into a myriad of jagged, picturesque fjords. Spending a day exploring the fjords on a wooden dhow is a must for any Dubai resident. Most of the trips originate from the region's capital, Khasab, and day trips from Khasab Travel & Tours (04 266 9950) cost around Dhs.200 per person and include lunch, soft drinks and an informative guide.

Alternately, you can access the famous Wadi Bih off-road route from Dibba and spend a weekend camping atop some of the region's most magnificent mountains. See the UAE Off-Road Explorer for information about the route.

### Nizwa

After driving deep into the Hajar Mountains, you'll find Nizwa, the largest city in Oman's interior. This oasis city offers fascinating sights and heritage, including the 17th century Nizwa Fort and the Jabrin Fort, notable for is secret passageways.

### Salalah

Home to several museums and souks, Salalah is best known for its lush landscape. The scenery is especially attractive during the summer months, when the area catches the Indian monsoon. Salalah is also a major frankincense producer and you can visit the farms along the Yemen border to witness how it is extracted. A 16 hour drive from Dubai, plan on spending a few days here to make the most of it.

Musandam

The site of the Six Senses Hideaway Zighy Bay, in the Sultanate of Oman, is a secluded fishing village on the Sultanate's northern Musandam Peninsula. It is designed with 82 pool villas, including the two-bedroom Retreats and the four-bedroom Reserve – all with butler service. There is an impressive wine cellar and a private marina. The setting is dramatic, with mountains on one side and a 1.6-kilometre sandy beach at Zighy Bay on the other.

Six Senses Hideaway Zighy Bay offers a choice of guest experiences at every turn – from diverse dining alternatives to inspiring excursions and activities. Sense on the Edge, a contemporary modern restaurant, presents a panoramic view over Zighy Bay from the top of the mountain – also the jump-off point for the award-winning paragliding activity. Zighy Deli serves light comfort meals and Dining on the Sand offering modern and local favorites. The focus on a superior level of service is evidenced by personal pool villa butlers.

The Six Senses Spa offers nine treatment rooms and focuses on holistic wellness and rejuvenation. It offers a full menu of treatments delivered by skilled international therapists, and includes the world famous Six Senses signature treatments plus Middle East features such as Hamams.

SIX SENSES
HIDEAWAY
ZIGHY BAY

Musandam Peninsula, Sultanate of Oman
T: +968 2673 5555   E: reservations-zighy@sixsenses.com   www.sixsenses.com

# MUSCAT

Sandwiched between spectacular rocky mountains and beautiful beaches, Muscat is one of the Middle East's most striking cities.

Muscat is one of the most attractive and charismatic cities in the Middle East, and once you've visited you'll understand why many count it as their favourite regional city. It is visually striking, perhaps because it looks so little like a normal city; rather than a bustling CBD characterised by countless skyscrapers, gridlocked traffic and dirty smog, Muscat has many separate areas nestling between the low craggy mountains and the Indian Ocean. There is no one area that defines Muscat on its own – each part has its own distinctive character and charm.

Great care has been taken to ensure that, while it is definitely a modern city, there is a cohesive and traditional Arabic element which has been retained. Visit the old town of Muscat or the Mutrah Souk for an idea of what life has been like for decades for the people that still live in the area.

Muscat is clean and features a lot more greenery than you may be used to in Dubai. With beautiful beaches, bustling souks, a collection of great restaurants and cafes, and some fascinating museums, you'll need at least a few days to fully discover this friendly city. The main areas worth exploring are around the old town and the fishing port of Mutrah, although taking long walks along the beach in Qurm or exploring the natural lagoons in Qantab are also worthwhile activities.

## The Old Town Of Muscat

The old town of Muscat is situated on the coast at the eastern end of the greater Muscat area between Mutrah and Sidab. It is quiet and atmospheric, based around a sheltered port that was historically important for trade. The area is home to some very interesting museums. Muscat Gate Museum is located in one of the fortified gates of the old city walls, and illustrates the history of Muscat and Oman from ancient times right up to the present day. The view from the roof over the old town is worth the visit alone. Bait Al Zubair is in a beautifully restored house and features major displays of men's traditional jewellery, including the khanjar, women's jewellery and attire, household items, and swords and firearms. The Omani French Museum celebrates the close ties between these two countries, and is on the site of the first French Embassy. Other highlights include the striking Alam Palace, home of Sultan Qaboos, and Jalali Fort and Mirani Fort overlooking the harbour.

## Other Areas

Although primarily a residential area, Qurm has some great shopping, good quality restaurants and cafes, the city's largest park (Qurm National Park) and arguably the best beach in Muscat. It is also home to some of the top hotels, all of which have superb leisure facilities.

The villages of Al Bustan and Sidab provide an interesting diversion from the main Muscat areas. Head south along Al Bustan Street out of Ruwi on the spectacular mountain

---

### Mutrah

Mutrah rests between the sea and a protective circle of hills, and has grown around its port, which today is far more vibrant than the port of Muscat's old town. Mutrah Corniche is lined with pristine gardens, parks, waterfalls and statues. Further east you'll find Riyam Park, where a huge incense burner sits on a rocky outcrop, while nearby is an ancient watchtower overlooking Mutrah – the view at the top is lovely and well worth the steep climb. One of Muscat's most famous shopping experiences lies in this area: the Mutrah Souk. It is always buzzing with activity and is renowned as one of the best souks in the region.

Sultan Qaboos Mosque

Mutrah Fort

Weekend Breaks
Oman & UAE

Get the
lowdown
on the best
weekend
breaks in Oman
and The UAE

road to get to the village of Al Bustan and the Al Bustan Palace Hotel, one of the most famous hotels in the region.

Further down the coast, the mountains increase in height and the landscape gets more rugged. However, this undulating rocky coastline hides a number of beautiful secluded coves. These bays, mostly reachable by roads winding over the mountains, are home to the beaches of Qantab and Jassah, the Oman Dive Center (www.omandivecenter.com) – one of the top dive centres in the world – and the new Shangri-La Barr Al Jissah Resort. Many of the bays in this area have stretches of sandy beach sheltered by the rocky cliffs, and crystal clear waters that are perfect for snorkelling, diving and fishing.

## Outside Muscat

Not much further out of Muscat than the Shangri-La Barr Al Jissah Resort, Yiti Beach, while once a popular daytrip from Muscat, is now sadly becoming off limits due to the construction of a huge development called Salam Yiti. As Sifah beach, a little further down the coast, is very popular. The well-travelled path past the last of the houses in As Sifah leads to a beach which slopes gently towards the ocean at low tide. If you're keen to snorkel, head towards the northern edge of the beach. If you enjoy hiking, you can explore the headlands on foot (and maybe even find a secluded beach or two further along).

There are some excellent off-road routes you can do from Muscat within a day, or on an overnight camping trip. For more information on off-roading in Oman, get a copy of the *Oman Off-Road Explorer*.

# Oman Hotels

## The Chedi
Nr Lulu Hypermarket Muscat +968 24 524 400
www.chedimuscat.com
This beautiful boutique hotel on the shore is famed for its clean lines, luxury and an impressive sense of calm. The stunning spa and outstanding restaurant don't hurt either. With an infinity pool, private beach and library, this is a destination for a break from bustle and perhaps isn't an ideal choice for families.

## Crowne Plaza Hotel Muscat
Bldg 1730 Qurum St Muscat +968 24 660 660
www.ichotelsgroup.com
This established hotel boasts cliff top views over Al Qurm and the beach below. Many of the 200 guest rooms benefit from the striking vistas and several of the restaurants also benefit from outdoor terraces. There's a large swimming pool, gym, spa and dolphin watching trips available, making this hotel a great choice for both those looking for relaxation and visitors who want an action packed break.

## InterContinental Muscat
Al Kharijiyah Street Muscat +968 24 680 000
www.ichotelsgroup.com
This is an older hotel that has recently undergone a major facelift. The InterContinental continues to be popular for its outdoor facilities, international restaurants and regular entertainment in the form of dinner theatres and visiting bands. Alfresco restaurant, Tomato, is a must-try. Trader Vic's, with its legendary cocktails, is perennially popular. All of the rooms have views of Qurm Beach, landscaped gardens or the mountains.

## Oman Dive Center
Bandar Al Jissah Qantab Muscat +968 24 824 240
www.omandivecenter.com
Just south of Muscat, a stay here is an amazing experience, whether you're a diver or not. You can book a barasti hut (they are actually made of stone, with barasti covering) for an average of RO.66 for two people (depending on season), including breakfast and dinner in the licensed restaurant. The centre offers dive training and excursions, as well as boat tours.

## Shangri-La's Barr Al Jissah Resort & Spa
Off Al Jissah St Muscat +968 24 776 666
www.shangri-la.com
With three hotels catering for families, business travellers and luxury-seekers, the Shangri-La is one of the most gorgeous resorts in the region. The hotels have several swimming pools and enough play areas to keep children occupied for a few days. The

exclusive, six-star Al Husn is incredibly luxurious and perfect for a weekend of out-of-town pampering.

## Six Senses Hideaway Zighy Bay > *p.297*
Zighy Bay, Musandam Peninsula Dabba
+968 26 735 555
www.sixsenses.com
Located in a secluded cove in Musandam, the resort has been designed in true rustic style and is made up of individual pool villas. Like all Six Senses resorts, the focus here is on relaxation. The spa treatments available are of the highest quality and expertly prepared dinners can be enjoyed from the comfort of your own villa, or from the mountainside restaurant with breathtaking views of the bay.

---

### Hoota Cave > *p.301*

Now open to the public, this cave has a large chamber with some amazing rock formations, an underground lake and a fascinating ecosystem. Facilities include a train that transports you into the cave, knowledgeable Omani guides, a restaurant and a natural history museum. Photography is not allowed. All visitors need to book at least 24 hours in advance, as only a limited number of people are allowed into the cave at a time. (+968 24 490 060, www.alhootacave.com).

---

# Bahrain
For a change of pace, head to nearby Bahrain, it is just a 50 minute flight away and small enough to be explored in a weekend. With traditional architecture, miles of souks, excellent shopping and some truly outstanding bars and restaurants, you can choose from a cultural escape or fun-packed break. Formula 1 fans won't want to miss the Grand Prix that usually takes place in March or April, with hotels booked up months in advance – see the *Bahrain Mini Visitors' Guide* for more on what to do there.

# Bahrain Attractions

## Bahrain Fort
Nr Karbabad Village Karbabad
This impressive 16th century Portuguese fort is built on the remains of several previous settlements, going back to the Dilmun era around 2800BC. There are several large, informative notices dotted around the area, and some information booklets are available in English. Entry is free and the fort is open from 08:00 to 20:00 every day including Friday. The village at the entrance to the fort is worth a visit on its own. Nearly every square inch of the place, from walls to satellite dishes, is covered in brightly coloured murals.

*Visit Oman*

**Sense Al Hoota Cave**

... a beauty beneath

Cave ▪ Geological Exhibition ▪ Zajal Restaurant ▪ Al Hoota Cafe ▪ Karma Souvenir Shop

ALHOOTA CAVE
كهف الهوتة

For reservations: Tel: +968 92 404444
Email: reserve@alhootacave.com
Website: www.alhootacave.com

Member

ISO 9001
ISO 14001
BUREAU VERITAS
Certification

Managed by:

## Bahrain National Museum

Nr Shaikh Hamad Causeway Manama
+973 1729 8777
www.bnmuseum.com
Situated on the corniche, this museum documents
Bahraini life before the introduction of oil. Children
will love the Hall of Graves and the museum often
hosts impressive international exhibits.

## Beit al Qur'an

Nr Diplomat Htl Manama +973 1729 0101
www.beitalquran.com
The building may not look like much from afar, but
a closer inspection reveals walls covered in beautiful
Arabic calligraphy. The museum displays examples
of historical calligraphy and Islamic manuscripts.
Entrance is free, but donations are welcome.

## The Burial Mounds

South of Saar Village, West of Ali Village,
Hamad Town
One of the most remarkable sights in Bahrain is the
vast area of burial mounds at Saar, near A'ali Village,
at Hamad Town and at Sakhir. The mounds were built
during the Dilmun, Tylos and Helenistic periods and
are anything from 2,000 to 4,000 years old. The largest
burial mounds, which are known as the Royal Tombs,
are found in and around A'ali Village, where the
traditional pottery kilns are located.

## La Fontaine Centre of Contemporary Art

92 Hoora Ave, Manama 306 Manama
+973 1723 0123
www.lafontaineartcentre.com
This place is a true architectural gem. The wind towers,
cool corridors, a Pilates studio that has to be seen to
be believed, world-class restaurant, extensive spa,
regular film screenings and art exhibitions make
La Fontaine a unique jewel in Bahrain's crown. The
enormous fountain in the courtyard is worth a visit.

## Bahrain Hotels

### Al Bander Hotel & Resort

Riffa +973 1770 1201
www.albander.com
Located at the southern end of Sitra, this resort has a
wide range of facilities including swimming pools and
watersports at their private beach. Rooms are either
cabana style or in chalets, and there are activities for
kids and a variety of food and dining options.

### Banyan Tree Desert Spa and Resort

Nr Al Areen Wildlife Park East Riffa +973 1784 5000
www.banyantree.com/bahrain
This all-villa resort is located close to the F1
International Circuit and offers a truly luxurious

hideaway. With the Middle East's most extensive spa,
outstanding restaurants and conference facilities, this
is the perfect place for both work and play.

### Novotel Al Dana Resort

Off Shk Hamad Causeway Manama +973 1729 8008
www.novotel-bahrain.com
The only city beach resort in Bahrain, the Novotel is
a great choice for families with both an indoor and
outdoor play area, a large pool and a small private
beach. The spa offers a large menu of treatments and
guests can rent jet skis, windsurfers and kayaks.

### The Ritz-Carlton Bahrain Hotel & Spa

Manama +973 1758 0000
www.ritzcarlton.com
The hotel has one of the best beaches in Bahrain, in a
man-made lagoon surrounded by lush gardens. The
600 metre private beach sweeps round the lagoon
with its own island and private marina. Along with
the nine quality dining venues and comprehensive
business facilities, hotel residents have access to all of
the club facilities, including the racquet sport courts,
the luxurious Spa and watersport activities.

## Kuwait

Kuwait may be one of the world's smallest countries
but its 500 kilometre coastline has endless golden
beaches that remain refreshingly tranquil. From the
Grand Mosque to the Kuwait Towers there are many
architectural splendours to explore, while Al Qurain
House, which still shows the scars of war with its
immortal bullet holes, gives you a fascinating insight
into the troubled times of the Iraqi invasion. There is
also Green Island, an artificial island linked by a short
bridge which is home to restaurants, a children's play
area and a great alternative view of Kuwait's shoreline.
For accommodation options, try the Four Points
by Sheraton (965 1835 555, www.starwoodhotels.
com), Courtyard by Marriott (965 229 97000, www.
marriott.com) or Radisson Blu (965 5651 999, www.
radissonblu.com).

## Qatar

Qatar once had something of a sleepy reputation, but
things are changing fast. The amount of development
and investment in the country means it is becoming
increasingly popular with visitors. With an attractive
corniche, world-class museums and cultural centres,
and plenty of hotels with leisure and entertainment
facilities, the capital Doha makes a perfect weekend
retreat. Away from the city, the inland sea (Khor Al
Udaid) in the south of the country also makes a great
day trip, usually as part of an organised tour. The
Qatar Mini Guide has details of all these activities and
includes a pull-out map.

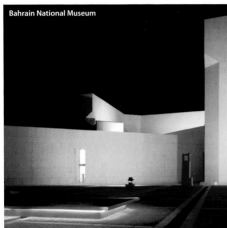
Bahrain National Museum

Financial Centre

Mutrah

Qatar Islamic Cultural Centre

Musuem of Islamic Art, Qatar

# Qatar Attractions

## Education City
**Al Luqta Street,** Doha
ww.qf.edu.qa
This massive complex contains some of the most tasteful contemporary architecture in the Middle East. Education City is home to some of the world's best universities and is a clear example of Qatar's plans for the future. A drive through the campuses will no doubt impress any architecture buffs.

## Museum Of Islamic Art
**The Corniche** Doha **+974422 4522**
www.mia.org.qa
Architect IM Pei has created an elegant home for this impressive collection. The building is beautifully subtle, with details drawn from a wide range of Islamic influences. The collection is showcased as a journey through time, countries and cultures, and the oldest piece dates from the ninth century.

## Souq Waqif
Doha
www.soukwaqif.com
The city's oldest market, Souk Waqif, was renovated in 2004 using traditional building methods and materials. The resulting complex is now one of the most beautiful and authentic modern souks in the Gulf. The most refreshing aspect of the souk area is its dual purpose – tourists can easily stroll the narrow alleys in search of souvenirs while locals can purchase everything from fishing nets to pots and pans. Aside from the many shops and restaurants, there is the Waqif Art Center, which houses several small galleries and craft shops.

# Qatar Hotels

## La Cigale
Doha **+974 428 8888**
www.lacigalehotel.com
La Cigale has a reputation for first-class hospitality and is an exclusive nightlife destination.

## Four Seasons Hotel
**The Corniche** Doha **+974 494 8888**
www.fourseasons.com/doha
One of the finest hotels in the city, the Four Seasons has an exclusive beach and marina, first-class service and incredible restaurants, including the Italian Il Teatro.

## Mövenpick Hotel Doha
Doha **+974429 1111**
www.moevenpick-hotels.com
This modern hotel boasts the breathtaking corniche as its vista, where guests can enjoy a morning jog or afternoon stroll. Popular with business travellers, this boutique-style hotel also attracts tourists with its excellent restaurants and leisure facilities which include a swimming pool, whirlpool and steam bath.

## Ramada Plaza Doha
Doha **+974 428 1428**
www.ramadaplazadoha.com
With a new wing and plenty of restaurants, bars and lounges, the Ramada is a staple of Doha's nightlife.

## The Ritz-Carlton, Doha
Doha **+974 484 8000**
www.ritzcarlton.com
The opulent Ritz-Carlton is a perfect stop-off point if you are sailing in the region, with its 235 slip marina and clubhouse. You can expect five-star touches as standard at this resort. All of the 374 rooms and suites have breath-taking views over the sea or marina. The beach club provides a great selection of water sports and there's a luxurious spa. You'll be spoilt for choice with nine restaurants serving a range of international and local cuisine, and you can finish the night with either a cigar at Habanos or a cocktail at the Admiral Club.

## Sharq Village & Spa
**Ras Abu Abboud St** Doha **+974 425 6666**
www.sharqvillage.com
Reminiscent of a traditional Qatari town, Sharq Village & Spa is another example of Qatar's insistence on spectacular architecture. The accompanying Six Senses Spa was constructed using traditional building techniques and the resort's restaurants are some of the finest in Doha.

## W Hotel & Residences
**Off Diplomatic St** Doha **+974 499 6530**
www.whotels.com
Adding a touch of fun to Doha's conservative luxury hotel scene, the W Hotel chain is known for its incredible level of service. Every inch of the hotel is an exercise in architectural minimalism, and its central location makes exploring Doha easy.

# Saudi Arabia
The Kingdom of Saudi Arabia has some incredible scenery, fascinating heritage and archaeological sites, and diving locations that are among the best in the world. Sadly, due to the difficulty in obtaining visas and the present security concerns, most expats are unlikely to ever experience this diverse and intriguing country. Recent press reports suggest that the Kingdom will issue more tourist visas in order to boost the tourism industry, and give better access to business travelers now that it is part of the WTO. Until then, take a look at www.sauditourism.gov.sa and www.saudinf.com to see what you're missing.

# Looking for beachwear? Turn the page for your

# 30% discount voucher...

## AL BOOM MARINE

Jumeirah Beach Road    04 394 1258
Nadd Al Hamar Road    04 289 4803
Dubai Marina Yacht Club    04 422 7178

Mall of the Emirates    04 341 0781

**RETAIL OUTLETS**

Spinneys Centre, Umm Suqeim    04 394-2977
Mercato Mall    04 349 0105
Emaar Springs Town Centre    04 360 8877
The Courtyard, Green Community    04 885 3244
Uptown Mirdiff    04 288 7416
Motor City    04 432 8392
Al Wahda Mall, Abu Dhabi    02 443 7201

Mall of the Emirates    04 341 0794
Mirdiff City Centre    OPENING SOON

**Terms & Conditions apply**
Offer valid on full price items only | Not valid in conjunction with any other in store offer | Not valid on Oakley eyewear or watches | Voucher must be surrendered upon purchase | Voucher not redeemable for cash | Valid until December 15th, 2010 | Al Boom Marine reserves the right to change these terms & conditions at any time

# AL BOOM MARINE

## BEYOND THE BEACH

Visit any of our store locations
for your favourite
beachwear and lifestyle brands

✂ - - - - - - - - - - - - - - - - - - - - - - - - - - - - - - - - - -

Present this voucher and receive 30% off your purchase
at any participating store location

# 30% OFF

see reverse for store locations

# Activities &
# Hobbies

# ACTIVITIES & HOBBIES

With so many different cultures converging in Dubai, it's little surprise that there is such a diverse range of activities to fill your free time with. Everything from jumping out of an airplane to scrapbooking is covered in this section, and for every traditional pursuit such as tennis or football, there is the opportunity to try something a little different, such as kitesurfing, yogilates or even caving.

For the adventurous, the UAE's diverse topography lends itself perfectly to a range of outdoor pursuits including rock climbing, mountain biking, dune bashing, wadi driving and skydiving. Thanks to the miles of coastline, watersports are particularly popular as well, with scuba diving, snorkelling, sailing, surfing and water-skiing all firm favourites.

Of course, not all activities require a dose of adrenaline or the great outdoors and there are an increasing number of groups that meet indoors for everything from scrabble to amateur dramatics. Whatever your hobby or interest, the chances are there are like-minded people in Dubai that would love to enjoy it with you. If you don't find what you're looking for, why not set up a club yourself? Social networking sites, like Facebook, are a great way to reach people with similar interest to you. For more information on fitness and well-being see p.207.

## American Football

On 'Any Given Tuesday' (the name of the league), Duplays' hosts its American football competitive men's league at the sports pitch next to the Metropolitan Hotel on Sheikh Zayed Road. From January 2010, girls can join in with the mixed recreational league which takes place on the pitch next door. Membership is Dhs.330 per season for individuals and Dhs.2,640 for a team. Find out more at www.duplays.com.

## Archery

### Dubai Archers
Sharjah Wanderers Golf Club Sharjah 050 558 0951
www.dubaiarchers.com
Meets at Sharjah Wanderers Golf Club on Fridays. Beginners from 09:00-12:30; Dhs.50 for non-Wanderers.

## Activity Finder

**Activities & Hobbies**

### Hatta Fort Hotel > *p.283*
Dubai – Hatta Rd Hatta **04 852 3211**
www.jebelali-international.com
The 25 metre range has eight targets and the
hotel hosts an annual archery competition. Dubai
Archers (above) also holds its annual tournament
here. Dhs.50 for 30 minutes target practice, with
equipment included.

### Jebel Ali Shooting Club
Nr Jebel Ali Golf Resort & Spa Jebel Ali **04 883 6555**
www.jebelali-international.com
As well as five outdoor floodlit clay-shooting
ranges, this club also boasts indoor and outdoor
archery ranges with equipment for both men and
women. The 5,000 square metre outdoor range
can accommodate up to 12 archers. Range use
costs Dhs.70 for 30 minutes. There's also a shooting
academy with professional coaching for individuals
and groups. No archery on Fridays and Saturdays; club
closed Tuesdays.

### Sharjah Golf & Shooting Club
Emirates Road, Nr Tasjeel Auto Village Sharjah
**06 548 7777**
www.golfandshootingshj.com
The shooting club's indoor range offers target practice
at Dhs.60 for 20 arrows. You can also try your hand at
pistol and rifle shooting.

## Art Classes

### Arthouse Marina
1101 Oceanic Tower, Trident Marinascape
Dubai Marina **055 723 7340**
www.arthousemarina.com
Map **1 K4** Metro **Dubai Marina**
Weekly art classes for kids aged 6 to12. An array
of materials and tools are provided for children to
explore ideas, learn about art and art history, and
discover new techniques such as printing, drawing,
painting and papier mache and clay modelling.
Classes are Dhs.85, including a healthy snack.
Workshops are from Sunday to Thursday.

### Bead Palace & Accessories
Jumeira Rd, Villa 504b, Nr Jumeirah Beach Park
Jumeira **04 395 2771**
beadpalace@regencyglobal.ae.
Map **2 D3** Metro **Business Bay**
Classes, workshops and kids crafty birthday parties,
ranging from T-shirt printing and decoupage to
painting and pottery. It also stocks a great selection
of beads including semi-precious beads and Austrian
Swarovski crystals. Open Saturday to Thursday from
10:00 to 19:00 and Friday from 14:00 to 18:00.

### Café Ceramique
Town Centre Jumeirah Jumeira **04 344 7331**
www.cafe-ceramique.com
Map **2 F3** Metro **Burj Dubai**
Indulge your creative streak with a choice of blank
pottery which the cafe will glaze and fire once
decorated. Events include Art4fun Workshops and the
Kidz4art Summer Camp. Also at Mall of the Emirates
(04 341 0144).

### Dubai Community Theatre & Arts Centre (DUCTAC)
Mall of the Emirates Al Barsha **04 341 4777**
www.ductac.org
Map **1 R5** Metro **Mall of the Emirates**
A cultural hub offering art classes for all ages. Decorative
arts, drawing, painting, photography, sculpture and
paper craft are just some of the activities offered to help
budding artists hone their creative talents. A variety
of artist-led classes are held at the centre, and details
are listed online. DUCTAC also has art galleries and
studios for art and crafts and dance. There's also a cafe,
art supplies shop and lending library. Open daily 09:00
to 22:00 and 14:00 to 22:00 on Fridays. Two-hour kids'
classes from Dhs.100; Adult classes from Dhs.165.

### Dubai International Art Centre
Nr Town Centre Jumeirah Jumeira **04 344 4398**
www.artdubai.com
Map **2 F3** Metro **Burj Dubai**
Villa-based art centre offering six to eight week courses
in over 70 subjects, including painting, drawing,
dressmaking, etching, pottery and photography.
Annual membership starts from Dhs.350 for adults,
Dhs.450 for families and Dhs.120 for under 18s.

### The Jam Jar
Exit 39 from Sheikh Zayed Rd, St 17a, Beh Dubai
Garden Ctr Al Quoz **04 341 7303**
www.thejamjardubai.com
Map **1 S6** Metro **First Gulf Bank**
A canvas, paints and the obligatory jam jar are yours
starting at Dhs.195 for four hours of self-inspired
creativity; all you need to bring is your inspiration. The
'Jam-To-Go' service brings the experience to you – a
novel idea for a garden party or corporate event. Open
weekdays from 10:00 to 20:00; Fridays 14:00 to 20:00;
closed on Sundays.

## Baseball

### Dubai Little League
Nr Nad Al Sheba Club Nad Al Sheba **050 293 3855**
www.eteamz.com/DubaiLittleLeague
Map **2 F10**
Parent volunteers field over 20 baseball teams for
boys and girls aged 5 to 16. Beginners are welcome.

# Basketball

Dhs.500 registration includes season fees, team picture, uniform and year-end trophy.

## Basketball

Dubai has a number of public basketball courts but getting a game on them can be tricky during the evenings as they are very popular with regular teams. There are courts near the Canadian University of Dubai, at Hamriya Park in Abu Hail and on Al Diyafah Street in Satwa, next to Rydges Plaza Hotel. You can also go to Safa Park (p.344) and get regular pick up games on Wednesday, Thursday and Sunday evenings. Air-conditioned indoor courts can be hired for Dhs.35 per person per hour at Insportz (www.insportzclub. com), behind Modern Bakery in Al Quoz. Duplays organises men's and women's recreational and competitive leagues (www.duplays.com).

### Basketball Academy Dubai
050 457 1706
www.badubai.com
A children's academy offering everything from slam dunking for beginners to basketball clinics, camps, leagues and pickup sessions. All of the highly qualified staff are properly trained in instructing children. Call Academy Administrator, Marlon Kustec, on 050 358 1603 for more info.

## Belly Dancing

The ancient art of belly dancing is a great way to keep fit. The Ballet Centre (04 344 9776) holds daily lessons for Dhs.40 from 10:00 to 11:00 and on Tuesdays from 19:00 to 21:00. Milla Tenorio teaches at the Shangri-La Hotel on Sundays and Tuesdays at 18:00; classes cost Dhs.50 (04 343 8888). Nora Dance Group also offers belly dancing classes (050 875 0111) and Exhale Fitness Studio offers belly dance fitness classes (www. exhaledubai.com).

## Birdwatching

Thanks to the ever-increasing greenery, Dubai attracts many bird species not easily found in Europe or the rest of the Middle East. Over 80 species breed locally, and during the spring and autumn months, over 400 species have been recorded on their migration between Africa and Central Asia. The many parks and golf clubs are often the best birdwatching sites, where parakeets, Indian rollers, little green bee eaters and hoopoe can easily be spotted. Other species found in the Emirates include the striated scops owl, chestnut bellied sandgrouse, Saunders' little tern and Hume's wheatear.

Outside Dubai, the mangrove swamps in Umm Al Quwain and Khor Kalba are good places for birdwatching. Khor Kalba is the only place in the world where you can spot a rare subspecies of the white-collared kingfisher. Canoe trips through the mangroves can be arranged by tour companies, such as Desert Rangers p.316 and Explorer Tours p.312t. The Ras Al Khor Wildlife Sanctuary at the end of Dubai Creek is the only wildlife park within the city and a great place to see many types of resident and migratory birds, including the famous flamingos, from the three bird hides.

### Emirates Bird Records Committee
www.uaebirding.com
Collates information on birds in the UAE and requests local and visiting birders to submit details of sightings. A weekly round up of bird sightings and a monthly report are available via email upon request from Tommy Pedersen at 777sandman@gmail.com.

## Boxing

### Al Nasr Leisureland
Nr American Hospital Oud Metha 04 337 1234
www.alnasrll.com
Map 2 L5 Metro Oud Metha
Boxing classes are held every Saturday, Monday and Wednesday from 19:00 to 21:00. A 12 lesson package costs Dhs.550. For more information on the different weight classes you can contact their resident coach Mr. Iraj Dortolouee on the above number.

## Colosseum Health & Fitness Club

Montana Centre Bld, Zabeel Rd Karama
04 337 2755
www.colosseumuae.com
Map 2 L5 Metro Oud Metha
Gym specialising in boxing, Muay Thai (Thai boxing),
kickboxing and street fighting. Group classes meet
daily between 20:30 and 22:00 and cost Dhs.450 for
12 sessions.

## Dubai Fight Academy

Al Rashidiya 050 650 1184
www.fightacademy.ae
Map 2 P10 Metro Rashidiya
The academy offers Thai boxing lessons and holds
tournaments. Membership is Dhs.500 per month
including use of gym and pool. Another branch is
located in Jumeira (050 650 1184).

# Bowling

There are a number of places that you can go bowling
– be they independent centres where the lanes are
cheap and you can have an alcoholic drink while you
play (see Al Nasr Leisureland below) or as a shopping
diversion (see Bowling City opposite). If you want to
join a bowling league contact the Dubai International
Bowling Centre (see opposite) and they will put you in
touch with Dubai's leagues.

## Al Nasr Leisureland

Nr American Hospital Oud Metha 04 337 1234
www.alnasrll.com
Map 2 L5 Metro Oud Metha
Eight lanes surrounded by fast food outlets and a bar
where you can buy alcohol. Booking is recommended.
First game costs Dhs.15, including shoe rental; games
thereafter are Dhs.10.

## Bowling City

Dubai Festival City Garhoud 04 232 8600
www.bowling-city.com
Map 2 M8 Metro Emirates
Bowling City on the balcony level of Dubai Festival
City has 12 bowling lanes as well as nine billiard tables
and a 24-station PC gaming network. After you've
had a few strikes you can take your adrenalin into a
karaoke cabin and belt out 'We Are the Champions'.

## Dubai Bowling Centre

Al Hadiqa St Al Quoz 04 339 1010
www.bowlingdubai.com
Map 2 D5 Metro Business Bay
With 24 professional series lanes for recreational and
professional bowling and a gaming area for kids, the
bowling centre has leagues for serious players as well
as those who bowl for fun. They cater for professional
tournaments, corporate events and kids' parties. Prices
are Dhs.20 per game or Dhs.130 per hour for a lane.

## Dubai International Bowling Centre

Opp Al Shabab Club & Century Mall Al Mamzar
04 296 9222
www.dubaibowlingcentre.com
Map 2 R5 Metro Al Quiadah
Dubai's biggest bowling centre boasts 36 state-of-the-
art computerised lanes as well as amusement games,
snooker, billiards and food outlets. Several of Dubai's
clubs and leagues are based here and the centre hosts
regular competitions.

## Magic Planet

Mall of the Emirates Al Barsha 04 341 4000
www.magicplanet.ae
Map 1 R5 Metro Mall of the Emirates
This branch of Magic Planet has a number of bowling
lanes in its games arcade. Prices per player per game
start at Dhs.20.

# Bridge

## Dubai Ladies Bridge Club

Dubai Intl Women's Club Jumeira 050 659 1300
Map 2 F3 Metro Burj Dubai
Ladies-only bridge mornings are held at 09:00 on
Sundays and Wednesdays. Contact Marzie Polad on
the number above or Jan Irvine on 050 645 4395.

# Canoeing & Kayaking

Canoeing and kayaking are great ways to get close
to marine and bird life in the UAE. Khor Kalba Nature
Reserve (p.292) on the East Coast is a popular
canoeing spot, as are the coastal lagoons of Umm
Al Quwain (p.289) and mangrove-covered islands
north of Abu Dhabi (p.274). Sea canoes can be used
in the Musandam (p.296) to visit secluded bays and

# Caving

spectacular rocky coastlines. There are a number of tour companies who offer canoeing and kayaking trips to all of these areas, including Desert Rangers. For more details, see Main Tour Operators p.268.

## Dubai Paddling School
**Mena Seyahi Watersports Club** Al Sufouh
www.dubaipaddlingschool.com
Map **1 M3** Metro **Nakheel**
This school offers lessons in surfskiing. Surfskis are long, open-top kayaks. Lesson prices are Dhs.160 for first hour-long lesson or Dhs.600 for a set of five. Training for the Shamaal International Surf Ski Race (www.dubaishamaal.com), held annually on National Day (2 December), is also available.

## Dubai Surfski & Kayak Club
**Nr Dubai Offshore Sailing Club** Jumeira
**050 640 6087**
www.dskc.net
Map **1 U3** Metro **Al Quoz**
Holds the annual Dubai Shamaal race and kayaking trips. Dhs.1,200 for membership with berth, Dhs.250 without.

## Explorer Tours
**Nr Rashidiya Civil Defence 2** Al Rashidiya
**04 286 1991**
www.explorertours.ae
Map **2 P10** Metro **Rashidiya**
Offers canoe and kayak trips to Khor Kalba from Dhs.300 per person with transportation or Dhs.175 without.

## Hilton Dubai Jumeirah Water Sports Center
**Opp Jumeirah Beach Residence** Dubai Marina
**04 399 9005**
www.hilton.com
Map **1 K3** Metro **Jumeirah Lakes Towers**
Kayaks are available for hire by the hour. Prices are Dhs.100 for a single and Dhs.150 for a double.

## Sandy Beach Hotel & Resort
Fujairah **09 244 5555**
www.sandybm.com
Chalet resort on the East Coast with equipment for rent or sale. Single kayaks are available for hire at Dhs.40 per hour, or you could go for a two-seater for Dhs.75.

# Caving

The cave network in the Hajar Mountains is extensive and much of it has yet to be explored. Some of the best caves are located near Al Ain, the Jebel Hafeet area and just past Buraimi near the Oman border. Many of the underground passages and caves have

spectacular displays of curtains, stalagmites and stalactites, as well as gypsum flowers. In Oman, the range includes what is believed to be the second largest cave system in the world, as well as the Majlis Al Jinn Cave – the second largest chamber in the world. To arrange caving trips in Oman, contact a local tour operator such as Gulf Leisure (+968 819 006, www.gulfleisure.com) or Muscat Diving & Adventure Center (+968 24 485 663, www.holiday-in-oman. com). Within the region, caving ranges from fairly safe to extremely dangerous and, as no mountain rescue services exist, anyone venturing out into mountains should always be well-equipped and accompanied by an experienced leader.

## Mountain High
**Dubai Media City** Al Sufouh **050 659 5536**
www.mountainhighme.com
Map **1 M4** Metro **Nakheel**
Offers guided tours in and around the caves of Al Ain plus canyoning and other adventures from Dhs.500 per person per day.

# Chess

## Dubai Chess & Culture Club
**Nr Al Mulla Plaza** Hor Al Anz **04 296 6664**
www.dubaichess.ae
Map **2 R6** Metro **Stadium**
Home of the UAE's national chess team, this club is involved in all aspects of chess. Members can play at the club seven nights a week and competitions are organised on a regular basis. The club promotes international competitions including Dubai International Open, Emirates Open and Dubai Junior Open. Membership costs Dhs.100.

# Climbing

For those who feel at home on a vertical plane, excellent climbing can be found in various locations around the UAE, including Ras Al Khaimah, Dibba, Hatta and the Al Ain/Buraimi region; more than 600 routes have been recorded since the 1970s. These vary from short outcrop routes to difficult mountain routes of alpine proportions. Most range from (British) Very Severe, up to extreme grades (E5). However, there are some easier routes for new climbers, especially in Wadi Bih and Wadi Khab Al Shamis. To meet like-minded people head to Wadi Bih where you're sure to find climbers nearly every weekend, or go to either of the climbing walls below, where most of the UAE climbing fraternity hangs around (ahem). For more information contact John Gregory on 050 647 7120 or email arabex@eim.ae. Another excellent resource is www.uaeclimbing.com, which features an active forum and wealth of information for anyone interested in climbing in the UAE.

## Climbing Dubai

**Dubai World Trade Centre** Trade Centre
**04 306 5061**
www.climbingdubai.com
Map **2 J5** Metro **Trade Centre**
The Middle East's biggest outdoor climbing wall can be found at Dubai World Trade Centre Apartments. Learn to scale its 16 metres with an introductory lesson for Dhs.75. Courses for adults (Dhs.300 for three classes) and kids (Dhs.250 for five classes) are available. A day pass costs Dhs.50. Climbing Dubai also has an eight metre climbing tower at Horizon School Dubai, next to Safa Park Gate 4 (050 659 8500).

## E-Sports Dubai

**The Aviation Club** Garhoud
**04 282 4540**
www.e-sportsdubai.com
Map **2 M7** Metro **GGICO**
E-Sports offers climbing lessons for children and adults at GEMS World Academy, Jumeirah Primary School and GEMS Wellington International School. E-Sports also organises climbing and hiking holidays to destinations such as the French Alps.

## Pharaohs' Club

**Pyramids** Wafi **04 324 0000**
www.wafi-health-leisure.com
Map **2 L6** Metro **Healthcare City**
The indoor climbing wall at Pharaohs' Club offers a range of courses for all abilities, as well as public sessions for experienced climbers. The wall has climbing routes of varying difficulty and crash mats are provided for bouldering. Lessons cost Dhs.55 per hour and are limited to six people per instructor.

# Cookery Classes

Eating out is a national pastime in Dubai and gastronomes can also learn how to cook a range of global cuisines. Many hotels provide this service, either by special request if you particularly like one of their dishes, or as an advertised activity. There are also wine tasting classes and courses for budding oenophiles or those just wanting to up their dinner party game.

The Shangri-La (04 343 8888) can organise classes at Hoi An from Dhs.375 per person. You can learn the art of sushi making at Nobu (04 426 0760) every first Saturday of the month; classes are priced at Dhs.1250 per person including lunch. Park Hyatt Dubai has classes at Traiteur (04 602 1234) for Dhs.295 or Dhs.495 with champagne, and at Al Bustan Rotana, the Blue Elephant's Thai cookery course on the first Monday of the month costs Dhs.140 (04 282 0000).

Further afield there's the Six Senses Resort in Dibba (p.297), who hold Arabic cooking classes for guests.

## Cin Cin

**Fairmont Dubai** Trade Centre **04 311 8559**
www.fairmont.com
Map **2 J4** Metro **Trade Centre**
Learn about notes, vintages and bouquets with wine master Matthew Jones, while nibbling on unlimited cheese. Four wines are sampled per class. Classes are usually held on the first Wednesday of the month from 19:30 to 21:30 and cost Dhs.185 per person.

## Cooking Sense

**Dubai Media City** Al Sufouh **04 882 1295**
www.cooking-sense.com
Map **1 M4** Metro **Nakheel**
This school offers classes in cooking, baking, children's cookery, table etiquette and diets for medical conditions like diabetes. Corporate cooking classes can also be arranged.

## Fashion Lounge

**Jumeirah Beach Residence, Amwaj 4** Dubai Marina
**04 427 0268**
www.fashionlounge.ae
Map **1 K3** Metro **Dubai Marina**
For Dhs.395, you'll be lead through one of four three-course mediterranean menus. Classes are held within the restaurant's kitchen, where space is at a premium meaning the chef does a lot of the cooking. The main skill required is in presenting the dishes as artfully as possible. The lounge itself is a great venue with white leather seats, beaded chandeliers and funky decor.

## L'atelier des Chefs

**Le Meridien Dubai** Garhoud **056 690 0480**
www.atelierdeschefsdubai.com
Map **2 N7** Metro **Terminal 1**
This French cooking school offers a wide range of classes including Arabic, Indian and French cuisine, plus sushi and pastry making. Classes cost from Dhs.120 for half an hour to Dhs.350 for three hours, depending on type of class.

## Tavola

**Century Plaza** Jumeira **04 336 4900**
www.tavola.ae
Map **2 G3** Metro **Emirates Towers**
Cake decoration, baking and chocolate making with an authorised Wilton method instructor. A course consists of four three-hour sessions and costs Dhs.700.

## Verre

**Hilton Dubai Creek** Deira **04 212 7551**
www.hilton.com
Map **2 N5** Metro **Al Rigga**
Gordon Ramsay protege Matthew Pickop shares his Michelin secrets with a three course master class at Dhs950 per person.

# Cricket

At the weekend you'll see informal cricket games spring up on scratchy patches of open space on the outskirts of the city. If you prefer a little more green for your stumps, Zabeel and Safa parks are favourite spots. There are several small-scale training centres such as the Emirates Cricket Training Centre (050 497 3461). International matches are regularly hosted in the Emirates, particularly at the brand new cricket ground in Dubai Sports City (www.dubaisportscity.ae) where it's possible to see some of the world's best teams in action.

### Chevrolet Insportz Club
Cnr Street 17, Beh Garden Centre Al Quoz
04 347 5833
www.insportzclub.com
Map 1 S5 Metro First Gulf Bank
Insportz has three main net courts with a scoreboard and one side court, available for playing a social game as part of a league, or just for practice.

### ICC Global Cricket Academy
Dubai Sports City 04 425 1111
www.dubaisportscity.ae
Map 1 L10
The ICC cricket academy will be opening in early 2010 in Dubai Sports City, offering cricket coaching for all ages with ICC-affiliated coaches and state-of-the-art facilities.

### Last Man Stands
Zabeel Park Zabeel 1 056 605 2905
www.lastmanstands.com
Map 2 J5 Metro Al Jafiliya
Amateur T20 cricket league. Registration fees are Dhs.640 per year. Matches are played at Zabeel Park.

# Cycling

Dubai is not particularly bicycle-friendly, but there are pleasant areas where you can ride, such as both sides of the creek and the cycle tracks at Mamzar Park and along Jumeira Open Beach and Jumeira Road. Dubai Municipality has plans to create a cycle network through key areas of the city and along the Metro route on Sheikh Zayed Road. The first stage of the project involves extensions to the existing tracks, due to be completed by mid 2010.

Jebel Hafeet, Hatta and the central area in the mountains near Masafi down to Fujairah or Dibba, offer interesting paved roads with better views. The new road from Hatta through the mountains to Kalba on the east coast is one of the most scenic routes in the country. On occasion, Dubai Autodrome has hosted cycling sessions thanks to the Facebook group, CyclesafeDubai, a community of cycling enthusiasts trying to open up safe spaces for Dubai's cyclists. Check the discussion threads for the next event. Wolfi's Bike Shop (04 339 4453) offers equipment and advice on improving technique.

For more on cycling as a mode of transport in Dubai, see Getting Around, p.53

### Dubai Roadsters
04 339 4453
www.dubairoadsters.com
A safe bike, cycling helmet, pump and spare tubes are the only membership requirements of the club, whose average distance covered on a Friday ride is 65km to 100km, with the weekday rides ranging from 30km to 50km. They also run special events for true enthusiasts, covering long distances and varying terrains. Don't worry though it's not all riding – a number of socials are also held throughout the year making the group a great place to meet likeminded people.

Activities & Hobbies

## Dance Classes

Whether your feet tap to classical or contemporary rhythms, all dancing tastes are catered for in Dubai. In addition to established dancing institutions, a number of health clubs, restaurants and bars hold weekly sessions in flamenco, salsa, samba, jazz dance, ballroom and more (see Salsa Dancing, p.335).

### The Ballet Centre

**Beh Jumeira Plaza** Jumeira **04 344 9776**
www.balletcentre.com
Map **2 H3** Metro **Emirates Towers**
Classes on offer include ballet, tap, modern, salsa, Irish, jazz and belly dancing. Adult's and children's classes are available, with youngsters aged 3 years and above accepted for enrollments. Training for the Imperial Society for Teachers of Dancing (ISTD) and the Royal Academy of Dance examinations is encouraged.

### Ceroc Dubai

**Dubai Knowledge Village** Al Sufouh **050 428 3061**
www.cerocarabia.com
Map 1 N4 Metro **Dubai Internet City**
Easy to learn and similar to salsa (without the fancy footwork), this modern jive can be danced to all kind of different music including club and chart hits, old classics, swing, Latin & rock n roll. Regular classes, workshops, social dance nights and private tuition are available (Dhs.50 per person).

### Disco Dance Dubai

**Kings' Dubai** Umm Suqeim **055 289 6735**
Map **1 S4** Metro **Mall of the Emirates**
Dance routines to Hannah Montana, Mamma Mia and songs from High School Musical are taught by RAD and IDTA trained director, Becky Kerrigan. Classes for girls aged 5 to 8 are every Tuesday, 14:30-15:15.

### Dance Horizons

04 360 7691
Dance Horizons is a specialist ballet school that offers the Royal Academy of Dance Examination syllabus for beginners and advanced dancers and a Specialized Music and Movement programme for age 4 and older. Classes are held at Horizon School and Safa School in Jumeirah (near Safa Park) in fully equipped ballet studios with sprung floor, barres and mirrors, and are led by highly qualified, RAD registered, teaching staff.

### Dubai Liners

**Safa Kindergarten 22nd Street, Off Al Wasl Rd**
Al Safa **050 654 5960**
Map **2 A4** Metro **Al Quoz**
It's not all country and western; here you can line dance to disco, rock 'n' roll, salsa, jazz, R&B, waltz and ballads. Beginner's classes are held on Saturdays from 09:30 to 11:30 and intermediates dance from 11:00 to 13:00.

### El Firulete BNF Dance Company Dubai

**Dubai Knowledge Village** Al Sufouh **04 364 4883**
www.elfiruletebnf.com
Map **1 N4** Metro **Dubai Internet City**
The National Ballet El Firulete (BNF) is a celebrated Columbian dance school and the Dubai branch offers private and group instruction in tango, salsa and belly dancing, among other styles, and puts on public performances.

### First International Dance Studio

**Nr Clock Tower** Deira **056 605 5265**
www.firstids.com
Map **2 N5** Metro **Deira City Centre**
Hip hop is the main dance discipline offered at this school, but other modern and classical styles are also available. Dhs.800 per month for thrice-weekly group classes; get a taster with a free introductory lesson.

### Nora Dance Group

050 875 0111
www.noradancegroup.com
Offers instruction in an array of international dance styles including hip-hop, ballet, jazz, tango, modern freestyle, as well as Eastern styles including belly dancing and Bollywood.

### Swing Dancing

050 428 3061
www.cerocarabia.com/lindyswing
Fans of Strictly Come Dancing and Dancing With The Stars will be familiar with swing dancing or Lindy Hop. This energetic form of dance involves intricate footwork and jazz steps from dances like the Charleston to music from jazz greats like Count Basie and Duke Ellington. Call Des for more details.

# Desert Driving Courses

## Tango Dubai
**Mall of the Emirates** Al Barsha **050 451 6281**
Map **1 R5** Metro **Mall of the Emirates**
Tuesday classes are held for beginners and advanced dancers at Evory Bar, Kempinski Hotel and at DUCTAC, Mall of the Emirates respectively. Call Eleanor on 050 451 6281 or Maya on 050 622 3679 for more info. Lessons cost Dhs.200 for four beginner's classes and Dhs.240 for advanced. Tango Dubai also runs the dance nights at Sezzam and Pachanga (see intro).

## Turning Pointe Dance Studios
**Russia Building V23** International City **800 32623**
www.turningpointe.ae
This dance centre has multiple studios throughout Dubai offering classes in ballet, tap, jazz, hip hop, modern and musical theatre for ages 3-19. The centre is affiliated to the Royal Academy of Dance (RAD) and Imperial Society of Teachers of Dancing (ISTD).

# Desert Driving Courses
Don't just do the school run – instead make the most of your 4WD and take a crash course in desert driving. With several organisations offering instruction from professional drivers, you'll quickly master the art of driving in the desert without getting stuck and learn how to get yourself out when you do. In addition, if you intend to go out camping anytime it is a really good idea to have some experience in desert driving.

## Al Futtaim Training Centre
**Nxt to Dubai Duty Free** Umm Ramool **04 285 0455**
www.traininguae.com
Map **2 N8** Metro **Emirates**
Classroom and practical tuition for off-road driving enthusiasts to venture safely into the desert.

## Desert Rangers
Oud Metha **04 357 2233**
www.desertrangers.com
Map **2 L5** Metro **Oud Metha**
Experience a four-hour desert driving safari with the chance to spend one hour behind the wheel. The costs are Dhs.1000 with own vehicle, or Dhs.1800 without.

## Emirates Driving Institute
**Nr Al Bustan Ctr** Al Qusais **04 263 1100**
www.edi-uae.com
Map **2 R7** Metro **Al Nahda**
Offers five-hour desert driving course from Dhs.500 or Dhs.550 on Fridays.

## Off-Road Adventures
**Shangri-La Hotel** Trade Centre **050 628 9667**
www.arabiantours.com
Map **2 G5** Metro **Financial Centre**
Instructor Karim has more than 20 years driving experience to share with 4WD owners wishing to hone their desert driving skills. Drivers meet at the Eppco station near Dragonmart (see website for timings). You need to drive your own vehicle and the charges per person are Dhs.500 or Dhs.350 for two people. The company also arranges drives, treasure hunts, tours and safaris.

## OffRoad-Zone
**Jebel Ali Shooting Club** Jebel Ali **04 339 2449**
www.offroad-zone.com
Training course with simulated obstacles lets drivers learn in a controlled environment. From deep water crossings to sandy descents, every kind of terrain is covered. You can bring your own 4WD or you can rent one from OffRoad-Zone from Dhs.850 per person for three hours.

Off-Roading

Quad Biking

**Activities & Hobbies**

# Diving Courses

There are plenty of dive companies in the UAE where you can improve your diving skills. Courses are offered under the usual international training organisations. For more information on Diving in the UAE see p.259.

## 7 Seas Divers
Nr Khor Fakkan Souk, East Coast Khor Fakkan
09 238 7400
www.7seasdivers.com
This PADI dive centre offers day and night diving trips to sites around Khor Fakkan, Musandam and Lima Rock. Training is provided from beginner to instructor level, in a variety of languages.

## Al Boom Diving
Al Wasl Rd, Nr Iranian Hospital Jumeira 04 342 2993
www.alboomdiving.com
Map 2 H3 Metro Emirates Towers
Al Boom's Aqua Centre on Al Wasl Road (there are centres in Fujairah, Dibba and Jebel Ali too) is a purpose-built school with a fully outfitted diving shop. There are diving trips daily. PADI certification starts from Dhs.1750 for Scuba Diver; novices can do a try dive experience for Dhs.150. Al Boom also runs the Diving With Sharks experience in Dubai Aquarium at Dubai Mall. For more details see www.thedubaiaquarium.com.

## Desert Sports Diving Club
Off Sheikh Zayed Rd, I/C 2, Street 40a Al Quoz
www.desertsportsdivingclub.net
Map 2 C6 Metro Al Quoz
Dubai's only independent diving group meets on Mondays and Wednesdays at the clubhouse near Sheikh Zayed Road to plan dives. The group has two boats in Dubai and one on the east coast. A Dhs.1650 fee entitles members to unlimited free dives on club boats. Guests pay Dhs.75 per dive.

## Divers Down
Oceanic Hotel Khor Fakkan 09 237 0299
www.diversdown-uae.com
This diving company offers courses for all abilities and organises dives in the Gulf of Oman. It's open seven days a week and transport can be provided. Check the website for rates and diving information.

## Explorer Member Card
Don't forget to register your member card (found at the back of the book) and check online for current offers. Discounts are updated on a monthly basis and cover a wide range of companies. www.liveworkexplore.com.

## Emirates Diving Association
Heritage & Diving Village Al Shindagha 04 393 9390
www.emiratesdiving.com
Map 2 M3 Metro Al Ghubaiba
This is a non-profit organisation that seeks to protect the UAE's marine resources. It runs a coral monitoring project and annual Clean-Up Arabia campaigns. Divers are encouraged to join for Dhs.100 per year.

## Nomad Ocean Adventures
Nr the Harbour, Al Biah Dibba 050 885 3238
www.discovernomad.com
Dive, dhow and overnight camp trips can be tailored for individual parties. A two-dive trip with equipment starts at Dhs.395, a beginner's trial dive costs Dhs.400 and the open water course (including nine dives and certification) costs Dhs.1800. Call Christophe on the number above or +968 99 834 256 for more info.

## The Pavilion Dive Centre
The Jumeirah Beach Hotel Umm Suqeim
04 406 8827
www.jumeirah.com
Map 1 S3 Metro Mall of the Emirates
This PADI Gold Palm IDC Centre is run by PADI course directors. Daily dive charters for certified divers are available in Dubai; charters to Musandam can be organised upon request from Dhs.650 with equipment. Discover Scuba costs Dhs.325; Open Water certification is Dhs.1,500.

## Sandy Beach Hotel & Resort
Fujairah 09 244 5555
www.sandybm.com
Located in a chalet beach resort, the centre, which sells dive equipment, is open year-round. Nearby Snoopy Island, alive with hard coral and marine life, is an excellent spot for snorkelling and diving.

## Scuba 2000
Al Badiyah Beach Dibba 09 238 8477
www.scuba-2000.com
This east coast dive centre provides daily trips to dive sites at Dibba and Khor Fakkan as well as a range of courses. The prices start at Dhs.500 for Discover Scuba rising to Dhs.2,350 for Open Water certification.

## Scuba Dubai
Al Khail Rd Al Quoz 04 341 4940
www.scubadubai.com
Map 1 S8 Metro First Gulf Bank
This dedicated dive store and been open since 1989 and sells wide range of equipment. If you are looking for underwater camera housings it has a range here. Its workshop services and repairs most brands of diving gear; you can also rent equipment which is charged on a 24 hour basis.

# Dodgeball

## Scubatec

Sana Bld Karama 04 334 8988
Map 2 L4 Metro Karama
Scubatec is a five-star IDC operator, licensed by PADI
and TDI, offering courses from beginner to instructor
level. Dive trips are available in Dubai and on the
east coast.

## Sharjah Wanderers Dive Club

Nxt to Sharjah English School Sharjah 06 566 2105
www.sharjahwanderers.com
This club is a member of the British Sub Aqua Club and
follows its training, certification and diving practices.
Clubhouse facilities include a training room, social
area, equipment room, compressors, dive gear and
two dive boats.

# Dodgeball

## Duplays

050 257 7359
www.duplays.com
Register a team for Dhs.2,700 or join as an individual
for Dhs.300 and be allocated to a team. The Duplays
mixed recreational league welcomes beginners and
you can learn to dip, duck, dive and dodge the soft
balls thrown by other contestants.

# Dragon Boat Racing

Training sessions in the ancient eastern sport of
dragon boat racing are held most mornings and
evenings at either Dubai Festival City or Le Meridien
Mina Seyahi. There are several teams based in Dubai
who regularly compete against each other and teams
from Abu Dhabi. Most accept new members with little
or no experience. The UAE Dragon Boat Association
lists all of the country's teams: for training times and
joining details, visit www.dubaidragonboat.com.
An annual dragon boating festival is held at Festival
Centre (see UAE Calendar, p.25).

## Dubai Flying Dragons

Le Meridien Mina Seyahi Al Sufouh
www.dubaiflyingdragons.com
Map 1 M3 Metro Nakheel
Holds training sessions at Le Meridien Mina Seyahi.
Email info@dubaidragons.com for info. Serious paddlers
can try out for international dragon boat competitions.

## Dubai Sea Dragons

Le Meridien Mina Seyahi Al Sufouh 055 584 0588
www.dubaiseadragons.com
Map 1 M3 Metro Nakheel
An independent dragon boating club, affiliated
with the International Dragon Boat Federation and
DBA Federation. It participates in regular local and
international competitions and newcomers are

welcome on Mondays and Wednesdays at 09:00 and
17:00. Call for more info.

# Drama Groups

## Drama Workshops Dubai

Dubai Community Theatre & Arts Centre (DUCTAC)
Mall of the Emirates Al Barsha 050 986 1761
www.dramaworkshopsdubai.com
Map 1 R5 Metro Mall of the Emirates
This school runs classes for both children and
adults that focus on the different aspects of acting.
School workshops in circus fighting, comedy and
Shakespeare (among others) are also offered. Private
tuition and corporate training can be arranged.

## Dubai Drama Group

Dubai Community Theatre & Arts Centre (DUCTAC)
Mall of the Emirates Al Barsha 050 509 4211
www.dubaidramagroup.com
Map 1 R5 Metro Mall of the Emirates
Members include actors, directors, singers, dancers,
and behind the scenes personnel. Four productions
are staged each year, and there are workshops,
monthly social events, and an internet forum. Annual
membership is Dhs.100.

## Manhattan Film Academy

Dubai Knowledge Village Al Sufouh
www.mfacademy.com
Map 1 N4 Metro Dubai Internet City
The Dubai branch of this New York film school offers
workshops in screenwriting, directing and acting.

## Scenez Group

Dubai Media City Al Sufouh 04 391 5290
www.scenezgroup.com
Map 1 M4 Metro Nakheel
Budding talents between 6 and 16 can get involved
with all kinds of theatre and backstage productions
through its workshops and events, including courses
on scriptwriting, costume design, acting and mime.

# Environmental Groups

In recent years, the determined clamour of
environmentally-conscious campaigners has begun
to make an impact in a country where concepts like
carbon-offsetting, recycling and re-using are still
nascent. In 1998, HH Sheikh Mohammed Bin Rashid
Al Maktoum, Crown Prince of Dubai, established an
environmental award which recognises an individual
or organisation for work carried out on behalf of
the environment. On an everyday level, there are
increasing numbers of glass, plastic and paper
recycling points around the city, mainly around
shopping centres (see Going Green, p.12). However,
overall, little seems to be done to persuade the

average citizen to be more environmentally active, for instance by encouraging the reduction of littering.

If you want to take action, there are a couple of groups that you can contact who always need volunteers and funds.

## Dubai Natural History Group

**Emirates Academy, Opp Wild Wadi** Umm Suqeim
**04 349 4816**
www.enhg.org
Map **1 S4** Metro **First Gulf Bank**
Monthly meetings feature lectures about flora, fauna, geology, archaeology and the natural environment of the emirates. Regular trips are organised and the group maintains a library of natural history publications. Annual membership is Dhs.100 for families and Dhs.50 for individuals. Contact chairperson Brien Holmes on 050 533 0579.

## Emirates Environmental Group

**Villa JMR 68, Nr Dubai Zoo** Jumeira **04 344 8622**
www.eeg-uae.org
Map **2 G3** Metro **Financial Centre**
This voluntary organisation is devoted to protecting the environment through education, action programmes and community involvement. Activities include evening lectures and special events such as recycling collections and clean-up campaigns. Annual membership costs Dhs.100 for adults and Dhs.50 for students.

# Fencing

## Dubai Fencing Club

**Mina A'Salam** Umm Suqeim **050 794 4190**
www.dubaifencingclub.com
Map **1 R3** Metro **First Gulf Bank**
This club offers individual (Dhs.200) and group training (Dhs.50) in epée and foil for all levels. Fencers receive basic equipment such as masks, gloves and weapons, with three fencing paths, electrical scoring systems and electrical weapons for advanced levels.

## UAE Fencing Federation

**Nr Ramada Hotel** Bur Dubai **04 269 9866**
www.uaefencing.org.ae
Map **2 L4** Metro **Khalid Bin Al Waleed**
This body organises and supervises fencing in the UAE and has affiliations with local competition organisers and the UAE national team. Call the number above or 050 445 1355 for more information.

# Fishing

The Dubai government has introduced regulations to protect fish stocks, however you can still fish, as long as you have the right permit or you charter a licensed tour guide. The best fishing is from September to April,

although it is still possible to catch sailfish and queen fish in the summer. Fish commonly caught in the region include king mackerel, tuna, trevally, bonito, kingfish, cobia and dorado. Beach or surf fishing is popular along the coast, and in season you can even catch barracuda from the shore; the creek front in Creekside Park is also popular, although you may want to think twice about eating your catch.

Alternatively, on a Friday, you can hire an abra for the morning at the Bur Dubai or Deira landing steps and ask your driver to take you to the mouth of the creek. You could also consider a deep-sea fishing trip with one of the charter companies listed. For more competitive anglers, the UAQ Marine Club (www. uaqmarineclub.com) sponsors a fishing competition twice a year in April and October. Call 06 766 6644 for more details. A good selection of all manner of fishing rods, tackle and equipment is available at Barracuda Dubai (www.barracudadubai.com). You can even post your catch of the day on their website, look through the gallery of catches and read features on different styles of fishing.

## Bounty Charters

**Le Meridien Mina Seyahi** Al Sufouh **050 552 6067**
Map **1 M3** Metro **Nakheel**
Offers full day sailfish sessions, half day bottom fishing and night fishing charters as well as three to five-day trips to Musandam.

## Club Joumana

**Jebel Ali Golf Resort & Spa** Jebel Ali **04 814 5555**
www.jebelali-international.com
Fishing trips with captain, tackle, equipment, food and drink included are organised by this club operating out of Jebel Ali Golf Resort & Spa.

## Dubai Creek Golf & Yacht Club

**Baniyas Rd, Opp Deira City Centre** Port Saeed
**04 295 6000**
www.dubaigolf.com
Map **2 M6** Metro **GGICO**
Charter the club's yacht, Sneakaway, and disappear into the Arabian Gulf to experience big game sport fishing. The 32 foot Hatteras carries up to six passengers and a Dhs.3,500 hire fee includes four hours at sea (or Dhs.4,500 for eight hours) plus tackle, bait, ice, fuel and a friendly crew.

## Dubai Fishing Trip

**Dubai Marina Yacht Club** Dubai Marina **04 432 7233**
http://dubaifishingtrip.com
Map **1 K4** Metro **Jumeirah Lakes Towers**
Two hour cruises and four hour fishing trips are available. A new 37 foot sport fishing boat operates out of the Dubai Marina Yacht Club.

### Oceanic Hotel
Beach Road Khor Fakkan 09 238 5111
www.oceanichotel.com
A fishing boat for up to five people costs Dhs.600 per
hour. Trips depart from 14:00. For hotel guests, the
catch of the day can be cooked by the hotel chef for a
nominal fee. Non-guests take their catch home.

### Soolyman Sport Fishing
Fishing Port 2, Jumeirah Beach Umm Suqeim
050 886 6227
www.soolymansportfishing.com
Map 1 T3 Metro First Gulf Bank
This company operates a fleet of fishing boats,
captained by experienced South African crew. Rates
are Dhs.2,300 for four hours (morning or afternoon),
Dhs.2,800 for six hours or Dhs.3,300 for eight hours.

---

**Licence To Krill**

Unless you set off with a registered fishing charter,
you'll need to obtain a fishing licence from the
Dubai government. There are different permits for
leisure boats and offshore fishing, but both are free
and can be applied for through the government
portal, www.dm.gov.ae. For details on how to get
your hands on the yearly permit, call 04 206 4260.

---

### Yacht Solutions
The Westin Dubai Mina Seyahi Al Sufouh
04 511 7130
www.yachtsolutionsllc.com
Map 1 M3 Metro Nakheel
Weekend fishing charters and 'seafaris' from DIMC.
Rates start at Dhs.650 per person.

## Flower Arranging

### Ikebana Sogetsu Group
Villa 13, 132 St 15, Al Waheda Karama
04 262 0282
Map 2 M4 Metro Khalid Bin Al Waleed
Ikebana is the art of Japanese flower arranging. This
Dubai-based group attempts to deepen cultural
understanding among the city's multinational society
through exhibitions, demonstrations and workshops.
Classes are taught by Fujiko Zarouni, a qualified
teacher from Japan.

## Flying

### Dubai Flying Association
Umm Al Quwain Airport Umm Al Quwain
050 625 8440
www.fly-dxb.com
A non-profit group that aims to provide flying time
to members at cost price. Annual membership is

Dhs.500. Please note it is not a flying school and does
not offer sightseeing or pleasure flights.

### Emirates Flying School
Dubai International Airport T2 Garhoud
04 299 5155
www.emiratesaviationservices.com
Map 2 Q6 Metro Airport Terminal 1
The only approved flight training institution in Dubai
offers private and commercial licences, and will
convert international licences to UAE. A Private Pilot
Licence course costs upwards of Dhs.48,500.

### Fujairah Aviation Academy
Fujairah International Airport Fujairah 09 222 4747
www.fujaa.ae
Facilities include single and twin-engine aircraft, an
instrument flight simulator and a repair workshop.
Training is offered for private and commercial
licences, instrument rating and multi-engine rating.
Pleasure flights, sightseeing tours and aircraft for hire
are also available.

### Jazirah Aviation
Dubai – Ras Al Khaimah Highway, Jazirat Al Hamra
Ras Al Khaimah 07 244 6416
www.jac-uae.net
The club is dedicated solely to microlight/ultralight
flying and also offers training and pleasure flights. A
Microlight Pilot's Licence course, with around 25 hours
flying time, costs Dhs.500 per hour.

### Micro Aviation Club
20km from the Emirates Rd Umm Al Quwain
055 212 0155
www.microaviation.org
Micro Aviation Club offers training courses in
microlight flying, paragliding and paramotoring. Their
office is located at Dubai Men's College, within Dubai
Academic City. Courses start from Dhs.3,500, with an
annual registration fee of Dhs.250.

### Umm Al Quwain Aeroclub
17km north of UAQ on the RAK Road
Umm Al Quwain 06 768 1447
www.horizonuae.ae
The Middle East's only skydiving centre offers skydive
boogies, tandem skydiving and an accelerated
freefall course.

## Football
Football (or soccer) is a much-loved sport here in the
UAE, with both impromptu kickabouts in parks and
more organised team practices and matches taking
place regularly. InSportz in Al Quoz has five indoor
five-a-side pitches, and some universities and schools
will rent out their outdoor and five-a-side pitches. See

Gyms & Fitness Centre, p.207 for more details. If you'd rather watch than play, the UAE's national league has regular fixtures in Dubai. See Spectator Sports, p.260. Gaelic Football fans should contact Dubai Celts GAA – details can be found in Gaelic Games on p.322. For American Football, see p.308.

### Dubai Amateur Football League

www.dxb.leaguerepublic.com
Known as the 'Expat League', it hosts two divisions of 12 teams. It runs an 11 a side league and cup games between September and April at various locations, and seven-a-side games during the summer.

### Dubai Football Academy

04 282 4540
www.esportsdubai.com
DFA provides comprehensive football training to youngsters at various locations. Players are encouraged to join one of the teams competing in the Dubai Junior Football League. A 20 week course costs Dhs.1,350 (one lesson per week) or Dhs.2,500 (two lessons per week).

### Dubai Irish

050 465 1087
Dubai Irish consists of players of all nationalities and participates in the Dubai Amateur Football League. Despite competing in the more competitive division one, the team welcomes players of all skill levels.

### Dubai Women's Football Association

Jebel Ali Shooting Club Jebel Ali 050 659 8767
www.dubaiwfa.com
17 women's teams compete across two divisions. Players train once a week, and have weekly matches.

### Duplays

050 257 7359
www.duplays.com
Duplays runs competitive and recreational five-a-side indoor and seven-a-side outdoor leagues, and has recently added a women's five-a-side league to its schedule, so whatever your level of skill, there's a league for you.

### International Football Academy

04 337 1698
www.intlfootballacademy.com
Offers training for 4-16 year olds by experienced internationally qualified coaches. The academy provides tailored coaching programmes at schools and in local communities as well as to existing teams.

### Manchester United Soccer School Dubai

Dubai Sports City 04 425 1125
www.muss.ae
Map 1 L10
MUSS trains youngsters to 'Play the United Way'. It offers a 30 week training programme lead by UK based Manchester United Soccer Schools Coaches, all of whom are UEFA or AFA licensed coaches. Students have the chance to represent Dubai in the soccer schools World Skills Final at Old Trafford.

### UAE English Soccer School Of Excellence

050 476 4877
www.soccerkidsdubai.com
Soccer Kids Dubai offers soccer training in a number of locations across Dubai for ages 3-17. Soccer camps during the school holidays and kids' parties are also available. Call James on 050 476 4877.

Dubai Creek Golf & Yacht Club

## Gaelic Games

### Dubai Celts GAA

**Safa Park** Al Wasl **050 558 1849**
www.dubaicelts.com
Map **2 D4** Metro **Business Bay**
Dubai Celts GAA holds games and organises training in men's and ladies' Gaelic football, hurling and camogie. In addition to monthly matches within the UAE, international tournaments are held in Bahrain (November) and Dubai (March) each year. Training sessions are held every Monday and Thursday at 18:45.

## Gardening

### Dubai Gardening Group

**Shk Rashid, Vila 52, Street 6C** Jumeira **04 344 5999**
Map **2 D4** Metro **Business Bay**
This group shares gardening know-how in a friendly and informal atmosphere, with seminars and practical demonstrations from experts, trips to nurseries and members' gardens also arranged. If you want advice on how to improve your garden or just want to mingle with other green fingered Dubaians then this group is for you.

For more information on Gardening, see p.108.

## Golf

With stars like Tiger Woods, Peter Harradine and Ernie Els all lending their star-power to Dubai's greens with their successful design collaborations, it is little surprise that the popularity of the city as a world-class gold destination has been cemented. Emirates Golf Club hosts the annual Dubai Desert Classic tournament, which is part of the European PGA Tour. It attracts big names including the aforementioned Woods and Els, along with other stars like Ian Woosnam and Colin Montgomerie. For amateur enthusiasts, there are local monthly tournaments and annual competitions open to all, such as the Emirates Mixed Amateur Open, the Emirates Ladies' Amateur Open (handicap of 21 or less), and the Emirates Men's Amateur Open (handicap of five or less).

To get your official handicap in the UAE you will need to register with the Emirates Golf Federation (see p.324) and submit three score cards. You will then be issued with a member card and handicap card enabling you to enter competitions.

Dubai Golf operates a central reservation system for those wishing to book a round of golf on any of the major courses in the emirate. For further information visit www.dubaigolf.com or email booking@dubaigolf.com. Just don't leave to the actual day you want to play or you may struggle to get a tee time.

If you don't want to join a golf club – as the fees are pretty steep – it might be an idea to join an amateur golf society (like the Kegs who play at the Emirates Golf Club every Tuesday evening, www.dubaigolf.com), or start one yourself with fellow players, as large groups can often get concessionary rates.

If it's a little too hot to take a swing outside, head to Scarlett's Gold Lounge at Emirates Towers (04 319 8768) where you can play over 50 international courses via the golf simulator. Full sets of clubs for right and left-handed players are available. The charges are Dhs.180 per hour for up to 8 people.

### Al Badia Golf Club

**Al Rebat St** Festival City **04 601 0101**
www.albadiagolfclub.ae
Map **2 M9** Metro **Emirates**
This Robert Trent Jones-designed course features a plush club house, 11 lakes and eco-friendly salt-tolerant grass, meaning the 7,250 yard, par 72 championship course can be irrigated with sea water.

### Al Hamra Golf Club & Resort > *p.323*

**Coast Rd (E11)** Ras Al Khaimah **07 244 7474**
www.alhamragolf.com
Although it's a bit of a drive, Al Hamra Golf Club offers a break from the city courses and their higher prices. Its 7,267 yard, par 72 links course, designed by Peter Harradine, surrounds a huge lagoon and features several interconnected lakes.

AL HAMRA
GOLF CLUB

*A taste of links Golf*

Al Hamra Golf Club *provides you with the first taste of* "Links Style" *golf in the Middle East, meandering along the shores and rolling waves of the Arabian Gulf, it is a truly unique experience for the region.*

*www.alhamragolf.com*

*Golf Reservations Tel.* +971 244 7474   *Emal:* golfreservation@alhamragolf.com

# Golf

## Arabian Ranches Golf Club

Arabian Ranches 04 366 3000
www.arabianranchesgolfdubai.com
Map 1 Q12
Designed by Ian Baker-Finch and Nicklaus Design, this par 72 grass course incorporates natural desert terrain and features indigenous plants. Facilities include a golf academy with a floodlit range, an extensive short game practice area, GPS on golf carts and a pleasant clubhouse which houses the popular Ranches Restaurant & Bar (p.490).

## Dubai Creek Golf & Yacht Club

Baniyas Rd, Opp Deira City Centre Port Saeed
04 295 6000
www.dubaigolf.com
Map 2 M6 Metro GGICO
The par 71 course features a challenging front nine designed by Thomas Björn and is open to players with a valid handicap certificate. Novices are encouraged to train with PGA qualified instructors at the golf academy. There is also a new nine-hole par three course, a floodlit driving range and extensive short game practice facilities. The iconic clubhouse features dining favourites The Boardwalk (p.463 ), QD's (p.514) and The Aquarium (p.456).

## The Els Club Dubai > p.viii – p.ix

Emirates Rd, Dubai Sports City
04 425 1010
www.elsclubdubai.com
Map 1 L10
The 7,538 yard, par 72 signature course was designed by Ernie Els and includes a Butch Harmon School of Golf for players of all ages and skills, and a Mediterranean club house, managed by Troon Golf.

## Emirates Golf Club

Int 5, Shk Zayed Rd Emirates Hills 04 380 2222
www.dubaigolf.com
Map 1 M4 Metro Nakheel
At Emirates Golf Club you can choose from two 18 hole courses: the 6,857 yard, par 71 Majlis Course – the first grass course in the Middle East and venue for the Dubai Desert Classic – or the Faldo Course designed by Nick Faldo and IMG Design. The club has a Peter Cowen Golf Academy, along with two driving ranges, practice areas and clubhouse.

## Emirates Golf Federation

The Clubhouse Arabian Ranches Golf Club
04 368 4988
www.emiratesgolffederation.com
Map 1 Q12
Affiliated to R&A and the International Golf Federation, this non-profit organisation is the governing body for amateur golf in the UAE and supports junior players

and develops the national team. They issue official handicap cards and have a hold in one club where golfers can record their glorious moments. The affiliate membership rate is Dhs.200 for one year. The EGF office is open between 09:00 and 17:00 on Sunday through to Thursday. They are closed on Friday, Saturday and public holidays.

## Jebel Ali Golf Resort & Spa

Nr Palm Jebel Ali Jebel Ali 04 814 5555
www.jebelali-international.com
This nine-hole, par 36 course has peacocks to keep golfers company and gulf views to distract them. It hosts the Jebel Ali Golf Resort & Spa Challenge, the curtain raiser to the Dubai Desert Classic (p.25).

## Jumeirah Golf Estates

Emirates Road, 04 375 2222
www.jumeirahgolfestates.com
Map 1 J10
Dubai's newest golf course and home to the Dubai World Championship (p.28). The golf club has four themed courses – Earth, Fire, Wind and Water, although only Fire and Earth were open for play at the start of 2010. Both designed by Greg Norman, the Fire course features desert terrain and greens, with red sand bunkers, and Earth is reminiscent of European parklands. Annual membership packages offer access to both courses.

## The Montgomerie Golf Club

The Address Montgomerie Dubai Emirates Hills
04 390 5600
www.themontgomerie.com
Map 1 L6 Metro Nakheel
Set on 200 acres of land, the 18 hole, par 72 course has some unique characteristics, including the mammoth 656 yard 18th hole. Facilities include a driving range, putting greens and a swing analysis studio, while the clubhouse is managed by The Address and boasts guest rooms, an Angsana spa (p.212), and various bars and restaurants including the excellent Nineteen (p.486).

## Sharjah Golf & Shooting Club

Emirates Road, Nr Tasjeel Auto Village Sharjah
06 548 7777
www.golfandshootingshj.com
The club sponsors a junior development programme for youngsters interested in improving their game, and floodlights have been added to the course for night play. Members pay Dhs.165 for 18 holes including kart at off peak times, Dhs.100 for nine holes. This is a popular option for Dubai residents who are not members of a golf club and want a more affordable 18 holes. Competitions are also held here is contact the club if you want to get involved.

# Gymnastics

Whether you're looking for professional coaching, something to keep the kids' active or just to try out a new activity, there are gymnast facilities and training for all. For baby and toddler gymnastics, see Kids' Activities p.143.

### Dubai Olympic Gymnastics Club

12A Street off Al Wasl Road Al Wasl 050 765 1515
www.uae-gymnastics.com
Map **2 E4** Metro **Business Bay**
Run by UK gymnastics champion Dean Johnstone, the club offers courses for gymnasts of all levels. Geared specifically towards children, classes correspond with school terms.

### DuGym Gymnastics Club

050 553 6283
www.dugym.com
Gymnastics and trampoline coaching for children of all abilities. The club operates at locations including the GEMS World Academy, Jumeirah English Speaking School and Emirates International School. Classes held from Sunday to Thursday. Contact Suzanne for more info.

# Hashing

Billed as 'drinking clubs with a running problem', Hash House Harriers is a worldwide network of social running clubs where the emphasis is on taking part, and socialising afterwards, rather than on serious running. Members run or walk around a course laid out by a couple of 'hares'. It's a fun way to get fit and meet new people.

### Creek Hash House Harriers

050 451 5847
www.creekhash.net
This group meets every Tuesday and runs last around 45 minutes.

### Desert Hash House Harriers

050 454 2635
www.deserthash.org
This group runs every Sunday, meeting an hour before sunset. The fee is Dhs.50 including refreshments.

# Hiking

If you've always wanted to get into hiking but are a little daunted about the prospect of setting out on your own, then going on an organised hike is the best way to introduce yourself to the UAE's great outdoors. It can be easy to live in Dubai and rarely walk anywhere so even the most gentle of hikes can be good for the heart. For more information on hiking see p.258.

East Coast

### Absolute Adventure

Nr Golden Tulip Hotel, Dibba 04 345 9900
www.adventure.ae
This adventure tour operator offers range of treks, varying in difficulty, including extreme trekking at Jebel Qihwi and an eight-hour coastal village trek. Prices for both start at Dhs.350. The activity centre located directly on Dibba's beach can accommodate 14 people for group stays with a barbeque on the beach. They also organise treks for serious hikers to far flung places like Nepal. Check their website for details of upcoming trips.

### Desert Rangers

Oud Metha 04 357 2233
www.desertrangers.com
Map **2 L5** Metro **Oud Metha**
Desert Rangers offer hikes for individuals and groups of up to 100 people by dividing them into smaller teams and taking different trails to the summit. A variety of routes are offered according to age and fitness. Locations include Fujairah, Dibba, Masafi, Ras Al Khaimah and Al Ain, with prices starting at Dhs.275 per person.

## Hockey

### Dubai Hockey Club
055 966 8762
www.dubaihockeyclub.com
Club training sessions take place on Sunday and Wednesday evenings. All abilities are welcome and both men and women can join. The club plays in local tournaments on grass and takes part in friendly games. International tours to locations such as Singapore, Hong Kong and the UK are also organised.

### Sharjah Wanderers Hockey Club
Sharjah Wanderers Sports Club Sharjah
06 566 2105
www.sharjahwanderers.com
The club's hockey section was the first mixed team in the Gulf. The approach at the club is to play sport within a friendly, but competitive, environment.

## Horse Riding

Horse riding is a national sport in the UAE and there are a number of excellent stables and equestrian clubs in Dubai. While keeping your own horse comes at huge expense, you may fine that horse riding lessons cost less in Dubai than in your home country. That said, many of the equestrian clubs are so in demand that they have waiting lists for lessons. There are a few places, such as The Desert Palm Riding School where you can take your kids for a horse ride – they will be trotted around the track for 10 minutes or so.

If you are a dressage rider and would like to get involved in shows in the UAE you can contact some of the stables, such as Godolphin (www.godolphin.com), the Abu Dhabi Equestrian Club (www.emiratesracing.com ), or the Al Zobair Stud Farm in Sharjah (www.alzobairstud.com)

Horse racing in Dubai is extremely popular, with most races, including the Dubai World Cup (p.26), the richest horse race in the world, taking place at the brand new Meydan racetrack.

### The Desert Equestrian Club
050 309 9770
If you've got your own horse, the Desert Equestrian Club offers livery services for Dhs.1,500 a month, while accomplished riders can pay Dhs.100 to use one of the stable's horses. Private lessons are Dhs.80 for adults and Dhs.50 for children under 16.

### The Desert Palm Riding Schools
Nr Dragonmart Al Awir 050 451 7773
www.desertpalm.ae
This riding school offers classes for all ages, in either groups, semi-private or one-to-one. Prices are Dhs.80 per 30 minutes for child beginners and Dhs.160 per hour for adults, including all equipment.

### Dubai Polo & Equestrian Club
Arabian Ranches 04 361 8111
www.poloclubdubai.com
Map 1 Q12
This club features a sandplast arena (sandplast is one of the best surfaces to ride on), a riding school and a polo club. Horse riding lessons are available for all abilities. Group polo lessons start at Dhs.500 for 40 minutes; a 1.5 hour introductory polo lesson is Dhs.700. If you don't fancy taking lessons you can always enjoy a picnic pitchside for their Chukkas, held every weekend during the winter. You can pack your own sandwiches or for bespoke picnics order through the website.

### Emirates Equestrian Centre
Nr Endurance City Nad Al Sheba 050 553 7986
www.emiratesequestriancentre.com
This centre is home to over 100 horses and facilities include an international size floodlit arena, a riding school, and dressage and lunging rings. It can cater for very small children and hosts regular competitions, gymkhanas and shows. The centre also has regular clinics and stable management courses.

### Jebel Ali Equestrian Club
Jebel Ali Village Jebel Ali 04 884 5101
www.jaec-me.com
Map 1 F4
Qualified instructors teach all levels of dressage, jumping, gymkhana games and hacking. Newcomers can try a one-day lesson, after which a 10 lesson package costs Dhs.800 for children and Dhs.1,000 for adults, plus a Dhs.120 annual registration fee.

### Jebel Ali Golf Resort & Spa
Nr Palm Jebel Ali Jebel Ali 04 814 5555
www.jebelali-international.com
The riding centre has 9 horses and air-conditioned stables. Instructors give private lessons for 45 minutes from Tuesday to Sunday and one-hour desert rides can be arranged for experienced riders. Children's 30 minute lessons cost Dhs.150.

### Riding For The Disabled
Desert Palm Polo Club Al Awir
www.rdad.ae
RDAD is a non-profit charity which uses therapeutic horse riding and hippotherapy to attain a variety of therapeutic goals for those suffering from disabilities including autism, cerebral palsy, Down's syndrome, spina bifida and learning disabilities. The aim is to improve poise, posture, strength and flexibility while boosting confidence. Classes are usually 45 minutes long but will vary according to the attention span, age and disability of the rider.

Activities & Hobbies

### Sharjah Equestrian & Racing Club

Al Dhaid Rd, Jct 6 Sharjah 06 531 1188
www.forsanuae.org.ae
Facilities at this club include a floodlit sand arena and paddock, a grass show jumping arena, hacking trails into the desert and a training centre. One hour group lessons start at Dhs.120, with five classes costing Dhs.350.

## Ice Hockey

Ice hockey has been a fixture on the local sports scene ever since Al Nasr Leisureland opened in 1979. With the opening of Dubai Ice Rink (p.327) in 2008, ice hockey teams now have two venues in Dubai to play. The Skate Shop next to the ice rink at Dubai Mall stocks ice hockey kit including skates, sticks, body armour, jerseys and helmets in both children's and adult sizes. Call the Dubai Ice Rink for stock details (04 448 5111).

### Dubai Mighty Camels Ice Hockey Club

Al Nasr Leisureland Oud Metha 050 450 0180
www.dubaimightycamels.com
Map 2 L5 Metro Oud Metha
This club has over 120 adult members and has regular social get-togethers from September to May. The club also hosts an annual tournament in April, which attracts up to 20 teams from the Gulf, Europe and the Far East.

### Dubai Sandstorms Ice Hockey Club

Al Nasr Leisureland Oud Metha 050 775 8713
www.dubaisandstorms.com
Map 2 L5 Metro Oud Metha
Practice sessions are held twice a week for youngsters aged 4 to 18. The emphasis is on teamwork and sportsmanship. Matches are played against teams from Dubai, Abu Dhabi, Al Ain Oman and Qatar. The Sandstorms website has a noticeboard for buying and selling ice hockey equipment.

## Ice Skating

### Al Nasr Leisureland

Nr American Hospital Oud Metha 04 337 1234
www.alnasrll.com
Map 2 L5 Metro Oud Metha
This olympic sized rink is part of the complex that also includes a bowling alley, squash and tennis courts, arcade games and shops. Entry is Dhs.10 for adults and Dhs.5 for children under ten, with skate hire at Dhs.15 per two hours. They have an ice skating school, teaching all ages, and put on Ice Shows for the public. If you intend to turn up for a skate you should call in advance to check the session times as the rink is sometimes closed for practice sessions.

### Dubai Ice Rink

The Dubai Mall Downtown Burj Dubai 04 448 5111
www.dubaiicerink.com
Map 2 F6 Metro Burj Dubai
The largest and newest rink in the UAE, this Olympic-size arena has daily public skating sessions, disco nights and special events. There are also daily group and private lessons.

### Galleria Ice Rink

The Galleria Residence Deira 04 209 6550
www.thegalleria.hyatt.com
Map 2 N3 Metro Palm Deira
Public skating costs Dhs.25 per person (including skate hire) or Dhs.15 with your own skates. Membership rates start at Dhs.300 per month, or Dhs.1,200 per year, with unlimited skating. Lessons are available for non-members and start at Dhs.100.

### Stargate

Zabeel Park Zabeel 800 9977
www.stargatedubai.com
Map 2 J5 Metro Al Jafiliya
An ice rink just for kids is one of the many attractions at this family entertainment and educational centre.

## Jetskiing

Previously jetskiers had free range on the public beaches of Dubai. However due to complaints of noise pollution and safety issues concerning swimmers the Dubai Municipality introduced regulations for jetskiing. You must now register and get a licence through the Marine Transport Agency (check the Marine section of www.rta.ae) and are allowed to jetski within restricted areas betweem sunrise and sunset. If you do go jetskiing, it may be worth checking that your medical insurance covers you for this potentially dangerous sport before you rev away, as accidents do happen. You may also want to consider whether you have any personal liability insurance in case you injure a third party.

## Karting

### Dubai Autodrome

Dubailand 04 367 8700
www.dubaiautodrome.com
The autodrome has a 500 metre indoor circuit plus a 1.2km outdoor track with 17 corners. After a safety briefing you'll take to your 390cc kart (there are 120cc karts for kids over 7 years) and hit the tarmac. There are timed races for the International Leisure Ranking plus the Dubai Autodrome Championship for serious racers. Races are Dhs.100, including kart and clothing, and last 15 minutes. Those with their own karts can use the track at certain times, and full garaging and maintenance packages are available.

# Kitesurfing

### Emirates Kart Centre

Nr Jebel Ali Golf Resort & Spa Jebel Ali
050 559 2131
www.emsf.ae

Operated by Emirates Motor Sports Federation, the floodlit, 0.8km track has straights, hairpins and chicanes. Professional and junior karts are available for Dhs.100 per half hour and the centre is open 15:00-22:00 daily.

---

#### Blokarting

Get involved with the latest extreme sports craze in Dubai. Blowkarting or landsailing, takes the principles of windsurfing and applies them on land – or to a buggy on land, to be specific. A Blowkarting experience for two costs Dhs.550 through Dreamdays (www.dreamdays.ae) and once you've got the bug, join Duplays' blowkart racing league at Jumeirah Beach Park. Find out more at www.duplays.com.

---

Kitesurfing on Jumeira Beach

## Kitesurfing

Kitesurfing is an extreme sport that fuses elements of windsurfing, wakeboarding, surfing and kite flying. While you may see kitesurfers practicing (and showing off) off various Dubai beaches, the kiting beach in Umm Suqeim is the only place where kiting is officially permitted. Dubai Municipality has recently installed showers at Kite Beach and has eased up restrictions on the sport, dropping the requirement for kiters to hold a licence. Whether this changes again in the future remains to be seen so it may be best to check with the Marine Transport Agency as they regulate all watersports (check the Marine section of www.rta.ae).

The Dubai Kite Forum (www.dubaikiteforum.com) is a good place to find out the latest on regulations. Kite People (www.kitepeople.net) and Kitesurfing in Dubai (www.dubaikiters.com) are good online resources for buying equipment and locating IKO instructors.

### AD Kitesurfing

050 562 6383
www.ad-kitesurfing.net

A number of International Kiteboarding Organisation instructors are available for kiteboarding lessons. An hour's instruction including equipment costs Dhs.300.

### Dubai Kitefly Club

Kite Beach Jumeira 050 254 7440
www.kitesurf.ae
Map 1 T3 Metro Mall of the Emirates

Kitefly offers groups lessons in kitesurfing starting at Dhs.250 and private tuition from Dhs.300 per hour, including all equipment.

### Duco Maritime

Various Locations 050 870 3427
www.facebook.com/DucoMaritime

Kitesurfing classes are available every day by request, at the public beach between Jumeirah Beach Park and Dubai Offshore Sailing Club and at kite beach. Two-hour lessons are available for beginners, charged at Dhs.300 per hour including equipment.

## Martial Arts

Aspiring Bruce Lees and Jacky Chans are well catered for with many centres offering courses in judo, aikido, karate, kick boxing and other martial arts. In addition, many fitness clubs and gyms offer thai boxing, kung fu, self-defence and other martial arts alongside their group exercise programmes. For Kids the Active Sports Academy (p.144) have an excellent range of disciplines for all ages and run after-school classes as well as holiday camps.

### Angsana Spa & Health Club Dubai Marina

Marina Walk Dubai Marina 04 368 4356
www.angsanaspa.com
Map 1 L4 Metro Dubai Marina

A Thai boxing class is held every Saturday at 19:00. Entry is Dhs.50; private classes can be arranged.

### Colosseum Health & Fitness Club

Montana Centre Bld, Zabeel Rd Karama
04 337 2755
www.colosseumuae.com
Map 2 L5 Metro Oud Metha

Classes are held daily from 20:30 to 22:00, except for Fridays. 12 sessions cost Dhs.450. Personal training is available for those over 8 years. Colosseum organises competitions between clubs in the area.

## Dubai Aikido Club
**Al Razi Boys' School** Al Safa **050 7952716**
www.aikido.ae
Map **2 C4** Metro **Business Bay**
Classes for both children and adults are held throughout the week at the Dubai Karate Centre. Lifetime registration costs Dhs.100; kids' classes are Dhs.300 for eight classes a month and adult training costs Dhs.400 for 12 sessions a month.

## Dubai Karate Centre
**Al Raizi Boys School Training Hall, Nr Medcare Hospital** Al Safa **050 855 7996**
www.dubaikarate.com
Map **2 C4** Metro **Business Bay**
The club is a member of the Japanese Karate Association (JKA) and a team of black belt, JKA qualified instructors teach shotokan karate, taekwondo, aikido, Muay Thai, judo, kudo, iado, wingtzun and courses in self defence. Registration is Dhs.100 with monthly membership from Dhs.330.

## EBMAS School Of Self Defense
**Dubai Community Theatre & Arts Centre (DUCTAC)** Al Barsha **055 605 8128**
www.ebmas-selfdefense.com
Map **1 R5** Metro **Mall of the Emirates**
EBMAS is a form of self-defence taught in more than 40 countries worldwide; this school teaches both armed and unarmed forms. Classes are held on Sundays and Wednesdays from 20:30 to 21:45.

## Golden Falcon Karate Centre
**Nxt to Choithram Supermarket** Karama **04 336 0243**
www.goldenfalconkarate.com
Map **2 K5** Metro **Karama**
Established in 1990, the centre is affiliated with the International Karate Budokan and the UAE Judo, Taekwondo & Karate Federation. The centre is open throughout the week and students can choose class times to suit their schedules. Training costs Dhs.150 for two classes per week.

## Golden Fist Karate Club
**Al Riffa Plaza, Nr Ramada R/A** Bur Dubai **04 355 1029**
www.goldenfistkarate.net
Map **2 L4** Metro **Al Fahidi**
This club provides flexible times for training in martial arts including karate and kung fu. A nine-month black belt crash course is available. Two and six classes a week, from Dhs.100 to Dhs.200 per month (plus a Dhs.30 admission fee). Yoga, swimming and aerobics classes are also offered.

## Raifet N Shawe
**Boulevard at Emirates Towers** Trade Centre **050495 4446**
Map **2 H5** Metro **Emirates Towers**
Raifet Shawe is a black belt teacher in karate, kickboxing, judo and Muay Thai and holds classes at Big Apple gym in the Emirates Towers (04 319 8660) on Mondays, Wednesdays and Saturdays from 17:30 to 18:30.

## Taekwondo
**The Ballet Centre** Jumeira **04 344 9776**
www.balletcentre.com
Map **2 H3** Metro **Al Jafiliya**
This martial art teaches mental strength and self-control. Adult classes are held on Tuesdays at 19:30 and cost Dhs.45.

# Mini Golf

## Hatta Fort Hotel > p.283
**Dubai – Hatta Rd** Hatta **04 852 3211**
www.jebelali-international.com
Set against the backdrop of the Hajar Mountains, the Hatta Fort Hotel has a mini golf course, chipping green, and driving range. Hotel guests can use the course for free, but there's a fee for day visitors.

## Hyatt Golf Park
**Hyatt Regency** Deira **04 209 6747**
www.dubai.hyatt.com
Map **2 N3** Metro **Palm Deira**
Bring your own clubs and golf balls for the nine-hole pitch and putt grass course (Dhs.30 for one round) or rent it all at the 18 hole crazy golf course (Dhs.15 per person). No membership required.

# Motocross

## Dubai Motocross
**Jebel Ali Motocross Park** Jebel Ali
www.mydubaimotocross.com
Dubai Motocross (DMX) runs classes for cadets, juniors, 65cc, 85cc, 125cc and adults. The facility features two tracks, one for juniors and one for seniors and organises eight championship events per year. The entry fee is Dhs.100 for members and starts at Dhs.200 for non-members.

# Motorcycling

## Harley Owners Group (HOG) Dubai
Various Locations **04 339 1909**
www.hogdubai.com
Harley owners meet at various locations for rides across the region, including the Middle East HOG Rally in Fujairah.

### UAE Motorcycle Club
Al Muraqqabat St, Above Al Tayer Motors Deira
04 296 1122
www.uaedesertchallenge.com
Map **2 N5** Metro **Al Rigga**
The club is the UAE's FIM representative. Regular motocross and off-road enduros are held between September and April, and activity centres at the DMX Club and in Umm Al Quwain host quad and drag races.

## Motorsports

### Dubai Autodrome
Dubailand 04 367 8700
www.dubaiautodrome.com
Dubai's motorsport home has six different track configurations, including a 5.39km FIA-sanctioned GP circuit, state-of-the-art pit facilities and a 7,000 seat grandstand. The venue hosts events including rounds of the FIA GT Championship.

### Emirates Motor Sports Federation
Nr Aviation Club Garhoud 04 282 7111
www.emsf.ae
Map **2 M7** Metro **GGICO**
Emirates Motor Sports Federation organises events throughout the year such as the 4WD 1000 Dunes Rally, the Champions Rally for saloon cars, road safety campaigns and classic car exhibitions. Membership including competition license is Dhs.300 per year; non-members can race for a fee.

## Mountain Biking
Away from the cities, the UAE has a lot to offer outdoor enthusiasts, especially mountain bikers. On a mountain bike it's possible to see the most remote and untouched places that are not even accessible in 4WDs. For hardcore, experienced mountain bikers there is a good range of terrain, from the super-technical rocky trails in areas like Fili and Siji, to mountain routes like Wadi Bih, which climb to over a thousand metres and can be descended in minutes. The riding is mainly rocky, technical and challenging. Even if you are an experienced biker, always be sensible and go prepared – the sun is strong, you will need far more water than you think, and it's easy to get lost. You'll find wide, knobbly tires work much better on the loose, sharp rocks. For further information on mountain biking in the UAE, including details of possible routes, refer to the UAE Off-Road Explorer.

### Hot Cog MTB
Various Locations
www.hot-cog.com
An active group of enthusiasts who organise weekend trips all over the country and midweek off-road night rides. They also camp, hike and barbecue, and new riders are always welcome.

## Music Lessons
There are a number of music schools in Dubai where you and your kids can have music lessons. In addition you may find that some schools offer additional music programmes (for a fee) for students.

### Centre For Musical Arts
Mall of the Emirates Al Barsha 04 341 4666
www.cmadubai.com
Map **1 R5** Metro **Mall of the Emirates**
The centre offers instruction in a number of string, woodwind and brass instruments, for all age groups

as well as piano tuition. Group lessons start at Dhs.865 and individual lessons (from Dhs.1,460) per 12 week term. There is another centre at the Gold & Diamond Park (04 341 8872).

## Dubai Music School
Stalco Bld, Zabeel Rd Karama 04 396 4834
www.dubaimusicschool.com
Map 2 L5 Metro Oud Metha
One-hour lessons in guitar, piano, organ, violin, brass, drums, singing and composing, leading to Trinity College of Music examinations.

## Juli Music Centre
Sheikh Zayed Rd, Al Wadi Bld, Nr Safestway Al Wasl
04 321 2588
Map 2 E5 Metro Business Bay
In addition to selling a wide variety of musical instruments including new and used pianos, brass, woodwind, strings, and percussion, Juli Music Centre also offers lessons in various instruments from Dhs.150 per hour.

## Jumeirah Music Centre
Jumeira Plaza Jumeira 04 349 2662
www.jumeirah-music.com
Map 2 H3 Metro Al Jafiliya
Lessons in piano, guitar, flute, violin, drums, and voice for all ages at Dhs.90 per half hour. All children are welcome to audition for the choir, which puts on a concert every year.

## The Music Institute
Dubai Knowledge Village Al Sufouh 04 424 3818
www.themusic-uae.com
Map 1 K4 Metro Jumeirah Lakes Towers
Piano, violin, guitar and drums lessons with musical theory for all ages, plus group guitar and violin lessons. Practice rooms available to hire and show recitals are also held.

## The Vocal Studio
Sheikh Zayed Road 050 698 0773
www.bravodubai.com
Vocal instruction for all ages. The centre offers the Associated Board of the Royal Schools of Music (ABRSM) and Trinity College of Music syllabi. Students are encouraged to take part in recitals and concerts, sometimes with visiting guest artists.

# Netball

## Dubai Netball League
The Sevens Mirdif 050 450 6715
www.dubainetballleague.com
The over 21 teams compete between September and May. Training is on Sundays or Mondays and league nights fall on Wednesdays. Players also have the chance to be selected for the Inter-Gulf Championships.

## Duplays
050 257 7359
www.duplays.com
Duplays' competitive women's league is held on Sundays, and he recreational league on Mondays. Players can sign up as individuals and be allocated to a team for Dhs.360 or enter a full team for Dhs.3,200 per season.

# Orchestras & Bands

## Centre For Musical Arts
Mall of the Emirates Al Barsha 04 341 4666
www.cmadubai.com
Map 1 R5 Metro Mall of the Emirates
The centre is home to a number of adult and children's musical groups including ensembles for string, flute, saxophone and guitar players. It also offers instrumental and choral tuition and has an instrument hire and repair service.

## Dubai Chamber Orchestra
Horizon English School Al Wasl 04 349 0423
www.dubaiorchestra.org
Map 2 D4 Metro Business Bay
Founded by a group of musicians residing in the UAE, the chamber orchestra aims to give at least two public performances a year. There are currently over 40 members from more than 15 countries.

## Dubai Classical Guitar Orchestra
Al Barsha
www.dcgo.ae
Map 1 R5 Metro Mall of the Emirates
This classical guitar ensemble rehearses at DUCTAC every Tuesday from 18:00 to 20:00. People of all ages and levels of skill are welcome.

## Dubai Drums
Various Locations 050 659 2874
www.dubaidrums.com
Famous around the city, Dubai Drums not only entertain school kids, delegates at various exhibitions and whoever happen to be in close proximity, but also African Djembe drumming circles are held every Monday so you can get involved. Beginners can learn the basics and regulars can jam for an hour. Classes are Dhs.50 with drums provided. On Saturdays, Kidz Drum Club is held at DUCTAC, from 10:15-11:15 and costs Dhs.50. Other events, such as full moon desert drumming and community beats, are held regularly at various locations including DUCTAC, Mall of the Emirates, and Barasti.

# Paintballing & Laser Games

### Dubai Wind Band
**Horizon English School** Al Wasl **050 651 8902**
Map **2 D4** Metro **Business Bay**
This is a gathering of over 50 woodwind and brass musicians. All ages and abilities are welcome. The band is in high demand during December for seasonal singing and music engagements at clubs, malls and hotels.

### UAE Philharmonic Orchestra
**Dubai College** Al Sufouh
www.uaephilharmonic.com
Map **1 P4** Metro **Nakheel**
The only full orchestra in the UAE, they consist of musicians from more than 20 countries who perform in public regularly, as well as for private events.

## Paintballing & Laser Games

### Laserdrome Dubai
**Dubai Autodrome** None **04 436 1422**
www.dubaiautodrome.com
Players wear special vests that detect their enemies' lasers. At the end of each round, contestants can see how many times they got shot and who shot them. The charges are Dhs.80 per person for 15 minutes.

### Pursuit Games
**WonderLand** Umm Hurair **04 324 4755**
www.paintballdubai.com
Map **2 L6** Metro **Healthcare City**
The Pursuit Games version of paintball is a combination of speedball and paintball and the arena capitalises on the desert terrain. Costs start at Dhs.85 for a two-hour session, including 100 paintballs and gear.

### Sharjah Paintball Park
**Sharjah Golf & Shooting Club** Sharjah **050 203 2288**
www.paintballuae.com
This paintball park has two arenas. The first is a woodland area strewn with army jeeps and plane carcasses; with sniper towers and plenty of obstacles to hide behind it calls for a strategic battle plan. The second is smaller and more open meaning that the paintball battles are more frantic. A variety of different packages are available ranging from Dhs.85 for 100 paintballs and basic equipment, to Dhs.500 for 500 balls plus extra body armour and equipment.

## Photography & Film
Photography and film are increasingly popular in the region. Although three film festivals, DIFF, MEIFF and Gulf Film Festival (see UAE Calendar, p.25) shine an encouraging spotlight on the region's film making, there is still a dearth of serious funding. However, for amateur film fans, there are several groups that bring the film making community together for screenings, workshops and presentations. Shelter (www.shelter. ae) has a small screening room and holds regular film nights which are open to non-members. The Alliance Francais (p.176) has its own francophonic cine club and award-winning filmmaker, Mahmood Kabour, holds a film series at the Jam Jar; details are available on the Mahmovies! group Facebook page. The Picturehouse at Reel Cinema in Dubai Mall screens art house films and documentaries that don't make it onto the main screens.

For photographers, UAE Photo (www.uae-photo. com) is a web-based community where local photography enthusiasts can exchange tips and ideas, post their pictures, and buy and sell equipment.

### Gulf Photo Plus
**Dubai Knowledge Village** Al Sufouh **04 360 2365**
www.gulfphotoplus.com
Map **1 N4** Metro **Dubai Internet City**
Gulf Photo Plus offers a range of digital photography classes for beginner and intermediate photographers, and organises workshops and events with master photographers. Introductory classes to Photoshop are also available if you want to learn how to touch up your shots. There is also a well-stocked store selling lenses, lights, literature and other photography kit.

### Lightform
Various Locations www.lightform.ae
Lightform is the International Filipino Photographer's Guild photographic society. It organises regular workshops, field trips and events for members focusing on camera work and camaraderie. Members must complete a basic class to join.

### Lomography UAE
www.lomography.ae
This group organises workshops and exhibitions for enthusiasts of the unpredictable Lomo LC-A cameras.

### SAE Institute
**Dubai Knowledge Village** Al Sufouh **04 361 6173**
www.sae-dubai.com
Map **1 M4** Metro **Dubai Internet City**
The largest worldwide private college for film and audio production, animation and multimedia offers a degree in filmmaking as well as photography bootcamps.

---

**Live Work Explore**

If we have missed your club or association and you would like to be listed on our website www.liveworkexplore.com, just contact info@explorerpublishing.com.

### The Scene Club

Dubai Media City Al Sufouh 04 391 0051
www.thesceneclub.com
Map **1 N4** Metro **Dubai Internet City**
Dubai's first official film club for true buffs offers workshops as well as screenings of films and documentaries that may not make the box office but are felt to be culturally significant.

## Pilates

### Club Stretch

Beh Capitol Hotel Al Satwa 04 345 2131
www.clubstretch.ae
Map **2 J3** Metro **Al Jafiliya**
Club Stretch offers Pilates classes taught by highly qualified instructors.

### Exhale Fitness Studio

Jumeirah Beach Residence 04 424 3777
www.exhaledubai.com
Map **1 K4** Metro **Dubai Marina**
This ladies-only centre specialises in Pilates and yoga. Prices start at Dhs.90 for a single Pilates Reformer class; a set of ten is Dhs.650 and is valid for two months.

### The Hundred Pilates Studio

Dubai Healthcare City Umm Hurair 04 429 8433
www.thehundred.ae
Map **2 L6** Metro **Healthcare City**
Personalised Pilates sessions are available as well as small group classes with a maximum four participants. Prices start at Dhs.90 for a single class.

### Zen Yoga

Emirates Hills 04 422 4643
www.yoga.ae
Map **1 K7**
Mat and Reformer Pilates (using a machine to increase workout intensity) are available. Yogilates, incorporating moves from yoga, is also offered, and expectant mums can join prenatal Pilates classes. A trial Reformer lesson costs Dhs.90, with five classes for Dhs.450. Emirates Hills (04 422 4643), Dubai Media City (04 367 0435), Jumeirah Town Centre (04 349 2933) and The Village Mall, (04 344 6551).

## Polo

### Dubai Polo & Equestrian Club

Arabian Ranches 04 361 8111
www.poloclubdubai.com
Map **1 N12**
With two full-size pitches, this is a regular venue for both local and international polo. Coaching is offered for all levels, from 40 minute lessons to six-day courses. An introductory 1.5 hour lesson is Dhs.800.

### Ghantoot Racing & Polo Club

Sheikh Maktoum Rd Abu Dhabi 02 562 9050
www.emiratesracing.com
Map **1 D2**
The club's extensive facilities include seven international standard polo fields (three of which are floodlit), two stick and ball fields, three tennis courts, a pool, gym, sauna and restaurant. It has 200 polo ponies which are supported by six fully equipped stables, five paddocks and an outdoor training ring.

#### Camel Polo

For a fun twist on the game, head to the Dubai Polo & Equestrian Club for a spot of camel polo. It might not be as fast-paced as the real thing, but you'll come away with plenty of stories. Any group of eight or more people is welcome to reserve a session. Call Lindsay on 04 404 5918 for reservations.

## Rollerblading & Rollerskating

Dubai's many parks provide some excellent locations for rollerblading. Creekside Park (p.246) and Safa Park (p.248) have wide pathways, few people and enough slopes and turns to make it interesting. Alternatively, check out both sides of Dubai Creek, the seafront near the Hyatt Regency Hotel or the promenades at the Jumeirah Beach Corniche and in Deira along towards Al Mamzar Beach Park (p.246), where the views are an added bonus. Burj Boulevard, running through the Downtown area, and The Walk at Jumeirah Beach Residences also have wide promenades which are great for skating. Inline skating can be done at both Rampworks (Al Quoz, 050 440 5857) and the Springs Village skate park (p.336).

Chukkas at the Dubai Polo & Equestrian Club

# Rugby

## Dubai Exiles Rugby Club
Dubai – Al Ain Rd Al Awir **050 253 0787**
www.dubaiexiles.com
The Exiles is Dubai's most serious rugby club and has a 1st and 2nd XV team that competes in the AGRFU leagues, as well as veterans, U19s, ladies, girls U17s and a minis and youth section. The Exiles also host the annual Dubai International Rugby 7s Tournament.

## Dubai Hurricanes
Al Ain Rd Nad Al Sheba **050 626 6107**
www.dubaihurricanes.com
Having started as a social outfit, the Hurricanes now compete in the Dubai Sevens. The club has a ladies' team and players of all abilities are welcome. Training is Mondays and Wednesdays at 19:00.

# Running
For over half the year, Dubai's weather is perfect for running and many groups and clubs meet up for runs on a regular basis. There are several running events, such as the Round the Creek Relay Race (contact John Harrington on 050 645 0587), the Dubai Marathon (www.dubaimarathon.org), and the Wadi Bih Race (jcyoung@eim.ae).

## Dubai Creek Striders
Various Locations **04 321 1999**
www.dubaicreekstriders.com
Established in 1995 the Striders meet every Friday morning (on the road opposite the Novotel next to the Trade Centre) for a long-distance run, with training geared at members taking part in the 42.2km Dubai Marathon in January. For more info you can email them on dubai.creek.striders@gmail.com.

## Dubai Road Runners
Safa Park Al Wasl **050 624 3213**
www.dubai-road-runners.com
Map **2 D4** Metro **Business Bay**
This running club meets on Saturdays at 18:30 by gate four of Safa Park to run 3.5km to 7km (the park charges Dhs.5 entrance fee). For fun, runners predict their times, with a prize for the winner.

## Mirdif Milers
Uptown Primary School Mirdif **050 652 4149**
www.mirdifmilers.blogspot.com
Map **2 P12** Metro **Rashidiya**
This friendly group meets for training runs every Monday evening at 19:00 outside Mushrif Park. It also organises longer runs leading up to marathons and half marathons.

## Stride For Life
Various Locations **050 657 7057**
www.strideforlife.com
Stride for Life offers aerobic walking and running for all abilities. Following a fitness assessment, a thrice-weekly programme is recommended. Stride for Life also does Nordic and mall walking, and 'training journeys' for novices preparing for long distance events. Fees are Dhs.1,600 for a one-year membership.

# Sailing Courses
Temperatures in winter are perfect for sailing, and taking to the sea in summer serves as an escape from the scorching heat. Membership at one of Dubai's sailing clubs allows you to participate in club activities and to rent sailing and watersports equipment. You can also use the leisure facilities and the club's beach, and moor your boat, at an additional cost. If you've not found your sea legs but would like to, there are a few places that will teach you to be your own captain.

There's a healthy racing scene for a variety of boat types, and long distance races such as the annual Dubai to Muscat race, held in March. The traditional dhow races (p.28) are an exciting spectacle as is the Powerboat Formula One Grand Prix (p.27). For further information on sailing in the region, check out Explorer's *Dubai Boating & Yachting*, available at www. liveworkexplore.com/shop.

## Dubai International Marine Club
Mina Seyahi Dubai Al Sufouh **04 399 5777**
www.dimc.ae
Map **1 L3** Metro **Dubai Marina**
One of the oldest sailing clubs, DIMC offers sailing lessons for children. For a 36 hour course you'll be set back by Dhs.1,800 for club members and Dhs.2,600 for non-members. Visit the website for more details on lessons and how to become a member.

### Dubai Offshore Sailing Club
Umm Suqeim Beach Umm Suqeim **04 394 1669**
www.dosc.ae
Map **2 B3** Metro **Al Quoz**
This Royal Yachting Association Training Centre offers dinghy and keelboat courses throughout the year.

## Salsa Dancing
If you fancy a bit of salsa there are a number of places you can get serious or just have a bit of fun. Check out www.dubaisalsa.com for more information.

### El Malecon
Dubai Marine Beach Jumeira **04 346 1111**
www.dxbmarine.com
Map **2 H3** Metro **Trade Centre**
This restaurant hosts Sunday night salsa from 20:00-21:00 for Dhs.35. If you order food, the dancing is free.

### Ritmo De Havana
Dubai Community Theatre & Arts Centre (DUCTAC) Al Barsha **050 696 3520**
www.ritmo-de-havana.com
Map **1 R5** Metro **Mall of the Emirates**
Del Piero is a certified instructor; his courses start from Dhs.650 per person and run in batches so check the web site for the most up-to-date timings.

### Salsa Dubai
Various Locations **050 848 7188**
Instructor Phil has 13 years experience in Cuban, New York and Spanish dance styles. Classes are tailored to the individual, so everyone can progress at their own speed and members can learn the famous La Rueda Cuban dance. Class schedules can be found on 'The Original Salsa Dubai' Facebook page.

### Savage Garden
Capitol Hotel Al Satwa **04 346 0111**
Map **2 J3** Metro **Al Jafiliya**
This Latin American restaurant and nightclub serves up Latino food and daily salsa and merengue classes (except Sundays). Beginners' lessons are from 20:00 to 21:00 and intermediate and advanced dancers take to the floor from 21:00 to 22:00. Classes are Dhs.40. Contact Ms Mari on 050 245 5774 for more details.

## Sandboarding & Skiing
Sandboarding or sandskiing down a big sand dune is not as fast or smooth as snowboarding, but it can be a lot of fun. Standard snowboards and skis are pretty similar to sandboards and skis. Alternatively you can use a plastic sled. However the terrain does make a big difference so don't expect a couple of lessons at Dubai Ski to have you set for the dunes. All major tour companies (p.262) offer sandboarding and skiing experiences with basic instructions.

## Scouts & Guides
Scouts and Guides groups are gaining popularity in Dubai, the majority of which are held at schools so check with your kids' school if you would like them to enrol. In addition, with each new group comes a need for adult volunteers. If you have experience with scout or guide groups, or you have a child that was once a member, call Mary Dunn (04 348 9849) or Dawn Tate (050 654 2180) to see how you can get involved.

### 1st Dubai Guides
The English College Al Safa **050 286 7501**
Map **2 B5** Metro **Al Quoz**
A member of British Guides in Foreign Countries, this group caters to girls aged 10 to 14 and teaches decision making skills and responsibility. It meets on Sundays from 18:00 to 20:00 to play games and sports, do arts and crafts and take part in community work. There is an overnight camping trip each school term. Membership is Dhs.150 per term.

### British Guides In Foreign Countries
Various Locations **04 348 9849**
www.bgifc.org.uk
Various groups for girls of different age ranges include Rainbows (5 to 7), Brownies (7 to 10), Guides (10 to 14), and Young Leaders and Rangers (14 to 26). For more information call Jane Henderson (04 340 8441) or Mrs Patsy (04 348 9767).

### Scouts Association (British Groups Abroad)
Various Locations **050 514 4049**
The Scouts' Association encourages the development of youngsters through weekly activities and outings for ages 6-18 and 18-25. Contact Gill for more information.

## Scrabble

### Dubai Scrabble League
Al Maskam Bld Karama **050 653 7992**
Map **2 K5** Metro **Karama**
This group meets once a month for friendly games between players of all levels. Regular competitions are held, and players also attend competitions overseas. The UAE Open (annually March or April) is the qualifier for the Gulf Open in Bahrain. For more information, contact Selwyn Lobo.

---

### Live Work Explore

If we have missed your club or association and you would like to be listed on our website www.liveworkexplore.com, just contact info@explorerpublishing.com.

# Scrapbooking

### Creative Hands
Various Locations 04 348 6568
www.dubaiscrapbookingshop.com
This is an online store that offers workshops and
sessions at various locations.

### Paper Lane
Umm Al Sheif St, Villa 2, Opp Spinneys Umm
Suqeim 04 395 5337
www.dubaiscrapbookstore.com
Map 1 S4 Metro Mall of the Emirates
One of the city's biggest scrapbooking shops, Paper
Lane carries all the materials you'll need to create a
memorable album, and hosts classes for all ages and
levels, with families welcome.

### Paper@ARTE
Time Square
www.arte.ae
Map 1 T5 Metro Al Quoz
Every second Friday of the month, Paper@ARTE is
part of Arte Souk, held at the Times Square Mall. All
scrapbookers are welcome to join the workshops.
Creative Hands (above) is present and brings supplies
for patrons to buy and use.

## Shooting

### Hatta Fort Hotel > p.283
Dubai – Hatta Rd Hatta 04 852 3211
www.jebelali-international.com
Clay pigeon shooting is one of activities (once you've
finished on the pitch and putt course) offered by the
hotel, which is a popular overnight retreat from Dubai.
See Hatta Fort Hotel (p.283) for more information.

### Jebel Ali Shooting Club
Nr Jebel Ali Golf Resort & Spa Jebel Ali 04 883 6555
www.jebelali-international.com
Five floodlit clay shooting ranges that consist of
skeet, trap and sporting. Professional instructors give
comprehensive lessons and experienced shooters are
welcome to try their hand at clay shooting or archery.
Members and non-members welcome.

### Ras Al Khaimah Shooting Club
Al Duhaisa, Nr RAK Airport Ras Al Khaimah
07 236 3622
RAK Shooting Club offers lessons in firing shotguns
or long rifles, as well as invites recreational visits for
people wishing to try their hand at shooting. The club
boasts a 50m indoor and 200m outdoor rifle range.
You can make group bookings by calling in advance.

### Sharjah Golf & Shooting Club
Emirates Road, Nr Tasjeel Auto Village Sharjah
06 548 7777
www.golfandshootingshj.com
The shooting range features indoor pistols, rifles &
revolvers, as well as 25m and 50m ranges. A fully
trained safety instructor is on hand at all times.
Beginner lessons cost Dhs.150 for 30 minutes with .22
caliber weapons; 25 shots with standard weapons are
charged at Dhs.95.

## Singing

### Dubai Harmony
Various Locations 04 348 4525
www.sweetadelineintl.org
A barbershop-style group with an all-female
ensemble. New members are always welcome and
musical training is not required. Find the right part for
your voice at weekly rehearsals.

### Dubai Singers & Orchestra
JESS Al Safa dubaisingers@gmail.com
www.dubaisingers.info
Map 2 C4 Metro Business Bay
This is a group of amateur musicians who meet
regularly to create music in a variety of styles,
including requiems, choral works, Christmas carols,
musicals and variety shows. Membership is open to
everyone; sheet music is provided.

## Skateboarding

### Rage Bowl
The Dubai Mall Downtown Burj Dubai 04 434 1549
www.rage-shop.com
Map 2 F5 Metro Burj Dubai
This indoor skateboarding bowl is open Sunday to
Thursday, 10:00 to 22:00 and 10:00 until midnight
at the weekends. Kids can use the area in two hour
sessions for Dhs.25; helmets can also be hired for
Dhs.10. Lessons are available at Dhs.100 per hour and
no previous experience is required. Check the website
for happy hour timings when skating is free, sign up
for newsletters, watch skills videos and meet other
skaters on the forum.

### The Springs Skate Park
Emirates Hills 050 915 5967
Map 1 L6 Metro Dubai Marina
Emirates Hills residents and Hayya Club members
can enjoy the skate park for free. It has four ramps,
obstacles and two half pipes, and accommodates
20 skaters at a time. Guest charges are Dhs.15 at
weekends and Dhs.10 during the week. The park is
open daily from 06:00 to 22:00.

Dreamland Aqua Park

Stargate

# Skiing & Snowboarding

## Dubai Ski Club
Ski Dubai Al Barsha www.dubaiskiclub.com
Map **1 R5** Metro **Mall of the Emirates**
The club has over 1,400 members and meets at
18:00 on the last Saturday of every month, next
to Ski Dubai's ticket counter, for social skiing or
snowboarding, race training and races, followed by
après ski. Membership benefits include a reduced fee
for the slope pass and use of the 'advance booking'
lane when purchasing tickets, plus special offers
on equipment, clothing, accessories and holidays.
Membership is Dhs.300.

## Ski Dubai > p.339
Mall of the Emirates Al Barsha **04 409 4000**
www.skidxb.com
Map **1 R5** Metro **Mall of the Emirates**
Ski Dubai is the Middle East's first and largest indoor
snow park, with more than 22,500 square metres of
real snow. The park is open to everyone; competent
skiers can choose between five runs which include
one of 400 metres. Alternatively, there is a huge
snowpark, freestyle area and après ski chalet.
 If you've never tried skiing or boarding before it
is probably best to get a lesson, as you will be asked
your competency level when you purchase a snow
pass. You can book Discovery Lessons (Dhs.150) by
calling in advance or online.
 Group lessons cost Dhs.220 for adults and Dhs.190
for children and last 90 minutes. A slope day pass
(Dhs.300 adult, Dhs.240 child) includes jacket, trousers,
boots, socks, helmets and either your skis and poles or
snowboard, but make sure you bring gloves as these
are charged additionally. Freestyle nights are held
every other week on Mondays from 20:00 to 23:00.

# Skydiving

## Umm Al Quwain Aeroclub
17km north of UAQ on the RAK Road Umm Al
Quwain **06 768 1447**
www.horizonuae.ae
In addition to pilot training, helicopter flying, hangar
and aircraft rental, paramotors and microlights, the
club operates a skydive school and boogie centre.

# Snooker

## Billiard Master
Sana Bld Karama **04 335 2088**
www.uaebilliard.com
Map **2 L4** Metro **Karama**
This club has 18 billiard tables and two private snooker
tables in spacious surroundings. It organises annual
inter-club leagues and international tournaments.

## Dubai Snooker Club
Nr Karama Post Office Karama, **04 337 5338**
www.dubaisnooker.com
Map **2 L5** Metro **Khalid Bin Al Waleed**
The club's facilities include 14 snooker tables, 13 pool
tables, two private snooker rooms and one private
pool room. Table charges are Dhs.20 per hour and
membership is not required.

# Softball

## Dubai Softball League
Metropolitan Downtown Burj Dubai **050 651 4970**
www.dubaisoftball.com
Map **2 D5** Metro **Business Bay**
Over 16s can join one of over 20 teams in three
leagues (two men's, one mixed) and take part in the
Middle East Softball Championships in April. The
season runs from September to December and from
January to May.

## Duplays
**050 257 7359**
www.duplays.com
Duplays runs a mixed recreational softball league on
Wednesdays. Matches are held at the sports field next
to the Metropolitan Hotel on Sheikh Zayed Road.

# Squash

## Dubai Squash League
Various Locations **050 688 7421**
www.dubaisquash.org
The league has been active in Dubai and Sharjah
since the 1970s and is run by the UAE Squash Rackets
Association. Around 250 competitors in 25 teams play
three 10 week seasons. Teams meet on Mondays at
19:30 and each team fields four players.

# Surfing
Dubai isn't well-known as a surfing destination
but if you're looking to catch some waves, you'll
find an enthusiastic community of surfers who are
out whenever there's a swell. You can sign up for
Swell Alerts through Surfing Dubai (below). Dubai
Municipality has periodically cracked down on surfing
at public beaches in the past – check with Surfing
Dubai for the latest before paddling out. Sunset Beach
(Umm Suqueim open beach) has smallish but decent
waves as does the Sheraton Beach between the Hilton
and Sheraton in Dubai Marina.
 Surfing season in Dubai is between October and
April, with the peak months being December to
February; surfers also head to the south of Oman
for the bigger waves between May and August.
The largest wave recorded in Dubai is 3.5m and the

A discovery lesson is all it takes to find how easy it can be.

Skiing, snowboarding and snowscoot lessons available at Ski Dubai.
Open everyday. To register, call 04 409 4129. Visit www.skidxb.com

SKI DUBAI سكي دبي

*an unforgettable snow experience*

# Swimming

average surf is between 0.5 and 1m in peak season. Manageable waves and year-round warm water makes Dubai a perfect location for beginners.

Equipment can be bought at Surf Shop Dubai (04 422 1232).

## Surfing Dubai

**Sunset Beach** Umm Suqeim
**050 504 3020**
www.surfingdubai.com
Map **1 T3** Metro **Mall of the Emirates**

Dubai's only surf school offers group lessons for beginner and intermediate surfers from Dhs.200, with board rental from Dhs.50 per hour. It also organises surfing packaged holidays to Sri Lanka, Bali, Japan, Morocco and the Philippines. The school's website is a useful resource – the weekly surf timetable shows when swells are predicted for Dubai's unreliable surf so that you can be sure you're there when the good waves come.

## Swimming

Dubai has some great swimming spots, whether it's at a public beach, a private pool, a beach club or one of the beach parks. The water temperature rarely dips below 20° to 30° in winter and during the summer it can feel like stepping into a bath. As with sea swimming elsewhere, rip tides and undertows can catch out even the strongest swimmer, so never ignore flags or signs ordering you not to swim. You might also run into jellyfish towards the end of the summer. Around the UAE there are occasional outbreaks of red tide, a naturally occurring algal bloom which turns the water red and gives it an unpleasant smell – but these are relatively uncommon in Dubai. Many hotels and clubs have swimming pools that are open for public use for a day entrance fee.

Lessons are widely available from health and beach clubs. For children's lessons, check with your school whether they offer any extra-curricular swimming coaching.

For keen swimmers you can sign up for the Wild Wadi Swim Around the Burj annual challenge (held in November), see www.swimburjalarab.com to register. The distance is around 1.1km and swimmers are given support from beach spectators.

## Active Sports Academy

**050 559 7055**
www.activeuae.com

Classes, held in various locations around Dubai, include water babies, parent and toddlers, and lessons for beginner to advanced swimmers.

## Arabian Gulf Swimming Academy

**Jumeirah English Speaking School,** Jumeira,
**050 420 3098**
www.agsadubai.com
Map **2 C4** Metro **Business Bay**

The academy offers swimming training for 3-18 year olds at Dubai College, Jumeirah English Speaking School, American School of Dubai and Dubai Mens' College. All levels of training are available up to competitive levels. Beginners' 12 week swimming programmes start from Dhs.600. For more details and registration, contact Ms Jane Barrell on the number above between 08:00 and 15:00, Sunday-Thursday.

## Australian International Swim Schools

**Various Locations, 04 372 1220**
www.aiswimschools.com

AUSTSWIM certified instructors provide swimming lessons at a number of pools around Dubai. This company also runs many of the schools' swimming

## Table Tennis

Table tennis can be played for Dhs.20 per hour, including equipment, at Insportz just behind Dubai Garden Centre, Sheikh Zayed Road; booking is required. Several of the older leisure clubs provide table tennis, although the equipment is usually a bit rusty. The UAE Table Tennis Association is based in Dubai (04 266 9362), and can provide some information on how to get into leagues and high level competitions, but unfortunately most of the local clubs only accept UAE Nationals.

## Tennis

Dubai is firmly established on the international tennis circuit, with the annual Dubai Tennis Championships attracting the best players in the world (p.26). There are plenty of venues around the city to enjoy a game. Outdoor courts are available at most health and beach clubs, many of which are floodlit. There are also indoor courts for hire at InSportz (04 347 5833).

programmes. Swim training is provided at all levels from parent and baby classes to adult triathlon squads.

### Baby Splash Dubai
Hayya, The Lakes Club, Emirates Hills
www.babysplashdubai.com
Map **1 M5** Metro **Nakheel**
Since 2003, Baby Splash has been giving parent and baby swimming lessons. Classes are held at the Hayya clubs in The Lakes and The Meadows, and at Dubai Ladies Club.

### Desert Swim Club
050 396 5747
www.desertsportservices.com
This club's programme is divided into four stages of learning from beginners to competitive squads. Training is held at Kings' Dubai and English College Primary School.

### Excel Sports
Various Locations **050 748 5631**
www.excelsportsuae.com
Excel sports offer coaching in swimming, cricket, soccer and gymnastics.

### Speedo Swim Squads
04 394 4898
www.speedodubai.net
This private swimming club offers tuition in swimming for all ages and abilities, from duckling to squad training. It teaches the British Amateur Swimming Association programmes. It also offers ASA teacher training and water polo classes. Lessons take place at a number of locations including Horizon School, Uptown High School, Dubai International Academy and Emirates International School.

### The Atlantis Tennis Academy > p.ii-iii
Atlantis The Palm Palm Jumeirah **04 426 1433**
www.atlantisthepalm.com
Map **2 A3** Metro **Nakheel**
This academy provides world-class coaching for all levels. The state-of-the-art facilities include the latest court surfaces plus video technology for technique analysis. The academy also organises social events such as tournament afternoons.

### Clark Francis Tennis Academy
Various Locations **04 282 4540**
www.esportsdubai.com
This tennis school offers group and individual tennis coaching for children and adults. A ladies' morning is held at the Grand Hyatt on Mondays from 08:15. Cardio Tennis classes (a cross between tennis and circuit training) are every Tuesday from 18:45 at the Aviation Club. It also organizes competitive leagues in a variety of categories including junior leagues. Ball kid training (for the Dubai Tennis Championships) is also available and the service centre can have your racket restrung and returned to you in 12 hours.

### Dubai Tennis Academy
American University in Dubai Al Sufouh
04 399 4539
www.dubaitennisacademy.com
Map **1 M4** Metro **Nakheel**
This academy provides training for all levels, with internationally qualified coaches, at American University Dubai, Dubai Men's College and Atlantis. The adult and junior programmes include private lessons, group clinics, competitions, ladies' tennis mornings and school holiday camps. Personal progress reports and video analysis also available.

# Triathlon

### Emirates Golf Club
Int 5, Shk Zayed Rd Emirates Hills **04 380 2222**
www.dubaigolf.com
Map **1 M4** Metro **Nakheel**
Open to non-members for coaching at all skill levels. The centre has four courts and coaching is provided by qualified USPTR professionals. The academy has two teams in the ladies' Spinney's League and one in the men's Prince League.

## Triathlon

### Dubai Triathlon Club
Various Locations **050 774 6581**
www.dubaitriclub.net
During the winter season (October to April), the club organises the Dubai Triathlon Series that comprises three or four triathlons, aquathons or duathlons.

## Ultimate Frisbee
Duplays (www.duplays.com) organises a friendly non-competitive league which you can enter as a team or individual and be placed in a team. Games are played on Monday nights on the games field next to the Metropolitan Hotel on Sheikh Zayed Road. Pickup games are held in Safa Park on Saturday afternoons.

## Volleyball

### EK Volleyball
050 358 1603
www.ekvolleyballclub.com
This club organises various events around Dubai including community pickup nights, indoor and beach volleyball. Prices vary but a two-hour community game starts from Dhs.25. Contact Marlon Kustec for more info.

# Watersports
Most beach hotels in Dubai offer watersports. Activities are often discounted to hotel guests and beach club members but day visitors may have to pay an extra fee to access the beach. Waterskiing, windsurfing, jet skiing, laser sailing, kayaking and wakeboarding are all available.

For more info on canoeing and kayaking, see p.311; for surfing, see p.338; for diving, see p.316 and for kitesurfing, see p.328.

---

## Dream Experiences

Want to try wadi bashing? Longing for Liwa? Dying to drive a Ferrari? Or promised someone special some pampering? Whatever you've got on your wishlist Dreamdays can make it come true with its gift experiences. Find out more at www.dreamdays.ae.

---

### Club Joumana > p.455
**Jebel Ali Htl** Jebel Ali **04 814 5555**
www.jebelali-international.com
Watersports including windsurfing, waterskiing, kayaking, catamaran and laser sailing, and banana boat rides are available from Club Joumana at Jebel Ali Golf Resort & Spa. Special rates are available for guests and club members. Non-residents are charged an additional fee for access to the beach and pools.

### Dubai International Marine Club
**Mina Seyahi Dubai** Al Sufouh **04 399 5777**
www.dimc.ae
Map **1 L3** Metro **Dubai Marina**
DIMC is the home of Mina Seyahi Watersports Club. Kayaks, surfskis, lasers, catamarans, wakeboards, jetskis and kneeboards are available to hire.

### Dubai Surfski & Kayak Club
**Near Dubai Offshore Sailing Club** Jumeira
050 640 6087
www.dskc.net
Map **1 U3** Metro **Al Quoz**
The club has a paddling school that offers training for surfski or kayak beginners, and individual coaching for

---

## Go West

Al Gharbia Watersports Festival is on 2-10 April 2010, on Mirfa Beach in Abu Dhabi's western region. It's a calendar highlight for watersports fans and last year's event included competitive kite board, surfski kayak and wakeboard events, and a sports photography competition. For more details, see www.algharbiafestivals.com/watersports.

---

Activities & Hobbies

## Club Stretch

**Beh Capitol Hotel** Al Satwa **04 345 2131**
www.clubstretch.ae
Map **2 J3** Metro **Al Jafiliya**
Club Stretch is the only studio in Dubai that offers
Bikram yoga, which is practiced in a hot room to aid
muscle warming and stretching. Pilates is also offered.
An unlimited 10 day introduction pass costs Dhs.100.

## Exhale Fitness Studio

**Jumeirah Beach Residence 04 424 3777**
www.exhaledubai.com
Map **1 K4** Metro **Dubai Marina**
This ladies-only fitness centre offers classes in
Vinyasa, Ashtanga and Power yoga, as well as yoga for
pregnant women and those who want to slim down.
The cost per session is Dhs.70, with packages of ten
costing Dhs.650 and valid for two months. One and
three month memberships are available.

advanced paddlers. The club runs activities including
the 10km DSKC Squall which takes place on the last
Friday of every month at Mina Seyahi.

## Gems Of Yoga

**White Crown Bld** Trade Centre 1 **04 331 5161**
www.gemsofyogadubai.com
Map **2 H4** Metro **Trade Centre**
Classes in Hatha, Ashtanga and Power yoga are offered
as well as classes just for ladies, children and elderly
adults. Prices vary according to which type of class
you pick but you can expect to pay around Dhs.500
for ten classes, or Dhs.950 for 20 classes. For the yoga
devotees there are also intensive half-day classes on
Fridays (10:00 to 15:00 and 15:00 to 20:00) for Dhs.500
per person.

## Sky & Sea Adventures

**Hilton Jumeirah Dubai,** Dubai Marina, **04 399 9005**
www.watersportsdubai.com
Map **1 K3** Metro **Jumeirah Lakes Towers**
This watersports company offers body boarding,
kayaking, waterskiing, snorkelling, parasailing,
windsurfing and wakeboarding. It also offers courses
in waterskiing, sailing and windsurfing. Rentals can be
hired from the Hilton Dubai Jumeirah (p.234) and the
Sheraton Jumeirah Beach (p.238).

## Hayya!

**Al Manzil Club, beh Al Manzil Hotel**
Downtown Burj Dubai **04 367 3282**
www.hayya.ae
Map **2 F6** Metro **Burj Dubai**
Great for those new to yoga Hayya runs Hatha classes
at the Hayya Club in Old Town on at 09:00 and 19:30
on Tuesdays and Thursdays. They also have Power
Yoga at 18:30 on Thursdays. Prices start at Dhs.45
for non members. Other locations for yoga are The
Meadows and Lakes branches.

## Yoga

Yoga is a low-impact (but deceptively challenging)
form of holistic exercise which has been practiced in
the eastern world for centuries. Yoga involves holding
sequences of poses, or 'asanas' that combined with
breathing exercises gently but powerfully help your
body to become stronger and more flexible, as well
as improving your mental wellbeing. Many health
and fitness clubs offer yoga as part of their weekly
schedule, catering to all levels of experience (see
Gyms & Fitness Clubs, p.207) as do some alternative
therapy centres (p.198).

## Zen Yoga

Various Locations **04 367 0435**
www.yoga.ae
Yoga and Pilates specialists Zen Yoga has four modern
centres featuring mirrored walls to help you check
you're getting the right posture, and they run classes
throughout the day. A one month unlimited trial for
yoga costs Dhs.700 and regular classes are Dhs.75.
The studios are located in Emirates Hills (04 422 4643),
Dubai Media City (04 367 0435), Jumeirah Town Centre
(04 349 2933) and The Village Mall, (04 344 6551).

## Artistic Yoga

Various Locations **04 398 1351**
www.artisticyoga.com
Bharat Thakur's school of yoga offers the latest twist
in this flexible form of inner and outer exercise which
combines ancient yogic techniques with modern
cardiovascular training. Morning and evening classes,
from Dhs.65, are held at Angsana Spa, Body & Soul Spa
Al Ghusais and Al Hana Centre.

# Walk This Way

There are plenty of great places in Dubai to stretch your legs if you're feeling cooped up indoors...

## Jumeirah Beach Residence

The largest single-phase residential development in the world has turned from a building site into a pleasant community. Boasting big name shops like Saks Fifth Avenue, Boutique 1 and Gallery One, an evening stroll could quickly turn into a shopping spree. The shorefront development covers 1.7km and there are also fountains, grassy areas and benches should you need a rest. See p.246

## Down By The Creek

From the embassy area stroll along the creek, taking photos of the much-loved NBD building opposite. From here walk towards the Majlis Gallery (p.244) and XVA Gallery (p.245) and stop for a much needed juice. Keep going passed the Dubai Museum (p.240), through the textile souk (p.397) and down towards the creek. Take an abra across the creek and you will find yourself at the entrance to the spice souk (p.397). You can then wander through the packed streets of Deira towards the gold souk (p.396).

## Safa Park

This huge park is a great place to exercise and escape the hustle. Tuesday is ladies' day, but there is also a permanent ladies' garden within the park. Entry costs Dhs.3 (free for children under 3 years old). There's a great 3km spongy running track around the park's perimeter, not to mention the countless paths that criss-cross the grassy space. See p.248.

## Ernie Els Club

If you're going to ruin a good walk, do it in style at the Ernie Els golf course. Located in Sports City, it is difficult with challenging putting surfaces, but visually sumptuous and full of mystery. Stretching over 7,538 yards, it features natural dunes and plants native to the UAE.

## Creekside Park

It may be in the heart of the city but Creekside Park (p.246) is a welcome slice of green with expansive gardens, fishing piers, jogging tracks, barbecue sites, children's play areas, restaurants and kiosks. From Gate Two, four-wheel cycles can be hired for Dhs.20 per hour. Admission costs Dhs.5.

## Jumeira Open Beach Running Track

An early morning walk on the beach got easier (and less sandy) when the 1.5km track on Jumeira Open Beach opened. With running and cycling lanes, distance markers and regular maintenance it is a fun and free way to get active while enjoying some people watching and sunshine. The track starts near Dubai Marine Resort and is open 24 hours.

**Downtown Burj Dubai**

Wander wide promenades, linger by the lake or get lost in the narrow passageways of Old Town; Dubai's newest residential community was designed for getting around on foot. With cafes, restaurants and coffee shops at every turn, there are plenty of pit-stop possibilities. See p.226.

## Creekside Souks

Explore the city streets on foot near the creek and you'll get a good workout while witnessing a Dubai far from the sterile malls. Hidden alleyways, secret shops and tiny cafes abound so get your bearings and take a tour. Fridays are the quietest, as are the early afternoons when stores often close for a break.

## Mirdif

Mirdif as a residential area is good for walking and is home to two community parks. Both have sprung walking tracks around their perimeter – perfect for wannabe yummy mummies; provided your kids are old enough to tackle the climbing frames on their own, you can walk a few laps, keeping them in sight the whole time. Uptown Mirdif Shopping Centre also makes a nice outdoor stroll – although you might spend more time shopping and eating than walking. See p.90

## Mall Walkers

Indulge in some (speedy) window shopping at Mall of the Emirates (before the crowds descend) with Mall Walkers. Simply register at the customer service desk on the ground floor near parking area A and turn up at first level, car park entrance A-F at 08:30 on a Saturday, Monday or Wednesday morning wearing proper running or walking shoes. See p.397.

# Friday Brunch at Saffron

With an impressive Friday Brunch and a vibrant atmosphere Saffron is the perfect place to socialise anytime of year. With over 20 chefs at special theatrical cooking stations bringing you zesty Asian flavours.

Friday Saffron Brunch: 1:00pm – 3:30pm

For restaurant reservations please call +971 4 426 2626
or email restaurantreservations@atlantisthepalm.com

ATLANTIS

# Shopping

# SHOPPING

The variety of shops on offer in Dubai is impressive and the contribution retail makes to the emirates' economy is not underestimated. The Dubai Shopping Festival, a month dedicated to consumerism, takes place annually with sweeping discounts, entertainment and promotions (although sales seem to happen all year round). Dubai's development is inextricably linked to shopping, and with each new development comes a new mall.

The city's shopping highlights include markets, boutiques, a few thrift stores and a plethora of designer names. Shopping revolves around the malls, both big and small (see p.397), but the expanding numbers of independent stores (see p.393) though harder to find, are invariably more original than anything the malls have to offer.

While shopping is definitely part of the tourism strategy in Dubai, you'll find that the focus is on offering a fantastic range of produce rather than offering surprisingly low prices. There are bargains to be had, particularly if you hold out for the sales, but fashion items are often more expensive than they are in other countries.

Practicality plays a large part in the mall culture, and during the hotter months they are oases of cool in the sweltering city – somewhere to walk, shop, eat and be entertained. From the smaller community malls, to the mega malls that have changed the skyline, shopping opportunities abound and most shops are open until 22:00 every night and even later at the weekends. The malls are particularly busy at the weekends, especially on Friday evenings. The various shopping areas, the closest that Dubai has to high streets, are great for their eclectic mix of shops.

Like many countries, the cost of living is increasing and while some of what is available is still cheaper than elsewhere, groceries seem to be more expensive every week. While average prices for most items are comparable, there are not many places that can beat Dubai's range and frequency of the sales. Cars are, on the whole, a good buy and petrol, though prices are rising, is still cheap enough to make large 4WDs practical for the school run.

Electronics can be cheaper but it depends what you are used to; and Dubai is the world's leading re-exporter of gold. The variety of goods on sale in the city means there is very little that is not available. For most items there is enough choice to fit any budget, from the streets of Karama with its fake designer goods, to the shops in the malls that sell the real thing.

One of the few retail sectors where Dubai is lacking is second-hand shops (see Second-Hand Items on p.383), although there are a few linked to various charities. With the population still being largely transitory, there is no shortage of second-hand goods, many of which are advertised on the notice boards in supermarkets, in the classified section of newspapers, and on websites (such as www.expatwoman.com).

Further afield, Sharjah's modern malls offer a similar selection of brands and they are convenient for those living on that side of the city. Sharjah's souks, the Al Arsah Souk (p.396) in particular, are more traditional than those in Dubai and are great for unique gifts. Sharjah is also renowned for its furniture warehouses, especially those selling Indian pieces, such as Lucky's, Pinky's and Khan's. Ajman is developing as the population grows, and has its own City Centre and an area with garment factories and their outlet shops. The traffic to both emirates can be heavy and they are more traditional, with many companies still working split shifts i.e. closing between 13:00 and 16:00.

## Online Shopping

The range of products you can find online, and perhaps the discounted prices, make online shopping more appealing, particularly for items you can't find locally. However, not all companies will ship to the UAE and if they do, the shipping charges can be prohibitive.

## Quick Reference

## Store Finder

The following pages detail key information about shopping in Dubai's shopping areas (p.386), malls (p.397) and souks (p.395). Use the Store Finder on p.414 to locate various stores; for the low-down on Dubai's most popular malls, including listings of their various outlets, see p.397.

The use of PayPal can often cause problems as the facility is only available to those with a US or UK credit card, but vendors on sites like eBay may be flexible if you explain the situation. Many sites will accept other forms of payment. Sites like Amazon should provide little difficulty, although its branded packaging may sometimes be opened at customs. Companies without representation in the region will sometimes agree to sell directly to individual customers, so it is worth sending them an email.

Online shopping in Dubai is still in its infancy and unlike in other countries, you won't find a huge catalogue of online fashion stores and you can't do your grocery shopping online.

Salt Street (www.saltstreet.com) is an online fashion store selling a variety of labels – it also offers free delivery in the UAE. Hellwafashion (hellwafashion. com) is an online resource providing information on the clothes on offer in Dubai's independent stores (p.393) and designer boutiques.

Jacky's Electronics (www.jackys.com) has a fairly comprehensive site with good online deals; Magrudy's website (www.magrudy.com) allows for both buying and reserving books; www.uaemall. com is a site which sells items from a number of companies. There are also sites based here that will arrange for gifts to be delivered both here and internationally, for example, www.giftexpressdubai. com, or www.papagiftexpress.com, which deals with India, Sri Lanka and the UAE. For books detailing the best off-road routes in the UAE or Oman or a guide to weekend breaks in the region, visit the online store at www.liveworkexplore.com.

Second-hand items can be bought through sites such as www.dubizzle.com, www.expatgossip.com, www.expatwoman.com, www.souk.ae, www.souq. com and www.websouq.com.

Aramex (see also Shipping p.349) provide a 'Shop & Ship' service which sets up a mailbox in both the UK and US, great for dealing with sites which do not offer international shipping. Borderlinx (www.borderlinx. com) also provides a similar service for stores that will only ship to the USA. Aramex also offers a Web Surfer card, a prepaid MasterCard for use online – this can be set up through the mailboxes and is a solution to PayPal problems.

## Refunds, Exchanges & Consumer Rights

The policies on refunds and exchanges vary from shop to shop. There is more chance of success with faulty goods rather than if you have simply changed your mind, and it is more common to be offered an exchange or credit note rather than a refund. Even with tags attached, many stores will not even consider an exchange unless you have the receipt. For some items, such as those in sealed packages, shops insist that the packaging should be intact so that the item can be resold. This is ok if the item was unwanted however it has been known for claims for faulty goods to be rejected as the packaging has been damaged but how could you know if it was faulty if you hadn't opened it?

If you are having no success with customer services, ask to speak to the manager, as the person on the shop floor is often not authorised to deviate from standard policy whereas managers may be more flexible.

## Shop On The Hop

The website www.quickdubai.com is a great online shopping resource that delivers food and items for the home to any Dubai address within 24 hours. You can even send a gift to someone in Dubai from anywhere in the world. If you need your shopping in a hurry, www.brownbag.ae offers a selection of goods ranging from pet food to iPods, and aims to deliver to any Dubai address within one hour. If you're thirsty, www.bebida.ae delivers a variety of soft drinks to your door.

The Consumer Protection Department of the UAE Ministry of Economy has been established to safeguard the interests of shoppers. The department tracks and regulates retail prices and has rejected planned price increases for staple goods. Consumers wishing to complain about a retailer can complete a form on the website www.economy.ae, send an email to consumer@economy.ae, or call the freephone hotline on 600 522225. The hotline is manned by non-English speakers so it may be best to stick to the other methods. In Dubai, the Consumer Rights Unit within the Dubai Economic Department (700 4000, www.dubaided.gov.ae), primarily deals with unfit food, but can be contacted to report faulty goods or to complain if a guarantee is not honoured.

## Shipping

Due to the number of international and local shipping and courier agencies, it is possible to transport just about anything. Both air freight and sea freight are available; air freight is faster and you can track the items, but it's more expensive and not really suitable for large or heavy objects. Sea freight takes several weeks to arrive but it is cheaper and you can rent large containers for larger items. It is worth getting a few quotes and finding out what will happen when the goods arrive; some offer no services at the destination while others, usually the bigger ones, will clear customs and deliver right to the door. Check for discounts during the Dubai Shopping Festival (p.25) or Dubai Summer Surprises (p.25). Empost (04 286 5000), the Emirates Postal Service, offer both local and international courier and air freight services – its prices are competitive and packages can be tracked.

Several courier companies can arrange for items to be delivered to Dubai, and Aramex (04 286 5050) offers a great service called 'Shop & Ship', for those wishing to buy online. If a site doesn't offer international delivery or their postage rates are high, for a one-off payment of $35, Aramex will set up a mailbox for you in both the UK and the US. The company will then arrange deliveries up to three times a week and packages can be tracked; rates for the first half kilo are Dhs.39 and Dhs.30 for additional half kilos.

## How To Pay

You'll have few problems parting with your money. Credit cards (American Express, Diners Club, MasterCard and Visa) and debit cards (Visa Electron) are accepted in shopping malls, supermarkets, and many independent shops. However, you can only pay with cash at petrol stations, for petrol or in the shops. You are never too far from an ATM in the city and it is preferable to pay with cash in souks and smaller shops – try to have a variety of denominations, because it is better to hand over close to the exact amount. US dollars and other foreign currencies are accepted in some larger shops (and in airport duty free).

DIFC Gate Village

## Bargaining

Bargaining is still common practice in the souks and shopping areas of the UAE; you'll need to give it a go to get the best prices. Before you take the plunge, try to get an idea of prices from a few shops, as there can often be a significant difference in prices. Once you've decided how much you are willing to spend, offer an initial bid that is roughly around half that price. Stay laidback and vaguely disinterested. When your initial offer is rejected (and it will be), keep going until you reach an agreement or until you have reached your limit. If the price isn't right, say so and walk out – the vendor will often follow and suggest a compromise price. The more you buy, the better the discount. When the price is agreed, it is considered bad form to back out of the sale.

### Buyer Beware

Traps for the unwary shopper do exist in Dubai. Some of the international stores sell items at prices that are far more expensive than in their country of origin (you can even still see the original price tags). This can be as much as 30% higher – so beware.

Bargaining isn't commonly accepted in malls and independent shops. However, use your discretion, as some shops such as jewellery stores, smaller electronics stores and eyewear optical centres do operate a set discount system and the price shown may be 'before discount'. Ask whether there is a discount on the marked price and you may bag a bargain.

## Sending Gifts Home

Sending gifts to your friends and family back home shouldn't be too taxing as there are several online stores that offer international delivery services. For cards and flowers, www.moonpig.com is a great online store where you can customise your own cards by uploading photos and have them sent to a variety of locations. Interflora (www.interflora.com) also delivers a selection of gifts internationally and can often accommodate same day or next day delivery.

## Shoes & Clothing Sizes

Figuring out your size isn't rocket science, just a bit of a pain. Firstly, check the label – international sizes are often printed on them. Secondly, check the store – they will often have a conversion chart on display. Otherwise, a UK size is always two higher than a US size (so a UK 10 is a US 6). To convert European sizes into US sizes, subtract 32 (so a European 38 is actually a US 6). To convert European sizes into UK sizes, a 38 is roughly a 10. As for shoes, a woman's UK 6 is a European 39 or US 8.5 and a men's UK 10 is a European 44 or a US 10.5. If in doubt, ask for help.

AMOUAGE

THE GIFT OF KINGS

EPIC

LEGENDS OF THE SILK ROAD ON WWW.AMOUAGE.COM

# Top 10 Things That Are Cheaper In Dubai

## Eating Out

Enjoying a three-course dinner and a few rounds of drinks in a fine-dining restaurant will probably cost more-or-less the same as in other cities, but cheap, street-side dining is one of Dubai's great bargains. Whether you snack on a Dhs.3 chicken shawarma at Al Mallah in Satwa, or feast on a Dhs.9 Thali lunch (refillable pots of yummy vegetarian curry) from Karama's Saravanna Bhavan, it's hard to find such delicious, authentic food at a cheaper price.

## Home Help

Having a cleaner come in a few times a week to hoover and dust would be an unaffordable luxury for most people living in the UK, but here in Dubai it is as normal as eating breakfast in the morning. For as little as Dhs.20 per hour, you can get a maid service in to do all the stuff you're too busy – or too lazy – to do. Frazzled parents can also rejoice at the bargain babysitters' rates available in Dubai. Call Molly Maid (04 398 8877) or Ready Maids (04 294 8345) for more info (also see p.106).

## Personal Grooming

Having pretty hands and feet comes cheap in Dubai, where there is seemingly a nail salon on every street corner, and you'll pay as little as Dhs.70 for a manicure and pedicure. Even the boys aren't left out: gents can enjoy a shampoo, a hot oil treatment, a haircut, a shave and a head massage all for around Dhs.40 at your typical Karama-based men's salon.

## Cigarettes

That Dhs.7 pack of Marlboro Lights would set you back the equivalent of over Dhs.30 in the UK, Dhs.15 in the USA, and Dhs.25 in Australia. It's good news for visiting relatives, who always want to take back a few sneaky cartons, and bad news for smokers, who have little financial incentive to quit here; but at least you don't have to charge your friends 50p every time they cadge a smoke off you.

## Taxis

In many of our home countries, a night on the tiles would involve an elaborate plan to recruit a designated driver, or a lengthy wait in a queue for a taxi. Here in Dubai, walking out of a restaurant or club to find a line of cabs ready and waiting to take you home, at a very reasonable price, never gets old. And just when you thought it couldn't get any cheaper, as of December last year, you don't even have to pay Salik charges in taxis. Bargain.

## Soft Drinks

Seemingly, since the beginning of time, a can of Coke or Pepsi has cost just one little dirham when you buy it from a cornershop, a petrol station or a supermarket. The price per can is even cheaper when you buy your favourite fizzy drink by the case. Unfortunately, this bargain price doesn't always survive the transition to restaurant menus, where that Dhs.1 can of pop can set you back a shocking Dhs.15 or more. That's quite a mark-up.

## Petrol

Filling up your car here is cheaper than in many other countries, and often significantly so. For a gallon of petrol you'll pay Dhs.6.25 at a Dubai pump, but the same would cost you the equivalent of around Dhs.10 in South Africa, Dhs.17 in the UK, Dhs.8 in America, Dhs.11.50 in Australia, Dhs.10.50 in Canada, Dhs.14 in India, and a whopping Dhs.19 in parts of Europe.

## Cinema Tickets

You'll pay between Dhs.30 and Dhs.40 for a cinema ticket in Dubai (Dhs.40 is usually for a 3D performance). A ticket will set you back around Dhs.50 in London, Dhs.45 in New York, Dhs.45 in Dublin and Dhs.67 in Tokyo. The downside is that here in Dubai, there are no concessions if you are a child, a student or a pensioner, and the ticket price is the same, no matter what time of day it is (whereas in other cities, morning and matinee shows are cheaper).

## Tailoring

Having a tailor whip up a made-to-measure piece of clothing is prohibitively expensive in cities such as London, where a simple shift dress could cost you as much as Dhs.1,000 and you'll need at least Dhs.5,000 for a bespoke suit. In Dubai, however, there are tailors who can whip up a long dress for around Dhs.100, a blouse for Dhs.50, and a suit starting from as little as Dhs.1,600.

## Trips To Oman

It's fast becoming one of the most popular Middle Eastern destinations for tourists from Europe, and it's not hard to understand why: Oman is a breathtaking country combining scenery, culture and luxury hotels. And it's just a four-hour drive to Muscat from Dubai, so you can visit without forking out high prices for a plane ticket. Regional visitors often get good rates on hotels too. For more information see Out Of The City, p.274.

**Shopping**

## Specialist Sizes

Clothing sizes in Dubai's stores usually range from a UK 8 to 16; however there are an increasing number of shops are offering plus-size and petite clothing. Petite ranges are available in many stores including Debenhams (p.390), Splash and Marks & Spencer, (p.391) while H&M, New Look, Wallis, Bhs, Debenhams (p.390), Liz Claiborne, Marks & Spencer, Splash and Woolworths all carry plus-size collections (look out for Evans in Debenhams and Scarlett's in Splash). For more exclusive lines for the fuller figure, try Oui (04 324 2167) or Charisma (04 324 0200) in the Beach Centre in Jumeira.

Men looking for larger sizes should head to Big & Tall (04 397 3873) on Bank Street and Jumeirah Beach Residence (04 438 9529) which caters for waist sizes from 40 plus and shirts up to 6XL.

## Laundry & Drycleaning

There are no self service laundrettes, but laundries are everywhere in the city. As well as dry cleaning and laundry, they also offer an ironing service. The standard of service is usually exceptional and you can often opt to pick up your clothes or have them delivered straight to your door. Compensation polices for lost or damaged items vary, but losses are rare, even in the places that look most disorganised. Large chains normally have a free delivery service. The prices for laundry are reasonable. Expect to pay Dhs.8 for a shirt, Dhs.25 for a suit and Dhs.35 for a quilt.

## Repairs & Cobbling

Dubai's multitude of tailors will repair or alter garments for a reasonable price, but there are fewer companies who mend shoes. Locksmiths in the city often offer the service and you'll find stores in Satwa and Kuwaiti Street in Karama. Minutes (p.421) offers shoe repairs in addition to its key cutting service and it has outlets located in many of the main malls. 60 Second Lock & Shoe Repair (04 355 2600) is located inside Spinneys (p.392) in Bur Dubai and Al Fareed Shoes (04 359 286) is located on Musalla Road.

## Tailoring & Bespoke Services

The best way to select one of Dubai's many tailors is by recommendation. They can be found in most areas, but there is a concentration of stores around the Dubai Museum in Bur Dubai and on the main street in Satwa. A good tailor can make a garment from scratch (rather than just make alterations), either from a photo or diagram or by copying an existing garment. They will also make alterations if the item isn't spot on.

Dream Girl Tailors (04 335 2582), in Meena Bazaar and Satwa, are popular and will take on all tailoring jobs from taking up trousers to making ball gowns. Skirts cost around Dhs.50 and dresses from around Dhs.80, depending on how basic the pattern is. For those living near Deira, Khamis Abdullah Trading & Embroidery (04 225 5940), in Rashidiya, is one of the least expensive in town, with skirts starting from around Dhs.30.

Dream Boy (04 352 1840), near the museum, is good for shirts and suits, as are Kachins (04 352 1386) and Whistle & Flute (04 342 9229); shirts usually start from Dhs.30 and suits from around Dhs.500. Stitches has stores in Jumeirah Beach Residence, Murjan 6, Plaza Level (04 437 0113), The Village Mall (04 342 1476) and in Jumeira (04 348 6110).

# WHAT & WHERE TO BUY

With so much choice there should be little problem finding what you need. From antiques to the latest technology, and from tools to toys, the aim of this section is to let you know what's out there and the best places to buy.

## Alcohol

It is legal for anyone over the age of 21 to buy alcohol in Dubai's restaurants and licensed bars, and some clubs, for consumption on the premises. This does not apply to all the emirates. If you wish to drink at home you will need a liquor licence (see p.42 for more information); how much you are permitted to buy is dependent on your monthly salary.

Two companies operate liquor stores in Dubai: African & Eastern (A&E) and Maritime & Mercantile International (MMI). Both have branches in several locations around the city, the most handy being the ones near supermarkets. The selection is decent, and prices are not so bad: wine costs from around Dhs.20 and upwards; vodka from Dhs.60; whisky from Dhs.80; and beer from Dhs.4 to Dhs.8 per can or Dhs.100 to Dhs.135 per case. Alcohol is, however, subject to 30% tax on top of the marked prices and, although this is not included in your allowance, it can be a bit of a shock at the till.

There is a good selection of alcohol (and several other products including perfume, confectionary and cosmetics) available at the airport Duty Free. The alcohol available at the airport is similar in price to the shops in town, but you don't pay the tax.

There are a number of 'hole in the wall' stores close to Dubai that sell duty-free alcohol to members of the public, even if you don't have a licence. Prices are reasonable and there is no tax. You can pick up a cheap bottle of wine from around Dhs.20, and most international brands of beer, wine and spirits are available. Certain brands are offered exclusively in certain stores, so it is worth comparing what's on offer, if you are looking for something different.

# Dubaı Duty Free

# WIN $2,000,000

## LIVE A NEW LIFE

# DOUBLE
## *Millionaire*

The World's No. 1 Duty Free brings you the opportunity to win US $2 million.
Simply purchase a Dhs 2000 (approx. US $550) ticket in the Dubai Duty Free Double Millionaire promotion.
Only 5000 tickets are available.
Visit dubaidutyfree.com for more details.

 Full of surprises.

You don't need to worry about being busted buying booze illegally, but you should be careful when driving home, because it is the transporting of alcohol that could get you into trouble, especially if you are stopped within the borders of Sharjah emirate. There have been reports of random police checks on vehicles driving from Ajman into Sharjah. Also, if you have an accident and you're found to have a boot full of liquor, your day could take a sudden turn for the worse.

## African & Eastern (A&E)

**Al Wasl Rd** Umm Suqeim **04 394 2676**
www.africanandeastern.com
Map **2 B4** Metro **Al Qouz**

Conveniently located in shopping areas and stocking a wide variety of products, A&E outlets remain a good place to purchase wine, spirits and beer. Its stores sell the typical brands and a few imports of Japanese and German beer. It is also worth checking out its regular promotions as a particular brand of beer or wine is selected each month for a tax-free promotion. For other locations see the Store Finder p.414.

## Al Hamra Cellar

Ras Al Khaimah **07 244 7403**
www.mmidubai.com

MMI-owned Al Hamra Cellar is around an hour's drive from Dubai along the Emirates Road. The store stocks an amazing selection of beers, spirits and award-winning wines from around the world – it also has properly chilled storage facilities and wine specially selected by guru Oz Clarke.

## Barracuda Beach Resort

**Nr Dreamland Aqua Park** Umm Al Quwain
**06 768 1555**
www.barracuda.ae

A tax-free, licence-free outlet that is popular with Dubai's residents. The store has recently undergone some renovation and the new building houses a bigger variety of stock. There is a superb selection, including the regular brands of beer, wine and spirits.

## Centaurus International RAK

Ras Al Khaimah **07 244 5866**
www.centaurusint.biz

This is another 'hole in the wall' outlet which offers a good range of products. You can view its range of a wine, beer and spirits on its online shop and it also offers a delivery service.

## Maritime & Mercantile International

**Nxt to Spinneys** Bur Dubai **04 352 3091**
www.mmidubai.com
Map **2 L4** Metro **Khalid Bin Al Waleed**

Similar to A&E, this store offers a broad selection of international brands and lesser known names. To

get the best value for money, select from its bin end discounts on wine which select new or lesser known brands for promotion. Its more exclusive store Le Clos in Emirates Terminal 3 offers a premium selection of alcohol that can only be pre-ordered on departure and collected on arrival at the terminal see the website (www.leclos.net) for more details or call (04 220 3633). For other locations see the Store Finder, p.421.

## Art

The art scene in Dubai, quiet for so long, is now enjoying rapid growth. Several of the galleries (p.241) in Dubai display traditional and contemporary art by Arabic and international artists which are also for sale.

### Arte Soukh

Artisans of the Emirates (ARTE) set up markets selling arts and crafts in Times Square Center (p.413), Aquaventure (p.248) and Dubai Festival City (p.401). Stalls sell a range of items including photography, jewellery and a variety of art. For more information, including dates, visit www.arte.ae.

Art Dubai (www.artdubai.ae) is a commercial art fair that draws together artwork from many of Dubai's galleries. The event will run from the 17-20 March in 2010 and is a great opportunity to check out the variety of art on offer in the city.

The Majlis Gallery (p.244) in Bastakiya is a great venue for fine art, handmade glass, pottery and other unusual pieces. For cutting edge art, check out the XVA Gallery (p.245) and Boutique 1 Gallery (www. boutique1.com). The Art Source in the Al Ghazal Mall in Satwa stocks a range of original artwork – it also offers a framing service. For funky, but inexpensive,

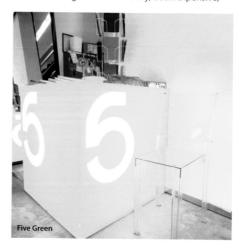

Five Green

WHETHER IT'S A PARTY WITH FRIENDS, A QUIET NIGHT IN OR A SPECIAL CELEBRATION, YOUR LOCAL A+E STORE IS HERE TO SERVE ALL YOUR WINE, BEER AND SPIRIT NEEDS.

**AL WASL RD**
NEXT TO UM SEQUIM SPINNEYS

**ARABIAN RANCHES**
AT THE COMMUNITY CENTRE

**JUMEIRAH 1**
BEACH ROAD BEHIND SPINNEYS

**BUR DUBAI**
BESIDE SPINNEYS AND THE RAMADA HOTEL

**KARAMA**
NEAR KARAMA MARKET

**MIRDIFF**
UPTOWN MIRDIFF NEXT TO SPINNEYS

**DEIRA**
OPPOSITE THE MAYFAIR HOTEL

**MARINA**
AT THE MARINA WALK

BUY ALCOHOL LEGALLY... FOR LICENCING ENQUIRIES VISIT
WWW.AFRICAN-EASTERN.NET OR DIAL 800 CHEERS

you'll find a limited selection in furniture stores like IKEA (p.371) and THE One (p.372).

Gallery One (www.g-1.com) sells a selection of stylish photographs and canvas prints and are particularly good if you want images of the region.

If your knowledge of art isn't up to speed, Police Pigalle (050 240 0521, www.policepigalle.com) offer art consultations and will help source artwork from within the UAE or abroad. You can also find information on art auctions, as well as information on art fairs and gallery openings online at www. artinthecity.com.

Souk Madinat Jumeirah has the largest concentration of boutiques selling art, glass and photographs, both originals and reproductions. The style and subjects are diverse, from traditional to modern, and Arabic to international.

### Magnificent Murals

Fiona MacKenzie has commercial experience on many Dubai hotel projects and can be commissioned to produce artwork and large scale murals for your home or commercial environment. She can also provide hand-painted pieces on printed canvasses for an original gift or to decorate your home or office. Contact Fiona on 04 341 9803 or see www.mackenzieart.com for more information.

Many of the galleries and showrooms have a framing service or can recommend one. There are some excellent framing shops on Plant Street in Satwa (p.388) and in Karama Market (p.388) – they can frame anything from prints to sports jerseys. You can also create your own piece of art by transferring your photos onto canvas. There are a few stores that offer the service including Riot Art (04 422 4166, www. riot-art.com), Captivate Art (055 999 3894, www. captivate-art.com) and Portfolio (www.portfolio-uae. com), which is located in Dubai Festival City.

## Art & Craft Supplies

A number of shops sell a good range of art and craft supplies and you should find there is enough choice, whether you need paints and crayons for children, or top quality oils. Particularly good places to find materials are Bin Sougat Mall in Rashidiya (p.410), and the Holiday Centre on Sheikh Zayed Road. Emirates Trading (04 284 4594) stocks everything from children's crayons to industrial spray booths and it is a supplier of Windsor & Newton and Daler-Rowney products. Elves & Fairies (04 344 9485) have a huge range of decorative stamps and stencils. Wasco White Star (04 342 2179) stocks craft supplies that are suitable for children's projects and difficult to find elsewhere. Prices can be expensive for some speciality

items, such as mosaic tiles, but art materials are reasonably priced. For DIY picture framing, Rafi Frame Store (04 337 6989), aka Al Warda Gallery, in Karama is the place to find the necessary equipment, including mountboard.

## Baby Items

The basic baby items are all available in Dubai and, while you may not find the range you would back home, you should find nursery essentials, like bottles, buggies, car seats, changing bags, cots, prams, rocking chairs and travel cots.

Supermarkets stock formula, nappies and wipes and many also sell bottles and feeding equipment. Choithram (p.392) has the best selection of formulas, stocking popular UK brands SMA and Cow & Gate. If you can't find an item, check with the store because some are kept behind the counter. A good range of jars of baby food are available but prices are slightly higher than what you'd pay at home. Pharmacies sell baby essentials and some have breast pumps.

The Organic Foods & Cafe (04 434 0577) in The Dubai Mall (p.402) and The Greens (04 361 7974), sells a wide selection of items including biodegradable and terry cloth nappies, wooden toys, organic baby food and children's mattresses made from organic fibre.

Toys R Us has doubled the size of its baby department and now stocks a wide range, from pushchairs to baby bottles, cots to travel accessories. The quality of the items is good and most conform to international safety standards. Britax and Maxi Cosi car seats are widely available and should fit most cars; all shops will offer to help fit car seats but the staff aren't always knowledgeable about what is most suitable. You can also rent car seats, buggies, strollers and other equipment from Rentacrib.ae – if you hire a car seat its staff will fit it for you free of charge.

### Second-Hand Stuff

Second-hand baby items are widely available in Dubai – you just need to know where to look. There are classifieds listings on www.expatwoman.com and www.expatgossip.com, and then of course there's always the supermarket noticeboards.

The range of slings on sale is pretty limited and backpacks to put your baby in are hard to find, so you may want to order these items from overseas or look online at Kid Eternity (www.kid-eternity.com), Bubs Boutique (www.bubsboutique.com) or Baby Souk (www.babysouk.com).

When it comes to clothing, there are several stores to choose from. The Dubai Mall (p.402) has a particularly good selection of well-known stores and a range high-end brands like Cacharel Paris, Burberry Children, Jacadi and Armani Junior. Online store

MANCHESTER HAS 140 DAYS OF RAIN A YEAR DUBAI HAS 6.

FOR MANY MORE REASONS TO BE CHEERFUL GET YOUR BEVERAGE LICENCE FROM MMI AND BE SHOWERED WITH REWARDS.

**VISIT OUR SHOPS AT** TRADE CENTRE RD • AL WASL • IBN BATTUTA MALL • BUR DUBAI • GREEN COMMUNITY • DEIRA
MALL OF THE EMIRATES • KARAMA • SHEIKH ZAYED ROAD • DUBAI SILICON OASIS • FESTIVAL CITY **Shop finder www.mmidubai.com**

DubaiBabies (www.dubaibabies.com) also stock a fabulous range of products for babies and parents. IKEA (p.372) has a small range of nursery furniture such as cots, changing tables and bathtubs. It also makes a selection of cot sheets and blankets and some baby-safe toys. Worth waiting for are Baby Shop's sales which they have several times a year. For more information on having a baby see p.141.

## Babyshop

**Mall of the Emirates** Al Barsha **04 341 0604**
www.babyshopstores.com
Map **1** R5 Metro **Mall of the Emirates**
Babyshop sells low-cost baby clothing and essentials; pick up feeding items, clothing, toys and even baby monitors here. It also stocks feeding pillows, safety rails and sterilisers. Its affordable newborn items come in value packs, perfect for the temporary items you can't live without, but know you won't keep. For other locations see Store Finder, p.415.

## DubaiBabies

**050 457 9698**
www.dubaibabies.com
You can shop at your leisure at this online boutique selling blankets, feeding essentials, slings and skincare products, among other items. The store also offers a good selection of gifts that are perfect for baby showers, such as cupcakes, gift baskets, balloons and books for new parents. It has also has small kiosks in Mercato Mall (p.406) and Mall of The Emirates (p.405) and offers free delivery within Dubai.

## Goodbaby

**Trade Centre Rd, Opp BurJuman** Bur Dubai
**04 397 5653**
www.goodbabydubai.com
Map **2** L4 Metro **Khalid Bin Al Waleed**
Goodbaby is a great store for key items like car seats, changing mats and a range of engaging toys for kids. You'll find a large selection of buggies too from Maclaren, Quinny and Phil & Teds. The store also stocks stair guards, walkers and cots.

## Just Kidding

**No 15, Street 26** Al Quoz 4 **800 5878**
www.justkidding-uae.com
Map **1** S7
Not for the budget conscious, but still worth a browse, Just Kidding sells a good range of baby items, furniture and clothes from Europe, including Bugaboo buggies, Little Company bags and Stokke high chairs. You'll find interesting toys for playtime and a catalogue of items that includes maternity wear, gift sets and slings. The store offers free delivery to Dubai and you can also sign up for its gift registry service for baby showers.

## Mamas & Papas

**Mercato** Jumeira **04 344 0981**
www.mamasandpapas.com
Map **2** F3 Metro **Burj Dubai**
This store has become a household name for providing well-designed, stylish products for babies and mums-to-be. The shop has several locations across Dubai including Wafi, The Dubai Mall, Dubai Marina Mall, Mercato Mall and a small concessions store in Harvey Nichols, Mall of the Emirates. The store stocks a good variety of items including toys, car seats, pushchairs, cribs, nursery items and decorations, maternity clothes and feeding items. Although this is one of the more costly options, it remains a popular spot for gifts and newborn essentials. For other locations see the Store Finder on p.421.

## Mothercare

**The Dubai Mall** Downtown Burj Dubai **04 339 9812**
www.mothercare.com
Map **2** F6 Metro **Burj Dubai**
Mothercare is a long-established store which remains a reliable place to shop for baby essentials. It has a particularly good selection of clothes and many of its larger stores stock cots, prams and car seats. You can order matresses in specific sizes and items you've seen online or in a UK catalogue can also be ordered, but the delivery time is a minimum of four weeks and often longer. There are several branches of this store, but its largest store, in The Dubai Mall, has a wide selection of goods and a fantastic parents' area with changing mats and bottle warmers. See the Store Finder on p.421.

# Bicycles

Dubai may not seem like the most bicycle-friendly city, but there is an active cycling scene. Road and mountain biking are popular and you can find an adequate (although sometimes expensive) range of equipment for both. For serious cyclists, an increasing number of shops, and brands, in town offer a good selection of bikes, safety equipment and any accessories you may need. The shops will also repair and service bikes. Kona has a store near Lamcy Plaza, and Rage (p.423) sells Giant and the sought-after Santa Cruz range of bikes. 360 Lifestyle (04 337 3013) in Oud Metha stocks a wide range of the excellent Specialized bikes, clothing and accessories (and also has a smaller range on show inside Studio R in Ibn Battuta, 04 366 9890); Trek (04 407 6641) shop in the Metropolitan Hotel. Bike 'n' Rack on Al Khail Road also stocks Giant and a range of Thule bike racks, the Cannondale shops stock Cannondale, Fuji, Mongoose and Schwinn, and Wolfi's stocks Scott, Felt, Merida and Storck.

For the casual cyclist, Toys R Us (p.378) and the larger sports shops sell more basic models at

reasonable prices. Go Sports (p.385) has a large bike section and a workshop in its Mall of the Emirates store. The 'sit-up-and-beg' models – popular with gardeners and delivery cyclists – can be found in the smaller bike shops all over the city (check out Karama and Satwa). Supermarket noticeboards and www. dubizzle.com are good places to look for second-hand bikes.

Children's bicycles are widely available in bike and sports shops, and shops like Babyshop (p.360), Toys R Us (p.378) and Goodbaby (p.360) have a range for tiny Lance Armstrong wannabes. If you want to make cycling a family activity, Cannondale in Oud Metha and Wolfi's and Go Sport (p.385) have a selection of children's seats, priced from Dhs.150 to Dhs.300, which its staff will fit for you. Both adults' and children's helmets are available at the main retailers.

## Rage Bike Shop
**The Dubai Mall** Downtown Burj Dubai **04 434 1549**
www.kinokuniya.co.jp/english/contents
Map **2 F6** Metro **Burj Dubai**
Specialising in BMX and mountain bikes, Rage has a good range of stock and will offfer advice on the most suitable bike for your needs. The store has a good selection for both serious cyclists and those who just need something for recreational use. There are three branches in Dubai (see Store Finder, p.423).

## Wolfi's Bike Shop
**Sheikh Zayed Road, Btn Jct 2 & 3** Al Quoz
**04 339 4453**
www.wbs.ae
Map **1 U5** Metro **Times Square**
Wolfi's is by far the most popular bike shop for the city's cycling enthusiasts. Its staff are well educated on the products it sells. The store will also repair and service your bike (although this is pricey). The shop sells bikes for every level of cyclist, from children to semi-pro road cyclists. As the main sponsor of the Dubai Roadsters road cycling group, Wolfi's tends to focus on the road cycling scene.

# Books
You'll find both international bookstores and good local stores in Dubai which stock a vast selection of international books and magazines. Virgin Megastore (p.380) carries an interesting selection of books related to music and popular culture. You will also find a small selection of books in larger supermarkets like Carrefour (p.391) and Géant (p.392).

All malls feature at least one book store and if you cannot find a publication, the larger stores often have customer service sections where you can search for titles, place an order or enquire whether it is available in another branch. Due to strict UAE laws on censorship, you may find some titles are not available in Dubai and any unacceptable images are covered up with black marker.

Popular online store Amazon also delivers to the UAE – it's usually better to order from the UK site (www.amazon.co.uk) than the US site (www. amazon.com), so that you can take advantage of cheaper delivery rates. Unless you choose the super-expensive express delivery it will take around two weeks to receive your order and your package may be inspected by UAE customs.

Dubai's transitory residents furnish the second-hand book shops – you'll find a wide range of books, particularly fiction, many of which have only been read once. Both House of Prose (p.362) and Book World (p.364), buy and sell, and they'll also give you back 50% of what you paid on books you've bought from them. There are regular charity book sales, the most notable being the ones organised by Medecins Sans Frontieres (www.msfuae.ae). They are held several times throughout the year, usually in the Dune Centre in Satwa. You can also buy books by Explorer Publishing in the below bookstores or online at www.explorerpublishing.com/shop.

## Books Plus
**Ibn Battuta Mall** Jebel Ali **04 368 5375**
Map **1 G4** Metro **Ibn Battuta**
A fairly comprehensive range of titles are stocked at this small bookstore. You'll find a good selection of titles and a several international magazines. This is a perfect place to pick up light reads and popular titles. For other locations see Store Finder,, p.415.

## Book World By Kinokuniya
**The Dubai Mall** Downtown Burj Dubai **04 434 0111**
www.kinokuniya.co.jp/english
Map **2 F6** Metro **Burj Dubai**
At over 65,000 square feet, Kinokuniya is one of the biggest bookshops in Dubai. The Japanese chain is a household name in many Asian countries but its new store in The Dubai Mall is its first in the Middle East. You will find a variety of international titles, including a particular good selection of Japanese books, which rivals many of the city's current big players, and a great selection of comics. The store also has a good stationary section and an extensive selection of magazines.

## Bookworm
**Beh Park n Shop** Jumeira **04 394 5770**
Map **2 C4**
A great store for inspiring kids to read, Bookworm has an extensive range of titles that cover everything from read-to books for very young kids up to young adults. In addition to its assortment of educational books, is also a stocks a good selection of toys and gifts. For other locations see Store Finder,, p.415.

www.borders.com

**Map 1 R5 Metro Mall of the Emirates**

This US chain has stores in Mall of the Emirates, Deira City Centre, Dubai Marina Mall, Ibn Battuta Mall and DIFC. The variety of books on sale is vast and its larger stores have a fantastic selection of the latest international magazines. The branches, in the Mall of The Emirates and Ibn Battuta, also have a Starbucks where you can peruse your purchases with a coffee. Borders stocks a good range of Paperchase stationery items, a small gift range, and one of the better selections of diaries and calendars. For other locations see Store Finder, p.416.

## Culture & Co

**API Tower, Sheikh Zayed Rd** Trade Centre
**04 331 3114**
www.culturecodubai.com
**Map 2 G4 Metro Financial Centre**

Located in the same building as the Consulate General of France, this bookshop sells a selection of French novels guidebooks, magazines and newspapers.

## House Of Prose

**Ibn Battuta Mall** Jebel Ali **04 368 5526**
**Map 1 G4 Metro Ibn Battuta**

If your reading habit is breaking the bank, head for House of Prose and spend an hour browsing through a huge collection of second-hand books. Most of the stock is in excellent condition, and you may be able to pick up a new release that has only been read once, for around half the price it would cost you if you bought it new. For other locations see Store Finder, p.419.

## Jashanmal > p.xiv, p.365

**Mall Of The Emirates** Al Barsha **04 347 1715**
www.jashanmal-uae.com
**Map 1 R5 Metro Mall of the Emirates**

Jashanmal's selection of books is wide-ranging and you'll find international books and magazines. Head here during the sales and you can grab some really good bargains. For other locations see Store Finder p.414.

## Magrudy's

**Ibn Battuta Mall** Jebel Ali **04 366 9770**
www.magrudy.com
**Map 1 G4 Metro Ibn Battuta**

This local chain has a wide selection covering new releases, reference, travel, fiction, children's books and

photographers can usually find most things in Dubai. Digital models dominate the shelves and can be bought in the city's electronics shops, hypermarkets, and photo processing outlets; all the major brands are represented. The jury's still out on whether cameras here are cheaper than elsewhere, it really depends on where else you are looking; the prices in Asia are often lower, and in most of Europe they will be higher. Within Dubai, prices will vary between the larger outlets, where prices are fixed, and the electronics shops of Bur Dubai (p.386). However, while you might be able to bag a bargain from the independent retailers using your superior powers of negotiation, you'll have more protection buying from the larger outlets. The most important consideration, if you are buying the camera to take to another country, is to ensure that your warranty is international: don't just take the retailer's word for it, actually ask to open the box and read the warranty to make sure.

For specialist equipment and a good range of film cameras, the main outlets are Grand Stores and Salam Studio. Grand Stores sells Fuji, Nikon, Canon and Mamiya; Salam Studio carries Bronica, Leica, Minolta and Pentax; they both sell a selection of filters, tripods and studio equipment. The alternative to buying locally is to use an online retailer. B&H Photo (www.bandhphoto.com) and Adorama (www.adorama.com), in New York, are extremely popular.

For second-hand equipment, www.gulfphotoplus.com has an active equipment noticeboard (as well as being a great source of information and a good networking site for locally based photography enthusiasts).

Should your equipment need to be repaired, Grand Stores offers a repair service. HN Camera Repairs (04 349 0971) offer an in house repair service for all makes of camera.

## Grand Stores

**The Dubai Mall** Downtown Burj Dubai **04 339 8614**
**Map 2 F6 Metro Burj Dubai**

This is the main retailer for Nikon cameras in Dubai; the store also stocks Fuji, Canon and Mamiya. You can also have you camera cleaned and repaired in its stores, which can be found in several locations across Dubai in (for other locations see Store Finder, p.419).

## M.K. Trading Co

**Baniyas Road** Deira **04 222 5745**
www.mktradingco.com

*" Today a Reader
Tomorrow a Leader "*

# JASHANMAL
# BOOKSTORES

Dubai: Mall of the Emirates, Tel: 3406789, The Village Mall, Jumeirah, Tel: 3445770,
Caribou Coffee, Uptown Mirdiff, Tel: 2888376, Dubai Marina Walk, Tel: 04 4222504,
Abu Dhabi: Abu Dhabi Mall, Level 3, Hamdan Street, Tel: 6443869, Sharjah: Sahara Centre, Tel: 5317898
Bahrain: Seef Mall, West Wing, Tel: 17581632, Al Aali Shopping Complex, Tel: 17582424

INCA/JNC/1191

### National Store
Khansaheb Bld, Al Fahidi St Bur Dubai 04 353 6074
www.jk.ae
Map 2 L3 Metro Al Fahidi
This store is a distributor of Canon products and
you'll find a good selection of cameras, printers and
camera accessories from the well-known brand. There
are several branches of this store in Dubai (see Store
Finder, p.421).

### Salam
Wafi Umm Hurair 04 704 8484
www.salams.com
Map 2 L6 Metro Healthcare City
Stocking a complete range of professional-grade
camera and studio equipment, this department store
is considered by many to be the most comprehensive
photography store in the city. The store carries Bronica,
Leica, Minolita and Pentax – there is also a good
selection of filters, tripods and studio equipment.

## Car Accessories
Cars and their accessories are big business in Dubai,
so you won't struggle to find the accessories you
need. ACE (p.381) and Carrefour (p.391) have large
departments selling everything from steering wheel
covers to fridges which run off the car battery and there
is a wide selection of tools in larger stores and in the
smaller shops in Satwa. You'll find a fantastic selection
of products in Yellow Hat in Times Square (p.413), or
head further out to Sharjah industrial area for slightly
cheaper outlets than you'll find in Dubai.

GPS systems are available from Picnico (04 394
1653) and Abdulla Mohammed Ibrahim Trading (04
229 1195) who recommend the Garmin brand, and
even from more mainstream shops like Plug-Ins
(p.374), Carrefour (p.391) and Sharaf DG (p.374). The
AAA (www.aaadubai.com) sells specialist sand tracks
and heavy duty jacks and winches – if your car is fitted
with a GPS system the company can rescue you from
the most remote dune or wadi. Car stereos are widely
available, and are sold by most electronics shops,
with some of the car dealerships stocking alternative
models for their cars. To have them fitted, head either
to the workshops of Rashidiya or Satwa, or AAA and
the dealers – it should cost around Dhs.500 if you are
providing all the parts.

Many car owners try to beat the heat by having
their car windows tinted. The legal limit is 30% tint; if
you get your windows tinted any darker you could be
fined, and your car won't pass its annual inspection.
The options range from the Dhs.75 plastic film from
the workshops in Satwa, to Dhs.1,300 to Dhs.1,500
at After Dark (covered a by a ten-year warranty), and
up to Dhs.5,000 at V-Kool (04 340 0092), which is also
covered by warranty, and its clear film is more heat
resistant than the tinted one.

If you are just looking for some memorabilia, or
if you simply love fast cars, the new Ferrari Store (04
232 9845) in Festival City (p.401) has a showroom and
it also sells memorabilia and accessories. Head to Al
Quoz and Rashidiya if you want to customise your car
by increasing its performance – West Coast Customs
(as featured on the MTV series Pimp My Ride) now has
a showroom and workshop in Al Quoz.

### Yellow Hat > p.50, p.367
Times Square Al Quoz 04 341 8592
www.yellowhat.ae
Map 1 T5 Metro Al Quoz
Yellow Hat is a one-stop shop for car accessories and
its comprehensive stock ranges from tyres and sound
systems, to more expensive engine tuning. Head here
to pick up breakdown kits, steering wheels, air filters
or alloy wheels. The store also offers car cleaning and
servicing.

## Carpets
Carpets are one of the region's signature items. The
ones on sale here tend to be imported from Iran,
Turkey, Pakistan and Central Asia. Carpets vary in price
depending on a number of factors such as its origin,
the material used, the number of knots, and whether
or not it is handmade. The most expensive carpets are
usually those hand-made with silk, in Iran.

Inspect carpets by turning them over – if the
pattern is clearly depicted on the back and the
knots are all neat, the carpet is of higher quality than
those that are indistinct. Try to do some research so
that you have a basic idea of what you are looking
for before you go, just in case you happen to meet
an unscrupulous carpet dealer who could take
advantage of your naivety. Fortunately, crooked
carpet conmen are rare, and most will happily explain
the differences between the rugs and share their
extensive knowledge with you. If you ask the dealer,
you can often garner some interesting information
about the carpets and where they were made – for
example some carpets have family names sewn into
the designs.

National Iranian Carpets have a section on their
website (www.niccarpets.com) about the history and
development of carpets from the various regions.

Ask to see a variety of carpets so that you can get
a feel for the differences between hand-made or
machine-made, silk, wool or blend carpets. Of course,
asking may not be necessary, since carpet vendors will
undoubtedly start unrolling carpets before you at a
furious pace.

Carpets range in price from a few hundred dirhams
to tens of thousands. It is always worth bargaining;
make sure the seller knows you are not a tourist, and
remain polite at all times to maximise the success of
your haggling.

# Car Accessories
# Auto Maintenance

## Car Accessories Available

Audio/Video Entertainment Systems
Navigation and Handsfree Gadgets
Alloy Wheels
Performance Tires
Window Tint Film
4x4 and Off-Road Equipment
Safety and Emergency Gear
Brake Discs
Performance Grade Suspension Kits
Sports Style Interior Upgrades
Interior and Exterior Accent Lighting
Car Care and Cleaning Products
Touch up and restoration kits
Car Interior Accessories

## AutoMaintenance Services Offered

Lube Services
Car Wash Services
Car Detailing Services
Window tinting
Paintless Dent Removal
Paint Protection film
Tire fitting and balancing
Wheel Alignment
Tire repair
Battery testing & replacement
Brakes Maintenance

## YellowHat
### Japan

Times Square Center Branch
Tel: 04 341 8593

Email: info@yellowhat.ae
www.yellowhat.ae

Nad Al Hamar Branch
Tel: 04 289 8060

# What & Where To Buy

Carpets

Deira Tower on Al Nasr Square has a huge number of carpet outlets under one roof, and the Blue Souk in Sharjah also has a great range. If you happen to venture further out, the road to Hatta (p.282) is lined with stalls selling carpets and the Friday Market in Fujairah is also a good place to pick them up.

Mall of the Emirates and The Dubai Mall have a good selection of shops selling traditional carpets, just bear in mind that prices may be steeper here.

Occasionally, you might get a travelling carpet seller ringing your doorbell – they usually drive around an area in a pickup that is packed to the roof with carpets. The quality isn't great, and if you show the slightest bit of interest they'll keep coming back.

Carpetland is a one-stop-shop for carpets, whether you're after a Persian antique or a shagpile. For something practical rather than decorative, head to Fabindia (p.393), IKEA (p.371), Carrefour (p.391) or THE One (p.372).

**Al Orooba Oriental Carpets**  04 351 0919
**National Iranian Carpets**  04 420 0264 (See also Store Finder, p.421)
**The Orientalist**  04 344 8811, *www.theorientalist.com*
**Persian Carpet House**  04 332 1161 (See also Store Finder, p.423)
**Pride Of Kashmir**  04 341 4477 (see also Store Finder p.423)
**Qum Persian Carpets & Novelties**  04 228 1848, *www.qumcarpets.com* (See also Store Finder, p.423)

## Computers

The latest computer equipment and technology is easy to find in the city and there's even a mall dedicated to it: Al Ain Mall in Bur Dubai. Every year Dubai hosts GITEX (the Gulf Information Technology Exhibition), the largest IT exhibition in the region. The phenomenally popular GITEX Computer Shopper is also a great place to bag the latest technology at lower prices (www.gitex.com).

Computer equipment is on sale in a surprising number of outlets, from Carrefour (p.391) to Plug-Ins (p.374), and all the main manufacturers are represented. You'll also find a row of stores, on the way to the Metro station, inside Mall of the Emirates. CompuMe has a great website where you can order products online (www.compume.com).

The market is dominated by PCs, but Macs are available from a growing number of stores including CompuMe, PACC, Virgin Megastore, the Mac Store in Ibn Battuta and Istyle (www.istyle.ae) in Dubai Festival Centre and The Dubai Mall.

The UAE government has been cracking down on the sale of pirated software, and consequently the software and hardware that is available is genuine and should be of good quality. If you have a poorly PC, contact St George Computers who provide all the assistance you need repairing equipment and with upgrades. For more information call Lee on 050 456 2821.

### Having Computer Issues?

WildIT provides total custom solutions for all your needs. Repairs, upgrades, new systems, networking your home – you name it, WildIT will sort it. Experienced, British-qualified technicians offer fast, competitive and secure services from the smallest virus removal to creating a state-of-the-art gaming powerhouse. Check out wildit.co.uk, email info@wildit.co.uk or call 050 871 0463

## Fashion

Clothes dominate Dubai's shopping scene; not only is the selection amazing, but its sweeping sales several times a year mean you can also bag great discounts on designer goods. The malls have their fair share of exclusive brands, but they also offer more affordable fashion. You'll find that areas of the larger malls are home to the likes of H&M (p.419), Forever 21 (p.418) and Topshop (p.426) and others feature premium designers like Donna Karan (p.417), Ralph Lauren (p.423), Hermes (p.419) and Matthew Williamson.

For those events when only the very best will do, Fashion Avenue in The Dubai Mall (p.402) is dedicated to high-end fashion. Then again, Saks Fifth Avenue in BurJuman, Boutique 1 (p.393) at The Walk, Jumeirah Beach Residence and Harvey Nichols in Mall of the Emirates, hold their fair share of cutting-edge couture. A recent addition to the scene is the Gate Village in Dubai International Financial Centre (p.387) which has a smattering of high-end names like Anya Hindmarch (04 382 5190), Nina Ricci (04 382 5240) and Vivienne Westwood (04 382 5140).

Luxcouture

Harvey Nichols

BRANDS
FOR LESS

Outlet Mall

Villa Moda

Mall of the Emirates (p.405) and The Dubai Mall are the big rollers, offering an astounding number of stores, boutiques and department stores. However, The Dubai Mall pips to the post with its large branches of Galeries Lafayette (p.390), Debenhams (p.390), Marks and Spencer (p.391), Paris Gallery (p.382) and Bloomingdales (www.bloomingdales.com) which is set to open in February 2010.

If you are looking for fashion that's less mainstream, head to stores like Kitsch, S*uce and Five Green for their eclectic mix of funky fashion (see Boutiques & Independent Stores p.393). Eve Michelle in Magrudy's Mall (p.364) has a loyal following for its range of exclusive European creations for ladies. Stores like Etoile La Boutique (p.418) Rodeo Drive (p.424), Villa Moda (p.395) and Ginger & Lace (p.418) combine a chic selection of high-end designer brands and are great if you like to splurge on labels. If you love designers but not the price tags, browse the selection online at www.mappochette.com. The online store stocks designer bags from Miu Miu, Versace and Prada and offers a rental service and will deliver one of its designer bags straight to your door.

For something a little different, you can get beautiful hand-crafted fabrics and traditional Indian clothing at Fabindia (see also p.393) on Al Mankhool Road, or Melangè (04 344 4721) in Jumeirah Plaza.

Men should head to Maktoum Road (between the Clock Tower Roundabout and Al Khaleej Palace Hotel) which is lined with stores selling men's designer clothing, and there are also plenty of options inside the Twin Towers Mall in Deira. There are a couple of suit shops along Al Diyafah Street in Satwa too. Of course, most of the shops loved by women also have excellent men's sections, such as Debenhams, Marks & Spencer, Next, Zara and Massimo Dutti.

Men can pick up funky T-shirts in H&M (p.419), Topman (p.426), Desigual (04 339 9408) and Zadig and Voltaire in Jumeirah Beach Residence. Soboho in Dubai Marina Mall has a great range of T-shirts with quirky graphics and Graniph (04 232 8531), a Japanese store, stocks a range of T-shirts that are anything but boring.

Bargain hunters have lots to choose from. The Dubai Outlet Mall (p.411) houses a number of well-known brands selling end-of-line stock at reduced prices. Try Sana Fashions (p.393), Carrefour (p.391) and Géant (p.392) for really good bargains – they receive regular deliveries of factory seconds and retailer overruns, and there are plenty of well-known brands available if you get there early, such as Gap, George and Cherokee. Lamcy Plaza (p.412) is a real bargain-hunter's mall – Mexx for Less, Peacocks and Factory Fashions (stocking overruns from Adams and Pumpkin Patch) are all excellent, as are Jennyfer and Mr Price.

The Karama Market (p.388) is perhaps the main contender for bargain shopping in Dubai. The area features rows and rows of shops selling designer labels, both the genuine article and some quite convincing knock-offs.

When it comes to shoes, the choice is enormous. Designer labels like Jimmy Choo (04 330 0404) and Gucci (p.419) mingle with middle-of-the-range creations from Bally (p.415), Milano (p.421), Faith (p.418) and Nine West (p.422), which also mingle with cheap-as-chips flip-flops and sandals in the big hypermarkets. For stylish shoes on a budget, Shoe Mart (p.424), Brantano Shoe City (p.416) and Avenue carry fashionable and practical shoes, as do the many shoe shops in Karama Market.

You'll probably find that sports shoes are cheaper than in your home country, but you might not be able to get the latest styles. Stadium (p.385) is good for active-wear shoes and sandals. Birkenstocks are widely available and Scholl shoes can be found in shoe shops and larger pharmacies. Pharmacies also stock supports, powders and specialist plasters.

Because of the weather, children spend a great deal of time in sandals, which are widely available. If you are planning a trip to colder climes, it can be hard to find good winter shoes for little feet – so if you see a pair, grab them.

## Petite & Plus Sizes

If you are frequently frustrated by the standard range (UK 8 to 16) of clothing sizes found in stores because items are always a little bit too big or a little bit too small, you will be relieved to know that retailers in Dubai are increasingly offering petite and plus-size lines. Petite ranges are available in Debenhams (p.390), Splash (p.425) and Marks & Spencer (p.391), while Bhs (p.415), Debenhams (p.390), Liz Claiborne (p.420), Marks & Spencer (p.391), Splash (p.425) and Woolworths (p.426) all carry plus-size collections (look out for Evans in Debenhams and Scarlett's in Splash). For more exclusive lines for the fuller figure, try Irene Sieber, Oui Plus and Samoon (all in Wafi), or Charisma in the Beach Centre in Jumeira.

It's not only women who are frustrated at not being able to find clothes that fit. Men looking for larger sizes should head to Big & Tall (04 397 3873) on Bank Street. They cater for waist sizes from 40 plus and shirts up to 6XL.

## Furniture

This is one of Dubai's most buoyant retail sectors, perhaps because of the unlimited supply of new villas and apartments all in need of furnishing. Most tastes are catered for, from ethnic pieces to the latest designer concepts and specialist children's furniture stores.

The industrial area between Junctions three and four of Sheikh Zayed Road is home to a number of furniture warehouses, many of which sell pieces crafted from Indonesian teak. Their hot, dusty warehouses are not the chicest of options, but prices are excellent and after a good polish the furniture looks fabulous. Genuine antiques are available but very rare (and therefore very expensive); many antique pieces come from Oman and Yemen.

The Walk, Jumeirah Beach Residence has a few independent homeware stores, and there is a good selection of stores in Mall of The Emirates and The Dubai Mall. You'll also find plenty of shops selling accessories to add the finishing touches to your home like @Home (p.414) and Fabindia (p.393).

Real investment pieces, that you'll want to keep and take back home, can be bought at Natuzzi (04 338 0777) in Al Quoz. For exotic designs, try Safita Trading Est (04 339 3230, Al Quoz) which stocks a range off items from India and the Far East.

House of the World provides advice on interior design and sells a range of art and photography, and Panache Furnishing (04 344 3677) offers design services and ready-made home accessories. Zara Home's (p.372) fresh, European designs are available in a number of malls, or try the stylish range of furniture at Crate & Barrel (p.372), BoConcept (04 341 4144), Traffic (04 341 8494) and Flamant (p.04 341 3862).

Next (p.391) has a small home accessories section and Debenhams (p.390) is good for homeware, bedding and kitchenware – this is where you can buy the entire range of Jamie Oliver's cookware. Kitchenalia junkies will love Tavola (p.425) and Harvest Home's (04 342 0225) mix of quirky items.

For children's rooms, Kidz Inc. (04 340 5059) in Al Quoz are the sole agents for Haba – its German, hand-made, wooden furniture doesn't come cheap but all pieces meet European and American safety standards and come with a warranty. Especially good is the range of themed beds (think pirate ships and flowery glades), with matching furniture and accessories.

If you need a hand painted design or gilding on your furniture. MacKenzie Art (04 341 9803, www.mackenzieart.com) specialise in a range of styles to add another dimension to your furniture and accessories, as well as providing commissioned art on canvases to complement your furniture scheme.

The transient nature of some of Dubai's population results in an active second-hand furniture market. Items are advertised in the classified sections of the local newspapers and on websites like www.dubizzle.com, but the supermarket noticeboards are the best source; this is also the place to find garage sales.

---

**Explorer Member Card**

Don't forget to register your member card (found at the back of the book) and check online for current offers. Discounts are updated on a monthly basis and cover a wide range of companies. www.liveworkexplore.com.

---

## General Furniture

### ID Design
**Mall of the Emirates** Al Barsha **04 341 3434**
www.iddesignuae.com
Map **1 R5** Metro **Mall of the Emirates**
ID Design sells a selection of modern furniture for the home or office and it also stocks a range of outdoor furniture. Both of its stores offer an interior design service and will reupholster furniture and custom-make curtains, pillows and other accessories for your home. The store also offers a gift registry and delivery service. For other locations see Store Finder, p.419.

### IKEA
**Festival Centre** Festival City **800 4532**
www.ikeadubai.com
Map **2 M8** Metro **Emirates Head Office**
IKEA's enormous showroom in the Festival Power Centre sells a great range of good value furniture. Its selection is suitable for most budgets, and it stocks everything from Dhs.1 tealight holders to Dhs.20,000 kitchens. The store also has a selection of reasonably priced kids' furniture (its range of bunkbeds is consistently popular).

### Move-in Emirates
**Al Quoz Industrial 4** Al Quoz **04 340 1994**
www.move-in-dubai.com
Map **2 S7**
If interior design isn't your forte, Move-in Emirates will fit out your new home with furniture, electronic goods and even cutlery, before you even walk through the door. The company offers a full service, from delivery to installation.

## Budget Furniture

### Home Centre
**Mall Of The Emirates** Al Barsha **04 341 4441**
www.homecentre.net
Map **1 R5** Metro **Mall of the Emirates**
Step into this store and you won't know which way to turn – a huge assortment of items fills the shop. You'll have to sort through its great range of bath towels, kitchenware and accessories before you arrive at its range of conservative wooden tables, sofas and bedroom furniture. For other locations see Store Finder, p.419.

### Pan Emirates
**Umm Suqeim Rd** Al Barsha **04 383 0800**
www.panemirates.com
Map **1 R5** Metro **Mall of the Emirates**
Kit out your home with a stylish range of modern furniture at this store – If your tastes are more traditional, its selection of wooden beds and furniture

will also appeal. The store also sells home accessories, rugs, mattresses and small range of garden furniture. For other locations see Store Finder, p.422.

## Contemporary Designer Furniture

**Aati**  Karama, 04 337 7825
**Armani Casa**  The Dubai Mall, 04 437 3131
**B&B Italia**  Mall of the Emirates, 04 340 5797, *www.bebitalia.it*
**Kartell**  Jumeira, 04 348 8169, *www.kartell.it*
**Natuzzi**  Al Quoz, 04 338 0777, *http://int.natuzzi.com*
**Objekts Of Design (OD)**  Al Quoz, 04 341 6061, *www.od.ae*
**Presotto Middle East**  Al Quoz, 04 340 6443, *www.presottome.com*
**Roche Bobois**  Al Barsha, 04 336 6172, *www.roche-bobois.com*
**Singways**  Mall of the Emirates, 04 340 9116, *www.singways.com*
**Traffic**  Al Barsha, 04 341 8494, *www.viatraffic.org*

## Modern Furniture & Home Decor

### THE One

Jumeira Rd  Jumeira  **04 345 6687**
www.theoneplanet.com
Map  **2 H3**

A favourite among the expat crowd, this store's only downfall is the fact that those divine cushions you bought will most likely pop up in your acquaintances' homes from time to time. But, there is a reason why it's so popular: its funky, modern style (that is highly decorative, but not gaudy) and good selection of home accessories can add a much-needed flourish to impersonal apartments.

**Artikel**  04 232 8339 (See also Store Finder, p.415)
**Crate & Barrel**  Mall of the Emirates, *www.crateandbarrell.com*
**Dwell**  04 232 5435 *www.liwastores.com* (See also Store Finder, p.417)
**IKEA**  Festival City, 800 4532, *www.ikeadubai.com*
**Index Living Mall**  The Dubai Mall 04 330 8132, *www.indexlivingmall.com*
**Indigo Living**  Al Quoz, 04 341 6305, *www.indigo-living.com*
**iwannagohome!**  The Dubai Mall, 04 339 8952, *http://iwannagohome.com.sg*
**Karma Creative Living**  The Walk at Jumeirah Beach Residence, *www.karma-deco.com*
**Zara Home**  04 359 5598, *www.zarahome.com* (See also Store Finder, p.426)

## Outdoor furniture

**ACE**  04 338 1416, *www.aceuae.com* (See also Store Finder, p.414)

**B&B Italia**  Mall of the Emirates, 04 340 5797, *www.bebitalia.it*
**Desert River**  Al Quoz, 04 323 3636, *www.desertriver.com*
**Kettal**  Oud Metha, 04 337 1870
**Nakkash Gallery**  Garhoud, 04 282 6767, *www.nakkashgallery.com*

## Wood furniture

### Lucky's

Sharjah, **06 534 1937**

Although this store is in Sharjah, it remains popular with expats looking well-priced furniture. The range of products is vast, but one of the staff will happily explain the origin and design of the pieces and they can also varnish, paint or make alterations.

### Marina Exotic Home Interiors

Mall Of The Emirates  Al Barsha  **04 341 0314**
www.marinagulf.com
Map  **1 R5**  Metro  **Mall of the Emirates**

Pick up key pieces that reflect the region at this popular store – the items here will add an exotic touch to your home. You can pick up large wardrobes, tables, ornate chests and various other types of wooden furniture. There is also a selection of garden furniture. For other locations see the Store Finder on p.421.

**Falaknaz – The Warehouse**  Jumeira, 04 347 0220, *www.falaknazthewarehouse.com*
**Khan's**  Sharjah, 06 562 1621
**Pinky's Furniture**  Al Barsha, 04 422 1720
**Zen Interiors**  Al Barsha, 04 340 5050, *www.zeninteriors.net*

# Gold & Diamonds

Dubai is the world's leading re-exporter of gold and you'll find at least one jewellery shop in even the smallest malls, and large areas dedicated to shops selling it in larger malls. Gold is available in 18, 21, 22 or 24 carats and is sold according to the international daily gold rate. This means that for an identical piece, whether you buy it in Emirates Towers or the Gold Souk, there will be very little difference in the price of the actual gold. Where the price varies is in the workmanship that has gone into a particular piece. While gold jewellery may be the most prevalent, silver, platinum, precious stones, gems and pearls are all sold, either separately or crafted into jewellery. Most outlets can make up a piece for you, working from a diagram or photograph. Just ensure that you are not obliged to buy it if it doesn't turn out quite how you had imagined.

Many of the world's finest jewellers are represented in Dubai; leading brands like Cartier, Tiffany & Co, Graff and De Beers can be found in the larger malls. Fabergé

Gold

jewellery is among the elite collection in Saks Fifth Avenue's jewellery department. For watches, whether it's a Rolex, Breitling, Tag Heuer, Swatch, Casio or Timex, you'll find a variety of models here.

### All That Glitters

The Gold & Diamond Park (at junction four on Sheikh Zayed Road) has branches of many of the same shops as the Gold Souk (p.396) but in a calmer, air-conditioned atmosphere. You can still barter, and there is an added bonus of cafes to wait in while the jeweller makes any alterations. This is also a good spot to head for if you are looking for engagement or wedding rings and, like the outlets in the souk, you are able to commission pieces.

The Gold Souk (p.396) is great in terms of choice. A traditional gift is a pendant with your name spelled out in Arabic, or some jewellery crafted with black pearls.

Costume jewellery and watches can be found in most department stores as well as Eve Michelle and the beautiful Swarovski range in Tanagra (04 324 2340), in Wafi. Several fashion stores also stock a small range of jewellery and branches of Accessorize and Claire's Accessories (which is great for children, with inexpensive jewellery and hair accessories) can be found in many of the malls. For Love 21 (04 294 3038), in Deira City Centre, has a great range which echoes the colours and fashions of the season.

**Al Fardan Jewels & Precious Stones**  04 295 3780, *www.alfardan.com* (See also Store Finder, p.414)
**Al Futtaim Jewellery**  04 295 2906, *www.watchesuae. com* (See also Store Finder, p.414)

**BinHendi Jewellery**  04 295 2544, *www.binhendi.com* (See also Store Finder, p.415)
**Damas**  04 352 5566, *www.damasjewel.com* (See also Store Finder, p.417)
**Golden Ring**  04 295 0373 (See also Store Finder, p.418)
**Liali Jewellery**  04 344 5055, *www.lialijewellery.com* (See also Store Finder, p.420)
**Mahallati Jewellery**  04 344 4771, *www. mahallatijewellery.com* (See also Store Finder, p.421)
**Mansoor Jewellery**  04 355 2110 (See also Store Finder, p.421)
**Paris Gallery**  04 295 5550 (See also Store Finder, p.422)
**Prima Gold**  04 355 1988, www.primagold.net (See also Store Finder, p.423)
**Pure Gold**  04 349 2400, www.pugold.com (See also Store Finder, p.423)
**Raymond Weil**  04 295 3254, www.raymond-weil.com (See also Store Finder, p.423)
**Ruane Jewellers**  04 327 9212 (see also Store Finder p.424)
**Silver Art**  Deira City Centre, 04 295 2414
**Tanagra**  04 324 2340 (See also Store Finder, p.425)

## Home Appliances

Whether you are setting up home in Dubai, or you are moving house, you'll have to spend some time looking for white goods. While you may be used to essential items like a cooker, washing machine or fridge, coming as part and parcel of a lease, in Dubai, unfurnished really means unfurnished and you'll have to fork out for the most standard items like curtain rails for your windows.

Unsurprisingly, there are several places for you to buy goods and several large international brands are sold here like LG, Samsung and Siemens. The Dubai Mall (p.402) and Mall of the Emirates (p.405) have a large selection of shops. You'll also find some high end brands like Gaggenau (04 394 4049) on Jumeirah Beach Road and Miele (04 398 9718) in Bur Dubai.

Many of the larger supermarkets and hypermarkets like Carrefour (p.391), Géant (p.392) and HyperPanda (p.392) stock a superb range of goods from well-known brands (and some lesser known ones that also do the job) and they usually offer a delivery and installation service. SharafDG (p.374), Jacky's Electronics (p.374), Jumbo Electronics (p.374) and Better Life (p.415) also stock a selection of home appliances. For stylish electronics for the kitchen, head to Tavola (p.425) and Galeries Lafayette (p.390).

You can buy coolers and water dispensers in the larger supermarkets or you can buy them directly from the companies that deliver bottled water (see p.102).

Competition is high, so prices are reasonable and most dealers will offer warranties – some will offer a warranty extension for an extra year or two. Check that the warranty is valid internationally if you wish to take items back to your home country. Also check that the item will work in all areas of the world and whether you will have to pay any import duty if you return back home. Also check who will service the items if there are problems. For second-hand items, check the adverts placed on supermarket noticeboards and online classifieds like www.dubizzle.com.

## Home Audio & Visual

When it comes to home entertainment, the stores in Dubai don't scrimp on size, quality or range. There are several stores dedicated to electronics in each of the larger malls and you'll find large sections in the supermarkets which stock top-of-the-range high-definition televisions, plasma screens, DVD players, games consoles and stereos.

### Mobile Phones

Mobiles are big business and you won't need to go too far to find one. Most of the larger supermarkets have areas dedicated to the popular brands. Handsets can be purchased directly from du (p.104) or Etisalat (p.102);it is often cheaper to purchase a phone from them as part of a package.

Whether or not the items sold here are cheaper than those sold in other countries depends on where you compare it too, but it does pay to wait for the sales as there can be a noticeable difference in prices.

Many of the stores displays of operational products so you can see or hear the quality of the products, and staff are often happy to explain the differences and benefits between models and brands. Bang & Olufsen (p.415) and Bose (p.416) offer a pricey, but undeniably stylish, range of goods for the home, but you'll find a stylish range of products in all of the electronic stores. Many stores also offer delivery and installation services, which take the hassle out of mounting a plasma screen or setting up your surround sound system.

### Dubai Audio Centre

Shk Zayed Rd, Nr Safestway Al Wasl **04 343 1441**
www.dubaiaudio.com
Map **2 E5** Metro **Business Bay**
Head to this store for a super stylish range of designer electronics from premium brands including Lexicon, Conrad Johnson and Linn. The range of stock on offer includes luxury home cinema and audio equipment and multi-room audio systems.

### Jacky's Electronics

The **Dubai Mall** Downtown Burj Dubai **04 434 0499**
www.jackys.com
Map **2 F6** Metro **Burj Dubai**
A wide range of electronics is stocked here including well-known brands – particularly Sony products. The

store offers home delivery and installation for some of its products as well as warranties and protection plans. For other locations see Store Finder, p.419.

### SharafDG

**Times Square** Al Quoz **04 341 8060**
www.sharafdg.com
Map **1 T5** Metro **Al Quoz**
This is many residents' first port of call because of its range of gadgets and good service. It stores carry everything from plasma televisions and laptop computers to mobile phones and irons. For other locations see the Store Finder p.424.

### Jumbo Electronics

**BurJuman** Bur Dubai **04 352 1323**
www.jumbocorp.com
Map **2 L4** Metro **Khalid Bin Al Waleed**
The selection on offer at this store is vast; head here for its popular brands, good deals and helpful staff. This is also a good place to head if you are looking for Sony LCD televisions and home theatre systems. For other locations see the Store Finder on p.419.

### Sound Solutions

If you are looking for ways to amp up your parties, or you want to set up a home cinema or sound system in your home, Sound Solutions ( 050 354 4842, www.soundsolutions.ae) offer all the advice and assistance you'll need. The company provide installation services for home audio equipment, projector systems and multi-room audio installation.

### Plug-Ins

**Festival Centre** Dubai Festival City **800 758 4467**
www.pluginselectronix.com
Map **2 M8** Metro **Emirates Head Office**
A comprehensive range of electronics is offered at this store, head here for Panasonic, Bose, Sony and LG products. For other locations see Store Finder, p.423.

## Hardware & DIY

With a number of companies offering handyman services (see Domestic Help on p.106), it may be easier and cheaper to find a 'man who can' rather than invest in the tools and materials you need for DIY jobs. However, ACE (p.381) and Speedex (04 339 1929) on Sheikh Zayed Road stock comprehensive ranges of tools, along with all the nails, nuts, bolts and screws you may need. Carrefour (p.391) has a DIY section and there are numerous independent shops selling a broad range of items in Satwa. Dragon Mart (p.411), in International City, has a section for builder's merchants and here you can find tiles, power tools and other hardware items.

# Health Food & Special Dietary Requirements

The range of health and speciality food is increasing, and although prices are generally high it is worth shopping around as costs vary from shop to shop. Shops selling sports supplements, energy bars and protein powders are often classified as health food shops and some are now diversifying into selling speciality foodstuffs.

Nutrition Zone (p.422) specialises in vitamins, health supplements and detoxifying products from Holland & Barrett. It also carries a range of health food, grains, gluten and wheat-free products, as well as Green & Blacks chocolate and some ecological household products. Its prices are reasonable and below those of the supermarkets for many items.

The main supermarkets stock increasing varieties of speciality foods and they all carry products for diabetics; Choithram (p.392) has possibly the widest range – it also stocks dairy-free, gluten-free and wheat-free products ranging from bread to icecream. A pricey, but wide selection of organic groceries can be bought at the Organic Foods & Cafe (p.392). Spinneys (p.392) carries a limited selection of organic fruit and vegetables and, through their partnership with Waitrose, an organic range which includes beans, pulses, biscuits and fruit juice. The store also stocks some items from Waitrose's 'Perfectly Balanced' calorie and fat counted range and some Weight Watchers products.

Park n Shop's (p.392) health food range includes breads made from spelt or rye flour; it even makes spelt hot cross buns and mince pies. Carrefour's (p.391) range is increasing and, as well as the basic items that most supermarkets carry, have some own-brand organic products.

Dubai hosts the annual Middle East Natural & Organic Products Expo, which sees over 300 companies from 35 countries exhibiting a range of natural products and treatments. See www.globallinksdubai.com for details.

# Kids' Items

There is a high concentration of shops selling toys and clothes for children and you'll find a good selection of well-known stores and smaller outlets. Magrudy's (p.364) sells toys for younger children and Park n Shop (p.392) has a great toy department with some good 'pocket money' toys, as does Book Worm (p.362). IKEA (p.371) and Kidz Inc in Al Quoz (04 340 5059) carry good quality toys that are built to last.

Most electronics stores stock a wide range of games for the various platforms. Try Geekay (p.418) and Carrefour (p.391) which have a good selection.

For inexpensive birthday presents and stocking fillers, Carrefour (p.391) and Géant (p.392) both have toy departments, and the little shops around Karama and Satwa are excellent for cheap toys (just don't expect them to last a long time).

Remember that not all toys conform to international safety standards and therefore should only be used under supervision.

When it comes to clothing, there is plenty of choice, whether it is high-end designer fashion like Christian Lacroix (04 351 7133) and Armani (p.415) or factory seconds from Sana (p.393). Many of the department stores (p.390) have children's departments and for real indulgence, The Dubai Mall (p.402) has a section dedicated to premium brands such as Armani Junior (p.415), Diesel Kids (p.417) and Cacharel (04 409 8888).

For babies and younger children, Babyshop (p.), Mamas and Papas (p.360), Mothercare (p.360), Woolworths (p.426) and Next (p.391) carry the essentials and have some great outfits at reasonable prices. Okaidi (p.422) and Pumpkin Patch (p.423) sell bright, colourful and practical clothes. Monsoon (p.421) has a great range of party clothes, particularly for girls.

---

## School Uniforms

Most schools will suggest a preferred supplier for its school uniforms, and Dar Al Tasmim Uniforms (04 394 1477) and Zaks (04 342 9828) produce uniforms for many of the schools in Dubai. You can also buy generic uniform from Marks & Spencer (p.391) and Magrudy's (p.364)

---

The majority of children's clothes shops also stock shoes and there are some specialist stores. Pablosky (p.422) stocks a range of colourful shoes for babies and children Shoe Mart (p.424) and Debenhams have children's sections. Adams (p.414) and The Athlete's Foot (p.425) and Shoe Mart (p.424) also carry a good range. Ecco (p.417) stocks a good range for children and adults shoes.

For party costumes check out the Early Learning Centre (p.375) or Toys R Us (p.378), year round, and Mr Ben's in Al Ghazal Mall. Supermarkets and hypermarkets (p.391) stock some items in the run up to festive events like Halloween and Christmas.

## Early Learning Centre

**Wafi** Umm Hurair **04 324 2730**
www.elc.com
Map **2 L6** Metro **Healthcare City**
Early Learning Centre stocks a good range of educational products and toys that stimulate play and imagination. There are several outlets in Dubai, but they are often rather small and quite cluttered. There are still some good buys to be had, including children's books and some wooden toys. For other locations see Store Finder, p.417.

# Places To Shop For Kids

Dubai is home to all manner of kids' items – from novelty t-shirts to toys galore. Get ready to spoil them!

Whether you need to get a gift, re-stock a wardrobe or fulfil a curriculum requirement, Shopping for your (or your friends') kids can be an expensive and exhausting task. But with a little bit of planning and a lot of imagination you can have the best-dressed, most-educated and well-occupied child in Dubai…

## Kids' Fashion

The good news is that Dubai has a wide variety of international brands (see Kids' Items, p.375) and many adult fashion stores have kids' ranges. H&M has a great range of on-trend kids clothes and shoes, while Marks & Spencer (p.391) and Next (p.391) have good quality ranges. Check out Women's Secrets for a unique baby and toddler wear, and Beyond the Beach for some super cool surf gear. For novelty t-shirts and babygrows ("My Dad's Cooler Than Yours" etc.) check out concession stalls found in most malls.

## Kids' Sportsgear

For swimming suits with built in floats check out Mothercare (p.360), Early Learning Centre (p.375) and most sports shops (p.384). Sun and Sand Sports (p.385) have a great range of sporting items for kids including roller blades, trampolines (also try Intersport, p.385 and Toys R Us p.378), bikes (see also p.360), miniature pool tables, tennis rackets and golf clubs. For specialists sportswear, like martial arts outfits and ballet outfits you will probably have to buy from one of the academies (see Kids' Activities p.143), although Marks & Spencer (p.391) sometimes carries ballet outfits.

## Musical Instruments

There are a number of specialists shops (see p.380) but you can also find basic drum kits and keyboards in Toys R Us, and Sharaf DG (p.374) have an excellent range of keyboards, as well as digital music games. You might also be able to pick up a second hand guitar or piano, check out www.dubizzle.com or put a notice on www.expatwoman.com. If you're looking for sheet music (often teachers will request parents to buy the required sheet music) Magrudy's has a large range, including exam papers, and can generally order specific books for you.

## Bedroom Design

If you want to decorate your kids room but don't want to paint it you can get family photos printed on canvas (see p.358), recreate a night time scene (with stars and a moon) or garden setting (with flowers and a ladybird) in wall lighting from Ikea (p.371). Alternatively go for wall stickers – Just Kidding stocks wall stickers for children from funky and friendly animal stickers for nurseries to flowers and rockets for young children's rooms. Order online at www.justkidding-me.com or pop into their store in Al Quoz (800 5878).

## Bags & Stationary

While a lot of schools have book bags as part of their uniform many kids also take their own school bag in order to fit in their gym kit and packed lunch. Pull along wheeled bags are popular and can be found in Toys R Us in all manner of characters, Uptown Mirdif has a dedicated store for kids at reasonable prices. If you're looking for pencil cases and the like Magrudy's, Toys R Us, Early Learning Centre (p.375) stock good ranges, whilst Dubai Library Distributors in Bin Sougat Centre (p.410) has a huge range of stationary items, pens, pads, arts and crafts etc.

## Affordable Gifts

Once your kids get to school age you will find that they will be invited to a birthday party nearly every month. So buying birthday gifts can get expensive – try Dragon Mart (p.411) for electronic cars, Candylicious in Dubai Mall (04 330 8700) for party bag ingredients, Daiso for all sorts of fun items like glow sticks and tattoos (in Lamcy Plaza, 04 3351532, Arabian Centre 04 284 5754) and the hypermarkets (p.391) are always a good bet.

## Hamleys

The Dubai Mall Downtown Burj Dubai **04 339 8889**
www.hamleys.com
Map **2 F6** Metro **Burj Dubai**
Hold on to your kids, this store is well known for offering the best, and the biggest, variety of toys. Hamleys' new store, in The Dubai Mall, lives up to expectations with its vibrant staff (who tantalise kids from the doorway) and plethora of toys for preschoolers through to early teens.

## Imaginarium

Wafi Umm Hurair **04 324 8055**
www.imaginarium.ae
Map **2 L6** Metro **Healthcare City**
This amusing store has two entrances – one for the grown ups and another for the real customers, the kids. The assortment of items on offer includes games, soft toys and arts and crafts. Many of the toys are fun and educational – perfect for stimulating young minds.

## The Toy Store

Mall Of The Emirates Al Barsha **04 341 2470**
Map **1 R5** Metro **Mall of the Emirates**
Recognisable by the large toy animals peering out of its open store front, The Toy Store is a great place to amaze kids. The store in the Mall of The Emirates is set over two floors and is filled with a broad variety of toys. For other locations see the Store Finder p.425.

## Toys R Us

Festival Centre Festival City **04 206 6552**
www.toysrus.com
Map **2 M8** Metro **Emirates Head Office**
This well-known emporium offers a good selection of products, whether you are looking for small toys to amuse kids or larger gifts like bikes, electronic games and play sets – its stores also have Ladybird concessions. For other locations see Store Finder, p.426.

# Maternity Items

Many retailers have jumped on the maternity fashion bandwagon and now offer fashionable outfits so that mums-in-training can look as stylish as everyone else. Dorothy Perkins (p.419), New Look (p.424), H&M (p.419) and Topshop (p.426) are great for fun, fashionable items, and Debenhams (p.390), Marks & Spencer (p.421), Mothercare (p.421), Mamas and Papas (p.421) and Woolworths (p.426) also stock good selections of maternity clothes. Formes (04 324 4856), Great Expectations (04 345 3155) and Jenny Rose (p.378) carry the latest styles, and are good places to find speciality items such as swimwear, underwear and evening wear. As well as buggies and nursery furniture, Just Kidding (www.justkidding-me.com) carries Noppies maternity wear from Holland. For other maternity items, like cool packs, creams and bras, you'll

have to shop around in Mothercare (p.421), Babyshop (p.360), Debenhams (p.390), Marks & Spencer (p.421) or Jenny Rose (p.378) – ranges vary and may be limited.

Baby Shop and Mothercare stock a range of breast pumps, or you could try one of the larger pharmacies if you want a really heavy duty one (you can also rent one, try Susi on 050 658 8905). Storage bags for breast milk are widely available (Playtex, Medela, and Avent brands). Boppy breastfeeding pillows are available in Toys R Us, and Arabian Home Health Care (www.arabianhomecare.com), opposite Rashid Hospital, also stock pillows for breast feeding – you need to ask for them when you go in.

Other essential accessories for pregnancy are available here – one example is a 'Bump Belt', which redirects your car seatbelt under your bump, which can be found in Mothercare and some Spinneys (p.392). For more information on having a baby see p.141.

## Blossom Mother & Child

The Dubai Mall Downtown Burj Dubai **04 272 6028**
www.blossommotherandchild.com
Map **2 F6** Metro **Burj Dubai**
A premium range of maternity items is sold at this store, all from well-known designers. The store also has a denim bar which features popular brands like J Brand Jeans and 7 For All Mankind, customised with the Blossom Band.

## Jenny Rose

Mall Of The Emirates Al Barsha **04 341 0577**
www.jennyrosematernity.com
Map **1 R5** Metro **Mall of the Emirates**
Fashionable mums should head to this store for classy clothes for the day or night. Its collection is particularly suitable for Dubai's warm climate and you'll find a good assortment of dresses, sleeveless tops and comfortable trousers. There is also a small selection of sports wear and lingerie.

# Music & DVDs

Unless you have particularly eclectic taste, you should find a satisfying collection of music in the city's supermarkets and record stores. The advantage of Dubai's multicultural society is that you can open yourself up to new genres – Arabic dance music for example, is very popular. Everything has to go through the censor, so any music or DVDs deemed offensive will not be sold here, unless it can be edited to make it more acceptable.

## Tune In

Rumour has it that iTunes may be making its way to the UAE and Dubai's residents could soon have the ability to purchase and download music, literature and films from its extensive online catalogue.

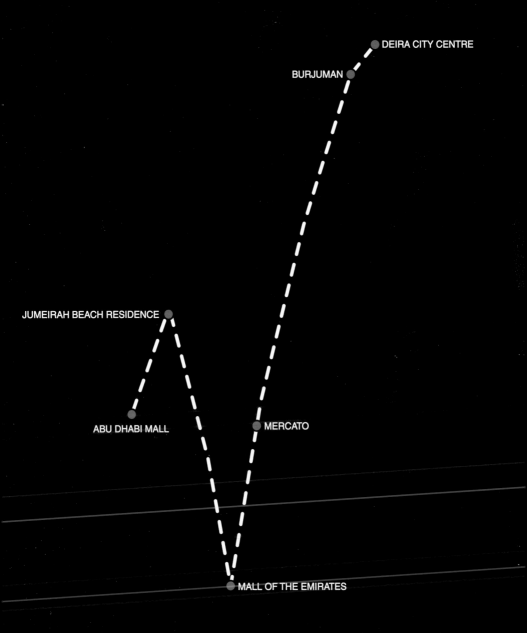

## DVD Rentals

There are a few places where you can rent DVDs in the city, Spinneys stores often have rental sections where you can sign up. Some supermarkets have a self service dvd dispenser from Moviebank (www.moviebankme.com) or Davina Box, where you pay to join and you are charged by the day – you simply return the DVD to the dispenser when you are finshed.

Hollywood blockbusters and mainstream titles can be picked up in many supermarkets. Music and DVDs are generally more expensive than they are in other countries. Disco 2000 (04 394 0139) stocks a good range of items, particularly BBC and children's titles – it also has a rental section. Carrefour has good value bargain bins and although they are usually filled with Hollywood titles, there are occasional gems and the odd BBC children's title. Bollywood films are extremely popular and available in most shops. In common with the rest of the world, video is being phased out, and DVD is now prevalent.

Retailers will order titles that are on the approved list for the UAE. Online shopping is an alternative if you can't find an item and you'll find more variety on sites like Amazon (www.amazon.com and www.amazon.co.uk). Amazon's postal charges are often fairly high and its branded packages are occasionally inspected at the post office (see online shopping p.348).

### Ohm Records
Opp Burjuman Centre Bur Dubai **04 397 3728**
www.ohmrecords.com
Map **2 L4** Metro **Khalid Bin Al Waleed**
Vinyl fans and those into electronic mixing should head to this speciality shop – a selection of its music comes from independent labels. The store also holds a selection of very mainstream DVDs and videos and few independent films. You can also buy processors and turntables, as well as record bags, accessories and a select line of street wear.

### Virgin Megastore
Mall Of The Emirates Al Barsha **04 341 4353**
www.virginmegame.com
Map **1 R5** Metro **Mall of the Emirates**
The widest selection of mainstream music is stocked at this store. Its sizeable range is well organised by genre and it holds an excellent range of DVD box sets. For other locations see Store Finder, p.426.

## Musical Instruments
Things are looking up for the Dubai's music scene; several new stores have opened and you should find a decent selection of products. Juli Music, on Sheikh Zayed Road, stocks a good range of instruments and can also arrange lessons (see Music Lessons p.330). Particularly useful is its 'hire before you buy' policy. Sowira Pianos offer rental and sales on a range of new and used pianos. The Music Room is run by an experienced music teacher, and has the widest range of sheet music in Dubai. Here you'll find a range of instruments including clarinets, flutes, violins, trumpets and guitars, and their associated accessories. The store is an agent for Steinway & Sons pianos, but if you don't have the space it also stocks Kawai grand, upright and digital pianos. Prices for pianos are considerably lower than elsewhere in the world. Music House has a wide range of mainly Yamaha instruments, from pianos to drum kits and guitars, and they also sell mixing desks and equipment for digital music-making (there is a branch in Ibn Battuta called Thomsun Pure Music). Sharaf DG, Carrefour, Géant and other large supermarkets stock basic keyboards and guitars, which are fine for beginners.

### The Music Institute
Dubai Knowledge Village Al Sufouh **04 424 3818**
www.themusic-uae.com
Map **1N4** Metro **Dubai Internet City**
A small range of items are stocked here such as digital pianos, guitars, violins and guitar accessories, but the range is primarily to support its students.

### Sadek Music
Souk Madinat Jumeirah Al Sufouh **04 368 6570**
www.sadek-music.com
Map **1 R4** Metro **Mall Of The Emirates**
Sadek Music stocks an assortment of eastern and western instruments. The store also offers a repair service, music lessons and you can also rent a selection of its instruments. Its branch in The Dubai Mall carries a good range of guitars. For other locations see the Store Finder on p.424.

### Zak Electronics
Zabeel Rd, Karama, **04 336 8857**
www.zakelectronics.com
Map **2 L4** Metro **Khalid Bin Al Waleed**
This store carries grand pianos, keyboards, amplifiers and guitar accessories. You'll also find a good range of brands including Roland, Kawai and Fender.

## Outdoor Goods
Exploring the great outdoors is a popular pastime in the UAE, especially when the weather cools. While there are no specialist camping shops, the basic gear is readily available in Carrefour (p.391), Go Sports (p.385), Géant (p.392) and ACE (p.381). Items are suitable for weekend campers, but would not withstand extremes, so if you are intending to do anything more strenuous you should consider ordering kit online. Go Sports produces its own range of camping equipment as well

as importing ranges from other suppliers.

Caveman Make Fire (04 347 6167, www.cavemanmakefire.com) produces a range of barbecues and heaters which you can pick up at Géant (p.392) or Spinneys (p.392) and HyperPanda (p.392), or you can have them delivered free of charge.

GPS equipment can be found in SharafDG – the Times Square branch has the biggest selection. For outdoor sports enthusiasts there are a number of options (see Sports Goods on p.384). Fishing equipment is widely available from shops such as Al Hamur Marine, Picnico (p.381) and Go Sports (p.385).

Serious climbers and hikers should consider getting their boots and equipment from overseas, as a very limited range of boots are available and are often aimed more towards the fashion market. You can order a good range of items from REI (www.rei.com) and Mountain Equipment Co-op (www.mec.ca). You can also buy boots from Timberland (p.426) and some of the stores in Karama (p.90). While hydration packs (backpacks that you can fill with water, complete with a long tube and mouthpiece) are becoming more widely available in sports shops, anything larger than a day pack should be bought overseas. Hiking accessories for those people with small children, such as backpack carriers, are not widely available here and should be bought online or from overseas.

### ACE > p.107
Sheikh Zayed Road Al Quoz 04 338 1416
www.aceuae.com
Map 2 B4 Metro Al Quoz
You can buy all the basic equipment you need for your jaunt in the desert at this store, including tents, sleeping bags and cool boxes. The store also stocks a good range of hardware and accessories.

### Picnico General Trading
Jumeira Rd, Nr Eppco Jumeira 04 394 1653
Map 2 C3 Metro Business Bay
Picnico are outdoor specialists, stocking a good range of Coleman and Campingaz equipment like cooler bags, tents and accessories. The store also stocks GPS systems and rock climbing gear. It has one of the largest ranges of hydration packs and it carries Dakine (kite surfing kit) sea kayaks and angling equipment.

## Party Accessories
Party accessories are available, on a small scale, in most supermarkets and toy shops but there are several specialist stores that stock everything for children's or adults' parties. If you want a party at home but without the bother, there are a number of companies who will do it for you (see Parties at Home, p.434). You can always go the easier route and have a party at one of the various play centres around town. Tickles & Giggles is a party zone for kids which also has a

well-stocked party store. Partyzone (04 344 4158) in Jumeira Plaza, covers the basics; Carrefour (p.391), Park n Shop (p.392) and Toys R Us (p.378) all sell themed party essentials, such as paper cups, gift bags, balloons and plates. The range isn't huge and tends to be either Winnie the Pooh, Barbie or Mickey Mouse, so if your child has a preference you may have to order online. For certain occasions, like Halloween and Easter, specialist shops and even supermarkets (Park n Shop, Carrefour and Spinneys) really get into the spirit of things, selling a range of costumes, sweets and accessories. Costume ranges tend to be a bit limited though. Mr Ben's Closet (04 345 3577), in Al Ghazal Mall, is dedicated to fancy dress, with costumes for children and adults available for purchase and hire.

Fabric is inexpensive and it doesn't cost much to hire the services of a tailor, so you can easily have a costume made (see Tailors, p.354).

For cakes, try Lenôtre (04 351 6953), Coco's (04 332 6333) or Boulevard Gourmet (04 222 7171) at the InterContinental for some yummy options. For children, you can get a customised cake made at Park n Shop (p.391); choose one of its own designs or take your own picture in and the staff will scan it onto edible paper and place it on top of your cake. Baskin Robbins (04 336 6636) makes a range of icecream party cakes and Caesars (04 335 3700) does some elaborately iced creations.

For party entertainment (see p.434), Flying Elephant (p.354) can provide bouncy castles, soft-play areas and more. Tumble Time (www.tumbletimedubai.com) are bouncy castle specialists, and Harlequin (www.harlequinmarquees.com) provide marquees and even outdoor cooling units. Planet Hollywood (p.489), Café Céramique (p.464) and The Jam Jar (p.244) all cater for children's parties, as do many of the hotel clubs. For entertainment at an adult's party, try Andy the Entertainer (050 840 1770) his acts range from the amazing (magic tricks and fire eating) to the bizarre (encasing his whole body in a big balloon).

### Balloon Lady
Jumeira Plaza Jumeira 04 344 1062
www.balloonladyuae.com
Map 2 H3 Metro Al Jafiliya
This store is the place to buy balloons and seasonal items; you can also hire bouncy castles and purchase costumes for special events. The store offers a balloon decoration service and can also customise balloons. For other locations see Store Finder, p.415.

### The Party Centre
Opp Welcare Hospital Garhoud 04 283 1353
www.mypartycentre.com
Map N6 Metro GGICO
The Party Centre is enormous and stocks pretty much everything you will need, no matter what the

occasion. This is a one-stop shop for decorations and party accessories, and it even sells children's fancy dress outfits.

# Perfumes & Cosmetics

Perfumes and cosmetics are big business here, from the local scents like frankincense and oudh, to the latest designer offerings. These perfumes and scents tend to be strong and spicy – you can often locate the stores by the smell of the incense they burn in their doorways. The department stores (Harvey Nichols, Saks Fifth Avenue and Debenhams) and local chains (such as Areej and Paris Gallery) stock the most comprehensive ranges of international brand perfumes and cosmetics.

The Body Shop (p.425), MAC (p.420), Bobbi Browm (p.415) and Red Earth (p.423) are found in many of the city's malls, while Boots now has several branches. Sephora (p.424) has a wide selection of brands and its staff will also offer tips on application. This sector has been joined by Pixi Cosmetics in Mall of the Emirates. L'Occitaine is also worth seeking out for their natural skincare products. Larger supermarkets and pharmacies stock skincare products and some make-up. Anti-allergenic ranges are available at some of the larger pharmacies. Most needs are covered but if yours aren't, specialist retailers often have online shopping facilities.

Ajmal and Arabian Oud outlets are found in most malls, but they cater to the Arab population and don't always have English-speaking shop assistants on duty.

Prices for perfumes and cosmetics are similar to those in some other countries, although certain nationalities might find perfume is cheaper here than in their home country. There are no sales taxes, so there is rarely a difference between Duty Free and shopping mall prices.

## Amouage

**Paris Gallery** Deira City Centre **04 295 5550**
www.amouage.com
Map **2 N6** Metro **Deira City Centre**
Amouage 'the world's most valuable perfume,' is made in Oman. The luxurious brand is sold exclusively in Paris Gallery stores (p.382) and Dubai and Abu Dhabi Duty Free. A standalone store is set to open in Dubai in February.

## Faces

**BurJuman** Bur Dubai **04 325 1441**
www.faces-me.com
Map **2 L4** Metro **Khalid Bin Al Waleed**
All manner of lotions and potions are sold in this store. Get all of your monthly makeup, perfume and skincare buys here, from brands like Clarins, Lancome, Givenchy and Clinique. There are several locations in Dubai (see Store Finder, p.418).

## Paris Gallery

**Ibn Battuta Mall** Jebel Ali **04 368 5500**
www.uae-parisgallery.com
Map **1 G4** Metro **Ibn Battuta**
Although it stocks a wide selection of perfumes and cosmetics (and a good range of shoes, eyewear and jewellery), its stores never feel too busy, which allows plenty of freedom to browse. For other locations see Store Finder, p.422.

# Pets

Most supermarkets carry basic ranges of cat, dog, bird and fish food, although the choice is limited. If your pet has specific dietary requirements, many of the veterinary clinics (p.148) carry specialist foods.

Some pet shops are a bit on the dismal side here – standards are low and animals are usually in tiny

cages without water for long periods. The pet shops along Plant Street in Satwa are notoriously the worst offenders and animals purchased there are often malnourished and diseased. Dubai Municipality has laid down regulations but if they are contravened the shop will often be closed down for just one day. Even the pet shops that most animal lovers can bear to go into have a long way to go before standards are acceptable. Petland (04 338 4040), in Al Quoz, Paws and Claws in Uptown Mirdiff, Petzone (04 321 1424) on Sheikh Zayed Road, and Animal World (04 344 4422), on Jumeira Beach Road, are the most acceptable. All sell a range of pet accessories, food, animals, birds and fish.

If you are looking for a family pet, consider contacting Feline Friends or K9 Friends (see p.124) who have hundreds of cats and dogs looking for homes.

## Second-Hand Items

There is an active second-hand market in Dubai, as people are always leaving, redecorating or downsizing and need to get rid of their stuff. Supermarket noticeboards are a great place to start, as many people post 'for sale' notices with pictures of all the items. Garage sales are also popular on Fridays and you'll notice signs going up in your neighbourhood from time to time.

For the Dhs.3 entry fee into Al Safa Park you can peruse the flea market which has stalls filled with furniture, books, clothing and a broad range of unwanted items and homemade crafts. The flea market is set up on the first Saturday of every month near Gate 5 (for more information see www.dubai-fleamarket. com). A car boot sale is held every Friday in the cooler winter months at the Autodrome (p.330); it's free for shoppers and Dhs.150 per car for those wishing to sell (see www.carbootuae.com for more details). There are also a number of websites with classifieds sections. Try www.expatwoman.com, www.dubizzle.com, www. souq.com, and www.websouq.com.

There are a number of second-hand shops, often linked to churches and special needs schools, but the opening hours can be somewhat eccentric. The Holy Trinity Thrift Shop (04 337 8192) gives you back 50% of what your items sell for, so you can even make money out of being charitable. It is good for high-quality items and books in particular, and proceeds go towards a number of orphanages supported by the church. The Al Noor shop raises funds for the Al Noor School for Special Needs and is good for second-hand clothing. All donations in good condition are accepted. The Dubai Charity Centre (04 337 8246), behind Choithram in Karama, is the biggest of the charity shops. This store supports the students who attend The Dubai Centre for Special Needs, and finances a number of places for those who are unable to afford them. It stocks a good range of clothes,

books and toys. The Rashid Paediatric Therapy Centre, behind the American Academic School in Al Barsha, has a decent range of items and raises money for projects at the centre.

If you are looking to clear some space on your bookshelves, Book World in Karama and Satwa, and House of Prose which has branches in Jumeira Plaza and Ibn Battuta, both buys books in good condition that they will be able to sell. Any books bought from them will be worth 50% of the purchase price if returned in good condition.

## Souvenirs

From typical holiday trinkets to tasteful keepsakes, there is a good range of souvenirs in Dubai. Many of the items are regional rather than local, and several are mass produced in India, Pakistan and Oman. You will find a good selection of traditional gifts like antique wooden wedding chests, or pashminas, and the typical holiday buys like fridge magnets, T-shirts and soft toys.

Tourist hotspots like Souk Madinat Jumeirah (p.408) and Mall of the Emirates (p.405) all sell a good selection of souvenirs, but warehouse stores like the Antiques Museum (p.384) and Pinky's (p.372) also stock a wide range. You'll also find a good selection of stores in Trade Routes in Festival City (p.401) and Khan Murjan (p.396). If you make it clear you are a resident and you'll be back for more if the prices are good, you should get a better price (see Bargaining p.350).

You'll find camels feature heavily in souvenir shops; wooden carvings, camel pot stands, and even carvings made from camel bones are all widely available and are great as novelty presents. Perhaps the tackiest souvenirs are plastic alarm clocks in the shape of a mosque – they only cost Dhs.10 and they wake you up with a loud call to prayer.

Coffee pots are symbols of Arabic hospitality and another popular souvenir item. Prices vary enormously from Dhs.100 for a brand new, shiny one, to several thousand dirhams for a genuine antique. Traditional silver items, such as the Arabic dagger (khanjar) and silver wedding jewellery, are excellent souvenirs, and are available both framed and unframed.

Wooden items are popular and representative of the region; trinket boxes (often with elaborate carvings or brass inlays) start from around Dhs.10. Elaborate Arabic doors and wedding chests, costing thousands, are also popular. The doors can be hung as art, or converted into tables or headboards.

While carpets are a good buy, it is worth doing some research before investing (see p.366 for more information). For a smaller, cheaper option, many shops sell woven coasters and camel bags, or you can buy a Persian carpet mouse pad.

You can hardly walk through a mall or shopping area without being offered a pashmina – they are available in an abundant range of colours and styles. Most are a cotton or silk mix and the ratio dictates the price. It is a good idea to check out a few shops before buying as prices vary and, as with most items, the more you buy the cheaper they are. For a decent quality pashmina, prices start from around Dhs.50. Shisha pipes make fun souvenirs and can be bought with various flavours of tobacco, such as apple or strawberry. Both functional and ornamental examples are on sale, prices start from around Dhs.75 in Carrefour.

## LIVE WORK EXPLORE SHOP

Listing all the stores in Dubai would make this already cumbersome book too big to handle. If your favourite shopping spot has not been mentioned, log on to www.liveworkexplore.com for a full list of stores, or to share your expertise.

Local scents like oudh and frankincense make good gifts and are widely available in outlets like Arabian Oud. These perfumes and scents tend to be strong and spicy – you can often locate these stores by the smell of incense they burn in their doorways. Amouage produces some of the world's most valuable perfumes, made with rare ingredients. Its products can be found in airports and branches of Paris Gallery (p.382). Ajmal and Arabian Oud outlets are found in most malls, but they cater to the Arab population and don't always have English-speaking shop assistants on duty.

Well-known perfume brands can be picked up in many of the department stores and local chains (such as Areej and Paris Gallery). Prices for perfume are similar to most countries, although some nationalities may find it cheaper than back home. There are no sales taxes, so there is rarely a difference between prices in Duty Free and the shopping malls.

For book lovers, there are a number of great coffee table books with stunning photos depicting the diversity of this vibrant city. Grab a copy of *Dubai: Tomorrow's City Today*, *Impressions Dubai*, or *Images of Dubai and the UAE*. *Dubai Discovered* is a concise pictorial souvenir of Dubai and is available in five languages (English, Japanese, French, German and Russian).

If you've scoured the souvenir shops in Dubai and still can't find what you're looking for, head for Souk Al Arsah in Sharjah, where you can shop for traditional items in a traditional setting.

### Al Jaber Gallery

The Dubai Mall Downtown Burj Dubai 04 339 8566
www.aljaber.ae
Map 2 F6 Metro Burj Dubai
Colourful accessories, souvenirs and carpets are sold at this eclectic store. This is the perfect spot to take out of town visitors, or if you need a few traditional items to spice up your home. For other locations see the Store Finder p.414.

### Antique Museum

Nr Kanoo Int Paints Al Quoz 04 347 9935
Map 1 S6 Metro First Gulf Bank
Upon entering this store's gilded doors, you'll be met by an eclectic mix of wooden furniture, soft furnishings and accessories and an impressive selection of decorative wooden statues. It has a large section devoted to teak Indian furniture and large collection of silver chests. The store also has a fantastic selection of token holiday tat – cheaper than you'll find in tourist havens like the Souk Madinat Jumeirah (p.408), but you can also pick up pashminas, Omani silver boxes and other traditional souvenirs. A guide will lead you through the store's maze of products, buried doorways and secret rooms – it's hard to shop alone as there are no prices.

### The Sultani Lifestyle Gallerie

Souk Al Bahar Downtown Burj Dubai 04 420 3676
Map 2 F6 Metro Burj Dubai
Head here for traditional souvenirs, carpets and exotic items from the region. The store also carries a good selection of postcards and elaborate home furnishings. For other locations see the Store Finder on p.425.

## Sports Goods

Sport is already big business in Dubai, but the development of Sports City (part of Dubailand) should heighten this interest. Several stores sell basic equipment, clothing and footwear, as well as equipment for 'core sports' like running, basketball, cricket, football, swimming, badminton, squash and tennis. The usual sports brands are sold in the larger sportswear stores and The Dubai Mall has a whole strip of stores featuring well-known brands such as Adidas (p.414), Nike (p.422), Puma (p.423) and Element (04 434 0638) for skateboarding gear. Stadium (p.385) stocks New Balance footwear and has a large Speedo and Reebok collection. Stylish boarding brands Quiksilver (p.423), Billabong (p.415) and Rip Curl (04 341 0794) all have stores in Dubai and you'll also find branches of Columbia (p.417) and Timberland (p.426).

Several stores in Karama Market (p.388) have decent ranges that are often cheaper than the bigger stores – just remember, if the item you are buying is much cheaper than normal, it could be a fake. Stylish active wear brand Lorna Jane and Capezio dancewear can be bought from Active Living (contact Belinda Reardon for more information, 050 352 7446).

Golf is extremely popular and clubs, balls and bags are available in most sports shops. Golf House (04 434 0655) and the pro shops are the best places for decent kit. Knight Shot Inc (04 343 5678), in Trade Center 1, specialise in pool and snooker tables and equipment.

Clubs that organise specialist sports, such as Dubai Surfski Kayak Club (www.dskc.net), can often be approached for equipment. Kite surfing equipment is stocked in several shops; Al Boom Marine (p.317) stocks North Kites at the Jumeira Beach Road showroom, and Picnico (p.381), next door, stocks Dakine. Al Boom also stocks equipment for other watersports, including waterskiing and diving. Magic Swell (www.magicswell.com), is an online shop which sells a wide range of watersport accessories such as wetsuits, harnesses and helmets.

### Go Sports
**Ibn Battuta Mall** Jebel Ali **04 368 5344**
Map **1 G4** Metro **Ibn Battuta**
Go Sport has the most comprehensive collection of sports goods. Its large stores in Ibn Battuta Shopping Mall and Mall of the Emirates sell equipment for popular sports like running, basketball and tennis and it also stocks cycling, camping and golfing gear. The range of products and brands on offer is very good but specialist advice is harder to come by – know exactly what you need before you head here. For other locations see Store Finder, p.418.

### Intersport
**Times Square** Al Quoz **04 229 6514**
www.intersport.com
Map **1 T5** Metro **Al Quoz**
Intersport is great for picking up essentials and well-known brands. It stocks a good selection of running apparel and football gear (such as shin pads, football

boots and replica football shirts). The brands on offer include the regulars like Nike, Adidas and Puma, in addition to New Balance, The North Face and Firefly. For other locations see Store Finder, p.419.

### Stadium
**Deira City Centre** Deira **04 295 0261**
www.billabong.com
Map **2 N6** Metro **Deira City Centre**
Stadium (previously known as Studio R) sells brands that cater to those with an active lifestyle. With a range of well-known clothing labels (Quiksilver, Rockport and Union Bay), and sports brands (Adidas, New Balance, Reebok and Speedo), Stadium has created its own niche. It also stocks Teva, which make a range of practical sandals. The store has sales throughout the year when prices are heavily discounted. For other locations see the Store Finder on p.425.

### Sun & Sand Sports
**Ibn Battuta Mall** Jebel Ali **04 366 9777**
www.sunandsandsports.com
Map **1 G4** Metro **Ibn Battuta**
This is one of the larger stores stocking sports goods in the city. You'll find a good range of home gym equipment, from treadmills to rowing machines, as well as a limited range of pool and snooker tables. Larger branches have Nike, Columbia and Timberland departments. For other locations see the Store Finder on p.425.

> ### Beach Wear
>
> Finding stuff for the beach shouldn't be too taxing, several stores in the city sell beachwear including Beyond The Beach > **p.305-306** which sells a good selection of swimming gear, wax for surfboards and clothes by major brands.

## Textiles & Haberdashery
You have three options if you are looking for fabric: the Textile Souk (near Al Fahedi Street), Satwa, or the shopping malls (most of which have at least one fabric outlet). Prices start from a few dirhams for a metre of basic cotton. The Textile Souk can get busy and parking is difficult, but the sheer range of fabrics makes it worth while. There are several haberdashery shops in the same area should you wish to buy matching buttons, bows or cotton.

Al Masroor Textiles (04 225 5343) in Deira has a good selection of fabric; Plant Street in Satwa is the place to go for upholstery fabrics. IKEA (p.372) and Fabindia (p.393) also stock a range of vibrant fabrics that can be used for cushions, curtains or bedding.

## Places To Shop

### Deepak's
Plant St Satwa **04 344 8836**
www.deepakstextiles.com
Map **2 H4** Metro **Emirates Towers**
Deepak's is well-stocked with a fantastic range of
frabrics – pick up anything from casual denim to more
glamorous silks, chiffons and pure linen at its stores.
For other locations see Store Finder, p.417.

### Regal Textiles
Opp Satwa parking Satwa **800 73425**
www.regaldubai.com
Map **2 H4** Metro **Emirates Towers**
This store stocks a good selection of fabrics including
French chiffon, printed silks, Swiss cotton and French
lace. Its range textiles are perfect for casual designs,
wedding gowns, or African and Asian fashion. For
other locations see the Store Finder on p.424.

### Rivoli Textiles
Zabeel Road Karama **04 335 0075**
www.rivoligroup.com
Map2 **L5** Metro **Karama**
This classy textile store has a broad range of fabrics
and a personalised tailoring service. Its store in Satwa
(04 344 6602) caters to women and stocks a good
range of fabrics. If you need a custom-made suit, men
or women can head to its Marina branch (04 422 1542).
For other locations see the Store Finder on p.424.

## Wedding Items
Many people choose to hold their wedding in Dubai,
so it shouldn't be too difficult to find the key items for
your big day. You can begin your wedding research by
looking up wedding etiquette, traditions and fashion
at Magrudy's (p.364), Book World by Kinokuniya
(p.362) and Marks & Spencer (p.391) which have a
limited range of books.
For dresses, head to Beach Road where you'll find
several bridal stores including The Bridal Room (04 344
6076) and Frost. For designer gowns head to Saks Fifth
Avenue's (p.391) bridal department which stocks the
latest off-the-peg designer wedding gowns by Vera
Wang and Reem Acra. The store keeps some gowns in
stock, but others can be ordered (allow around four
months for delivery). The bride will need to attend a
number of fittings, but alterations are done in-house
and are up to couture standards. Cocoon (04 295
4133) in Deira City Centre (p.400) has a good, but
unusual, selection of designs.
There are several specialist bridal designers with
workshops in Dubai, but Arushi (04 344 2277) is
renowned as one of the best. You can select the fabric
yourself or it can be selected during the first meeting
with the designer. Gowns take around one month
to make, but as Arushi is so popular, there is often a
waiting list. Some of the city's tailors are also able to

work from pictures to create your ideal dress.
Bridal accessories and shoes are available at Saks
Fifth Avenue (p.391). For the groom, there are several
shops where formal wear can be hired, including
The Wedding Shop, Elegance, and Formal Wear,
on Al Diyafah Street. Bridesmaid's dresses are sold
in the children's department of Saks Fifth Avenue.
Debenhams (p.390) and Monsoon (p.421) both sell
suitable ranges, as does Cocomino (04 286 1514) in the
Bin Sougat Centre; if the style or shade you are looking
for aren't available, you can also have them made up
by a tailor (p.354). Mothers of the bride and groom,
and guests, are well catered for at Coast, Debenhams
and Monsoon among many others.
Amal & Amal in the Jumeirah Centre and Chic Design
(050 744 3634) both make bespoke wedding stationery
and Cadorim, in the Village Mall, do tailor-made favours
and ring boxes. Magrudy's (p.364) and Susan Walpole
(p.425) stock invitations, guest books and photo
albums. Debenhams and THE One both offer wedding
list services. For any items that you can't find here,
www.confetti.co.uk accepts international orders. For
more information see Getting Married on p.140.
As well as offering wedding planning services,
several of the hotels can be commissioned to make the
wedding cake; Lenôtre also creates them. Most of the
city's florists can turn their hands to wedding bouquets
and arrangements; discuss your requirements with
them to find out what will be available.

### Frost
Palm Strip Jumeira **04 345 5690**
www.frostdubai.com
Head here for contemporary wedding dresses from
US and European designers. The store has a great
set-up for trying dresses on and very friendly staff are
on hand to help. There's also a decent selection of
evening gowns and bridesmaid dresses.

### The Wedding Shop
Jumeira Plaza Jumeira **04 344 1618**
**www.theweddingshop.ae**
You'll find everything but the cake here, and itis a
great place to get your confetti, guest books and
photo albums. Some of the designers stocked here
may be a little dated or a little flamboyant for some
brides' tastes.

# PLACES TO SHOP
## Shopping By Area

### Al Faheidi Street
Nr Astoria Hotel Bur Dubai
Map **2 L3** Metro **Al Fahidi**
Al Fahedi Street is part of the commercial area that
runs from the Bastakiya area all the way to Shindagha

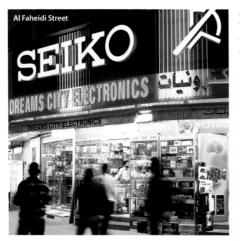

Al Faheidi Street

and takes in Dubai Museum, the electronics souk and the Textile Souk. A great place to wander round in the cooler evenings, it's perfect for a bit of local colour and some great shopping. There is a good range of inexpensive places to eat, including some fantastic vegetarian restaurants near the museum, and the outlets in the Astoria (04 353 4300) and Ambassador hotels (04 393 9444). This area is always busy but it really comes to life at night – if you're not sure you're in the right place, just head for the neon lights. The electronics souk has several shops selling top global brands such as Canon, JVC, LG, Panasonic, Philips and Sony. Prices are negotiable and competitive but the vendors know the value of what they're selling. To get the best deal, don't make your purchases at the first store you come to; instead, compare product ranges and prices between a few stores before you buy. Although goods are often cheaper here, if you are making a big purchase it may be worth paying a little bit extra at a major retailer, so that you have more security if something goes wrong.

### Downtown Burj Dubai & Dubai Mall

Downtown Burj Dubai www.thedubaimall.com
Map **2 F6** Metro **Burj Dubai**

This area has dusted off the sand and grown into a key place to eat, meet and shop. Dubai Mall currently has over 1,000 stores and it will eventually hold 1,200 shops. Those keen to spend won't be disappointed with the extensive store listing, although several stores still have 'coming soon' facades. Nonetheless, those looking for high-street fashion will be happy with its range of favourites like Topshop, GAP, S*uce (p.394), and a superb branch of Forever 21. It also has large department stores: Galeries Lafayette (p.390), Debenhams (p.390), Marks & Spencer (p.391) and Paris Gallery (p.382); well-known American

department store, Bloomingdales, is also on its way. The high end market is also catered for with a range of designer stores such as Tiffany & Co., Chanel, Dior, and Jimmy Choo.

For a more laidback atmosphere, Souk Al Bahar's passageways, resembling a traditional souk, hold shops selling Arabian wares such as carpets, ornaments, paintings, jewellery, clothes and perfumes. You'll also find that there are a number of useful outlets catering for residents such as banks, a branch of Jacky's electronics and Spinneys. Many of the shops cater to tourists, but you will find a few international brands and the odd funky boutique like Kitsch (04 367 4504) and 50°C (04 420 0414). The souks never feel too busy and most folk seem to head here for the views of the Burj Dubai and the range of eateries. To round off a day's shopping, try the Rivington Grill for British dining and great Burj views, New York's gourmet cafe Dean & DeLuca (04 420 0336), The Meat Co. (p.484) for great South African steaks, or The Mezza House (p.484) for Arabic cuisine with an international flavour.

### Dubai International Financial Centre (DIFC)

The Gate Village Trade Centre
Map **2 G5** Metro **Financial Centre**

While it may not be the first place that springs to mind when you have the urge to browse the shops, the Gate Village area of DIFC does house a select, but interesting, range of high-end boutiques. Top of the list and a must for anyone in search of the source of Dubai's glam is Villa Moda (p.395), which has accumulated top-class designers and ultra-chic couture in its glass confines. The theme continues with boutiques for famed designers Issey Miyake (04 382 5180), Marni (04 382 5120), Dries Van Norten (04 382 5130) and Vivienne Westwood (04 382 5140). Also in the area are a few convenience stores, a branch of Boots (p.415), Emirates Post and a Fitness First (p.210). There is also a branch of NStyle (p.207), and Urban Male Lounge – personal grooming for men. A few art galleries are also located in the area including Opera Gallery (p.245) and Artspace.

When you need to make a pitstop, there are several eateries to choose from whether you wish to go all out at Zuma (p.505) and Café Floirian or head for more demure surrounds at Caribou (04 363 7455), Dome (04 363 7455) and Gourmet Burger Kitchen (p.474).

### Jumeira Beach Road

Jumeira Road Jumeira
Map **2 H3**

The community feel of this area is a pleasant contrast to the large malls shoppers are used to in Dubai. While you may not be able to walk the whole strip (Beach Road stretches from Souk Madinat Jumeirah up to Al Diyafah Street), head to the cluster of stores near Dubai Zoo (p.250), the Beach Centre (p.410) and Jumeira Plaza. As you head down the road, you'll notice several stores located in villas; these are mostly spas, dentists, and a selection of clinics which offer cosmetic surgery and enhancement. As well as the range of outlets in the malls, you'll find a few independent stores selling Middle Eastern and Asian clothing along the strip and several bridal stores like Frost (p.386) and The Wedding Shop (p.386). There is a collection of smaller community malls, including Palm Strip (p.413), which has high-end boutiques, The Village (p.413) and Jumeirah Centre (p.412). At the far end of the strip is and Mercato (p.406) which has several high-street shops. There is a particularly good branch of THE One (p.372) which also includes THE One Restaurant (p.487) and a branch of Magrudys (p.364). When you are done perusing the shops, pitch up at one of the cafes – Lime Tree Cafe (p.480) is popular with residents and Arz Lebanon is particularly good for people watching.

## Karama Shopping Complex

Karama
Map **2 K5** Metro **Karama**

Karama is one of the older residential districts in Dubai, and it has a big shopping area that is one of the best places to find a bargain. The best spot is the Karama Complex, a long street running through the middle of the district that is lined by shops on both sides. The area is best known for bargain clothing, sports goods, gifts and souvenirs, and it is notorious for being the hotbed of counterfeit items in Dubai. As you wander round you will be offered 'copy watches, copy bags' with every step, and if you show any interest you will be whisked into a back room to view the goods. If you're not interested, a simple 'no thank you' will suffice, or even just ignore the vendor completely – it

may seem rude, but sometimes it's the only way to cope with the incessant invitations to view counterfeit items. Two of the most popular shops are Blue Marine (04 337 6806) and Green Eye (04 337 7721, while Asda is around the corner, and offers high quality handbags and accessories crammed into two floors. It's pretty claustrophobic but the range is excellent.

There's a huge range of T-shirts, shoes, shorts and sunglasses at very reasonable prices in Karama. There are several shops selling gifts and souvenirs, from toy camels to mosque alarm clocks and stuffed scorpions to pashminas. Gifts Tent (04 335 4416) is one of the larger outlets and has a wide range, including every colour of pashmina imaginable. The staff are happy to take most of them out so you can find exactly the right shade. With loads of small, inexpensive restaurants serving a range of cuisines, you won't go hungry while pounding the streets of Karama. Try Chef Lanka (p.466), Aryaas (p.456) or Saravana Bhavan (p.492). For fresh produce, head for the large fish, fruit and vegetable market.

## Satwa

**Btn Trade Centre & Jumeira** Satwa
Map **2 G4** Metro **Trade Centre**

Satwa, one of Dubai's original retail areas, has something of a village feel about it. Primarily arranged over four roads, the area is best known for its fabric shops and tailors, but it holds a real mix or stores. Although parts of Satwa have been demolished, many of the retail outlets still remain and the area tends to cater to the lower end of the market and is great fun to look around. Popular reasons to visit Satwa include buying traditional majlis seating and getting your car windows tinted. The pick of the fabric shops is Deepaks (p.386), with an amazing range, reasonable prices and helpful staff.

Shop around, because whatever you are looking for there's bound to be more than one outlet selling it and prices vary. There are a number of shops on 'Plant Street' with good indoor and outdoor plants. This is also the street for upholstery and paint, with Dulux, Jotun and National Paints' outlets and several upholstery shops. Animal lovers should probably avoid the pet shops – conditions are awful, despite regulations, and the animals are often in a sorry state.

Al Diyafah Street is a great place for an evening stroll. There's an eclectic mix of shops and fastfood outlets but, for some reason, there is a fairly high shop turnover so don't count on finding the same outlets twice. Al Mallah (p.452), the popular Lebanese restaurant, recognisable by its green umbrellas and neon lighting, is highly recommended for delicious and authentic local food (the best falafel in Dubai). Along Al Diyafah Street you'll also find an off-road motorbike gear shop and a shop hiring formal evening wear, both men's and women's.

Karama

Satwa is renowned for its fastfood outlets and reasonably priced restaurants. Ravi's (p.490) is an institution in Dubai, serving good Pakistani food at incredible prices; Mini Chinese (04 345 9976) has been going for years and serves great Chinese food. Rydges Plaza Hotel (04 398 2222) has a number of popular, licensed bars and restaurants.

Satwa is also home to some great salons, where you can get various treatments at low prices. They might not be as smooth as the upper-end salons, but they are great for a quick treatment. Try Pretty Lady (04 398 5255) or Honeymoon (04 398 3799).

## Sheikh Zayed Road
Btn Trade Centre & Jebel Ali Trade Centre
Map 2 H5 Metro Trade Centre
More than just the highway connecting Abu Dhabi and Dubai, Sheikh Zayed Road, between the Trade Centre and Jebel Ali, is the artery for many of Dubai's shopping districts. The area that runs alongside the road is surrounded by a mixture of industrial and retail units which house some of the city's larger independent stores.

Beginning at the Trade Centre end, this portion of the highway is flanked by some of Dubai's tallest buildings – it is worth checking out the stores at ground level. On the left side are Emirates Towers (home to Boulevard at Emirates Towers – see p.411), a number of sports shops and an Axiom Telecom repair centre; while on the right are the Holiday Centre, Lifco supermarket, and a number of cafes and fastfood outlets.

The left-hand side of the stretch between Junction One (Defence Roundabout) and Junction Two (Safa Park) is home to Emaar's new Downtown district, Burj Dubai (p.387) and The Dubai Mall (p.402). On the right-hand side are Safestway supermarket, the Mazaya Centre and a number of used-car dealers.

After Junction Two, the right-hand side of the road is residential while on the left-hand side there are a number of retail outlets and car dealerships. Behind the Pepsi factory is Safita, which sells well-priced wooden Indian furniture. For those looking to make improvements to their homes, ACE (p.372) and Speedex (04 339 1929) will have the equipment to do the job. The area between Junctions Three and Four has some real gems waiting to be discovered including the new Oasis Centre (p.412) and Wolfi's Bike Shop (p.360). Kidz Inc (04 340 5059) sells furniture, puzzles and toys for children – it's not cheap but everything is built to last. Just Kidding (p.360) has all the latest baby equipment, furniture and fashion from Europe as well as maternity wear. The Courtyard (p.469), near the Spinneys warehouse, is home to a collection of interesting shops and galleries; there's even a coffee shop. This is also the area to head for if you have green fingers or enjoy the alfresco lifestyle; Dubai Garden Centre (04 340 0006) has everything for

the garden pretty much covered. The Gold & Diamond Park (p.373), right by junction four, has almost as much to offer as the Gold Souk (p.396), but you can browse in air-conditioned comfort.

Mall of the Emirates (p.405) is the place to enjoy shopping and skiing. There is little else other than high rise-buildings but there are a few shops around the Greens, including a branch of Organic Foods & Café (p.392). The Walk, a new outdoor shopping area beneath the Jumeirah Beach Residence is where you'll find the Covent Garden Market (p.395) and a number of shops and eateries; Dubai Marina Mall (p.411) is also nearby. It's then not far to Ibn Battuta Mall (p.404). After that you'll be hard pressed to part with your cash until you reach Abu Dhabi; be sure to have a copy of the *Abu Dhabi Residents' Guide* on hand when you arrive.

## Uptown Mirdif
Mirdif
Map 2 R12
While this isn't a key shopping destination, Uptown does have a sense of community that attracts plenty of families living in the area, in the late afternoon. The mall has the essentials: a Spinneys, an A&E, a money exchange, a bank (Lloyds), a pharmacy, a branch of Fitness First and nutritionists VLCC (www.vlccinternational.com). There is a limited selection of fashion but Gant, Bedu and Kamiseta have a great range of clothes, and Pumpkin Patch, Adams and Mothercare will keep the kids dressed to the nines. There is a good selection of shoe stores including Aldo and Nine West and you'll find a good range of accessories at Beyond the Beach. 2XL has some lovely furniture and Howard's Storage World and Stokes are great for kitchen items.

There is also a good selection of cafes; particularly popular are Caribou Coffee, Central Perk (which has a healthy food menu), Starbucks and Le Pain Quotidien. There's a great foodcourt, a branch of Gourmet Burger Kitchen, Da Shi Dai for innovative Chinese cooking, and Pane Caldo for interesting Italian food.

## The Walk, Jumeirah Beach Residence
Jumeirah Beach Residence
Map 1 K3 Metro Dubai Marina
A solution to the age old gripe – there aren't enough places to walk in Dubai, The Walk, Jumeirah Beach Residence moves away from glitzy mall interiors to street-side shops and cafes. The fully pedestrianised area stretches 1.7 kilometres along the beachfront attracting beach strollers, wandering window shoppers and guests from the nearby hotels. Outlets are located either on the ground level or on the plaza level of six clusters of towers called Murjan, Sadaf, Bahar, Rimal, Amwaj and Shams. There is a concentration of stores at the ground level of Murjan

and Sadaf, but other stores are dotted further along The Walk. The plaza level of each cluster can be accessed from large staircases, or by the lifts at ground level and in the carpark.

Fashion forward shoppers will be pleased with stores like Boutique 1 (p.393), Saks Fifth Avenue (p.391), which mainly carries men's fashion – although a small women's section has emerged, and Zadig Voltaire (Dubai Mall 04 339 9186). There is also a branch of ACT Marine (04 424 3191), which sells a good range of equipment for watersports, and a few convenient stores for nearby residents such as Al Maya Supermarket (p.391). Many of the outlets are yet to open – you will need to become a regular if you want to keep up-to-date with new store openings.

In the afternoons, people congregate in the cafes along The Walk (particularly popular are Le Pain Quotidien (04 437 0141) and Starbucks (04 367 5468), and there are plenty of restaurants to dine in come the evening. Parking is available along the beach near Bahar, or you can also park in designated areas of the Murjan carpark. Many of the shops open at 10:00 and close at 22:00.

Harvey Nichols

## Department Stores

Department stores anchor some of Dubai's biggest malls and you'll find anything from the epitome of chic, Saks Fifth Avenue, to stalwarts like Marks & Spencer that provide the essentials. Renowned department store Bloomingdale's (www.bloomingdales.com) is also set to join the mix in February.

### Debenhams

Deira City Centre Deira 04 294 0011
www.debenhams.com
Map 2 N6 Metro Deira City Centre
A stalwart of the British high street, Debenhams has four stores in Dubai: Deira City Centre, Ibn Battuta, Mall of the Emirates and The Dubai Mall. All stores stock perfumes, cosmetics, and clothing for men, women and children. There are also several concessions including Evans, for plus-size clothing, Motivi, Warehouse, Oasis and Dorothy Perkins. Its branch at The Dubai Mall also has the only range of fashion brand Miss Selfridge in Dubai. There's also a good selection of homeware, including Jamie Oliver's cookware. Debenhams' reputation for selling good quality items at reasonable prices is continued in its Designers at Debenhams ranges by John Rocha, Jasper Conran and Pearce Fionda.

### Fitz & Simons

Ibn Battuta Mall Jebel Ali 04 368 5598
www.fitzandsimons.com
Map 1 G4 Metro Ibn Battuta
Head to Fitz & Simons for its range of high-quality, exclusive, European brands. The store stocks fashion for men and women, as well as lingerie, and a good range of kitchware and homeware. The store's brands include Gerry Weber, Oui and Olsen, Camel Active and Windsor Man, Luisa Cerano, Sem Per Lei and Windsor Woman. Casa Marrakesh has interesting home accessories.

### Galeries Lafayette

The Dubai Mall Downtown Burj Dubai 04 339 9933
Map 2 F6 Metro Burj Dubai
Galeries Lafayette adds more designer brands to The Dubai Mall's extensive store list. Whether you are after a glamorous frock or stylish shoes, this French department store has it all including cosmetics, children's wear, lingerie and a home ware section. The store will eventually house Lafayette Gourmet food store and French restaurant The Red Box.

### Harvey Nichols

Mall of the Emirates Al Barsha 04 409 8888
www.harveynichols.com
Map 1 R5 Metro Mall of the Emirates
The epitome of chic shopping, Harvey Nick's' (as it is affectionally called) offers a large selection of high-rolling fashion (for men, women and kids), beauty and homeware brands. Here's where you'll find Jimmy Choo, Diane Von Furstenburg, Juicy Couture, Hermes and Sergio Rossi, rubbing shoulders with other swish brands. Take note of its animated (and very realistic) mannequins, good range of designer denim and its extensive collection of designer shoes and handbags. There is a lingerie section hidden at the back of the ladies section which also sells a great range of swimwear. There is also a small selection of gourmet products in the Foodmarket on the first floor next to swish restaurant Almaz by Momo (04 409 8877); a great place for a mid-shop pit stop.

## Marks & Spencer

**Festival Centre** Festival City **04 206 6466**
www.marksandspencerme.com
Map **2 M8** Metro **Emirates Head Office**
M&S, as it is also known, is a well-known UK brand which sells clothes and shoes for men, women and children, along with a small, but ever popular, selection of food. The Dubai stores carry selected ranges of its chic Per Una brand as well as its more classic lines and its revered lingerie line. The cafe is a great place to sit and relax; the food is good and the portions generous, particularly the children's menu. As well as offering fashion and homeware, its largest store, in the Festival Centre (p.401), also has an espresso bar, a restaurant and a bakery. For other locations see the Store Finder on p.421.

## Next

**Deira City Centre** Deira **04 295 5025**
www.next.co.uk
Map **2 N6** Metro **Deira City Centre**
Next is a popular British chain that has several stores in the UAE. On sale are clothes for men, women and children, as well as shoes, underwear, accessories and homeware. It's a great place to go clothes shopping for all occasions. The kids' clothing section has a great selection for all ages. For other locations see Store Finder, p.422.

## Saks Fifth Avenue

**BurJuman** Bur Dubai **04 351 5551**
www.saksfifthavenue.com
Map **2 L4** Metro **Khalid Bin Al Waleed**
Anchoring the extension to BurJuman is the second-largest Saks Fifth Avenue outside the US. Even in Dubai's cultured retail sector, this store has an added air of sophistication. The first level is all about pampering,

with cosmetics and perfumes, designer sunglasses and the Saks Nail Studio; it also houses the D&G Boutique, the children's department (with designer clothes for little ones), the men's store, and the chocolate bar and cafe. The second level holds designer boutiques including Christian Dior, Jean Paul Gaultier and Prada. This is where to head for accessories, jewellery – including Tiffany and Fabergé – and an exclusive bridal salon which stocks Vera Wang gowns. There is also a branch of racy lingerie store Agent Provocateur. The Fifth Avenue Club is a personalised shopping service, where members can browse the store with the guidance of a consultant. A smaller branch has opened at The Walk, Jumeirah Beach Residence which only caters for men (04 435 5681).

## Salam

**Wafi** Umm Hurair **04 704 8484**
www.salams.com
Map **2 L6** Metro **Healthcare City**
This local department store has swanky decor and a good mix of brands. While its spacious store in Wafi seldom sees customers arriving in their droves, it does stock a good selection of homeware, jewellery and clothing and you'll have ample opportunity to browse. The store also has a particularly good selection of photography accessories from well-known brands. Designer names on offer include Betsey Johnson, Roberto Cavalli, Prada and Missoni. The store also sells a range of clothes from LA brand Gypsy 05 – great for maxi dresses and summer essentials.

# Supermarkets & Hypermarkets

## Al Maya Supermarket

**The Walk, Jumeirah Beach Residence** Dubai Marina **04 437 0166**
www.almayagroup.com
Map **1 K4** Metro **Dubai Marina**
This store servicing the Dubai Marina area and Jumeirah Beach Residence is part of a city wide chain. Its stores carry a good range of items, a bakery and fresh meat and fish. It also has a pork section selling a wide range of items. Many of its branches are open 24 hours and offer free home delivery. For other locations see the Store Finder on p.414.

## Carrefour

**Deira City Centre** Deira **04 295 1600**
www.carrefouruae.com
Map **2 N6** Metro **Deira City Centre**
Branches of this French hypermarket chain can be found throughout the city. As well as food, each large store carries fairly comprehensive ranges of electronics, household goods, luggage, mobile phones, and white goods. Camping gear and car accessories are also on sale here, in addition to clothes and shoes for men,

Saks Fifth Avenue

women and children, garden furniture, hardware, music and DVDs, and stationery. The store offers a good range of French products (it's the best place to get crusty, freshly baked French sticks) and it has a small health food section. Carrefour is renowned for its competitive pricing and special offers. For other locations see the Store Finder on p. 416.

### Choithram
Al Mankhool Rd, Opp Ramada Hotel Al Mankool
04 352 6946
www.choithram.com
Map **2 L3** Metro **Al Fahidi**
With 15 branches, Choithram is technically Dubai's largest supermarket chain (the 'mothership' is on Al Wasl Road next to Union Coop). Its stores are renowned for stocking British, American and Asian product that can't be found elsewhere, but they are also known for being expensive. Its stores also have excellent frozen sections and a great range of baby products – particularly food and formula. For other locations see the Store Finder on p. 417.

### Géant
Ibn Battuta Mall Jebel Ali 04 368 5858
www.geant-dubai.com
Map **1 G4** Metro **Ibn Battuta**
Géant stocks a massive selection of produce that is similar to that of Carrefour. It is well worth a visit for the cheap fruit and vegetables and the huge selection of nuts (great almonds). You'll also find a massive selection of very reasonably priced towels and bedding, a good selection of electronics, a car accessories section and it's also a good destination for DVD boxsets. The store is particularly handy for the residents of Jebel Ali and Dubai Marina.

### HyperPanda
Festival Centre Festival City 04 232 5566
Map **2 M8** Metro **Emirates Head Office**
HyperPanda is enormous, however it is a lot quieter than similar stores, so it's a good choice when you need hypermarket shopping without the hyperactive crowds. The store's selection of produce isn't as extensive as some of the other hypermarkets, but it does have a healthcare department, a good electronics department and more than the basic range of goods. The parking is good and it allows easy access to other outlets.

### Lifco
Nr Al Moosa Tower Trade Centre 04 332 7899
www.lifco.com
Map **2 H4** Metro **Emirates Towers**
Although not the largest of the city's supermarkets, Lifco stocks a great range of items in terms of convenience. It is a good place to go for fresh olives. The

store has regular specials offers where you can buy two or three items banded together for a discount. For other locations see the Store Finder on p. 420.

### Lulu Supermarket
Nr Dubai Municipality Karama 04 336 7070
www.luluhypermarket.com
Map **2 L5** Metro **Karama**
The store is great for those on a budget; its hot food counters, salad bars and fish monger are particularly good value. Stores have an Aladdin's cave quality about them and there's not much that they don't sell – from luggage and electronics to food and clothing. Each store stocks a good range of home appliances and an area selling colourful saris. For other locations see the Store Finder on p.420

### Organic Foods & Café
The Greens Emirates Hills 04 361 7974
www.organicfoodsandcafe.com
Map **1 N4** Metro **Dubai Internet City**
Do something good for the environment and for your body by shopping at the only certified organic supermarket in Dubai. With two branches (also in The Dubai Mall, p.402), it's easy to stock up on fresh organic fruit, veg, meat, fish and bread every week. If you think organic food is too pricey think again; they offer weekly specials and the prices might surprise you. The adjoining cafe serves food prepared with organic ingredients and is a popular spot.

### Park n Shop
Al Wasl Rd Al Wasl 04 394 5671
www.parkshopdubai.com
Map **2 C4** Metro **Al Quoz**
Although it is small, and just one shop (rather than a chain), Park n Shop is worth a trip simply because it has the best bakery and butchery in the city. The bakery sells a range of wheat-free breads (made with alternatives such as spelt), as well as a range of delicious and incredibly fresh goodies, including reputedly the best jam doughnuts in Dubai. Famous for its birthday cakes, come Christmas time this is where you'll get your mince pies. The butchery sells a range of marinated cuts ideal for the barbecue, and it also has a Christmas ordering service for your turkey and ham. Prices are competitive and it has products you won't always find elsewhere.

### Spinneys
Trade Centre Road Bur Dubai 04 351 1777
www.spinneys-dubai.com
Map **2 L4** Metro **Khalid BinAl Waleed**
With branches across Dubai, from Mirdif to the Marina, you're never far from this well-known store. Products are competitively priced (although many items are more expensive in Spinneys than they are at one of the

larger hypermarkets). They have a great range of South African and Australian, as well as British and American items. They stock a selection of Waitrose products (a supermarket renowned in the UK for its quality), and the freezer section and vegetarian options are both good. Also worth a try are items from the deli counter which are great for picnics, along with the ever popular roasted chickens – if you stay in town for Christmas you can order your seasonal goodies from here. For other locations see the Store Finder on p. 424

### Union Co-operative Society
Nr Rashidiya Police Station Al Rashidiya 04 286 2434
www.ucs.ae
Map 2 N10 Metro Rashidiya
It may lack the dazzling shine of other hypermarkets, but this is an essential place to shop if you're trying to shave a few dirhams off your grocery bill. The huge fruit and veg section is packed with farm-fresh produce at great prices, and because it is very popular with locals, it has a super selection of Arabic cheeses, olives, and family size bargain packs. There are several branches, but the one on Al Wasl Road is open 24 hours a day. For other locations see the Store Finder on p. 426

### Waitrose
The Dubai Mall Downtown Burj Dubai 04 362 7500
www.waitrose.com
Map 2 F6 Metro Burj Dubai
UK supermarket Waitrose is well known for its premium range of British produce and gourmet goods. Its stores offer a good range of items; including basic household goods, glassware, flowers and a good selection of books and DVDS. It has a well-stocked deli filled with hot and cold selections of pre-made dishes, perfect for picnics, and its selection or baked goods, meat and cheese are some of the best in Dubai. For other locations see Store Finder, p.426.

## Boutiques & Independent Shops
Independent stores and boutiques are opening, predominantly in converted villas, all over the city. A few stores have opened in some of the larger malls and shopping areas, but the biggest cluster of stores are along Jumeirah Beach Road. Modern souks like Khan Murjan (p.396), Souk Al Bahar (p.396) and Souk Madinat Jumeirah (p.408) also hold a few independent outlets.

### Ayesha Depala Boutique
The Village Jumeira 04 344 5378
www.ayeshadepala.com
Map 2 H3 Metro Al Jafiliya
Ayesha studied at London's prestigious, Central St Martins College of Art & Design, and is now based in Dubai. Her boutique holds all of her own creations. Pick up glamorous couture frocks, shimmering fabrics

and feminine accessories. As well as items fit for the catwalk, the store offers a bridal service, ready-to-wear pieces and vintage dresses and accessories.

### Boutique 1
The Walk, Jumeirah Beach Residence Dubai Marina
04 425 7888
www.boutique1.com
Map 1 K4 Metro Dubai Marina
A regular haunt for many fashion foragers, Boutique 1's Dubai Flagship store holds sought after designer brands, elegant evening wear, cosmetics and clothing for men and women. The store also has a gallery on the first floor, a small cosmetics section, a chic range of furniture, a small cafe and a spa (p.207). This isn't an option for the budget conscious – products here are high-end and high-priced.

> #### Fashion For Less
> If you need to save the pennies, but don't want to scrimp on fashion, head to Karama (p.388) for its range of fake designer goods; Dubai Outlet Mall (p.411) has outlet stores for well-known brands, and Matalan (04 284 5555) for its well-priced essentials. Avenue (04 397 9983) stocks the basics and Sana Fashions (04 337 7726) offers a superb range of low-cost branded clothing.

### Fabindia
Al Mankhool Rd, Nashwan Building Bur Dubai
04 398 9633
www.fabindia.com
Map 2 L3 Metro Al Fahidi
Fabindia's clothing ranges for men, women and children combine Indian and western styles – from capri pants to kurtas, the cotton-based designs are guaranteed to add a splash of colour to any wardrobe. You can also pick up soft furnishings and a beautiful range of rugs and hard-wearing dhurries to liven up dreary white floor tiles. The rolls of fabric, sold by the metre, are a great alternative to standard upholstery. Its products are handcrafted in villages, creating a livelihood for many and supporting rural communities. Considering this, its prices are very reasonable – shirts start from around Dhs.40, large table cloths from Dhs.120 and quilts from Dhs.300.

### Five Green
Garden Home Center Oud Metha
www.fivegreen.com
Map 2 L5 Metro Oud Metha
This is one of the best independent clothes shops in Dubai. Styled as an urban living boutique, it's the place to go for cutting-edge fashion and art. Street chic jeans, printed tees, shirts and trainers from labels including

# Places To Shop

Paul Frank, GSUS and Boxfresh mix with creations from Dubai-based designers. The soundtrack to your retail experience is provided by top US labels like BBE, Compost and Soul Jazz. Five Green's inspiring space plays host to a number of exhibitions throughout the year from both home-grown and international talent. It may be expensive, but it is a unique spot in Dubai.

## Luxecouture

**Souk Madinat Jumeirah** Umm Suqeim **04 423 0633**
www.shopluxecouture.com
Map **1 R4** Metro **Mall of the Emirates**
Buyers from this fresh, stylish store regularly head to New York to ensure Dubai's discerning shoppers stay on trend. Get a slice of red carpet glamour with dresses from Carmen Marc Valvo, bags by Goldenbleu, and individually designed jewellery pieces.

## O'de Rose

**Al Wasl Rd** Umm Suqeim **04 348 7990**
Map **1 T4** Metro **First Gulf Bank**
O'de Rose arrived on the city's shopping scene with a feminine flounce. The gorgeous boutique, in a spacious villa, is devoted to clothing, art and furniture, with embellished kaftans, clutch bags and homeware at every turn. Minimal it is not. With pieces from all over the world, a trip to O'de Rose is as good as a mini-break – with better souvenirs.

## Ounass

**Boulevard at Emirates Towers** Trade Centre
**04 330 0617**
Map **2 H5** Metro **Emirates Towers**
Ounass (which means 'people' in Arabic) appeals to the sophisticated party people of Dubai with lines from Diane Von Furstenburg, Marchesa and Alberta Ferretti. As well fashionable creations and designer treats,

shoppers can also pick up original pieces by Arabic artists. The walls in this modern store are lined with artwork, so you can buy beautiful creations for your home as well as your wardrobe. For other locations see Store Finder, p.422.

## Reem's Closet

**Mazaya Centre** Al Wasl **04 343 9553**
www.reemscloset.com
Map **2 F5** Metro **Burj Dubai**
Tucked away in the decidedly non-flashy Mazaya Centre off Sheikh Zayed Road, is a second-hand haven, packed to the rafters with quality designer clobber at astonishing prices. Bring in the 'it bag' you've tired of, pick up some vintage pieces or discover an unwanted item from last season. The store accepts designer pieces or items off the high street; what is essential is that they offer the same attractive quirky high-fashion as the store's stock. What you won't find are Karama's finest genuine fakes – quality control is uncompromised so you can buy with confidence.

## S*uce

**The Village** Jumeira **04 344 7270**
www.shopatsauce.com
Map **2 H3** Metro **Al Jafiliya**
You can't pick up your basic white T-shirt or simple plastic flip-flops at this shop. The items at S*uce are anything but basic, but you can peruse the funky accessories, quirky high-fashion and individual pieces at this eclectic boutique. Fashionistas head here for token buys that are less likely to be seen on anyone else. You'll find clothes by international designers such as Chloè. The store also offers a loyalty card, and personal shopper for those needing advice on the seasons key buys. For other locations see Store Finder, p.424.

Villa Moda

## Villa Moda

Dubai International Financial Centre (DIFC)
Trade Centre **04 382 5150**
Map **2 G5** Metro **Financial Centre**
This store is where want meets need, where you spend those dirhams reserved for key fashion buys. You'll find top-class designer togs from well-known designers and the odd selection from emerging talent. Its store for women in DIFC is fabulously chic and a glorious display of ornate chandeliers adorns its ceiling. There is an equally stylish range of brands in its men's store (Gate Village, Building 04). A branch of the store is also located at The Avenues at Atlantis (04 422 1346).

# Markets & Souks

There are a number of souks and markets in Dubai. The souks are the traditional trading areas, some more formally demarcated than others. In keeping with tradition, bargaining is expected and cash gives the best leverage.

The Gold, Spice and Textile Souks line either side of the creek, but parking is limited, so if possible it is better to go to these areas by taxi or, if you are visiting all three, park on one side of the creek and take an abra (p.55) to the other side.

Western-style markets are becoming more popular: they are usually based around crafts and are often seasonal. The Covent Garden Market (p.395) is set up along The Walk, Jumeirah Beach Residence, during the cooler months, and Bastaflea, a market near the XVA Gallery (p.245), runs on Saturdays between 10:00 and 19:00. Both are great launch pads for local talents, with artists, jewellers and other crafty types displaying their wares.

Global Village (www.globalvillage.ae), on the Emirates Road near Arabian Ranches, is a huge collection of stalls, food and entertainment from all over the world. It runs from November to February and is a good spot to pick up everything from Chinese lanterns to honey from Yemen. Organised by country, you can spend hours exploring the wares before enjoying a unique range of dishes in the international foodcourt. Just don't overdo dinner before getting on the fairground rides. Global Village is open from16:00 to midnight, Saturday to Wednesday, and until 01:00 on Thursday and Friday. Entrance costs Dhs.5 and is free for children under 2 years old.

## Covent Garden Market Dubai

The Walk at Jumeirah Beach Residence Dubai
Marina **050 244 5795**
www.marinamarket.ae
Map **1 L4** Metro **Dubai Marina**
The vibrancy of this street market comes from its street entertainers, open stalls and morning strollers along Jumeirah Beach Residence's cobbled beachfront promenade. You can pick up canvas or watercolour paintings from emerging artists for a rock bottom price. You will also find stalls selling fashion items, handmade jewellery, confectionary and kids' toys. The market is located in the Rimal sector of JBR on Wednesdays and Thursdays 17:00 till midnight and Fridays and Saturdays 10:00 to 21:00.

## Dubai Flea Market

Safa Park Al Wasl
www.dubai-fleamarket.com
Map **2 D4** Metro **Business Bay**
This flea market is a great place to take advantage of Dubai's transient population. As people pack up and move on, an escapee's excess baggage could become a bargain hunter's treasure. For the Dhs.3 entry fee into Al Safa Park, or Dhs.5 fee into Al Mamzar Beach Park, you can peruse the stalls covered with furniture, books, clothing and a broad range of unwanted items and homemade crafts. The flea market is set up on the first Saturday of every month at Al Safa Park and every third Saturday at Al Mamzar Beach Park. A new market has also been introduced on the second Saturday of every month in Sharjah. Al Qasba Flea Market (www.alqasbamarket.com) is free to enter and you can pick up genuine second-hand luxury goods.

## Fish Market

Nr Shindagha Tunnel Deira
Map **2 N3** Metro **Palm Deira**
The Fish Market in Deira is hard to ignore if you're in the area, especially during the hotter months – maybe not the best place to visit if you don't like the smell of fish. To get the freshest fish for your evening meal, and to experience the vibrancy of this working market, head down early in the morning or late at night as the catch is coming in. There is an incredible range of seafood on display. The emphasis is on wholesale but the traders are usually more than happy to sell to individuals and, for those of a squeamish disposition, the fish can be cleaned and gutted for you.

## Fruit & Vegetable Market

Dubai – Hatta Rd, nr Used Car Market Nad Al Sheba
Map **2 K12**
There are a number of small fruit and vegetable markets around the city, like the one in Karama. The main market is now located off Emirates Road in Al Awir. It is a wholesale market but, like the Fish Market (p.395), the traders are usually happy to sell by the kilo rather than the box. There is a huge variety of produce on offer and it is usually fresher than in the supermarkets. Be sure to haggle, you can often tell if you have paid more than the trader thinks the goods are worth if they give you freebies. The location is not convenient for most people but take a look if you are out that way. It is well signposted as you drive along the Dubai-Hatta Road. Mornings are the best time to visit.

# Places To Shop

## Gold Souk

**Baniyas Rd** Deira
Map **2 M3** Metro **Al Ras**

This is Dubai's best-known souk and a must-do for every visitor. It's a good place to buy customised jewellery for unique souvenirs and gifts at a reasonable price.

On the Deira side of the creek, the meandering lanes are lined with shops selling gold, silver, pearls and precious stones. These can be bought as they are or in a variety of settings so this is definitely a place to try your bargaining skills – but don't expect a massive discount. Gold is sold by weight according to the daily international price and so will be much the same as in the shops in malls – the price of the workmanship is where you will have more bargaining power. Most of the outlets operate split shifts, so try not to visit between 13:00 and 16:00 as many will be closed.

The Gold Souk is always busy, and it is shaded, but there is added sparkle when you visit in the evenings as the lights reflect on the gold and gems. If you are more interested in buying than enjoying the souk experience, visit the Gold & Diamond Park (04 347 7788, www.goldanddiamondpark.com), by Interchange Four on Sheikh Zayed Road. There are branches of many of the outlets that are also found in the Gold Souk but here they are quieter and the area is fully air-conditioned.

## Khan Murjan

**Wafi** Umm Hurair **04 327 9212**
www.wafi.com
Map **2 L6** Metro **Healthcare City**

For something a little different, head to Wafi's underground souk. Khan Murjan's magnificent stained glass ceiling (which stretches 64 metres) and long curved arches help make this an atmospheric place to shop. The souk features over 150 stalls selling jewellery, antiques, Arabic perfume and souvenirs. It is particularly good if you wish to spice up your home with traditional arts and crafts; there are workshops where artisans can create various bits of arts and crafts on site. In the centre of the souk, you'll find an open air marble courtyard which houses the highly recommended Khan Murjan Arabic restaurant (04 324 4555).

## Sharjah Central Souk

**Nr Corniche** Sharjah
www.sharjah-welcome.com

Situated beside the lagoon, the Sharjah Central Market, or Blue Souk, is an unmissable sight. Consisting of two long, low buildings running parallel to each other and connected by footbridges, the souk is intricately decorated and imaginatively built according to Islamic design.

Each building is covered and air-conditioned to protect shoppers from the hot sun, with one side selling a range of gifts, knick-knacks, furniture, carved wood and souvenirs, and the other given over almost entirely to jewellery stores. There are over 600 individual shops, and the upper floors have a traditional souk feel with narrow passages and staircases. The souk also has shops selling a fabulous range of carpets from all over the world. For visitors and residents, a half-hour trip into the Blue Souk can easily turn into half a day.

## Souk Al Arsah

**Nr Bank St** Sharjah

This is probably the oldest souk in Sharjah. It has been renovated in recent years, so although the shops are still in a style reminiscent of old market places, the souk is covered (to provide shelter from the sun) and air-conditioned. Around 100 tiny shops line a labyrinth of peaceful alleyways, selling goods such as silver jewellery, perfumes, spices, coffee pots and wedding chests. There is a small coffee shop where you can get Arabic coffee and sweets. Shop closing times do vary, with some closing by 20:30 and others remaining open until 22:00.

## Souk Al Bahar

**Old Town** Downtown Burj Dubai **04 362 7011**
www.emaar.com
Map **2 F6** Metro **Burj Dubai**

While this isn't a souk in the conventional terms, Souk Al Bahar, in Downtown Burj Dubai, is an Arabian-style mall similar to the souk at Madinat Jumeirah (p.408). Although many of the outlets serve the tourist market, Souk Al Bahar also has shops for the more discerning shopper. Designer style can be found at Roccobarocco (04 361 9015) and Kitsch Boutique (04 367 4504), with Indian designer labels at Samsaara and Manish Malhotra. For exclusive beachwear head to Pain de Sucre (04 420 0142) or vogue swimwear chain Vilbrequin (04 420 0152), and pick up a pair of famously comfortable flip-flops at the Havaianas store (04 420 0150). Marina Interiors (04 420 0191) or Sia (04 423 0914) sell contemporary home furnishings and interior design, or try Pride of Kashmir (04 344 8570), Fortix (04 420 3680) or Emad Carpets (04 368 9576) for a more Arabian look. Sadek Music (04 367 4530) has a wide array of eastern and western instruments.

There are also several food outlets; you can grab light bites at Dean & Deluca and Shakespeare & Co. or something heartier at Margaux (p.482) and the Rivington Grill (p.491). Hive Lounge Bar & Restaurant (p.510) and Left Bank (p.512) are perfect for a post-shop cool down. For information on other shopping possibilities in Downtown Burj Dubai see p.387.

Spice Souk

## Spice Souk

**Nr Gold Souk** Deira
Map **2 M3**

The Spice Souk's narrow streets and exotic aromas are a great way to get a feel for the way the city used to be. The number of spice shops is diminishing, due in part to hypermarkets like Carrefour having areas dedicated to spices and supermarkets selling a wider range. Most of the stalls sell the same range and the vendors are usually happy to give advice on the types of spices and their uses. You are unlikely to shop here on a regular basis, but the experience of buying from the Spice Souk is more memorable than picking a packet off a shelf. You may even be able to pick up some saffron at a bargain price. The shops operate split shifts but, whether you visit in the morning or the evening, this is a bustling area of the city.

## Textile Souk

**Nr Abra Station** Bur Dubai
Map **2 M3** Metro **Al Ghubaiba**

The Textile Souk in Bur Dubai is stocked with every fabric and colour imaginable. The textiles are imported from all over the world, with many of the more elaborate coming from the subcontinent and the Far East. There are silks and satins in an amazing array of colours and patterns, velvets and intricately embroidered fabrics. Basic cottons can sometimes be harder to find but you can always try Satwa (p.388). Prices are negotiable and there are often sales, particularly around the major holidays of Eid and Diwali, and the shopping festivals. It is worth having a look in a few shops before parting with your cash as they may have different stock and at better prices. The mornings tend to be a more relaxed time to browse.

Meena Bazaar (04 353 9304) is the shop that most taxi drivers head for if you ask for the Textile Souk. It has

an impressive selection of fabrics but prepare to haggle. Rivoli (04 335 0075) has a range of textiles for men on the ground floor and for women upstairs. The assistants are keen to offer the 'best discount', but it is always worth bartering to see if the price will drop further.

A number of tailors are located around the Textile Souk, including a branch of Dream Girl (p.354) which is renowned for its service. See p.354 for more information on tailors.

## Shopping Malls

Shopping malls are not just places to shop; a definite mall culture exists here and they are places to meet, eat and mingle. Many malls provide entertainment and people of all ages can spend hours in them. Recent changes to the law have resulted in a smoking ban in all of Dubai's malls (and some of the bars attached to them) which has been welcomed across the city.

With so much choice out there, malls make sure they can offer something unique to shoppers to draw the crowds. In terms of architecture, Ibn Battuta is remarkable – six distinct architectural styles reflecting the sights of Egypt, China, India, Persia, Tunisia and Andalusia. Mall of the Emirates has got their unique selling point covered – a community theatre and a huge ski slope has made this one of the busier malls. The Dubai Mall, is a spectical, beacause of its size and its selection of shops (covering both the high-end and the high-street markets), entertainment and eateries. Deira City Centre is the old kid on the block and yet is still consistently popular because of its excellent range of outlets, huge cinema multiplex and wide range of food outlets. Wafi City and BurJuman have cornered the market for exclusive boutiques and designer labels.

### Mall Parking

At the time of going to print, Mall of the Emirates and Deira City Centre are the only malls which charge for parking. Other malls are expected to introduce charges once their Metro stations are open to discourage commuters from parking at the mall for extended periods. Parking in the Mall of the Emirates (p.405) and Deira City Centre (p.400) is free for the first four hours and charged at Dhs.20 per hour thereafter. Parking is also free on Fridays, Saturdays and public holidays.

Special events are held during Dubai Shopping Festival, Dubai Summer Surprises and Ramadan, with entertainment for children and some special offers in the shops. These are peak shopping times and an evening in the larger malls at this time is not for the faint-hearted. Most of the malls have plenty of parking – often stretched to the limits at the weekends; all have taxi ranks and many are handy for bus routes.

## Places To Shop

### BurJuman  > p.399

Trade Centre Rd Bur Dubai **04 352 0222**
www.burjuman.com
Map **2 L4** Metro **Khalid Bin Al Waleed**

BurJuman is renowned for its blend of designer and
high-street brands attracting many a well-heeled
shopper. There are enough designer shops to
keep even the most dedicated label hunter happy,
including Shanghai Tang, Hermes, Fendi and Christian
Dior. The mall houses many famous brands such as
Gap, Whistles and Escada, as well as some interesting
smaller shops and legendary New York department
store Saks Fifth Avenue. For everyday fashion,
Massimo Dutti and Zara lead the way. If you are into
music or DVDs, the independent music shops sell
a good range and they often have sales. There is a
Fitness First gym with a pool on site too.

BurJuman has been active in organising activities
for the Dubai Shopping Festival and Dubai Summer
Surprises and is also heavily involved with the Safe &
Sound breast cancer awareness programme; during
October (breast cancer awareness month) it gets
decked out in pink ribbon and organises a walkathon.

The outlets within the mall are a mixture of
clothing, electronics, home decor and sports goods.
There are a few shops on the ground level that are
often overlooked, including ACE (hardware & DIY
store) and a pharmacy. There's also branches of Yo!
Sushi, and Dôme on the same level.

There is a branch of Virgin Megastore – you can

also pick up tickets here for local events. Home decor
stores include THE One and Zara Home.

There are two foodcourts and numerous cafes, well
arranged for people watching, including the popular
Pavillion Gardens on the third floor, and Paul on the
ground floor, where you can dine outside during the
cooler months. The mall can be accessed directly from
the Dubai Metro and there is plenty of underground
parking and a taxi rank just outside the mall (this gets
pretty congested after 18:00 and at weekends).

## BurJuman Stores

| Department Stores | Escada | Promod | Furniture & Home Appliances |
|---|---|---|---|
| Saks Fifth Avenue | Esprit | Quiksilver | Bhs |
| Next | Etoile | Ralph Lauren | Descamps |
| | Fendi | Rodeo Drive | Grand Stores |
| **Electronics & Computers** | Gap | Ted Baker | Hermes |
| Bang & Olufsen | Giordano | Versace | Jadhafs |
| Braun | Guess | Whistles | Kas Australia |
| Cellucom | Hermes | X.O.X.O. | Little Things |
| Digital (Grand Stores) | Hugo Boss | Zara | Reshi Arts & Crafts |
| Jumbo Electronics | Just Cavalli | | Sharief |
| Virgin Megastore | Kenneth Cole | **Footwear** | Tanagra |
| | Kenzo | AK Anne Klein | THE ONE |
| **Fashion** | La Perla | Aigner | Villeroy & Boch |
| BCBGMAXAZRIA | La Senza | Aldo | Zara Home |
| Bebe | Lacoste | Baldinini | |
| Bhs | Laurel | Burberry | **Perfume & Cosmetics** |
| Blumarine | Levi`s | Chanel | Arabian Oud |
| Bossini | Loewe | Dune | Faces |
| Burberry | Mango | Gianfranco Ferre | MAC |
| Chanel | Marina Rinaldi | Nine West | Mikyajy |
| Christian Lacroix | Massimo Dutti | Saks Fifth Avenue | Paris Gallery |
| CK Calvin Klein | Monsoon | Salvatore Ferragamo | Rasasi Perfumes |
| Diesel | New Look | Tod's | The Body Shop |
| Dior | Paul & Shark | Versace | |
| DKNY | Paul Smith | Vincci | |
| Dolce & Gabbana | Pierre Cardin | Sketchers | |

# A BETTER CLASS OF SHOPPING.

With over 340 of the world's finest brands, including Saks Fifth Avenue, you'll always be spoilt for choice.

burjuman.com  04-352 0222

BURJUMAN

## Places To Shop

### Deira City Centre
Ittihad Rd Deira 04 295 1010
www.deiracitycentre.com
Map 2 N6 Metro Deira City Centre

A stalwart of Dubai's mall scene, this centre attracts the most cosmopolitan crowd. Deira City Centre is popular with residents and visitors alike, particularly at the weekends. The three floors offer a diverse range of shops where you can find anything from a postcard to a Persian carpet. There's an 11 screen cinema, a children's entertainment centre, a jewellery court, a textiles court and an area dedicated to local furniture, gifts and souvenirs. It is all anchored by a huge Carrefour hypermarket, a Debenhams department store, Paris Gallery and a large Magrudys bookshop. Most of the high-street brands are represented, including Gap, Warehouse, Topshop, Forever 21, New Look and River Island. A number of designer boutiques can be found mostly of the top floor. The City Gate section (on the same level as car parks P2 and P3) is dominated by electronics retailers, although there is also a pharmacy and information desk. The mall has two foodcourts: one on the first floor, next to Magic Planet, serving mainly fastfood, and one on the second floor, featuring several good sit-down restaurants such as Noodle House and Japengo. The opening of the Deira City Centre Metro station means

that it is even easier to get to and from, which is great because the taxi queues can get very long, especially during weekends and in the evenings. Another City Centre mall is under construction in Mirdif (www.macegroup.com); the mall is rumoured to open in early autumn.

## Deira City Centre Stores

**Books & Stationery**
Borders
Carlton Cards
Gulf Greetings
Magrudys

**Department Stores**
Carrefour
Debenhams
Paris Gallery
Stadium
Woolworths

**Electronics & Computers**
Axiom
Cellucom
Eros Digital Home
Grand Stores Digital
Harman House
Jacky's Electronics
Jumbo Electronics
SharafDG

**Fashion**
Armani Exchange
Balmain
Banana Republic
Bebe

Bershka
Burberry
Calvin Klein Underwear
Club Monaco
Diesel
DKNY Jeans
Dockers
Duchamp
Esprit
Forever 21
French Connection
Gant
GAP
Giordano
Guess
H&M
Hugo Boss
Jane Norman
Jennyfer
Karen Millen
Kookai
La Senza
Lacoste
Levi's
Lucky Brand Jeans
Mango
Massimo Dutti
Mexx

Monsoon
Morgan
Nautica
New Look
Next
Pepe Jeans
Pimkie
Promod
Pull & Bear
Replay
River Island
Sisley
Springfield
Stradivarius
Ted Baker
Ted Lapidus
Tommy Hilfiger
Topshop
United Colors of Benetton
Warehouse
Wrangler
Zara

**Footwear**
Aldo
Bata
Clarks
Ecco

Geox
Havaianas
Kurt Geiger
Nine West
Pretty Fit
Shoe Mart
Valencia
Vincci

**Furniture & Home Appliances**
Sia
The White Company
Villeroy & Boch
Zara Home

**Kids' Items**
Adams
Bhs
Carter's
Early Learning Centre
GAP
Geekay Toys & Games
Mothercare
Okaidi
Pablosky
The Cartoon Magic-Disney Store

## Dubai Festival City

**Al Rebat St Nr Garhoud Bridge** Festival City
04 213 6213
www.dubaifestivalcity.com
Map **2 M8** Metro **Emirates**

Dubai Festival City incorporates the Festival Centre and The Festival Waterfront Centre. The area features around 600 retail outlets (including 25 flagship stores) and 100 restaurants including 40 alfresco dining options.

The need for retail therapy can be sated by the broad range of fashion, electronics and homeware outlets spread over 2.9 million square feet of retail space. Some of the biggest names in homeware, such as The White Company and the largest IKEA in the UAE are featured and it is home to HyperPanda (p.392), a large Plug-Ins and the largest ACE store outside of North America. There is also a 25,000 square foot modern gold souk where you can peruse gold from all over the world. The mall also features Brit favourite Marks & Spencer, high-street brands Ted Baker and Reiss and designer stores like Marc by Marc Jacobs. You'll find a branch of the Dubai London Clinic here too, a pharmacy, banks and dry cleaners.

It's not just shopping though; The Festival Waterfront Centre has dramatic water features and performance spaces, there is a Grand Cinema (04 232 8328) and a

ten-lane bowling alley on site. You can happily spend an entire day here, dining at Romano's Macaroni Grill (04 232 6001) or Steam Sum Dim Sum (p.495) before relaxing in the Belgian Beer Cafe (p.507).

# Dubai Festival City Stores

**Books & Stationery**
Book Plus
Gulf Greetings
Magrudy's
News Centre

**Department Stores**
Hyper Panda
Marks & Spencer

**Electronics & Computers**
Axiom
Bose
Cellucom
Dell
Grand Stores Digital
I-Style
LG
Panasonic
Plug Ins
Samsung
Jumbo Electronics

**Fashion**
Aftershock
Balmain
Bebe
Bench

Bendon
Bhs
Bossini
Bugatti
Calvin Klein Underwear
Carolina Herrera
Diesel
DKNY
Dockers
Dunhill
Esprit
Forever 21
Fred Perry
French Connection
Gas
Giordano
Guess
Hobbs
Hugo Boss
Jeanswest
Karen Millen
Kenneth Cole
Kenzo
K-Lynn
Koton
La Senza
Lacoste
Laura Ashley

Levis
Liu Jo
Mango
Marc By Marc Jacobs
Massimo Dutti
Merc
Monsoon
Nautica
New Yorker
Nougat Of London
Oysho
Paul & Joe
Paul Smith
Phat Farm
Pierre Cardin
Porsche Design
Raoul
Reiss
River Woods
Rodeo Drive
Stradivarius
Ted Baker
Ted Lapidus
Vero Moda
Women's Secret

**Footwear**
Aldo

Baldinini
Charles & Keith
Chic Shoes
Clarks
Dune
Ecco
Geox
Kurt Geiger
Naturalizer
Nine West
Spring
Valencia

**Furniture & Home Appliances**
Howard Storage House
IKEA
Marina Home Interiors
The Sultani Lifestyle Gallerie
The White Company

**Kids' Items**
Adams
Build A Bear
Diesel Kids
Early Learning Center
Geekay Games
Toys 'R' Us

## Places To Shop

### The Dubai Mall

**Doha St, nr Interchange 1** Downtown Burj Dubai
04 437 3200
www.thedubaimall.com
Map **2 F6** Metro **Burj Dubai**

Anyone who thinks Dubai has enough shopping malls will be stunned by this colossus. The Dubai Mall holds 1,000 retail outlets and over 160 eateries. The complex also houses an Olympic size ice skating rink, a catwalk for fashion shows, an enormous aquarium, a 22-screen cinema, an indoor theme park called SEGA Republic (p.254), a luxury hotel, and a children's 'edutainment' centre. The shopping highlights are manifold, but unique to Dubai Mall are the regional flagship stores for New York department store Bloomingdales, French department store Galeries Lafayette (p.390), and the world-renowned toy shop Hamleys (p.378). You'll find all of the haute couture designer brands along Fashion Avenue, several high street favourites like Topshop, New Look, Express and Forever 21, and a sprawling gold souk with over 220 gold and jewellery outlets. When you need to check your funds, you'll also find branches of the major banks on the ground floor. For refreshment, there is a huge variety of fastfood outlets, cafes and restaurants. Check the store listings on the website before you tackle this mall as a number of the outlets are yet to open.

If you are there for some late night shopping, don't miss the fountain show beside the Burj Dubai that starts around 18:00 every night. For a complete contrast, cross the wooden bridge over the Burj Lake to Souk Al Bahar (p.396). The tranquillity of its dimly lit passageways offer a more relaxing stop after the onslaught of the mall.

## The Dubai Mall Stores

| | | | |
|---|---|---|---|
| **Books & Stationery** | Bedo | Levi's | Oasis |
| Kinokuniya | Blumarine | Missoni | Oscar de la Renta |
| Magrudy's | Burberry | Mango | S*uce |
| The Paper Room | Calvin Klein | Marc By Marc Jacobs | Stella McCartney |
| | Chanel | Massimo Dutti | Temperley |
| **Department Stores** | Chloe | Moschino | Zadig & Voltaire |
| Bloomingdale's | Coast | Nautica | |
| Debenhams | Desigual | Next | **Furniture & Home** |
| Galeries Lafayette | Diesel | Paul Smith | **Appliances** |
| Marks & Spencer | Dior | Pepe Jeans | @ Home |
| Paris Gallery | Dockers | Ralph Lauren | Ethan Allen |
| Al Khazana | Dolce & Gabbana | Reiss | Hermes Arts De La Table |
| | Escada | River Island | La Maison Coloniale |
| **Electronics & Computers** | Esprit | Roberto Cavalli | The White Company |
| Grand Stores Digital | Express | Rodeo Drive | Villeroy & Boch |
| iStyle Apple Computers | Fendi | Salvatore Ferragamo | Zara Home |
| Jacky's Electronics | Forever 21 | Ted Baker | |
| Jumbo Electronics | Fred Perry | Thomas Pink | **Kids' Items** |
| LG Digital | Gap | Tommy Hilfiger | Adams |
| Plug-Ins Electronix | Guess | Topshop | Armani Junior |
| SharafDG | H&M | United Colors Of Benetton | Baby Guess |
| | Hugo Boss | Versace | Baby Shop |
| **Fashion** | Jean Paul Gaultier | Von Dutch | Bubbles & Giggles |
| 7 For All Mankind | Joseph | Zara | Burberry Children |
| Agent Provocateur | Just Cavalli | Mango | Cacharel Paris |
| Alexander McQueen | Karen Millen | Matthew Williamson | Diesel Kids |
| Banana Republic | Kenneth Cole | Monsoon | Geekay Games |
| BCBGMAXAZRIA | Lacoste | New Look | Hamleys |

## Places To Shop

### Ibn Battuta Mall

The Gardens, Sheikh Zayed Rd, Btn Int 5 & 6
Jebel Ali 04 362 1901
www.ibnbattutamall.com
Map 1 G4 Metro Ibn Battuta

This mall is divided into six zones each based on a region that explorer Ibn Battuta visited in the 14th century (China, India, Egypt, Tunisia, Andalusia and Persia). Guided tours that illuminate the mall's unusual features, such as the full-size replica of a Chinese junk and Al Jazari's Elephant Clock, are available.

There is a good range of mostly international stores and several anchor stores such as Debenhams and Géant hypermarket. Shops are loosely grouped: China Court is dedicated to entertainment, with several restaurants and a 21 screen cinema – with an IMAX screen which is often used to show regular films as well as blockbusters. The fashion conscious should head for India Court for H&M, Forever 21, Oasis, Topshop and Splash. Persia Court is styled as the lifestyle area, anchored by Debenhams – when you get to Starbucks, look up to see the ceiling detail. Egypt Court is for sporty types; Géant is the hub of Tunisia Court and the place to head for your weekly shop. Andalusia Court covers life's necessities such as banking, dry cleaning, key cutting, and DVD and video rental.

Foodcourts are located at either end of the mall. There are several restaurants in China Court (including the excellent Finz) and a group of fastfood outlets in

Tunisia Court. Several restaurants and coffee shops are also dotted around other areas of the mall. To reward the kids for trailing round after you, there's a Fun City in Tunisia Court. It is an enjoyable mall to wander around, but it can be a long way back if there's something you've missed. There are 10 carparks (the numerical order is a little eccentric), so remember which zone you came in through – and taxi ranks at either end of the mall.

## Ibn Battuta Mall Stores

| Books & Stationery | Fashion | Companys | Furniture & Home |
| --- | --- | --- | --- |
| Books Plus | Arrow | Element | Appliances |
| Gulf Greetings | B C Bulgari | Elle | @home |
| House of Prose | Daniel Hechter | Ginger & Lace | Bayti |
| Magrudy's | Forever 21 | Le Chateau | Pan Emirates |
| | Guy Laroche | Nayomi | Howards Storage World |
| Department Stores | Joe Bloggs | Oasis | |
| BHS | Pierre Cardin | Plus It | Kids' Items |
| Debenhams | Ted Lapidus | Wallis | Giordano Junior |
| Fitz & Simons | Verri | | Gocco |
| Geant | Bauhaus | Footwear | H&M |
| Grand Stores | Bench | Aldo | Iana |
| Lifestyle | Evisu | Charles & Keith | La Senza Girl |
| Paris Gallery | Giordano | El Dantes | Max |
| Woolworths | H&M | Faith | Mini Me |
| | Lacoste | Geox | Mothercare |
| Electronics & Computers | Levi's | Milano | Nautica |
| LG | Max | Naturalizer | Next |
| Axiom Telecom | Nautica | Nicoli | Pablosky |
| Cell-U-Com | Next | Nine West | Sanrio |
| Digicom | River Island | Prince Shoes | Tammy |
| I Style | Splash | Rodo | The Toy Store |
| Jacky's Electronics | Topshop/Topman | Shoe Mart | Tuc Tuc |
| Jumbo Electronics | Wrangler | Skechers | Wizz |
| Sharaf DG | Peacocks | Tosca Blu | |
| Sharaf Digital | Betsey Johnson | Zu | |

## Mall of the Emirates

**Sheikh Zayed Rd, Exit 39, Int 4** Al Barsha
04 409 9000
www.malloftheemirates.com
Map **1 R5** Metro **Mall of the Emirates**

This is more than a mall, it's a lifestyle destination. Mall of the Emirates houses an indoor ski slope (Ski Dubai, see p.338), the Kempinski Mall of the Emirates Hotel (p.234) and the Dubai Community Theatre & Arts Centre (p.435). There are over 400 outlets selling everything from forks to high fashion here. Label devotees should head for Via Rodeo for designer labels like Burberry, Dolce & Gabbana, Salvatore Ferragamo, Tod's and Versace. If you're more into street chic, there are two H&M stores, Fat Face, Phat Farm and Forever 21, while Rampage and Staff stock the coolest styles for the ski slopes.

The mall is anchored by Carrefour hypermarket, Dubai's largest branch of Debenhams, trendy department store Harvey Nichols, and Centrepoint, which is home to Baby Shop, Home Centre, Lifestyle, Shoemart and Splash. There is also a Cinestar cinema which offers Gold Class film showings (with comfy leather armchairs and waiter service throughout). The entertainment centre, Magic Planet includes a bowling alley, and a myriad of games and rides.

When it comes to homeware Home Centre, Marina Gulf, BoConcept, B&B Italia, THE One, and Zara Home are just a few of the stores on offer. While Jacky's

Electronics and Jumbo Electronics offer an extensive range of electronics. Should you fancy a marathon shopping trip, Mall of the Emirates is open from Sunday to Wednesday 10:00 to 22:00, Thursday to Saturday 10:00 to midnight and Carrefour opens 09:00 to midnight every day. You'll need to keep your energy up exploring this mall, so it's fortunate there is a wide range of dining options from the Swiss chalet feel of Après (p.456) to the three separate foodcourts.

## Mall of the Emirates Stores

| | | | |
|---|---|---|---|
| **Books & Stationery** | Bershka | Mexx | Camper |
| Borders | Betty Barclay | Miss Sixty | Charles & Keith |
| Carlton Cards (Jashanmal) | Bhs | Missoni | Clarks |
| Gulf Greetings/Hallmark | Carolina Herrera | Monsoon | Dune |
| Jashanmal | CK Jeans | Morgan | Ecco |
| | Columbia | Next | Kenneth Cole |
| **Department Stores** | Diesel | Paul Smith | Nine West |
| Babyshop | DKNY | Pepe Jeans | PrettyFIT |
| Carrefour | Dolce & Gabbana | Phat Farm | Shelly's |
| Centrepoint | Emporio Armani | Pimkie | |
| Debenhams | Esprit | Promod | **Furniture & Home** |
| Harvey Nichols | Etoile | Pull & Bear | **Appliances** |
| Lifestyle | Forever 21 | Ralph Lauren | B&B Italia |
| | French Connection | Reiss | BoConcept |
| **Electronics & Computers** | Gucci | River Island | Bois & Chiffons |
| Bose | Guess | Roberto Cavalli | Bombay & Zone |
| CompuMe | H&M | Rodeo Drive | Flamant Home Interiors |
| Eon Digital | Hugo Boss | Tommy Hilfiger | Grand Stores Home |
| Grand Stores Digital | Kenneth Cole | United Colors of Benetton | Home Centre |
| Jacky's Electronics | La Senza | Whistles | ID Design / Better Life |
| Jashanmal | Lacoste | Zara | La Maison Coloniale |
| Jumbo Electronics | Levi's | | Marina Exotic Home |
| Radio Shack | Loewe | **Footwear** | Interiors |
| Virgin Megastore | Lucky Brand Jeans | Aldo | Sia |
| | Mango | Alfred Dunhill | Tavola |
| **Fashion** | Marc Jacobs | Bally | THE One |
| BCBG Max Azria | Massimo Dutti | Brantano Shoe City | The White Company |

# Places To Shop

## Mercato  > p.407

> p.407

**Jumeira Rd** Jumeira **04 344 4161**
www.mercatoshoppingmall.com
Map **2 F3** Metro **Burj Dubai**

Mercato is the largest mall in Jumeira, with over 120 shops, restaurants, a cinema and cafes. As you drive along the Jumeira Beach Road, the Renaissance-style architecture really makes the mall stand out, and once inside, the huge glass roof provides a lot of natural light enhancing its Mediterranean feel. The layout is more interesting than many of the malls and it's worth investigating the 'lanes' so you don't miss anything. The mall is anchored by Spinneys which has a dry cleaners, photo lab and music shop; a large Virgin Megastore (that has a decent book department) Laura Ashley Home and Gap. There are also a few good options for kids such as Early Learning Centre, Toy Store Express and Armani Junior. The mix of designer boutiques and high-street brands mean you can peruse the reasonably priced Pull and Bear then find yourself amongst the more exclusive range at Hugo Boss. Shoes and accessories are covered by favourites like ALDO and Nine West, while cosmetics can be picked up at MAC.

There is a foodcourt and a number of cafes and restaurants, including Paul, a French cafe renowned for its patisserie, and Bella Donna, an Italian restaurant where you can dine alfresco. The Grand Mercato cinema and large Fun City play area near the food court should keep most of the family occupied. There is a mother and baby room, tucked away near Costa Coffee on the upper floor, in addition to ATMs, a money exchange, and a branch of HSBC (it doesn't handle money but can offer advice and do the paperwork) and a key cutting and shoe repair shop.

## Mercato Stores

**Books & Stationery**
Gulf Greetings (Hallmark)
Virgin Megastore

**Electronics & Computers**
Axiom Telecom
Sharaf Digital
Virgin Megastore

**Fashion**
Armani Jeans
Bershka
Beyond the Beach
Cube Boutique
Diesel
Fleurt
GAP
GF Ferre
Hugo Boss Men & Women
IVY
La Senza Lingerie
Laura Ashley

Mamas & Papas
Mango
Massimo Dutti
Nayomi
Next
Nike
Polo Jeans
Promod
Pull & Bear
River Woods
TopShop
Triumph
Tru Trussardi
Vittorio Marchesi
Zin Zin

**Footwear**
Aldo
Ecco
Geox
HOBBs
Lacoste

Milano
Nine West
PrettyFIT
Skechers

**Furniture & Home
Appliances**
@ home
KAS Australia
Laura Ashley Home
Pride of Kashmir
Tavolino by Tavola
Zone

**Jewellery & Accessories**
Aldo Accessories
Damas
Paul Frank
Pure Gold Jewellers
Rivoli

**Kids' Items**
Adams
Armani Junior
Damas Kids
Early Learning Centre
GAP
Next
Nougat
Pablosky
River Woods
Sparkles
The Toy Store Express

**Perfume & Cosmetics**
Areej
MAC
Red Earth

**Supermarkets**
Spinneys

## SPEND SOME QUALITY MERCATO TIME

Isn't it time you re-discovered the pleasures of shopping?
The enjoyment of browsing along cobbled streets and
taking your time down quaint alleyways. The pleasure of
knowing you will always find everything you came for.
The delight of buying that special something, then relaxing
over a romantic dinner or a great movie. Why not spend some
time at Mercato and experience it all.

Mall timings: Daily 10am - 10pm. Call (04) – 3444161
www.MercatoShoppingMall.com

## MERCATO
### The Good Life

# Places To Shop

### Souk Madinat Jumeirah

**Al Sufouh Road** Umm Suqeim **04 366 8888**
www.madinatjumeirah.com/shopping
Map **1 R4** Metro **Mall of the Emirates**

Souk Madinat Jumeirah is a recreation of a traditional souk, complete with narrow alleyways, authentic architecture and motorised abras. The blend of outlets is unlike anywhere else in Dubai, with boutique shops, galleries, cafes, restaurants and bars. The souk is best appreciated if you have time to walk around and enjoy the experience. During the cooler months the doors and glass walls are opened to add an alfresco element and there is shisha on offer in the courtyard.

The layout can be a little confusing; there are location maps throughout and the main features are signposted. If you're really lost, a member of staff will be able to point you in the right direction.

With an emphasis on unique brands, there are a large number of speciality outlets that aren't found anywhere else in Dubai. The souk is home to a concentration of art boutiques, including Gallery One (p.418) which sells photos with a local flavour and Mirage Glass (04 368 6207). The stalls in the outside areas sell souvenirs, some tasteful and some tacky. Eye-catching, but expensive, swimming gear can be found at Vilebrequin (04 368 6531), Rodeo Drive (04 368 6568) is good for label hunters or head to Tommy Bahama (04 368 6031) for some tropical flavour. There are more than 20 waterfront cafes, bars and

restaurants to choose from, including some of Dubai's hottest night spots and you'll find Left Bank (p.512), Shoo Fee Ma Fee (p.494), Jambase (p.512) and Bar Zar (p.507) to name a few. There's also the impressive Madinat Theatre (www.madinattheatre.com) which sees international and regional artists perform everything from ballet to comedy.

## Souk Madinat Jumeirah Stores

**Art & Photography**
Foto Fun
Gallery One
Sadek Music
Spirit of Art Gallery

**Arts & Crafts Supplies**
Al Jaber Gallery
Indian Emporium
Kashmir Cottage Arts
Kenza Art Gallery
Orient Spirit
Scarabee
Sinbad
Tarrab Trading

**Beachwear**
Grain De Sable
Havaianas
Sun & Sands
Vilebrequin
Sun & Sands Sports

**Carpets**
National Iranian Carpets
Persian Carpet House

**Eyewear & Opticians**
Al Jaber Optical Centre
Yateem Optician

**Fashion (Men)**
Paris Moda
Tie Shop

**Fashion (Unisex)**
Converse
Kuna by Alpaca 111
Louise Harrison Couture
Rodeo Drive
Sun & Sands Sports
Tommy Bahamas
Tough & Espadrille
Vilebrequin

**Fashion (Women)**
Cotton Club
Ounass
Yasmine

**Footwear**
Havaianas

**Furniture & Home Appliances**
Kashmir Cottage Arts
Marina Gulf Trading
Miri
Pride of Kashmir
Sinbad
Toshkhana

**Jewellery & Accessories**
Azal
Damas
Ferini Jewels
GB Jewellery
Hour Choice
La Marquise Diamond & Watches
Le Paris Diamond
Liali Jewellery
Luxe Cuture
Mademoiselle Accessories
Pure Gold
Rivoli
Tejori
Three Star Jewellery
Zayoon

**Kids' Items**
Bon Point
Early Learning Centre

**Perfume & Cosmetics**
Al Quraishi
Caravella
Henna Heritage
NStyle

**Services & Utilities**
Royal Fashions
National Bank of Dubai
Panacea

**Souvenirs & Gifts**
Al Dukan
Modern Antiques
The Camel Company
Smokers Centre

**Textiles & Haberdashery & Tailoring**
Indian Emporium

## Wafi

**Oud Metha Rd** Umm Hurair **04 324 4555**
www.wafi.com
Map **2 L6** Metro **Healthcare City**

Wafi's Egyptian theme, designer stores and layout make this one of the more interesting malls to wander around, and it rarely feels busy. The distinctive building has three pyramids forming part of the roof and a large stained glass window. Two of the pyramids are decorated with stained glass, depicting Egyptian scenes – best viewed during daylight.

Wafi past extensions added Raffles Dubai hotel, an underground carpark and 90 new shops. Its store directory now reads like a who's who in design, be it jewellery or couture, and the likes of Versace, Kitson, and Nicole Farhi mix with well-known high-street shops like Topshop (the largest in the UAE), Monsoon and a large branch of UK stalwart Marks and Spencer. There is a large branch of Jashanmal to browse in, and Imaginarium, a children's toy shop, has some great traditional toys (and a separate kid-sized door). For something differen head to Khan Murjan, the mall's impressive underground souk. Its magnificent stained glass ceiling and atmospheric archways house over 150 stalls selling an eclectic mix of items, including jewellery, antiques, perfume and souvenirs. The area is particularly good for spicing up your home with traditional arts and crafts – there are workshops where artisans can create pieces onsite.

There are also a number of cafes and restaurants,

including Biella and the highly recommended Khan Murjan Arabic restaurant (04 324 4555), where you can enjoy your meal in an alfresco dining area. The children's entertainment area, Encounter Zone, is very popular and has age-specific attractions.

If you feel the need for pampering, or an evening out, head across to the Pyramids complex where there are some excellent bars, restaurants, a club and a renowned spa.

## Wafi Stores

| | | | |
|---|---|---|---|
| **Books & Stationery** | Chanel | Sixty | Edra |
| Gulf Greetings | Club Monaco | Ted Lapidus | Frette |
| Montblanc | Daniel Hechter | Tigerlily | Genevieve Lethu |
| Montegrappa | Desert Rose | Topshop/Topman | La Murrina |
| Rivoli | dunhill | Tru Trussardi | Le Boudoir |
| | Ed Hardy | Versace JC | Memoires |
| **Department Stores** | Escada | Vintage 55 | Petals |
| Jashanmal | Etoile La Boutique | Zilli) | Point a la Ligne |
| Marks & Spencer | Ferre | | Tanagra |
| Paris Gallery | Gant | **Footwear** | THE One |
| Philipp Plein | Ginger & Lace | Alberto Guardiani | The White Company |
| Salam | Jaeger | Comfort Shoes | VGnewtrend |
| | John Galliano | Opera Shoes | Villeroy & Boch |
| **Electronics & Computers** | Kenneth Cole | Organdy | |
| Axiom Telecom | Kitson | Pointure | **Kids' Items** |
| Digi-Com/Nokia | LiuJo | Rossini | Angels |
| Jumbo Electronics | Miss Sixty | Sebago | Calvin Klein |
| | Oasis Fashion | Umberto Bilancioni | Christian Audigier |
| **Fashion** | Oilily | Via Rossi | Early Learning Centre |
| Baby Phat | Oui | Walter Steiger | Ed Hardy Kids |
| Betty Barclay | Ounass | | Gap Kids |
| Bugatti B More | Pal Zileri | **Furniture & Home** | Imaginarium |
| Calvin Klein | Pierre Cardin | **Appliances** | Kitson |
| Canali | Roberto Cavalli | Bombay | La Coquette |
| Cerruti 1881 | Roccobarocco | Crystalline | Oilily |

# Places To Shop

## Al Ghazal Complex & Shopping Mall

Cnr Al Diyafah & Al Wasl Rd Al Wasl 04 345 3053
Map 2 J3 Metro Al Jafiliya

The Al Ghazal Centre is a low-key shopping hub just finding its place on the Dubai shopping map. It's situated in a large office building and can often feel deserted, but the ground floor is used occasionally at weekends for craft fairs featuring stalls with jewellery, photography and home accessories, which get the crowds through the doors. Although the mix of stores won't rival the big players in town, what is on offer is enough smaller stores to make it a worthwhile pit stop for those little essentials and treats. There is a good branch of Carrefour Express, head to Alina Baby's Dream for kid's clothes or pick up costumes at Mr Ben's Closet. You can also visit Giordano for high-street clothes or get your toes pampered at NStyle. Other outlets include: Carrefour, China Star, Claire's, Cutest Fashion, Daphne, FAE, Le Carmen, Marble Slab, Redstar, and Watch Me.

## Al Ghurair City

Al Riqqa Rd Deira 04 222 5222
www.alghuraircity.com
Map 2 N4

One of the biggest draws for this area is Deira City Centre but, for a change of scene, Dubai's oldest mall is also worth a look. Al Ghurair City houses an eight-screen cinema, a Spinneys, and a good range of shops. The layout of the two-storey mall has the maze-like quality of a souk. There are a number of international brands, including Bhs, Book Corner and Mothercare, along with smaller boutiques. When you need a break, there are coffee shops and food outlets, and a Fun Corner to keep children occupied. Other outlets include: Aldo, Bhs, Bossini, Esprit, French Connection, Guess, La Senza, Mexx, Nine West, Paris Gallery, Plug-

Al Ghurair City

ins, Red Earth, Starbucks, Sun & Sand Sports, Swatch and Triumph.

## Arabian Center

Al Khawaneej Road Mirdif 04 284 5555
www.arabiancenter.ae
Map 2 S12

This mall may be smaller than its counterparts but it still manages to tick all the boxes when it comes to convenience, packing in well-known high-street brand so that Mirdif dwellers don't have all the essentials onb their doorstep. The mall has a selection of ove 200 stores where you can pick up home essentials (Oat Homes r Us, Sharaf DG and Eros Digital) and reasonably priced fashion at New Look, Splash, Topshop, Mango and H&M. For real budget buys, head to Daiso (p.425) and Matalan (a brilliant department store with a great range of low cost fashion and home accessories). The mall features a good selection of sport stores including Sport's Market, Adidas and Footlocker. Also at the mall is a cinema, hypermarket, Fun City play area for kids and Spaces Ladies Salon & Spa.

## Beach Centre

Jumeira Rd, Nr Dubai Zoo Jumeira 04 344 9045
Map 2 G3 Metro Al Jafiliya

This unassuming mall on Jumeira Beach Road has a number of interesting independent shops selling everything from books to furniture and jewellery. Notably, the mall includes two branches of White Star Bookshop, one stocks craft materials and the other specialises in teachers' supplies. It also houses Charisma, an independent plus-size womens' clothes shop, and the Music Room, at the back on the second floor, has the largest supply of sheet music in Dubai and a selection of instruments. With Kuts 4 Kids, a children's hairdressers, and an opticians, pharmacy and Cyber Café, this is a good community mall. Other outlets include: Bossini, Crystal Gallery, Dubai Desert Extreme, Kids to Teens, Party Zone, Sports House, Studio Al Aroosa, Yateem Opticians.

## Bin Sougat Centre

Airport Rd Al Rashidiya 04 286 3000
Map 2 P10 Metro Emirates Head Office

Anchored by a comprehensive branch of Spinneys (p.392), this mall is particularly convenient for Mirdif dwellers. There is an interesting mix of stores including Emirates Trading, which sells a great range of professional art supplies and equipment and Dubai Library Distributors which is excellent for stationery. Head to the basement for Orient Curios Furniture or RelaxSit which sells beanbag chairs. There is a small branch of Jumbo Electronics, Nugoosh ladies salon and Secrets Boutique which sells a limited range of lingerie in larger sizes. There are several food outlets in the mall and ample parking, except on Fridays when the mosque next door is busy. Other outlets include: Al Ansari Money Exchange, Damas Jewellers, Cocomino, London Café, Kuts 4 Kids, San Marco, The Balloon Lady, and Union National Bank.

## Boulevard at Emirates Towers
Sheikh Zayed Rd Trade Centre **04 330 0000**
www.jumeirah.com
Map **2 H5** Metro **Emirates Towers**
The Boulevard houses some of Dubai's most exclusive boutiques, popular restaurants and bars. The area links the Emirates Towers Hotel and Emirates Towers Offices, and is accessible from both. Boutiques include Cartier, Gucci, Yves Saint Laurent and Jimmy Choo shoes – so exclusive it has its own entrance from the carpark). If you're into more than shopping, there's also a health club and 1847, a men-only spa.

There are cafes (some with wireless internet access), licensed restaurants (Scarlett's and The Noodle House), and the ever-popular early evening hangout, The Agency. Head here for high fashion at high prices – the steep parking charge (first hour is free, thereafter it is Dhs.20 per hour) says it all. Other outlets include: Bottega Veneta, Bvlgari, Chloe, Damas, Ermenegildo Zegna, Flower@towers, Gucci, N-Bar, Paper Room, Rodeo Drive, Sergio Rossi.

## Dragon Mart
Emirates Rd, International City Al Awir **04 368 7205**
www.dragonmart.ae
Map **2 C3**
Dragon Mart reportedly has the largest concentration of Chinese traders outside China. At over one kilometre in length, it takes about three hours to have a good look round. The mall is divided into zones by commodity, but these demarcations have been blurred. From building materials to toys, household items to quad bikes, everything is available – and cheaper than elsewhere in the city. The centre is open from 10:00 to 23:00, but many of the shops don't open till 17:00. The quality isn't great, but if you're looking for something cheap and for the short haul, you can't go wrong. There is no foodcourt as such, although there is a restaurant, a cafe, and several little foodstands at regular intervals.

## Dubai Marina Mall
Dubai Marina **04 436 1000**
www.dubaimarinamall.com
Map **1 K4** Metro **Dubai Marina**
Located in Dubai Marina's thriving community, and within walking distance of The Walk, Jumeirah Beach Residence p.389, this new mall's 160 outlets will offer a mix of plush designer goods and high-street regulars. Many stores are now opening, with shops like New Look (04 399 7740), Reiss (04 399 7664), Karen Millen and Accessorize anchor its offering of reasonably priced

Dubai Outlet Mall

fashion. Get your shoes made to order at Morgan Miller (04 434 2700) and pick up kids' items at Mamas & Papas (04 399 7807). There is a large foodcourt with many of the usual suspects and several restaurants, including T.G.I Fridays (04 434 2686), Gourmet Burger Kitchen and Yo! Sushi. The Favourite Things Mother and Child play area (p.144) provides plenty of entertainment for kids, and you can leave your kids there so they can enjoy supervised play while you shop. Yet to open is an eight-screen cinema and the Gourmet Tower, which will offer world-class cuisine with waterfront views.

## Dubai Outlet Mall
Dubai – Al Ain Rd (Route 66), Dubailand
**04 367 9600**
www.dubaioutletmall.com
In a city where the emphasis in on excess, it is refreshing (not only for the wallet) to find a mall dedicated to saving money. Dubai's first 'outlet' concept mall may be a way out of town, (20 minutes down the Al Ain road) but it's worth the drive. Big discounts on major retailers and labels are available with price tags seemingly missing a zero; think T-shirts for under Dhs.30 and Karama-esque prices for Marc Jacobs handbags. High street shops including Massimo Dutti and Dune sit alongside designer names such as Tommy Hilfiger and DKNY, with city style and sports casual equally catered for. Pick up trainers from

# Places To Shop

Adidas, Nike and Puma, reduced eyewear from Al Jaber or Magrabi, jewellery from Damas, cosmetics from Paris Gallery and a range of electronics and homewares from more than 10 different outlets. There are several pharmacies, a barber, Starbucks, Stone Fire Pizza Kitchen and Automatic as well as the usual foodcourt suspects. And to keep the little ones engaged there's Chuck E Cheese – a US institution serving up ample portions of food and entertainment. Other outlets include: Adams, Aldo, Converse, Diesel, Espirit, Fashion For Less, G-Star, Giordano, Guess, Kenneth Cole, Levi's, Mango, Monsoon, Nine West, Phat Farm, Pierre Cardin, Planet Nutrition, Price Less, Pumpkin Patch, Replay, Samsonite, Sports Direct Outlet, Stadium and Timberland.

## Jumeira Plaza

Jumeira Rd, Nr Jumeira Mosque Jumeira
04 349 7111
Map 2 H3 Metro Al Jafiliya

The 'pink mall' on Jumeira Beach Road has an interesting range of independent shops. It is dominated on the ground floor by a play area (for young children) and the Dôme Cafe. Downstairs, there are outlets selling everything from furniture to greeting cards. House of Prose is a popular second-hand book shop; there are also a number of home decor, trinket and card shops, and a small branch of the Dubai Police – great for paying fines without having to queue. Upstairs, Aquarius sells silk paintings of local scenes and Melangé has an interesting selection of clothing, jewellery and soft furnishings from India. This is a busy area and parking spaces can be hard to find; there is parking under the mall but the entrance is a squeeze – especially for larger cars or four wheel drives. Other outlets include: Art Stop, Balloon Lady, Blue White, Falaknaz Habitat, Girls' Talk Beauty Centre, Kashmir Craft, KKids, Susan Walpole, Safeplay and The Warehouse.

## Jumeirah Centre

Jumeira Rd, Nr Jumeira Mosque Jumeira
04 349 9702
Map 2 H3 Metro Al Jafiliya

This mall packs a lot into a small space. There are branches of several established chains including Benetton, Mothercare, Stadium and Sun & Sand; and a number of independent shops. Kazim, on the ground floor, has a good range of stationery and art supplies. Upstairs, independent shops abound and include Elves & Fairies (a crafts and hobbies shop), Panache (for accessories made only from natural materials), Sunny Days (a boutique selling a range of gift items), and the Wedding Shop.

There are also some interesting clothes shops, and a gallery here. Harvest Home has shops on both levels selling gifts and kitchenalia. For refreshment, head to

Coffee Bean & Tea Leaf which has a terrace where you can enjoy an alfresco coffee. Other outlets include: Blue Cactus, Caviar Classic, Cut Above, Kazim Gulf Traders, Lunnettes, Nutrition Centre, Photo Magic, Rivoli, Sunny Days, The Barber Shop and Thomas Cook

## Lamcy Plaza

Nr EPPCO HQ Oud Metha 04 335 9999
www.lamcyplaza.com
Map 2 K5 Metro Oud Metha

Home to five floors of open-plan shopping, and open at 09:00 seven days a week, Lamcy is consistently popular. The mall has a great variety of shops in close quarters; entertainment dominates the ground floor, with a huge foodcourt and Loulou Al Dugong', a play area for children. There is also a pharmacy, a money exchange, a florist and a post office counter, as well as a fascinating feng shui shop that is crammed with interesting knick-knacks. Also on the ground floor is a photo developing outlet, a key cutting service and a branch of Belhasa Driving Center. The first floor is for women's fashion and shoes and includes Dorothy Perkins (good value fashion), Guess, Monsoon and Hush Puppies. The second floor is great for mums and kids, with Mothercare, Pumpkin Patch and Adams. Mexx for Less sells discounted clothing for men, women and children, and Peacocks and Mr Price sell reasonably priced fashion. Factory Fashions is well worth a look as it carries Adams and Pumpkin Patch overstocks. Men's clothing and sports shops are located on the third floor. This is the destination for bargain hunters too; Daiso is a Japanese store where almost everything costs Dhs.6. The top floor is dedicated to the Hypermarket which sells everything from kitchenware and bedding to clothes and groceries. Other outlets include: Aldo, Athlete's Foot, Books Plus, Bhs, Bossini, City Sports, Giordano, Golf House, Hang Ten, Hush Puppies, La Senza, Nine West, Peacocks, Shoe Mart, Swatch and Watch House.

## Oasis Centre

Shk Zayed Rd Al Quoz 04 515 4000
www.oasiscentremall.com
Map 2 H5 Metro Al Qouz

It may not have the size or the glamour of some of Dubai's other mega malls, but the new Oasis Centre (the old building was destroyed by fire in 2005) is now bigger and better than before. The mall offers a good selection of outlets including a Home Centre, New Look, Carrefour Express and a Centrepoint. There is a small foodcourt which offers the usual fastfood outlets, but for something different, head to Gourmet Station which sells a good range of deli items, cooked food and sandwiches. Other outlets include: Adidas, Bossini, Claires, Damas, Game King, Joyallukas, Koton, Lifestyle, Max, Mothercare, Nike, Q Home Decor, Rage Bike Shop, Sun & Sands Sports, Splash, Springfield.

## Palm Strip

Jumeira Rd, Opp Jumeira Mosque Jumeira
04 346 1462
Map **2 H3** Metro **Al Jafiliya**
Palm Strip is across the road from Jumeira mosque, and is more of an arcade than a mall. Upmarket boutiques dominate; there are also speciality shops for Arabic perfumes (Rusasi), maternity wear (Great Expectations) and chocolate (Jeff de Bruges). There are two beauty salons and a walk-in branch of N-Bar. Palm Strip is often quiet during the day, getting a little livelier in the evenings with the popular Japengo Café. If the shaded parking at the front is full, there's an underground carpark, with access from the side. Zara Home has an outlet selling bright and stylish accessories. Other outlets include: Beyond the Beach, Elite Fashion, Gulf Pharmacy, Hagen-Dazs, Little Me, Mask, My Time Ladies Salon, Oceano, Starbucks and Zara Home.

## Reef Mall

Salahuddin St Deira 04 224 2240
www.reefmall.com
Map **2 N4** Metro **Salahudin**
This surprisingly large mall is anchored by Home Centre, Lifestyle, Splash and Babyshop. Among many other outlets are branches of Cellucom, i2, and Athlete's Foot. There's a huge Fun City here, a great place where kids (toddlers to teens) can burn off a bit of energy. There's a small foodcourt, several cafes and a supermarket. Other outlets include: Aldo Accessories, The Athlete's Foot, Babyshop, Bossini, Charles & Keith, Damas, Digi 4 U, Grand Optics, Karisma, McDonald's, Nayomi, Nine West,, Splash, Dome Café.

## Spinneys

Cnr Al Wasl Rd Umm Suqeim 04 394 1657
www.spinneys-dubai.com
Map **2 B4** Metro **Al Quoz**
This small mall, just off Al Wasl Road, centres around a large Spinneys supermarket. There are a small number of other shops including Early Learning Centre and Mothercare, Tavola (for kitchenalia), and Disco 2000, which is one of Dubai's better music and DVD shops. There are branches of both MMI and A&E, along with cafes and a large Fun Corner play area for children. It gets quite busy at weekends and the small carpark is nearly always full. Other outlets include: Arabella Pharmacy, Areej, Axiom Telecom, Baskin Robbins, Beyond the Beach, Books Plus, Café Havana, Champion Cleaners, Damas, Emirates Bank, Gulf Greetings, Hair Works, The Healing Zone, Starbucks and Uniform Shop.

## Times Square

Skh Zayed Rd, Btn Jct 3 & 4 Al Quoz 04 341 8020
www.timessquarecenter.ae
Map **1 T5** Metro **Al Quoz**
The large branch of Sharaf DG, and its moderately sized foodcourt, is the biggest draw for this small, but modern, mall. Several of the stores have closed, but you'll find a large branch of Intersport, Toys R Us, Yellow Hat (for car accessories) and V-Moto. Head to the Chillout ice lounge (unlicensed), if only for the novelty, for sub-zero mocktail. In addition to the foodcourt, there is Sun Cafe, Caribou Coffee and Extreme Freshies Café. There's also a pharmacy and a few children's clothes stores. Other outlets include: Bayti, InWear, Joe Bloggs, Ladybird, Sanrio (Hello Kitty), Sharaf DG, Toys R Us, Watch Square and Yellow Hat.

## Town Centre Jumeirah

Jumeira Rd Jumeira 04 344 0111
www.TownCentreJumeirah.com
Map **2 F3** Metro **Burj Dubai**
Town Centre is a community mall on Jumeira Beach Road, next to Mercato. There is an interestign blend of outlets and several cafes, including Café Céramique where you can customise a piece of pottery while you dine. For pampering, there's Feet First (reflexology and massage for men and women), Kaya Beauty Centre, Nail Station and SOS Salon. There are also clothing shops including Heat Waves (for beachwear) and Anne Klein (fashion accessories) a large branch of Paris Gallery, an Empost counter and an Etisalat machine.

Other outlets include: Al Jaber Optical, Bang & Olufsen, Bateel, Books Plus, Bayti, Damas, Marie Claire, Nine West, Nutrition Zone, Papermoon, Paris Gallery, Zen Yoga, Little Luxurious.

## The Village

Jumeira Rd Jumeira 04 344 4444
www.thevillagedubai.com
Map **2 H3** Metro **Al Jafiliya**
The Village Mall, with its Mediterranean theme, has more of a community feel than many of the malls in Dubai. The niche boutiques are great if you're looking for something different, whether it's clothing or something for the home, and there are some audaciously feminine outlets like S*uce, Ayesha Depala and Shakespeare & Co. (a cafe that embraces chintz). Peekaboo, the children's play area, is bright and fun for younger children – it also runs activities. There are a number of places to eat, including Thai Time (04 344 8034), and the Shakespeare & Co (04 344 6228). Other outlets include: Ayesha Depala, Books Gallery, Boots, Irony Home, Julian Hairdressing for Men, Offshore Legends, OXBOW Sportswear, Sugar Daddy's Bakery, Sisters Beauty Lounge and Sensasia Urban Spa (p.216).

# STORE FINDER

**@Home** Dubai Marina Mall, The Dubai Mall, Ibn Battuta Mall, Mercato

**Accessorize** Arabian Center, BurJuman, Deira City Centre, Dubai Marina Mall, The Dubai Mall, Festival Centre, Lamcy Plaza, Mall of the Emirates, Uptown Mirdif

**ACE** Festival Centre, The Market Mall (Green Community), Sheikh Zayed Rd (Btn Interchange 1 & 2)

**Adams** Al Ghurair City, Arabian Center, BurJuman, Deira City Centre, The Dubai Mall, Festival Centre, Lamcy Plaza, Mercato, Uptown Mirdif

**Adidas** Al Ghazal Complex & Shopping Mall, Al Ghurair City, Arabian Center, BurJuman, Deira City Centre, Dubai Outlet Mall, Festival Centre, Ibn Battuta Mall, Mall of the Emirates, Uptown Mirdif

**African & Eastern (A&E)** Karama (Nr Karama Market), Al Wasl Rd (Nxt to Spinneys, Umm Suqeim), Arabian Ranches (Community Centre), Bur Dubai (Spinneys, nr Ramada Htl), Deira (Opp Mayfair Htl), Dubai Marina (Marina Walk), Jumeirah 1 (Beh Spinneys, Jumeira Rd), Uptown Mirdif (Nxt to Spinneys, Mirdif)

**Aftershock** The Dubai Mall, Festival Centre, Mall of the Emirates, Souk Al Bahar

**Aigner** BurJuman, Deira City Centre, The Dubai Mall, Mall of the Emirates

**Ajmal Perfumes** Al Ghurair City, Bin Sougat Centre, BurJuman, Deira (Al Dagaya, Nr Kuwaiti Mosque), Deira City Centre, Emirates Co-operative (Al Mizher), Gold Souq (Deira), Mall of the Emirates, Murshad Bazaar (Deira), Satwa Rd, Union Co-operative Society (Al Wasl), Wafi

**AK Anne Klein** BurJuman, Festival Centre

**Al Boom Marine** Dubai Marina Yacht Club, Jumeira Rd, Nadd Al Hamar Rd

**Al Fahidi Stationery** Al Faheidi St (Bur Dubai), Al Nasr Square, Al Ras, Murshad Bazaar (Deira)

**Al Fardan Jewels & Precious Stones** Deira City Centre, The Dubai Mall, Hamarain Centre, InterContinental Dubai Festival Centre, Mall of the Emirates

**Al Futtaim Jewellery** BurJuman, Deira City Centre, The Dubai Mall, Festival Centre, Lamcy Plaza, Mall of the Emirates

**Al Jaber Gallery** Deira City Centre, The Dubai Mall, Dubai Marina Mall, Gold Souk (Deira), Mall of the Emirates, Souk Madinat Jumeirah

**Al Jaber Optical Centre** Al Ghurair City, Arabian Center, Bin Sougat Centre, Deira City Centre, Dubai Outlet Mall, The Dubai Mall, Dubai Marina Mall, Emaar Town Centre (Emirates Hills), Festival Centre, Ibn Battuta Mall, Lamcy Plaza, Mall of the Emirates, Meena Bazaar (Bur Dubai), Sheikh Zayed Rd (Nxt to Coco's Restaurant), Souk Al Bahar, Souk Madinat Jumeirah, Town Centre Jumeirah, Wafi

**Al Kamda** Al Wasl (Nxt to Mazaya Centre), Salahudhin Rd (Deira)

**Al Maya Supermarket** Al Mamzar, Downtown Burj Dubai (Boulevard 8), Dubai Marina (Dream Tower), Nr Al Murooj Rotana Htl, Reef Mall, The Walk at Jumeirah Beach Residence (Bahar, Tower 6), The Walk at Jumeirah Beach Residence (Al Sadaf)

**ALDO** Al Ghurair City, Arabian Center, BurJuman, Deira City Centre, The Dubai Mall, Dubai Marina Mall, Dubai Outlet Mall, Festival Centre, Ibn Battuta Mall, Lamcy Plaza, Mall of the Emirates, Mercato, Uptown Mirdif

**ALDO Accessories** Al Ghurair City, Arabian Center, BurJuman, Deira City Centre, The Dubai Mall, Festival Centre, Ibn Battuta Mall, Lamcy Plaza, Mall of the Emirates, Mercato, Reef Mall, Dukkan Al Manzil Souk (Downtown Burj Dubai), Uptown Mirdif

**Amouage** Available in Paris Gallery stores: Al Bustan Centre, Al Ghurair City, Arabian Center, BurJuman, Burj Al Arab, Deira City Centre, The Dubai Mall, Festival Centre, Hamarain Centre, Ibn Battuta Mall, Lamcy Plaza, Town Centre Jumeirah, Uptown Mirdiff, Wafi

**Aptec Mobiles** Al Ghurair City, Arabian Ranches (Community Centre), Danat Al Khaleej Bld (Deira), The Dubai Mall, Lamcy Plaza

**Arabian Oud** Al Bustan Centre, Al Ghurair City, Al Manal Centre 1, Al Manal Centre 2, BurJuman, Deira City Centre, Dubai Concorde Hotel & Residence, Dubai Outlet Mall, The Dubai Mall, Gold Souk (Naif), Hamarain Centre, Ibn Battuta Mall, Souk Al Bahar, Wafi

**Areej** Dubai Marina Mall, The Dubai Mall, Emirates Towers Hotel, Ibn Battuta Mall, Mall of the Emirates, Mercato, Spinneys (Umm Suqeim)

**Shopping**

**Armani** Deira City Centre, The Dubai Mall, Boulevard at Emirates Towers, Mall of the Emirates, Mercato

**Armani Junior** BurJuman (Saks Fifth Avenue), The Dubai Mall, Mall of the Emirates (Harvey Nichols), Mercato

**Artikel** Festival Centre, Mall of the Emirates

**Axiom Telecom** Al Ghurair City, Arabian Center, Bin Sougat Centre, Century Mall, Deira City Centre, Dubai International Financial Centre (DIFC), Dubai Internet City, Dubai Marina Mall, Dubai World Trade Centre, The Dubai Mall, Emarat Station (Various Locations), BurJuman, Emirates Hills, Festival Centre, Grand Cineplex (Umm Hurair), Hyatt Regency Hotel, Ibn Battuta Mall, Town Centre Jumeirah, Mall of the Emirates, Mercato, Sheikh Zayed Rd (Nr Dusit Thani Dubai), Spinneys (Nr Ramada Htl, Bur Dubai), Spinneys (Umm Suqeim), Wafi

**Babyshop** Abu Hail Center, Al Ghurair City, Centrepoint (Bur Dubai), The Dubai Mall, Mall of the Emirates (Centrepoint), Reef Mall, Zabeel Rd (Karama)

**Baldinini** BurJuman, Dubai Outlet Mall, The Dubai Mall, Festival Centre

**Balloon Lady** Bin Sougat Centre, Jumeira Plaza

**Bally** The Dubai Mall, Mall of the Emirates

**Balmain** Deira City Centre, Dubai Marina Mall, Festival Centre

**Banana Republic** Deira City Centre, The Dubai Mall

**Bang & Olufsen** BurJuman, The Dubai Mall, Town Centre Jumeirah

**Barakat Optical** Dubai Outlet Mall, Festival Centre, Jumeira Plaza, Jumeirah Beach Residence, The Dubai Mall, Umm Suqeim, Uptown Mirdif

**Basler** BurJuman, Deira City Centre, Ibn Battuta Mall, Mall of the Emirates

**Bata** Deira City Centre, The Dubai Mall, Mall of the Emirates

**BCBG Max Azria** BurJuman, The Dubai Mall, Mall of the Emirates

**Bebe** BurJuman, Deira City Centre, Dubai Marina Mall, The Dubai Mall, Festival Centre

**Bendon** Arabian Center, Dubai Outlet Mall, The Dubai Mall, Festival Centre, Mall of the Emirates,

**Bershka** Deira City Centre, The Dubai Mall, Mall of the Emirates, Mercato

**Better Life** Al Ittihad Rd (Deira), Karama, Jumeirah Beach Residence, Mall of the Emirates

**Beyond the Beach** Al Bahar Showroom (nr Picnico, Jumeirah), Emaar Town Centre (Emirates Hills), Green Community, Grosvenor House, Ibn Battuta Mall, Le Royal Meridien Beach Resort, Mercato, Motor City, One&Only Royal Mirage, Sheraton Jumeirah Beach Resort, Spinneys (Umm Suqeim), Town Centre (The Springs), Uptown Mirdif

**Bhs** Al Ghurair City, BurJuman, Dubai Outlet Mall, Festival Centre, Ibn Battuta Mall, Lamcy Plaza, Mall of the Emirates

**Billabong** Dubai Marina Mall, The Dubai Mall, Festival Centre

**BinHendi Boutique** Jumeirah Beach Hotel, Sheikh Rashid Bld (Deira), Wafi

**BinHendi Jewellery** Burj Al Arab, BurJuman, Deira City Centre, Dubai International Financial Centre (DIFC), The Dubai Mall, Jumeirah Beach Hotel, Mall of the Emirates

**Blush** Al Ghurair City, Festival City

**Bobby Brown** BurJuman (Paris Gallery), Dubai Marina Mall, The Dubai Mall, Deira City Centre (Debenhams), Festival Centre (Paris Gallery), Mall of the Emirates (Harvey Nichols)

**Boboli** BurJuman, Dubai Outlet Mall, The Dubai Mall, Festival Centre,

**Bombay** Mall of the Emirates, Mercato, Wafi

**Book World** Karama, Al Satwa

**Books Plus** Arabian Center, Arabian Ranches, Festival Centre, Green Community, The Greens, Ibn Battuta Mall, Lamcy Plaza, Spinneys (Umm Suqeim), Spring Community Centre, Uptown Mirdif

**Bookworm** Jumeirah (Beh Park & Shop), The Meadows

**Boots** Al Diyafa Rd (Al Satwa), Al Wasl Hospital, Arabian Center, Boulevard at Emirates Towers, Choitram (Al Wasl Rd), Deira City Centre, Dubai

# Store Finder

International Financial Centre (DIFC), Dubai Marina Mall, The Dubai Mall, Ghadeer Tower (Sheikh Zayed Rd), Ibn Battuta Mall, Lamcy Plaza, Mall of the Emirates, Residence Tower 1 (Downtown Burj Dubai), The Village Mall, The Walk at Jumeirah Beach Residence, Wafi

**Borders**  Deira City Centre, Dubai International Financial Centre (DIFC), Dubai Marina Mall, Ibn Battuta Mall, Mall of the Emirates

**Bose**  The Dubai Mall, Festival Centre, Mall of the Emirates

**Bossini**  Al Ghurair City, Al Manal Centre, Arabian Centre, Beach Centre (Jumeirah), BurJuman, The Dubai Mall, Festival Centre, Lamcy Plaza, Mall of the Emirates, Meena Bazaar, Oasis Centre, Reef Mall, Souk Al Kabir (Bur Dubai)

**Braccialini**  The Dubai Mall, Festival Centre, Holiday Centre Mall (Trade Centre), Mall of the Emirates

**Brantano**  Mall of the Emirates, Uptown Mirdif

**Breitling**  Deira City Centre, Dubai International Airport (Terminal 1), Dubai International Airport (Terminal 3), Kunooz Jewellers (Festival Centre), Kunooz Jewellers (The Ritz-Carlton, Dubai), Kunooz Jewellers (Sheraton Dubai Creek Hotel & Towers), Kunooz Jewellers (The Westin Dubai Mina Seyahi Beach Resort & Marina), Kunooz Jewellers (Wafi), Le Meridien Mina Seyahi Beach Resort & Marina (04 399 3090), Mall of the Emirates,

**Burberry**  BurJuman, Deira City Centre, Dubai Outlet Mall, The Dubai Mall, Mall of the Emirates,

**Bvlgari**  Boulevard at Emirates Towers, Dubai International Airport (Terminal 1), Dubai International Airport (Terminal 3), The Dubai Mall, Mall of the Emirates

**Café Cotton**  Dubai Outlet Mall, The Dubai Mall, Festival Centre, Mall of the Emirates

**Calvin Klein**  Al Ghurair City, BurJuman, The Dubai Mall, Mall of the Emirates, Wafi

**Calvin Klein Underwear**  Deira City Centre, Festival Centre, Mall of the Emirates

**Camaieu**  Arabian Center, The Dubai Mall, Festival Centre, Lamcy Plaza, Mall of the Emirates

**Canali**  BurJuman, The Dubai Mall, Wafi

**Carl F. Bucherer**  The Dubai Mall, Festival Centre, Rivoli (Burj Al Arab), Rivoli (BurJuman), Rivoli (Deira City Centre), Rivoli (Dubai Marina Mall), Rivoli (Mall of the Emirates), Rivoli (Mercato), Rivoli (Wafi), Rivoli (Souk Madinat Jumeirah)

**Carlton Cards**  Deira City Centre, Lamcy Plaza, Mall of the Emirates (Jashanmal)

**Carolina Herrera**  The Dubai Mall, Festival Centre, Mall of the Emirates

**Carrefour**  Al Shindagha, Century Mall, Deira City Centre, Mall of the Emirates

**Carrefour Express**  Al Ghazal Complex & Shopping Mall, Oasis Centre, Wafi

**Cartier**  Atlantis The Palm, BurJuman, Dubai International Airport (Terminal 1), The Dubai Mall, Emirates Towers Hotel, Gold & Diamond Park, Gold Souk (Deira)

**Casadei**  BurJuman, Deira City Centre, Wafi

**Cellucom**  BurJuman, Deira City Centre, Dukkan Tamarhind (Yansoon 9, Downtown Burj Dubai), Emaar Town Centre (Emirates Hills), Festival Centre, Green Community Center (Dubai Green Community), Ibn Battuta Mall, Jumeirah Centre, Mall of the Emirates, Reef Mall, The Dubai Mall

**Centrepoint**  Mall of the Emirates, Trade Centre Rd (Bur Dubai)

**Cerruti**  BurJuman, Mall of the Emirates, Mercato, Wafi

**Cesare Paciotti**  BurJuman, Dubai Outlet Mall, The Dubai Mall, Wafi

**Chanel**  BurJuman, The Dubai Mall, Wafi

**Charles & Keith**  Al Manal Centre, Al Ghurair City, Arabian Center, The Dubai Mall, Festival Centre, Ibn Battuta Mall, Mall of the Emirates, Reef Mall, Uptown Mirdif

**Chevignon**  Festival Centre, Mall of the Emirates

**Chopard**  Atlantis The Palm, Burj Al Arab, BurJuman, Deira City Centre (Ahmed Seddiqi & Sons), Deira Tower (Ahmed Seddiqi & Sons), The Dubai Mall, Emirates Towers Hotel (Ahmed Seddiqi & Sons), Festival Centre (Ahmed Seddiqi & Sons), Grand Hyatt Dubai (Ahmed Seddiqi & Sons), Grosvenor House (Ahmed Seddiqi & Sons), Jumeirah Beach Hotel (Ahmed Seddiqi & Sons), Le Royal Meridien Beach Resort (Ahmed Seddiqi &

Sons), Mall of the Emirates, Murshad Bazaar, Deira (Ahmed Seddiqi & Sons), Souk Madinat Jumeirah (Ahmed Seddiqi & Sons), Wafi

**Choithram** Al Fahidi St (Bur Dubai), Garhoud, Karama, Al Mankhool Rd (Al Mankhool), Al Nasr Square, Al Wasl Rd (Al Wasl), Green Community, The Greens, Holiday Centre, Hyatt Regency Dubai (The Galleria), Jebel Ali, Jumeira Rd (Jumeirah), The Lakes, The Springs, Umm Suqeim

**Claire's** Al Ghazal Complex & Shopping Mall, Al Ghurair City, Arabian Center, Deira City Centre, The Dubai Mall, Emaar Town Center (Emirates Hills), Festival Centre, Ibn Battuta Mall, Lamcy Plaza, Mall of the Emirates, Mercato, Uptown Mirdif, Wafi

**Clarks** Al Ghurair City, Deira City Centre, The Dubai Mall, Festival Centre, Mall of the Emirates, Wafi

**Club Monaco** Deira City Centre, Wafi Mall,

**Coach** Boulevard at Emirates Towers, Deira City Centre, The Dubai Mall, Mall of the Emirates (Harvey Nichols)

**Coast** The Dubai Mall, Ibn Battuta Mall, Mall of the Emirates (Debenhams)

**Columbia** Deira City Centre, The Dubai Mall, Festival Centre, Ibn Battuta Mall, Mall of the Emirates

**Damas** BurJuman, Deira City Centre, Dubai International Financial Center (DIFC), The Dubai Mall, Festival Centre, Hamarain Centre, Holiday Centre Mall, Ibn Battuta Mall, Mall of the Emirates, Mercato, Souk Madinat Jumeirah, Spinneys, Town Centre Jumeirah, Umm Suqueim, Uptown Mirdif, Wafi

**Danier** The Dubai Mall, Festival Centre

**Dar Al Tasmim Uniforms** Al Rashidiya, Spinneys, Umm Suqeim

**De Beers** Dubai International Financial Center (DIFC), Mall of the Emirates

**Debenhams** Deira City Centre, The Dubai Mall, Ibn Battuta Mall, Mall of the Emirates

**Deepak's** Al Satwa (Opp Emarat Gas Station), Dubai Outlet Mall, Plant St (Al Satwa), Oasis Centre

**Diesel** BurJuman, Deira City Centre, Dubai Marina Mall, Dubai Outlet Mall, The Dubai Mall, Festival Centre, Mall of the Emirates, Mercato

**Dior** Al Ghurair City (Paris Gallery), Burj Al Arab (Paris Gallery), BurJuman (Saks Fifth Avenue), Deira City Centre (Paris Gallery), Dubai International Airport (Terminal 1), The Dubai Mall, Festival Centre (Paris Gallery), Ibn Battuta Mall (Paris Gallery), Mall of the Emirates (Watch Gallery), Town Centre (Paris Gallery), Uptown Mirdif (Paris Gallery), Wafi (Paris Gallery)

**DKNY** BurJuman, Deira City Centre, Festival Centre, Mall of the Emirates

**Dockers** Deira City Centre, The Dubai Mall, Festival Centre

**Dolce & Gabbana** BurJuman, The Dubai Mall, Mall of the Emirates

**Domino** Al Ghurair City, Mercato, Wafi

**Dorothy Perkins** Ibn Battuta Mall, Lamcy Plaza, Mall of the Emirates

**Dune** Arabian Center, BurJuman, Dubai Outlet Mall, The Dubai Mall, Festival Centre, Mall of the Emirates

**Dream Girl** Karama, Al Satwa, Meena Bazaar

**Dubai Library Distributors** Al Satwa Rd, Al Yasmeen Bldg (Salahudhin Rd), Bin Sougat Centre, Nad Al Rashida Bldg (Al Rashidiya), Naif Rd (Deira), Nasr Lootha Old Bldg (Al Qusais), Sheikh Zayed Rd (Nr Abu Dhabi Commercial Bank)

**Dwell** The Dubai Mall, Festival Centre, Uptown Mirdif

**Early Learning Centre** Arabian Center, Al Ghurair City, BurJuman, Deira City Centre, Dubai Marina Mall, Dukkan Al Manzil Souk (Downtown Burj Dubai), The Dubai Mall, Festival Centre, Mall of the Emirates, Mercato, Souk Madinat Jumeirah, Spinneys (Uptown Mirdiff), Spinneys (Umm Suqeim), Wafi

**Ecco** Al Ghurair City, Deira City Centre, Dubai Marina Mall, Dubai Outlet Mall, The Dubai Mall, Festival Centre, Mall of the Emirates, Mercato, Reef Mall

**Ed Hardy** Dubai Marina Mall, The Dubai Mall, Festival Centre, Wafi

**Elle** Deira City Centre, Ibn Battuta Mall, Reef Mall

**Emirates Trading Est.** Bin Sougat Centre, Oud Metha (Nr Al Nasr Cinema), Mall of the Emirates, Jumierah (Nr Town Centre Jumeirah)

# Store Finder

**EROS Electricals** Karama (Abdul Aziz Mirza Bldg), Baniyas Rd (Deira), Deira City Centre, Mall of the Emirates (Centrepoint)

**Escada** BurJuman, The Dubai Mall, Mall of the Emirates, Wafi

**Esprit** Al Ghurair City, BurJuman, Deira City Centre, Dubai Outlet Mall, The Dubai Mall, Festival Centre, Mall of the Emirates

**Etoile** BurJuman, Mall of the Emirates, Wafi

**Etro** BurJuman, The Dubai Mall, Mall of the Emirates

**Evans** Al Ghurair City, Deira City Centre (Debenhams), Ibn Battuta Mall (Debenhams), Mall of the Emirates (Debenhams)

**Fabi** The Dubai Mall, Festival Centre, Mall of the Emirates

**Faces** Atlantis The Palm, BurJuman, The Dubai Mall, Festival Centre, Ibn Battuta Mall, Mall of the Emirates, Uptown Mirdif

**Faith** The Dubai Mall (Debenhams), Deira City Centre (Debenhams), Ibn Battuta Mall, Mall of the Emirates (Debenhams)

**FCUK** Al Ghurair City, Deira City Centre, Festival Centre, Mall of the Emirates

**Feshwari** Al Hudheibah Rd (Al Satwa), Sheikh Zayed Rd (Smark Bldg)

**Fila** The Dubai Mall, Deira City Centre, Ibn Battuta Mall, Mall of the Emirates

**Folli Follie** BurJuman, The Dubai Mall, Dubai Marina Mall, Festival Centre, Mall of the Emirates

**Fono** Arabian Center, Deira City Centre, The Dubai Mall, Festival Centre, Mall of the Emirates, Uptown Mirdif

**Forever 21** Deira City Centre, The Dubai Mall, Festival Centre, Ibn Battuta Mall, Mall of the Emirates

**Fossil** BurJuman, Deira City Centre, Lamcy Plaza, Nasr Square

**Furla** BurJuman, The Dubai Mall, Mall of the Emirates

**G2000** Al Ghurair City, BurJuman, The Dubai Mall, Festival Centre, Lamcy Plaza, Mall of the Emirates, Reef Mall

**Gallery One** Mall of the Emirates, The Dubai Mall, Souk Al Bahar, The Walk at Jumeirah Beach Residence, Souk Madinat Jumeirah

**Gant** BurJuman, Deira City Centre, The Dubai Mall, Festival Centre, Jumeirah Beach Residence, Mall of the Emirates, Wafi, Uptown Mirdif

**GAP** BurJuman, Deira City Centre, The Dubai Mall, Mercato, Wafi

**GAS** Festival Centre, Mall of the Emirates,

**Geekay Games** BurJuman, Deira City Centre, The Dubai Mall, Festival Centre, Mall of the Emirates

**Genevieve Lethu** Mercato, Wafi

**Geox** Deira City Centre, The Dubai Mall, Festival Centre, Ibn Battuta, Mall of the Emirates, Mercato

**GF Ferre** BurJuman, The Dubai Mall, Mercato, Mall of the Emirates

**Gianfranco FERRE** BurJuman, The Dubai Mall, Mall of the Emirates, Mercato, Palm Strip (Jumeirah)

**Gianni Martinelli** Deira City Centre, The Dubai Mall, Wafi Mall

**Ginger & Lace** Ibn Battuta Mall, Wafi Mall

**Giordano** Al Ghazal Complex & Shopping Mall, Al Ghurair City, Al-Manal Center, Al-Nasr Square, Al Sabkha Corner, Al Satwa Rd (Al Satwa), Arabian Plaza, BurJuman, Century Mall, Deira City Centre, Dubai Marina Mall, Dubai Outlet Mall, The Dubai Mall, Festival Centre, Ibn Battuta Mall, Jumeirah Beach Residence, Karama Centre, Lamcy Plaza, Mall of the Emirates, Reef Mall, Wafi

**Glitter** Al Ghurair City, BurJuman, Deira City Centre, The Dubai Mall, Festival Centre, Ibn Battuta Mall, Lamcy Plaza, Reef Mall

**Go Sports** Ibn Battuta Mall, Mall of the Emirates, Uptown Mirdif

**Golden Point** Deira City Centre, The Dubai Mall, Mall of the Emirates

**Golden Ring** Deira City Centre, The Dubai Mall

**Golf House** BurJuman, Deira City Centre, The Dubai Mall, Ibn Battuta Mall, Lamcy Plaza, Mall of the Emirates

**Grand Optics** Al Shindagha (Carrefour), Arabian Ranches, Deira City Centre, Dukkan Al Manzil Souk (Downtown Burj Dubai), The Dubai Mall, Festival Centre, Jumeirah Beach Residence, Mall of the Emirates, Meadows Community Centre, Reef Mall

**Grand Stores** BurJuman, Deira City Centre, Dubai Outlet Mall, Dubai Marina Mall, The Dubai Mall, Festival Centre, Maktoum St, Ibn Battuta Mall, Mall of the Emirates

**Gucci** The Dubai Mall, Mall of the Emirates (Harvey Nichols), Mall of the Emirates (Via Rodeo), Boulevard at Emirates Towers

**Guess** Al Ghurair City, BurJuman, Deira City Centre, Dubai Outlet Mall, Festival Centre, Dubai Outlet Mall, The Dubai Mall, Ibn Battuta Mall, Mall of the Emirates

**Guess Accessories** Deira City Centre, The Dubai Mall, Festival Centre, Hamarain Centre,

**Gulf Greetings** Al Bustan Centre, Al Khaleej Centre, BurJuman, Century Mall, Deira City Centre, Dubai Marina Mall, The Dubai Mall, Festival Centre, Green Community, Ibn Battuta Mall, Lulu Centre (Al Qusais), Mall of the Emirates, Mazaya Centre, Meadows Town Centre, Mercato, Oasis Centre, Spinneys (Trade Centre Rd), Spinneys, Umm Suqeim, Uptown Mirdif, Wafi

**H&M** Arabian Center, Deira City Centre, The Dubai Mall, Ibn Battuta Mall, Mall of the Emirates

**Falaknaz Habitat** Jumeira Plaza, Al Quoz (Nr Spinneys Distribution Centre)

**Hamac** Dubai Marine Beach Resort & Spa, The Dubai Mall, Jumeirah Beach Hotel

**Hang Ten** Al Ghurair City, Al Khaleej Center, Baniyas Square, BurJuman, Century Mall, Deira City Centre, Dubai Outlet Mall, The Dubai Mall, Lamcy Plaza, Festival Centre, Ibn Battuta Mall, Mall of the Emirates

**Harman House** Al Hawai Tower (Sheikh Zayed Rd), Baniyas Complex (Al Nasr Square), Deira City Centre, Festival Centre, Mall of the Emirates

**Havaianas** Deira City Centre, Souk Al Bahar, Souk Madinat Jumeirah

**Heatwaves** Dubai Marina Mall, Le Meridien Mina Seyahi Beach Resort & Marina, Town Centre Jumeirah

**Hermes** BurJuman, The Dubai Mall

**Hobbs** Deira City Centre, Festival Centre, Mercato

**Hour Choice** Al Ghurair City, Arabian Center, Arabian Ranches, BurJuman, Deira City Centre, Dubai Marina Mall, The Dubai Mall, Festival Centre, Ibn Battuta Mall, Lamcy Plaza, Lulu Centre (Al Barsha), Mall of the Emirates (Debenhams), Mercato, Oasis Centre, Reef Mall, Souk Madinat Jumeirah, Town Centre (The Springs), Wafi

**Home Centre** Mall of the Emirates, Mercato, Oasis Centre, Reef Mall

**Homes r Us** Arabian Center, Mazaya Centre

**House of Prose** Ibn Battuta Mall, Jumeira Plaza

**Hugo Boss** BurJuman, Deira City Centre, The Dubai Mall, Festival Centre, Mall of the Emirates, Mercato

**ID Design** Al Ittihad Rd (Nr Gargash Showroom), Mall of the Emirates

**Indigo Living** Al Quoz (Showroom 45, Road 8, Street 19), Jumeirah Beach Residence, Mall of the Emirates (Home Design)

**Intersport** Festival Centre, Times Square

**iStyle** The Dubai Mall, Festival Centre, Ibn Battuta Mall

**Jack & Jones** The Dubai Mall, Festival Centre (Vero Moda), Mall of the Emirates

**Jacky's Electronics** Airport Rd (Garhoud), Al Nasser Square, Deira City Centre, The Dubai Mall, Ibn Battuta Mall

**Jacky's Express** Century Mall, The Dubai Mall, Mall of the Emirates, Souk Al Bahar,

**Jashanmal** Al Ghurair City, Dubai Marina Mall, Mall of the Emirates, The Village Mall (Jumeirah), Uptown Mirdif (Caribou Coffee), Wafi

**Jashanmal Bookstores** Mall of the Emirates, Dubai Marina (Caribou Coffee, Marina Tower), Uptown Mirdif (Caribou Coffee), The Village Mall (Jumeirah)

**Jeanswest** Al Ghurair City, Arabian Center, BurJuman, The Dubai Mall, Festival Centre

**Jumbo Electronics** Karama (Opp Fish Market), Al Nasr Square (Baniyas Square), Bur Dubai (Al Mankhool Rd), BurJuman, Deira City Centre, The Dubai Mall, Festival Centre, Ibn Battuta Mall, Mall of the Emirates, Shk Zayed Rd, Wafi

**Just Cavalli** BurJuman, The Dubai Mall

# Store Finder

**Just Optic**  BurJuman, Ibn Battuta Mall

**Karen Millen**  Deira City Centre, Dubai Marina Mall, The Dubai Mall, Festival Centre, Palm Strip (Jumeirah)

**Kenneth Cole**  BurJuman, Dubai Outlet Mall, The Dubai Mall, Festival Centre, Mall of the Emirates, Wafi

**Kenzo**  BurJuman, The Dubai Mall, Festival Centre

**Kipling**
Deira City Centre, The Dubai Mall, Festival Centre, Wafi (Jashanmal)

**Koton**  The Dubai Mall, Festival Centre, Mall of the Emirates

**Kurt Geiger**  Deira City Centre, Dubai Marina Mall, The Dubai Mall, Festival Centre, Mall of the Emirates

**La Perla**  BurJuman, The Dubai Mall, Mall of the Emirates

**La Senza**  Al Ghurair City, Arabian Center, BurJuman, Deira City Centre, Dubai Marina Mall, The Dubai Mall, Festival Centre, Lamcy Plaza, Ibn Battuta Mall, Jumeirah Beach Residence, Mall of the Emirates, Mercato, Palm Strip, Uptown Mirdif, Wafi

**La Senza Girl**  Al Ghurair City, Arabian Center, Deira City Centre, The Dubai Mall, Festival Centre, Ibn Battuta Mall

**Lacoste**  BurJuman, Deira City Centre, The Dubai Mall, Festival Centre, Ibn Battuta Mall, Mall of the Emirates, Mercato

**Lancel**  The Dubai Mall, Festival Centre, Wafi

**Laura Ashley**  Festival Centre, Mercato

**Le Chateau**  The Dubai Mall, Festival Centre, Ibn Battuta Mall

**Leather Palace**  Al Ghurair City, Al Manal Centre, BurJuman, Hamarain Centre, Mall of the Emirates

**Levi's**  Al Ghurair City, Al Khaleej Center, Arabian Centre, BurJuman, Deira City Centre, Dubai Outlet Mall, The Dubai Mall, Festival Centre, Ibn Battuta Mall, Lamcy Plaza, Mall of the Emirates

**LG**  The Dubai Mall, Festival Centre, Ibn Battuta Mall

**Liali Jewellery**  Community Center (Arabian Ranches), BurJuman, The Dubai Mall, Dubai Outlet Mall, Festival Centre, Gold & Diamond Park, Ibn Battuta Mall, Jebel

Ali Golf Resort & Spa, Jumeirah Centre, Mall of the Emirates, Mercato, Souk Madinat Jumeirah, Spinneys (Al Ghurair City), Spinneys (Trade Centre Rd, Bur Dubai), Spinneys (Nr Ramada Htl, Bur Dubai), Springs Village Community Center, (The Springs), Town Center (The Meadows), Uptown Mirdif

**Lifco**  Al Nahda (Opp NMC Hospital), International City (England Cluster), Mirdif (Uptown R/A), Sheikh Zayed Rd (Zabeel Tower), Garhoud (Nr Welcare Hospital)

**Life Style Fine Jewelry**  Al Ghurair City, Arabian Center, Dubai Outlet Mall, The Dubai Mall, Gold Centre, Gold & Diamond Park, Ibn Battuta Mall, Lamcy Plaza

**Lifestyle**  Bur Dubai, Ibn Battuta Mall, Mall of the Emirates, Oasis Centre

**Lifestyle Nutrition**  Al Ghurair City, Al Mulla Plaza, BurJuman, Deira City Centre, The Dubai Mall, Festival Centre, Mall of the Emirates, Meadows Town Centre

**Limited Too**  Ibn Battuta Mall, Mall of the Emirates

**Liu.Jo**  The Dubai Mall, Festival Centre, Wafi

**Liz Claiborne**  Deira City Centre, Ibn Battuta Mall, Mall of the Emirates (Monet & Co.)

**L'Occitaine**  Deira City Centre, Dubai Marina Mall, The Dubai Mall, Festival Centre, Ibn Battuta Mall, Mall of the Emirates, Mercato, Uptown Mirdiff

**Loewe**  BurJuman, The Dubai Mall, Mall of the Emirates

**Louis Vuitton**  BurJuman, The Dubai Mall, Mall of the Emirates

**Lutfi Optical Centre**  Abraj Bld (Sabkha, Deira), Baniyas Square, The Dubai Mall, Festival Centre, Reef Malll, Sheikh Latifa Bld (Baniyas St, Deira), Wafi

**Lulu Hypermarket**  Al Barsha, Al Qusais, Karama

**Lulu Center**  Karama, Deira

**Luxecouture**  The Walk at Jumeirah Beach Residence, Souk Madinat Jumeirah

**M.A.C.**  Arabian Center, BurJuman, Deira City Centre, Dubai International Airport (Terminal 3), Dubai Marina Mall, The Dubai Mall, Ibn Battuta Mall, Mall of the Emirates (Harvey Nichols), Mercato, Wafi

**Magrabi Optical**  Arabian Center, BurJuman, Dubai Healthcare City, Dubai Marina Mall, Dubai Outlet Mall,

The Dubai Mall, Festival Centre, Ibn Battuta Mall, Mall of the Emirates, The Village (Jumeira Rd)

**Magrudy's** BurJuman, Festival Centre, The Dubai Mall, Deira City Centre, Fen House (Jumeirah 1), Ibn Battuta Mall, Jumeira Rd (Jumeirah)

**Mahallati Jewellery** The Dubai Mall, Gold Souk (Deira), Mall of the Emirates, Mercato, Wafi

**Make Up For Ever** Al Bustan Centre, Al Ghurair City, Arabian Plaza (Vavavoom), Bin Sougat Centre (Karisma), BurJuman, Deira City Centre, The Dubai Mall (Debenhams), Festival Centre, Hamarain Centre, Ibn Battuta Mall, Lamcy Plaza, Mall of the Emirates (Debenhams & Faces), Reef Mall (Karisma), Town Centre Jumeirah, Uptown Mirdif, Wafi

**Mamas & Papas** Dubai Marina Mall, The Dubai Mall, Mall of the Emirates (Harvey Nichols), Mercato, Wafi

**Man & Moda** Deira City Centre, Dubai International Financial Centre (DIFC), Dubai Outlet Mall, Mall of the Emirates

**Mango** Arabian Center, BurJuman, Deira City Centre, Dubai Outlet Mall, The Dubai Mall, Festival Centre, Mall of the Emirates, Palm Strip (Jumeirah), Mercato

**Mansoor Jewellery** BurJuman, Mall of the Emirates, Wafi

**Marc Jacobs** The Dubai Mall, Festival Centre, Mall of the Emirates

**Marina Exotic Home Interiors** Festival Centre, Souk Al Bahar, Souk Madinat Jumeirah, Mall of the Emirates, Spinneys (Umm Suqeim), Umm Suqeim Rd (Al Barsha), Umm Suqeim Rd (Al Quoz 3)

**Maritime & Mercantile International (MMI)** Al Hamra Cellar (Ras Al Khaimah), Karama (Cellar Saver), Al Wasl Rd (Next to Spinneys, Al Wasl), Bur Dubai (Cellar Saver, Khalid Bin Al Waleed St), Dnata Airline Bld (Deira), Dubai Investment Park (Green Community), Dubai Silicon Oasis (Community Centre), Festival Centre, Ibn Battuta Mall, Le Clos (Dubai International Airport, Terminal 3), Mall of the Emirates, Saeed Tower 2 (Sheikh Zayed Rd), Trade Center Rd (Nxt to Spinneys)

**Marks & Spencer** The Dubai Mall, Festival Centre, Al-Futtaim Centre (Deira), Wafi

**Marlin** Port Rashid Rd, Karama, Sheikh Zayed Rd

**Massimo Dutti** BurJuman, Deira City Centre, Dubai Outlet Mall, The Dubai Mall, Festival Centre, Ibn Battuta Mall, Mall of the Emirates, Mercato

**Max** Deira (Nxt to Abu Hail Center), Al Ghurair City, Ibn Battuta Mall, Khalid Bin Al Waleed St (Bur Dubai), Oasis Centre

**Mexx** Deira City Centre, Mall of the Emirates

**Mikyajy** Al Dhiyafah Rd (Al Satwa), Arabian Center, Bin Sougat Centre, BurJuman, Century Mall, Deira City Centre, The Dubai Mall, Festival Centre, Hamarain Centre, Ibn Battuta Mall, Lamcy Plaza, Mall of the Emirates, Reef Mall, Souk Madinat Jumeirah

**Milano** Al Ghurair City, Arabian Centre, Deira City Centre (Debenhams), Ibn Battuta Mall, Mall of the Emirates, Mercato, Uptown Mirdif

**Minutes** Ibn Battuta Mall, Mall of the Emirates, Mercato, The Dubai Mall, Deira City Centre

**Miss Sixty** Dubai Marina Mall, The Dubai Mall, Mall of the Emirates, Wafi

**Monet & Co.** Mall of the Emirates, Souk Al Bahar, Wafi

**Monsoon** Arabian Center, BurJuman, Deira City Centre, Dubai Marina Mall, Dubai Outlet Mall, The Dubai Mall, Festival Centre, Lamcy Plaza, Mall of the Emirates, Uptown Mirdif, Wafi

**Montblanc** BurJuman, Deira City Centre, The Dubai Mall, Festival Centre, Grand Hyatt Dubai, Ibn Battuta Mall, Jumeirah Beach Hotel, Mall of the Emirates, Wafi

**Mothercare** Al Ghurair City, BurJuman, Deira City Centre, Dubai Marina Mall, The Dubai Mall, Emaar Town Center (Emirates Hills), Ibn Battuta Mall, Jumeirah Beach Residence, Jumeirah Centre, Lamcy Plaza, Mall of the Emirates (Debenhams), Spinneys (Al Wasl Rd), Uptown Mirdif

**Mr Price** Arabian Center, Lamcy Plaza, Reef Mall

**Mumbai Se** Dubai Marina Mall, The Dubai Mall, Festival Centre

**National Iranian Carpets** Al Nasr Square (Deira Tower), The Dubai Mall, Mall of the Emirates, Mercato, Souk Madinat Jumeirah

**National Store** Al Fahidi St (Bur Dubai), Baniyas Square, Hamarain Centre, Union Co-operative Society (Al Awir), Union Co-operative Society (Al Wasl)

**Naturalizer** Al Ghurair City, Arabian Center, Dubai Outlet Mall, The Dubai Mall, Festival Centre, Ibn Battuta Mall, Mall of the Emirates, Reef Mall, Town Centre Jumeirah

**Nautica** Deira City Centre, Dubai Marina Mall, The Dubai Mall, Festival Centre, Ibn Battuta Mall, Jumeirah Beach Residence

**Nayomi** Al Ghurair City, Bin Sougat Centre, Century Mall, Dubai Outlet Mall, The Dubai Mall, Festival Centre, Ibn Battuta Mall, Lamcy Plaza, Mall of the Emirates, Mercato, Reef Mall, Times Square, Uptown Mirdif, Wafi

**New Look** BurJuman, Deira City Centre, Dubai Marina Mall, The Dubai Mall

**New Yorker** The Dubai Mall, Festival Centre

**Next** BurJuman, Deira City Centre, The Dubai Mall, Ibn Battuta Mall, Lamcy Plaza, Mall of the Emirates, Mercato

**Nike** Arabian Center, BurJuman, Dubai Marina Mall, The Dubai Mall, Festival Centre, Ibn Battuta Mall, Mall of the Emirates, Mercato

**Nine West** Al Ghurair City, Arabian Center, BurJuman, Deira City Centre, Dubai Outlet Mall, The Dubai Mall, Festival Centre, Ibn Battuta Mall, Lamcy Plaza, Mall of the Emirates, Mercato, Reef Mall, Town Centre Jumeirah, Uptown Mirdif

**Nutrition Zone** Ibn Battuta Mall, The Dubai Mall, Town Centre Jumeirah

**Oasis** Deira City Centre (Debenhams), The Dubai Mall, Ibn Battuta Mall, Mall of the Emirates (Debenhams)

**Okaidi** BurJuman, Deira City Centre, Dubai Marina Mall, The Dubai Mall, Festival Centre, Mall of the Emirates

**Omega** BurJuman, Deira City Centre, The Dubai Mall, Wafi

**Opera** BurJuman, Dubai Outlet Mall, Ibn Battuta Mall

**Opera Shoes** The Dubai Mall, Mall of the Emirates, Wafi

**Optifashion/Optivision** Al Fahidi St (Bur Dubai), Al Khaleej Centre, BurJuman, Deira City Centre, Dubai Outlet Mall, The Dubai Mall, Festival Centre, Ibn Battuta Mall, Mall of the Emirates, Palm Strip

**Organic Foods & Café** The Dubai Mall, The Greens

**Oriental Stores** Al Fahidi St (Bur Dubai), Al Khaleej Centre (Bur Dubai), Al Khor (Bur Dubai), Baniyas St (Deira), Deira City Centre, Festival Centre, Ibn Battuta Mall, Mall of the Emirates, Sabhka (Deira), Souk Al Kabir (Bur Dubai)

**Osh Kosh B'gosh** The Dubai Mall, Mall of the Emirates

**Ounass** Boulevard at Emirates Towers, Souk Madinat Jumeirah, Wafi

**Oysho** BurJuman, The Dubai Mall, Festival Centre, Mall of the Emirates

**Pablosky** BurJuman, Deira City Centre, The Dubai Mall, Festival Centre, Ibn Battuta Mall, Lamcy Plaza, Mall of the Emirates, Mercato, Reef Mall

**Pairs** Deira City Centre, The Dubai Mall, Mall of the Emirates

**Pal Zileri** Al Reem Tower (Maktoum St), BurJuman, The Dubai Mall, Festival Centre, Mall of the Emirates, Wafi

**Pan Emirates** Umm Suqeim Rd (Al Barsha), Ibn Battuta Mall, TechnoPark

**Papermoon** Al Ghurair City, Al Mina Rd (Al Satwa), Town Centre Jumeirah

**Paris Gallery** Al Bustan Centre, Al Ghurair City, Arabian Center, BurJuman, Burj Al Arab, Deira City Centre, The Dubai Mall, Festival Centre, Hamarain Centre, Ibn Battuta Mall, Lamcy Plaza, Town Centre Jumeirah, Uptown Mirdiff, Wafi

**Patrizia Pepe Firenze** Dubai Marina Mall, The Dubai Mall, Festival Centre, Holiday Centre Mall (Nr Crowne Plaza)

**Paul & Shark** BurJuman, Dubai Marina Mall, The Dubai Mall, Mall of the Emirates

**Paul Smith** BurJuman, The Dubai Mall, Festival Centre, Mall of the Emirates

**Peacocks** The Dubai Mall, Ibn Battuta Mall, Lamcy Plaza

**Peak Performance** The Dubai Mall, Mall of the Emirates

**Pearle Opticians** Ibn Battuta Mall, Mall of the Emirates

**Pepe Jeans** Deira City Centre, The Dubai Mall, Mall of the Emirates

**Persian Carpet House** Festival Centre, Holiday Centre Mall, Mall of the Emirates, Souk Madinat Jumeirah

**Pet's Delight** Arabian Ranches, Town Centre (Emirates Hills)

**Phat Farm** Deira City Centre, Festival Centre, Mall of the Emirates

**Pierre Cardin** Al Dhiyafah Rd (Al Satwa), Arabian Center, BurJuman, Century Mall, Deira City Centre, Dubai Outlet Mall, The Dubai Mall, Festival Centre, Hamarain Centre, Ibn Battuta Mall, Lamcy Plaza, Twin Towers (Deira), Uptown Mirdif, Wafi

**Pinky's Furniture** The Dubai Mall, Festival Centre, Mall of the Emirates

**Pixi** The Dubai Mall, Festival Centre, Mall of the Emirates

**Planet Nutrition** Deira City Centre, Dubai Marina Mall, Dubai Outlet Mall, The Dubai Mall, Ibn Battuta Mall

**Plug-Ins** Al Ghurair City, The Dubai Mall, Festival Centre

**Plus IT** Dubai Marina Mall, The Dubai Mall, Festival Centre, Ibn Battuta Mall

**Pollini** BurJuman, The Dubai Mall, Mall of the Emirates

**Polo Jeans** Deira City Centre, Mercato

**Porsche Design** Atlantis The Palm, Deira City Centre, Dubai International Financial Centre (DIFC), The Dubai Mall, Festival Centre, Jumeirah Beach Hotel, Mall of the Emirates

**Premaman** Arabian Center, The Dubai Mall, Uptown Mirdif

**PrettyFIT** Deira City Centre, Mall of the Emirates, Mercato

**Pride Of Kashmir** Deira City Centre, Festival Centre, Mall of the Emirates, Mercato, Souk Al Bahar, Souk Madinat Jumeirah

**Prima Gold** Al Ghurair Centre, Burj Al Arab, BurJuman, Deira City Centre, The Dubai Mall, Gold Souk (Deira), Grand Hyatt Dubai, Mall of the Emirates

**Principles** Deira City Centre (Debenhams), Ibn Battuta Mall (Debenhams), Mall of the Emirates (Debenhams)

**Promod** BurJuman, Deira City Centre, Mall of the Emirates, Mercato

**Pull & Bear** Deira City Centre, The Dubai Mall, Mall of the Emirates, Mercato

**Puma** Deira City Centre, The Dubai Mall, Festival Centre

**Pumpkin Patch** Al Ghurair City, Arabian Center, BurJuman, Dubai Outlet Mall, The Dubai Mall, Festival Centre, Jumeirah Beach Residence, Lamcy Plaza, Mall of the Emirates, Uptown Mirdif

**Pure Gold** Al Fahidi St (Bur Dubai), Arabian Center, Bin Sougat Centre, Deira City Centre, The Dubai Mall, Festival Centre, Gold Centre Bld (Deira), Habtoor Grand Resort & Spa, Ibn Battuta Mall, Karama Shopping Complex, Lamcy Plaza, Lulu Shopping Center (Karama), Mall of the Emirates, Meena Bazaar (Bur Dubai), Mercato, Reef Mall, Souk Madinat Jumeirah, Uptown Mirdif

**Quiksilver** BurJuman, Dubai Marina Mall, The Dubai Mall, Festival Centre, Mall of the Emirates

**Qum Persian Carpets & Novelties** Sheraton Dubai Creek Hotel & Towers, Taj Palace Hotel

**Rage** The Dubai Mall, Festival Centre, Mall of the Emirates

**Rage Bike Shop** The Dubai Mall, Festival Centre, Oasis Centre

**Ralph Lauren** BurJuman, The Dubai Mall, Mall of the Emirates

**Raoul** Festival Centre, Mall of the Emirates

**Rasasi** Al Bustan Centre, Al Ghurair, Al Ghurair Bld (Deira), Al Manal Centre, Arabian Center, BurJuman, Century Mall, Deira City Centre, Festival Centre, Fakhree Market (Deira), Mall of the Emirates, Murshad Bazaar (Deira), Palm Strip (Jumeirah), Union Co-operative Society (Al Wasl), Union Co-operative Society (Rashidiyah)

**Raymond Weil** Al Futtaim Jewellery (See p.414), Al Nasr Square, BurJuman (The Watch House), Deira City Centre, The Dubai Mall, Festival Centre

**Red Earth** Al Ghurair City, Bin Sougat Centre, Deira City Centre, Ibn Battuta Mall, Mercato

# Store Finder

**Regal Textiles** Al Fahidi St (Bur Dubai), Karama (Opp Al Attar Centre), Al Satwa (Opp Satwa parking), Murshid Bazaar (Deira)

**Reiss** Dubai Mariina Mall, The Dubai Mall, Festival Centre, Galeries Lafayette (The Dubai Mall), Mall of the Emirates

**Replay** BurJuman, Deira City Centre, Dubai Outlet Mall, The Dubai Mall

**River Island** Deira City Centre, The Dubai Mall, Ibn Battuta Mall, Mall of the Emirates

**Rivoli** Al Fahidi St (Bur Dubai), Al Ghurair City, Arabian Center, Atlantis The Palm, BurJuman, Deira City Centre, Festival Centre, Dubai Marina Mall, The Dubai Mall, Gold & Diamond Park, Ibn Battuta Mall, Jebel Ali Hotel, Jumeirah Beach Residence, Jumeirah Centre, Lamcy Plaza, Mall of the Emirates, Mercato, Souk Al Bahar, Souk Madinat Jumeirah, Wafi, The Westin Dubai Mina Seyahi Beach Resort

**Rivoli Arcade** Dubai International Financial Centre (DIFC), Dusit Thani Dubai, Grosvenor House, Media Rotana, One&Only Royal Mirage, Uptown Mirdif

**Rivoli Prestige** Burj Al Arab, Deira City Centre, Festival Centre, Boulevard at Emirates Towers, Jumeirah Beach Hotel, Mall of the Emirates

**Rivoli Textiles** Al Satwa (Nr Lal's Supermarket), Dubai Marina, Zabeel Rd (Karama)

**Roberto Cavalli** The Dubai Mall, Mall of the Emirates, Wafi

**Roccobarocco** Dubai Marina Mall, The Dubai Mall, Waf

**Rodeo Drive** Al Bustan Rotana Hotel, Atlantis The Palm, Boulevard at Emirates Towers, Burj Al Arab, BurJuman, Dubai Outlet Mall, The Dubai Mall, Festival Centre, Grand Hyatt Dubai, Grosvehouse House, Holiday Centre Mall, Hyatt Regency Dubai, Jumeirah Beach Hotel, Mall of the Emirates, Souk Madinat Jumeirah

**Rolex** Deira City Centre, The Dubai Mall, Mall of the Emirates, Wafi

**Rossini** Festival Centre, Mercato, Wafi

**Ruane Jewellers** The Dubai Mall, Wafi (Khan Murjan)

**Rugland** Dubai Outlet Mall, Festival Centre, Ibn Battuta Mall, Lamcy Plaza

**S*uce** Bastakiya (Bur Dubai), The Dubai Mall, Jumeirah Centre, The Village (Jumeirah)

**Sacoche** BurJuman, Deira City Centre, Dubai Outlet Mall, Ibn Battuta Mall

**Sacoor Brothers** Festival Centre, Mall of the Emirates, Dubai Marina Mall The Dubai Mall

**Sadek Music** The Dubai Mall, Festival Centre, Omar bin Al Khattab St (Deira), Souk Madinat Jumeirah

**Saks Fifth Avenue** BurJuman, The Walk at Jumeirah Beach Residence

**Salsa Jeans** BurJuman, Deira City Centre, Festival Centre, Mall of the Emirates

**Salvatore Ferragamo** BurJuman, The Dubai Mall, Mall of the Emirates

**Samsonite** BurJuman, Deira City Centre, Dubai Outlet Mall, The Dubai Mall, Festival Centre

**Sana Fashion** Abu Hail Centre, Karama

**Sanrio** Deira City Centre, The Dubai Mall, Ibn Battuta Mall

**Sephora** Dubai Marina Mall, The Dubai Mall, Festival Centre

**Sharaf DG** Al Mankhool Rd (Al Raffa), Deira City Centre, Dubai International Airport (Terminal 1 & 3), Dubai Marina Mall, The Dubai Mall, Ibn Battuta Mall, Times Square, Union Co-operative Society (Beh Shangri-la Htl, Al Satwa)

**Shoe City** Deira City Centre, Mall of the Emirates, Uptown Mirdiff

**Shoe Mart** Arabian Center, Centrepoint (Bur Dubai), Deira City Centre, The Dubai Mall, Ibn Battuta Mall, Mall of the Emirates, Oasis Centre, Lamcy Plaza, Bur Dubai (Nr Jumbo Showroom)

**Skechers** Arabian Center, BurJuman, Dubai Outlet Mall, The Dubai Mall, Festival Centre, Ibn Battuta Mall, Mercato, Sheikh Zayed Rd (Trade Centre)

**Solaris** Arabian Center, Deira City Centre, The Dubai Mall, Ibn Battuta Mall (Debenhams), Mall of the Emirates (Debenhams)

**Spinneys** Al Ghurair City, Al Mankhool Rd (Bur Dubai), Bin Sougat Centre, Dubai Marina Mall, Jumeira Rd (Jumeirah), Mazaya Centre, Mercato, Trade Centre Rd

(Bur Dubai), Cnr Al Wasl & Umm Al Sheif Rd (Umm Suqeim), Town Centre (The Springs), Uptown Mirdiff

**Spinneys Market** Emaar Residence (Downtown Burj Dubai), Festival Centre, Dubai Silicon Oasis, Mirdif Community Centre, Oud Metha (Nr Lamcy Plaza), Souk Al Bahar

**Splash** Al Bustan Centre, Al Ghurair City, Arabian Center, Centrepoint (Bur Dubai), Deira City Centre, Ibn Battuta Mall, Mall of the Emirates (Centrepoint), Karama (Nr Maktoum Bridge), Oasis Centre, Reef Mall

**Spring** Arabian Center, The Dubai Mall, Festival Centre, Ibn Battuta Mall, Lamcy Plaza, Mall of the Emirates, Reef Mall

**Springfield** Deira City Centre, Dubai Marina Mall, The Dubai Mall, Festival Centre

**Stradivarius** Deira City Centre, The Dubai Mall, Festival Centre, Mall of the Emirates

**Stadium** Deira City Centre, Dubai Marina Mall, The Dubai Mall

**Strandbags** Dubai Outlet Mall, The Dubai Mall, Festival Centre, Ibn Battuta Mall, Mall of the Emirates

**Studio R** BurJuman, Dubai Outlet Mall, Ibn Battuta Mall, Jumeirah Beach Hotel, Jumeirah Centre

**Sun & Sand Sports** Al Ghurair City, Al Nasr Square (Deira), Deira City Centre, Ibn Battuta Mall, Jumeirah Centre, Oasis Centre, Souk Madinat Jumeirah

**Sunglass Hut** Arabian Center, BurJuman, Deira City Centre, Mall of the Emirates, Wafi

**Susan Walpole** Atlantis The Palm, Dubai Marine Beach Resort, The Dubai Mall, Festival Centre, Jumeirah Beach Hotel, Jumeira Plaza, Mall of the Emirates, Mercato, One&Only Royal Mirage, Park n Shop, The Ritz-Carlton Dubai

**Swarovski** Al Ghurair City (Allied Enterprises), BurJuman (Tanagra), Deira City Centre (Tanagra), The Dubai Mall, Festival Centre, Ibn Battuta Mall (Allied Enterprises), Mall of the Emirates (Tanagra), Wafi

**Swatch** Al Ghurair City, BurJuman, Deira City Centre, The Dubai Mall, Festival Centre, Ibn Battuta Mall, Mall of the Emirates, Wafi

**TAG Heuer** BurJuman, The Dubai Mall, Wafi Mall

**Tanagra** Al Ghurair City, BurJuman, Deira City Centre, Mall of the Enmirates, Wafi

**Tavola** Century Plaza, Mall of the Emirates, Spinneys Centre (Umm Suqeim), Town Center (The Springs)

**Ted Baker** BurJuman, Deira City Centre, The Dubai Mall, Festival Centre

**Ted Lapidus** Deira City Centre, Festival Centre, Ibn Battuta Mall, Wafi

**Tehran Persian Carpets & Antiques** The Dubai Mall, Festival Centre

**The Athlete's Foot** Dubai Outlet Mall, Festival Centre, Greens Community Shopping Centre, Ibn Battuta Mall, Lamcy Plaza, Mall of the Emirates, Meadows Community Centre, Reef Mall, Salahuddin Road (Deira), Uptown Mirdif

**The Bike Shop** Jebel Ali (Nxt to Ibn Battuta Mall), Sheikh Zayed Rd (Nxt to BMW Showroom)

**The Body Shop** Al Ghurair City, Arabian Center, BurJuman, Deira City Centre, Dubai Marina Mall, The Dubai Mall, Festival Centre, Ibn Battuta Mall, Jumeirah Centre, Lamcy Plaza, Mall of the Emirates, Wafi

**The Daiso** Arabian Center, Lamcy Plaza

**THE One** BurJuman, Dubai Outlet Mall, Jumeira Rd, Mall of the Emirates, Wafi

**The Music Institute** Dubai Knowledge Village, The Walk at Jumeirah Beach Residence

**The Sultani Lifestyle Gallerie** Dukkan Al Manzil Souk, Festival Centre, The Dubai Mall, Grand Millennium Dubai, The Palace – The Old Town (La Boutique), The Walk at Jumeirah Beach Residence, Meadowns Town Centre, Souk Al Bahar,

**The Toy Store** Deira City Centre, Ibn Battuta Mall, Mall of the Emirates, Mercato

**The Watch House** Al Nasser Square, Arabian Center, BurJuman, Deira City Centre, The Dubai Mall, Festival Centre, Lamcy Plaza, Mall of the Emirates

**The White Company** Deira City Centre, The Dubai Mall, Festival Centre, Mall of the Emirates, Wafi

**Thomsun Music** Ibn Battuta Mall, Deira (Nr Fish R/A), Salahuddin St (Deira), Wafi

**Tiffany & Co.** Atlantis The Palm, BurJuman (Saks Fifth Avenue), Deira City Centre, The Dubai Mall, Mall of the Emirates, Wafi

# Store Finder

**Timberland** Arabian Center, The Dubai Mall, Ibn Battuta Mall, Mall of the Emirates

**Tod's** BurJuman, The Dubai Mall (Galeries Lafayette), Mall of the Emirates

**Tommy Bahama** Mall of the Emirates, Souk Madinat Jumeirah

**Tommy Hilfiger** Deira City Centre, Dubai Outlet Mall, The Dubai Mall, Festival Centre, Mall of the Emirates

**Topman** Deira City Centre, Ibn Battuta Mall, Wafi

**Topshop** Arabian Center, Deira City Centre, Dubai Marina Mall, The Dubai Mall, Ibn Battuta Mall, Mercato, Wafi

**Toys R Us** Festival Centre, Salahuddin Rd (Deira), Times Square

**Triumph** Arabian Center, Deira City Centre, Mercato

**Tru Trussardi** BurJuman, The Dubai Mall, Festival Centre, Mercato, Wafi

**Union Co-operative Society** Abu Hail Rd (Al Hamriya), Al Nahda Rd (Al Twar), Al Rashidiya (Nr Rashidiya Police Station), Al Satwa (Beh Shangri-la Htl), Al Satwa (Opp Rydges Plaza), Al Wasl Rd (Opp Safa Park), Ras Al Khor (Al Awir), Sheikh Khalifa Bin Zayed Rd (Al Mankhool)

**United Colors of Benetton** Deira City Centre, The Dubai Mall, Factory Outlet, Jumeirah Centre, Mall of the Emirates

**Valencia** Al Maktoum St (Deira), Deira City Centre, The Dubai Mall, Festival Centre, Jumeirah Centre, Mall of the Emirates, Twin Towers

**Valentino** BurJuman, The Dubai Mall

**Vero Moda** The Dubai Mall, Festival Centre, Mall of the Emirates

**Verri** BurJuman, Deira City Centre, Ibn Battuta Mall, Wafi

**Versace** BurJuman, The Dubai Mall, Mall of the Emirates, Wafi

**Vertu** BurJuman, Deira City Centre, The Dubai Mall, Grand Hyatt Dubai, Rivoli (See p.424), Wafi

**Vilebrequin** Festival Centre, Souk Al Bahar, Souk Madinat Jumeirah

**Villa Moda** Atlantis The Palm, Dubai International Financial Centre (DIFC)

**Villeroy & Boch** BurJuman, Deira City Centre, Dubai Outlet Mall, The Dubai Mall, Mall of the Emirates, Wafi

**Vincci** BurJuman, Deira City Centre, The Dubai Mall

**Virgin Megastore** BurJuman, Deira City Centre, Jumeirah Beach Residence, Mall of the Emirates, Mercato

**Waitrose** Dubai Marina Mall, The Dubai Mall

**Wallis** Arabian Center, Deira City Centre (Debenhams), Ibn Battuta Mall, Mall of the Emirates (Debenhams)

**Watch Gallery** BurJuman, The Dubai Mall, Mall of the Emirates

**Whistles** BurJuman, Mall of the Emirates

**Wizz** Deira City Centre, Festival Centre, Ibn Battuta Mall, Mall of the Emirates, Souk Madinat Jumeirah

**Women'secret** Deira City Centre, The Dubai Mall, Festival Centre, Lamcy Plaza

**Woolworths** Deira City Centre, Ibn Battuta Mall

**XOXO** BurJuman, Dubai Outlet Mall, The Dubai Mall, Festival Centre

**Yas** The Dubai Mall, Festival Centre, Ibn Battuta Mall, Wafi

**Yateem Optician** Al Dhiyafah Rd, Al Fahidi St, Al Ghurair City, Al Rigga St, Arabian Center, Boulevard at Emirates Towers, BurJuman, Dubai Media City, The Dubai Mall, Beach Centre (Jumeirah), Holiday Centre Mall, Lamcy Plaza, Mall of the Emirates, Souk Madinat Jumeirah

**Yellow Hat** Nad Al Hamar, Times Square

**Zak Electronics** Salahuddin Rd (opp Muraqabat Police Station, Deira) Zabeel Rd (Karama)

**Zara** BurJuman, Deira City Centre, The Dubai Mall, Mall of the Emirates

**Zara Home** BurJuman, Deira City Centre, Jumeirah Beach Residence, The Dubai Mall, Mall of the Emirates, Palm Strip

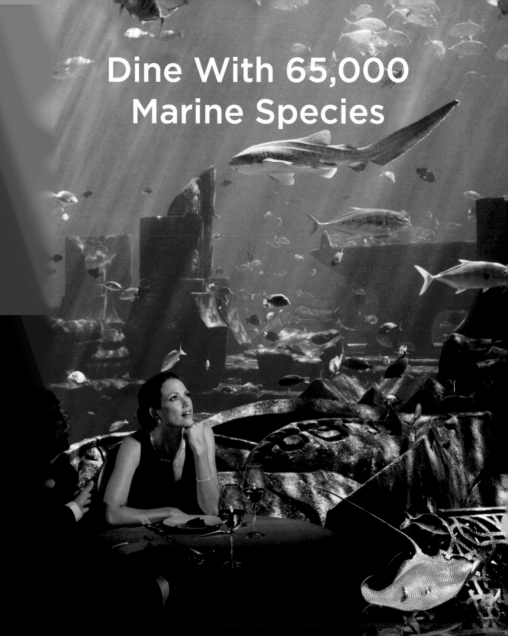

# Dine With 65,000 Marine Species

i Santamaria, the three star Michelin Chef, offers gourmet seafood and a seductive
iance in the underwater world of Atlantis. In his first venture outside Europe, the
hitect of Food' offers an intensity of flavours and a focus on technique with his
lan cuisine in an elegant space inspired by the ocean depths.

restaurant reservations please call +971 4 426 2626
mail restaurantreservations@atlantisthepalm.com

**ATLANTIS**

# Going Out

# GOING OUT

Dubai's gastronomic landscape is expansive. At one end of the spectrum, celebrity chefs, picturesque cocktail lounges and mammoth clubs compete for your hard-earned dirhams. At the other end, bargain ethnic eateries, drink-deal bars and plenty of bang-for-your-buck brunches are there to help at the end of the month. Dubai's social scene revolves around club nights, raucous brunches and laid-back shisha cafes, so expect to go out more than you ever did back home.

## Dressing Up

Generally speaking shorts and T-shirts are a no-no for Dubai's bars and restaurants, and even some pubs will frown at your beach-bum attire. While trainers aren't strictly outlawed it will depend on the whole ensemble, and many places don't let you in wearing filp-flops – even if they're nice ones. Dubai's dress code is on the smarter side – more beautiful than bohemian – so shine your shoes when you're stepping out.

Thursday and Friday nights are the big ones, with reservations required in the restaurants and international DJs packing out the clubs. During the week you'll find drinks deals across the city and all manner of dining promotions, so the town is still buzzing. Since alcohol can only be served in hotels and sports clubs, chances are you won't have a 'local' at the corner. Instead, you might have a roster of four or five favourites within a 10 minute taxi drive. Most of the city's most popular restaurants are located in hotels for the same reason – but don't let the absence of a wine list deter you from exploring the many outstanding independent restaurants that Dubai has to offer.

The live entertainment scene lags other cities, but with the opening of new theatres and venues, and more big names such as Kanye and Kylie being lured over to perform, it is improving all the time.

## Opening Hours

In general, cafes and restaurants close between 23:00 and 01:00, with bars and nightclubs split between those that close 'early' at 01:00 and those that go on until 03:00. The legal drinking age is 21, and it's best to avoid getting staggeringly drunk as it may land you behind bars. Most importantly, don't even think about getting behind the wheel of a car after drinking – Dubai maintains a strict zero tolerance stance on drunk driving. Respect the laws and you'll have nothing to worry about – apart from your dwindling finances. Dubai certainly knows how to throw a party so don't forget your glad rags because over-the-top is par for the course in this town.

## Ramadan Timings

During Ramadan, opening and closing times of restaurants change considerably. Because eating and drinking in public is forbidden during daylight hours, many places only open after sunset then keep going well into the early hours. Restaurants in some hotels remain open, but will be screened off from public view. Live entertainment is not allowed, so while some nightclubs remain open, all dancefloors are closed.

# EATING OUT

Many of Dubai's most popular restaurants are located within hotels and leisure clubs, and their popularity is partly down to the fact that these are virtually the only outlets where you can drink alcohol with your meal. Almost all other restaurants are unlicensed. If you're the type who requires a glass of vino to make a meal complete, it's best to phone ahead to check whether the establishment serves alcohol. There's quite a hefty mark-up on drinks, with a decent bottle of wine often costing as much as your meal.

The city has some superb independent restaurants and cafes that shouldn't be ignored just because they don't serve booze. Bottled water also seems to rocket in price in the five-star venues, and if you ask for water you'll often be given an imported brand, costing up to Dhs.40 a bottle. You should specify 'local' water when ordering, but even then you can expect to pay Dhs.10 or Dhs.20 for a bottle of water that costs less than Dhs.2 in the supermarket.

## Stretch In Style

If you're feeling a bit flash (or are on a stag or hen party), you can rent a stretch Hummer, Lincoln or even Mercedes Limo Van from Dubai Exotic Limo (www.dubaiexoticlimo.com) so that you can arrive at your destination in style. They are fully equipped with TV screens and a stereo system, with neon or leopard skin interiors, so you can make your journey as eventful as your destination.

## Hygiene

Food and drink outlets are subject to regular checks by Dubai Municipality, and unclean outlets are warned to either scrub up or shut down. You can be fairly confident that restaurants within hotels and most independent restaurants meet basic health and hygiene requirements. The city isn't immune to the odd food poisoning incident, however, so if a place looks like it might have some hygiene issues, it's best to avoid it. If you feel a restaurant you have visited could use an inspection, you can call the Municipality Food Control Department (04 705 6256).

New Asia Bar

## Food Allergies

If you suffer from food allergies, take extra care when eating out in Dubai's restaurants. A lack of clearly-marked menus and a serving culture that is trained to tell customers what they think they want to hear can combine to form a dangerous situation. Don't hesitate to inform servers about the seriousness of your allergies if you don't think they are catching the drift of your questioning.

## Taxes & Service Charges

Look out for the small print at the bottom of your menu and you may spot the dreaded 'prices are subject to 10% service charge and 10% municipality tax'. In most hotel restaurants and bars these extras are already included, but in an independent outlet they may appear as an additional charge. The 10% service charge is perhaps incorrectly named as often it isn't passed on to the staff, and you have no option of withholding it if you receive poor service. If you want to reward the waiting staff directly then the standard rule of a 10-12.5% tip will be appreciated, but give them cash if you can, or your tip may go straight in the till.

## Vegetarian Food

Vegetarians should be pleasantly surprised by the variety available to them in Dubai's restaurants. Dubai is home to a large population from the subcontinent who are vegetarian by religion, and numerous Indian restaurants offer a range of cooking styles and tasty vegetarian dishes. Try Saravana Bhavan (p.492) and Aryaas (p.456) in Karama. In other restaurants (even in steakhouses), you'll often find at least one or two vegetarian options. Arabic cuisine, although heavy on meat-based mains, offers a great range of mezze that are mostly vegetarian.

Dubai's cafes are also great for vegetarian food. Of particular note are the Lime Tree Café (p.480), THE One (p.487) and Celebrities (p.466), which offers fine dining and a completely separate vegetarian menu. Magnolia (p.480) in Madinat Jumeirah is particularly notable for its high-class organic, vegetarian food.

## Cultural Meals

Bastakiya is a great place to eat while soaking up local culture. This traditional part of the city is best experienced by strolling through the streets, visiting the museums and dining at one of the many cafes. A cultural and culinary experience rolled into one. The Department of Tourism & Commerce Marketing is working closely with the Emirates Culinary Guild and a few chefs to revive Emirati cuisine in Dubai's restaurant scene. Truly local food has several distinct flavours, thanks to the country's trading past. Look out for tangs of cinnamon, saffron and turmeric along with nuts (almonds or pistachios), limes and dried fruit in the different mouthfuls.

A word of warning: if you are a strict veggie, confirm that your meal is completely meat free. Some restaurants cook their 'vegetarian' selection with animal fat or on the same grill as the meat dishes. Also, in some places you may need to check the ingredients of the vegetarian items before ordering.

## Street Food

Shawarma is a popular local snack consisting of rolled pita bread filled with lamb or chicken carved from a rotating spit, vegetables and tahina sauce. You'll see countless roadside stands offering shawarma for as little as Dhs.3 each, and they make a great alternative to the usual fast-food staples. In residential areas, the small cluster of shops beside a mosque is often a good place to look for your local shawarma outlet. These cafes and stands usually sell other dishes, such as falafel (or ta'amiya), which are small savoury balls of deep-fried chickpeas, also sold separately or in a pita bread sandwich. Many also offer freshly squeezed fruit juices for around Dhs.10. For a really unique version, check out Al Shera'a Fisheries Centre, next to Marks & Spencer in Deira (04 227 1803), the only place in town that offers fish shawarmas.

## Independent Restaurants

While hotel restaurants tend to draw in the crowds, especially at the weekend, Dubai's independent choices are not to be missed. Areas like Oud Metha, Karama and the Jumeira strip are home to restaurants serving everything from authentic Arabic kebabs (Al Mallah, p.452) and tempting pad thai (Lemongrass, p.479) to crispy Peking duck (Lan Kwai Fong, p.479) and fiery Pakistani curry (Karachi Darbar, p.477). Whether you pop in for a hearty lunch or have a teetotal evening you shouldn't ignore the culinary, and affordable, delights of these independents.

# NIGHTLIFE

## Bars, Pubs & Clubs

You can't expect authenticity from Dubai's pubs, but then when they're mostly in hotels, in the desert, in the Middle East, that won't come as a surprise. What you can look forward to is some inviting, friendly spots with a decent selection of draught and bottled beers, and reliably good bar grub. Many of these mostly English and Irish places are popular when there's a big game on. And they're all comfortable, raucous and smoky enough to feel like the real thing.

Century Village

### Sporting Life

The glitz and glamour of Dubai's bars is all very well, but sometimes you just want a joint where you can catch the big match and enjoy a pint with your mates. These venues are recommended for supping and spectating: Aussie Legends (p.506), Boston Bar (p.508), Champions (p.509), Double Decker (p.509), Dubliners (p.509), Fibber Magee's (p.509) Irish Village (p.510), Nezesaussi (p.513), The Underground (p.516) and Scarlett's (p.514).

## Door Policy

Certain bars and nightclubs have a 'selective' entry policy. Sometimes the 'members only' sign on the entrance needs a bit of explaining. Membership is usually introduced to control the clientele frequenting the establishment, but is often only enforced during busy periods. At quieter times, non-members may have no problems getting in, even if not accompanied by a member. Some places seem to use the rule to disallow entry if they don't like the look of you or your group. Large groups (especially all males), single men and sometimes certain nationalities may be turned away without explanation. You can avoid the inconvenience, and the embarrassment, by breaking the group up or by going in a mixed-gender group.

If you do find yourself being discriminated against it's not worth arguing with the doorman – it won't work. Most companies do everything to avoid bad publicity, so try taking the issue up with the local media instead.

Some of the city's most popular hotspots, such as 360° (p.506), can be nearly impossible to enter on certain nights unless you're on the guest list. Several of the top clubs maintain electronic guest lists via

Platinum List (www.platinumlist.ae). To get onto one of these virtual guest lists you'll need to register with the website and then sign up for the 'events' you want to attend. Pre-booking a table is another way to ensure entrance into a popular club. Keep in mind that table reservations usually come with a required minimum spend.

## Dress Code

While many bars have a reasonably relaxed attitude towards dress code, some places will not allow you in if you are wearing shorts and sandals, while others require a collared shirt and have a 'no jeans or trainers' policy. In general, nightclubs are more strict, so dress to impress.

## Under Age

The law in Dubai states that drinkers must be 21 or over. If you're lucky enough to look like you barely remember the 80s, make sure to carry some form of ID that shows your age – a passport or driving licence is best. Even if you think you're flattering your slightly wrinkled self, it's better to be safe than sorry. Otherwise you'll be on lemonade all night, or, worse still, left outside alone.

### Safe Driver

If you've enjoyed a few drinks with dinner then leave the car and contact Safe Driver. Not only will you be breaking the law if you drive after even one drink, but this clever service means you avoid the hassle of picking up the car in the morning. Simply call 04 268 8797 with your location and the time you wish to be picked up. A driver will come to take you and your car home then be on his merry way.

## Driving Under The Influence

Drinking and driving is illegal in Dubai. There is zero tolerance; if you are caught with even a hint of alcohol in your system you will be sent to prison. Be responsible and always take a taxi – they're cheap, reliable and plentiful – or book Safe Driver to take you and your car home. For more information on drink driving and the law, see p.58.

## Cinemas

There are a number of cinemas around Dubai – many of them situated in shopping malls and run by either Cinestar (www.cinestarcinemas.com) or Grand Cinemas (www.grandcinemas.com). Aside from Dubai Mall, which has opened an arthouse cinema called The Picturehouse, Dubai tends to show mainly mainstream films with multiple screenings (check www.liveworkexplore.com). The biggest cinemas include a 22 screen outlet in Dubai Mall (Reel Cinemas) and a 21 screen cinema at Ibn Battuta Shopping Mall (Grand Megaplex) – the latter has the region's first IMAX screen.

There are cinema annoyances – freezing air conditioning, people chatting to each other or talking on their mobile phones, and the heavy hand of the censor can all affect your experience. Also the sound quality can be a little off and Arabic (as well as often French) subtitles cover the bottom of the screen.

A definite cinematic highlight is Dubai International Film Festival (p.25). The event runs for a week in December across various locations and showcases an impressive mix of mainstream, world and local cinema, from shorts to full features.

## Alternative Screenings

While most of the cinema multiplexes only show big Hollywood movies, several bars and clubs put on screenings of older, foreign and independent films, usually early in the week and free of charge. Check out Movies Under The Stars at Wafi (04 324 4100), Movies & Munchies at Desert Palm (04 323 8888), Dubai Polo & Equestrian Club (04 361 8111) or the Cine-Club Alliance Française auditorium (04 335 8712). It is also worth looking in local listings magazines for details of one-off screenings at some of the city's more progressive art spaces, such as The Jam Jar (p.244).

### CineStar
**Mall of the Emirates** Al Barsha **04 341 4222**
www.cinestarcinemas.com
Map **1 R5** Metro **Mall of the Emirates**

### Grand Cinecity
**Al Ghurair City** Deira **04 228 9898**
www.century-cinemas.com
Map **2 N4** Metro **Union**

Hilton Dubai Creek

Going Out

### Grand Cineplex
**Garhoud Rd, Nr Grand Hyatt Dubai** Umm Hurair
**04 324 2000**
www.grandcinemas.com
Map **2 L7** Metro **Jaddaf**

### Grand Festival Cinemas
**Festival Centre** Festival City **04 232 8328**
www.grandcinemas.com
Map **2 M8** Metro **Jaddaf**

### Grand Mercato
**Mercato** Jumeira **04 349 9713**
www.grandcinemas.com
Map **2 F3** Metro **Financial Centre**

### Grand Metroplex
**Metropolitan** Downtown Burj Dubai **04 343 8383**
www.grandcinemas.com
Map **2 D5** Metro **Business Bay**

### Lamcy Cinema
**Lamcy Plaza** Oud Metha **04 336 8808**
Map **2 K5** Metro **Oud Metha**

### Plaza Cinema
**Nr Carrefour, Al Ghubaiba Bus Station** Bur Dubai
**04 393 9966**
Map **2 L3** Metro **Al Ghubaiba**

### Reel Cinemas
**The Dubai Mall** Downtown Burj Dubai **04 449 1988**
www.reelcinemas.ae
Map **2 F6** Metro **Burj Dubai**

## Comedy Nights
Comedy nights in Dubai are popular with the expat crowd but events tend to be semi-regular, rather than weekly. The Laughter Factory organises monthly events, with comedians from the UK's Comedy Store coming over to play various venues throughout the Gulf. In Dubai these venues include Zinc (p.516) at the Crowne Plaza, Jambase (p.512) at Madinat Jumeirah, Rainbow Room at the Aviation Club (p.514), and the Courtyard Marriott at the Green Community. Keep an eye on www.thelaughterfactory.com for details of future shows. There are also several one-off events featuring comedians from around the world. Remember that a lot of comedy is regional, so unless you're familiar with the comedian's country, you might not get the joke.

## Concerts & Live Music
Dubai hosts a number of concerts each year, and it seems to be attracting bigger and bigger names. Past acts to play here include Kylie, Robbie Williams, Mariah Carey and Muse. These big name acts usually play at outdoor venues such as the Tennis Stadium, Dubai Autodrome, Dubai Festival City and the amphitheatre at Media City.

Big acts such as Paul Weller, Kanye West, Mika, Ziggy Marley, Joss Stone and Madness have appeared at the Desert Rhythm festival in recent years, while another regular event that attracts major names is Dubai Desert Rock Festival (www.desertrockfestival.com), which in 2009 gave the region's rock fans a multi-band ear bashing with Motorhead headlining.

In addition to artists at the height of their fame, Dubai also plays host to a string of groups that may be past their prime, but nonetheless provide good entertainment (think Human League, Tony Hadley, Go West and Deacon Blue).

There's also been a recent rise in the number of alternative and slightly lesser-known (basically 'more cool') acts coming over for some sun, including Groove Armada, 2ManyDjs, Super Furry Animals and Soulwax.

A new event in 2009 was Dubai Sound City, a three-day music festival which brought together a wide range of well-known, lesser-known and local bands for an extravaganza across multiple venues.

If you don't mind travelling a bit, Abu Dhabi also attracts some huge names. The past few years have seen performances by Justin Timberlake, Beyonce, Kings of Leon, Aerosmith, The Killers, Coldplay, and Shakira. Most of the concerts are held at a huge amphitheatre outside Emirates Palace (p.278), although the Abu Dhabi Grand Prix in 2009 hosted several of the previously mentioned headliners.

## Parties At Home
There are several companies in Dubai that can do all the cooking, decorating and cleaning up for you, leaving you with more time to concentrate on your witty after-dinner anecdotes. All of the companies listed offer a complete service from event organisation to the hiring of performers and equipment rental. For a novel outdoor party idea, you can get your own shawarma stand set up in the garden, complete with shawarma maker. Several Arabic restaurants provide this service, which works out as a very reasonable and easy way to sustain hordes of party guests. Also many popular Indian restaurants (such as Open House, listed opposite) offer catering services at great prices. You can order off the menu and specify the number of guests (although the general rule is reduce it by a few unless you want to be eating curry for a week).

In addition to specialist companies, many hotels and restaurants have catering departments, so pick your favourite and ask if they can help out. Depending on what you require, caterers can provide just the food or everything from crockery, napkins, tables, chairs, waiters, doormen and a clearing up service afterwards.

## Caterers

### Eat & Drink
**Nr Choithrams** Garhoud **04 394 3878**
Map **2 NL** Metro **GGICO** www.eatanddrinkgroup.com
Provides catering contracts and one-off parties.

### Flying Elephant
**Sheikh Zayed Rd** Al Quoz **04 347 9170**
www.flyingelephantuae.com Map **1 U5** Metro **Al Quoz**
Offers everything from entertainment for kids'
birthday parties to theme decoration and catering.

### Harlequin Marquees & Event Services
Al Quoz **04 347 0110** www.harlequinmarquees.com
Map **1 S5** Metro **Al Quoz**
Everything you need for an outdoor event, including
marquees, tables, chairs, and even outdoor A/C units.

### The Lime Tree Café
**Jumeira Rd, Nr Jumeira Mosque** Jumeira
**04 349 8498** www.thelimetreecafe.com
Map **2 H3** Metro **Al Jafiliya**
Tasty, fresh catering from this popular restaurant.

### Mad Science
**Zabeel Rd** Karama **04 337 7403**
www.madscience.org/uae
Map **2 L5** Metro **Karama**
Interactive, science-based shows for kids' parties.

### Maria Bonita's
**Umm Al Sheif St, Nr Spinneys Centre** Umm Suqeim
**04 395 4454** Map **2 B4** Metro **Al Quoz**
Catering from one of the best Mexican restaurants in
Dubai, which serves excellent margaritas.

### Open House
**Nr Pyramid Bld** Karama **04 396 5481**
Map **2 L5** Metro **Oud Metha**
Catering service providing tasty Indian food, perfect
for small to medium-sized parties.

### Sandwich Express
**Sheikh Zayed Rd,** Trade Centre **04 343 9922**
Map **2 G5** Metro **Financial Centre**
Catering service specialising in sandwiches and salads.

## Theatre
The theatre scene in Dubai has always been rather
limited, with fans relying chiefly on touring companies
and the occasional amateur dramatics performance.
However, as the city grows so does its thirst for culture,
and with an increase in modern facilities over the
past couple of years, theatre lovers are finally finding
something to cheer about. The First Group Theatre at
Madinat Jumeirah hosts a variety of performances,
from serious stage plays to comedies and musical
performances to pantomimes. Cirque du Soleil has
set up its massive big-top at Ibn Battuta each spring
for the past few years and is always a big hit. The
city's newest performance venue, the Palladium
(www.thepalladiumdubai.com), is located in Media
City and should see some promising shows in the
near future. Young budding thespians can receive
training in acting, mime, script writing and costume
design through the Scenez Arts & Drama Academy
(www.scenezgroup.com) and Kidsworks (www.
kidstheatreworks.com, p.144).

### Dubai Community Theatre & Arts Centre (DUCTAC)
**Mall of the Emirates** Al Barsha **04 341 4777**
www.ductac.org
Map **1 R5** Metro **Mall of the Emirates**
In addition to rehearsal spaces, workshops, and
exhibition halls, the complex features two fully
equipped theatres. The Centrepoint Theatre can seat
543 people, while the smaller Kilachand Studio Theatre
has a capacity of 196 people. The theatres aim to
present a variety of entertainment, from drama, opera
and classical music to comedy and children's shows.

### First Group Theatre at Madinat Jumeirah
**Souk Madinat Jumeirah** Umm Suqeim **04 366 8888**
www.madinattheatre.com
Map **1 R4** Metro **Mall of the Emirates**
The theatre's well planned design and space
(424 seats), has witnessed an impressive list of
performances. From 'treading the boards' classics to
musicals and innovative comedy shows, make sure
you keep your eyes open for what's coming into town
next and chances are you won't be disappointed.

# Where To Go For What

Dubai is a pick'n'mix of eateries, drinking spots and entertainment options vying to please a highly diverse audience. Whether you want a daytime binge of five-star cuisine, a raucous night out dancing to live music, an evening of brain teasers or an early morning rendition of 'I Will Survive' you will find it all within Dubai's restaurants, cafes, pubs, bars and nightclubs.

## Alfresco

Between late October and early May the weather in Dubai is perfect for alfresco dining and beachfront drinking. Popular spots for dinner with a waterfront view are: on stilts over the creek at The Boardwalk (p.463); overlooking the beach at Bussola (p.463); a collection of intimate restaurants at Century Village, including Da Gama's and Mazaj (p.484); the mix of cuisines by the water at Madinat Jumeirah featuring the likes of Left Bank (p.512) and Zheng He's (p.505); on the terrace at Souk Al Bahar and the neighbouring Dubai Mall; and finally the streetside eateries of Marina Walk and The Walk, JBR (p.517).

## Fish & Chips

You may not find a 'chippy' on every street corner in Dubai, but if you're really hankering for some good old fish and chips there are a few choices at your disposal. The Fish & Chips Room (04 427 0443) at Jumeirah Beach Residence is a rising star, and already has a legion of loyal fans. It stays open until the wee hours of the morning too. Fish Supper (04 284 5551) in the Arabian Centre on the Al Khawaneej Road is a good option for Mirdif dwellers, as is Fish & Chip Mirdif, 26c Street, near the mosque on 15 Street (04 288 1812). The Irish Village (p.510), Barasti (p.507), The Boardwalk (p.463), the Dhow & Anchor (p.509) and Aprés (p.456) all deserve a special mention for the quality of their fish and chips. More Café (p.485) also has excellent fish and spicy chunky chips.

## Dancing

There is a whole host of clubs to boogie the night away in (see p.506), as well as a few places for impromptu dance routines. Should you fancy wiggling to something slightly more alternative while out on the town, check out Step On on Friday nights at Chi@The Lodge (p.509), which offers some British flavour with classic indie tunes. On the same night but in the Garden is Cheese (check out the group on Facebook) with DJ Tim Cheddar and his get-up-and-dance mix of pop classics. For a more eclectic selection try the Adidas sponsored Audio Tonic on Fridays at 360° (p.506) or the new Ocean Club at the Sheraton Jumeirah (you will need to get on the guestlist at www.platinumlist.ae for both).

Waxy's

## Late & Lively

In addition to the dedicated clubs listed in this chapter, Dubai's nightlife scene also includes several bars and restaurants which transform late evening into lively joints with hopping dancefloors. These include Barasti (p.507), Boudoir (p.508), Buddha Bar (p.508), Malecon (p.470), Rock Bottom (p.514), Jambase (p.512), and The Warehouse (p.502).

## Karaoke Bars

There are a few places in Dubai where you can show off your vocal abilities, or even just belt out a comedy version of Ice Ice Baby. Harry Ghatto's (p.510) in Emirates Towers is a popular haunt, with the small space filling fast, while the post-brunch karaoke sessions at Double Decker (p.509) range from the sublime to the ridiculous. For a unique night, try 'curryoke' at It's Mirchi (04 334 4088) in the Ramee Royal Hotel, Bur Dubai, which serves up Indian fare with an enormous multi-language song book. On the other side of the creek, Kisaku (p.478) is a good option, with private rooms for groups.

## Ladies' Nights

Lucky ladies in this fair city can go out almost any night of the week and enjoy free drinks. Of course, this isn't a charitable venture by Dubai's bar scene; where ladies are drinking, the men and their wallets inevitably follow. Tuesday is the biggest ladies' night with many bars and pubs offering at least two free drinks. The most legendary venues are Scarlett's (p.514), Oeno (p.513), The Agency (p.506) and Waxy's (p.516), while Boudoir (p.508) is very lady friendly, with free bubbly or cocktails nearly every night of the week.

## Quiz Nights

If you want to test your brain power and knowledge of useless trivia then head to one of Dubai's many quiz nights. Try Boston Bar (p.508) or Player's Lounge (04 398 8840) on Mondays, or Tuesdays at Fibber Magee's (p.509), which features a plasticine model-making round. If you don't mind fierce competition, give the quiz at the Arabian Ranches Golf Club (p.324) a go.

## And The Rest...

Dubai is full of fun alternatives for when you need a break from the bar and restaurant scene. You can enjoy the slides and lazy river in between trips to the bar at Aquaventure at Atlantis The Palm (p.248), which offers a night pass from 20:00 to midnight for Dhs.175. The ancient bowling alley at Al Nasr Leisureland (04 337 1234, www.alnasrll.com) is the only one in the city that serves booze (at cheap prices too), and reservations can be made for large parties. For an especially memorable night out, you could charter a yacht from Dubai Marina Yacht Club. Dhs.1,500 will buy you two hours for up to 10 people and you can bring your own food and drink on board. If you'd rather sit back and relax, Peanut Butter Jam at the Wafi Rooftop (www.wafi.com) happens on Fridays from 20:00 to midnight.

### Celebrity Chefs

Does food prepared by famous hands really taste better? To find out head to Frankie's (p.473) to sample Marco Pierre White's menu, Verre (p.500), Gordon Ramsay's restaurant, Pierre Gagnaire's Reflets (p.490), Mezzanine by Gary Rhodes (p.490) or at Atlantis try Nobu Matsuhisa's offering (p.486), Ronda Locatelli (p.491), Santi Santamari's Ossiano (p.487) and Michel Rostang's French restaurant (p.491). For a more reasonably priced option try Sanjeev Kapoor's Khazana (p.478).

# RESTAURANTS BY CUISINE

## Cuban
**El Malecon**, Dubai Marine Beach — p.470

## Dinner Cruises
**Al Mansour Dhow**, Radisson Blu Hotel, Deira — p.452
**Bateaux Dubai**, Bur Dubai — p.460
**Creekside Leisure**, Bur Dubai — p.469
**Tour Dubai**, Bur Dubai — p.498

## European
**25°55°**, Dubai Marina Yacht Club — p.450
**Focaccia**, Hyatt Regency — p.473
**Nineteen**, The Address Montgomerie Dubai — p.486

## Far Eastern
**Bamboo Lagoon**, JW Marriott Hotel — p.460
**Beachcombers**, The Jumeirah Beach Hotel — p.460
**Chimes**, Seven Sands Hotel Apartments — p.468
**Eauzone**, One&Only Royal Mirage — p.470
**Thai Chi**, Pyramids — p.498
**The Noodle House**, Emirates Towers — p.486
**Veda Pavilion**, Palm Jumeirah — p.500
**Wox**, Grand Hyatt Dubai — p.504
**Yum!**, Radisson Blu Hotel, Deira — p.505

## Filipino
**Tagpuan**, Karama Centre — p.496

## French
**Bistro Domino**, Deira City Centre — p.462
**Bistro Madeleine**, InterContinental DFC — p.462
**Café Chic**, Le Meridien Dubai — p.464
**Entrecôte Café de Paris**, The Dubai Mall — p.471
**La Baie**, The Ritz-Carlton, Dubai — p.478
**La Maison d'Hôtes**, Jumeira — p.478
**Le Classique**, Emirates Golf Club — p.479
**Margaux**, Souk Al Bahar — p.482
**Reflets par Pierre Gagnaire**, InterCon DFC — p.490
**Rostang**, Atlantis The Palm — p.491
**Signatures**, Jebel Ali Htl — p.494
**St Tropez**, Century Village — p.495
**Verre**, Hilton Creek — p.500

## German
**Brauhaus**, Jumeira Rotana — p.463
**Der Keller**, The Jumeirah Beach Hotel — p.469
**Hofbräuhaus**, JW Marriott Hotel — p.474

## Greek
**Elia**, Majestic Hotel Tower — p.470

## Indian
**Aangan**, Dhow Palace Hotel — p.450
**Antique Bazaar**, Four Points by Sheraton — p.454
**Aryaas**, Kuwait St — p.456
**Asha's**, Pyramids — p.457
**Ashiana**, Sheraton Hotel & Towers — p.457
**Coconut Grove**, Rydges Plaza Hotel — p.468
**Foodlands**, Opp Ramada Continental Hotel — p.473
**Gazebo**, Nr Meena Plaza Hotel — p.473
**Handi**, Taj Palace Hotel — p.474
**Indego**, Grosvenor House — p.476
**India Palace**, Al Hudda Bld — p.476
**iZ**, Grand Hyatt Dubai — p.476
**Jaipur**, Burj Residences — p.476
**Khazana**, Al Nasr Leisureland — p.478
**Masala**, Bab Al Shams Desert Resort & Spa — p.484
**Nina**, One&Only Royal Mirage — p.486
**Sai Dham**, Saleh Bin Lahej Bld, Oud Metha Rd — p.492
**Saravana Bhavan**, Karama Park Square — p.492
**The Bombay**, Marco Polo Hotel — p.463
**The Rupee Room**, Marina Walk — p.492
**Zaika**, Al Murooj Rotana Hotel & Suites — p.505

## International
**Al Dawaar**, Hyatt Regency — p.450
**Al Forsan**, Bab Al Shams Desert Resort & Spa — p.450
**Al Shindagah**, Metropolitan Palace — p.454
**Après**, Mall of the Emirates — p.456
**Arboretum**, Al Qasr Hotel — p.456
**Blue Orange**, The Westin Dubai Mina Seyahi — p.463
**Cascades**, Fairmont Dubai — p.464
**Celebrities**, One&Only Royal Mirage — p.466
**Chalet**, Jumeirah Rd — p.466
**Chef's House**, Radisson Blu Hotel, DMC — p.466
**Choices**, Al Bustan Rotana — p.468
**Conservatory**, Al Manzil Hotel — p.469
**Entre Nous**, Novotel World Trade Centre — p.471
**Fazaris**, The Address Downtown Burj Dubai — p.472
**Fire & Ice – Raffles Grill**, Raffles Dubai — p.472
**Five Dining**, Jumeira Rotana — p.472
**Flavours On Two**, Towers Rotana — p.473
**Glasshouse Brasserie**, Hilton Creek — p.473
**Golf Academy**, Creek Golf Club — p.474
**Inferno Grill**, Dubai Marina — p.476
**Japengo Café**, Mall Of The Emirates — p.476
**Mizaan**, The Monarch Dubai — p.485
**Nasimi**, Atlantis The Palm — p.486
**Promenade**, Four Points by Sheraton — p.489
**Ranches Restaurant**, The Desert Course — p.490
**Rotisserie**, One&Only Royal Mirage — p.491
**Saffron**, Atlantis The Palm — p.492
**Seasons**, Mall of the Emirates — p.493
**Sezzam**, Mall of the Emirates — p.493
**Sketch**, Metropolitan Palace — p.494
**Spectrum On One**, Fairmont Dubai — p.495
**Teatro**, Towers Rotana — p.496
**The Boardwalk**, Creek Golf Club, — p.463
**The Cellar**, The Aviation Club — p.466
**The Edge**, Dubai International Financial Centre — p.470
**The Junction**, Traders Hotel, Deira — p.477
**The Kitchen**, Hyatt Regency — p.478
**The Observatory**, Dubai Marriott Harbour — p.487
**Warehouse**, Le Meridien Dubai — p.502

# Restaurants By Cuisine

# BARS, PUBS & CLUBS

## Bars

# VENUES BY LOCATION

## Al Barsha

## Al Sufouh

Going Out

## Venues By Location

**Going Out**

**Going Out**

# Venues By Location

## Jebel Ali

## Jumeira

## Karama

## Mirdif

## Oud Metha & Umm Hurair

**Going Out**

# Venues By Location

## Shangri-La Hotel
Amwaj, Seafood — p.454
Balcony Bar, Bar — p.507
Hoi An, Vietnamese — p.474
Marrakech, Moroccan — p.484
Shang Palace, Chinese — p.494

## The Monarch Dubai
Arcadia, Afternoon Tea — p.456
Mizaan, International — p.485
Okku, Japanese — p.487
Ruth's Chris Steak House, Steakhouse — p.491

## Independent Restaurants & Cafes
Al Borz, Persian — p.450
Al Safadi, Arabic/Lebanese — p.454
Bento-Ya, Japanese — p.462
Fibber Magee's, Pub — p.509
French Connection, Cafe — p.473
Shakespeare & Co, Cafe — p.494
Bento-Ya, Japanese — p.462

## Umm Suqeim

### Al Qasr Hotel
Al Hambra, Spanish — p.452
Arboretum, International — p.456
Koubba, Bar — p.512
Magnolia, Vegetarian — p.480
PaiThai, Thai — p.487
Pierchic, Seafood — p.489

### Burj Al Arab
Al Mahara, Seafood — p.452
Al Muntaha, Mediterranean — p.454
Majlis Al Bahar, Mediterranean — p.482
Sahn Eddar, Afternoon Tea — p.492
Skyview Bar, Bar — p.515

### Mina A'Salam
Al Muna, Buffet — p.454
Bahri Bar, Bar — p.506
The Wharf, Seafood — p.504
Zheng He's, Chinese — p.505

### Souk Madinat Jumeirah
Bar Zar, Bar — p.507
Jambase, Bar — p.512
Pisces, Seafood — p.489
Segreto, Italian — p.493
Shoo Fee Ma Fee, Moroccan — p.494
Trader Vic's, Polynesian — p.500

## The Jumeirah Beach Hotel
360°, Bar — p.506
Beachcombers, Far Eastern — p.460
Carnevale, Italian — p.464
Der Keller, German — p.469
Dhow & Anchor, Pub — p.509
Go West, American — p.474
La Parrilla, Argentinean — p.479
La Veranda, Italian — p.999
Marina, Seafood — p.482
The Apartment Lounge + Club, Nightclub — p.506
Uptown Bar, Bar — p.516
Villa Beach, International — p.500

## Independent Restaurants & Cafes
Café Havana, Cafe — p.464
Maria Bonita's, Mexican — p.482

## Out Of The City

### Bab Al Shams Desert Resort & Spa
Al Forsan, International — p.450
Al Hadheerah, Arabic/Lebanese — p.452
Le Dune Pizzeria, Italian — p.479
Masala, Indian — p.484

### Desert Palm Dubai
Epicure, Cafe — p.471
Rare Restaurant, Steakhouse — p.490

### Dubai Outlet Mall
Stone Fire Pizza Kitchen, Pizzeria — p.495

Going Out

# Your guide to living in and loving the UAE

**Liveworkexplore**

The one-stop magazine for expats in the UAE, from the publishers of the No.1 best selling Dubai Explorer - Live Work Explore.

www.liveworkexplore.com

# RESTAURANTS & CAFES

## 25°55°                                European

Marina-side views and an oceanic theme

25° 55° are the nautical coordinates of Dubai, and the marina-side view and gentle decor of the restaurant create an oceanic theme, with tasty staples like pasta, sandwiches and salads rounded off nicely with languid desserts such as warm strawberries in Pimm's.
**Dubai Marina Yacht Club** Dubai Marina **04 362 7955**
www.dubaimarinayachtclub.com
Map **1 K4** Metro **Jumeirah Lakes Towers**

## Aangan                                Indian

Traditional decor, live music and excellent kebabs

Traditionally decorated in rich wood with many elaborate ornaments nailed to the walls, the atmosphere and live in-house music mingle well with the authentic food. Savour its range of biryanis, special curries and kebabs from the charcoal-smoked clay oven, plus excellent desserts.
**Dhow Palace Hotel** Al Mankool **04 359 9992**
www.dhowpalacedubai.com
Map **2 L4** Metro **Karama**

## Al Bandar                              Seafood

Tradition, seafood and camels by the creek

With an idyllic creekside location and good international seafood, Al Bandar is the perfect venue to ease visitors into the Arabian experience. It caters for a dress-down clientele, making a change from the usual five-star hotel feel. It's good value, and the nearby resident camels make an excellent photo opportunity.
**Heritage & Diving Village** Al Shindagha **04 393 9001**
www.alkoufa.com
Map **2 M3** Metro **Al Ras**

## Al Basha                            Arabic/Lebanese

Fine set menu options, with nimble belly dancers

Al Basha offers fine Lebanese food, with live music from 21:30. You can order al a carte, but the set menus are wide-ranging; wafer-thin pitta, cheese rolls and grilled meat start from Dhs.220 per person up to Dhs.350 with prawn and lobster. Alcohol is available but very expensive.
**Metropolitan Resort** Dubai Marina **04 399 5000**
www.habtoorhotels.com
Map **1 L3** Metro **Dubai Marina**

## Al Borz                                Persian

An ideal introduction to Iranian fare on SZR

Renowned as one of Tehran's best kebab houses, Al Borz serves up its famous kebabs and rich rice specialities in a family setting. A buffet lunch, large portions and moderate prices mean it's popular with Iranians and Persian food novices alike. Takeaway and delivery are available.
**Al Durrah Tower, Sheikh Zayed Rd** Trade Centre **04 331 8777**
Map **2 H5** Metro **Emirates Towers**

## Al Dahleez                          Arabic/Lebanese

Cavernous shisha cafe with juices and Arabic grills

Packed nearly every night of the week, Al Dahleez serves some of the best shisha in Dubai, and its bizarre, faux-cavern interior is a great place to spend a few hours playing cards or backgammon. Large grilled sandwiches, traditional Arabic grills and fresh juices dominate the extensive menu.
**Al Boom Tourist Village** Umm Hurair **04 324 3000**
www.alboom.ae
Map **2 L7** Metro **Jaddaf**

## Al Dawaar                           International

Quality buffet food that makes the world go round

Surprisingly sophisticated for a revolving restaurant, the decor here is minimalist and the buffet ample rather than over the top. Enjoy dainty starters, a la carte-style main dishes and an unrivalled dessert table, plus changing views over Deira and out to sea.
**Hyatt Regency** Deira **04 317 2222**
www.dubai.regency.hyatt.com
Map **2 N3** Metro **Palm Deira**

## Al Dhiyafa                         Arabic/Lebanese

Rustic decor and meat galore

Brass ceiling fans, the warm red glow from table lamps, and a tantalising aroma of roasting meats fill Al Dhiyafa. The buffet food themes change daily, and the splendid array of fresh, imaginative food remains constant, particularly the meat dishes.
**Metropolitan Resort** Dubai Marina **04 399 5000**
www.habtoorhotels.com
Map **1 L3** Metro **Dubai Marina**

## Al Diwan                           Arabic/Lebanese

Fantastic cuisine with Arabic music

Enjoy traditional Lebanese food and belly dancing from 23:00 at this cosy restaurant. The selection of wine, Montecristo cigars and Beluga caviar provide a special treat, but the hummus Al Diwan and the Oriental mixed grill are not to be missed.
**Metropolitan Palace** Deira **04 227 0000**
www.habtoorhotels.com
Map **2 N5** Metro **Al Rigga**

## Al Forsan                           International

Magical atmosphere amid the desert dunes

A small but perfectly formed buffet offers Arabic and international dishes, while the a la carte option also has a great selection for kids. The magical, Arabian

# One&Only
## Royal Mirage, Dubai

Dubai's most romantic beach resort

The Palace    *Residence & Spa    Arabian Court

For reservations or more information please contact
One&Only Royal Mirage, Dubai, UAE.  Telephone + 971 4 399 99 99   oneandonlyroyalmirage.com
*Member of The Small Leading Hotels of the World

atmosphere, helped along by the rich decor, and surrounding dunes, is worth the 45 minute drive from Dubai.
**Bab Al Shams Desert Resort & Spa 04 809 6100**
www.jumeirah.com
Map **1 E2**

### Al Fresco                                Italian
A taste of Italy in the heart of Dubai
A great little Italian serving exciting and authentic pastas and risottos. Be sure to leave room for dessert; the tiramisu is delicious. The casual vibe in this cosy nook makes it perfect for al fresco dining with friends.
**Crowne Plaza** Trade Centre **04 331 1111**
www.ichotelsgroup.com
Map **2 H5** Metro **Emirates Towers**

### Al Hadheerah                    Arabic/Lebanese
Delightful dining: great food and entertainment
A buffet of traditional Arabic (including Emirati) food is served here, amid a variety of elaborate performances. Enjoy grilled seafood, meat and desserts; henna painting and shisha are available for an extra charge. Prices start from Dhs.395 for adults and Dhs.275 for children.
**Bab Al Shams Desert Resort & Spa 04 809 6100**
www.jumeirah.com
Map **1 E2**

### Al Hambra                              Spanish
Tasty dishes that fuse Andalusia with Morocco
A mariachi duo, exposed brickwork and vaulted ceilings set the mood at this excellent Spanish restaurant. The seafood paella served here is a must, but there are few options for vegetarians. The pricey menu may mean reserving this restaurant for those special occasions.
**Al Qasr Hotel** Umm Suqeim **04 366 6730**
www.jumeirah.com
Map **1 R4** Metro **Mall of the Emirates**

### Al Koufa                         Arabic/Lebanese
Great food and live performances
In true Arabic style, Al Koufa comes alive around 23:00 when the huge restaurant starts to fill. Enjoy great traditional Arabic food and fruit juices, including some lesser known and Emirati dishes. A charge of Dhs.30 covers the live performances.
**Nr Al Nasr Leisureland** Oud Metha **04 335 1511**
www.alkoufa.com
Map **2 L5** Metro **Oud Metha**

### Al Mahara                              Seafood
Superlative seafood in a sub-marine setting
Your visit starts with a simulated submarine ride 'under the sea', arriving at an elegant restaurant curled around a huge aquarium. The superlative fine dining menu is

predominantly seafood and boasts prices to match. Gentlemen are required to wear a jacket for dinner.
**Burj Al Arab** Umm Suqeim **04 301 7600**
www.jumeirah.com
Map **1 S3** Metro **Mall of the Emirates**

### Al Mallah                         Arabic/Lebanese
Fab Arabic fastfood at this no-frills institution
Watch the world go by on Al Diyafah from this popular pavement Arabic joint, as you sample excellent shawarmas, fruit juices and some of the biggest and best falafel in Dubai. The incongruous 'Diana' and 'Charles' shakes are also recommended.
**Al Diyafah Rd** Satwa **04 398 4723**
Map **2 J3** Metro **Al Jafiliya**

### Al Mansour Dhow > p.239         Dinner Cruise
All aboard for traditional food and music
This two-hour creek trip features dinner aboard a traditional dhow operated by Radisson SAS. Great views, atmospheric oud music, a traditional buffet spread and shisha on deck make this a memorable evening. The ship sails at 20:30, and the price is Dhs.185 per adult.
**Radisson Blu Hotel, Dubai Deira Creek** Al Rigga **04 222 7171**
www.radissonblu.com/hotel-dubaideiracreek
Map **2 N4** Metro **Union**

Al Mahara

# Time Out award winning Indian restaurant!

Come and experience authentic North Indian culinary flavours. Our experienced chefs practice the art of blending freshly ground spices and herbs while preparing delicacies to perfection in a home-style way. Watch our chefs prepare mouth watering dishes such as tender kebabs and breads, baked in our clay tandoor oven. You can also relish the different variety of curries and Biryanis and lots more.

Evenings become more lively with traditional music as you settle down to your meal. Live entertainment is provided by our resident musicians "Santosh & Jyotsna".

Our private dining room is available for special requests.

Open 12:30pm till 3:30pm for lunch
7:00pm onwards for dinner
For reservations, call 04 359 9992

فـنـدق داو بـالاس
DHOW PALACE HOTEL

# Restaurants & Cafes

## Al Muna — Buffet
*Buffet bonanza in plush Madinat surroundings*
Al Muna offers a mouthwatering buffet of international cuisine, as well as a 24 hour a la carte menu catering to those who want a more personal experience. Like everything in the Madinat it comes in a nice posh package with elegant decor and an inviting terrace to match.
**Mina A'Salam** Umm Suqeim **04 366 6730**
www.jumeirah.com
Map **1 R3** Metro **Mall of the Emirates**

## Al Muntaha — Mediterranean
*Great views, reasonable dining at the top of the Burj*
The breathtaking coastline view from this restaurant at the top of the Burj Al Arab goes some way to excusing the eccentric decor; thankfully, the European menu is more conservative than the interior. You may feel you're paying for the name more than anything else.
**Burj Al Arab** Umm Suqeim **04 301 7600**
www.jumeirah.com
Map **1 S3** Metro **Mall of the Emirates**

## Al Nafoorah — Arabic/Lebanese
*Busy Lebanese place that's perfect for group dining*
A crisp, colonial and busy Lebanese restaurant, equally suited to a power lunch or elegant dinner. The food is excellent and the menu is extensive, with pages and pages of mezze and mains to tantalise, so come in a group and share the wide selection.
**Boulevard at Emirates Towers** Trade Centre
**04 319 8088**
www.jumeirah.com
Map **2 H5** Metro **Emirates Towers**

## Al Safadi — Arabic/Lebanese
*No-frills dining where the food outshines the venue*
Function rules over form at big and busy Al Safadi, but it's the high quality Arabic food that people come here for. Street-side tables are perfect for more relaxed dining, shisha and people watching. Another branch is on Al Rigga Road in Deira (04 227 9922).
**Al Kawakeb Bld, Sheikh Zayed Rd** Trade Centre
**04 343 5333**
Map **2 G5** Metro **Financial Centre**

## Al Shindagah — International
*Umm's the word at this reliable restaurant*
Expect bountiful buffets and consistently good food at this restaurant. During Ramadan the focus here shifts from international to delicious Middle Eastern treats (including its fabulous umm ali). The buffet costs Dhs.110, which includes soft drinks.
**Metropolitan Palace** Deira **04 227 0000**
www.habtoorhotels.com
Map **2 N5** Metro **Al Rigga**

## Almaz by Momo — Moroccan
*A richly decorated restaurant, perfect for lounging*
The subdued atmosphere inside this Moroccan restaurant is a contrast to the retail buzz outside. Settle down with a mocktail and enjoy its stews, tender lamb and fluffy couscous. With the tempting menu you won't be going anywhere fast – the service is as laidback as the vibe.
**Mall of the Emirates** Al Barsha **04 409 8877**
www.altayer.com/companies/food
Map **1 R5** Metro **Mall of the Emirates**

## Amaseena — Arabic/Lebanese
*Exotic Arabian dining under the stars*
A torch-lit entrance, sounds of the oud, the aroma of shisha, and exotic belly dancing under the stars make this a truly magical Arabian experience. The food – an all you can eat Arabic buffet – is excellent, and you can sit in your own private majlis.
**The Ritz-Carlton, Dubai** Dubai Marina **04 399 4000**
www.ritzcarlton.com
Map **1 K3** Metro **Dubai Marina**

## Amwaj — Seafood
*Top food and service – real fine-dining find*
Amwaj is a Dubai must. The service couldn't be more attentive or unobtrusive, and the chef is an expert at combining seemingly contrasting flavours into dishes that work so well you'll find yourself licking the plate. Priding itself on perfectly prepared seafood, Amwaj's meat and vegetarian dishes are equally impressive.
**Shangri-La Hotel** Trade Centre **04 405 2703**
www.shangri-la.com
Map **2 G5** Metro **Financial Centre**

## Andiamo! — Italian
*Enticing pizzas straight from the exciting oven*
This chic, relaxed Italian features Miro-style lamps, with an abundance of mirrors, wood and stark colours, and an eye-catching pizza oven. The starters are pretty, delicious and generous while pizzas are thin, crispy, fresh and tasty. Prices are a little above average.
**Grand Hyatt Dubai** Umm Hurair **04 317 1234**
www.dubai.grand.hyatt.com
Map **2 L7** Metro **Healthcare City**

## Antique Bazaar — Indian
*A musical extravaganza and a feast of curry*
Antique Bazaar offers a full range of curried delights to ever-present musical accompaniment. When in full swing, the live music show is a memorable cultural experience, but can detract from the great food. Arrive early for conversation, late to party.
**Four Points by Sheraton Bur Dubai** Bur Dubai
**04 397 7444**
www.starwoodhotels.com
Map **2 L4** Metro **Al Fahidi**

Going Out

# Explore the endless possibilities
# at Dubai's only true resort

The 800 metre strip of palm-lined private beach at one of Dubai's most fabulous beach and leisure destinations, is just one of many reasons to visit the award-winning Jebel Ali Golf Resort & Spa. Unwind at leisure by booking your own annual beach club membership, or simply visit at your convenience to experience any of the more than 50 facilities and activities. Twelve restaurants and bars, two hotels, three swimming pools, a 9-hole golf course, spa, horse riding stables, marina, diving centre, seaplane flights and even a shooting range make a visit to Dubai's Only True Resort truly unforgettable.

A MEMBER OF

JEBEL ALI INTERNATIONAL
HOTELS

For reservations, please call +971 4 814 5555
E-mail jagrs@jaihotels.com ✆ www.jebelali-international.com

JEBEL ALI GOLF RESORT & SPA
Dubai's Only True Resort

# Restaurants & Cafes

## Applebees
*American*

Tex-Mex galore at this family-pleasing favourite
An all-American family restaurant serving up huge portions of Tex-Mex, burgers, and crowd pleasers. Smiling staff, big screen TVs, and great kids' and dessert menus keep the whole clan happy. The Oreo milkshake is a fine way to end your calorie overload.
**Sheikh Issa Tower, Sheikh Zayed Rd** Trade Centre**04 343 7755**
www.applebees.com
Map **2 H5** Metro **Emirates Towers**

## Après
*International*

Party like you're on the piste at this apres-ski spot
This cosy alpine ski lodge has a comfortable bar area and an unrivalled view of the Ski Dubai slope. The varied menu offers wholesome fare including steaks, fondue and excellent pizzas. During the day it's great for families, but at night the laidback vibe and wide-ranging cocktail list encourages both chilled dining and socialising.
**Mall of the Emirates** Al Barsha **04 341 2575**
www.emiratesleisureretail.com
Map **1 R5** Metro **Mall of the Emirates**

## Aquara
*Seafood*

Classy Marina terrace spot to take in the yachts
Aquara is chic but understated, allowing the view of million-dirham yachts to speak for itself. It specialises in seafood, most of which is served with an Asian twist. Friday brunch is excellent value at Dhs.180, or Dhs.250 with house drinks. The centrepiece is the seafood bar with lobster, oysters, prawns, crab, clams, sushi and sashimi. A great terrace too.
**Dubai Marina Yacht Club** Dubai Marina **04 362 7900**
www.dubaimarinayachtclub.com
Map **1 K4** Metro **Jumeirah Lakes Towers**

Al Forsan

## Aquarium Restaurant
*Seafood*

Consistently good food in a swanky setting
This is one of Dubai's old time favourites, but it still serves up tasty seafood dishes beside a glorious view of the creek. If you can pull yourself away from the view, enjoy the well-priced menu inspired by the countries surrounding the Pacific Rim.
**Creek Golf & Yacht Club** Deira **04 295 6000**
www.dubaigolf.com
Map **2 N6** Metro **GGICO**

## Arboretum
*International*

Tempting variety in an impressive setting
Enjoy Asian, Middle Eastern and western salads and appetisers here before tackling seafood, meat or pasta dishes and the fantastic desserts. The buffet (with a live-cooking station) is available at traditional meal times, or you can order a la carte throughout the day.
**Al Qasr Hotel** Umm Suqeim **04 366 6730**
www.jumeirah.com
Map **1 R4** Metro **Mall of the Emirates**

## Arcadia
*Afternoon Tea*

High class high tea at 1 Sheikh Zayed Road
For an afternoon of refinery, the relaxing atrium at The Monarch is the perfect place to be ensconced with your scones. The high tea experience starts with a tower of sandwiches and a bottomless teapot, before moving on to scones and finally the patissier's platter – all for Dhs.120.
**The Monarch Dubai** Trade Centre **04 501 8888**
www.themonarchdubai.com
Map **2 J4** Metro **Trade Centre**

## Armani Dubai Caffe
*Cafe*

Armani by name, Armani by nature
Classy Italian dishes are served up with the kind of style and flair you'd expect from this cafe's designer namesake, and the surroundings certainly live up to the label, with moody reds and dark wooden tones creating an ambience that is at once welcoming and effortlessly stylish.
**The Dubai Mall** Downtown Burj Dubai **04 339 8396**
Map **2 F6** Metro **Burj Dubai**

## Aryaas
*Indian*

A veggie thali feast of unbeatable value
This Indian chain has been serving up excellent fare since 1959, and, despite its prison-like austerity, the food is excellent. The house speciality is thali, small pots of different flavours into which you dip endless naan bread or rice. Around Dhs.10 will buy enough food to fill you up for the whole day.
**Kuwait St** Karama **04 335 5776**
Map **2 L5** Metro **Karama**

## Asado
Argentinean

*Argentinean gem that really raises the steaks*
A combination of moody lighting, passionate music, and a meat lovers' dream menu cement Asado's top steakhouse position. Excellent meat and an enormous wine selection, with terrace views of Burj Dubai thrown in, make this Argentinean restaurant something special.
**The Palace – The Old Town** Downtown Burj Dubai
**04 428 7888**
www.theaddress.com
Map **2 F6** Metro **Burj Dubai**

## Asha's
Indian

*Atmospheric Indian with superstar status*
Indian superstar Asha Bhosle has put a lot of love into this restaurant. Beautifully decorated, the quality of the atmospheric interior is equalled by the eclectic menu, which includes Indian classics, Asha's signature dishes inspired by her travels, and some fusion choices concocted by the resident chef. Great cocktails too.
**Pyramids** Wafi **04 324 4100**
www.wafi.com
Map **2 P6** Metro **Healthcare City**

## Ashiana
Indian

*Top-notch curries and kebabs in an eclectic setting*
Dimmed lights and live music set the tone for the ambling, relaxed Indian meal to come. The staff have perfected the art of subtle attentiveness, and the kitchen seems to nail each item on its vast menu, from seafood curries to massive meats from the tandoor.
**Sheraton Hotel & Towers** Deira **04 207 1733**
www.starwoodhotels.com
Map **2 M4** Metro **Union**

## Asiana Restaurant
Asian

*Accessible Asian with the special Raffles touch*
Feast on a host of Asian-inspired dishes (including a remarkable pad thai) while savouring beautiful city views at this atmospheric venue. With a cool, classy interior, a breathtaking balcony and fine dining at non-exorbitant prices, Asiana ticks all the right boxes.
**Raffles Dubai** Wafi **04 314 9888**
www.dubai.raffles.com
Map **2 K6** Metro **Healthcare City**

## At Home
Mediterranean

*Comfortable dining above Sheikh Zayed Road*
At Home overlooks the bustle of Sheikh Zayed Road, and you can gaze out at the traffic from a comfy armchair while perusing the decent-sized wine list.
**Four Points by Sheraton Sheikh Zayed Road**
Trade Centre **04 354 3333**
www.starwoodhotels.com/fourpoints
Map **2 G5** Metro **Financial Centre**

## Atrium Café
Cafe

*Sandwich sophistication, great for business lunches*
Offering the best in business cafe sophistication, with its leather seats, international newspapers and beautifully presented cake and sandwich counter, this cafe is a good choice for breakfast or lunch.
**JW Marriott Hotel** Deira **04 607 7009**
www.marriottdiningatjw.ae
Map **2 P5** Metro **Abu Baker Al Siddque**

## Automatic
Arabic/Lebanese

*Fresh, tasty Arabic delights in a casual setting*
This popular chain continues to serve high quality Arabic food in various locations in Dubai. The vast range of mezze is accompanied by mountainous portions of salad, and grilled meat, fish and kebabs. The atmosphere is minimalist but clean and bright, with family friendly amenities and good service.
**Beach Centre** Jumeira **04 349 4888**
Map **2 G3** Metro **Financial Centre**

## Awafi Arabic Café
Arabic/Lebanese

*Poolside Arabic cuisine on the roof of the Marriott*
Situated around the Marriott's rooftop pool, you can enjoy top-quality Arabic food underneath the stars with traditional music soundtracking your evening. The menu includes the usual fare, with an ample selection of hot and cold mezze, grilled items, and dishes from the tandoor oven.
**JW Marriott Hotel** Deira **04 607 7009**
www.marriottdiningatjw.ae
Map **2 P5** Metro **Abu Baker Al Siddque**

## Awtar
Arabic/Lebanese

*Stylish Arabian decor and moreish mezze*
Gold-swathed booths and low lighting gives the feeling of opulent Arabic elegance at this Lebanese restaurant. The starters and desserts steal the show from the mains, so load up your plate from an appealing selection of well-presented mezze. A belly dancer makes an appearance after 22:00.
**Grand Hyatt Dubai** Umm Hurair **04 317 1234**
www.dubai.grand.hyatt.com
Map **2 L7** Metro **Healthcare City**

## az.u.r
Mediterranean

*Fresh, organic dining with a Marina view*
Az.u.r serves a cornucopia of wholesome high-end dishes using organic food wherever possible. It offers a range of hearty meat, fish and seafood dishes, fresh vegetables and even organic wine. The food is excellent with rich combinations of ingredients, and there's a great Marina view from the terrace.
**Dubai Marriott Harbour Hotel & Suites**
Dubai Marina **04 319 4000**
www.marriott.com
Map **1 L4** Metro **Dubai Marina**

# Let's Do Brunch

Al Mahara

Brunch may have been invented in the States, given kudos in New York, and be setting itself a place mat in the hipper centres of western Europe, but in this particular Middle Eastern city, it's a hobby, a social skill, a weekend institution. It's the calorific glue that holds the weekend together.

Far from the genteel image of croissants, scrambled eggs and good coffee over the day's newspapers, brunch in Dubai is synonymous with triumphantly eating your own body weight in food and washing it down with free-flowing champagne. And all for a set price. Having eaten and quaffed the entire day away, brunchers are renowned for then throwing themselves into misguided rampages around the city's nightspots, and suffering spirit-crushing hangovers the following morning. New arrivals are quickly asked whether they've been to a brunch yet, typically by an expat with more Dubai-years under their (loosened) belt, and a knowing glint in their eye.

So why is this gluttonous sport so popular in Dubai? This city's predominantly expat community probably has plenty to do with it. There are more work-hard, play-even-harder young singles looking to blow off steam and mingle, so Dubai has a more sociable culture than most. The fact that you boil alive if you venture outside for more than 10 minutes during at least three months of the year also helps keep people inside and ingesting at the weekends.

Whatever the reason, brunch has become quite the art form; one which diners master by flexing their (softening) stomach muscles at the masses of competitive, creative and uniquely reasonable deals available from the city's fleet of five-star hotels. Formerly purely a Friday fun-for-all, the pursuit is now spreading through the week, almost to the point where brunch becomes a round-the-clock way of living, rather than just a way of eating.

If you want to throw yourself in at the deep end and push your liver to its very limits, head to Waxy's (p.516) on a Friday or Saturday. Here, you can buy five drinks, a greasy breakfast buffet and carvery banquet (effectively lunch and dinner – 'linner'?), and a dignity bypass for a rock bottom price. Roll up at 17:00 on either day and you'll find brunch victims rocking out to Bruce Springsteen or clinging to the walls for mercy. Also contributing to brunch's bad name are Double Decker (p.509), which offers a similar deal, and Spice Island (p.495) – a place that boasts the booziest of brunch deals: Dhs.199 for absolutely all-you-can-eat (from British breakfast

Brunch. You might think the word is self-explanatory: a portmanteau of 'breakfast' and 'lunch' – a meal you have between the two more accepted dining anchors. If so, you clearly haven't lived in Dubai that long.

to Chinese, Japanese, Mexican and Arabic), and absolutely all-you-can-drink for less than a basketful at Choithram.

Once you've flaunted your daytime partying prowess, you might want to prove your worth when it comes to tackling sheer food volume and variety. The 12-hour Friday buffet option at JW Marriott is a killer. For one price you set up a base in either The Market Place (p.484), Hofbrauhaus (p.474), or Bamboo Lagoon (p.460), then pilfer as much as you like from the buffet available within each. You can even leave the hotel, have a nap, and return when your digestive system's partially recovered.

Then there's the other end of the brunching spectrum – namely, Spectrum on One (p.495). The deal at this Fairmont favourite epitomises Dubai's posh and pricey all-inclusive. For a higher fee you can feed on the entire world (from Japan to Europe via India), swig a champagne flute all afternoon, and feel slightly classier about your splurge than your Waxy-going counterparts might. Yalumba and Al Qasr are equally high-minded affairs.

Somewhere in the middle of this brunch-ometer lies a trove of average-priced bargains that take the feasting mission slightly less seriously, and are therefore ideal for a laidback meal with chums or a family outing. Glasshouse (p.473) is a subtly sophisticated example, with a la carte options rather than the standard buffet relay, while More (p.485) is ideal for a non-alcoholic brunch in the traditional sense: cakes, homemade breads,

Lotus One

coffee and pancakes (with salads, curries and sandwiches in there somewhere as well). The Cellar (p.466) and Carter's (p.508) are both child-friendly, offering smaller portions and a less alcohol-orientated atmosphere, while Legends (p.479) serves up a tasty view of the creek along with its munch fest. If you're sick and tired of mixing your dishes, there are plenty more cuisine-specific brunches to be tasted too, such as the self-explanatory Thai Kitchen (p.498) and Organic Foods & Café (p.392), and the deliciously Japanese Momotaro (p.485).

And so there it is. Brunching in Dubai is as big as football in the UK, sumo wrestling in Japan and basketball in the US. So raise your fork and join in.

# Restaurants & Cafes

## Bamboo Lagoon                                      Far Eastern
Grass-skirted singers and a brilliant buffet
Bamboo Lagoon's staggering range of exquisite fusion
cuisine demands a repeat visit. The bottomless buffet
with numerous stalls offers everything from sushi
to curries and grills, and an abundance of oriental
trappings dominate the decor. At 21:00 a band takes
to the stage and grass-skirted singers serenade diners
with Polynesian tunes and entertaining covers.
**JW Marriott Hotel** Deira **04 607 7009**
www.marriottdiningatjw.ae
Map **2 P5** Metro **Abu Baker Al Siddque**

## Barry's Bench                                        Mexican
Top quality Tex-Mex in large portions
Barry's Bench serves up Tex-Mex cuisine with views
of Bur Dubai and Dubai Museum. Its large portions
of Mexican-style breakfasts, fajitas, grills, burgers and
desserts can be enjoyed with a cerveza or one of its
fantastic margaritas. A fast-food version is in Times
Square's food court (04 341 8118).
**Arabian Courtyard Hotel & Spa** Bur Dubai
**04 351 6646**
www.jackberrys.com/barrysbench
Map **2 M3** Metro **Al Fahidi**

## Basta Art Café                                          Cafe
Atmospheric escape from the Bur Dubai bustle
This courtyard cafe and gallery offers quiet sanctuary
amid atmospheric Bastakiya. Sit on majlis-style cushions
or under a canopy while choosing from the healthy
dishes, each of which has a description of its vitamins,
minerals and calories. A sister outlet at Arabian Ranches
(04 362 6100) has a similarly rustic atmosphere.
**Bastakiya** Bur Dubai **04 353 5071**
Map **2 M3** Metro **Al Fahidi**

## Bastakiah Nights                              Arabic/Lebanese
Magical place celebrating local cuisine and culture
This spot offers a perfect amalgamation of great
location and delectable food.  Choose from the fixed
menus or various a la carte offerings – there's no alcohol
on the menu, but you'd be a fool to let that put you off.
**Bastakiya** Bur Dubai **04 353 7772**
Map **2 M3** Metro **Al Fahidi**

## Bateaux Dubai > p.461                        Dinner Cruise
More than just your average creek cruise
This sleek, glass-topped vessel offers three-course fine
dining from a varied international menu, with five-star
surroundings to match. Intimate lighting, with cosy
tables and splendid views of the city make for a top
pick for romance or a special tourist treat.
**Nr British Embassy** Al Hamriya **04 399 4994**
www.bateauxdubai.com
Map **2 M4** Metro **Khalid Bin Al Waleed**

## Beach Bar & Grill                                     Seafood
Seafood by the seashore for true romantics
Seafood lovers must make a trip to this opulent,
romantic beach bar. Terrace tables are candle-lit, and
the fresh fish is cooked simply but with style. Seafood
platters to share and surf and turf options are available
for people who simply can't pick just one dish.
**One&Only Royal Mirage** Al Sufouh **04 399 9999**
www.oneandonlyresorts.com
Map **1 M3** Metro **Nakheel**

## Beach House Cabana                            Latin American
Tapas and good times all the way
A good choice for a laidback evening spent with
friends. Casual seating, hot and cold tapas, hearty
mains, reasonable prices and a good cocktail selection
add to the convivial feel.
**Clubhouse Azraq, Shoreline Apartments**
 Palm Jumeirah **04 361 8856**
www.emiratesleisureretail.com
Map **2 A3** Metro **Al Quoz**

## Beachcombers                                        Far Eastern
Decadent Oriental cuisine in a memorable location
This breezy shack has an idyllic location right on the
beach with fantastic views of the Burj Al Arab. Expect
excellent far eastern buffets with live cooking stations
for stir-fries and noodles. The Peking duck, curry
hotpots and satay are highly recommended.
**The Jumeirah Beach Hotel** Umm Suqeim
**04 406 8999**
www.jumeirah.com
Map **1 S3** Metro **Mall of the Emirates**

## Bella Donna                                            Italian
Reasonably priced cuisine from a bygone era
Bella Donna has a vaguely 1920s feel. Its low-cost
Italian fare includes homemade pasta and classic
pizzas like the margarita or the more unusual
capricciosa (with a cooked egg and potatoes). There is
no kids menu but there is plenty to keep them happy.
**Mercato** Jumeira **04 344 7701**
www.binhendi.com
Map **2 F3** Metro **Financial Centre**

## Benihana                                              Japanese
Full-on food entertainment at its best
Knife-tossing, food-flipping chefs and live cooking
tables are Benihana's main attractions. Don't come
expecting to be blown away by exotic flavours –
Benihana does the basics very well and leaves the rest
to the entertainment factor. There are food specials
nearly every night of the week and reservations are
mandatory.
**Al Bustan Rotana** Garhoud **04 282 0000**
www.rotana.com
Map **2 N7** Metro **GGICO**

**bateaux dubai**
*A Unique Cruise Experience*

A MEMBER OF

JEBEL ALI INTERNATIONAL
HOTELS

# A Unique Dinner Cruise Experience

Discover the historic sights and modern architecture along Dubai Creek onboard the elegant and fully licensed Bateaux Dubai – a unique cruise experience which serves freshly prepared gourmet cuisine as part of its à la carte menu. The sleek design of this glass-enclosed air-conditioned vessel, personalised service and panoramic views, make a Bateaux Dubai cruise as inspiring as the city itself.

Time:        Bateaux Dubai cruises every evening from 8.30pm to 11pm.
             Also available for private breakfast, lunch and dinner charters.

Location:    Moored opposite the British Embassy in Bur Dubai.
             Nearby Khalid Bin Waleed (Burjuman) metro station.

For reservations, please call 04 399 4994 or visit **www.bateauxdubai.com**

## Restaurants & Cafes

Going Out

### Benjarong — Thai
Perfect Thai served in mediocre surroundings
The decor is in a regal Thai style, the food is deliciously
concocted and perfectly presented, but the
atmosphere is a little lacking. The menu is tempting
though, with classics and a few inventive twists, and if
you love Thai food you'll certainly enjoy it.
**Dusit Thani Dubai** Trade Centre **04 343 3333**
www.dusit.com
Map **2 G5** Metro **Financial Centre**

### Bento-Ya — Japanese
Quick, fresh and authentic bento on SZR
Bento-Ya's popularity with Dubai's Japanese expats
vouches for the authenticity of its fresh, good quality
maki, sushi and bento boxes. The teriyaki pan-fried
beef is particularly recommended. The compact,
double storey restaurant is well-priced and ideal for a
quick, casual bite.
**Al Kawakeb Bld** Trade Centre **04 343 0222**
Map **2 G5** Metro **Financial Centre**

### BiCE — Italian
Excellent cuisine, great wine and live music
With excellent food and a delightful atmosphere, BiCE
is hugely popular. A great mix of traditional Italian
comfort food and nouvelle cuisine is served in good-
sized portions, while an extensive wine list, 1930s art
deco furnishings and live piano music all complement
the fine fare.
**Hilton Jumeirah** Dubai Marina **04 399 1111**
www.hilton.com
Map **1 K3** Metro **Jumeirah Lakes Towers**

### Biella — Italian
Tasty Italian and a perfect shopping pit stop
An Italian staple in malls across town, put down your
shopping and tuck into tasty favourites served by
friendly staff. The extensive menu includes salads and
pasta, but the pizzas top the bill. The terrace at the
Wafi branch is a perfect spot to recharge on coffee
and cake.
**Wafi** Umm Hurair **04 324 4666**
www.waficitirestaurant.com
Map **2 L6** Metro **Healthcare City**

### Bistro Domino Restaurant & Bar — French
Reasonably priced fare in low-key surrounds
A hearty selection of dishes is served here that will
leave you warm, satisfied and wishing you where
tucking into your meal in a rustic chateau. The menu
is an authentic mix of typical French dishes (including
deliciously buttery escargot) and fabulously rich
desserts.
**Novotel Deira City Centre** Port Saeed **04 292 5200**
Map **2 N6** Metro **Deira City Centre**

Blue Elephant

### Bistro Madeleine — French
Reasonably priced fare in laidback surroundings
Bistro Madeline's tasty French cuisine offers a more
down-to-earth alternative to the InterContinental's
high-end Reflets Par Pierre. The menu includes well-
cooked, understated meals and a good selection of
fresh bread, pastries and desserts.
**InterContinental Dubai Festival City**
Festival City **04 701 1111**
www.intercontinental.com/dubai
Map **2 M8** Metro **Jaddaf**

### Blades — Asian
Fine dining but child-friendly too, a parent's dream
Delicious Asian noodles, steaks and tasting platters
feature prominently in this fine-dining eatery that
also welcomes children with a healthy kids' menu and
colouring books. Excellent service for all ages and not
a chicken nugget or plastic toy in sight.
**Al Badia Golf Club** Festival City **04 601 0101**
www.albadiagolfclub.ae
Map **2 M9** Metro **Creek**

### Blue Elephant — Thai
Jungle Book interior and plenty of tasty Thai
Bringing the outdoors indoors, Blue Elephant is a lush
space of greenery, bamboo and waterfalls. The buffet
nights on Mondays, Tuesdays, Thursday and Saturdays
offer the chance to sample spring rolls, prawn
crackers, fragrant curries, spicy salads and delicate rice
dishes while enjoying unlimited beer, house wines
and soft drinks.
**Al Bustan Rotana** Garhoud **04 282 0000**
www.rotana.com
Map **2 N7** Metro **GGICO**

### Blue Orange · International
Food from all around the world, around the clock
A lively open kitchen serves up breakfast, lunch and dinner at this 24 hour hotel restaurant. The menu is international: choose from dishes such as Japanese sushi, Arabic mezze, Chinese dim sum and Belgian waffles. Family friendly and reasonably priced.
**The Westin Dubai Mina Seyahi Beach Resort & Marina** Al Sufouh **04 399 4141**
www.starwoodhotels.com
Map **1 M3** Metro **Nakheel**

### Bluefields Caribbean Restaurant · Caribbean
A modest spot to enjoy down-to-earth food
The Caribbean menu served here features a mix of curries, rice and grilled meat that is wholly satisfying and deliciously seasoned. While the casual atmosphere encourages you to enjoy a leisurely meal, the service may be a little slower than you'd like.
Oud Metha **04 335 7377**
Map **2 K5** Metro **Oud Metha**

### The Boardwalk · International
Fine menu in a prime location
Overlooking the creek, on wooden stilts, Boardwalk's close-up views of the water are unmatched. The menu features an array of generous and well-presented starters and mains including seafood and vegetarian options. The restaurant doesn't take reservations but you can grab a drink at QD's (p.514) while you wait.
**Creek Golf Club** Deira **04 295 6000**
www.dubaigolf.com
Map **2 N6** Metro **GGICO**

### The Bombay · Indian
A casual spot to enjoy tasty fare
An unassuming restaurant that packs quite a punch, the Bombay is a favourite destination for Indian food lovers in the know. Dishes are well-priced, generous and among the best in the city, and the atmosphere lends itself to a convivial night out with friends.
**Marco Polo Hotel** Hor Al Anz **04 272 0000**
www.marcopolohotel.net
Map **2 P4** Metro **Salahudin**

### Brauhaus · German
Beers, bratwurst and Bavaria abound at Brauhaus
Join German expats and those seeking well-cooked, authentic Bavarian food in this informal restaurant. The sought after semi-private booths are the choice spot to enjoy substantial portions of well-cooked schnitzels, bratwursts and sauerkraut. Top it off with the selection of imported German beers.
**Jumeira Rotana** Satwa **04 345 5888**
www.rotana.com
Map **2 J3** Metro **Al Jafiliya**

### Bussola · Italian
Beachside pizza and cocktails under the stars
Adventurous, delicious Sicilian-influenced pizzas served alfresco on a terrace by the sea – Arabia doesn't get much more Mediterranean than this. Upstairs the open-air deck offers a relaxed atmosphere, with more formality and a fuller menu downstairs. The desserts are excellent whatever floor you're on.
**The Westin Dubai Mina Seyahi Beach Resort & Marina** Al Sufouh **04 399 4141**
www.starwoodhotels.com/westin
Map **1 M3** Metro **Nakheel**

### Butcher Shop & Grill · Steakhouse
White aprons slicing prime cuts to go or eat in
Despite its mall location this unique meat lovers restaurant has a traditional butchers stocking the best in Australian cuts. You can also savour some surprisingly good vegetarian dishes and diet-destroying desserts. Also on The Walk, JBR.
**Mall of the Emirates** Al Barsha **04 347 1167**
Map **1 R5** Metro **Mall of the Emirates**

### Cactus Cantina · Tex Mex
Burritos, margaritas and potential for a great night
The portions here are muy grande, with the emphasis leaning more toward the Tex than the Mex (refried beans and melted cheese with everything). The lively atmosphere is aided by a pumping soundtrack and energetic staff. Weekends see the joint jumping, with crowds attracted by meal deals and generous jugs of margaritas.
**Rydges Plaza Hotel** Satwa **04 398 2274**
www.cactuscantinadubai.com
Map **2 J4** Metro **Al Jafiliya**

The Boardwalk

# Restaurants & Cafes

## Cafe Arabesque · Arabic/Lebanese
Excellent Arabic in romantic, creekside surrounds
Whether you go buffet or a la carte, linger over a cold mezze spread, succulent wood-fired kebabs and fantastic Lebanese, Syrian and Jordanian dishes, as you take in marvellous views of the creek. With romantic, soft lighting, the perfect evening awaits – finished with a stroll along the creek.
**Park Hyatt Dubai** Deira **04 602 1234**
www.dubai.park.hyatt.com
Map **2 M6** Metro **GGICO**

## Café Ceramique · Cafe
Typical cafe treats in a creative setting
Reserve this cafe for when you, or the kids, need to release your creativity. Turn up, choose an item and decorate it using the paints and stencils – it will then be glazed for collection at a later date. The menu has a good choice of light snacks, kids choices and hot and cold drinks. It's also a popular choice for kids parties with special birthday menus. There's another branch in Mall of the Emirates (04 341 0144).
**Town Centre Jumeirah** Jumeira **04 344 7331**
www.cafe-ceramique.com
Map **2 F3** Metro **Burj Dubai**

## Café Chic · French
More of a great restaurant than a chic cafe
With dishes such as lamb rack with parmesan polenta, black olive and citrus essence, this is more than your average cafe. Add to that faultless service, a parade of beautifully presented amuses bouches, and an outstanding dessert selection, and Café Chic really is a gem of a restaurant.
**Le Meridien Dubai** Garhoud **04 282 4040**
www.lemeridien-dubai.com
Map **2 N7** Metro **GGICO**

Café Ceramique

## Café Havana · Cafe
A step up from standard mall foodcourt offerings
Dotted all over Dubai, including branches in Deira City Centre (04 295 5238) and Ibn Battuta (04 366 9923), this chain offers consistently good cafe-style food with a Middle Eastern twist. Quality is high, prices reasonable and the service spot on.
**Spinneys** Umm Suqeim **04 394 1727**
www.binhendi.com
Map **2 B4** Metro **Al Quoz**

## Carluccio's · Italian
Stylish venue with super fountain and Burj views
From the chalked-up specials board to the shelves laden with cookery books and deli produce, Carluccio's is a family-friendly slice of Europe. The high ceilings and modern white interior and alfresco dining are stylish modern rather than cosy trattoria, while the terrace has great views of Dubai Fountain.
**The Dubai Mall** Downtown Burj Dubai **04 434 1320**
www.carluccios.com
Map **2 F6** Metro **Burj Dubai**

## Carnevale · Italian
Family friendly Italian in the shadow of the Burj
Carnevale offers upmarket Italian food, swift service and views of the Burj Al Arab from the adjoining indoor terrace. Despite its exclusive, Venetian-themed interior, families and children are well catered for.
**The Jumeirah Beach Hotel** Umm Suqeim
**04 406 8999**
www.jumeirah.com
Map **1 S3** Metro **Mall of the Emirates**

## Casa Mia · Italian
Well-prepared Italian fare and a massive wine list
A quality restaurant, the standard Italian menu is nothing if not consistent, and the temperature-controlled wine cellar holds more than 400 Italian wines. Portions are generous, and most of the dishes are available either as a main or a side, allowing you to broaden your selection.
**Le Meridien Dubai** Garhoud **04 282 4040**
www.lemeridien-dubai.com
Map **2 N7** Metro **GGICO**

## Cascades · International
Decent dining in a venue you'll fall for
Tumbling water features dominate the Fairmont's breathtaking lobby where this international restaurant serves dishes to suit every palate and devilishly tempting desserts to finish. Head here for a trendy dinner, business lunch, extended brunch or an indulgent cocktail while elevator watching.
**Fairmont Dubai** Trade Centre **04 332 5555**
www.fairmont.com
Map **2 J4** Metro **Trade Centre**

Asado

Al Muntaha

Arz Lebanon

Chandelier

Asha's

## Restaurants & Cafes

### Celebrities                    International
Well crafted European dishes in a romantic setting
This elegant restaurant offers romantic views of softly
lit gardens from tables peppered with rose petals and
iridescent stones. The well-priced European menu
contains dainty but filling dishes such as sea-bass
and baked rack of lamb, or try the tasting menu for
Dhs.245.
**One&Only Royal Mirage** Al Sufouh **04 399 9999**
www.oneandonlyroyalmirage.com
Map **1 M3** Metro **Nakheel**

### The Cellar > p.467              International
Lively but elegant, simple but sophisticated
The Cellar offers lovely dining among soaring arches,
stained glass and soft gauze curtains. The international
menu features favourites and innovations, with wine
bargains on Saturday and Sunday evenings. The
relaxed outside space has just a hint of the raucous
Irish Village next door.
**The Aviation Club** Garhoud **04 282 9333**
www.aviationclub.ae
Map **2 N7** Metro **GGICO**

### Certo                               Italian
Impressive menu with an eye-catching wine cellar
Certo's tasty, creative menu and floor-to-ceiling, glass
encased wine cellar bring to life what would otherwise

The Cellar

be a fairly non-descript business hotel restaurant.
Excellent starters and mains combine with good,
attentive service to make this one of the best Italians
in the area.
**Radisson Blu Hotel, Dubai Media City** Al Sufouh
**04 366 9111**
www.radissonblu.com
Map **1 M4** Metro **Nakheel**

### Chalet                          International
Firm favourite of residents and tourists alike
Clean, modern and compact, this Beach Road eatery
offers a culinary world tour with Chinese noodles
and Indian curries, but the main draws are the sturdy
Arabic offerings. Expect a clientele as eclectic as the
menu but beware the unisex toilet.
**Jumeira Rd, Nr Jumeirah Beach Hotel** Jumeira
**04 348 6089**
Map **1 T3** Metro **Mall of the Emirates**

### Chandelier                 Arabic/Lebanese
Great outdoor venue, good food and shisha
Set in the lively Marina Walk, Chandelier has a modern
interior and a great outdoor section overlooking the
marina. The service is leisurely, but with an interesting
mix of fare and a full range of mocktails and juices
served no one really cares.
**Marina Walk** Dubai Marina **04 366 3606**
Map **1 L4** Metro **Dubai Marina**

### Chef Lanka                      Sri Lankan
Dubai's best place to try Sri Lankan cuisine
This is a smart, clean, little Sri Lankan restaurant
offering good value and tasty food. Eat from the buffet
for just Dhs.8 at lunch and Dhs.20 at dinner, or order a
la carte for authentic dishes modified to your desired
level of spiciness.
**Opp Lulu Supermarket** Karama **04 335 3050**
Map **2 L5** Metro **Karama**

### Chef's House                  International
Eat your way around Asia in Media City
Choose from a range of south-east Asian, Indian and
Middle Eastern a la carte dishes, while various themed
buffet nights and a Saturday brunch provide all-you-
can-eat options. The decor is contemporary, with an
open kitchen, and fans of exotic ice cream will be in
their element.
**Radisson Blu Hotel, Dubai Media City** Al Sufouh
**04 366 9111**
www.radissonblu.com
Map **1 M4** Metro **Nakheel**

### Chili's                          American
Burgers, ribs and paraphernalia a-plenty
Around the world and all over Dubai, Chili's delivers
its winning formula for inexpensive, all-American

...delightfully delectable gastronomy

Saturday Brunch. Wine Evenings. Friday Brunch.
Contact Chris at 04 282 9333

The Aviation Club - P.O.Box 55400, Dubai, U.A.E - Tel. 04 282 4122 - Fax. 04 282 4751 - www.aviationclub.ae

tucker in huge portions and in family-friendly surrounds. Takeaway and home delivery (04 282 8303) are also available.
**Saleh Bin Lahej Bld** Garhoud **04 282 8484**
www.chilis.com
Map **2 N6** Metro **GGICO**

## Chimes Far Eastern
*Asian eatery that lures the locals*
The minimal decor emits a delicious aroma that entices local residents in from outside, while visitors from further afield will be pleasantly surprised by its well-cooked curries, seafood, noodles and fried rice. If you're after substance rather than flair, you'll be more than happy with its delicious Singapore pepper mud crab, Thai green curry and nasi goreng.
**Seven Sands Hotel Apartments** Al Barsha
**04 323 4211** www.chimesdubai.com
Map **2 R5** Metro **Mall of the Emirates**

## The China Club > *p.239* Chinese
*A tucked-away place to duck in for Peking duck*
A chic space with subtle touches of authenticity, The China Club serves a mix of recognisable favourites and new creations. The Peking duck, carved at the table, is recommended. Lunchtimes boast a Dhs.95 tasting menu, while Friday brunch for Dhs.140 (excluding alcohol) is great value.
**Radisson Blu Hotel, Dubai Deira Creek**
Al Rigga **04 222 7171**
www.radissonblu.com
Map **2 N4** Metro **Union**

## China Sea Chinese
*A hidden gem with oceans of authenticity*
Head to China Sea for traditional Chinese food at reasonable prices. The fresh noodles are recommended but the crab tanks and open kitchen make it a great venue for watching as much as for eating. Private karaoke rooms are available.
**Al Maktoum Rd** Deira **04 295 9816**
Map **2 N5** Metro **Deira City Centre**

## China Times Chinese
*Affordable Asian treats, in a tranquil atmosphere*
This restaurant brings you closer to China with its soothing music, water statues and flashes of red and black. Its tempting sushi bar is only a small part of the menu, which packs an assortment of dim sum, stir-frys, and noodles. Also located at Jumeirah Plaza (04 344 2930).
**Deira City Centre** Deira **04 295 2515**
www.binhendi.com
Map **2 N6** Metro **Deira City Centre**

## Choices International
*Elegant eat all you can venue – stuff yourself in style*
The comfortable and elegant dining areas at this all-day dining restaurant host a differently themed buffet each night of the week, including Shanghai, French, Mexican, seafood and international. Unlimited beer, wine and soft drinks are included in the price, and breakfast and lunch buffets are also served.
**Al Bustan Rotana** Garhoud **04 282 0000**
www.rotana.com
Map **2 N7** Metro **GGICO**

## Circle Cafe
*The perfect venue to meet up for a girlie gossip*
Light, bright and gloriously feminine, the decor at Circle suits its menu of bagels, salads, smoothies and puddings. Walls are lined with mirrors and quirky photos, dishes include smoked salmon and cream cheese or salads with goat's cheese, pumpkin and pine nut, and there's even a resident goldfish.
**Jumeirah Beach Plaza, opp Jumeira Beach Park**
Jumeira **04 342 8177**
www.circlebagels.com
Map **1 S3** Metro **Mall of the Emirates**

## Coconut Grove Indian
*Fairly priced and perfect for a casual curry*
The slightly surly service doesn't deter patrons who return to this modestly decorated restaurant located in the heart of Satwa for its excellent Goan and Sri Lankan delicacies such as the kingfish curry. If you're planning a night in Aussie Legends you might find yourselves in here after.
**Rydges Plaza Hotel** Satwa **04 398 3800**
www.rydges.com
Map **2 J4** Metro **Al Jafiliya**

The China Club

## Conservatory — International
A relaxing oasis at any time of day
Uncomplicated and reasonably priced, this buffet restaurant features European, Arabic and Asian flavours. Choose between the airy but stylish indoors and the atmospheric outdoor courtyard. Mound your plate with tasty morsels but remember to save room for the delicious desserts.
**Al Manzil Hotel** Downtown Burj Dubai **04 428 5888**
www.almanzilhotel.com
Map **2 F6** Metro **Burj Dubai**

## Counter Culture — Cafe
Homely deli fare, available around the clock
Deli delights lie within this gem which features relaxing leather chairs, wooden shelves and a contemporary colour scheme. Counter Culture serves up fresh bread baked on the premises (you can watch), daily hot and cold specials, huge salads, chunky sandwiches and homemade icecream. Licensed and open 24 hours.
**Dubai Marriott Harbour Hotel & Suites**
Dubai Marina **04 319 4000**
www.marriott.com
Map **1 L4** Metro **Dubai Marina**

## The Courtyard — Arabic/Lebanese
Atmospheric restaurant serving tasty Arabic treats
A typical selection of hot and cold mezzes, soups and mixed grills are served in this licensed, outdoor restaurant. Five items from the mezze menu cost Dhs.90 or individual portions can be ordered for Dhs.18 each. A broad a la carte menu is also available if you fancy poultry, fish or steak.
**Al Manzil Hotel** Downtown Burj Dubai **04 428 5888**
www.almanzilhotel.com
Map **2 F6** Metro **Burj Dubai**

## Creekside — Japanese
All you can eat in a modern wood and glass setting
One of the best Japanese restaurants in the city, Creekside now runs 'theme nights' every night of the week. In other words, it has become an all-you-can-eat paradise. The restaurant's clean lines and bright interior make a great setting for large groups, and the food, though limited in variety, far exceeds the buffet norm.
**Sheraton Hotel & Towers** Deira **04 207 1410**
www.starwoodhotels.com
Map **2 M4** Metro **Union**

## Creekside Leisure — Dinner Cruise
A relaxing way to enjoy a meal along the creek
This authentic dhow has a delightful upper deck where guests relax with a drink and enjoy the view. Downstairs, the good international buffet (with an Arabic slant) is served halfway through the two-hour

cruise which drifts to Shindagha, then Maktoum Bridge, and finally back to its mooring by the Twin Towers in Deira.
**Opp Dubai Municipality HQ** Deira **04 336 8407**
www.tour-dubai.com
Map **2 N4** Metro **Union**

## Cubo Pasta — Italian
Busy eatery for hungry conference delegates
Cubo Pasta dishes up serviceable Italian fare to hungry Trade Centre conference goers. There's pizza, secondi and pasta, but the innovative antipasti is the highlight. Wednesdays and Thursdays feature a good value all-you-can-eat-and-drink buffet. It can get cramped so arrive early for lunch.
**Ibis World Trade Centre** Trade Centre **04 332 4444**
www.ibishotel.com
Map **2 H5** Metro **Trade Centre**

## Cucina — Italian
Great pizza and pasta in faux-Tuscan surroundings
A solidly traditional menu and a reasonably priced wine list make up for the faux-rural Tuscan decor. The pizzas are great and the pasta dishes are good Italian staples. Be sure to get there in time for the staff's renditions of Italian tunes.
**JW Marriott Hotel** Deira **04 607 7009**
www.marriottdiningatjw.ae
Map **2 P5** Metro **Abu Baker Al Siddque**

## Da Shi Dai — Chinese
Contemporary design and dim sum delights
Enjoy the 'lighter side of Chinese dining' with fresh and delicately arranged dishes like crystal prawns, kung po chicken and a selection for vegetarians. Alfresco dining, reasonable prices and a fast, friendly service guarantee return visits. Also at Jumeirah Beach Residence (04 426 4636).
**Uptown Mirdif Mall** Mirdif **04 288 8314**
www.da-shi-dai.ae
Map **2 Q12** Metro **Rashidiya**

## Da Vinci's — Italian
Reliable food and novel decor
This rustic trattoria features wholesome decor, with checked tablecloths and even a dummy pianist. The food is reliably hearty and straightforward; there are three-course lunch deals and early evening discounts, and the drinks are affordable.
**Millennium Airport Hotel** **04 282 3464**
www.millenniumhotels.com
Map **2 N7** Metro **GGICO**

## Der Keller — German
Der Keller ist sehr gut for German fare
From pretzels to schnitzels, frankfurters to fondue, the popular Der Keller delivers fine German cuisine and

beer in a cosy pseudo-subterranean setting with a Burj view. Try to resist the fresh bread as the starters are as big as mains and the mains bigger than Austria.
**The Jumeirah Beach Hotel** Umm Suqeim **04 406 8999**
www.jumeirah.com
Map **1 S3** Metro **Mall of the Emirates**

### The Dhow                                      Seafood
Romantic venue that will float your boat
The gentle sway of this softly lit restaurant moored off the shore encourages you to take your time over a menu offering a broad range of seafood; try the large seafood platter with lobster or the fresh sushi. Although pricey, it's perfect for a relaxed, romantic evening.
**Le Meridien Mina** Al Sufouh **04 399 3333**
www.lemeridien-minaseyahi.com
Map **1 M3** Metro **Dubai Marina**

### Ding Xiu Xuan                                  Chinese
Tasty Chinese cuisine that transcends the norm
If you want to stay within the confines of standard Chinese dishes then you'll miss out on the eclectic range offered here. The pleasant surrounds provide a casual spot for patrons to enjoy a full menu of typical treats or fresh deviations, like cold jellyfish and bean soup dessert.
**Al Khaleej Palace Hotel** Deira **04 223 1000**
Map **2 N4** Metro **Al Rigga**

### Don Corleone                                    Italian
Decent but dated; more grandfather than Godfather
With its red and white table cloths and plastic vines, Don Corleone may not have reached kitschdom yet, but it's not far away. Excellent home-made pasta dishes make up for the dated style, and the al fresco area retains a certain cheesy holiday charm.
**Metropolitan** Downtown Burj Dubai **04 343 0000**
www.habtoorhotels.com
Map **2 D5** Metro **Business Bay**

### Dynasty                                         Chinese
Chinese that's good enough but doesn't dazzle
A mix of Szechuan, Cantonese and Peking dishes allow diners to explore China's culinary landscape. A choice of set menus let novices experiment without committing to the comprehensive a la carte menu. Ultimately, the food and service doesn't match the superior setting.
**Ramada Hotel** Bur Dubai **04 506 1148**
www.ramadadubai.com
Map **2 L4** Metro **Khalid Bin Al Waleed**

### Eauzone                                     Far Eastern
Stylish place for teppanyaki and sake
Dine beneath softly lit canopies overlooking a network of waterways for a truly romantic meal. The

Thai and Japanese fusion dishes are best accompanied by an unusual sorbet such as chilli and raspberry, or some sake. Groups should try the teppanyaki station, from Dhs.225 per head.
**One&Only Royal Mirage** Al Sufouh **04 399 9999**
www.oneandonlyresorts.com
Map **1 M3** Metro **Nakheel**

### The Edge                                  International
Modern food, stylish interior, plastic-melting prices
Every detail in this stylish restaurant has been deliberated to ensure a professional reception. Settle into the ostentatious lounge area or red velvet-curtained dining area and choose your menu: it varies depending on available ingredients, with prices ranging from Dhs.400 to a crisp Dhs.1,200. The service is sharp and the food is pristinely presented.
**Dubai International Financial Centre (DIFC)** Trade Centre **04 363 7770**
www.theedge.ae
Map **2 G5** Metro **Trade Centre**

### El Malecon                                       Cuban
Salsa dancers, Cuban food and great drinks
Graffiti-covered turquoise walls and low lighting creates a sultry Cuban atmosphere that builds up during the evening, helped along by live music and Salsa dancers. Big windows overlook the glowing Dubai Marine lagoon, and Malecon's doors are constantly swinging, so it's a great place to start or end the night.
**Dubai Marine Beach** Jumeira **04 346 1111**
www.dxbmarine.com
Map **2 H3** Metro **Trade Centre**

### Elements                                          Cafe
Industrial art warehouse vibe in Wafi
Walls crammed with paintings give Elements the feel of an industrial art warehouse. Lunchtime is always busy thanks to the bargain three-course buffet, while the shisha terrace fills up in the evenings as diners dig into sushi, tapas to pasta and Arabic dishes.
**Wafi** Umm Hurair **04 324 4252**
www.wafi.com
Map **2 L6** Metro **Healthcare City**

### Elia                                              Greek
Great Greek treats packed with flavour
Sit inside the slightly over-airconditioned dining area or better, out on the terrace, which manages to be serene despite looking out over Bur Dubai. The selection of Greek dishes are served with zesty olive oils, fluffy breads and include succulent meatballs and moreish dolma.
**Majestic Hotel Tower** Bur Dubai **04 359 8888**
www.dubaimajestic.com
Metro **Karama**

### Entre Nous
**International**

Short on character but excellent value buffet

The restaurant has few distinguishing features, but excels with its value-for-money themed buffets. Fill your plate everyday with tasty, high-quality fare from Dhs.129. The atmosphere is businesslike, but if you're in the neighbourhood, Entre Nous puts on a great spread.
**Novotel World Trade Centre** Trade Centre
**04 332 0000**
www.novotel.com
Map **2 H5** Metro **Trade Centre**

### Entrecôte Café de Paris
**French**

Like steak? Come here. Don't like steak? Move along

Steak-frites is the only order of the day here; diners must simply decide on the grade and age of the steak, which comes bathed in a secret recipe sauce. Tokenistic lampshades and chandeliers, plus a waterfall muffling the shoppers' hum, mean you can almost forget you're in a mall.
**The Dubai Mall** Downtown Burj Dubai **04 434 0122**
www.ghospitality.ae
Map **2 F6** Metro **Burj Dubai**

### Epicure
**Cafe**

Gourmet deli that focuses on freshness

This licensed gourmet deli serves freshly baked bread, fruit compotes, and a range of cooked breakfasts while you gaze out over the Desert Palm's swimming pool and polo fields. The staff take their time with the service, which makes it perfect for lunchtime lounging. A delicious range of lunch dishes and light snacks are also available, along with excellent juices and hot drinks.
**Desert Palm Dubai 04 323 8888**
www.desertpalm.ae
Map **2 C3**

### Esca
**Italian**

Good value international and Italian buffet fare

Esca has a sharp, designer atmosphere, with a huge metallic oven behind the live cooking station. Food is buffet style, with international offerings for breakfast and lunch, while dinner has an Italian theme. The evening buffet costs Dhs.149, excluding drinks. Outdoor dining is available.
**Qamardeen Hotel** Downtown Burj Dubai
**04 428 6888**
www.qamardeenhotel.com
Map **2 F6** Metro **Burj Dubai**

### ET Sushi
**Japanese**

Great pre-karaoke sushi venue

A buzzy sushi restaurant serving dishes around a conveyor belt, with busy chefs slicing delicate morsels of fish. The sister restaurant of tokyo@thetowers (p.498), it also does grilled, fried and cold dishes and excellent desserts.
**Boulevard at Emirates Towers** Trade Centre
**04 319 8088**
www.jumeirah.com
Map **2 H5** Metro **Emirates Towers**

### Ewaan
**Arabic/Lebanese**

The most archetypical Dubai shisha joint in town

Surrounding the palm-lined pool in the Arabian-themed Palace Hotel, the private cabanas at this shisha joint sit directly beneath the towering Burj Dubai. Customers can stretch out on Arabic seating while a musician plays the oud and attentive staff serve up shisha and tasty mezze.
**The Palace – The Old Town** Downtown Burj Dubai
**04 428 7951**
www.theaddress.com
Map **2 F6** Metro **Burj Dubai**

El Malecon

### The Exchange Grill — Steakhouse

A treat for meat lovers and fans of fine dining
Exchange Grill is the epitome of excess with outsized
leather armchairs, modern art installations and a
floor-to-ceiling chandelier. The menu strikes a balance
between the classic and the innovative, and both
lunch and dinner menus offer the best quality beef.
**Fairmont Dubai** Trade Centre **04 332 5555**
www.fairmont.com
Map **2 J4** Metro **Trade Centre**

### FAI — Thai

Posh surrounds and a pleasing menu
Book early and enjoy your meal on the veranda of
this stylish restaurant and you'll be afforded a view
of the Burj lake and the fantastic fountain show. As
you'd expect from a Palace eatery, the Thai dishes are
packed with flavour and artfully presented.
**The Palace – The Old Town** Downtown Burj Dubai **04
428 7961**
www.theaddress.com
Map **2 F6** Metro **Burj Dubai**

### Fakhreldine — Arabic/Lebanese

Get your glad rags on for some stylish Lebanese
From your first dip into the creamy hummus to the
last crumb of Arabic sweets, the quality is apparent
and the bill isn't too painful. Choose from rarer Arabic
dishes and old favourites as you watch the gyrating
belly dancer.
**Mövenpick Hotel Bur Dubai** Oud Metha **04 336 6000**
www.moevenpick-hotels.com
Map **2 K6** Metro **Oud Metha**

### Fazaris — International

Varied menu and a romantic Burj view setting
With 12 pages of mouth-watering dishes from Japan,
south-east Asia, India, Arabia and the Mediterranean,
this is a menu that tries to cater for everyone. Inside is
cavernous and bright, while outside is more romantic,
with views of The Palace hotel and the Burj Dubai.
**The Address Downtown Burj Dubai** Downtown Burj
Dubai **04 436 8888**
www.theaddress.com
Map **2 F6** Metro **Burj Dubai**

### Finz — Mediterranean

Cheerful seafood in Ibn Battuta's China Court
The open-to-the mall setting means Finz won't win
many romantic accolades, but come here if you want
to choose from an eclectic mix of Portuguese, Italian,
Spanish and South American fare. Seafood dominates
the menu, while the signature Espetada beef dish is
recommended. Unlicensed.
**Ibn Battuta Mall** Jebel Ali **04 368 5620**
Map **1 G4** Metro **Ibn Battuta**

Fakhreldine

### Fire & Ice – Raffles Grill — International

Extreme concept venue, not for the conservative
A conceptual restaurant offering unusual dishes from
two set menus: the seven-course Ice menu (Dhs.1,000)
features the likes of foie gras on a bed of popping
candy and crab cakes with a bubble bath-type
topping, while the Fire menu (Dhs.500) is a little tamer.
Each course comes with its own wine.
**Raffles Dubai** Wafi **04 314 9888**
www.dubai.raffles.com
Map **2 K6** Metro **Healthcare City**

### The Fish Market > p.239 — Seafood

Choose your seafood straight from the market stall
This novel restaurant lets diners pick raw ingredients
from a large bank of fresh, raw seafood and
vegetables. Choose anything from tiger prawns and
Omani lobster to red snapper, and then request your
cooking style preference. The food is not outstanding
but the concept is entertaining.
**Radisson Blu Hotel, Dubai Deira Creek** Al Rigga **04
222 7171**
www.radissonblu.com/hotel-dubaideiracreek
Map **2 N4** Metro **Union**

### Five Dining — International

Buffet delights and a lively atmosphere
This lively, relaxed venue has a well-chosen buffet
where the theme changes daily between favourites
that include seafood and pasta. The ambience is more
suitable for groups than romancing couples. Good
value for the mid-market price range.
**Jumeira Rotana** Satwa **04 345 5888**
www.rotana.com
Map **2 J3** Metro **Al Jafiliya**

## Flavours On Two
**International**

Dinner-brunch favourite with a new Flavour nightly
This stylish, busy 'dinner brunch' venue focuses on a
different global cuisine each night, including British
and Italian. The wide range of dishes includes cold
starters, hot grills and delicious desserts. Free-flowing
alcohol is included in the reasonable cover charge
(Dhs.169), or you can upgrade to champagne.
**Towers Rotana** Trade Centre **04 343 8000**
www.rotana.com
Map **2 G5** Metro **Financial Centre**

## Focaccia
**European**

Home-style decor and cooking in a casa setting
Book a table in the kitchen, library, dining room, or
cellar of this homely Italian, or catch a glimpse of the
sea from the terrace. Tasty pasta dishes dominate,
but save room for the delicious desserts. The brunch
option has a wider menu with Iranian options.
**Hyatt Regency** Deira **04 209 6704**
www.dubai.regency.hyatt.com
Map **2 N3** Metro **Palm Deira**

## Foodlands
**Indian**

High quality and low prices; a great independent
Among the many cheap and cheerful independent
restaurants in town, Foodlands deserves a special
mention thanks to the excellent quality and awesome
array of Indian, Persian and Arabic dishes. The window
into the kitchen will get your mouth suitably watering
before your fresh, sizzling meal arrives.
**Opp Ramada Continental Hotel** Hor Al Anz
**04 268 3311**
Map **2 Q5** Metro **Abu Hail**

## Frankie's
**Italian**

Jockey-owned joint that's no one-trick pony
Grab a vodka martini and pizza in the bar at this stylish
joint, co-owned by Frankie Dettori and Marco Pierre
White, then head into the main restaurant for Italian
classics and new favourites such as duck ravioli. With a
sultry interior, pianist and good Friday brunch, this is a
classy establishment.
**Al Fattan Towers** Dubai Marina **04 399 4311**
www.frankiesitalianbarandgrill.com
Map  Metro **Dubai Marina**

## French Connection
**Cafe**

Onsite bakery guarantees a great breakfast venue
Survey Sheikh Zayed Road as you relax in this cheerful
cafe. Expertly prepared coffee and freshly baked
pastries, breads and cakes top the menu which
also offers a full English breakfast, salads and tasty
sandwiches. Free Wi-Fi is available at this and the sister
branch behind Spinneys next to BurJuman.
**Wafa Tower** Trade Centre **04 343 8311**
Map **2 G5** Metro **Financial Centre**

## Gazebo
**Indian**

Indian food at its very best
Choosing from the vast menu is a challenge,
but whether you order from the charcoal grilled
specialities, mouth-watering curries and biryanis, fresh
salads, tasty breads or deliciously sweet lassis and
kulfis, you'll be served an authentic dish packed with
flavour. The elegantly clad staff are genuinely friendly
and the service is top notch. A great value Indian
experience.
**Nr Meena Plaza Hotel** Bur Dubai **04 359 8555**
Map **2 L4** Metro **Khalid Bin Al Waleed**

## Gerard's
**Cafe**

Jumeira institution that draws yummy mummies
The courtyard setting gives this popular coffee spot
its unique atmosphere and there's a good selection
of croissants, pastries and chocolate covered dates;
takeaway trade is brisk. Also at Al Ghurair City
(04 222 8637).
**Magrudys** Jumeira **04 344 3327**
Map **2 H3** Metro **Al Jafiliya**

## Glasshouse Brasserie
**International**

Sophisticated atmosphere, good food and prices
Managed by the team behind Gordon Ramsay's Verre,
Glasshouse is a chic brasserie serving up modern
Mediterranean cuisine at reasonable prices. It is a
good spot for a business lunch or a lively group dinner.
The interior is stylish – glass walls, dark woods and
tasteful colours – and they run drink deals during the
week. Check out the Monday Madness when drinks
are one dirham when having a two course meal.
**Hilton Creek** Deira **04 227 1111**
www.hilton.com
Map **2 N5** Metro **Union**

Glasshouse Brasserie

# Restaurants & Cafes

## Go West                                    American

Tex-Mex with a wild west twist

A well-priced menu includes the signature angus beef, which complements a big drinks menu. A band plays from 19:30 every night (except Sundays) so reserve a spot indoors or on the terrace if you fancy a dining experience with a Western twist.
**The Jumeirah Beach Hotel** Umm Suqeim
**04 406 8999**
www.jumeirah.com
Map **1 S3** Metro **Mall of the Emirates**

## Golf Academy                              International

Take the smooth with the rough at this golf cafe

A wide assortment of international appetisers, sandwiches, salads, main courses and beverages of all sorts is available in this snack bar overlooking Dubai Creek's golf course; a cheerful colour scheme fits in well with the view of luscious greens and happy golfers.
**Creek Golf & Yacht Club** Deira **04 205 4666**
www.dubaigolf.com
Map **2 N6** Metro **GGICO**

## Gourmet Burger Kitchen                     American

Burgers at their best

This popular chain serves up a winning formula – good juicy meat, fresh produce, a diverse choice of toppings and sauces, and hearty portions of fries in trendy canteen-style surrounds. The delivery service has saved many a hungry couch potato. See the website for other locations around Dubai.
**Uptown Mirdif** Mirdif **04 288 9057**
www.gbkinfo.com
Map **2 Q12** Metro **Rashidiya**

## Hakaya Cafe                                Arabic/Lebanese

Quirky late-night shisha spot

With seating on the first floor arranged around a huge plastic tree, this shisha cafe offers a diverse menu serving everything from steak to pizza and specialising in fruit juices and flavoured coffees. Go late for live Arabic music.
**Bank St, Nr York International** Bur Dubai
**04 352 8213**
Map **2 L3** Metro **Al Fahidi**

## Handi                                      Indian

Handi crafts a mean curry

An elaborate thali offers four curries and kebabs for Dhs.90, including biryani, salad, dessert and lassis. The lamb curry with cashew and cardamom is particularly good and biryani fans will love the individual copper pots sealed to keep the flavour in. Live music and private dining rooms add to the atmosphere.
**Taj Palace Hotel** Deira **04 223 2222**
www.tajpalacehotel.co.ae
Map **2 N5** Metro **Al Rigga**

## Haru Robatayaki                            Japanese

An authentic Japanese experience on The Walk

Hidden away on The Walk, Haru still draws a crowd for its fresh, delicious Japanese food and amazing grilled 'robatayaki' specialities. Bright lights, Japanese pop music and knowledgeable, friendly staff keep the feel upbeat. Also at Green Community (04 885 3897).
**The Walk, Jumeirah Beach Residence**
Dubai Marina **04 437 0134**
www.haru.ae
Map **1 K4** Metro **Dubai Marina**

## Hofbräuhaus                                German

Super sausages and strudels in this brauhaus

From the sauerkraut to the white sausage with sweet mustard and the strudel, everything is top notch. Add in the great German beer, Bavarian garb for the staff and accordion music, and you have a fun night out.
**JW Marriott Hotel** Deira **04 607 7977**
www.marriottdiningatjw.ae
Map **2 P5** Metro **Abu Baker Al Siddque**

## Hoi An                                     Vietnamese

Intimate, traditional Vietnamese with western twist

Compact and stately, Hoi An's teahouse-inspired space is perfect for exploring the exotic Vietnamese flavours that come out of the kitchen. Novices should opt for the set meal, in which each dish is explained by the well-informed staff.
**Shangri-La Hotel** Trade Centre **04 343 8888**
www.shangri-la.com
Map **2 G5** Metro **Financial Centre**

## Hukama                                     Chinese

A fresh and fancy eatery offering well-cooked fare

More fine dining Chinese than comforting carb-fest, this sophisticated eatery offers glorious views of Burj Dubai from its terrace, and a menu which consists of the usual and the unexpected (such as wontons on soy infused crushed ice).
**The Address Downtown Burj Dubai** Downtown Burj Dubai **04 436 8888**
www.theaddress.com
Map **2 F6** Metro **Burj Dubai**

## Hunters Room & Grill                       Steakhouse

Stylish surrounds and succulent dishes

A veritable meat feast is offered at this restaurant, so come prepared for the hearty portions of fine steaks from North America, Australia and Brazil. The meat is tender, the selection on offer is broad, and as you'd expect from The Westin, the restaurant has a fresh contemporary vibe.
**The Westin Dubai Mina Seyahi Beach Resort & Marina** Al Sufouh **04 399 4141**
www.westin.com/dubaiminaseyahi
Map **1 M3** Metro **Nakheel**

Hoi An

# Restaurants & Cafes

## Il Rustico — Italian
*Relaxed, unpretentious, with decent fare*
It may not be classy, but Il Rustico is the type of Italian restaurant that doesn't need a special occasion. The pasta, pizzas and salads are all freshly made on the premises, and the desserts taste as good as they look. The wine list won't disappoint either.
**Rydges Plaza Hotel** Satwa **04 398 2222**
www.rydges.com
Map **2 J4** Metro **Al Jafiliya**

## Indego — Indian
*Serves up one of Dubai's most upmarket curries*
Run by Vhineet Bhatia, the first Indian chef in over a century to win a Michelin star, it is little surprise to discover that this pricey restaurant elevates Indian cooking to art form. Its red velvet armchairs and tastefully restrained decor make this a fine dining restaurant with food you'll want to take away.
**Grosvenor House** Dubai Marina **04 399 8888**
www.grosvenorhouse.lemeridien.com
Map **1 L4** Metro **Dubai Marina**

## India Palace — Indian
*Mouth-watering food in atmospheric surrounds*
Surrounded by elaborately carved wood and strains of traditional sitar music, you'll be transported back to the Moghul Dynasty. Cosy booths and private dining rooms make for an intimate scene. The food is excellent and diners are spoilt for choice.
**Al Hudda Bld, Nr Al Tayer Motors** Garhoud
**04 286 9600**
www.sfcgroup.com
Map **2 N7** Metro **GGICO**

## Indochine — Vietnamese
*Exotic eastern flavours in a well-designed setting*
Choose from a blend of exotic Vietnamese, Thai, Cambodian and Laosian dishes, offering some exciting and unusual a la carte choices, especially the imaginative salads and expertly seasoned soups. The predominantly dark wood and bamboo decor complements the food well. Evenings only.
**Grand Hyatt Dubai** Umm Hurair **04 317 1234**
www.dubai.grand.hyatt.com
Map **2 L7** Metro **Healthcare City**

## Inferno Grill — International
*Varied menu and a Marina-view terrace*
With a terrace that offers a stunning night-time view of the marina, this is a perfect venue for a relaxing dinner. The reasonably-priced menu includes steaks, seafood, pizza and a variety of grilled Lebanese-style meats. If it's too hot to sit outside, the modern interior has live music.
**Marina Walk** Dubai Marina **04 343 7710**
Map **1 L4** Metro **Dubai Marina**

## Italian Connection — Italian
*Great family-run neighbourhood Italian*
A friendly cafe-restaurant, run by an Italian family with a flair for interior design, Italian Connection is colourful and fresh, just like the food. Freshly made pasta comes with tasty sauces and the pizzas are thin, crisp and delicious.
**Nr Lamcy Plaza** Oud Metha **04 335 3001**
Map **2 K5** Metro **Oud Metha**

## iZ — Indian
*Stylish setting for contemporary tandoori tapas*
IZ's dark, contemporary interior is beautifully designed, complete with hardwood screens, sculptures and private rooms. The perfectly prepared Indian dishes are presented tapas style, with tandoori items served by the piece – ideal for sampling several flavours. Expect gourmet Indian cuisine that respects tradition.
**Grand Hyatt Dubai** Umm Hurair **04 317 1234**
www.dubai.grand.hyatt.com
Map **2 L7** Metro **Healthcare City**

## Jaipur — Indian
*Northern Indian specialities to eat in or take out*
Familiar dishes sit alongside delicious specialities from Rajasthan and northern India, and the friendly sets a relaxing atmosphere. A busy delivery service means that the ingredients are always fresh, and an alfresco terrace offers great views of the mighty Burj Dubai.
**Burj Residences, Bld One** Downtown Burj Dubai
**04 422 6767**
www.theroyalorchid.com
Map **2 F5** Metro **Burj Dubai**

## Japengo Café — International
*Sushi, salads and sandwiches and a whole lot more*
A Japanese-western hybrid menu that impresses with top-notch food in a neon bright, minimalist setting. Other Locations include Ibn Battuta, Wafi Mall, Palm Strip, Souk Madinat Jumeirah and Dubai Festival City.
**Mall of the Emirates** Al Barsha **04 341 1671**
www.binhendi.com
Map **1 R5** Metro **Mall of the Emirates**

## Johnny Rockets — American
*Classic American diner that guarantees happy days*
This 1950s inspired American diner, with its classic decor and coin-operated jukeboxes, transforms a casual meal into a novelty experience. Fresh hamburgers, great shakes, reasonable prices, and impromptu outpourings of dance by friendly staff will brighten up anybody's evening. Other locations include Dubai Mall (04 434 1526) and Dubai Marina (04 368 2339).
**Juma al Majid Center** Jumeira **04 344 7859**
www.johnnyrockets.com
Map **2 G3** Metro **Burj Dubai**

### The Junction — International
Buffet delights in Deira
The Junction's speciality is the buffet, with breakfast and lunchtime deals at reasonable prices, while weekend evenings feature a themed buffet. Friday is seafood and the prawns are recommended, with numerous methods of cooking on offer including battered, barbecue and tandoori.
**Traders Hotel, Deira** Deira **04 265 9888**
www.shangri-la.com
Map **2 P5** Metro **Abu Baker Al Siddque**

### JW's Steakhouse — Steakhouse
Everything you'd expect from a good steakhouse
Chefs can be seen cleaving huge chunks of meat in the open kitchen of this steak restaurant. It's a good introduction to the meat and seafood you'll soon enjoy from your leather armchair. Salads are prepared fresh at your table and the simple and generous desserts are worth it.
**JW Marriott Hotel** Deira **04 607 7977**
www.marriottdiningatjw.ae
Map **2 P5** Metro **Abu Baker Al Siddque**

### Kabab-ji Grill — Arabic/Lebanese
So-so venue, so good food
Although the inoffensive decor and laminated menus scream 'chain' at this JBR joint, the food is excellent.

The service is fast, and the prices won't make you flinch. Its take on fatoush is incredible, one of the best in Dubai, and the grills are juicy and consistent, especially the veal.
**Rimal, The Walk, Jumeirah Beach Residence** Dubai Marina **04 437 0122**
www.kabab-ji.com
Map **1 K4** Metro **Dubai Marina**

### Kaleidoscope > p.ii-iii — Mediterranean
International cuisine in an airy Atlantis setting
Of the two buffet restaurants at Atlantis, this is the low-key option. A bright, sunny dining area draws in poolside crowds. A deli sandwich counter, a rustic Italian station, and offerings from Asia, India and Europe make this a well-rounded dining experience that is satisfying but not overwhelming.
**Atlantis The Palm** Palm Jumeirah **04 426 2626**
www.atlantisthepalm.com
Map **2 A3** Metro **Nakheel**

### Kan Zaman — Arabic/Lebanese
Enjoy traditional Emirati fare by the creek
Kan Zaman offers an excellent Arabic menu and a chance to try some local food. Traditional Emirati dishes include local breads served either with honey and dates or cheese. Portions are large and prices are low – perfect for sharing. Dine outdoors for great views of the creek.
**Heritage & Diving Village** Al Shindagha **04 393 9913**
www.alkoufa.com
Map **2 M3** Metro **Al Ghubaiba**

### Karachi Darbar — Pakistani
Perennial favourite for cheap, tasty, quality food
The simple decor, plain menus, and utilitarian settings may not pull visitors in off the street, but that's their loss. With Pakistani dishes on the menu, it offers a little something different to other restaurants from the subcontinent. There are several branches around old Dubai; this one offers outside dining.
**Karama Shopping Centre** Karama **04 334 7272**
Map **2 K5** Metro **Karama**

### Khan Murjan Restaurant — Arabic/Lebanese
Atmospheric, popular with a vibrant crowd
Located in the heart of the underground souk, the restaurant is set within in an open courtyard and offers a range of Arabic dishes from across the region. The traditional architecture creates a tranquil setting to fuel up before exploring the souk.
**Khan Murjan** Wafi Mall **04 324 4555**
www.wafi.com
Map **2 L6** Metro **Healthcare City**

Il Rustico

# Restaurants & Cafes

## Khazana                                      Indian
*Celebrated cuisine from this Indian celebrity chef*
Indian celebrity chef Sanjeev Kapoor's eatery
specialises in cuisine from north India. Try the grilled
tandoori seafood and gravy-based dishes, as well as
Anglo-Indian novelties like 'British raj railroad curry'.
**Al Nasr Leisureland** Oud Metha **04 336 0061**
www.sanjeevkapoorskhazanadubai.com
Map **2 L5** Metro **Oud Metha**

## Kiku                                         Japanese
*Japanese diners flock to this sushi-teppanyaki joint*
Kiku is regularly packed with Japanese guests. There
is a choice of dining areas, from the traditional private
tatami rooms to the teppanyaki bar, sushi counter and
regular tables. The menu is diverse, and particularly
worth trying are the set meals.
**Le Meridien Dubai** Garhoud **04 702 2703**
www.lemeridien-dubai.com
Map **2 N7** Metro **GGICO**

## Kisaku                                       Japanese
*Traditional Japanese in a unique setting*
A mix of dining settings, from sitting at the sushi bar
to chairs with no legs and standard tables for the
unadventurous, add to the Kisaku experience. With
celebrity chef Chitoshi Takahashi at the helm the food
is of a very high standard and the service impeccable.
**Al Khaleej Palace Hotel** Deira **04 223 1000**
www.ghospitality.ae
Map **2 N4** Metro **Union**

## The Kitchen                                  International
*International food cooked before your eyes*
The open kitchen is the centrepiece of this intimate
spot, which serves a mix of Thai, Lebanese and
European divided into styles of cooking – wok,

charcoal grill, wood burning oven and tandoor.
**Hyatt Regency** Deira **04 317 2222**
www.dubai.regency.hyatt.com
Map **2 N3** Metro **Palm Deira**

## Kitsune                                      Japanese
*Fancy venue with a touch of the wow factor*
Leather, polished gold trim and dark red florals make
this a surreal yet beautiful space. Pricey Japanese
favourites dominate the menu – black cod, wagyu
beef, sushi – and make this a perfect place to impress.
**Fairmont Dubai** Trade Centre **04 332 7660**
www.kitsunerestaurant.com
Map **2 J4** Metro **Trade Centre**

## La Baie                                      French
*Chic French fare by the sea*
This chic, expensive French restaurant specialises in
excellent fish dishes. Both the menu and the food is
captivatingly presented, and the wine list extensive
but expensive. The serene balcony offers pleasant sea
air or cigarettes depending on how the wind blows.
**The Ritz-Carlton, Dubai** Dubai Marina **04 399 4000**
www.ritzcarlton.com
Map **1 K3** Metro **Dubai Marina**

## La Maison d'Hôtes                            French
*Gourmet Français at a tres bien price*
The decor is Middle East meets Morocco, with its
covered terrace, chunky furniture and cushioned
benches, but in taste it's gourmet Français, and
reasonably priced at that. The menu is deliciously light
with foie gras, beef carpaccio and goats' cheese.
**Villa 18, Street 83B, beh Al Rabee Kindergarten**
Jumeira **04 344 1838**
www.lamaisondhotesdubai.com
Map **2 F3** Metro **Burj Dubai**

Kiku

Kitsune

## La Moda > p.239 — Italian
Simple Italian food in a lively setting
La Moda serves great Italian food, both unpretentious and generous in portion. The lively ambience and big tables make it perfect for an evening of pizza swapping with friends, while the small, pretty terrace is more romantic.
**Radisson Blu Hotel, Dubai Deira Creek** Al Rigga
**04 222 7171**
www.radissonblu.com/hotel-dubaideiracreek
Map **2 N4** Metro **Union**

## La Parrilla — Argentinean
Great steaks, worked off on a vibrant dancefloor
Well-known for its range of steaks in every conceivable cut and origin, La Parilla's live band entices diners away from their tables and onto the dance floor for a post-dinner tango. The vibe is pure Argentina and the decorative cart wheels and traditional wooden furniture only add to the charm.
**The Jumeirah Beach Hotel** Umm Suqeim
**04 406 8999**
www.jumeirah.com
Map **1 S3** Metro **Mall of the Emirates**

## La Veranda — Italian
Unpretentious fare that won't break the bank
This cosy restaurant serves large portions of inexpensive pizza, pasta and seafood alongside marina views. Children are well catered for with typical treats like burgers and fish fingers from the menu.
**The Jumeirah Beach Hotel** Umm Suqeim
**04 406 8999**
www.jumeirah.com
Map **1 S3** Metro **Mall of the Emirates**

## La Villa — Mediterranean
Good spot for a working lunch
Warm yellow walls enclose beautifully appointed tables with fresh flowers, under subtle lighting. The Business Lunch, served Saturday to Wednesday, is a hit with diners who can then round off their meal with a winning dessert and choice of satisfying beverages.
**City Centre** Port Saeed **04 294 1222**
www.pullmanshotels.com
Map **2 N6** Metro **Deira City Centre**

## Lan Kwai Fong — Chinese
Inexpensive and popular, so don't mind the decor
If you judge a good Chinese restaurant by the number of Chinese inside, then Lan Kwai Fong is worth exploring. Located between Lamcy Plaza and the Mövenpick Hotel, the restaurant's exhaustive menu includes a vast array of dim sum, clay pot, seafood, meat, duck and noodle dishes.
**Nr Lamcy Plaza** Oud Metha **04 335 3680**
Map **2 K5** Metro **Oud Metha**

## Latino House — Latin American
Smart and seductive South American restaurant
Latino House uses heavy drapes, marble decor and dim lighting to intoxicate before the food even appears. Succulent steaks, modernised classics and imaginative new creations make up the small but tempting menu. Surrender to the Latin vibe with dancing on Mondays.
**Al Murooj Rotana Hotel & Suites** Trade Centre
**04 321 1111**
www.rotana.com
Map **2 G5** Metro **Financial Centre**

## Le Classique — French
Country-club dining with pianist and dress code
Le Classique, the dining equivalent of championship golf at Emirates Golf Club, asks gentlemen to dress in coat and tie. Beginning with beverages in the handsome lounge, patrons move into the lavish country-club dining room. A pianist sings old standards, while the staff serve from a delicious menu.
**Emirates Golf Club** Emirates Hills **04 380 2222**
www.dubaigolf.com
Map **1 M4** Metro **Nakheel**

## Le Dune Pizzeria — Italian
Romantic desert dining, Italian style
Perfect for a romantic getaway, Pizzeria la Dune brings the smells and tastes of rustic Italy to the heart of the desert. The welcoming antipasti buffet offers a taste of everything but save room for the tiramisu trio.
**Bab Al Shams Desert Resort & Spa 04 809 6100**
www.jumeirah.com
Map **1 E2**

## Legends Steakhouse — Steakhouse
Luxury dining by the creek
Relaxing atmosphere, deep comfortable seats and good quality food that includes a range of steaks and seafood, accompanied by an extensive wine list. The decor is modern, with a ceiling that stretches right to the top of the distinctive white sails. Golfers enjoy the portion sizes.
**Dubai Creek Golf & Yacht Club** Deira **04 295 6000**
www.dubaigolf.com
Map **2 N6** Metro **GGICO**

## Lemongrass — Thai
A sound favourite with Thai lovers
One of the better – and cheapest – Thai restaurants in Dubai, the menu offers a typical range of decently executed Siamese dishes. There's no alcohol, but the fruit mocktails compensate. The setting is bright, inviting and comfortable, and the service unobtrusive. Also at Ibn Battuta Mall (04 368 5616).
**Nr Lamcy Plaza** Oud Metha **04 334 2325**
Map **2 K5** Metro **Oud Metha**

### Levantine > p.481                     Arabic/Lebanese

Lavish Lebanese, complete with belly dancer
With a very high ceiling and large sweeping red curtains, Levantine is a lavish affair. Indulge in a banquet of classic Lebanese dishes as you watch a talented belly dancer make her rounds. Finish your meal by sharing a shisha in the upstairs terrace bar with relaxed floor seating and views of Dubai.
**Atlantis The Palm** Palm Jumeirah **04 426 2626**
www.atlantisthepalm.com
Map **2 A3** Metro **Nakheel**

### The Lime Tree Café                              Cafe

Wholesome food in a relaxed setting; a classic
A Dubai institution whose food nods towards Mediterranean cuisine, with roast vegetables, halloumi cheese and roast chicken paninis, as well as delicious salads, satay kebabs and quiches. Don't leave without sharing an enormous slice of the superlative carrot cake. Good alfresco options too. Also at Ibn Batutta Mall (04 366 9320).
**Jumeira Rd, Nr Jumeira Mosque** Jumeira
**04 349 8498**
www.thelimetreecafe.com
Map **2 H3** Metro **Al Jafiliya**

### Lipton T-Junction                               Cafe

Cheery venue that's got tea down to a T
Tea, in its many forms, finds its way into nearly every drink and dish on the menu here. Go for the salads or sandwiches, some of which feature chicken cooked in green tea. The signature spice cha' and cha'latte drinks are well worth trying.
**Boulevard at Emirates Towers** Trade Centre
**04 330 0788**
www.thomaskleingroup.com
Map **2 H5** Metro **Emirates Towers**

Lemongrass

### The Lobby Lounge                        Afternoon Tea

Fine china and silver spoons; tea at its most refined
Tea at the Ritz is an exquisite experience. Delicate finger sandwiches and dainty pastries, succulent scones with clotted cream and a selection of jams, a fabulously colonial selection of teas and the fine china are all deliciously regal. It feels exclusive, but everyone is welcome.
**The Ritz-Carlton, Dubai** Dubai Marina **04 399 4000**
www.ritzcarlton.com
Map **1 K3** Metro **Dubai Marina**

### Luciano's                                    Italian

Family friendly poolside Italian
Good quality, family friendly dishes are served at this reasonably priced poolside Italian. Standard menu items are done well, and if you don't mind a slight chlorine smell and the weather is conducive, ask for a table outside underneath the fairy-light bedecked palm trees.
**Metropolitan Resort** Dubai Marina **04 399 5000**
www.habtoorhotels.com
Map **1 L3** Metro **Dubai Marina**

### M's Beef Bistro                             Steakhouse

Good steakhouse with some French classics
M's Beef Bistro is an unpretentious affair with an opulent feel in the mid-price range. Ideal for a smart lunch or dinner, the wine list is comprehensive and the menu offers excellent steaks and French dishes; look out for le classiques including french onion soup and burgundy snails.
**Le Meridien Dubai** Garhoud **04 702 2700**
www.lemeridien-dubai.com
Map **2 N7** Metro **GGICO**

### Magnolia                                    Vegetarian

Top vegetarian food, appealing to all
Magnolia is Dubai's first fine dining vegetarian restaurant. Its complimentary appetisers, amuse-bouches and main courses are imaginatively concocted using home-grown vegetables and herbs and are accompanied by delicious fresh juices and cocktails. There's also a wine list if you need something sinful to counteract the spa cuisine.
**Al Qasr Hotel** Madinat Jumeirah **04 366 6730**
www.madinatjumeirah.com/al_qasr
Map **1 R4** Metro **Mall of the Emirates**

---

### Explorer Member Card

Don't forget to register your member card (found at the back of the book) and check online for current offers. Discounts are updated on a monthly basis and you can search by area and cuisine type. www.liveworkexplore.com.

# True Taste Of Arabia

Levantine restaurant is a true taste of Arabia featuring the cuisine of the region with live Arabic entertainment surrounded by explosive colours and scents of the Middle East. Enjoy the Levantine Bar and Terrace serving a variety of drinks and shisha every night of the week.

For restaurant reservations please call +971 4 426 2626
or email restaurantreservations@atlantisthepalm.com
atlantisthepalm.com

ATLANTIS
THE PALM, DUBAI

# Restaurants & Cafes

## Mahi Mahi
**Seafood**

Modestly spectacular seafood spot

Live mud crab from Africa, langoustines from Norway, fresh red snapper, local helwayoo, hammour and more, offered in a choice of delicious sauces at this prize catch of a restaurant. Portions are plentiful and served with smiles and organic vegetables in a beautiful setting.

**Wafi** Umm Hurair **04 324 4100**
www.wafi.com
Map **2 L6** Metro **Healthcare City**

## Majlis Al Bahar
**Mediterranean**

Views to take your breath away, prices to match

Part of the Burj Al Arab, Majlis al Bahar offers front row seats to the iconic hotel's nightly light show. The meaty Mediterranean cuisine isn't exceptional but the mini barbecues are a novel attraction, and the salads are well executed.

**Burj Al Arab** Umm Suqeim **04 301 7600**
www.jumeirah.com
Map **1 S3** Metro **Mall of the Emirates**

## Manga
**Japanese**

Tokyo trendy with a decor unseen elsewhere

As the name suggests this Japanese eatery is all about Japan's cult comics, from the large screen showing Manga movies to the artworks on the walls. You may feel like you've drifted into Tokyo, where traditional fare has a modern edge. If you're looking for something a little different, you'll find it here.

**Beach Park Plaza, Jumeira Beach Road** Jumeira **04 342 8300**
Map **2 D3** Metro **Business Bay**

## Mango Tree
**Thai**

Decent Thai tucker with tantalising views

The menu offers something different to the standard Thai fare and includes grilled specialities, plentiful seafood, and signature dishes from the original Bangkok restaurant. The service is quiet but attentive and the beautifully designed location has arguably the best views in Downtown.

**Souk Al Bahar** Downtown Burj Dubai **04 426 7313**
Map **2 F6** Metro **Burj Dubai**

## Manhattan Grill
**Steakhouse**

Steaks and sophistication at this fine dining find

Soft lighting, plush seating, smooth music and an excellent selection of succulent steaks make this one of the finest fine-dining venues in town. There are seafood and vegetarian dishes on the menu too for non-meat eaters. It's on the pricey side, but you certainly get what you pay for here.

**Grand Hyatt Dubai** Umm Hurair **04 317 1234**
www.dubai.grand.hyatt.com
Map **2 L7** Metro **Healthcare City**

## Mannaland Korean Restaurant
**Korean**

Authentic Korean, full of flavour and atmosphere

A real find, this Korean restaurant in Satwa offers traditional floor seating and excellent, authentic food cooked at your table. Wash it all down with a teapot of 'special brew'. Great value too.

**Mina Road** Satwa **04 345 1300**
Map **2 J3** Metro **Al Jaffiliya**

## Margaux
**French**

Breathtaking views and belly-pleasing cuisine

Despite overlooking the Burj Dubai and its huge fountain display, the undisputed star of the show remains the menu, which includes a delectable mozzarella and tomato starter, steaks, fish, an interesting gold risotto and delicious penne, broccolini and fat, juicy scallops; leave room for the cheesecake, arguably the best in Dubai.

**Souk Al Bahar** Downtown Burj Dubai **04 439 9755**
Map **2 F6** Metro **Burj Dubai**

## Maria Bonita's
**Mexican**

Friendly neighbourhood Mexican, a tortilla thriller

Maria Bonita stands out as a friendly, well-worn neighbourhood eatery serving traditional Mexican and Tex-Mex dishes that include flavourful nachos, quesadillas and fajitas, served in a laid back atmosphere. Also at The Green Community (Casa Maria) (04 885 3188)

**Umm Al Sheif St, Nr Spinneys Centre** Umm Suqeim **04 395 4454**
Map **2 B4** Metro **Al Quoz**

## Marina
**Seafood**

Plush seafood place at the end of the pier

Marina features a selection of seafood cooked largely under Asian influence. Take a ride on a golf cart along the walkway to the pier-end building that also houses 360°. The view can't be seen from inside the restaurant, but the food compensates for this.

**The Jumeirah Beach Hotel** Umm Suqeim **04 406 8999**
www.jumeirah.com
Map **1 S3** Metro **Mall of the Emirates**

## The Market Café
**Buffet**

A creative, fun twist on buffet dining

Wander from station to station selecting your style of food as well as your specific starters, mains, desserts and drinks. Mix and match or stay within the Italian, Asian, Arabic or international cuisines on offer. Great food and great service, however, this restaurant mainly caters to hotel guests, although it is a good option for lunch for those in the area..

**Grand Hyatt Dubai** Umm Hurair **04 317 1234**
www.dubai.grand.hyatt.com
Map **2 L7** Metro **Healthcare City**

Elite

## Restaurants & Cafes

### The Market Place                                  Buffet
Excellent all-you-can-eat with free-flowing drinks
Free flowing drinks make revellers feel at home at
this bistro-style restaurant – but it is the five-star
food that distinguishes this buffet eatery, featuring
several live-cooking stations and an impressive array
of starters and desserts. This is a great place for group
celebrations and is packed at the weekends.
**JW Marriott Hotel** Deira **04 607 7977**
www.marriottdiningatjw.ae
Map **2 P5** Metro **Abu Baker Al Siddque**

### Marrakech                                        Moroccan
Tranquil surroundings and earthy flavours
Smooth arches and lamps add to an overwhelming
sense of tranquillity, while a duo belts out traditional
tunes on a small stage. Starters such as wedding pie
with pigeon, crushed almonds and icing sugar, are
served on blue ceramics. For mains try the lamb tagine
with fluffy, fragrant rice. Afterwards, a light orange
salad is the perfect ending.
**Shangri-La Hotel** Trade Centre **04 343 8888**
www.shangri-la.com
Map **2 G5** Metro **Financial Centre**

### Masala                                            Indian
Delicious Indian in a desert setting
Masala serves tasty versions of all you might expect
from the tandoor, curries and rice dishes. Tables in
alcoves surround a central kitchen from where the
slapping of naans accompanies the sounds of tabla
and sitar. Arrive early at Bab Al Shams to enjoy a desert
sundowner before dinner.
**Bab Al Shams Desert Resort & Spa 04 809 6100**
www.jumeirah.com
Map **1 E2**

Market Place

### Mazaj > p.497                                  Arabic/Lebanese
An atmospheric alfresco Arabic experience
From the sweet smell of shisa to the twinkle of
the fairy lights, Mazaj is a highly chilled Lebanese
restaurant with all the standard menu options. You can
also play board games and listen to the dulcet sounds
of an oud player and Arabic singer. The starters shine,
while the mains are generous.
**Century Village** Garhoud **04 282 9952**
www.centuryvillage.ae
Map **2 N7** Metro **GGICO**

### The Meat Co                                    Steakhouse
Meat and drink for steak fans
The terrace here offers excellent views of the Burj
Dubai while you decide which country you want your
steak to come from, the cut and how you want it
basted. The meat is aged, ensuring plenty of flavour.
Also at Madinat Jumeirah (04 368 6040).
**Souk Al Bahar** Downtown Burj Dubai **04 420 0737**
www.themeatco.com
Map **2 F6** Metro **Burj Dubai**

### Medzo                                              Italian
A taste of the Amalfi coast in Wafi
Outdoor air conditioning units make the terrace
at Medzo an alfresco option even in the summer,
while the inside dining area gives a more intimate,
sophisticated experience. There is a good range of
regional food on the menu, including superb seafood.
**Pyramids** Umm Hurair **04 324 4100**
www.wafi.com
Map **2 P6** Metro **Healthcare City**

### Meridien Village Terrace                          Buffet
Great outdoor buffet with different themed nights
Set in the middle of Le Meridien's outdoor dining area,
the huge buffet switches nightly between culinary
themes. Numerous live-cooking stations keep the
food wonderfully fresh, and a great choice of drinks
are replenished with alarming regularity. Definitely
one of the better buffets in town.
**Le Meridien Dubai** Garhoud **04 217 0000**
www.lemeridien-dubai.com
Map **2 N7** Metro **GGICO**

### Mezza House                                   Arabic/Lebanese
Popular Levant place with an atmospheric setting
Mezza House specialises in classic Levant cuisine. The
fresh flavours are complemented by a welcoming
atmosphere, value for money and delicious fruit
cocktails. The outdoor shisha lounge is the perfect
place to round off your meal with Arabic coffee.
**Yansoon Quarter, Old Town** Downtown Burj Dubai
**04 420 5444**
www.mezzahouse.com
Map **2 F5** Metro **Burj Dubai**

## Minato > *p.239* — Japanese

*Authentic Japanese restaurant with live cooking*
Dubai's oldest Japanese restaurant features intricately painted vases, rice paper doors and soft lighting, creating a personal yet traditional atmosphere. A sushi bar, tatami rooms, and teppanyaki tables liven up pricey dishes. Sushi and sashimi buffets are served on Mondays and Thursdays.
**Radisson Blu Hotel, Dubai Deira Creek** Al Rigga
**04 222 7171**
www.radissonblu.com/hotel-dubaideiracreek
Map **2 N4** Metro **Union**

## Mirai — Japanese

*Stylish interior and standout dishes*
The latest contender in Dubai's ongoing battle for contemporary Japanese supremacy boasts a cold and hot appetiser mix of standards and jaw-dropping standouts, like the roasted scallops with foie gras and jalapeno dressing. The illuminated red wall decor is straight from an interior design coffee table book.
**Souk Al Bahar** Downtown Burj Dubai **04 439 7333**
Map **2 F6** Metro **Burj Dubai**

## Miyako — Japanese

*Superb teppanyaki that will lure you back for more*
Small yet chic, Miyako combines a laid-back ambience with a genuinely exciting menu. The speciality is a delicate seafood broth served in a paper bowl and heated over a naked flame, while the tender slivers of teppanyaki are excellent.
**Hyatt Regency** Deira **04 317 2222**
www.dubai.regency.hyatt.com
Map **2 N3** Metro **Palm Deira**

## Mizaan — International

*International cuisine and a worldly wine list*
This hotel restaurant serves a range of international cuisine, from Indian and Thai curries to grilled Mediterranean vegetables, to guests and Dubai residents. The accompanying wine list is great value compared with similar venues in Dubai.
**The Monarch Dubai** Trade Centre **04 501 8888**
www.themonarchdubai.com
Map **2 J4** Metro **Trade Centre**

## Momotaro — Japanese

*Expansive menu, elegant dishes and helpful staff*
The tasteful interior of dark wood, red lighting and white square tables is a fitting residence for the elegant fare that include sashimi, maki rolls and sushi dishes. The menu is vast, so you'll appreciate the help of Momotaro's well-versed staff.
**Souk Al Bahar** Downtown Burj Dubai **04 425 7976**
www.momotaro.ae
Map **2 F6** Metro **Burj Dubai**

Miyako

## More Café — Cafe

*Fashionable family favourite that gives that bit More*
Known for its non-boozy brunches, outstanding sandwiches and imaginative salads, More attracts both families and fashionable media types. A stylish industrial interior, speedy service and extensive menu makes More enduringly popular in Dubai. Also at Al Murooj Rotana (04 343 3779) and Gold & Diamond Park (04 323 4350).
**Nr Welcare Hospital** Garhoud **04 283 0224**
www.morecafe.biz
Map **2 N6** Metro **GGICO**

## Mosaico — Italian

*Fine buffet, great for both high fliers and families*
Open 24 hours a day, Mosaico blends Italian flavours with Spanish flamboyance. The Mediterranean buffet incorporates freshly prepared tapas, pastas and pizzas made to order, and honey-drizzled profiteroles. Polish it off with a glass or three of traditional Italian wine.
**Emirates Towers** Trade Centre **04 319 8088**
www.jumeirah.com
Map **2 H5** Metro **Emirates Towers**

## Munchi — Thai

*Relaxing bamboo hut restaurant with great food*
Munchi offers great Thai food and sushi, with excellent service. Dine alfresco on the patio in the green hotel grounds, or inside at this stylish bamboo hut-style restaurant. The starter sharing platter gets the juices flowing, and there's live cooking for the showpiece dishes.
**Metropolitan Resort** Dubai Marina **04 399 5000**
www.habtoorhotels.com
Map **1 L3** Metro **Dubai Marina**

NA3NA3

### NA3NA3 — Arabic/Lebanese
Stylish surrounds and a good selection of dishes
NA3 NA3 (pronounced 'na na') is a demure all-day dining restaurant that is yet to appeal to the masses. A tasty range of stews, salads and deserts are on offer as well as a live cooking station serving seafood, grilled meat and shawarmas.
**The Address Dubai Mall** Downtown Burj Dubai
**04 423 8888**
www.theaddress.com
Map Metro **Burj Dubai**

### Nando's — Portuguese
Cheap, cheerful chicken, also with wings
Famous for its peri-peri chicken, which ranges from mild to extra hot. The takeaway option is popular (extra points for the 'poultry in motion' slogan on the delivery bikes). Also at Al Ghurair City (04 221 1992), The Greens Centre (04 360 8080), and Burj Residences (04 422 4882).
**Sheikh Zayed Rd, Nr Crowne Plaza Hotel**
Trade Centre **04 321 2000**
www.nandos.com
Map **2 H5** Metro **Emirates Towers**

### Nasimi > p.ii-iii — International
Incredible alfresco dining overlooking the Palm
Considering its location in the fantastical surroundings of Atlantis, Nasimi surprises with its simplicity – it offers a small, delectable menu of seafood and meat dishes, all expertly prepared, and one of the best alfresco settings in the city.
**Atlantis The Palm** Palm Jumeirah **04 426 2626**
www.atlantisthepalm.com
Map **2 A3** Metro **Nakheel**

### Nina — Indian
Romantic but slightly expensive Indian option
Nina's striking decor and soothing background music create a great setting for a candlelit dinner for two. The menu largely features the usual Indian suspects, with one or two surprises such as frogs' legs, and is complemented by a good wine list. It's not cheap.
**One&Only Royal Mirage** Al Sufouh **04 399 9999**
www.oneandonlyroyalmirage.com
Map **1 M3** Metro **Nakheel**

### Nineteen — European
Fine dining that puts the glamour into golf
The dark interior of the Montgomerie's flagship restaurant is lit by 70s kitsch lampshades, and subtle lights that single out your table. In contrast, the show kitchen is loud and proud. Choose from a perfectly balanced Thai-influenced menu.
**The Address Montgomerie Dubai**
Emirates Hills **04 363 1275**
www.themontgomerie.com
Map **1 L5** Metro **Dubai Marina**

### The Noble House — Chinese
Chinese dishes elevated to works of art
High-backed chairs and a sunken ceiling, in an austere setting worthy of its Raffles home, make this Chinese restaurant a truly fine dining experience. Showcasing traditional dishes with a contemporary twist, the fine details of Chinese cuisine have been preserved well.
**Raffles Dubai** Umm Hurair **04 324 8888**
www.dubai.raffles.com
Map **2 K6** Metro **Healthcare City**

### Nobu > p.ii-iii — Japanese
Unreal sushi and sashimi made by the best
Nobuyuki Matsuhisa, the godfather of sushi, has upped the ante for Japanese food aficionados, who will love the exceptional quality, attention to detail and huge menu of sushi, sashimi and tempura. Despite its reputation, Nobu is not restricted to celebrities – as long as you can get a reservation.
**Atlantis The Palm** Palm Jumeirah **04 426 2626**
www.atlantisthepalm.com
Map **2 A3** Metro **Nakheel**

### The Noodle House — Far Eastern
Simple, tasty dishes and a laid-back set up
A refreshingly relaxed affair – grab a seat at one of the communal tables, place your order by ticking off your choice on a list of soups, noodles and stir-fries, and then see your food arrive in record time. Also at Madinat Jumeirah and Deira City Centre.
**Boulevard at Emirates Towers**
Trade Centre **04 319 8088**
www.jumeirahemiratestowers.com
Map **2 H5** Metro **Emirates Towers**

## Noodle Sushi — Japanese
Seafood specials on Sheikh Zayed Road
Noodle Sushi is one of four themed restaurants surrounding Sea World. Sit at the live sushi station and watch the artistry, or order from a varied menu that includes reasonably priced bento boxes and a wide assortment of sushi, sashimi and tempura.
**Above Safestway** Al Wasl **04 321 1500**
Map **2 E5** Metro **Business Bay**

## The Observatory — International
Breathtaking views, sophisticated cocktails
It's all about the views at this atmospheric 52nd floor gastro-lounge. Spectacular 360° vistas over the Marina and The Palm accompany the concise (but tasty) menu, while the cocktails are excellent. Come just before sunset then stay for the evening to get the full benefit of the amazing panorama.
**Dubai Marriott Harbour Hotel & Suites**
Dubai Marina **04 319 4000**
www.marriott.com
Map **1 L4** Metro **Dubai Marina**

## Oceana — Buffet
Cruise the world at this international eatery
The decor at Oceana is akin to glamorous dining rooms of 1930s cruise ships – lots of chrome and wood with Art Moderne furniture and lighting fixtures. Different nights feature different cuisines – choose from seafood, Arabic, French and Mexican.
**Hilton Jumeirah** Dubai Marina **04 399 1111**
www.hilton.com
Map **1 K3** Metro **Jumeirah Lakes Towers**

## Okku — Japanese
Join the hip crowd at this stylish Japanese
From the slick cocktail bar with a tank of neon jellyfish to the elegant staff, Okku starts strong. Lovers of luxury will be thrilled with dishes like yellow fin tuna carpaccio, wagyu beef, foie gras sushi and black cod, and as the evening progresses, Dubai's bold and beautiful fill this achingly hip restaurant.
**The Monarch Dubai** Trade Centre **04 501 8777**
www.okkudubai.com
Map **2 J4** Metro **Trade Centre**

## Olive House — Mediterranean
Grab and go, or sit and stay at this quick-fix eatery
The tables at this Mediterranean marvel are always full and the prompt service makes it ideal for a quick meal in or a takeaway. Order a filling sandwich, pizza, mezze or salad, and round it off with some tasty icecream. A gem of a place if you like simple and delicious cuisine.
**No. One Tower, Sheikh Zayed Rd** Trade Centre
**04 343 3110**
Map **2 G5** Metro **Financial Centre**

## Olives — Italian
Slip into Mediterranean mode at the One&Only
Sturdy wicker furniture, lots of archways, indoor foliage and white ceramic tiles on the walls help to set the scene in Olives. Pizzas and pastas are the stars of the Mediterranean menu, and there's a lovely outdoor terrace overlooking the gardens and pool area.
**One&Only Royal Mirage** Al Sufouh **04 399 9999**
www.oneandonlyroyalmirage.com
Map **1 M3** Metro **Nakheel**

## THE One — Cafe
This could be THE One for funky cafe fans
Tucked away on the first floor of THE One furniture store, this funky cafe features an extensive menu that is imaginative, but also offers reliable classics if you're not feeling particularly adventurous. The food is high quality; the freshly squeezed juices are fabulous and the cakes outstanding. There's also a good kids' menu.
**Jumeira Rd** Jumeira **04 345 6687**
www.theoneplanet.com
Map **2 H3** Metro **Al Jafiliya**

## Ossiano > p.428 — Seafood
Superb seafood from a three-starred Michelin chef
Three Michelin-star chef Santi Santamaria serves up Catalan-inspired simple, delicate seafood dishes at this impeccable eatery. Glistening chandeliers and floor-to-ceiling views of the enormous Ambassador Lagoon provide a formal but romantic setting to enjoy the incredible, and incredibly priced, fare.
**Atlantis The Palm** Palm Jumeirah **04 426 2626**
www.atlantisthepalm.com
Map **2 A3** Metro **Nakheel**

## Pachanga — Latin American
Meat and greet at this tango restaurant
Choose from the Havana-style bar, Brazilian barbecue, Mexican lounge or Argentinean terrace that surround the dancefloor at this Latin American hotspot. Start with fresh guacamole prepared at your table, then move onto the wide selection of mains: the seafood is delicious but the real winners are meat-eaters.
**Hilton Jumeirah** Dubai Marina **04 399 1111**
www.hilton.com
Map **1 K3** Metro **Jumeirah Lakes Towers**

## PaiThai — Thai
Fantastic Thai cuisine in a truly romantic setting
You'll have a night to remember at PaiThai, from the abra ride to the restaurant to the nouvelle Thai cuisine. The outdoor seating area boasts delightful views in the winter months and the menu provides the odd twist on familiar favourites.
**Al Qasr Hotel** Umm Suqeim **04 366 8888**
www.madinatjumeirah.com
Map **1 R4** Metro **Mall of the Emirates**

Pachanga

## The Palermo Restaurant　　　Seafood

Remote fine dining, great for special occasions
It may be a drive to the Polo Club from most parts of town, but the quiet, elegant dining room and excellent food make it worth it. The original appetisers and quality meats and seafood will not disappoint. Perfect for an intimate meal or business dinner, it's an unexpected mini-escape from the city.
**Dubai Polo & Equestrian Club** Arabian Ranches
**04 361 8111**
www.poloclubdubai.com
Map **3 B3**

## Palm Grill > p.239　　　Steakhouse

Classic steaks and classical music
Palm Grill cooks up juicy steaks in an open-plan kitchen to the accompaniment of a live pianist. The steaks are a tender delight, cooked precisely to order and big enough to satisfy the most ravenous meat lover – so time is required to savour each bite.
**Radisson Blu Hotel, Dubai Deira Creek** Al Rigga
**04 222 7171**
www.radissonblu.com/hotel-dubaideiracreek
Map **2 N4** Metro **Union**

## Pane Caldo　　　Italian

Bright, trendy trattoria, great for people-watching
With a decor so white and funky, eating at Pane Caldo is like dining in an iPod. Touted as a 'different' Italian, the menu is innovative and varied enough to suit every taste, and there's a take-away service that includes freshly baked bread, sauce and pasta.
**Uptown Mirdif** Mirdif **04 288 8319**
www.pane-caldo.ae
Map **2 Q12** Metro **Rashidiya**

## Panini　　　Cafe

Decent pit stop for lunch on the go
Set among the tropical indoor 'rainforest' in the impressive lobby of the Grand Hyatt, complete with lush greenery and jungle mist, Panini is a good place to meet up with friends or business associates for a lunch on the run. The food is average but convenient.
**Grand Hyatt Dubai** Umm Hurair **04 317 2222**
www.dubai.grand.hyatt.com
Map **2 L7** Metro **Healthcare City**

## Pars Iranian Kitchen　　　Persian

Traditional Iranian food and laid-back shisha vibe
This branch of Pars offers a traditional, laid-back atmosphere a million miles from the modernity suggested by the garish neon sign outside. The menu includes standard regional favourites, while a delightful front garden, enclosed by a fairy light-entwined hedgerow, is home to soft, cushioned bench seats, perfect for shisha. Call for other locations.
**Nr Rydges Plaza** Satwa **04 398 4000**
Map **2 J4** Metro **Al Jafiliya**

## Pax　　　Italian

Pick 'n' mix Italian with SZR views
Pax does traditional Italian dishes in less than traditional sizes to give punters a pick 'n' mix of tastes. It is a style they call bocconcini (little delicacies), and with appetisers starting at Dhs.15, and most mains costing less than Dhs.70, a hearty feed is not prohibitively expensive.
**Dusit Thani Dubai** Trade Centre **04 343 3333**
www.dusit.com
Map **2 G5** Metro **Financial Centre**

## Peppercrab　　　Singaporean

Authentic Singaporean fare, impeccable service
One of Dubai's best Asian restaurants, the noodles and chilli crab are so authentic you'll feel like you're sitting in the middle of Newton's Circus in Singapore. Service is exceptional and the price, while on the high side, is worth it for this classy venue.
**Grand Hyatt Dubai** Umm Hurair **04 317 2222**
www.dubai.grand.hyatt.com
Map **2 L7** Metro **Healthcare City**

## Pergolas　　　Cafe

A venue that changes to match the food
Perfect for a romantic evening, the international buffet is based around changing theme nights. The terrace is overlooked by fairytale architecture and the decor changes throughout the week to reflect themes, including seafood and 'orient express' evenings.
**Al Murooj Rotana Hotel & Suites**
Trade Centre **04 321 1111**
www.rotana.com
Map **2 G5** Metro **Financial Centre**

### Persia Persia
Persian

*Irresistible Iranian food and company at Wafi*
Located at the top of the Wafi Pyramids, Persia Persia's interior is simple yet elegant. Choose from flavour-packed appetisers that are great for sharing, alongside regional favourites such as kebabs and lamb stew. The fact that it's a regular hangout for many Iranians reflects its quality.
**Pharaohs' Club** Wafi **04 324 4100**
www.wafi.com
Map **2 L6** Metro **Healthcare City**

### Pierchic
Seafood

*Quite possibly Dubai's most amazing restaurant*
Situated at the end of a long wooden pier that juts into the Arabian Gulf, Pierchic offers unobstructed views of the Burj Al Arab, which probably reflects in the heftier price tag. The superior seafood is meticulously presented and the wine menu reads like a sommelier's wish list.
**Al Qasr Hotel** Umm Suqeim **04 366 8888**
www.madinatjumeirah.com/al_qasr
Map **1 R4** Metro **Mall of the Emirates**

### Ping Pong
Chinese

*Tip-top Ping Pong dim sum*
Sleek and urban, Ping Pong is softened with dark wood and bench seating. An extensive dim sum menu offers a tantalising selection of steamed, baked and fried options and the flowering teas are a unique twist. Whether popping in for a savoury treat for one, or sharing a meal with friends, you'll find yourself bouncing back again soon.
**The Dubai Mall** Downtown Burj Dubai **04 4339 9088**
www.pingpongdimsum.ae
Map **2 F6** Metro **Burj Dubai**

Pane Caldo

### Pisces
Seafood

*Plush seafood restaurant that scores 10 out of 10*
Flawless in every sense, Pisces could be the perfect seafood restaurant. Professional service, delicious, artistically presented food and beautifully set, intimate tables all score full points. The winning detail is the outdoor bar with a breathtaking view of the Madinat waterways.
**Souk Madinat Jumeirah** Umm Suqeim **04 366 6313**
www.madinatjumeirah.com
Map **1 R4** Metro **Mall of the Emirates**

### Planet Hollywood
American

*Burgers and blaring decor – one for the kids*
With bright colours, lots of space and friendly staff, this is a popular place to take the kids. The menu features huge, American-style portions, plus a kids menu. Friday brunch is popular thanks to the movies, toys and face painting.
**Wafi** Umm Hurair **04 324 4777**
www.planethollywood-dubai.com
Map **2 L6** Metro **Healthcare City**

### Prego's
Italian

*A true Italian through and through*
Prego's takes one cuisine for its buffet – Italian – and specialises in it. From soups with shavings of parmesan and an antipasti station laden with marinated vegetables, to hearty pastas and pizzas for mains, the authentic dishes are all extremely satisfying and expertly prepared.
**Media Rotana** Al Barsha **04 435 0000**
www.rotana.com
Map **1 P5** Metro **Dubai Internet City**

### Promenade
International

*Average fare, not savoir-faire*
The selection of dishes from the a la carte menu of this French-style cafe is limited and the international buffet is basic. The mains are rather expensive, but the various cuts of meat and the seafood selection are cooked on the grill to specific requirements.
**Four Points by Sheraton Bur Dubai**
Bur Dubai **04 397 7444**
www.starwoodhotels.com
Map **2 L4** Metro **Al Fahidi**

### Pronto
Cafe

*Deli-style cuisine worthy of a lingering lunch*
Fairmont's Pronto should not be pigeonholed into Dubai's lacklustre hotel cafe culture. Its deli-style cuisine is worthy of a lingering lunch, with sushi and Arabic selections, alcohol and incredible cakes. It also offers complimentary Wi-Fi.
**Fairmont Dubai** Trade Centre **04 332 5555**
www.fairmont.com
Map **2 J4** Metro **Trade Centre**

## Restaurants & Cafes

### Ranches Restaurant
**International**

Above-par golf restaurant out in suburbia

Set within the elegant golf club building, Ranches serves unpretentious fare in comfortable surroundings, with a focus on traditional British dishes. The outdoor terrace offers a more intimate dining experience overlooking the course. Tuesday is quiz night, and there are themed buffets during the week.

**The Desert Course** Arabian Ranches **04 360 7935**
www.arabianranchesgolfdubai.com
Map **2 B3**

### Rare Restaurant
**Steakhouse**

Romantic steakhouse for meat lovers

Rare is slowly gaining attention as one of the best steakhouses in the city. It's not cheap, but there's enough choice to please both the serious carnivore and the picky gourmand. Book a table outside on the gorgeously contemporary terrace overlooking the polo fields to take advantage of the boutique hotel's isolated setting.

**Desert Palm Dubai 04 323 8888**
www.desertpalm.ae
Map **2 C3**

### Ravi's
**Pakistani**

Great cuisine at this popular cheap eatery

Ravi's has legendary status among western expats, and is one of the cheapest eateries in town. This 24 hour diner offers a range of Pakistani curried favourites and rice dishes. The prices are cheap at double the price and the dishes keep punters coming back for more. The venue is basic and dining is available inside or outside.

**Satwa Rd, Nr Satwa R/A** Satwa **04 331 5353**
Map **2 J4** Metro **Al Jafiliya**

### Reem Al Bawadi
**Arabic/Lebanese**

An Arabic favourite – great mezze, grills and shisha

Semi-isolated booths with thick Arabic cushions surround the perimeter, while tables lined with armchairs fill the dark, bustling dining area. The grills and mezze coming out of its kitchen are as appealing as the setting.

**Jumeira Rd, Nr HSBC** Jumeira **04 394 7444**
www.reemalbawadi.com
Map **2 E3** Metro **Burj Dubai**

### Reflets par Pierre Gagnaire
**French**

Parisian pomp with sculptured dishes

From the Michelin-starred grandfather of molecular gastronomy comes a magical, imaginative and highly conceptual dining experience. Bold purple carpet and pink chandeliers along with floor-to-ceiling mirrors and white tablecloths are the backdrop to a menu that strives to be a work of art.

**InterContinental Dubai Festival City** Festival City **04 701 1199**
www.intercontinental.com/dubai
Map **2 M8** Metro **Jaddaf**

### Rhodes Mezzanine
**British**

Classic British dishes with a modern twist

You expect nothing less than perfectly created dishes full of richness and flavour from Gary Rhodes, and his pristine restaurant, with white table cloths and exquisite finishings, certainly doesn't disappoint. The menu might not be expansive but you'll still be hard pressed to make a choice, especially when it comes to the superbly traditional desserts.

**Grosvenor House** Dubai Marina **04 399 8888**
www.grosvenorhouse.lemeridien.com
Map **1 L4** Metro **Dubai Marina**

Rib Room

### The Rib Room — Steakhouse
High-class place with beautifully prepared dishes
Friendly chatter, ambient lighting, dark wood and a flash of red make enjoying a plate of tasty wagyu beef with peppercorn sauce or a large plate of surf and turf an even classier affair. The food and fine wine doesn't come cheap but sometimes you need a proper steak.
**Emirates Towers** Trade Centre **04 319 8088**
www.jumeirahemiratestowers.com
Map **2 H5** Metro **Emirates Towers**

### Rivington Grill — British
Elegance and perfection to satisfy sweet tooths
Straight out of London, this white table-clothed, intimate eatery brings the best in European cuisine with dishes that are sculptured to perfection. The terrace is the perfect spot for watching the impressive Dubai Fountain displays and you'll want to linger once you've seen the desert menu.
**Souk Al Bahar** Downtown Burj Dubai **04 423 0903**
www.rivingtongrill.ae
Map **2 F6** Metro **Burj Dubai**

### Roadster Diner — American
Burgers and Americana; the quintessential US diner
Classic American diner serving huge portions of cheese-slathered Tex-Mex, juicy burgers, filling pasta dishes, hearty salads and loaded desserts. The Oreo shake is a glass of pure indulgence. There's also a classic breakfast menu, so if you're pining for pancakes and maple syrup, its cosy booth interior is the place to head.
**Jumeirah Road** Jumeira **04 345 9536**
Map **2 H3** Metro **Al Jafiliya**

### Rodeo Grill — Steakhouse
A steak-lover's heaven, excellent wine to match
Smoke a Montecristo cigar, sip a cool draught ale, and choose your selection from the grill while you relax in the snug little bar where the chef works from an open kitchen. The steaks are exceptional, the desserts delightful and the wine list expansive (and expensive).
**Al Bustan Rotana** Garhoud **04 282 0000**
www.rotana.com
Map **2 N7** Metro **GGICO**

### Ronda Locatelli > p.ii-iii — Italian
Popular Atlantis venue with a celebrity Italian chef
Run by celebrity chef Giorgio Locatelli, the cavernous interior seats hundreds in raised alcoves or at tables surrounding a huge stone-built wood-fired oven. The casual menu offers a good range of starters, pasta and mains, as well as a selection of small dishes that are perfect for sharing.
**Atlantis The Palm** Palm Jumeirah **04 426 2626**
www.atlantisthepalm.com
Map **2 A3** Metro **Nakheel**

### Rostang > p.ii-iii — French
Traditional bistro fare from a Michelin-starred chef
Rostang's wood trim, leather bench seating and dim lighting perfectly mimics the decor of a 1930s bistro. Two-star Michelin chef Michel Rostang's seasonal menu, based on different French regions, is full of comforting dishes that shy away from experimentation and concentrate on preparation and presentation.
**Atlantis The Palm** Palm Jumeirah **04 426 2626**
www.atlantisthepalm.com
Map **2 A3** Metro **Nakheel**

### Rotisserie — International
Filling buffet in the grounds of the Royal Mirage
All-you-can-eat buffet with exquisite Arabic and Mediterranean dishes. Ranging from mezze to an excellent lamb tagine, the only problem is finding room to sample everything on offer. Ask for a table outside or by the window so you can enjoy the view.
**One&Only Royal Mirage** Al Sufouh **04 399 9999**
www.oneandonlyresort.com
Map **1 M3** Metro **Nakheel**

### Royal Orchid — Thai
Popular Thai restaurant by the marina
Thai and Chinese food at reasonable prices, featuring the 'magic wok', where the chef will prepare your favourite meat, fish or vegetables in your chosen sauce. Portions are on the large side so arrive hungry and try a starter, like the stir-fried black pepper chicken wings. Also does takeaway.
**Marina Walk** Dubai Marina **04 367 4040**
Map **1 L4** Metro **Dubai Marina**

### Ruby Tuesday — American
Burgers and booths in this kid-friendly joint
Private booths make this an ideal place to relax with friends and family. High quality Angus beef burgers and steaks are the speciality, and the affordable menu also includes ribs and seafood. There's a salad bar and kids' menu too. Also in Jumeira Beach Park Plaza and Dubai Mall.
**Jumeirah Beach Residence** Dubai Marina **04 424 3771**
www.rubytuesday.com
Map **1 L4** Metro **Dubai Marina**

### Ruth's Chris Steak House — Steakhouse
Steak, the stylish way
With white leather sofas, red and dark panelling, and slick service, Ruth's Chris Steak house tops it off by delivering superior steaks cooked to precise temperatures, served with an extensive selection of accompaniments.
**The Monarch Dubai** Trade Centre **04 501 8666**
www.ruthschris.ae
Map **2 J4** Metro **Trade Centre**

## Restaurants & Cafes

### The Rupee Room · Indian
Excellent curry venue with live Indian music

Offers a wide selection of tasty north Indian dishes in relaxed surroundings. The glass-fronted kitchen allows you to keep an eye on the action and there is often a great trio of live musicians playing. There are a handful of tables outside offering marina views.

**Marina Walk** Dubai Marina **04 390 5755**
www.therupeeroom.com
Map  Metro **Dubai Marina**

### Russian Home Restaurant · Russian
Comforting home cooking, Russian style

This 24 hour restaurant lacks a bit of atmosphere, but is a great place to go for Russian home cooking. Relax in diner-style booths while enjoying favourites like borsht and filled breads. The service is very friendly, despite the language barrier.

**Nr Lamcy Plaza** Oud Metha **04 334 6050**
Map **2 K5** Metro **Oud Metha**

### Saffron > p.ii-iii · International
Buffet concept, Atlantis style: bigger and better

At Saffron, the sheer size and variety of the buffet stations is staggering. From sushi and Singaporean noodle soups to Sunday roasts and steaming dim sum, there's lots to sample. Leave room for the dessert section, which features a chocolate fountain and ice-cream stand.

**Atlantis The Palm** Palm Jumeirah **04 426 2626**
www.atlantisthepalm.com
Map **2 A3** Metro **Nakheel**

### Sahn Eddar · Afternoon Tea
Definition of luxury: afternoon tea at the Burj

It may be an expensive cuppa, but this is the ultimate afternoon tea. It begins with a glass of bubbly and continues with course after course of dainty sandwiches and fine pastries. Sahn Eddar is on the first floor, but to make it really memorable you can go to the Skyview Bar to enjoy the stunning vistas (p.515).

**Burj Al Arab** Umm Suqeim **04 301 7600**
www.jumeirah.com
Map **1 S3** Metro **Mall of the Emirates**

### Sai Dham · Indian
Great vegetarian food in an impressive setting

With gold textured walls and stylish wooden furniture, the tardis-like interior of Sai Dham defies expectations from outside. Serving superb vegetarian food that 'celebrates purity', it uses no garlic or onion, and only gentle spices, so the fresh taste of all ingredients comes through. Great value too.

**Saleh Bin Lahej Bld, Oud Metha Rd** Oud Metha
**04 336 6552**
www.sai-dham.com
Map **2 K5** Metro **Oud Metha**

### Sails · Mediterranean
Pick your catch, have it cooked the way you like it

Sails may look a little dated, but the food is good. Choose your seafood at the market-style counter and the chef who will cook it and recommend sides and sauces. The seafood buffet runs from Wednesday to Sunday, with surf 'n' turf on Mondays and Tuesdays.

**Renaissance Dubai** Deira **04 262 5555**
www.renaissancehotels.com
Map **2 P5** Metro **Salahudin**

### Sakura · Japanese
Sushi and sake in a memorable setting

Sakura offers one of Dubai's widest varieties of Japanese food, from sushi and teppanyaki to the less well-known shabu shabu. The two weekly buffet nights are excellent value. Seating is available at the cooking tables themselves, standard tables, or in one of the private tatami rooms – great for enjoying sake.

**Crowne Plaza** Trade Centre **04 331 1111**
www.ichotelsgroup.com
Map **2 H5** Metro **Emirates Towers**

### Salmontini · Seafood
Abundance of salmon in sophisticated surrounds

Salmontini's chic interior is fashioned around large windows overlooking the mall's indoor ski slope. Choose from a selection of Scottish salmon, worked in every possible way (from smoked and grilled to cured and poached). There are some good all-inclusive deals offered during the week.

**Mall of the Emirates** Al Barsha **04 341 0222**
www.lamaisondusaumon.com
Map **1 R5** Metro **Mall of the Emirates**

### Sana Bonta · Italian
Customisable menus and decent Italian fare

Sana Bonta's completely customisable Italian menu is a bit of a novelty, but will appeal to picky eaters and those who feel the need to take control. Separated into antipasti, pastas and pizzas, diners tick off the ingredients they want and wait for the results.

**Dubai International Financial Centre (DIFC)**
Trade Centre **04 425 0326**
Map **2 F5**  Metro **Trade Centre**

### Saravana Bhavan · Indian
Terrific thali at bargain prices

This is arguably the best of the area's south Indian restaurants. Saravana prefers elbow-to-elbow dining on tables decorated only with a bottle of mineral water. The menu is long but it's the thalis that draw big crowds – for around Dhs.12 you can get a plate packed with colour and incredible flavours.

**Karama Park Square** Karama **04 334 5252**
www.saravanabhavan.com
Map **2 L5** Metro **Karama**

## Sea World — Seafood
Fresh, simple seafood, cooked to perfection
It's a simple concept: choose your 'catch' from the market stall, and have it cooked to perfection by the talented chefs. The service and food is excellent, as is the price, which is considerably lower than you'd pay for the same thing elsewhere.
**Above Safestway** Al Wasl **04 321 1500**
Map **2 E5** Metro **Business Bay**

## Seafire > *p.ii-iii* — Steakhouse
Top seafood and steak at Atlantis
Dinner starts with a list of extravagant sounding and deliciously tasting appetizers. When it comes to the main, try to resist the succulent fillet, T-bone or the seafood grill – the Atlantis strip sirloin is one of the finest steaks you'll taste. The service is impeccable but refreshingly friendly and the stylish dining room manages to retain an intimate feel despite its size.
**Atlantis The Palm** Palm Jumeirah **04 426 2626**
www.atlantisthepalm.com
Map **2 A3** Metro **Nakheel**

## Seasons — International
Healthy lunchtime snacks to go
Swiftly swarming every area in Dubai, Seasons is a chain of cafes serving healthy, reasonably priced dishes to hungry shoppers and lunch-breakers. Also at Dubai Internet City (04 391 8711) and Ibn Battuta (04 368 5630).
**Mall of the Emirates** Al Barsha **04 341 2483**
Map **1 R5** Metro **Mall of the Emirates**

## Segreto — Italian
An Italian secret in the heart of Madinat
Candle-lit lamps lead you through the walkways to this hidden gem. Start the evening with a glass of prosecco on the terrace by the canal, then head into the stylish, modern interior. Segreto suits both dinner with friends and a romantic date. The food is aesthetically appealing, but the portions are more suited to a catwalk model than a rugby lad.
**Dar Al Masyaf** Umm Suqeim **04 366 6730**
www.madinatjumeirah.com
Map **1 R3** Metro **Mall of the Emirates**

## Seoul Garden Restaurant — Korean
Private rooms with in-table barbecues
Each of the private rooms is equipped with a traditional Korean barbecue, which you can put to use by ordering a beef dish. Order as many of the small starters as you can, as they're all delicious. Cool ginger tea and a sweet melon dessert round off a delicious meal perfectly.
**Zomorrodah Bld** Karama **04 337 7876**
Map **2 L5** Metro **Karama**

## Seville's — Spanish
Drinks and tapas in a special atmosphere
The atmosphere at Seville's is buzzing. Share tapas or feast on the heartier dishes available. Live music adds to the ambiance and the rustic decor has a cosy, homely feel. Reasonable prices help keep the atmosphere busy and the outdoor terrace creates a tranquil spot for alfresco dining.
**Wafi** Umm Hurair **04 324 7300**
www.waficityrestaurants.com
Map **2 L6** Metro **Healthcare City**

## Sezzam — International
Large restaurant with a range of dining options
Sezzam's open-plan concept may seem a little confusing, but once you've got the hang of it you can indulge in some excellent, varied food. There are three kitchens: 'Bake' serves up pizzas, lasagne and roasts; 'Flame' offers grilled meats and seafoods; and 'Steam' serves up Asian cuisine.
**Mall of the Emirates** Al Barsha **04 341 3600**
www.kempinski-dubai.com
Map **1 R5** Metro **Mall of the Emirates**

## Shabestan > *p.239* — Persian
The opulence of Persia in a traditional setting
This Persian restaurant is just as much about the decor as it is about the food. Ornate tables and chairs, decorative trinkets and traditional cooking stations combine to give a regal experience. The freshly baked breads set the scene for the quality of food and the dishes are plentiful.
**Radisson Blu Hotel, Dubai Deira Creek** Al Rigga **04 222 7171**
www.radissonblu.com/hotel-dubaideiracreek
Map **2 N4** Metro **Union**

## Shahrzad — Persian
Mouth-watering kebabs with live Persian music
Shahrzad's interior seems a bit dated, but the live Persian music and copper-clad open kitchen give it an exciting atmosphere. Start with the interesting ash irishta noodle soup, then move on to the equally tasty appetiser platter before digging in to some of the best kebabs in town.
**Hyatt Regency** Deira **04 317 2222**
www.dubai.regency.hyatt.com
Map **2 N3** Metro **Palm Deira**

---

### Explorer Member Card
Don't forget to register your member card (found at the back of the book) and check online for current offers. Discounts are updated on a monthly basis and you can search by area and cuisine type. www.liveworkexplore.com

# Restaurants & Cafes

Shang Palace

## Shakespeare & Co — Cafe
Shabby chic decor and a good menu range
Shakespeare & Co is uniquely eccentric, with a mix of floral designs with lace and wicker. The food is equally eclectic, combining Arabic, Moroccan and continental dishes with a splendid selection of sandwiches and smoothies. Other locations include The Village Mall (04 344 6228), Al Wasl Road (04 394 1121), Gulf Tower (04 335 3335) and Souk Al Bahar (04 434 0195).
**Al Attar Business Tower, Sheikh Zayed Rd**
Trade Centre **04 331 1757**
www.shakespeareandco.ae
Map **2 G5** Metro **Financial Centre**

## Shang Palace — Chinese
Dim sum and then some at this excellent Chinese
The food at Shang Palace is delicious and the knowledgeable staff will guide you through the huge menu. Tuck into shark fin soup, live seafood and dim sum while people-watching from the balcony overlooking the Shangri-La's bustling entrance, or take a quieter position inside the circular dining room.
**Shangri-La Hotel** Trade Centre **04 405 2703**
www.shangri-la.com
Map **2 G5** Metro **Financial Centre**

## Shoo Fee Ma Fee — Moroccan
Authentic Moroccan with unexpected flavours
This is perhaps the only place in Dubai where you can choose between traditional Moroccan dishes of lamb, chicken, goat and camel. After eating your fill head to the terrace for pastries, shisha, live entertainment and a mesmerising postcard-perfect vista.
**Souk Madinat Jumeirah** Umm Suqeim **04 366 6730**
www.madinatjumeirah.com
Map **1 R4** Metro **Mall of the Emirates**

## Shooters > *p.455* — American
Modern saloon that gives you its best shot
This modern western saloon with denim-clad waiters is surprisingly quiet despite the gunfire from the five floodlit shooting ranges below (visible through a glass wall panel). The menu is simple yet sophisticated, mainly offering fish and steak. King-size prawns and lobster tails are firm favourites.
**Jebel Ali Hotel** Jebel Ali **04 883 6555**
www.jebelali-international.com

## Siamin — Thai
Low-key Thai eatery on the quiet side of the Marina
The unlicensed Siamin is unlikely to draw the crowds from other parts of town, but as a quiet, local Thai venue for Marina east-siders it fits the bill. The interior is ornate and intimate, the service excellent, and the dishes well flavoured with some good sharing options.
**The Radisson Blu Residence** Dubai Marina
**04 435 5000**
www.siamindubai.com
Map **1 M4** Metro **Dubai Marina**

## Signatures — French
Elegant venue, strong wine, ideal for special nights
This French restaurant has something for everyone in terms of choice. The atmosphere is sophisticated both inside and out and, whether the weather permits alfresco dining or not, you'll feel like you are dining under the stars. It's a bit on the expensive side, but the experience is a special one.
**Jebel Ali Hotel** Jebel Ali **04 814 5555**
www.jebelali-international.com

## Singapore Deli Café — Singaporean
Authentic, home-style cuisine in a relaxed venue
From bowls of steaming noodles to traditionally cooked nasi goreng, the authentic dishes available at Singapore Deli Café are consistently excellent. The casual atmosphere and home-style cooking draws a large crowd of regular customers who come for a taste of home.
**Nr BurJuman Centre** Bur Dubai **04 396 6885**
Map **2 L4** Metro **Khalid Bin Al Waleed**

## Sketch — International
Artsy venue with a quirky menu
Dishes like fillet steak with spicy chocolate sauce and hammour with pea tzatsiki lend a slight quirkiness to Sketch. The atmosphere is enhanced by the incongruous spotlights, which cast the scarlet walls with a theatrical glow, making it feel like its run by a group of experimental artists. Good cocktails too.
**Metropolitan Palace** Deira **04 227 0000**
www.habtoorhotels.com
Map **2 N5** Metro **Al Rigga**

### Smiling BKK
Thai

*Cheerful Thai joint with a cheeky attitude*

This outstanding Thai pad is a rare thing: a restaurant that serves great food with a side of good humour. The cheekily named dishes are reasonable at around Dhs.30, but with gossip mag pages for place mats and ingenious theme nights such as 'sing for your supper', it's the atmosphere that sets Smiling BKK apart.

**Al Wasl Rd** Jumeira **04 349 6677**

Map **2 E4** Metro **Burj Dubai**

### Spectrum On One
International

*Possibly the biggest menu in Dubai*

Divided into some of the world's most delicious regions – India, China, Thailand, Europe, Japan and Arabia – you need a good half hour to absorb the menu. The surroundings are spacious, with intimate spots for couples and room for groups to mingle and a tucked-away bar.

**Fairmont Dubai** Trade Centre **04 332 5555**

www.fairmont.com

Map **2 J4** Metro **Trade Centre**

### Spice Island
Buffet

*A Dubai favourite, great for kids*

A trip to the Spice Island buffet creates a few dilemmas with so many cuisines begging to be picked up from the live cooking stations and cuisine divided areas. There's a choice of alcoholic and non-alcoholic packages, and the kids can hang out in a designated play area, where they can make you a desert. Entertaining the adults is a singing trio, who pass around the tables and buffet area.

**Renaissance Dubai** Deira **04 262 5555**

www.renaissancehotels.com

Map **2 P5** Metro **Salahudin**

### Splendido
Italian

*High-class Italian for a quiet, romantic evening out*

Head to Splendido for a large menu (literally) featuring some excellent, classic Italian fare. Tasty mains and delicious desserts are all generously portioned, and the tone is quietly classy. There's a good wine list and it's great location for a stroll along the beach afterwards.

**The Ritz-Carlton, Dubai** Dubai Marina **04 399 4000**

www.ritzcarlton.com

Map **1 K3** Metro **Dubai Marina**

### St Tropez > *p.497*
French

*Home-cooked French food on a charming terrace*

Authentic French food with frogs' legs and snails on the menu, as well as superb steaks that keep diners coming back for more. Choose to eat inside the cosy restaurant, offset by hundreds of black and white framed photos of celebrities, or on the fairy-light illuminated terrace.

**Century Village** Garhoud **04 286 9029**

www.centuryvillage.ae

Map **2 N7** Metro **GGICO**

### Steam Sum Dim Sum
Chinese

*Mouthwatering delights in an intimate setting*

Forget the shopping mall location (and you will once you arrive), this modern Asian restaurant serves a tantalising array of steamed and fried dim sum with tasty noodles and salads as well as exotic mocktails. Make sure you go with an appetite as you'll want to order numerous dishes.

**Festival Centre** Festival City **04 232 9190**

www.steamsum.com

Map **2 M8** Metro **Creek**

### Stefano's Restaurant
Italian

*Classic Italian dishes in a relaxed alfresco setting*

Dining tables and sofas fill Stefano's position along the water's edge at Marina Walk, offering excellent views and home-cooked classic Italian dishes. The menu includes traditional items such as bruschetta, spaghetti and pizza calzone with fresh juices and shisha.

**Marina Walk** Dubai Marina **04 422 2632**

www.reginapasta.com

Map **1 L4** Metro **Dubai Marina**

### Stone Fire Pizza Kitchen
Pizzeria

*Traditional pizzas and successfully bizarre options*

Stone Fire Pizza Kitchen serves the most original pizza in the UAE – and is so Dubai. Not only does it produce superb Italian fare from the freshest ingredients, it also comes up with some bizarre combinations. The Norwegian salmon white pizza with caviar and avocado is a delectable example.

**Dubai Outlet Mall** **04 425 5817**

**www.stonefirekitchen.com**

Map **2 C3**

St Tropez

# Restaurants & Cafes

## Sukhothai
**Thai**

*Excellent food and a beautiful interior*
With dark wood-panelled walls and authentic Thai artefacts, it's a great venue for a romantic occasion or a special treat. The extensive and expensive menu offers all the favourites and the seafood is top notch. There's an outdoor area, but the interior is unbeatable.
**Le Meridien Dubai** Garhoud **04 702 2307**
www.lemeridien-dubai.com
Map **2 N7** Metro **GGICO**

## Sumibiya > p.239
**Korean**

*Feasting fun at this eatery where you're the chef*
Eating is a social affair at this yakiniku (Korean grilled meat) eatery, where diners use the gas grill in the middle of every table to sear, grill and charcoal bite-size morsels. It's informal, fun and tasty; if your food is overdone, you only have yourself to blame.
**Radisson Blu Hotel, Dubai Deira Creek** Al Rigga **04 222 7171**
www.radissonblu.com/hotel-dubaideiracreek
Map **2 N4** Metro **Union**

## Sumo Sushi & Bento
**Japanese**

*Brilliant bento boxes that fit the bill perfectly*
You can almost imagine a Tokyo executive eating a lunch like yours: sticky beef atop rice and vegetables, with a little cup of green tea. It's simple, healthy stuff and while Sumo might not win culinary awards, it does what it sets out to do very well.
**Town Centre Jumeirah** Jumeira **04 344 3672**
www.sumosushi.net
Map **2 F3** Metro **Burj Dubai**

## Sushi
**Japanese**

*Simple name, simple concept – high-quality sushi*
Artfully prepared in the open kitchen of this petite venue, sushi and sashimi portions are determined by the number of pieces you feel like indulging in. The careful preparation and the melt in your mouth morsels are high quality.
**Grand Hyatt Dubai** Umm Hurair **04 317 2222**
www.dubai.grand.hyatt.com
Map **2 L7** Metro **Healthcare City**

## Sushi Sushi > p.497
**Japanese**

*Top sushi and tempura at reasonable prices*
This intimate venue offers a comprehensive menu of sushi and sashimi, while non-sushi eaters are equally well catered for with alternative Japanese dishes. Tuesday nights see an all you can eat offer for Dhs.169. Reservations are recommended. There's also a fabulous outdoor terrace.
**Century Village** Garhoud **04 282 9908**
www.centuryvillage.ae
Map **2 N7** Metro **GGICO**

## Switch
**Mediterranean**

*Swish interior, good menu, stands out from the mall*
The space age, experimental interior by designer Karim Rashid gives this mall food outlet a touch of the wow factor, while the food is good. Exemplary seared tuna loin with citrus sauce, beautifully presented goats cheese tarts and a range of salads, mains and sandwiches are all beautifully executed.
**The Dubai Mall** Downtown Burj Dubai **04 339 9131**
www.meswitch.com
Map **2 F6** Metro **Burj Dubai**

## Tagine
**Moroccan**

*Atmospheric interior, melt-in-the mouth dishes*
Duck down and enter through the tiny carved wooden doorway into a beautiful Moroccan den of embroidered hangings, glowing lanterns and sultry music. The food is deliciously authentic, and the meat dishes so tender. The intimate cushioned booths are the best seats in the house.
**One&Only Royal Mirage** Al Sufouh **04 399 9999**
www.oneandonlyroyalmirage.com
Map **1 M3** Metro **Nakheel**

## Tagpuan
**Filipino**

*Home-style Filipino cooking at great prices*
The tiny tables inside tiny Tagpuan fill up quickly, but the outside area on the terrace offers more space. Come here to try simple but tasty versions of Filipino home favourites including adobong pusit (squid), fried tilapia (fish) or pinakbet (mixed vegetables).
**Karama Centre** Karama **04 337 3959**
Map **2 K5** Metro **Karama**

## Teatro
**International**

*A popular classic on the buzzing SZR strip*
Perennially popular Teatro offers a fusion of tastes, with dishes from Japan, China, India and Europe. Whether you go for pizza, noodles, sushi or a curry, the food is guaranteed to please. There are great views over Sheikh Zayed Road, and a half-price discount if you order before 19:15.
**Towers Rotana** Trade Centre **04 343 8000**
www.rotana.com
Map **2 G5** Metro **Financial Centre**

## Terra Firma
**Italian**

*Fine steaks and wines keep you on course*
For golfers who want to tuck into David Blackmore Wagyu and internationally renowned wines with majestic views over the Al Badia course, Terra Firma has the perfect scorecard. Private rooms can be hired out making this the perfect spot for a special occasion, golf or not.
**Al Badia Golf Club** Festival City **04 601 0101**
www.albadiagolfclub.ae
Map **2 M9** Metro **Rashidiya**

# Serving the world's favourite dishes.

From the delights of the Orient to the delicacies of Continental Europe and Asia, Century Village takes your taste buds on a tour of the world's best cuisines.

MASALA CRAFT, SARBAND, THE SAPPHIRE, SUSHI SUSHI, ST. TROPEZ, CHINA WHITE, MAZAJ, LA VIGNA, DA GAMA AND THE PLAICE.

Next to the Tennis Stadium, Garhoud. Visit: www.centuryvillage.ae ( FREE VALET PARKING)

# Restaurants & Cafes

## The Terrace — International
Versatile, quality Deira restaurant

The Sheraton Deira's main restaurant sits behind the entryway in a massive, tree-lined atrium. Faux columns along the walls create isolated booths perfect for both an intimate date and a raucous evening with friends. The buffet and live cooking stations change based on the nightly theme; the selection is extensive.
**Park Hyatt Dubai** Port Saeed **04 317 2222**
www.dubai.park.hyatt.com
Map **2 M6** Metro **GGICO**

## Thai Chi — Far Eastern
A double dose of Asia at this Thai-Chinese favourite

Choose from the Thai-inspired bamboo lounge or the regal dinner room straight out of China at this double-flavoured Asian. The menu features excellent appetisers, meats, poultry, seafood and vegetarian options from both the Thai and Chinese kitchens. The shared platters are favourites with the regulars.
**Pyramids** Wafi **04 324 4100**
www.waficityrestaurants.com
Map **2 P6** Metro **Healthcare City**

## The Thai Kitchen — Thai
Classy Thai place in the delightful Park Hyatt

Set around four live-cooking areas, the decor is stylish and modern with dark walls and teak wood floors contrasting well with the large soft lights. Although relatively small, the menu consists of a range of Thai delicacies prepared to maximise the rich authentic flavours. Portions are purposely small so that you can share.
**Park Hyatt Dubai** Port Saeed **04 317 2222**
www.dubai.park.hyatt.com
Map **2 M6** Metro **GGICO**

## Thai Terrace — Thai
A hidden gem straight from the alleys of Bangkok

This cheap and cheerful Thai eatery is a solid choice, especially if you happen to be in the area. Its renditions of favourites such as spring rolls and green curries are all very good, and the pretty outdoor seating area makes a pleasant spot to grab a budget bite.
**Trade Centre Rd** Karama **04 396 9356**
Map **2 L4** Metro **Karama**

## Thiptara — Thai
Fresh-from-the-tank seafood and Burj views

Expect fresh and spicy seafood at this quality Thai restaurant overlooking the Burj Dubai and lake. There's a lively lobster tank from which to take your pick, while the wine list is extensive. A hard location to beat for impressing visitors and business associates.
**The Palace – The Old Town** Downtown Burj Dubai **04 428 7961**
www.thepalace-dubai.com
Map **2 F6** Metro **Burj Dubai**

## tokyo@thetowers — Japanese
Modern dining with private rooms and lively tables

With elegantly partitioned tatami rooms, lively teppanyaki tables and an eclectic menu, tokyo@thetowers offers diners enough options to keep things interesting. The private rooms all have traditional floor cushions and you can dine by the windows overlooking the mall if you need a view.
**Boulevard at Emirates Towers** Trade Centre **04 319 8088**
www.jumeirahemiratestowers.com
Map **2 H5** Metro **Emirates Towers**

## Topkapi — Turkish
A rare slice of Turkey in Dubai, cheap and cheerful

Topkapi, with its Istanbul-style interior and traditionally dressed waiters, is one of only two Turkish restaurants in Dubai. An average-tasting menu includes mezze with a Turkish twist. The decor is pleasing, featuring an open kitchen and cushion-laden benches.
**Taj Palace Hotel** Deira **04 223 2222**
www.tajhotels.com
Map **2 N5** Metro **Al Rigga**

## Tour Dubai > p.499 — Dinner Cruise
Dhow dining for something a bit different

For dinner with a difference, take to the creek on a traditional dhow. Majlis seating, regular and buffet dining and cocktail receptions all await. Alternatively, for a romantic evening, charter a personal dhow, complete with your own butler, roses for your partner, champagne, five-star dining and a limousine.
**Oud Metha 04 336 8409**
www.tour-dubai.com
Map **2 L5** Metro **Oud Metha**

tokyo@thetowers

## Dubai's First
## Arabian Dhow Cruises

# *Floating Functions - A unique experience for every event.*

- Sail on the creek with Dubai's premier Dhow cruise operator
- Exclusive Dhow charters - Fully licenced to serve beverages
- Dhow capacities ranging from 15 to 275 guests
- Choice of catering options - Arabic entertainment options
- Fitted with Govt. approved safety equipment

**DAILY DINNER CRUISES**
- 2 Hours Cruising - 5 Star Buffet Dinner
- Incl. Mineral water / Soft Drinks
Transfers can be arranged on request

**GUIDED CREEK TOURS**
Four times daily : 11.30, 13.30, 15.30, 17.30
Pre-recorded commentary in English
Incl. Mineral water or soft drink

## *Also available: Safaris & Sightseeing Tours*

**Tel: 04 3368407 / 9 Fax 04 3368411**
Email: admin@tour-dubai.com Web: www.tour-dubai.com

# Restaurants & Cafes

### Trader Vic's
**Polynesian**

*Legendary lively joint with lethal cocktails*

Until you've experienced Trader Vic's, you can't consider yourself a seasoned Dubai night-lifer. Delicious Asian-inspired dishes and moreish snacks are available or you can jump straight to the famously exotic cocktails, served in ceramic skulls and seashells. Head to the Crowne Plaza branch (04 331 1111) for live Cuban music every night. See Trader Vic's Mai-Tai for an even livelier version (p.516).

**Souk Madinat Jumeirah** Umm Suqeim **04 366 5646**
www.tradervics.com
Map **1 R4** Metro **Mall of the Emirates**

### Traiteur
**International**

*A brasserie menu in a fine dining setting*

Previously a decadent mix of European dishes that required a bank loan, Traiteur introduced a new French Brasserie menu in late 2009. The elegant setting remains, with the terrace that commands impressive views of the marina and beyond, and for wine lovers the bill will still stack up.

**Park Hyatt Dubai** Port Saeed **04 317 2222**
www.dubai.park.hyatt.com
Map **2 M6** Metro **GGICO**

### Troyka
**Russian**

*Russian regulars served in an intimate surrounding*

Troyka's old world charm creates an intimate mood to enjoy tasty cuisine. The Tuesday night buffet is all-inclusive and comprises time-honoured delicacies from Russian cuisine. A band plays every night from 22:30 and an extravagant live Vegas-style cabaret begins at 23:30.

**Ascot Hotel** Bur Dubai **04 352 0900**
www.ascothoteldubai.com
Map **2 L3** Metro **Al Fahidi**

Verre

### Veda Pavilion
**Far Eastern**

*Laidback post-beach hangout with amazing views*

Chic yet comfortable, this is a great place to head after a day at the beach. The substantial drinks list and affordable far eastern inspired menu are suited to casual lunches, dinners with groups of friends, or just a lazy beer on the poolside terrace, with views of the Burj Al Arab and the Arabian Gulf.

**Clubhouse Al Nafura, Shoreline Apartments**
Palm Jumeirah **04 361 8845**
www.emiratesleisureretail.com
Map **1 N2** Metro **Nakheel**

### Verre
**French**

*Simple interior, stunning food from Gordon Ramsay*

At Verre, Gordon Ramsay's first foray outside the UK, it's all about the food. The exciting menu is not huge, but contains some stunning culinary creations. Faultless service, delightful canapes and palate cleansers make this a memorable but pricey dining experience.

**Hilton Creek** Deira **04 212 7551**
www.hilton.com
Map **2 N5** Metro **Union**

### Vienna Café
**Cafe**

*Austrian-style cafe in the middle of the JW Marriott*

The wood panelling and delicate tablecloths are not readily associated with Deira, but it blends well with the grandeur of the JW Marriott. There is a good selection of food, from light salads to steaks, but the real draw is people watching while enjoying a good cuppa.

**JW Marriott Hotel** Deira **04 607 7977**
www.marriottdiningatjw.ae
Map **2 P5** Metro **Abu Baker Al Siddque**

### Villa Beach
**International**

*Probably the most upmarket beach shack, ever*

Mediterranean fare within cork-popping distance of the sea and Burj Al Arab. The wooden-decked terrace and hanging lanterns give Villa Beach a laidback feel, but the quality is anything but. Delicious dishes include warm goats cheese, prosciutto and figs, tender steaks and Bailey's tiramisu, and the service is worthy of a fine-dining venue.

**The Jumeirah Beach Hotel** Umm Suqeim
**04 406 8999**
www.jumeirah.com
Map **1 S3** Metro **Mall of the Emirates**

### Vivaldi
**Italian**

*Romance on the creek, with great food and wine*

Perched over the sparkling Dubai Creek, Vivaldi is a clear contender for one of the most romantic restaurants in Dubai. Spectacular views from both inside the warmly lit restaurant and the two outdoor terraces, an experimental Italian menu and a

Yum

Villa Beach

Wox

Wagamama

Spectrum On One

**Going Out**

comprehensive wine list will have you coming back to try all the delicious selections on offer.
**Sheraton Hotel & Towers** Deira **04 228 1111**
www.starwoodhotels.com
Map **2 M4** Metro **Union**

### Vu's
Mediterranean
Excellent modern fare, great views
A stylish and elegant eatery, Vu's offers one of the most sensational views in town. The modern European menu is finely compiled with dishes certain to impress, and each plate is exquisitely presented in more manageable portions than you might find elsewhere. Be warned, the location and quality might be sky high but so are the prices.
**Emirates Towers** Trade Centre **04 319 8088**
www.jumeirah.com
Map **2 H5** Metro **Emirates Towers**

### Wafi Gourmet
Arabic/Lebanese
A wide variety of deli-cious Arabic delights
Deliciously prepared traditional Lebanese dishes, along with pastries, sweets, ice creams, exotic juices and hot drinks, make Wafi Gourmet a great sustenance stop when on a shopping spree. Make sure you browse around the delicatessen and you're sure to leave with more bags than you arrived with.
**Wafi** Umm Hurair **04 324 4433**
www.wafi.com
Map **2 L6** Metro **Healthcare City**

### Wagamama
Japanese
Modern Japanese dining done in a funky style
Modelled on a traditional Japanese ramen bar, with communal tables, Wagamama's streamlined design works well for a quick bite. Orders are immediately and freshly prepared; if you want to linger over your meal, it is wise to order a course at a time. Also at Crowne Plaza (p.230) and The Greens (04 361 5757).
**Al Fattan Towers** Dubai Marina **04 399 5900**
www.wagamama.ae
Map Metro **Dubai Marina**

### Warehouse > p.503
International
Eat, drink and dance all in one stylish venue
Warehouse, a restaurant-pub-wine bar-vodka bar-lounge club, is a stylish addition to the old-school side of the Creek. There is a beer bar and garden on the ground floor serving fish and chips and the likes, while up the spiral staircase you'll find a dual-personality restaurant – half fine dining and half sushi – where the food is deliciously inventive. There is also an intimate nightclub should you want to continue the night.
**Le Meridien Dubai** Garhoud **04 702 2560**
www.lemeridien.com/dubaiwarehouse
Map **2 N7** Metro **GGICO**

### Water Lemon
Cafe
Worthy place for some quick shopping relief
The canteen-feel ambience of this Dubai Mall venue, with its bright lighting and modern furniture, isn't the most relaxing of spaces, but walk through to the back and you'll find a quiet outdoor area, lovely in the evening, with a staggering view of The Address hotel. The emphasis is on quick healthy fare with a fantastic choice of vitamin-packed juices.
**The Dubai Mall** Downtown Burj Dubai **04 434 0450**
www.h2o-lemon.com
Map **2 F6** Metro **Burj Dubai**

### Waterside Seafood Restaurant
Seafood
Small but cosy poolside fish restaurant
True to its name, even if the water is courtesy of Al Murooj's maze of pools and walkways, this small restaurant is all about the sea. There is a fish market where you can select your dish and the way in which you would like it cooked. The cocktails are elegant and the dimmed lighting make this a good location for a romantic dinner. There is also a pleasant terrace for the cooler months.
**Al Murooj Rotana Hotel & Suites** Trade Centre **04 321 1111**
www.rotana.com
Map **2 G5** Metro **Financial Centre**

The Warehouse

# wareHOUSE
## BARS • RESTAURANTS • LOUNGE

MALT BAR

CELLAR

RESTAURANT

LOUNGE

## GREAT FOOD, CREATIVE DRINKS AND FANTASTIC MUSIC

Start your evening early at the European style café bar and garden where you can enjoy an array of International beverages or a glass of grape beverage at the stylish bar.

Make your way to the upper level for a touch of sophisticated fusion cuisine. Indulge your senses in a captivating setting at the chic cocktail bar and on to the lounge where the resident DJ plays the best of house, dance and top hits.

5.00 pm to 3.00 am
Warehouse Sale from 5.00 pm to 8.00 pm

For reservations, please call
T +971 4 702 2560

### Le MERIDIEN

LE MERIDIEN
DUBAI
N 25° 14' E 55° 20'
T +971 4 217 0000
F +971 4 282 4672
lemeridien.com/dubaiwarehouse

### Wavebreaker — International
Relaxed beach bar perfect for sunset drinks

A beach bar that serves snacks, light meals, kids' meals, barbecue grills and a variety of cocktails and mocktails. It's a perfect place for a laidback afternoon, while at sunset, it's quiet, cool and the beach view is stunning, making you linger for more than just one of their sophisticated sundowners.

**Hilton Jumeirah** Dubai Marina **04 399 1111**
www.hilton.com
Map **1 K3** Metro **Jumeirah Lakes Towers**

### The Western Steakhouse — Steakhouse
Homely venue that serves up great food

Western Steakhouse is great for meat lovers to line their stomachs before a night on the town. It's an unpretentious venue that provides a refreshing change with its homely atmosphere and decor, serving up large portions of great quality fare in a comfortable setting.

**Crowne Plaza** Trade Centre **04 331 1111**
www.ichotelsgroup.com
Map **2 H5** Metro **Emirates Towers**

### The Wharf — Seafood
Excellent location, which you pay for

The Wharf faces the magical waterways of Madinat, and while the outdoor deck and sailing paraphernalia are appealing, the menu is not as mesmerising. There's steak and a smattering of Arabic dishes, alongside plentiful pizza, and while the food is well presented the prices are a little steep. If you do sit outside be prepared for the obsessive taking of photos and comings and goings of the abras.

**Mina A'Salam** Umm Suqeim **04 366 6730**
www.jumeirah.com
Map **1 R3** Metro **Mall of the Emirates**

### White Orchid — Asian
Delightful eastern cuisine that's worth the trip

Some of the best eastern flavours in Dubai are served up at this contemporary Asian restaurant which focuses on Thai and Japanese dishes. Mix sushi platters and green curries, or try something from the teppanyaki table. The decor is styled on a Thai bamboo hut, there's a spacious outdoor terrace, and service is impeccable.

**Jebel Ali Hotel** Jebel Ali **04 814 5604**
www.jebelali-international.com

### Wild Peeta — Arabic/Lebanese
Healthy eatery, locally owned and widely enjoyed

This Emirati-owned fusion shawarma restaurant created a huge buzz on its opening in October 2009: fresh, healthy shawarmas, salads and juices, served by some of the friendliest staff in Dubai, has made it popular in a short time. The Moroccan salad and Thai shawarma are both recommended. Takeaway and delivery available.

**Dubai Healthcare City** Umm Hurair **04 800 9453**
www.wildpeeta.com
Map  Metro **Healthcare City**

### Wox — Far Eastern
Watch your food sizzle and steam before tucking in

Sit at the noodle bar or one of the individual tables, place your order from the simple (but comprehensive) menu and watch the flurry of sizzling woks and steaming pots as your food is prepared in front of you.

**Grand Hyatt Dubai** Umm Hurair **04 317 1234**
www.dubai.grand.hyatt.com
Map **2 L7** Metro **Healthcare City**

### Xennya — Arabic/Lebanese
Great for guests who want an Arabic experience

Combining the best of Arabic and North African cuisine this subtly decorated restaurant has private dining rooms which may be preferable to the packed-in main seating area. Traditional live music and dancing adds to the atmosphere.

**Holiday Inn Al Barsha  04 323 4333**
www.hialbarshadubai.com
Map **1 Q5** Metro **Sharaf DG**

### Yakitori — Japanese
Authentic diner that draws a knowledgeable crowd

Laid out in the red and black style of a Japanese diner and with a huge menu of sushi, tempura, noodles, set meals, and the signature yakitori dish, this restaurant offers unrivalled choice.

**Ascot Hotel** Bur Dubai **04 352 0900**
www.ascothoteldubai.com
Map **2 L3** Metro **Al Fahidi**

### Yo! Sushi — Japanese
Fresh, fun sushi straight from the conveyor belt

Sushi addicts and first-timers will find something here, with both traditional and unconventional sushi available. Friendly staff explain the types of sushi on the conveyor belt and the different coloured plates indicate the price of the dish. Branches are also in Dubai Festival City, BurJuman, Dubai Marina Mall, Dubai Mall and DIFC.

**Dubai Internet City** Al Sufouh **04 36254 70/1**
www.yosushi.com
Map **1 M4** Metro **Nakheel**

---

**Explorer Member Card**

Don't forget to register your member card (found at the back of the book) and check online for current offers. Discounts are updated on a monthly basis and you can search by area and cuisine type. www.liveworkexplore.com.

### Yum! > *p.239* — Far Eastern

*International cuisine that's in Deira, but not dear*

Catering to an especially busy lunch crowd, the focus is on fresh, high quality Asian food cooked swiftly. Good-sized dishes are offered from Thailand, Malaysia and other regions, with healthy options highlighted on the menu for the body conscious. If you do intend to go for a group work lunch then it's a good idea to book in advance.

**Radisson Blu Hotel, Dubai Deira Creek** Al Rigga
**04 222 7171**
www.radissonblu.com/hotel-dubaideiracreek
Map **2 N4** Metro **Union**

### Zaika — Indian

*Atmospheric, classy Indian with great set menus*

Intimate upmarket Indian set in a characterful split-level rotunda building. Private booths occupy the upper level while Buddha statues and candles sit among the tables downstairs. The a la carte selection is based on traditional Indian flavours, with some good set menu options. The large sweeping staircase keeps the restaurant intimate for romantic diners.

**Al Murooj Rotana Hotel & Suites** Trade Centre
**04 321 1111**
www.rotana.com
Map **2 G5** Metro **Financial Centre**

### Zheng He's — Chinese

*Deliciously inventive Chinese with great views*

Zheng He's superb take on Chinese delicacies serves up exciting combinations of dim sum and mini starters, traditional dishes and marinated fish and stir-fried meats with arguably the best duck in town. The wine is a little on the pricey side but the waterside view makes it worthwhile.

**Mina A'Salam** Umm Suqeim **04 366 6730**
www.jumeirah.com
Map **1 R3** Metro **Mall of the Emirates**

### Zuma — Japanese

*Stylish Japanese venue that draws the DIFC crowds*

The stunning multi-level space is elegantly lit, with clean lines of wood and glass creating a restaurant and bar that has stepped straight out of London. It's buzzy, stylish and perfect for a first date or business lunch. Food arrives from the open kitchen and sushi bar artistically presented in classic Japanese style – like the decor, it is all about simplicity and flair. It's not cheap so if dinner is beyond your budget it's still worth going for a drink at the packed bar.

**Dubai International Financial Centre (DIFC)**
Trade Centre **04 425 5660**
www.zumarestaurant.com
Map **2 G5** Metro **Trade Centre**

Zheng He's

# BARS, PUBS & CLUBS

### 360° — Bar
*Lazy lounging, rebellious partying, ocean views*
This two-tiered circular rooftop bar situated above Marina seafood restaurant (p.482), boasts all-round views of the Arabian Gulf and Burj Al Arab. House DJs spin at the weekends, and late afternoon loungers smoking shisha give way to scruffily chic stylistas supping cocktails as the tempo rises. Open from 16:00. Closed in summer.
**The Jumeirah Beach Hotel** Umm Suqeim
**04 406 8999**
www.jumeirah.com
Map **1 S3** Metro **Mall of the Emirates**

### The 400 — Nightclub
*Showy club that's not to everyone's taste*
Home of dark corners and big bar bills, this club isn't to everyone's taste but serves a purpose for fans of excessive hair gel, plastic surgery and loud music. Negotiate the doormen, enter the underground venue via a stately staircase then get involved in the Arabic, house and R&B music, watching out for popping champagne corks. You can't help but notice when someone orders something special; the bottle is paraded around the club on a velvet cushion surrounded by sparklers.
**Fairmont Dubai** Trade Centre **04 332 4900**
www.the400nightclub.com
Map **2 J4** Metro **Trade Centre**

### The Agency — Bar
*Popular wine bar that enhances any night out*
Proving that wine bars aren't just a fad, The Agency continues to attract crowds. If overwhelmed by the 33 page wine menu, try one of the 'flights' (a selection of four different wines) to get yourself in the swing. Also serves tasty tapas-style snacks. There's another Agency at Madinat Jumeirah (04 366 6730).
**Boulevard at Emirates Towers** Trade Centre
**04 319 8088**
www.jumeirah.com
Map **2 H5** Metro **Emirates Towers**

### The Apartment Lounge + Club — Nightclub
*The place for mingling, with extra bubbles*
Look out for the popping of champagne corks and cameras snapping away for local society mags. Yes, this is The Apartment, home to a few high rollers and many beautiful people that fill up two decadent rooms. The soundtrack leans towards house, hip-hop and R&B.
**The Jumeirah Beach Hotel** Umm Suqeim
**04 406 8000**
www.jumeirah.com
Map **1 S3** Metro **Mall of the Emirates**

### Alpha — Nightclub
*High ceilings, hipster crowds, great hip-hop*
Alpha's high, white interior was formerly a Greek restaurant and its design elements still prevail. A packed schedule of international DJs, special events and drink deals attract a hip, low-key crowd. By spinning some of the best house and hip-hop in Dubai, Alpha raises the musical bar.
**Le Meridien Dubai** Garhoud **04 702 2640**
www.alphaclub.ae
Map **2 N7** Metro **GGICO**

### Aussie Legends — Pub
*Pool, live music, sports, party-time atmosphere*
Like any friendly local, Aussie Legends regularly hosts live bands and musicians. The small dance floor tends to kick off quite early at the weekends, and the pool table is popular. The grub is decent and the large TVs keep sports fans occupied.
**Rydges Plaza Hotel** Satwa **04 398 2222**
www.rydges.com
Map **2 J4** Metro **Al Jafiliya**

### Bahri Bar — Bar
*Cookie-cutter perfection in the shape of a bar*
This might just be the perfect bar: stunning views of the Burj Al Arab and the sparkling ocean beyond grace the spacious terrace, while inside lavish but comfortable furnishings create an intimate atmosphere. A selection of delicious drinks and nibbles, plus live music at the weekends, complete a picture of perfection.
**Mina A'Salam** Umm Suqeim **04 366 6730**
www.jumeirah.com
Map **1 R3** Metro **Mall of the Emirates**

The Agency

## Balcony Bar
Bar

Cocktails, vintage whiskies, and leather armchairs

Dark, masculine wooden panelling and black leather armchairs dominate this sophisticated cocktail bar. The drinks list is extensive, and each cocktail is artfully presented. For the extravagant pocket, there are some eye-wateringly expensive champagnes and vintage whiskies, while teetotallers can choose from a basic selection of booze-free beverages.

**Shangri-La Hotel** Trade Centre **04 343 8888**
www.shangri-la.com
Map **2 G5** Metro **Financial Centre**

## The Bar
Bar

A good spot to whet your whistle in Deira

Encased in glass and furnished with a mix of high tables, bar stools and soft leather armchairs, the interior of The Bar is unobtrusive and relaxed. The well-stocked bar dispenses some interesting aperitifs and after-dinner liqueurs, as well as decent cocktails, wines and bottled beers.

**Hyatt Regency** Deira **04 317 2222**
www.dubai.regency.hyatt.com
Map **2 N3** Metro **Palm Deira**

## Bar 44
Bar

An ideal place to start or end the evening

Good things come at high prices, or so it seems in this classy spot. From the bar's lofty location on the 44th floor, enjoy magnificent views of the Marina and the excellent selection of wine and cocktails.

**Grosvenor House** Dubai Marina **04 399 8888**
www.grosvenorhouse-dubai.com
Map **1 L4** Metro **Dubai Marina**

## Bar Below
Bar

Hidden Marina bar that's yet to take off

A classy but quiet bar area tucked away at the back of Le Royal Meridien, dishing up good (but pricey) cocktails accompanied by run-of-the-mill tunes. While the large chandelier and classy decor does raise an eyebrow, Bar Below rarely draws a big crowd.

**Le Royal Meridien** Dubai Marina **04 399 5555**
www.leroyalmeridien-dubai.com
Metro **Dubai Marina**

## Bar Zar
Bar

Slick, urban-feel bar with a few surprises

This funky two-tiered bar hits the balance between laidback cool and noisy revelry, with the added attraction of live bands. Eclectic drinks, such as beer cocktails, are paired with more traditional offerings in the cocktail, lager and bar snacks departments.

**Souk Madinat Jumeirah** Umm Suqeim **04 366 6730**
www.jumeirah.com
Map **1 R4** Metro **Mall of the Emirates**

Barasti

## Barasti
Bar

Beachside magnet for expat sun and fun hunters

Expats flock to lively beachside Barasti in flip-flops or their Friday finery – so arrive early. Stars of the underrated menu include particularly good seafood, ribs and steak. The view, big screens, split level seating, beach beds, live music and a friendly crowd make this a reliable spot for a good night out.

**Le Meridien Mina Seyahi** Al Sufouh **04 399 3333**
www.lemeridien-minaseyahi.com
Map **1 M3** Metro **Dubai Marina**

## Belgian Beer Cafe
Bar

Beer, Brussels and mussels

One of the best beer-drinking spots in town. On top of all manner of European amber nectar delights, there's good food, especially the moules frites, Belgian sausages, chocolate mousse and tempting waffles. The traditional decor features Victorian-style tiles and chunky furniture, and there's a nice terrace with creek views.

**Crowne Plaza Festival City** Festival City **04 701 2222**
www.intercontinental.com
Map **2 M8** Metro **Creek**

## BidiBondi
Bar

Great local bar, if you're lucky enough to live there

Typically relaxed and informal, this Aussie bar on Palm Jumeirah has a beach diner feel complemented by poolside perches. The menu offers hefty burgers, salads, bar snacks, breakfast and kids' specials alongside a great range of mocktails, cocktails, beers and wines.

**Clubhouse Al Manhal, Shoreline Apartments** Palm Jumeirah **04 427 0515**
www.emiratesleisureretail.com
Map **1 N2** Metro **Nakheel**

# Bars, Pubs & Clubs

Going Out

### Blue Bar
Bar

*A hidden gem for jazz fans*
Dark wood, low lighting and a smoky atmosphere create the perfect setting for live jazz on Thursdays. Mingle with the business crowd from Trade Centre over post-work drinks and bar bites. There's live music on Wednesdays and Fridays as well.
**Novotel World Trade Centre** Trade Centre
**04 332 0000**
www.novotel.com
Map **2 H5** Metro **Trade Centre**

### The Boston Bar
Bar

*Post-work hangout with several theme nights*
Slightly dingy but great for after-work drinks and watching sports. Theme nights include sports on Saturday and Sundays, a tricky yet popular Monday quiz, Tuesday ladies' night, Wednesday two-for-one, Thursday ladies' night, and a Friday breakfast binge.
**Jumeira Rotana** Satwa **04 345 5888**
www.rotana.com
Map **2 J3** Metro **Al Jafiliya**

### Boudoir
Nightclub

*Ladies' nights, big queues, and Parisian decor*
This exclusive spot can be as difficult to get into as a lady's chamber, but once inside you will be treated to a Parisian-style club with opulent fabrics, hypnotic tunes and moody lighting. The music selection changes throughout the week and there are drink deals for ladies almost every night of the week.
**Dubai Marine Beach** Jumeira **04 345 5995**
www.myboudoir.com
Map **2 H3** Metro **Al Jafiliya**

### Buddha Bar
Bar

*A flamboyant bar that attracts a glamorous crowd*
Half restaurant, half bar, this nightspot never fails to impress with its moody lighting, gigantic statue of Buddha and marina views. If the waiter can hear you over the funky Buddha bar beats, then order from it's sublime selection of cocktails.
**Grosvenor House** Dubai Marina **04 399 8888**
www.grosvenorhouse.lemeridien.com
Map **1 L4** Metro **Dubai Marina**

### Calabar
Bar

*A high-class vibe straight out of Latin America*
A large sweeping bar serving all manner of drinks from international brews to unique cocktails inspired by Latin America, is the centre piece of this chic lounge bar. Asian, Japanese and Arabic nibbles make a great accompaniment to sundowners on the terrace.
**The Address Downtown Burj Dubai**
Downtown Burj Dubai **04 436 8888**
www.theaddress.com
Map **2 F6** Metro **Burj Dubai**

Cavalli Club

### Carter's
Bar

*Gastro pub food; a good weekend watering hole*
The oversized wooden ceiling fans, hunting trophies and colonial-style paraphernalia lend Carters a slightly 'themed' quality, but don't be put off. The food is decent gastro-pub fare, and the large bar and live music make this a popular place for a good time at the weekend.
**Pyramids** Wafi **04 324 4100**
www.wafi.com
Map **2 P6** Metro **Healthcare City**

### Cavalli Club
Nightclub

*Catwalk fashion comes first, substance second*
Roberto Cavalli took a blank canvas and splattered it with leopard print, Swarovski crystal curtains and over-the-top opulence. Thrown in together is an Italian restaurant, cocktail lounge (with cigars of course), a sushi bar, wine bar and even a boutique shop. All to be enjoyed if you can get through the door.
**Fairmont Dubai** Trade Centre **04 332 9260**
www.fairmont.com/dubai
Map **2 J4** Metro **Trade Centre**

### Chameleon
Bar

*Vibrant bar, refreshment and entertainment on tap*
Depending on when you visit, the mood at this stylish bar will be set by a live pianist or a hip DJ. Relax on comfy couches, or on bar stools, to enjoy the reasonably priced selection of cocktails and signature Chameleon drinks.
**Traders Hotel, Deira** Deira **04 265 9888**
www.shangri-la.com
Map **2 P5** Metro **Abu Baker Al Siddque**

## Champions Pub
Classic US sports bar: pool, games, cheap drinks
Just what you'd expect from a sports bar – big screens,
pool tables, quiz nights, American pub grub and even
a little late night boogie. Daytime food deals make this
a good choice for lunch as well.
**JW Marriott Hotel** Deira **04 607 7977**
www.marriottdiningatjw.ae
Map **2 P5** Metro **Abu Baker Al Siddque**

## Chi@The Lodge Nightclub
Fun night spot for up-for-it partygoers
Chi@The Lodge is always busy with its indoor and
outdoor dancefloors, lots of seating, large screens and
VIP 'cabanas'. Regular fancy dress nights are popular as
are the legendary 'Cheese' nights with DJ Tim Cheddar.
It's easy to get taxis outside, there's a shawarma stand
in the carpark and entrance is free before 22:30 on
most nights.
**Al Nasr Leisureland** Oud Metha **04 337 9470**
www.lodgedubai.com
Map **2 L5** Metro **Oud Metha**

## Churchill's Pub
Good for escaping your shopping significant other
While it might not be the kind of place you go out of
your way to visit, this traditional English pub complete
with TVs, pool table and dartboard, has one distinct
advantage – it is attached (via the Sofitel Hotel) to
Deira City Centre so when shopping loses its appeal
you can nip in for a quick half.
**Deira City Centre** Port Saeed **04 294 1222**
www.accorhotels.com
Map **2 N6** Metro **Deira City Centre**

## Cin Cin Bar
As bling as Beyonce in a diamond-coated catsuit
With a stylish backdrop of warehouse-high wine
shelves, and walls fashioned like falling water, it's easy
to get carried away ordering imaginative cocktails
and fine wines, but brace yourself for the bill – this is
expense account territory.
**Fairmont Dubai** Trade Centre **04 311 8559**
www.fairmont.com
Map **2 J4** Metro **Trade Centre**

## Crossroads Cocktail Bar & Terrace Bar
Refined Raffles bar with a new Sling twist
Home of the Dubai Sling, an imaginative mix of
coriander, chilli, fig and lemon, and the drink of choice
for surveying the nearby sparkling skyline. With
extremely knowledgeable staff, well-executed bar
snacks and a dizzying choice of drinks, you won't mind
paying above-average prices for the experience.
**Raffles Dubai** Umm Hurair **04 314 9888**
www.dubai.raffles.com
Map **2 K6** Metro **Healthcare City**

## Dhow & Anchor Pub
Good pub grub in a relaxed setting
Dhow & Anchor's bar is a popular spot, particularly
during happy hour and sporting events – try the
outdoor terrace if you are dining and enjoy glimpses
of the Burj Al Arab. The menu includes the usual range
of drinks and terrific curries, pies, and fish and chips.
**The Jumeirah Beach Hotel** Umm Suqeim
**04 406 8999**
www.jumeirah.com
Map **1 S3** Metro **Mall of the Emirates**

## Double Decker Pub
The ultimate crowd-pleasing pub
Adorned with London transport memorabilia, this two
storey bar serves upmarket pub grub including plenty
of stodgy choices and tasty sharing platters. It is packed
on Fridays with revellers attracted by its lively, bargain
brunch. Weekly karaoke and ladies' nights plus big
screen sports ensure there is something for everybody.
**Al Murooj Rotana Hotel & Suites** Trade Centre
**04 321 1111**
www.rotana.com
Map **2 G5** Metro **Financial Centre**

## The Dubliner's Pub
Perfect for watching sports, eating or telling stories
Cosy and lively, this Irish pub has a weekly quiz, good
music and plenty of screens for watching sports. The
menu is full of fresh, tasty and reasonably priced
dishes. Save room for the Bailey's cheesecake.
**Le Meridien Dubai** Garhoud **04 702 2508**
www.lemeridien-dubai.com
Map **2 N7** Metro **GGICO**

## Eclipse Bar Bar
Pulling out all the stops to attract a cool clientele
On the 26th floor, Eclipse is all about glamour, with
red leather padded walls, marble tables and a huge
bar serving hundreds of different cocktails. A cigar
humidor, premium liquers and elegant little canapés
strive to make this a first choice for Dubai's hip crowd.
**InterContinental Dubai Festival City**
Festival City **04 701 1111**
www.intercontinental.com/dubai
Map **2 M8** Metro **GGICO**

## Fibber Magee's Pub
Characterful Irish pub with all the essentials
Succeeding where many bars on foreign shores
fail, Fibber's has the unpolished feel of a true pub.
Televised sport, DJs, themed entertainment evenings
(including the Easy Tiger quiz on Tuesdays), great
value food and drink promotions make it popular.
**Beh White Swan Bldg** Trade Centre **04 332 2400**
www.fibbersdubai.com
Map **2 H4** Metro **Trade Centre**

# Bars, Pubs & Clubs

### Ginseng
Bar

Calling all Carries: cocktails and glamour, NYC style
A great spot for a girls' night out, Ginseng manages to be dressy yet relaxed. The cocktails are a delight, with a variety of sweet, strong concoctions that slip down (too) easily, while the menu is full of tempting Asian treats perfect for sharing. There's two-for-one cocktails on Tuesdays and Champagne promotions on Fridays making this a great choice for groups.
**Pyramids** Wafi **04 324 4777**
www.wafi.com
Map **2 P6** Metro **Healthcare City**

### Harry Ghatto's
Karaoke Bar

Release your inner singer at this fun karaoke joint
The singing in this cosy karaoke bar starts at 22:00, so you've got time to muster up some Dutch courage. There's a great drinks list with a limited range of light meals and over 1,000 songs to choose from, so whether you croon like Sinatra or rap like Eminem you'll find your anthem.
**Boulevard at Emirates Towers** Trade Centre
**04 319 8088**
www.jumeirah.com
Map **2 H5** Metro **Emirates Towers**

### Harvesters
Pub

Middle-of-the-road English pub
The decor is as you would expect from a themed English pub, as is the drinks menu. What you come for though is the pub-style menu which is classically hearty, with a chicken tikka masala that would put many Indian restaurants to shame.
**Crowne Plaza** Trade Centre **04 331 1111**
www.crowneplaza.com
Map **2 H5** Metro **Emirates Towers**

### Hibiki Music Lounge
Karaoke Bar

Sing your heart out for the lads, or just your friends
This cosy karaoke lounge features a small stage, comfy seating areas, and a central bar, plus three private rooms, with Japanese, Singaporean and Thai themes. Singers have around 8,000 songs to choose from, and it makes for a great night out. Happy hour is from 19:30 to 22:00 nightly.
**Hyatt Regency** Deira **04 209 6701**
www.dubai.regency.hyatt.com
Map **2 N3** Metro **Palm Deira**

### Hive
Bar

The honey pot to Dubai's social bees
Hive draws the crowds with its funky design, cool terrace lounge, and Balearic beats that keep the crowd mingling until the small hours. The food, a range of pizzas, steaks, sushi and Asian dishes, is all exquisitely presented and, impressively, the three mini burgers taste even better than they look.
**Souk Al Bahar** Downtown Burj Dubai **04 425 2296**
www.hive.ae
Map **2 F6** Metro **Burj Dubai**

### Icon Bar
Bar

Slick after-work spot in the heart of Media City
This icon for stylish post-work boozers draws the Media City crowds. The carefully styled ambience – red leather chairs, sequined drapes and expensive looking ceramics – is book-ended by big screens showing football. Bar snacks and great pizzas help keep the stamina up.
**Radisson Blu Hotel, Dubai Media City** Al Sufouh
**04 366 9111**
www.radissonblu.com
Map **1 M4** Metro **Nakheel**

### Irish Village > p.511
Pub

Cold pints, tasty food and good craic
Should you fancy fish and chips (in Guinness batter) or a steak with your favourite ale, you can get it in the relaxed environment of the 'IV'. Be it for a quick pint, hearty meal, up even a spot of local talent (musical that is), the Irish Village, with its cubby holes and large outside seating area, is like a dear old friend.
**The Aviation Club** Garhoud **04 282 4750**
www.aviationclub.ae
Map **2 N7** Metro **GGICO**

> ### Explorer Member Card
>
> Don't forget to register your member card (found at the back of the book) and check online for current offers. Discounts are updated on a monthly basis and you can search by area and cuisine type. www.liveworkexplore.com.

Irish Village

THE AVIATION CLUB

...irrepressibly Irish

TOBACCONIST

THE IRISH VILLAGE

04 282 4750

The Irish Village
Dubai

The Aviation Club - P.O.Box 55400, Dubai, U.A.E - Tel. 04 282 4122 - Fax. 04 282 4751 - www.aviationclub.ae

# Bars, Pubs & Clubs

## Issimo
Bar

*Enjoy a touch of James Bond in Deira*

The long, narrow jazz bar has a retro-futuristic feel with stark chrome, black leather, and large slanted Japanese-style panels. There's a superb selection of (pricey) martinis and cocktails, while the clientele is an interesting blend of moneyed hotel guests, Mafioso lookalikes, and hip young clubbers.

**Hilton Dubai Creek** Deira **04 227 1111**
www.hilton.com
Map **2 N5**

## Jambase
Nightclub

*Great fun jazz club-wedding reception mash up*

A tempting drinks selection and generous portions of food is enough to kick off a good night at this Dubai favourite, but all this plays second fiddle to the storming live band that has everyone jostling for the dancefloor. The decor oozes a 50s jazz bar vibe, while the music is funky turn-of-the-century.

**Souk Madinat Jumeirah** Umm Suqeim **04 366 6730**
www.jumeirah.com
Map **1 R4** Metro **Mall of the Emirates**

## Karma Kafé
Bar

*Big Buddha's little sister*

Inside this dark and very cool bar, an array of devilish cocktails are waiting to be discovered. The little sister of Buddha Bar (p.508), it shares the same stylish decor and funky feel, but its Burj Lake view terrace is the trump card. The terrace is popular so arrive early.

**Souk Al Bahar** Downtown Burj Dubai **04 423 0909**
www.buddha-bar.com
Map **2 F6** Metro **Burj Dubai**

## Kasbar
Nightclub

*Atmospheric club with an air of exclusivity*

Kasbar combines the mystique and luxury of regal Arabia with the feel of an exclusive dance party. In keeping with the Arabian decor of the Royal Mirage, this is a sultry, candlelit nightclub perfect for liaisons, as well as dancing and chilling out.

**One&Only Royal Mirage** Al Sufouh **04 399 9999**
www.oneandonlyroyalmirage.com
Map **1 M3** Metro **Nakheel**

## Keva
Bar

*Perfect mix of dining, lounging and cocktails*

A great spot for a pre-clubbing dinner or drink (thanks to its neighbour Chi, p.509), Keva's mix of open booths, bar stools and more formal dinner tables are busy with a well-dressed crowd. Its strapline 'eat play lounge' says it all and the European and Asian cuisine is as elegant as the interior of darkwood and splashes of red.

**Al Nasr Leisureland** Oud Metha **04 334 4159**
www.keva.ae
Map **2 L5** Metro **Oud Metha**

## Koubba
Bar

*Ultra decadent, ultra cool and amazing views*

One of the most stunning views in Dubai awaits from the terrace of this sumptuous cocktail bar. Just off the terrace is the Armoury Lounge, where you can indulge in Cuban cigars surrounded by wooden screens, lavish carpets, and antique Indian weaponry.

**Al Qasr Hotel** Umm Suqeim **04 366 6730**
www.jumeirah.com
Map **1 R4** Metro **Mall of the Emirates**

## Left Bank
Bar

*A taste of hip New York in Dubai*

You'll feel like you're in a secret lounge in hip New York at Left Bank, with its black wallpaper, red velvet booths and white leather couches. The stylish food and cocktails fit well with the swanky surroundings, and the 'small plates' menu begs to be explored with a cocktail in hand. There's another, more low-key venue at Madinat Jumeirah.

**Souk Al Bahar** Downtown Burj Dubai **04 368 4501**
www.emiratesleisureretail.com
Map **2 F6** Metro **Burj Dubai**

## Library Bar & Cigar Lounge
Bar

*Cocktails and cigars in an English country setting*

With its dark wood, comfy sofas and dimmed lighting, the Library Bar could be in the study of an English country house. The bar serves light bites, main meals and a good range of cocktails, and of course top quality cigars.

**The Ritz-Carlton, Dubai** Dubai Marina **04 399 4000**
www.ritzcarlton.com
Map **1 K3** Metro **Dubai Marina**

## Loca
Bar

*Revamped venue that guarantees a good night out*

Formerly El Paso, this rebranded bar and restaurant has retained its Mexican flavour, serving up excellent fare that is a cut above standard mall-based Tex-Mex offerings. If your party of friends has got a thirst, bar tables now come with their own Heineken taps to ensure you're permanently topped up.

**Dubai Marine Beach** Jumeira **04 304 8120**
www.dxbmarine.com
Map **2 H3** Metro **Al Jafiliya**

## Long's Bar
Bar

*Looking for a party? Come along to Long's*

A firm favourite with long time expats and glammed-up singles alike, Long's is often crowded and smoky but dull moments are not on the menu: there are happy hours, theme nights, a brunch and two ladies' nights. Serves decent pub grub too.

**Towers Rotana** Trade Centre **04 343 8000**
www.rotana.com
Map **2 G5** Metro **Financial Centre**

## Lotus One — Bar
Gorgeous modern interior, full of fashionistas
Lotus One is at the top of the it-list. The shiny chrome bar and intimate tables for two with swinging chairs complement the selections made by the groovy house DJ. Beyond the bar is the spacious restaurant with an exquisite menu that jumps from Asian to Aussie.
**Dubai International Convention Centre**
Trade Centre **04 329 3200**
www.lotusonedubai.com
Map **2 J5** Metro **Trade Centre**

## Media Lounge — Bar
Media by name, media by nature in this stylish bar
The Media Lounge lives up to its name as a quiet but trendy hangout for creative types. Coffee, juices and Wi-Fi attract people in work mode during the day, while cocktails are the evening draw.
**Radisson Blu Hotel, Dubai Media City**
Al Sufouh **04 366 9111**
Map **1 M4** Metro **Nakheel**

## Nelson's — Pub
Busy British boozer in Barsha
Pitch up to this unpretentious bar if you want to watch football, tuck into traditional English dishes and enjoy some British banter. The bar in the centre resembles a typical Victorian pub, and punters can settle into large armchairs, prop themselves up on bar stools, or cluster around widescreen televisions.
**Media Rotana** Al Barsha **04 435 0000**
www.rotana.com
Map **1 P5** Metro **Dubai Internet City**

## Neos — Bar
Glorious views and surprisingly well-priced drinks
Seriously glamorous, this sky high bar on the 63rd floor boasts views and a drinks menu to make your jaw drop. Drag your eyes from the twinkling vista and you'll see modern chandeliers, a touch of 1920s art deco and throne-like chairs.
**The Address Downtown Burj Dubai**
Downtown Burj Dubai **04 436 8888**
www.theaddress.com
Map **2 F6** Metro **Burj Dubai**

## New Asia Bar — Bar
Tip top Raffles hangout
A giant stone head, oversized velvet armchairs and Night Fever-style underlit dancefloor are part of the uber-slick treasures to be found in this bar located at the tip of the Raffles Hotel pyramid. Pricey cocktails and spectacular views are enjoyed by a sophisticated crowd. Temporarily closed for renovations at the start of 2010.
**Raffles Dubai** Umm Hurair **04 314 9888**
www.raffles.com
Map **2 K6** Metro **Healthcare City**

Lotus One

## Nezesaussi — Bar
Antipodean sports bar for the tri-nations crowd
Celebrating the sport and cuisine of the tri-nations, Nezesaussi is a popular sports bar with rugby paraphernalia and 13 big screens. Great food and a comprehensive menu offers appeal to more than just sports fans. Meaty mains include South African sausages, New Zealand lamb and Australian steaks.
**Al Manzil Hotel** Downtown Burj Dubai **04 428 5888**
www.southernsunme.com
Map **2 F6** Metro **Burj Dubai**

## Oeno Wine Bar — Bar
Stylish wine bar that's far from cheesy
The fine wines, 50 plus cheeses and excellent service set Oeno apart. The decor is stylish and the wine wall, complete with library- style bookshelf ladder, adds a sense of decadence. Food is served tapas-style, and Tuesday nights bring three free glasses of sparkling wine for ladies from 18:00 to 21:00.
**The Westin Dubai Mina Seyahi** Al Sufouh
**04 399 4141**
www.starwoodhotels.com
Map **1 M3** Metro **Nakheel**

## Oscar's Vine Society — Bar
A cosy hideaway for wine and cheese
Wine cask tables and dim lighting set the mood for indulging in full-bodied reds and ripe cheeses. Special dining offers throughout the week offer good value for great French dishes such as cassoulet and moules mariniere. Friendly bar tenders and a cheese master are happy to explain the selections.
**Crowne Plaza** Trade Centre **04 331 1111**
www.ichotelsgroup.com
Map **2 H5** Metro **Emirates Towers**

### Plan B — Nightclub

For a laid-back night out, make Plan B your plan A
Aimed at people looking for a relaxed late night hang-out (no cover charge or ridiculous drinks prices), Plan B is a refreshing change to Dubai's increasingly exclusive nightlife. The music is wide ranging, with happy hour enlivening the fervour of Saturday nights.
**Pyramids** Wafi **04 324 4777**
www.wafi.com
Map **2 P6** Metro **Healthcare City**

### QD's — Bar

Location, location, location and a cocktail or two
Sitting so close to the water's edge that you can almost dip your toes in, you can watch the passing abras as the sun sets. Elegant bar snacks accompany an excellent cocktail list and as the night wears on, the live band keeps the shisha-smoking crowd entertained.
**Dubai Creek Golf & Yacht Club** Deira **04 295 6000**
www.dubaigolf.com
Map **2 N6** Metro **Deira City Centre**

### Rainbow Room — Bar

A laidback lounge lies at the end of this rainbow
Rainbow Room's pretty wooden deck, outdoor pool and spacious lounge are great for a drink and quick bite, with a small and straightforward menu. More chilled retreat than buzzing hotspot, it livens up to host Laughter Factory evenings (www.thelaughterfactory.com).
**The Aviation Club** Garhoud **04 282 4122**
www.aviationclub.ae
Map **2 N7** Metro **GGICO**

### The Red Lion — Pub

A good spot for homesick Brits who miss their local
The Red Lion is about as close to a traditional British Pub that you'll find in Dubai, and one of the oldest. From the endearing pub grub to their bad carpets and ornate wooden bar you'll certainly feel at home here (if you're a Brit of course). The beer garden barbecues are a favourite and sport is always on the TV.
**Metropolitan** Downtown Burj Dubai **04 343 0000**
www.habtoorhotels.com
Map **2 D5** Metro **Business Bay**

### Rock Bottom — Bar

Sweaty, messy, dirty: an essential Dubai experience
Your Rock Bottom experience depends on your time – or condition – of arrival. Early on, it draws a respectable crowd enjoying the reasonably priced dinner or a game of pool, before undergoing a nightly transformation into the sweaty home of the legendary Bullfrog cocktail and a cracking cover band.
**Regent Palace Hotel** Bur Dubai **04 396 3888**
www.ramee-group.com
Map **2 L4** Metro **Khalid Bin Al Waleed**

### Rooftop Lounge & Terrace — Bar

Kick back your kitten heels, relax under the stars
Rooftop is a hangout for the beautiful people, so expect to pay high prices for your tall drinks. That aside, the views of The Palm are superb and cleverly placed Arabic cushion seats promote interaction between the clientele in one of the most chilled-out bars.
**One&Only Royal Mirage** Al Sufouh **04 399 9999**
www.oneandonlyresorts.com
Map **1 M3** Metro **Nakheel**

### Sanctuary > p.ii-iii — Nightclub

Achingly cool Atlantis party spot
Modern and glam with a suspended catwalk, Sanctuary's got lashings of cool. It hosts a mixed crowd, from hotel guests to dedicated clubbers. On Fridays it kicks off with a blend of house, R&B and Arabic music, and the outdoor terrace fills up early.
**Atlantis The Palm** Palm Jumeirah **04 426 2626**
www.atlantisthepalm.com
Map **2 A3** Metro **Nakheel**

### Scarlett's — Bar

Sport and shared platters
Scarlett's is great for big groups who want to eat, drink and be merry with a satisfying menu, deals on throughout the week which include one of most popular ladies' nights in town on Tuesdays, and big screens and a golf simulator for the boys.
**Boulevard at Emirates Towers** Trade Centre **04 319 8088**
www.jumeirahemiratestowers.com
Map **2 H5** Metro **Emirates Towers**

### Senyar — Bar

A miss-match bar but great cocktails
This bar comes in four sections – a private lounge with widescreen TV, a mezzanine level with quirky furniture, a comfortable terrace, and a main room with a dated fibre optic bar – and lacks cohesion but the cocktails are executed expertly and are topped off with tapas-style bar snacks.
**The Westin Dubai Mina Seyahi**
Al Sufouh **04 399 4141**
www.starwoodhotels.com
Map **1 M3** Metro **Nakheel**

### Sho Cho — Bar

A terrace made for lounging and sipping cocktails
It may be a Japanese restaurant with delicate and imaginative dishes but the huge terrace, and sunshine holiday vibe are what attract the beautiful clientele. The mix of house and trance music and a gorgeous view of the shoreline make this a must.
**Dubai Marine Beach** Jumeira **04 346 1111**
www.dxbmarine.com
Map **2 H3** Metro **Al Jafiliya**

### Skyview Bar
Bar

Drinks at the top of the Burj: a Dubai must-do

A cocktail here can easily run into triple figures and you have to book well in advance – there's a minimum spend of Dhs.275 per person just to get in. But it is worth it for special occasions or to impress out-of-town visitors. The views are amazing, as you would expect. You can also take afternoon tea here (p.492)

**Burj Al Arab** Umm Suqeim **04 301 7600**

www.jumeirah.com

Map **1 S3** Metro **Mall of the Emirates**

### Studio One
Bar

Sport, beer and chips – sometimes it's all you want

Over-salted burgers and greasy fries are the perfect accompaniment to a night in front of the big game at this sport watcher's paradise. TVs scattered around the bar provide punters with a multi-screen sport marathon. The price of beer isn't off-putting, and the selection is good.

**Hilton Jumeirah** Dubai Marina **04 399 1111**

www.hilton.com

Map **1 K3** Metro **Dubai Marina**

### Submarine > *p.453*
Nightclub

Underground dance music and an alternative vibe

Submarine has filled a bit of the alternative dance void that exists in the city. It doesn't start to fill up until midnight, and the spaceship-meets-submarine decor might miss the mark, but Submarine's DJs will quickly remind you how diverse club music can be.

**Dhow Palace Hotel** Al Mankool **04 359 9992**

www.dhowpalacedubai.com

Map **2 L4** Metro **Karama**

### Tamanya Terrace
Bar

Good views, not bad nibbles and decent drinks

Business visitors, tourists and media locals mingle in a trendy mix of concrete and chrome. It's popular as a stopping-off point after work, and as night falls the cocktail bar gets busy with merriment and music.

**Radisson Blu Hotel, Dubai Media City**

Al Sufouh **04 366 9111**

www.radissonblu.com

Map **1 M4** Metro **Nakheel**

### The Terrace Lounge Bar
Bar

Rooftop chilling, media-style

This rooftop bar is the perfect alfresco drinking spot, with the option of perching at the long bar or relaxing in the garden style furniture. Food is served during the day but after 17:00 it is just drinks and shisha and the chill-out tunes of the resident DJ.

**Media Rotana** Al Barsha **04 435 0000**

www.rotana.com

Map **1 P5** Metro **Dubai Internet City**

Sho Cho

# Bars, Pubs & Clubs

## Tiki Bar — Bar
*Drop in for a tropical tipple en route to Spice Island*
This is a welcoming – if slightly sad and quiet – little place to grab a tropical cocktail if you happen to be in the vicinity and in need of coconut-infused cheer. It might not get much attention, but you could do worse than to start – or end – your evening at Tiki.
**Renaissance Dubai** Deira **04 262 5555**
www.marriott.com
Map **2 P5** Metro **Salahudin**

## Trader Vic's Mai-Tai Lounge — Bar
*More of the same strong Trader Vic's cocktails*
The livelier cousin of the Crowne Plaza and Madinat eateries (p.500), this large bar is decked out in Polynesian style. Mai-Tai's totally tropical cocktail list is accompanied by tasty, if expensive, bar snacks and the spacious dancefloor provides a clubby feel.
**Al Fattan Towers** Dubai Marina **04 399 8993**
www.tradervics.com
Map **1 L3** Metro **Dubai Marina**

## The Underground — Pub
*Football, beer, pub grub and the Tube*
Themed on the Tube, the order of the day in this popular pub is (expensive) beer, burgers and ball sports which attract a large crowd of regulars. There are numerous screens to ensure you can get a good view of the live sports action, plus a dartboard and pool tables.
**Habtoor Grand** Dubai Marina **04 399 5000**
www.grandjumeirah.habtoorhotels.com
Map **1 L3** Metro **Dubai Marina**

## Uptown Bar — Bar
*Shaken not stirred sundowners and fine views*
The 24th floor location affords great terrace views of the Burj Al Arab and beyond, and the interior is classy enough – in a James Bond kind of way. An extensive menu of cocktails with price tags to match is complemented by tapas and bar snacks.
**The Jumeirah Beach Hotel** Umm Suqeim **04 406 8999**
www.jumeirah.com
Map **1 S3** Metro **Mall of the Emirates**

## Viceroy Bar — Bar
*The stereotypical British pub*
A familiar, pokey British pub with authentic tobacco smoke, a cast of middle-aged regulars and corner televisions tuned to different sports channels. It serves up reasonably priced, generously portioned British, Tex-Mex, Thai and Indian food with daily happy hours.
**Four Points by Sheraton Bur Dubai** Bur Dubai **04 397 7444**
www.starwoodhotels.com
Map **2 L4** Metro **Khalid Bin Al Waleed**

## Vintage — Bar
*A cheese and wine aficionado's dream*
Vintage draws up an exclusive list of cold meat and cheese platters, costly vintages, burgundies and champagnes but manages to retain the feel of a friendly local. The bar is a small space, so arrive early or very late to bag a sofa.
**Pyramids** Wafi **04 324 4100**
www.wafi.com
Map **2 P6** Metro **Healthcare City**

## Vista Lounge — Bar
*Music, cocktails and a breathtaking backdrop*
With fabulous views over the creek from the relaxed terrace, a romantically lit piano bar and a modern cocktail bar, Vista is a welcome addition to the 'other side of the creek'. They also have a small food menu serving mainly sandwiches and salads.
**InterContinental Dubai Festival City**
Festival City **04 701 1111**
www.intercontinental.com/dubai
Map **2 M8** Metro **GGICO**

## Vu's Bar — Bar
*Give your guests a slice of the high life*
The doors open on to the 51st floor to reveal what feels like a private members' club, and the prices echo that suspicion. Through oddly-shaped windows you can glimpse fabulous views of Dubai. The beer and wine lists are huge, but the cocktails steal the show.
**Emirates Towers** Trade Centre **04 319 8088**
www.jumeirah.com
Map **2 H5** Metro **Emirates Towers**

## Waxy's — Pub
*Not high society – but expect a great time*
This faux Irish pub successfully staves off homesickness for British and Irish expats. Its legendary weekend brunch costs Dhs.85 for five drinks, a full English breakfast and then a carvery dinner. At 18:00 the lights go down, the music goes up and the party starts.
**Ascot Hotel** Bur Dubai **04 352 0900**
www.ascothoteldubai.com
Map **2 L3** Metro **Al Fahidi**

## Zinc — Nightclub
*The slinky superclub experience*
The soundtrack is R&B, house and hip-hop, with Housexy (Ministry of Sound) and Kinki Milinky ferrying over UK DJs. Design-wise, there are shiny flatscreens, lounge areas and glitzy mirrored walls, as well as a big dancefloor sectioned off by a mammoth bar.
**Crowne Plaza** Trade Centre **04 331 1111**
www.ichotelsgroup.com
Map **2 H5** Metro **Emirates Towers**

# Walk The Walk

Got the munchies? Head to The Walk, Dubai's latest place to be that's packed with a multitude of restaurants and cafes.

One of the most popular areas in Dubai for eating out is The Walk, the 1.7km pedestrian-friendly boulevard that lies between the JBR residential development and the beach. You won't find any fine dining establishments here, but that's not the main draw; crowds come for the atmosphere and the relaxed, alfresco eating and drinking. In the cooler months, hundreds of people of all nationalities – families, friends, couples, tourists – stroll the strip before settling down at a table to sociably while the night away.

There are dozens of cafes and restaurants on The Walk, serving up pretty much every popular cuisine available. If you can't decide what you're in the mood for, just go for a wander and you'll soon stumble upon something that takes your fancy. Starting at the Dubai end of the strip, the first JBR court is Murjan. This is the more upmarket side of The Walk, where the designer boutiques and home accessory stores congregate. There's also a cluster of international options to choose from here: The Noodle House and Da Shi Di (both Chinese); Umi Sushi (Japanese); Suvoroff (Russian); Scoozi (Italian-Japanese fusion); The Fish & Chip Room (British); and On The Border (Mexican). There's also a cigar lounge here, La Casa Del Habano, for a refined end to the evening.

The next court, Sadaf, has its main culinary treats tucked away up on the plaza level, including branches of the excellent Lebanese chain Automatic, Indian Pavillion and fun burger-and-shake joint Fuddrukers.

Wedged among the JBR courts is Oasis Beach Tower, which contains some popular (and, unlike the JBR outlets, licensed) restaurants, including Frankie's, Wagamama and Trader Vic's Mai-Tai Lounge.

JBR continues with Bahar and Rimal courts, which feature a great stretch of alfresco eating. Packed tables spread out onto the wide pavement, and it is perhaps The Walk's busiest section in the evenings and for leisurely weekend breakfasts. Highlights include Il Caffé Di Roma, Paul, Le Pain Quotidien, Butcher Shop & Grill, Sarai, Sukh Sagar, El Chico, Ruby Tuesday and Indian Pavillion.

Things descend into more of a fastfood frenzy by Amwaj and Shams courts, with a selection of the usual suspects – Hardee's, Cinnabon, KFC, Pizza Hut – plus decent breakfast spot Coco's.

And if the seemingly endless options along The Walk are not enough to satisfy your appetite, there are plenty more cafes and restaurants by the water at Marina Walk, while the beachfront hotels – Habtoor Grand, Le Royal Meridien, Ritz-Carlton, Hilton and Sheraton – house a more upmarket selection of higher-class restaurants and bars.

The delights of JBR

# EXPLORER

# Explorer Products

## Live Work Explore Residents' Guides

## Mini Visitors' Guides

## Mini Maps

# Check out www.liveworkexplore.com/shop

## Photography Books

## Maps

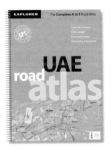

## Lifestyle Guides

## Magazine

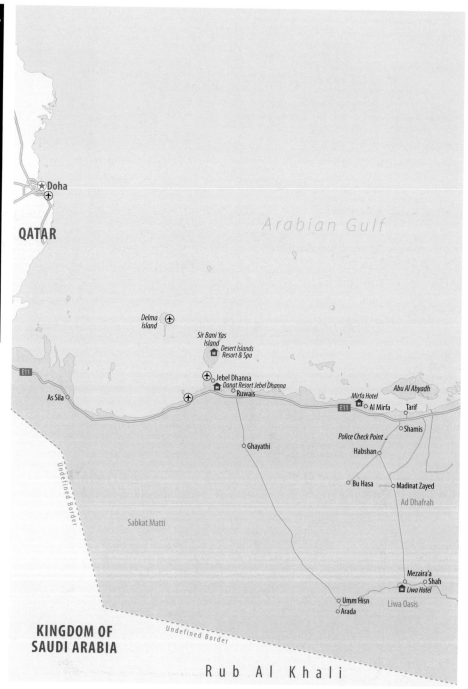

Doha
QATAR

Arabian Gulf

Delma Island

Sir Bani Yas Island
Desert Islands Resort & Spa

Jebel Dhanna
Danat Resort Jebel Dhanna
Ruwais

As Sila

E11

Mirfa Hotel
Al Mirfa
Tarif

Abu Al Abyadh

Shamis

Police Check Point
Habshan

Ghayathi

Bu Hasa
Madinat Zayed

Ad Dhafrah

Sabkat Matti

Undefined Border

Mezaira'a
Shah
Liwa Hotel
Umm Hisn
Arada
Liwa Oasis

KINGDOM OF
SAUDI ARABIA

Undefined Border

Rub Al Khali

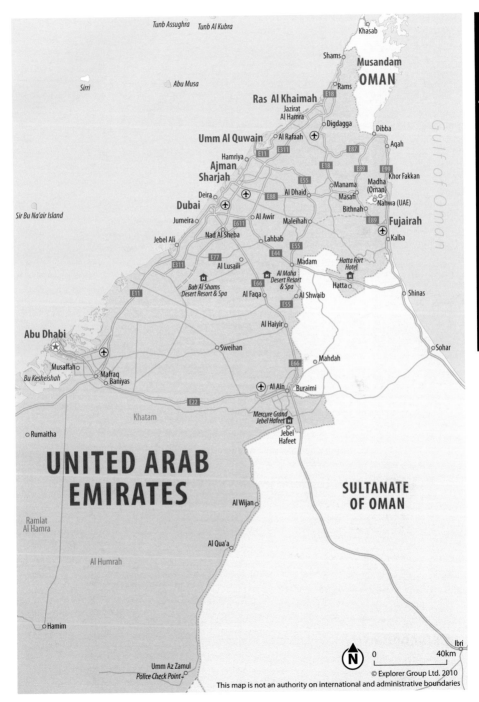

Tunb Assughra   Tunb Al Kubra

Khasab

Shams

Musandam
OMAN

Rams

Sirri   Abu Musa

Ras  Al Khaimah
Jazirat
Al Hamra

Dibba

Diggagga

Aqah

Umm Al Quwain   Al Rafaah

E87

Hamriya   E11   E311

E18   E89   E99

Ajman

Sharjah

E55   Manama   Madha   Khor Fakkan
(Oman)

Deira   Al Dhaid   Masafi

Dubai   E88

Bithnah   Nahwa (UAE)

Jumeira   Al Awir   Maleihah

E611   E89   Fujairah

Jebel Ali   Nad Al Sheba   Lahbab   Kalba

Sir Bu Na'air Island

E77   Al Lusaili   E44   Madam   Hatta Fort
Hotel

E311   Al Maha
Desert Resort
& Spa

E66   Hatta

E11   Bab Al Shams
Desert Resort & Spa   Al Faqa   Al Shwaib   Shinas

E55

Al Haiyir

Sweihan   Mahdah   Sohar

Abu Dhabi

E66

Musaffah   Mafraq   Al Ain   Buraimi
Bu Kesheishah   Baniyas

E22

Khatam   Mercure Grand
Jebel Hafeet

Rumaitha   Jebel
Hafeet

UNITED ARAB
EMIRATES   SULTANATE
OF OMAN

Al Wijan

Ramlat
Al Hamra

Al Qua'a

Al Humrah

Hamim

Ibri

N   0   40km

© Explorer Group Ltd. 2010
This map is not an authority on international and administrative boundaries

Gulf of Oman

# EXPLORER

## Dubai Explorer – 14th Edition

**Written and edited by** Claire England, Jake Marsico, Jane Roberts, Pamela Afram, Siobhan Campbell, Tom Jordan
**Freelance contributions by** Jola Chuddy, Kelly Whitehead, Sultan Sooud Al Qassemi
**Proofread by** Jo Holden MacDonald
**Data managed by** Anas Abdul Latheef, Derrick Pereira, Ingrid Cupido, Kathryn Calderon, Mimi Stankova, Shedan Ebona
**Designed by** Jayde Fernandes, Pete Maloney, Shawn Zuzarte
**Maps by** Sunita Lakhiani, Zainudheen Madathil
**Photographs by** Henry Hilos, Pamela Grist, Pete Maloney, Victor Romero

## Publishing
**Publisher** Alistair MacKenzie
**Associate Publisher** Claire England

## Editorial
**Group Editor** Jane Roberts
**Lead Editor** Tom Jordan
**Deputy Editors** Jake Marsico, Pamela Afram, Siobhan Campbell
**Production Coordinator** Kathryn Calderon
**Senior Editorial Assistant** Mimi Stankova
**Editorial Assistant** Ingrid Cupido

## Design
**Creative Director** Pete Maloney
**Art Director** Ieyad Charaf
**Account Manager** Chris Goldstraw
**Layout Manager** Jayde Fernandes
**Junior Designer** Didith Hapiz
**Layout Designers** Mansoor Ahmed, Shawn Zuzarte
**Cartography Manager** Zainudheen Madathil
**Cartographers** Noushad Madathil, Sunita Lakhiani
**Traffic Manager** Maricar Ong
**Traffic Coordinator** Amapola Castillo

## Photography
**Photography Manager** Pamela Grist
**Photographer** Victor Romero
**Image Editor** Henry Hilos

## Sales & Marketing
**Group Sales Manager** Peter Saxby
**Media Sales Area Managers** Laura Zuffa, Pouneh Hafizi
**PR & Marketing Manager** Annabel Clough
**Marketing Assistant** Shedan Ebona
**International Retail Sales Manager** Ivan Rodrigues
**Retail Sales Area Manager** Mathew Samuel
**Senior Retail Sales Merchandisers** Ahmed Mainodin, Firos Khan
**Retail Sales Merchandisers** Johny Mathew, Shan Kumar
**Retail Sales Coordinator** Michelle Mascarenhas
**Drivers** Shabsir Madathil, Najumudeen K.I.
**Warehouse Assistant** Mohamed Riyas

## Finance & Administration
**Office Manager** Shyrell Tamayo
**Junior Accountant** Cherry Enriquez
**Accounts Assistant** Soumyah Rajesh
**Personnel Relations Officer** Rafi Jamal
**Office Assistant** Shafeer Ahamed

## IT & Digital Solutions
**Digital Solutions Manager** Derrick Pereira
**Senior IT Administrator** R. Ajay
**Web Developer** Anas Abdul Latheef

## Contact Us

### Explorer Member Card
Register your member card and take advantage of monthly discounts and competitions.
Log on to **www.liveworkexplore.com/members**

### General Enquiries
We'd love to hear your thoughts and answer any questions you have about this book or any other Explorer product.
Contact us at **info@explorerpublishing.com**

### Careers
If you fancy yourself as an Explorer, send your CV (stating the position you're interested in) to
**jobs@explorerpublishing.com**

### Designlab & Contract Publishing
For enquiries about Explorer's Contract Publishing arm and design services contact
**designlab@explorerpublishing.com**

### PR & Marketing
For PR and marketing enquiries contact
**marketing@explorerpublishing.com**

### Corporate Sales
For bulk sales and customisation options, for this book or any Explorer product, contact
**sales@explorerpublishing.com**

### Advertising & Sponsorship
For advertising and sponsorship, contact
**sales@explorerpublishing.com**

**Explorer Publishing & Distribution**
PO Box 34275, Dubai, United Arab Emirates
www.liveworkexplore.com
www.explorerpublishing.com

**Phone:** +971 (0)4 340 8805
**Fax:** +971 (0)4 340 8806